"Ken Bailey is already widely known for s
Middle Eastern Eyes.' He has taught in x
East, as well as in America and Europe. This commentary is more than a conventional, largely repeated exegesis of 1 Corinthians. Bailey shows the relevance of prophetic and rabbinic forms of language, uses Arabic, Coptic and Syriac sources, and rightly stresses the coherence of this epistle, and its theology of the cross. He is alert to intertextual resonances and offers distinctive ideas. Especially for those who look for more than a conventional commentary, I warmly commend this work."

**Anthony C. Thiselton,** Professor of Christian Theology, University of Nottingham

"Professor Kenneth E. Bailey has authored a scholarly, creative and lucid commentary on Paul's first letter to the Corinthians. Bailey argues that Paul is not addressing, somewhat haphazardly, a series of disjointed issues. Rather, Bailey perceives Paul as providing a well-crafted series of essays that display a rhetorical and structural style, which allows him to address fundamental gospel concerns with persuasion, conviction and clarity. This volume will benefit not only scholars but especially undergraduates and graduates."

**Thomas G. Weinandy, O.F.M., Cap.,** Executive Director for the Secretariat for Doctrine, United States Conference of Catholic Bishops

"Bailey's warm pastoral style, up-to-date scholarship and attention to theology make for an excellent exposition of Paul's argument in 1 Corinthians. His unparalleled knowledge of the New Testament in Arabic translation, coupled with his lifetime of experience in the Middle East, gives Bailey a unique perspective on the biblical text. Highlighting Paul's rhetorical argument and extensive use of Jewish Scriptures, Bailey's work is a rare commentary that serves both pastor and layperson. This book sets a high standard for clarity and practical wisdom in the field of biblical exposition."

**Lynn H. Cohick,** Professor of New Testament, Wheaton College

"A veteran student and observer of the Middle East, Ken Bailey has distilled his knowledge and experience in this work of deep pastoral sensitivity, allowing Paul the apostle to come into his own in a way that a conventional reading of the apostle does not allow or encourage. Bailey's work teems with learning and insight, and buoyed by a clear, lively style, it instructs as well as it illuminates and elevates. The book is a model of biblical scholarship freed of the cobwebs of the study and consecrated to the life-giving work of the church. It is a 'double-decker sandwich,' to use Bailey's own figure, in which the sandwich is no less nourishing than the meat between the sandwich. I began reading it and couldn't put it down. Go and do thou likewise."

**Lamin Sanneh,** Professor of World Christianity, Yale Divinity School

"Kenneth Bailey sets forth a courageous proposition that Paul's first letter to the Corinthians was in fact written as a circular letter for all the churches. As he works through the letter, Bailey, drawing on neglected Syriac commentaries and his Middle Eastern experiences, presents a gem-laden exposition of 1 Corinthians that engages topics of Christian unity, the cross, living in a pagan culture, men and women in worship, and the resurrection. This is a study on 1 Corinthians like none other I have seen. A truly unique approach to studying a Pauline letter."

**Michael F. Bird,** Lecturer in Theology, Crossway College, Australia

"A rich and original study of 1 Corinthians, which draws on ancient Middle Eastern sources to shed fresh light on this great epistle. We are in Kenneth Bailey's debt for this work of scholarship."

**Lord Carey,** former Archbishop of Canterbury

"New Testament scholars recognize Kenneth Bailey as that rare interpreter with intimate knowledge of Middle Eastern culture, ancient and modern. His latest volume now reveals rumination of the rhetoric that serves Paul's theology and ethics. Bailey's signal achievement is to rebut readings of 1 Corinthians as a haphazard document, obscurely reasoned. At once learned and deeply personal, this commentary will surely stimulate productive debate in the exegesis of one among Paul's weightiest letters."

**C. Clifton Black,** Otto A. Piper Professor of Biblical Theology, Princeton Theological Seminary

"Yet another commentary on 1 Corinthians? Hardly. Bailey's work opens a new genre in the rhetorical analysis of this famous and difficult NT letter. He argues that 1 Corinthians consists of five essays and each has a common ancient rhetorical structure ("ring composition") missed by most exegetes. Paul was a trained rabbi, had memorized vast amounts of his scriptures, and knew how to write a polished public letter using ancient Hebrew forms (particularly from Isaiah). But in addition Bailey is using tools unavailable to the average New Testament scholar: twenty-two ancient translations of 1 Corinthians into Arabic, Syriac and Hebrew, as well as commentaries dating as far back as ninth-century Damascus. This book is a gold mine of astonishing new discoveries, crosscultural insight and sound pastoral wisdom. It will inevitably join the ranks of the 'great and important books' on this epistle."

**Gary M. Burge,** Professor of New Testament, Wheaton College

"Kenneth Bailey has transformed the way in which the parables and sayings of Jesus have been received and understood. Now he delves into the Pauline letters, and it becomes clear that a whole new perspective emerges. The view of Middle Eastern Christians is placed before us in its stark truthfulness . . . provid[ing] a window into the world of 1 Corinthians that is majestic in the vista it offers. . . . With the skill of a biblical surgeon, Kenneth opens up the layers of meaning present. This commentary will bring many hours of reflection and insight for the edification of the reader and will be a blessing to God's church."

**The Most Rev. Roger Herft,** Archbishop of Perth and Metropolitan of Western Australia

"Well-known for his numerous works on Jesus and the Gospels through Middle Eastern eyes, Kenneth Bailey now turns his attention to Paul's writing as he provides a powerful and passionate reading of 1 Corinthians within its Jewish and eastern Mediterranean contexts. . . . Particularly worth noting is Bailey's reading of this epistle through the lens provided by Arabic, Syriac and Hebrew translations from the fourth century up to the modern period. To students of the New Testament text, this provides an invaluable resource for the history of the reception of Paul's message to the Corinthian believers."

**David W. Pao,** Chair and Associate Professor of New Testament,
Trinity Evangelical Divinity School

"Ken Bailey is pure gold. No writer I can think of has been a greater help for teaching the Scriptures with freshness and clarity. What a gift to have his insights on Paul."

**John Ortberg,** Menlo Park Presbyterian Church

# Paul Through Mediterranean Eyes

## CULTURAL STUDIES IN 1 CORINTHIANS

KENNETH E. BAILEY

IVP Academic

An imprint of InterVarsity Press
Downers Grove, Illinois

*InterVarsity Press*
*P.O. Box 1400, Downers Grove, IL 60515-1426*
*World Wide Web: www.ivpress.com*
*E-mail: email@ivpress.com*

*InterVarsity Press® is the book-publishing division of InterVarsity Christian Fellowship/USA®, a movement of students and faculty active on campus at hundreds of universities, colleges and schools of nursing in the United States of America, and a member movement of the International Fellowship of Evangelical Students. For information about local and regional activities, write Public Relations Dept., InterVarsity Christian Fellowship/USA, 6400 Schroeder Rd., P.O. Box 7895, Madison, WI 53707-7895, or visit the IVCF website at <www.intervarsity.org>.*

*The Scripture quotations quoted herein are from the Revised Standard Version of the Bible (with occasional alternatives based upon the author's preferred translation), copyright 1946, 1952, 1971 by the Division of Christian Education of the National Council of the Churches of Christ in the U.S.A. Used by permission. All rights reserved.*

*Design: Cindy Kiple*
*Images: Portrait of a young man: Adrian Weinbrecht/Getty Images*
   *St. Paul arriving at Malta: St. Paul arriving at Malta by Pieter the Younger at Alan Jacobs Gallery, London, UK/The Bridgeman Art Library*

*ISBN 978-0-8308-3934-6*

*Printed in the United States of America* ∞

**Library of Congress Cataloging-in-Publication Data**

*Bailey, Kenneth E.*
 *Paul through Mediterranean eyes: cultural studies in 1 Corinthians*
*/ Kenneth E. Bailey*
  *p. cm.*
 *Includes bibliographical references and indexes.*
 *ISBN 978-0-8308-3934-6 (pbk.: alk. paper)*
 *1. Bible. N.T. Corinthians, 1st—Commentaries. I. Title.*
 *BS2675.53.B35 2011*
 *227'.2077—dc22*

                  *2011013672*

**P**   21   20   19   18   17   16   15   14   13   12   11   10   9   8   7   6   5   4

**Y**   28   27   26   25   24   23   22   21   20   19   18   17   16   15   14   13

To

**Bill Crooks**

**Dave Dawson**

**Bill McKnight**

faithful and beloved companions in the Way

المحبة

لا تسقط أبداً

"Love Never Falls" (13:8)

*"For we write to you nothing but what you can read and understand;
I hope you will understand fully, as you have understood in part."*

2 COR 1:13-14

# Contents

# Abbreviations

*ABD*  David Noel Freedman, editor, *The Anchor Bible Dictionary*, 6 vols. (New York: Doubleday, 1992).

BAGD  Walter Bauer, W. F. Arndt, F. Wilber Gingrich, Frederick W. Danker, eds., *A Greek-English Lexicon of the New Testament and Other Early Christian Literature* (Chicago: University of Chicago Press, 1979).

Barrett, *First Epistle*
    C. K. Barrett, *A Commentary on the First Epistle to the Corinthans* (New York: Harper, 1968).

Bishr ibn al-Sari, *Pauline Epistles*
    Bishr ibn al-Sari, *Pauline Epistles*, trans. Harvey Staal, *Mt. Sinai Arabic Codex 151, Corpus Scriptorum Christianorum Orientalium*, vol. 452-453 (Lovanii: In Aedibus E. Peeters, 1983).

Chrysostom, *First Corinthians*
    John Chrysostom, *Homilies on the Epistles of Paul to the Corinthians*, First Series, vol. XII, trans. Talbot W. Chambers, in *Nicene and Post-Nicene Fathers*, ed. Philip Schaff (Grand Rapids: Eerdmans, 1975).

Conzelmann, *1 Corinthians*
    Hans Conzelmann, *1 Corinthians* (Philadelphia: Fortress, 1975).

Fee, *First Epistle*
    Gordon D. Fee, *The First Epistle to the Corinthians* (Grand Rapids: Eerdmans, 1987).

Findlay, *First Epistle*
>G. G. Findlay, "St Paul's First Epistle to the Corinthians," in *The Expositor's Greek Testament,* ed. W. Robertson Nicholl, vol. 2 (New York: George Doran Company, 1900).

Garland, *I Corinthians*
>David E. Garland, *I Corinthians* (Grand Rapids: Baker, 2003).

Hays, *First Corinthians*
>Richard Hays, *First Corinthians* (Louisville: John Knox, 1997).

JB    Jerusalem Bible

Lightfoot, *First Corinthians*
>John Lightfoot, *A Commentary on the New Testament from the Talmud and Hebraica, Matthew—I Corinthians, Volume 4, Acts—I Corinthians* (Grand Rapids: Baker, 1979, reprinted from the 1859 English ed.; original Latin, 1658-1674).

Kistemaker, *1 Corinthians*
>Simon J. Kistemaker, *1 Corinthians* (Grand Rapids: Baker, 1993).

KJV   King James Version of the Bible

LSJ, *Greek-English Lexicon*
>H. G. Liddell, Robert Scott and H. S. Jones, *A Greek-English Lexicon*, rev. J. S. Jones (Oxford: Clarendon, 1966).

LVTL, *Lexicon*
>*Lexicon in Veteris Testamenti Libros,* ed. L. Koehler and W. Baumgartner (Leiden: J. J. Brill, 1958).

M. & M. James H. Moulton and George Milligan, *The Vocabulary of the Greek Testament Illustrated from the Papyri and Other Non-literary Sources* (Grand Rapids: Eerdmans, 1963).

Moffatt, *First Epistle*
> James Moffatt, *The First Epistle of Paul to the Corinthians* (London: Hodder and Stoughton, 1947).

Murphy-O'Connor, *1 Corinthians*
> Jerome Murphy-O'Connor, *1 Corinthians* (Wilmington, Del.: Michael Glazier, 1979).

NIV          New International Version of the Bible

NRSV          New Revised Standard Version of the Bible

Orr/Walther, *I Corinthians*
> William F. Orr and James A. Walther, *I Corinthians*, The Anchor Bible, vol. 32 (New York: Doubleday, 1976).

Robertson/Plummer, *First Epistle*
> Archibald Robertson and Alfred Plummer, *A Critical and Exegetical Commentary on the First Epistle of St Paul to the Corinthians*, ICC (Edinburgh: T & T Clark, 1914).

RSV          Revised Standard Version of the Bible

*TDNT*          *Theological Dictionary of the New Testament*, ed. Gerhard Kittle and G. Friedrich, 10 vols. (Grand Rapids: Eerdmans, 1967-1976).

Thiselton, *First Epistle*
> Anthony C. Thiselton, *The First Epistle to the Corinthians: A Commentary on the Greek Text* (Grand Rapids: Eerdmans, 2000).

Wright, *Resurrection*
> N. T. Wright, *The Resurrection of the Son of God* (Minneapolis: Fortress, 2003).

# Preface

As with many books, this work evolved in stages. Some forty years ago I noted that 1 Corinthians 13 was composed in the following manner:

> Love and the spiritual gifts (13:1-3)
> > Love defined positively (4a)
> > > Love defined negatively (4b-6)
> > Love defined positively (7)
> Love and the spiritual gifts (8-13)

A few years later I observed that this same chapter was encased within two discussions of "the spiritual gifts" (1 Cor 12 and 14:1-25). After another decade I became aware of a yet wider format that came to a climax in the chapter on "love." This involved 11:2–14:40 and is as follows:

1. Men and women *leading* in worship (11:2-16)
2.    Disorder in worship—Holy Communion: *Sacrament* (11:17-34)
3.       The spiritual gifts—In theory (12:1-31)
4.          Love (13:1-13)
5.       The spiritual gifts—In practice (14:1-15)
6.    Disorder in worship—Preaching: *Word* (14:16-33a)
7. Women and men *worshiping* (14:33b-40)

These seven sections are clearly a single essay focused on conflict and confusion in worship and the need for love. The Corinthians were quarreling over the place of men and women in worship, disorders in both sacrament (cameo 2) and word (cameo 6), and over the spiritual gifts and their use (cameos 3 and 5). None of these problems could be solved without the "love" that forms the center of the seven sections (cameo 4). Presenting the various parts of the discussion in this carefully balanced way was clearly important for Paul as he tried to communicate with his readers. The *women worshipers* were chatting in church (cameo 7) and failing to listen to the *women* (and men) *prophets* who were addressing the congregation (cameo 1). In short: Some women were preaching—and other women were not listening to them! But the reader would not catch this connection between cameo 1 and cameo 7 without awareness of the structure of the overall essay that began in chapter 11 and concluded at the end of chapter 14. More of this below.

Observing the construction of this "essay" was a turning point in my journey with 1 Corinthians. If Paul had gone to the effort to put chapters 11–14 together in this thoughtful way, the question became "what about the rest of the epistle?" Ever so slowly the composition of the other chapters in the epistle appeared like a magnificent castle emerging into bright sunlight with the gradual lifting of a dense fog (that was in my mind). More years of study and reflection were necessary before I cautiously dared to commit my findings to paper. My interest was not merely biblical theology as it relates to rhetorical structure, but also the Middle Eastern cultural context of the entire epistle.

A huge, usually neglected source for New Testament studies is the Oriental Versions. As always, to translate is to interpret. Over four decades, I taught New Testament in English and in Arabic in Egypt, Lebanon and then in Jerusalem. Gradually I came to appreciate the amount of interpretive content that is encoded in the Middle Eastern versions of the New Testament in Syriac, Arabic and Hebrew. For more than thirty years I collected twenty-three versions of 1 Corinthians in those three languages that were translated across more than 1,600 years. Gradually these versions became an ever more important part of my journey.[1] At critical points in the text, I have asked, "How did Middle Eastern Christians across the centuries understand this text?" Their translations provide an important key to the answers to that question. What then of Middle Eastern commentaries?

The early centuries of Middle Eastern Christian scholarship reflected in John Chrysostom and others is well known. The last of the Eastern fathers who wrote in Greek was John of Damascus (d. A.D. 750). With his passing, to a large extent, Middle Eastern Christian scholars and people disappeared

---

[1]An annotated list of these versions appears in "Description of the Oriental Versions" at the end of this study.

from the mind of Western Christianity primarily because their major theological language became Arabic.

As to Middle Eastern commentaries written in Coptic, Syriac or Arabic, much has been lost. Ibn al-Salibi (d. 1171) left us Syriac language commentaries on the Gospels that were translated into Arabic and published. In his introduction to those volumes, Ibn al-Salibi mentions his sources and lists: Ephraim the Syrian, Ya'qub al-Sarrugi, Filiksinus al-Manbaji, Sawirus al-Antaqi, Watha al-Takriti, Ya'qub al-Sawahiri, Andarawus al-Urushalimi, Zur'a al-Nasibini, Danial al-Suluhi, Yu'annus al-Dari and others.[2] To my knowledge, of this list, only Ephraim the Syrian has survived. Centuries of persecution caused the irreplaceable loss of many resources. In 1957 I was privileged to visit the Monastery of St. Anthony in the desert between the Nile Valley and the Red Sea. On that occasion the monks told me that over the centuries their monastery had been overrun and burned seven times. In 1849 Austen H. Layard published a detailed account of the massacres of Nestorian Christians in Northern Iraq by Kurds and Turks. He discusses what he personally witnessed and what is known of the long centuries of persecution. The destruction of Christian books was a significant part of that continuing tale of suffering.[3] Yet, as noted, in spite of monumental losses, numerous translations of the New Testament into Arabic from Greek, Syriac and Coptic have survived.

Printing did not arrive in the Middle East until the nineteenth century, and any Christian Arabic book published before 1900 is considered by Western librarians to be a "rare book." The one commentary on 1 Corinthians known to me that has survived was completed in A.D. 867 by Bishr ibn al-Sari, a Syrian Orthodox scholar who translated the Acts, the Epistles of Paul and the Catholic Epistles from Syriac into Arabic and then wrote an Arabic commentary on those same books. The only known copy is housed in the library of the Monastery of St. Catharine in Mt. Sinai. Harvey Staal transcribed, edited and translated the text and commentary which has been published.[4] In the modern period, Fr. Matta al-Miskin of the Coptic Orthodox Church has produced a

---

[2]Dionesius ibn al-Salibi, *Kitab al-Durr al-Farid fi iafsir al-'Ahd al-Jadid* (The Book of Rare Pearls of Interpretation of the New Testament, 2 Volumes), edited and published by the monk 'Abd al-Masih Dawlabani of the Syrian Orthodox Church (n.d., n.p.), introduction, p. 3.

[3]Austen Henry Layard, *Nineveh and Its Remains: With an account of a visit to the Chaldaean Christians of Kurdistan, and the Yezidis or Devil-worshippers; and an inquiry into the Manners and Arts of the Ancient Assyrians, Vol. I* (New York: George Putnam, 1848), pp. 148-72, 203-24.

[4]Bishr Ibn al-Sari, *The Pauline Epistles,* ed. and trans. Harvey Staal, CSCO Vol. 452-453 (Lovanii: In Aedibus Peeters, 1983).

large volume titled al-Qiddis Bulus al-Rasul: Hayatuhu, Lahutuhu, A 'maluhu
([Arabic] *Saint Paul the Apostle: His Life, his Theology and his Ministry*).[5]

As noted, in the wider Christian world, Middle Eastern Christians are
often forgotten. The current discussion of the emergence of the Christian
"Global South" (Africa, Asia and South America) and its numerical domi-
nance over Christians in Western Europe and North America, overlooks the
Middle East entirely. Having already discussed a few topics in the Gospels in
the light of important Middle Eastern Christian sources,[6] this volume intends
to focus similar attention on 1 Corinthians.

I am deeply indebted to my teachers in New Testament, who include Mar-
cus Barth, Fredric K. W. Danker, Edgar Krentz, William Orr, Martin Schar-
lemann, Theophilus Taylor and James Walther, who both taught me and set
for me a high standard of excellence. Colleagues and friends near and far who
across the years have encouraged me in this journey include Fahim Aziz,
Craig Blomberg, Gary Burge, George Carey, James Dunn, Craig A. Evans,
Edith Humphrey, Howard Marshall, 'Atif Mehenne, Cecil McCullough,
Lesslie Newbigin and N. T. Wright. I am indebted to Victor Makari for his
efforts in checking the numerous quotations from the Arabic Gospels noted
throughout the book and in the Oriental Versions Index. I am deeply indebted to The Bodleian Library, Oxford, the Cambridge University Library
and the British Museum Library for allowing me access to their Oriental resources and for the microfilms that they graciously produced for my use.
Other libraries to whom I owe thanks are the Borgianus Vatican Library and
the National Libraries of both Paris and Berlin. Father Justin, the head librar-
ian at St. Catherine's Monastery, has been most kind in filming for me important rare texts unique to their famous collection.

Every commentator on the Scriptures writes in a context and out of a series
of deep commitments. I am a confessing Christian with a high reverence for
the Bible as the inspired Word of God, which I approach with awe and gratitude. Many of the ideas formulated in this work come out of the non-Western
world and have been presented by me in Arabic and in English to numerous
audiences around the globe for more than forty years. The larger context in
which I spent decades of teaching was that of a series of wars "From Beirut to
Jerusalem" and beyond that stretched from 1956 to 2006. For years, staying

---

[5]Matta al-Miskin, *al-Qiddis Bulus al-Rasul: Hayatuhu, Lahutuhu, A'maluhu* (Monastery of St.
Maqar, wadi al-Natron, Box 2780, Cairo: Monastery of St. Maqar, 1992), p. 783.
[6]Kenneth E. Bailey, *Jesus Through Middle Eastern Eyes* (Downers Grove, Ill.: IVP Academic,
2008).

alive in the midst of heavy cannon fire was an almost daily and nightly pre-occupation. The result of these modest efforts is not intended to be a "Commentary on First Corinthians" modeled after the forty-seven extended commentaries on the desk before me. "Cultural Studies" intends to suggest a more modest enterprise.

Beirut and Jerusalem face both East and West. I am writing for native English speakers, but also looking to the new Global South where the majority of the world's Christians now live. Thiselton, Garland, N. T. Wright, Hays, Kistemaker, Orr/Walther, Barrett, Fee and many others have nobly discussed the many questions raised in the massive literature available in the West. I am deeply indebted to that detailed discussion from which I have learned much and which I have followed at a distance with respect and appreciation. Years of war made engagement with it nearly impossible.

In this study I have three basic concerns. The first has to do with Hebrew rhetorical style. I will present evidence for the fact that in 1 Corinthians, Paul, a Middle Easterner Jewish Christian, uses rhetorical styles that were available to him in the writing of the Hebrew prophets (particularly Isaiah and Amos). This study will investigate the significance this has for understanding Paul's thought. The second concern is, as much as possible, to bring to life Paul's metaphors and parables. Such word pictures are not illustrations of concepts, but rather primary modes of theological discourse. As he uses these metaphors and creates these parables Paul is creating meaning, not simply illustrating it. Middle Eastern life and literature will be of assistance in this attempted recovery.

The third is to examine twenty-three representative samples of the long and illustrious heritage of translations of 1 Corinthians into Syriac, Arabic and Hebrew. On numerous occasions critical words and phrases will be traced in those versions to see how Middle Eastern Christians across 1,600 years have read and understood the text. The Syriac Peshitta was finalized in the fourth-fifth centuries. The Arabic versions begin to appear in the ninth century. The two Hebrew versions available to me are from the nineteenth and twentieth centuries. The evidence from these versions appears in the notes and the original texts are set out in appendix II.

I wish also to thank students and countless audiences across America, South Asia, Europe and the Middle East who over five decades have patiently listened to my lectures on 1 Corinthians, stimulated my thought with their questions and encouraged me to undertake this project. I am also grateful to

Harvest Communications of Wichita, Kansas, and its director, Mr. Ray Dorsett, who gave me the opportunity to travel to ancient Corinth and record video lectures on 1 Corinthians while there. My editor, Michael Gibson, has rendered invaluable help and I am indebted to him for his patience, understanding, diligence and care throughout the editorial process. My thanks goes out also to Rev. George Bitar of Lebanon who created the beautiful and expressive Arabic calligraphy that appears on the dedicatory page. Most of all I wish to thank Sara B. Makari for her long hours working with my manuscript. To her no expressions of thanks are adequate.

For decades The Foundation for Middle Eastern New Testament Studies, now in partnership with the World Mission Initiative at Pittsburgh Theological Seminary, has provided funding for research travel (to many locations from Oxford to Mt. Sinai). It has financed the editorial assistance and the acquisition of books and microfilms needed for this manuscript. Without its help this book would not have been written. Special thanks also must be expressed to Dr. Atif Mehenni, president of Cairo Evangelical Seminary, for his friendship and partnership in the great task of trying to reclaim the biblical insights of the thousand years of unknown and forgotten New Testament scholarship of the Arabic-speaking Christians of the Middle East. The New Center for the Study of Middle Eastern Christianity that has come to life under President Atif's leadership offers hope and encouragement for our journey together along this long forgotten way.

My dear wife, Ethel, has patiently supported and endured a husband whose mind was "always somewhere else," focused on "the book" for far too long. To her my gratitude can never be fully expressed.

It is my fervent prayer that this modest effort may help others to discover a little more of St. Paul's original intent, who with great care, wrote this epistle for the Corinthians and "for all those in every place upon whom is called the name of *our Lord Jesus Christ*."

*Soli Deo Gloria,*
*Kenneth E. Bailey*

# Introduction

THE PREACHER IN ECCLESIASTES considers "wisdom and madness and folly" and then seems to accept his fate as he bemoans, "What can the man do who comes after the king? Only what he has already done."[1]

With the indescribable richness of many recent major commentaries on 1 Corinthians stretching for over a hundred years from Robertson/Plummer[2] to Thiselton,[3] what else can possibly be said about 1 Corinthians that has not been said?

This study will make no systematic attempt to review or interact with all the magisterial work currently available. Rather, with deep gratitude for what has already been accomplished, this book will attempt a fresh look at what can be called "Paul's most contemporary letter" and see if there is a layer of meaning that remains to be uncovered.

The lenses I intend to use for this purpose are *the rhetorical styles of 1 Corinthians that can be traced to the writing prophets* of the Hebrew Scriptures, and the *culture of the eastern Mediterranean* world as it can be recovered. The rhetorical styles I refer to are not directly related to the classical Greek rhetoric so ably described by Aristotle[4] and reviewed in its relationship to 1 Corinthians by Thiselton[5] who comments, "The literature on this subject has now become breathtakingly immense."[6] More exactly, as noted, my own decades of study of the epistle have led me to an extensive use by St. Paul of

---

[1]Eccles 2:12.
[2]Robertson/Plummer, *First Epistle*.
[3]Thiselton, *First Epistle*.
[4]Aristotle, *The "Art" of Rhetoric*, trans. J. H. Freese (1926; reprint, Cambridge, Mass.: Harvard University Press, 2006).
[5]Thiselton, *First Epistle*, pp. 46-52.
[6]Ibid., p. 47 n. 253.

rhetorical patterns traceable to the writing prophets of the Hebrew Scriptures. These patterns are formed from the well-known parallelisms of the Hebrew Bible where ideas are set out in pairs. In this type of writing the author presents an idea and then adds a second line that may repeat the first line, or present the opposite of the first line. It may illustrate the first line or simply complete it.[7] The Psalms, and almost all of the writings of the Prophets, are composed of these Hebrew parallelisms and modern translations format the text accordingly. Our concern here is to see how Paul has arranged *collections of Hebrew parallelisms* into larger patterns that are important to identify for a deeper understanding of his intent. In the following chapter I will set forth the three basic types of these collections of parallelisms with a few examples from the prophets. This raises the question: Does Paul always write this way?

First Corinthians exhibits this style of writing throughout its chapters with a few exceptions, which will be noted. These exceptions are either "asides" or connectives between two rhetorical homilies. But the carefully balanced rhetorical homilies that we will examine in this study are not Paul's "default" style. There are examples in 2 Corinthians of this classical Hebrew style, but most of it appears to be straightforward prose.[8] First Corinthians is different. Why so?

Every interpreter of 1 Corinthians is obliged to make a watershed decision as he/she examines the first three verses of the first chapter. In Romans Paul writes, "To all God's beloved in Rome" (1:7). In Galatians 1:2 he says, "To the churches of Galatia." Philippians opens with, "To all the

---

[7]Kenneth E. Bailey, "Inverted Parallelism and Encased Parables in Isaiah and Their Significance for Old and New Testament Translation and Interpretation," in *Literary Structure and Rhetorical Strategies in the Hebrew Bible*, ed. L. J. de Regt et al. (Assen, The Netherlands: Van Gorcum, 1996), pp. 14-30; idem, "Parallelism in the New Testament—Needed: A New Bishop Lowth," *Technical Papers for the Bible Translator* 26 (July 1975): 333-38; Adele Berlin, "Parallelism," in *The Anchor Bible Dictionary, Volume 5* (New York: Doubleday, 1992), pp. 155-62; C. F. Burney, *The Poetry of Our Lord* (Oxford: Clarendon, 1925); Mitchell Dahood, "Pairs of Parallel Words in the Psalter and in Ugaritic," in *The Anchor Bible Psalms III 101-150* (New York: Doubleday, 1970), pp. 445-56; John Jebb, *Sacred Literature* (London: T. Cadell, 1820); James L. Kugel, *The Idea of Biblical Poetry: Parallelism and Its History* (New Haven: Yale University Press, 1981); George Buchanan Gray, *The Forms of Hebrew Poetry*, Prolegomenon by David Noel Freedman (n.p.: KTAV Publishing House, 1972, c. 1915); Nils Lund, *Chiasmus in the New Testament* (Peabody, Mass.: Hendrickson: 1992, c. 1942).
[8]Second Corinthians has no great "hymns" such as the hymn to the cross (1:17–2:2), the hymn to love (chap. 13) and the hymn to the resurrection (chap. 15).

saints in Christ Jesus who are at Philippi" (1:2).[9] Second Corinthians is addressed to "the church of God which is at Corinth, *with all the saints who are in the whole of Achaia*" (1:1). In this last instance, the readers of 2 Corinthians are not a single church in one urban center. Rather, the letter is written for the church at Corinth and for all believers in the surrounding district. The intended readership of 1 Corinthians is, however, broader.

Paul addressed 1 Corinthians to the Corinthian Christians "together with all those in every place on whom is called the name of our Lord Jesus Christ, both their Lord and ours" (1:2, my translation). Paul states openly and boldly that *this letter is addressed to the entire church*. Is he serious?

Ambrosiaster (fourth century), writing in Latin, affirmed, "Paul writes to the church as a whole."[10] A few years later John Chrysostom, writing in Greek, made the same identification in his first homily on 1 Corinthians.[11] In the ninth century, Bishr ibn al-Sari completed his own translation of the letters of Paul into Arabic with thoughtful notes.[12] Writing in A.D. 867, Bishr comments on 1:2 and explains Paul to be saying, "That is, we are writing this letter not only to you, Oh assembly at Corinth, but also to all the people of every country who profess the name of Jesus Christ, those who love him."[13] John Calvin of Geneva, in his commentary on 1 Corinthians, concurs.[14] There is, therefore, a strong witness across the centuries that sees 1 Corinthians as a letter to the Corinthians *and to the whole church*. But in the modern period this view is often set aside.

Many interpreters have argued that of all Paul's letters, 1 Corinthians is the most "occasional."[15] That is, unlike other letters, in 1 Corinthians Paul mentions names and particular incidents, some scandalous. In addition to discussing special problems like getting drunk at Holy Communion and a man sleeping with his father's wife, 1 Corinthians appears to

---

[9]The same designation of recipients appears in Colossians and in 1 and 2 Thessalonians.

[10]Ambrosiaster, *Commentaries on Romans and 1-2 Corinthians*, trans. and ed. Gerald L. Bray (Downers Grove, Ill.: IVP Academic, 2009), p. 120.

[11]Chrysostom, *I Corinthians*, pp. 3-4.

[12]Bishr ibn al-Sari, *Pauline Epistles*.

[13]Ibid., p. 51 n. 4.

[14]John Calvin, *The First Epistle of Paul the Apostle to the Corinthians* (Grand Rapids: Eerdmans, 1960), pp. 19-20.

[15]For a more extensive discussion of this topic see Kenneth E. Bailey, "The Structure of I Corinthians and Paul's Theological Method with special reference to 4:17," *Novum Testamentum* 25, no. 2 (1983): 152-81.

be disjointed as though it were written in a great hurry. Conzelmann writes of its "loose construction" and of "breaks and joins."[16] Héring and Schmithals feel that these "breaks and joins" demonstrate that various letters compiled at various times have been brought together by an editor.[17] Barrett, Conzelmann and Orr/Walther cautiously affirm unity for the entire book as it now stands.[18] Orr/Walther mention the traditional outline, which is:

> A. Subjects raised with Paul orally by messengers from Corinth, 1–6.
> B. Subjects about which the Corinthians have written, 7–16.

Orr/Walther then observe a series of inserts placed into the topics of the letter and note:

> One has to decide whether these inserts are to be connected with the topics from the letters Paul is answering or are to be interpreted as independent items—and this in turn bears upon the editorial unity of the epistle.[19]

Barrett discusses the same problem, follows the same twofold division suggested above, and notes that Paul was a busy man with little time for writing. Barrett states,

> This means that the writing of the letter will have been spread over some time; it may well have been laid aside from time to time, and taken up again after an interval. A letter written in such circumstances may be expected to show occasional inconsistencies and passages in which the same topic is looked at from different points of view. Fresh news may reach the writer; plans may change with changing needs and opportunities.[20]

Coupled with the above rationale for the supposed disjointedness of 1 Corinthians, the comment is often made that the book is a *practical letter,* not a theological treatise. Thus naturally, no careful, ordered presentation of material is expected. Again Barrett writes,

[16]Conzelmann, *1 Corinthians*, p. 2.
[17]Jean Hering, *The First Epistle of Saint Paul to the Corinthians* (London: Epworth, 1962), pp. xiii-vx; W. Schmithals, *Paul and the Gnostics* (New York: Abingdon, 1972), pp. 245-53.
[18]Barrett, *First Epistle*, pp. 14-17; Conzelmann, *1 Corinthians*, pp. 2-3; Orr/Walther, *I Corinthians*, pp. 120-22.
[19]Orr/Walther, *I Corinthians*, p. 122.
[20]Barrett, *First Epistle*, p. 15.

I Corinthians is anything but a work of systematic theology. It is a practical letter addressed to a single, though complex situation, aimed at telling its readers not so much what they ought to think as what they ought to do—or ought not to do.[21]

At the same time Barrett also observes, "The practical advice, however, is consciously grounded in theological principles which can usually be detected." Yet, in spite of this latter admission, the conclusion that Barrett and many others come to is that the book is, as it were, "written on the run," and that its outline is dictated by the list of questions that came first orally (1–6) and then in writing (7–16) from Corinth. It is practical, not theological, we are told; occasional, not universal in outlook. Commenting on 11:2-16, Richard Hays represents many when he writes,

His [Paul's] reasoning is notoriously obscure, . . . because the line of argument is—by any standard—labored and convoluted.[22]

I am not sure that even Paul's opponents in Corinth would have agreed. He records them saying about him, "His letters are weighty and strong" (2 Cor 10:10). With deep respect for the above mentioned modern position, I would offer an alternative. The view presented in this study is that the entire book has a carefully designed inner coherence that exhibits amazing precision in composition and admirable grandeur in overall theological concept. This study will argue that the outline of 1 Corinthians is as precise as any of Paul's letters and that it falls into five carefully constructed essays, which themselves showcase a discernible theological method, both internally as individual essays and together as a collection.[23] The overall outline of the five essays, reduced to their simplest form and to their dominant themes, is as follows:

---

[21]Ibid., p. 17.
[22]Hays, *First Corinthians*, p. 183.
[23]Toward the end of the nineteenth century G. G. Findlay, in *The Expositor's Greek Testament*, proposed a sixfold division of 1 Corinthians. With the exception of including 4:17-21 in his first section, his first five divisions are identical to my proposal for five essays. The internal structure of each essay, the relationships between essays and the theological method the essays exhibit Findlay did not observe. Yet, prior to the twentieth century debate, most of this suggested overall outline was noted. Cf. Findlay, *First Epistle*, p. 754. In 1889 F. L. Godet combined chapters 5-10 under the title "Five Moral Questions," but otherwise his outline is identical to that of Findlay. Cf. F. L. Godet, *Commentary on First Corinthians* (1893; reprint, Grand Rapids: Kregel Publications, 1979), pp. 27-31.

I.    The Cross and Christian Unity 1:5–4:16
II.    Men and Women in the Human Family 4:17–7:40
III.    Food Offered to Idols (Christian and pagan) 8:1–11:1
IV.    Men and Women in Worship 11:2–14:40
V.    The Resurrection 15

---

**Figure Int.1. Summary of 1 Corinthians**

When the complementary pairs of essays are placed together it is evident that Paul has three principle ideas on his mind. These are:

1. The cross and the resurrection (I, V)

2. Men and women in the human family and in worship (II, IV)

3. Christians living among pagans: To identify or not to identify (III)

Some of the Corinthians' questions (oral and written) are worked into *Paul's outline*, instead of the other way around. *He* sets the agenda, not the Corinthians. Rather than 7:1 being a critical shift from oral reports to a written report, 11:34 looms large. At the end of that verse Paul says, "About the other things I will give directions when I come." This important aside makes it clear that there are problems in Corinth relating *only to the Corinthians*. Ergo, the rest of the book relates to the Corinthians *and to others*. This in turn leads us to conclude that Paul is deadly serious when he affirms that his intended readers are the Corinthians and all Christians everywhere.

What then is the meaning of the "hinge" in 7:1 where Paul appears to turn from problems he has heard about *orally* to problems that came to him in *writing?* We note that this verse appears in the middle of Paul's essay on acceptable and unacceptable patterns of human sexual practice (4:17–7:40). Paul opens this topic with a discussion of the sordid incident where a man was sleeping with his father's wife and some of the Corinthians were proud of this behavior (chapters 5–6). In chapter 6, he also discusses sleeping with prostitutes and like matters. It is clear that the Corinthians *did not write to Paul* about these incidents. They most likely hoped that he would never find out about them. Their attempt to hide this behavior failed; Paul found out anyway. They did however write to him asking for his advice on the topics that appear in chapter 7. They wrote about divorce, remarriage after the death of the spouse, marriage to unbelievers and the like. While they presented their "polite" problems to Paul in writing, at the same time they concealed the unpleasant cases that had erupted in their midst. This understanding of 7:1 harmonizes with the "other matters" mentioned in 11:34 and with the clear affirmation in 1:2 that this letter is for the whole church. The message of 1 Corinthians cries out to all Christians.

Are we to imagine that questions such as

- Christian divisions and the need for unity
- How to understand the cross
- Standards for Christian sexual practice
- How to live the Christian life in the midst of a pagan world
- How to understand and celebrate the Eucharist
- The place of women and men in worship leadership
- Understanding and using the spiritual gifts
- The centrality of costly love and how it is to be defined
- How to understand the resurrection

were unique to Corinth? Granted we are here making an assumption. But surely at least most of this list of problems was of deep concern across the church. We can hope that there were no other cases of incest in the churches, but were the Corinthians alone in their struggle over meat offered to idols? Did all the churches already have a deep theological foundation for sexual ethics? These are critical issues debated around most of the Christian world in our time. How, in Paul's day, could they have been problems that erupted only in Corinth?

Building on the above, it appears that Paul looked at the specific problems that surfaced in Corinth and selected some of them. The topics he chose were those that the new Christian communities were debating in many places. He then composed 1 Corinthians and sent a copy to Corinth *and to churches everywhere*. He *did* address the Corinthians and at the same time, he invited the rest of the Church to "listen in" on his "phone conversation" hoping to serve the entire church.

If this is the case, would we not expect Paul to have composed this letter with great care? The evidence indicates that he did so. Using his own Jewish literary tradition, he built on the rhetoric of the classical writing prophets and composed a series of masterpieces on the topics selected. As we will see, each essay is composed of a series of shorter homilies each of which has its own interior structure. Paul's basic methodology for constructing each of the five essays is largely the same. That methodology appears below in figure Int.2.

1. *The tradition.* (This is at times quoted and on other occasions referred to in passing.) The idea of *reminding* and *remembering* in connection with the tradition is mentioned at the beginning of three of the five essays. In the other two, the tradition is quoted directly.

2. *A practical/ethical problem* is presented (in bold negative colors).

3. *A foundational theological statement* is carefully composed and presented as a place where the church can stand to address the problem. This foundation is usually presented as two interlocking aspects of a single theme.

4. *The practical/ethical problem is restated* (usually more positively) and is generally discussed in the light of the theological statements just made.

5. *A personal appeal* concludes each of the five essays. Two of these have the "imitate me" theme; two reflect "I have the Spirit/command of the Lord," and two include the imperative "therefore, my beloved brethren, etc." The appeal at the end of the fourth essay has two of these components. Twice a summary of the essay in included in the personal appeal.

---

**Figure Int.2. Paul's outline for the essays in 1 Corinthians**

In short Paul does not say:

> Here is the problem!
> Here is what you must do!

Instead he writes:

> You have received the tradition from me.
>     Here is the problem.
>         Consider the following theological foundation
>         on which a solution can be built.
>     Look at the problem again in the light of this theology.
> Imitate me/I think I have the Spirit of the Lord.

When the five essays (noted above) are observed and the above methodology discerned[24] the apparent "confusion" disappears. Yes, there is repetition. The discussion "Paul, Apollos and Cephas" occurs in chapter 1 and again in chapter 4, but this is a deliberately constructed order that fits into the outline of the essay. The same is true for the double discussion of food offered to idols seen in chapter 8 and again in chapter 10. Chapters 12 and 14 discuss the spiritual gifts. All of this is deliberate. But there is a remaining question.

Written before 1 Corinthians, the letter to the Galatians opens with three chapters on *theology* which are followed by three chapters on *ethics*. In his letter to the Romans Paul opens with eight chapters on theology. This is followed

---

[24]Note the table of contents.

by three chapters in which Paul discusses Christians and Jews. The epistle concludes with four densely packed chapters on how we should live in the light of the theology set out in the opening chapters. With this first-theology-then-ethics pattern in use before and after the writing of 1 Corinthians, why does Paul compose a letter using the finely balanced construct of ethics and theology that appears in 1 Corinthians and then not use it again?

I do not know, but a conjecture is possible. Perhaps Paul, writing his first "general letter," tried this clear, yet sophisticated way to "do theology and ethics" and some readers were confused by it.

This possibility is in harmony with Paul's statement in 2 Corinthians 1:13-14 where he says, "For we write you nothing but what you can read and understand; I hope you will understand fully, as you have understood in part." Most likely Paul is referring to the reception 1 Corinthians received in Corinth. Thus we are obliged to ask: Why does Paul feel the need to make such a statement? Clearly, some of his readers had complained that they were *not able to follow* what he wrote to them. Paul is perhaps replying:

> Do not say you cannot understand. You can! I engaged a brother with good handwriting to make sure the copy I sent to you was easy to read, and I was careful not to use words you do not know. I included many metaphors and parables (from your world) and I repeated most of the major topics to assist comprehension. You *can* indeed read my long letter—and you *can understand it*. It is actually very clear. You have already understood *part* of it. Keep trying and you will be able to understand *all* of it!

A further concern is the presence of the often noted "asides" in 1 Corinthians. Why in the middle of a discussion of patterns of sexual practice (in harmony with the gospel) does Paul suddenly open a discussion of "the circumcised and the uncircumcised" and add to it a discussion of "slavery and freedom"? At times these "asides" interrupt a very carefully structured "apostolic homily." Sometimes they are more like a parenthesis between homilies. Some are serious statements of some length. Others appear to be "marginal notes." Each of these is a special case and each in turn will be discussed when it appears in the text.

In regard to the epistle as a whole, it is quite possible that some of the "set pieces" that make up an essay may have been composed by Paul at an earlier stage and were, so to speak, "in the file." The author of 2 Timothy instructs Timothy to bring "the books and above all the parchments" (2 Tim 4:13). It is hard to imagine that a scholar like Paul did not have *some* prepared material that, with a bit of adaptation, he could incorporate into a larger document. Paul was lecturing in the Hall of Tyrannus every day for two years (Acts 19:9). The Western text of Acts adds, "from the fifth hour to the tenth." Metzger suggests that this latter reading "may represent an accurate piece of information."[25] The time reference is from 11:00 a.m. to 4:00 p.m. For most of the year, those hours would have been "siesta" time. Few would have wanted to rent the hall in the heat of the early afternoon, and the cost of doing so would have been much lower. Did Paul have *no* notes, or carefully prepared material for *any* of those classes?

By way of summary, it appears that when a long list of problems surfaced in Corinth, Paul selected those of general concern and addressed both the Corinthians and the church at large in a single letter. For this extraordinarily well-constructed, important document Paul reached back into his own Jewish past and co-opted rhetorical styles sanctified by the classical writing prophets.[26] Occasionally his mind moved sideways to bring in related topics, and once in a while he added a few "notes" to a homily readily available in his mind or among his papers. The result was one of Paul's finest efforts and it can indeed be called "Paul's most contemporary epistle."

Throughout this study Paul's use of metaphor and parable will be noted. It is easy to see these metaphors as "illustrations" brought in to elucidate a point. But to make this assumption in studying a biblical text is to miss much of what the Middle Eastern author is trying to say. Middle Easterners *create meaning* through the use of simile, metaphor, parable and dramatic action. They do not simply *illustrate* concepts. Jesus used metaphors, parables and dramatic actions in this way. Paul's parables and metaphors can also be seen as primary theological statements.

Some of Paul's metaphorical language is buried in our traditional translations. Thiselton has written, "Most English translations, especially NRSV and often NIV, simply abstract the conceptual content of the metaphor from its forceful emotive imagery."[27] Thomas Friedman has astutely ob-

---

[25]Bruce Metzger, *A Textual Commentary on the Greek New Testament* (New York: United Bible Societies, 1971), p. 470. See M.-E. Bosmard et A. Lamouille, *Le Texte Occidental des Actes des Apotres: Reconstitution et Rehabilitation* (Paris: Editions Recherche sur les Civilisations, 1984), pp. 3-11; J. M. Wilson, *The Acts of the Apostles: Translated from the Codex Bezae with an Introduction on its Lucan Origin and Importance* (London: SPCK, 1924), pp. 1-37.

[26]Paul's letter may well have also overlapped with various Greek rhetorical styles. We will note a relationship between 1:17–2:2 and Pericles. However, as noted, a general investigation of Greek rhetoric as a background to the letter is beyond the scope of this study.

[27]Thiselton, *First Epistle*, p. 1053.

served that when you "opt for a big metaphor . . . you trade a certain degree
of academic precision for a much larger degree of explanatory power."[28]
Often this is what Paul has done. But to recover the impact of that "explanatory power" we must penetrate as deeply as possible into his metaphorical and cultural world. How can that best be accomplished?

In this study my goal is to allow Paul's metaphors and parables to exert
their full strength as they appear in the text. Ancient and modern Middle
Eastern sources, as available, will be utilized in attempting to achieve this
goal. John Chrysostom left us a full commentary on 1 Corinthians. As
noted in the preface, a translation of 1 Corinthians from Syriac into Arabic (with commentary) was completed by Bishr Ibn al-Sari of Damascus in
A.D. 867. That fine work is now also available in English. Matta al-Miskin
(d. 2008) has left us a weighty tome of 783 pages titled *St. Paul the Apostle: His Life, His Theology and His Ministry*.[29] There are many references
in this study to 1 Corinthians, but the book does not focus on any particular letter.

Beyond these few sources are the many translations of 1 Corinthians into
Arabic, Syriac and Hebrew that stretch from the fourth through fifth centuries up to the present. Over a lifetime, I have managed to acquire twenty-three such translations and have consulted them throughout the writing of
this book.[30] Translation is always interpretation and these versions open an
important window into how Middle Eastern Christians across the last 1,600
years have understood 1 Corinthians. Many of them add short interpretive
phrases to the text by way of interpretation. Such phrases intensify the character of these versions as mini-commentaries. Translated out of Greek, Syriac
or Coptic, these versions are important for this search.

The New Testament can be likened to a vast ocean. There are two well
known ways to sail upon it. One is to set the sails to the prevailing winds and
currents and to use great caution in any deviation from them. The other is to
move through uncharted waters, explore neglected islands and inlets and then
return and attempt a faithful report on the journey. I have chosen the second.

It is important now to turn aside to take a brief look at a few cases of the
kinds of "prophetic homilies" that were available to Paul as models for his

---

[28]Thomas L. Friedman, *The World Is Flat* (New York: Picador/Farrar, Straus & Giroux, 2007),
p. x.
[29]Matta al-Miskin, *al-Qiddis Bulus al-Rasul* [Arabic: Saint Paul the Apostle] (Cairo: Al Maqar
Monastery, 1992).
[30]A full annotated list of these versions is available as a part of the bibliography.

first letter to the Corinthians. After a careful examination of the Hebrew writing prophets, two decades ago I chose Isaiah as a rich mine for a study of biblical rhetorical styles.[31] To a small part of that great prophetic witness we now turn.

[31]For my study of the rhetoric of Isaiah 40–66, see www.shenango.org/Bailey/Isaiah.htm.

# Prelude

*The Prophetic Homily Rhetorical Style and Its Interpretation*

To BEGIN THIS TOPIC, a brief overview of the history of "rhetorical criticism" may be helpful.

In 1969, in his presidential address to the Society of Biblical Literature, James Muilenburg issued a call for moving beyond form criticism to what he titled "rhetorical criticism." He said that his primary interest was:

> in exhibiting the structural patterns that are employed for the fashioning of a literary unit, whether in poetry or in prose, and in discerning the many and various devices by which the predications are formulated and ordered into a unified whole. Such an enterprise I should describe as, rhetoric and the methodology as rhetorical criticism.[1]

Although the name "rhetorical criticism" was new, the interest in discovering the interrelatedness of ideas in a single passage of biblical literature was not. In the eighteenth century Bishop Robert Lowth broke new ground with his influential work, *De sacra Poesi Hebraeorum*.[2] His work was followed by Bishop John Jebb (1820),[3] Rev. Thomas Boys (1825)[4] and Professor of Oriental Languages, John Forbes (1854).[5] In the twentieth century the dis-

---

[1]James Muilenburg, "Form Criticism and Beyond," *JBL* 88 (1969): 8.

[2]Robert Lowth, *De sacra Poesi Hebraiorum* (Oxford: n.p., 1753), ET *Lectures on the Sacred Poetry of the Hebrews* (London: n.p., 1787).

[3]John Jebb, *Sacred Literature; comprising a review of the principles of composition laid down by the late R. Lowth . . . in his Praelections and Isaiah: and an application of the principles so reviewed, to the illustration of the New Testament; in a series of critical observations on the style and structure of that Sacred volume* (London: n.p., 1820).

[4]Thomas Boys, *A Key to the Book of Psalms* (London: L.B. Steely and Sons, 1825); idem, *Tactia Sacra, An attempt to develop and to exhibit to the eye by tabular arrangements a general rule of composition prevailing in the Holy Scriptures* (London: T. Hamilton, 1824).

[5]John Forbes, *The Symmetrical Structure of Scripture; or, the principles of Scripture parallelism*

cussion was moved forward by C. F. Burney (1925)[6] and N. W. Lund (1942).[7] The entire book of Hebrews was analyzed by Vanhoye in 1964[8] and, in 1966, John Bligh published a rhetorical study of Galatians.[9] In this current study I build on my previous essay on the outline of 1 Corinthians.[10] More recently Victor Wilson published *Divine Symmetries: The Art of Biblical Rhetoric*. That volume provides thoughtful material on the topic and includes an excellent recent bibliography.[11]

Our working assumption in this study of 1 Corinthians is as follows: Paul, as a trained rabbinic scholar, would have memorized at least most of the Torah and the Prophets.[12] Thus he would have been familiar with the various literary styles developed by the writing prophets.[13] Composing a major work for the entire church, Paul would have wanted to produce a polished epistle. I am convinced that Paul fell back on his own sacred literary heritage in the Hebrew prophets. What then were the major building blocks of the rhetorical patterns available to him?

The well-known Hebrew parallelisms were widely used in ancient Hebrew literature.[14] When the author is repeating or reversing individual words we catch it easily. But at times the biblical author is creating a "rhyme of ideas." In the Isaiah 28 passage examined below, the prophet repeats or reverses some of his ideas as he presents his case. The claims of the rulers in Jerusalem are mocked on one side, and God's answer is presented on the other side. Then in the center of the homily Isaiah sets out "the building material" in the third cameo in the homily and then affirms the need for "builder's tools" in order to build the future house promised by God. These

*exemplified, in an analysis of the Decalogue, The Sermon on the Mount, and other passages of the Sacred writings* (Edinburgh: n.p., 1854).

[6]C. F. Burney, *The Poetry of Our Lord* (Oxford: Clarendon, 1925).

[7]N. W. Lund, *Chiasmus in the New Testament* (Chapel Hill: University of North Carolina Press, 1942).

[8]Albert Vanhoye, *A Structured Translation of the Epistle to the Hebrews*, trans. from the Greek and the French by James Swetnam (Rome: Pontifical Biblical Institute, 1964).

[9]John Bligh, *Galatians in Greek: A Structural Analysis of St. Paul's Epistle to the Galatians* (Detroit: University of Detroit Press, 1966).

[10]K. E. Bailey, "The Structure of I Corinthians and Paul's Theological Method with Special Reference to 4:17," *Novum Testamentum* 25 (1983): 152-88.

[11]Victor M. Wilson, *Divine Symmetries: The Art of Biblical Rhetoric* (Lanham, Md.: University Press of America, 1997).

[12]Birger Gerhardsson, *Memory and Manuscript: Oral Tradition and Written Transmission in Rabbinic Judaism and Early Christianity* (Copenhagen: Ejanr Munksgaard, 1961), *passim*.

[13]Cf. note 15.

[14]James L. Kugel, *The Idea of Biblical Poetry: Parallelism and Its History* (New Haven: Yale University Press, 1981).

two cameos are also clearly "parallel." The type of parallelism is not easy to specify—but it is there. Here is where the work of James Kugel is extremely helpful. He argues convincingly that what the ancient Hebrew author was trying to say was, "A, and what's more, B."[15] The author presents one idea (slight pause), and then offers a related idea (longer pause). Kugel shows that there are hundreds of ways in which the second line is related to the first. Instead of insisting on a few strict categories like "synonymous parallelism" and "antithetical parallelism" one must allow for a *rhyme of ideas* that hold two lines or sets of lines together. In modern Bibles, the individual pairs of ideas are already set out for us in the Psalms and the Prophets. The same development has yet to take place in the New Testament. But more than that, we are looking for how sets of lines come together in a unit (cameo) and how that cameo is matched, balanced or completed by a second cameo somewhere else in the homily. The numbers in our Bibles only help us to find our place. They often work against any attempt to understand the larger units we have called "homilies."

The centuries-old number system in our Bibles inevitably presses the average reader into assuming that the material was composed in a "straight-line sequence" of "this after that." This pattern does occur and can be seen in Isaiah 55:6-7 below.

1. A. [55:6]Seek *the Lord* while he may be *found*,      SEEK THE LORD
   A. call upon him while he is *near*;      Call on Him

2. B. [7]let the wicked forsake his *way*,      HIS WAYS
   B. and the unrighteous man his *thoughts*;      His Thoughts

3. C. let him *return* to the *Lord*, that he may have *mercy* on him,      TO LORD—MERCY
   C. and to our *God*, for he will abundantly *pardon*.      To God—Pardon

**Figure 0.1. Straight-line parallelism (Is 55:6-7)**

The key words on the right attempt to summarize and highlight the ideas that repeat. The indentations on the page are simply a visual device to help the reader's eye catch the repetitions and inversions in their various patterns.[16]

---

[15]Ibid., p. 58.
[16]Cf. K. E. Bailey, "Methodology (2): Four Types of Literary Structures in the New Testament," *Poet and Peasant, A Literary Cultural Approach to the Parables in Luke* (Grand Rapids: Eerdmans, 1976), pp. 44-75. One rhetorical form that is common in 1 Cor, which is not described in the above essay, I have chosen to call "the encased parable." (The word *parable* is used here in the Hebrew sense of <u>*mashal*</u>, which includes the simile, the metaphor and the

Figure 0.1 above presents a set of three parallelisms. In each, an idea is stated and then repeated. The three pairs move in a *straight-line sequence*. Granted, there is an inversion of ideas as well. Summarized, the six lines do indeed say:

- A. Seek/call upon the Lord
  - B. Forsake wicked ways/thoughts
- A. Return to the Lord/God

That is, the final pair of lines picks up ideas from the first pair and repeats them. But there is also progression. The last two lines in the series of six announce *the result* of the seeking and calling. Those who "seek, call and return" will receive *mercy and pardon*. Thus we have a "counterpoint" in these six lines. Indeed the pairs have an A-B-A structure as noted. At the same time they exhibit an A-B-C movement which seems to dominate. The climax comes at the end with the promise of *mercy* and *pardon*. In these six lines, the prophet is the speaker.

This passage in Isaiah continues with what has historically been called "chiasm" or "inverted parallelism." More recently this second rhetorical style has been labeled "ring composition." In this case God is the speaker. The text reads:

4. A. [8]For *my thoughts* are not *your thoughts*,　　　　THOUGHTS
    - B. neither are *your ways my ways*, says the Lord.　　Ways
      - C. [9]For as the *heavens* are higher than the *earth*　　Parable
    - B. so are *my ways* higher than *your ways*　　Ways
- A. and *my thoughts* than *your thoughts*.　　　　THOUGHTS

---

**Figure 0.2. Inverted parallelism (Is 55:8-9)**

The center of figure 0.1 (noted above) focuses on "ways" and "thoughts" *of the wicked*. Here in figure 0.2 those twin ideas of "ways" and "thoughts" are repeated, only this time they are the "ways" and "thoughts" *of the Lord*. The repetition and movement of the words "ways" and "thoughts" tie the two stanzas (cameos) together. Also, figure 0.2 uses "ring composition." The five lines interrelate using an A-B-C-B-A pattern. *Thoughts* and *Ways* form two outer "envelopes" and in the center the prophet places a "parable" in the form of a concrete image of *the heavens and the earth*. The metaphors of "the heavens and the earth" become an "an encased parable."

---

parable.) This "encased parable" style is where a parable is encased in the middle of two or more matching blocks of material that are informed/illustrated/communicated/clarified by the parable.

However, this second set of lines creates a theological problem. In figure 0.1 the prophet tells the reader to *seek the Lord*. Now in figure 0.2 the reader discovers that *God is not available*. God is in the heavens with his *thoughts* and *ways*, and the reader/listener is trapped on the earth with the *ways* and *thoughts* of the *wicked*. What is the solution to this dilemma? The third rhetorical section (cameo) comes to the rescue.

| | | |
|---|---|---|
| 5. a.[10]For as the *rain* and the *snow* come down from *heaven*, | THE RAIN | |
|     b.  and *return not* thither but *water the earth*, | Not Return | |
|         c.  making it bring forth and sprout, | Result | |
|            giving *seed to the sower* and *bread to the eater*, | | |
| | | |
| 6. a.[11]so shall *my word* be that goes forth from my mouth; | MY WORD | |
|     b.  it shall *not return* to me *empty*, | Not Return | |
|         c.  but it shall *accomplish* that which I purpose, | Result | |
|            and *prosper* in the thing for which I sent it. | | |

**Figure 0.3. Step parallelism (Is 55:10-11)**

The ordering of the above eight lines I have called "step parallelism." The ideas are presented in a series of matching steps. Rain comes down—it doesn't return—here are the results. Like the rain, God's word comes down—it does not return—it also produces results. We are obliged to ask: What results? The answer is clear; the assumed results are the "mercy" and "pardon" promised at the end of the first section of this prophetic homily. The crisis created by the impassable distance between the believer and God (cameo 4) is bridged by the coming down of the Word of God (cameo 6) to deliver the promised mercy and pardon. (I can hear Christmas bells ringing in the background.)

From this third cameo of the homily it is obvious that Isaiah has again taken the center of one stanza (figure 0.2) and used it as a building block for the following stanza (figure 0.3). In figure 0.2 "the heavens" and "the earth" form the metaphorical climax in the center of the five lines. Here in figure 0.3 Isaiah starts with these two concrete images and creates a mini-parable with moving parts. The rain comes down from the *heavens* and falls upon the *earth*. Like the Word of God, it does not return but accomplishes its purpose. These comparisons are put together with "step parallelism."

These deceptively simple eleven lines of text form a very sophisticated piece of literature that skillfully uses three different ways of presenting parallels to the reader/listener (straight-line parallelism, inverted parallelism and step parallelism). These literary tools were already available and in use more than 500 years before the time of Paul.

But moving even further back in history, Isaiah of Jerusalem penned the following rhetorical masterpiece about 701 B.C.

28:14Therefore *hear the word of the Lord*, you scoffers, who *rule* this people *in Jerusalem!*

15Because you have said,

1. a. "We have made a *covenant with death*,
 b. and *with Sheol we have an agreement*;   COVENANT WITH
 c. when the *overwhelming scourge passes through* Death, Sheol—affirmed!
 d. it will *not come to us;*      Scourge avoided (?)

2.  a. for we have made *lies* our *refuge*,   REFUGE
  b. and in *falsehood* we have *taken shelter*"; Shelter

   16therefore thus says the Lord God,
3.   "Behold, I am laying in *Zion* for a *foundation* BUILDING
  a *stone*, a *tested stone*,     Material
  a *precious cornerstone*, a sure *foundation:*

4.    'He who *believes* (in it—LXX)  BELIEVER
   will *not be shaken.*'     Not shaken

5.    17And I will make *justice the line*,  BUILDING
   and *righteousness* the *plummet;*  Tools

6.   a. and *hail* will *sweep away the refuge of lies*, REFUGE
  b. and *waters* will *overwhelm the shelter.*" Shelter

7. a. 18Then *your covenant with death* will be *annulled*,
 b. and your *agreement with Sheol* will *not stand;* COVENANT WITH
 c. when the *overwhelming scourge passes through* Death, Sheol—canceled!
 d. you will be *beaten down by it.*17   Scourge beats down

**Figure 0.4. Isaiah's parable of the two buildings (Is 28:14-18)**

In this prophetic homily Isaiah is criticizing the government of Judea in Jerusalem for its covenant with Egypt that he calls "a covenant with death."

Initially we note that the entire passage makes sense when read as a "straight-line sequence" of parallelisms. But there is also a "counterpoint" at

17With one change, N. W. Lund observed this same structure. See N. W. Lund, *Chiasmus in the New Testament* (Peabody, Mass.: Hendrickson, 1992, c. 1942), p. 45. I discovered Lund's analysis some years after my own study of the passage.

work. The material falls into seven "cameos" that use "ring composition." Furthermore, cameo 1 is composed of four lines that are precisely reversed by the four lines of cameo 7 using "step parallelism." Working with two line cameos, cameo 2 is contradicted by cameo 6, again using step parallelism. In short, the homily makes sense as a *straight-line sequence*. As a whole it exhibits *inverted parallelism*, and in two cases the various cameos relate to each other using *step parallelism*.

Moving to the center, the prophetic homily is so well constructed that if cameos 3-5 were missing the reader would not notice their absence. The affirmations in cameos 1 and 2 are neatly contradicted in cameos 6 and 7. But the message of "doom and gloom" is not the entire prophetic message. All is not lost. The climax of the homily is the future hope that is expressed in the center. Cameo 3 describes the building material that God will provide and cameo 5 identifies the tools needed for the new foundation stone to be placed "in Zion." Those tools are *justice* and *righteousness*. This is a rare case of the use of two metaphors (line and plummet) that are identified at once in the text itself. The climax appears in the very center in the form of a motto to be inscribed on the new foundation stone. That motto will read:

He who believes
Will not be shaken.[18]

The first line of this motto raises the question: Believe in what? What precisely is the reader/listener expected to believe? The answer to this question appears in the first line of cameo 1 where the word "covenant" appears. Indeed, the covenant mentioned is "a covenant with death" (read: Egyptians). But the reader knows that Israel has *another covenant*—with God, and if they will return to that covenant and trust in the one who made it (rather than trusting in the Egyptians) all will yet be well.

The second line of this climactic center assures the one who "believes" (in the covenant) "will not be shaken." This second line is illuminated by the last line in cameo 7 where those who are trusting in the "covenant of death" will "be beaten down by it." That is, the rhetorical center of the homily relates on the deepest level to the beginning and to the end. This is a common feature of "ring composition."

The use of seven inverted cameos (the perfect number) with a climax in the

---

[18]I am concurring here with the translation offered by Frederick Moriarty, "Isaiah 1-39," in *The Jerome Biblical Commentary*, vol. I (Englewood Cliffs, N.J.: Prentice-Hall, 1968), p. 278.

center is so common it deserves a name. I have chosen to call it "the prophetic rhetorical template," and I have found seventeen of these prophetic rhetorical templates in the Gospel of Mark alone. Psalm 23 uses this same form and Paul employs it many times in 1 Corinthians. As seen here in Isaiah 28:14-20 both "step parallelism" and "inverted parallelism" appear in a single passage and are woven together with great skill.

My own rhetorical analysis of Isaiah 40–66 has uncovered extensive use of these forms of parallelism. They form the "backbone" of many "prophetic homilies."[19] A few more examples from Isaiah (and before his time) may be helpful to illuminate the literary tools available to Paul in his own Jewish heritage. Psalm 23, mentioned above, is structured as follows:

| | | |
|---|---|---|
| 1. [23:1]The *Lord* is my *shepherd*,<br>I shall *not want*; | LORD—SHEPHERD<br>No Wants | |
| 2. [2]he makes me lie down<br>in *green pastures*.<br>He leads me beside *still waters*; | FOOD &<br>Drink (animals) | |
| 3. [3]He *brings me back*/he causes me to *repent*.<br>He leads me in *paths of righteousness*<br>for his name's sake. | RESCUE &<br>Security | |
| 4. [4]Even though I walk through<br>the valley of the shadow of death<br>I fear *no evil*,<br>for thou art with me. | DEATH<br>Sin | |
| 5. Thy *rod*<br>and thy *staff*<br>they *comfort* me. | SECURITY &<br>Comfort | |
| 6. [5]Thou preparest a *table* before me<br>in the presence of my enemies.<br>Thou anointest my head with oil,<br>my *cup* overflows. | FOOD &<br>Drink (people) | |
| 7. [6]Surely *goodness* and *mercy*<br>shall follow me all the days of my life;<br>and I will dwell in the *house* of the *Lord*<br>for the length of the days.[20] | GOODNESS AND MERCY<br>LORD—House | |

**Figure 0.5. Prophetic rhetorical template (Ps 23)**

---

[19]See www.shenango.org/Bailey/Isaiah.htm.
[20]This final line is my own literal translation of the Hebrew. This translation dominates the Arabic versions.

This psalm uses the "prophetic rhetorical template" with its seven inverted stanzas. The "Lord" is mentioned by name only in cameos 1 and 7. In cameo 1 the psalmist refers to his wants. Security, food, drink and freedom from fear are all discussed, but his deepest wants are for the "goodness and mercy" of God that are mentioned in cameo 7. Food and drink for animals (cameo 2) are parallel to food and drink for people (cameo 6). Two matching cameos on security appear in cameos 3 and 5. The climax is (as usual) in the center where the psalmist declares his freedom from both death and sin (evil). The beginning (cameo 1) and the end (cameo 7) are related to the center (cameo 4) in that only in these three sections does the *first person* appear. The third person (he) appears in cameos 2 and 3 while the second person (thou) occurs in cameos 5 and 6. If the ascription to David is historical, this psalm demonstrates that the prophetic rhetorical template style was at least a thousand years old by the time of Paul.

Two shorter rhetorical pieces of interest are recorded in the famous suffering servant songs that appear in Isaiah. The first of these is found in the second of these songs (Is 49:5-6) and is as follows.

1. [49:5]And now the Lord says,
   who formed me from the womb to be his servant,
   GOD SAYS: His Servant

2. to bring Jacob back to him,
   and that Israel might be gathered to him,
   JACOB—RETURN Israel—Gathered

3. for I am honored in the eyes of the Lord,
   and my God has become my strength -
   SERVANT HONORED Made Strong

4. [6]he says: "It is too light a thing,
   that you should be my servant
   HE SAYS: TOO LIGHT My Servant

5. to raise up the tribes of Jacob
   and to restore the preserved of Israel;
   JACOB—RAISED Israel—Preserved

6. I will give you as a light to the nations,
   that my salvation may reach to the end of the earth."
   TO NATIONS Salvation to All.

Figure 0.6. Step parallelism (Is 49:5-6)

Here Isaiah uses "step parallelism" as a framework for his ideas. The special servant of God opens the passage with a speech. He, the servant, is aware of his task. He knows (cameo 1) why he was formed in the womb. His calling (cameo 2) was to bring "Jacob back to him [God]" and to "gather Israel to him

[God]." The text does not say that the servant's task is to bring Jacob and Israel back *to Jerusalem!* Rather he is to lead Jacob and Israel back *to God.* In cameos 1-3 (above) the servant accepts this destiny. It is also clear that the servant is not the community. Rather, the servant is an individual whose task is to *restore* Israel to God.

The three matching cameos (4-6) then affirm that the above amazing assignment is *not enough* for this particular servant. His mandate reaches far beyond the confines of Jacob and Israel. Indeed, that task, although valid, is "too light" for this extraordinary servant. His larger mandate is to be "a light to the nations," the *goyim* (who have oppressed Israel). The final vision is of a salvation that reaches "to the end of the earth." This extraordinary message, rare in the Hebrew Scriptures, is presented in "step parallelism" and the rhetoric highlights and clarifies the message.

A second brief prophetic homily appears in Isaiah 53:3-4 and is as follows:

1. [53:4] He was despised     DESPISED
   and rejected by others;     By Others

2.     a man of sorrows,     ACQUAINTED WITH
   and acquainted with grief;     Sorrow/Grief

3.       and as one from whom others hide their faces     PARABLE OF
   he was despised, and we esteemed him not.     A Person Despised

4.     [4]Surely he has borne our griefs     HAS BORNE OUR
   and carried our sorrows;     Grief/Sorrow

5. Yet we esteemed him stricken,     ESTEEMED NOT
   smitten by God, and afflicted.     Smitten by God

**Figure 0.7. Isaiah 53:3-4**

The ring composition of the text is obvious (note the indentations formatted above). As noted in Isaiah 55:8-9 so here this brief rhetorical homily has a simile in the center. This is another example of an "encased parable."

The point of special emphasis in the center of ring composition is often filled with one of three types of sayings. These are:

1. A nature miracle
2. A simile/parable
3. A Scripture quotation (or a reference to an earlier sacred tradition)

In 1 Corinthians, Paul used the second and third of this series. Here in Isaiah 55:3-4, as is common, the center is related to the outside. When the beginning, the center and the end are compared the following is evident.

> Beginning: Others despise the servant
> Center: We despise the servant
> End: (We thought that) God despises the servant

At the end the people "esteemed him smitten by God." That is, the people thought God was punishing him. But the text is careful to leave that possibility as a conjecture in the minds of the people. Isaiah wanted his readers to face their personal responsibility for rejecting the servant. The issue was not "others" or "(perhaps) God" but rather "*we*" despised the servant even though he bore our griefs and carried our sorrows. Thus "we despise the servant" appears in the center.

There is also a progression between cameos 2 and 4. In cameo 2 the servant endures *sorrows* and *griefs*, while in cameo 4 that same servant endures *sorrows* and *grief—for us*. This illustrates a further feature of "ring composition." The author often presents his/her case in a series of stanzas. That series comes to a climax in the center. Just past the center, where the series begins to repeat backwards, there is often a *point of emphasis* or a *point of turning*. Even so, in this figure, the servant is despised also by us (3) and at the point of turning (4) we find that in spite of our having joined those who despise him, he yet bears our griefs and carries our sorrows. Awareness of these rhetorical features is an important aid to interpretation.

A number of times Paul composes a homily using what I have called "the high jump format." This can be simply described as "ring composition with an introduction." It can also be seen to have four distinct parts. These are like a "high jump." The high jumper starts with a *short sprint*. Then comes the *ascent*, the *crossing of the bar* and the *descent* on the far side. The climax of the jump is the crossing of the bar. In like manner, a biblical homily is at times composed of (1) an introduction (the sprint) followed by (2) a series of ideas (the jump) that come (3) to a climax (the crossing of the bar) and conclude (4) with a presentation in reverse order of the original series of ideas (the descent to the ground). Paul uses this style often. It also appears in Isaiah. A clear case of this "high jump format" appears in Isaiah 43:25—44:5. The text reads:

1. [43:25]I, I am He who blots out your transgressions
   for my own sake,                                  MERCY
   and I will not remember your sins.

2. [26]Put me in remembrance, let us argue together;
   set forth your case, that you may be proved right.
   [27]Your first father sinned,
   and your mediators transgressed against me.       JUDGMENT
   [29]Therefore I profaned the princes of the sanctuary,
   I delivered Jacob to utter destruction
   and Israel to reviling.

3. [44:1]But now hear, O *Jacob* my servant,          JACOB MY SERVANT
   *Israel* whom I have chosen!                       Israel
   [2]Thus says the Lord who made you                 (I choose you)
   who formed you from the womb and will help you:
   Fear not, O *Jacob* my servant,
   *Jeshu'run*[21] whom I have chosen.

4. [3]For I will pour water on the thirsty land,       PARABLES OF
   and streams on the dry ground;                     Water/Streams

5. I will pour my Spirit upon your descendants,        MY SPIRIT
   and my blessing on your offspring.                  My Blessing

6. [4]They shall spring up like grass amid waters,     PARABLES OF
   like willows by flowing streams.                    Water/Streams

7. [5]This one will say, "I am the Lord's,"            JACOB
   another will call himself by the name of *Jacob*,  ISRAEL
   and another will write on his hand, "The Lord's,"  (You choose me)
   and surname himself by the name of *Israel*.[22]

**Figure 0.8. Judgment/mercy on Jacob/Israel (Is 43:25–44:5)**

This text shows that when Paul uses this "high jump format" he has models in his Jewish heritage.

Isaiah 56:1-8 is our final example and it appears in figure 0.9.

---

[21]A poetic reference to Israel that occurs only here and in Deut 32:15; 33:5; 33:26.
[22]The Dead Sea Isaiah Scroll has a major break between Is 44:5 and 44:6 which unites Is 44:1-5 with what comes before it rather than what follows. See John C. Trever (photographer), *Scrolls from Qumran Cave I: The Great Isaiah Scroll, The Order of the Community, The Pesher to Habakkuk* (Jerusalem: The Albright Institute and the Shrine of the Book, 1972), pp. 88-89.

1. [56:1]Thus says the Lord:

   "*Keep justice*,

    and do *righteousness*,                   THE BELIEVER'S PIETY

       for soon *my salvation* will come,       God

       and *my deliverance* be revealed.        Saves

  [2]*Blessed is the man* who does this,      THE BELIEVER'S PIETY

    and the *son of man* who *holds it fast*,

2. who keeps the Sabbath, not profaning it,     THE SABBATH

  and keeps his hand from doing any evil."

                                  THE FOREIGNER

3.     [3]Let not the *foreigner* who has joined himself to the Lord say,

      "The Lord will surely separate me from his people";

4.     and let not the *eunuch* say,          THE EUNUCH

      "Behold, I am a dry tree."         (no children)

5.      [4]For thus says the Lord:         FAITHFUL TO:

      "To the eunuchs who *keep my Sabbaths*,   My Sabbaths

      who *choose* the things that *please me*    My Covenant

      and *hold fast my covenant*,         GOD GIVES

      [5]*I will give* in *my house* and within my walls   Monument/Name

      a *monument and a name*.

6.     *Better* than *sons and daughters;*

    I will give them an *everlasting name*     (TO THE EUNUCH)

    which shall *not be cut off*.           Better than children

7.     [6]And the *foreigners* who join themselves to the Lord,

    to minister to him, to love the name of the Lord,

    and to be his servants,            THE FOREIGNER

8. every one who keeps the *Sabbath*, and does not profane it,

  and holds fast to my covenant—        THE SABBATH

9. [7]these *I will bring* to my holy mountain,    GOD SAVES

  and *make them joyful* in my house of prayer;

    *their* burnt *offerings* and their *sacrifices*   The Believer's

    will be *accepted on my altar*;         Piety

    for my house shall be called *a house of prayer*

    for *all peoples*."

  [8]Thus says the *Lord God*,

  who *gathers the outcasts of Israel*,      GOD SAVES

  "*I will gather yet others* to him        Outcasts and Others

  *besides those already gathered*."

---

**Figure 0.9. Isaiah 56:1-8**

This remarkable prophetic homily exhibits a sophisticated use of the rhetorical devices noted above. Initially we observe that the first cameo (1) and the last cameo (9) form an outer envelope within which is placed a seven-cameo prophetic rhetorical template. An interest in the sabbath appears at the beginning (2), in the middle (5) and at the end (8) of these seven cameos. These language markers create a balanced whole out of the seven cameos. Its outline is as follows:

> *Sabbath*
>     Foreigner
>         Eunuch
>             *Sabbath,* covenant faithfulness
>             & its rewards
>         (Eunuch)
>     Foreigner
> *Sabbath*

---

**Figure 0.10. Summary of Isaiah 56:1-8**

The parallels are clear and strong. They come to a climax in the center with its reference to holding fast to the *sabbath* and to the covenant. But then, two carefully balanced (extended) cameos are added to the beginning and the end of this prophetic rhetorical template. When seen side by side, they appear as follows:

Thus says the Lord:
1. [56:1]"*Keep justice,*
    and do *righteousness,*                                      THE BELIEVER'S PIETY
        for soon *my salvation* will come,                          God
        and *my deliverance* be revealed.                           Saves
    [2]*Blessed is the man* who does this,                       THE BELIEVER'S PIETY
    and the *son of man* who *holds it fast,*

    ----------------------------------------

9.    [7]these *I will bring* to my holy mountain,              GOD SAVES
    and *make them joyful* in my house of prayer;
        *their* burnt *offerings* and their *sacrifices*          The Believer's
        will be *accepted on my altar*;                            Piety
    for my house shall be called *a house of prayer*
    for *all peoples.*
    [8]Thus says the *Lord God,*                                GOD SAVES
    who *gathers the outcasts of Israel,*                        Outcasts and Others
    *I will gather yet others* to him
    *besides those already gathered.*"

---

**Figure 0.11. Isaiah 56:1-2 and 7-8**

The organization of the material in cameo 1 is reversed in cameo 9. This can be traced as follows:

| *The first of these presents* | *The second sets forth* |
|---|---|
| 1. The Believer's Piety | 9. God Saves |
|     God Saves |     The Believer's Piety |
|     The Believer's Piety |     God Saves |

Obviously in cameo 9 Isaiah has reversed the order of his presentation of the two themes of "God saves" and "the believers piety" that he set out in cameo 1. Furthermore, the nature of the "believer's piety" in cameo 1 has to do with social acts of "justice and righteousness" while the "believer's piety" in cameo 9 focuses on "offerings, sacrifices and prayers." The first discusses a concern for *justice* in the *extended community*. The second focuses on *acts of piety in worship* in the *gathered community*. Each is incomplete without the other. They form a pair. Isaiah assumes that at least the more astute of his readers can follow all of this, otherwise he would not have bothered to put together such a sophisticated homily.[23]

In a similar manner, in cameo 1 God's acts to save are non-specific references to "salvation and deliverance." Then in cameo 9 God acts in history by bringing the people to "my holy mountain" along with a pledge that after gathering "the outcasts of Israel" he will bring in *others* "besides those already gathered."

In passing we can also note that this particular creative expansion of the prophetic rhetorical template (to my knowledge) does not occur again in Isaiah 40–66.[24] This shows that "variations on a tune" were acceptable, and perhaps even anticipated. The various rhetorical building blocks could be used in different ways in the presenting of a message.

At the same time, as noted, Isaiah has a prophetic rhetorical template in the center of the homily. He then adds two balancing sections to the beginning and to the end. This creates a larger homily of three parts. This same literary style reappears with (with one variation) in 1 Corinthians 1:17–2:2. There in the hymn to the cross Paul also composes a center of seven cameos to which he adds three extra cameos to the beginning and three matching cameos to the end. Paul opens with an A-B-C format which he repeats (backwards) at the end. Isaiah, however, chooses an A-B-A pattern which he balances with a B-A-B as we have seen. Each author has seven cameos in the

---

[23]Not every listener catches Bach's counterpoint.
[24]For a full rhetorical analysis of Isaiah 40–66, see www.shenango.org/Bailey/Isaiah.htm.

center and three units of material at the opening and the closing of the homily. A great deal of artistic skill is involved in the composition of each homily. The two authors are offering variations on a single melody.[25]

This remarkable prophetic homily had a strong influence on the New Testament. It stands behind "the Jew first and also to the Greek" (Rom 1:16) in that "the foreigners" are singled out for special assurance of welcome (cameos 2 and 6) and God's house is designated as "a house of prayer for all peoples/nations." This latter text is quoted by Jesus in his dramatic act of "cleansing the Temple" (Mk 11:17). Furthermore, Jesus may have built his parable of the great banquet on this text (Lk 14:15-24).[26] In that parable, outcasts from within the community are gathered. The master then orders the servant to bring in others from *beyond the community*. All of this points to the influence this particular prophetic homily may have had on Jesus and Paul.

These short prophetic homilies offer a whiff of the rhetorical heritage that was a part of Paul's bloodstream. If indeed, like any learned rabbi, he had large portions of the sacred Hebrew writings memorized, would we not expect a strong influence from those sources to appear in his own writing, especially when he sat down to compose an important document for the entire church? But, as noted, this was not "simply the way Paul wrote." When Paul offers an aside, such as his comment on who baptized whom, his language appears to be straightforward prose (1:14-16). How then can we best unlock the treasures of this kind of rhetoric?

Traditionally we have often assumed a "this after that" straight-line sequence for most of 1 Corinthians. Some of the homilies in the epistle do indeed follow in that order. But when "ring composition" is used the average modern reader has a special problem. Sometimes the ring composition is short, as in the case of Luke 16:13 that reads:

| | | |
|---|---|---|
| 1. | No servant can serve *two masters;* | Two Masters |
| 2. | For either he will *hate* the one | Hate |
| 3. | And *love* the other | Love |
| 4. | Or be *devoted* to the one | Love |
| 5. | And *despise* the other | Hate |
| 6. | You cannot serve *God and Mammon.* | Two Masters |

**Figure 0.12. Luke 16:13**

[25]Paul also composes an extended homily made up of three parts (with a climax in the center) in 11:17-34a and in 13:1-13.
[26]K. E. Bailey, *Jesus Through Middle Eastern Eyes* (Downers Grove, Ill.: IVP Academic, 2008), pp. 318-19.

Clearly cameos 1 and 6 are a pair and the reader can easily remember the "two masters" of cameo 1 and mentally wait for their identification in cameo 6. When Jesus says "two masters" in cameo 1 he means "God and Mammon" mentioned in cameo 6. But what if the passage is a prophetic rhetorical template with seven cameos such as we noted in Isaiah 28:14-18? In this case cameo 1 is very carefully matched by cameo 7 but it is easy for the modern reader to miss the connection due to the distance between them on the page. What can be done to make this connection clear to modern readers?

To ease the making of these connections, I have opted to repeat the text and print the matching cameos side by side, starting from the outside and working toward the center. That is, if the homily under study has seven cameos (as in the case of the Is 28 passage) it seems right to examine the various pairs of cameos one at a time beginning from the outside [see figure 0.13].

1.  a. ²⁸:¹⁵We have made a *covenant with death*,
    b.    and *with Sheol we have an agreement*;        COVENANT WITH
    c.    when the *overwhelming scourge passes through*   Death, Sheol—affirmed!
    d.    It will *not come to us*;                      Scourge Avoided (?)

-------------------------------------------------------

7.  a.  ¹⁸Then *your covenant with death* will be *annulled*,
    b.    and your *agreement with Sheol* will *not stand*;   COVENANT WITH
    c.    when the *overwhelming scourge passes through*   Death, Sheol—Canceled!
    d.    you will be *beaten down by it*.                Scourge Beats Down

**Figure 0.13. Is 28:15, 18**

After reflecting on these two carefully matched cameos we would then turn to cameos 2 and 6. Finally, the three center cameos would be examined together.

If a modern English language text refers to do-re-mi-fa-so-la-ti-do, the reader is able to "hear the tune" as he/she reads the words. No one needs to tell us that the beginning and the end are the same note an octave apart. In like manner, an ancient, literate (and illiterate) Hebrew listening to or reading a text such as the Isaiah passage presented above would be able to "hear" the 1-2-3-4-3-2-1 and would naturally compare the two cameos numbered 1 on the outside and then the pair of cameos numbered 2 and so forth. Current estimates are that not more than 10 percent of the people in New Testament times could read. Learned Jews would be able to follow Paul's prophetic style "tunes" and explain them to non-Jewish believers. Furthermore, this is not the only aspect of 1 Corinthians in which Jewish believers would have needed to explain things to Greek believers.

In 1 Corinthians 10 Paul writes, "our fathers were all under the cloud, and all passed through the sea" (10:1). Paul does not explain what he is talking about. Unless they were "God fearers" worshiping with the Jews, Greeks would not be able to follow this kind of a discussion without help from Jewish Christians who knew the appropriate stories. We modern Christians may have the Old Testament stories in the backs of our minds, but not their literary "tunes." The longer the "tune" the more difficult it is for us to hear it.[27] By first presenting the entire homily and then examining it (one "envelope" at a time) it is my hope that the reader will be able follow Paul's argument with relative ease. The longest and most complex of all the homilies in the epistle appears near the beginning in 1:17–2:2. For that homily in particular I beg the readers' patience. In a lecture, armed with some study sheets and a few histrionics, I can make all of this easy for a Western audience to follow—I have been doing it for decades. Gold is available where you find it. Sometimes one must dig to mine it. I will do my best.

A further question remains: Why bother? This kind of analysis may be seen by some as "interesting" and "artistically intriguing" but is it significant for interpretation? To this important question we must turn briefly because if it is not, it can be ignored. For centuries the church has generally seen most of the texts examined in this study as having a straight-line "this after that" order.[28] What difference does it make if we observe Paul using the classical rhetoric of his Jewish past? A few comments on this important question may be helpful.[29]

1. If the author is presenting his/her case using an ABC-CBA structure, then half of what he/she has to say about (A) will appear at the beginning and the other half will appear at the end. The same is true of the first (B) and the last (B) which again form a pair. To miss this pairing of ideas is to miss an important part of the author's intent. The larger the ring composition, the harder it is for the modern mind to follow the parallels without some assistance.

---

[27]Sometimes the "tunes" are available to us and yet recognized only by the trained ear. Professional musicians have told me that the sonata-allegro form in classical music is composed of: Introduction + Exposition + Development + Recapitulation + Coda. This is a "musical ring composition" that follows the A + B + C + B + A structure. I cannot hear it without help.

[28]I hasten to add that some major voices in the study of 1 Corinthians have shown considerable interest in cases of extended parallelism. These include: Gordon Fee, *First Epistle*; Jerome Murphy-O'Connor, *1 Corinthians*; and N. T. Wright, *Resurrection*.

[29]This list is revised from Bailey, *Jesus Through Middle Eastern Eyes*, pp. 16-18.

2. Biblical "ring composition" usually places the climax in the center, not at the end. We saw cases of this "center climax" in the texts examined above. Our centuries-old "default" assumption is that the climax appears at the end of *any* discussion. If the author has placed his/her conclusion elsewhere, the reader should have a chance to observe and ponder that climax. In the case of ring composition, rhetorical analysis offers that opportunity.

3. Where a particular text begins and ends can often be determined with greater certainty when the rhetorical form is uncovered. Paul's hymn to the cross appears in 1:17–2:2. Our chapter numbers do not assist us in noting either the beginning or the end of this great hymn.[30] Particularly our chapter 2 division is in the wrong place. Paul's hymn opens with reference to the preaching of Christ crucified. Christ crucified is restated in the middle and again at the end.[31] The rhetorical style identifies the beginning and the end of this masterpiece and allows us to reflect on it as a whole. (Obviously the people who gave us the chapter numbers did not see the hymn with its threefold reference to preaching the cross.)

4. When the structure of a homily is identified, the smaller cameos maintain their integrity rather than becoming fragmented or absorbed into other verses.

5. Rhetorical analysis delivers the reader from the tyranny of the centuries-old number system. The text is allowed its own ordering of ideas. However useful they are for finding one's place, the numbers subtly dictate to the reader, "You *will* see these ideas or stories as a straight line sequence that follows the numbers!"

6. At times the rhetorical makeup of a particular homily is a key internal component to help choose between variant Greek readings of a text. External evidence related to which texts are the oldest and most reliable is very important. Internal evidence of the rhetorical style involved also needs consideration. We will observe one text in 1 Corinthians where the rhetoric of the passage is significant in selecting a reading (see below on 3:5).

7. Noting the parallels (straight-line, inverted or stepped) between cameos or within cameos often unlocks important meanings otherwise lost. In the Isaiah 28 passage noted above, the prophet presents the government's case in cameos 1-2 and then demolishes it line by line in cameos 6-7. We need to be able to observe him engaging in this dialogue and critique.

---

[30]The same is true for Isaiah 43:25–44:5 noted above.
[31]K. E. Bailey, "Recovering the Poetic Structure of I Corinthians i 17-ii 2: A Study in Text and Commentary," *Novum Testamentun* 17 (October 1975): 265-96.

8. Occasionally in 1 Corinthians there are carefully balanced sets of lines, to which some "footnotes" have been added. Three such "notes" appear in 1:17–2:2. These explanatory remarks can be spotted when the basic rhetorical structure is identified. Paul may be adding notes to homilies composed at some earlier time. Isaiah 47:1-7 also includes an extra "note."[32]

9. As noted, the rhetorical styles that appear can be traced to the writing prophets and beyond. The reappearance of these styles in 1 Corinthians makes clear that Paul was deeply embedded as a writer in his Jewish heritage.

10. When one observes the sophisticated, thoughtful and artistic precision of these rhetorically shaped passages Paul emerges as a skilled writer and indeed as a "poet" in the Jewish tradition. We have long noted *history, theology* and *ethics* in 1 Corinthians. "Art" has been seen in the great hymn to love in chapter 13. Some have admired the majesty of the final "ode to the resurrection" (chapter 15). Can we not also be moved and enlightened by the literary art that appears throughout the epistle?

11. The rhetoric of 1 Corinthians encourages the reader to rethink our understanding of the epistle as a whole. The various homilies here examined and their use in the creation of essays exhibits great care in composition.

Before we proceed, a few words of caution seem appropriate. Engaging in the rhetorical analysis of biblical texts is like playing the saxophone: it is easy to do poorly. In the name of "quality control" the following can be noted:

1. The goal of this work is to illuminate Paul's message. This is not "art for art's sake." You, gentle reader, will be the judge of any success or failure in this regard.

2. My chosen focus is on the *cameo* and the *homily*. In rhetorical analysis it is very easy to allow one's attention to shift to short phrases and individual words.[33] This can become a sort of "word game" that has its own fascination, but is minimally relevant to the sacred task of interpretation. It is like taking one of Churchill's great wartime speeches and diagramming each sentence. The exercise might be an engaging grammatical exercise but would probably distract rather than add to an understanding of what Churchill was trying to say to his listeners.

3. The ideas in one cameo that appear to repeat in another cameo must be the *major* ideas in the two cameos. If they are not, one must exercise great

[32]See Isaiah 47:1-7 in www.Shenango.org/Bailey/Isaiah.htm.
[33]The work of Niles Lund is often flawed in this regard. See Niles Lund, *Chiasmus in the New Testament* (Peabody, Mass.: Hendrickson, 1992, c. 1942).

caution in affirming that the two cameos are "parallel." Subtlety must be avoided.

4. We will examine various types of homilies in 1 Corinthians that Paul uses again and again. When the same style (in the work of a given author) appears repeatedly the interpreter is reassured of being on the right track. Rarities must be examined with special caution lest they be imaginary.

5. This kind of close work requires a knowledge of the original languages. The words and phrases in modern English translations are naturally arranged to provide smooth idiomatic English. To discover how Paul organized his phrases one must read the Greek text. Furthermore, occasionally the same Greek word ties two cameos together in the original text, but the translators have not used the same English word for both of them and thereby the connection is lost in English. The reverse is also true. An English word that appears in two cameos may have two Greek words behind it.

6. On rare occasions I have suggested that Paul has added a comment to his own text. This possibility introduces an option that can be abused easily. It is effortless to mark off one section as "original" and another section as "secondary." The result can fragment the text and lead nowhere. The possibility that Paul has added a "comment" to his own homily must be considered with caution.

7. The basic presupposition of this study is that Paul's *Hebrew literary heritage* profoundly influences Paul's rhetorical style. If that proves to be the case, that literary heritage becomes an important lens through which to examine 1 Corinthians.

The rhetorical analysis in this book suggests new approaches to well-known texts. The work here is offered with great appreciation for the extensive work of others and with openness to further refinement.

With the above prophetic heritage in mind, and with the chosen methodology in focus we turn to the text of 1 Corinthians with the hope of uncovering a fresh layer of meaning that is encoded in the homilies Paul composed for his readers in Corinth and for the church at large.

# Greeting and Prayer of Thanksgiving

PAUL'S LETTER OPENS WITH an identification of the senders (Paul and Sosthenes) and the receivers (the Corinthians, and all Christians). He then offers his introductory prayer. These two sections are tied together by their rhetorical form and by their theological content with its focus on God, Christ Jesus and the believing community. The text is displayed in figure 1.0(1).

### The Greeting (1:1-3)

1. ¹:¹Paul, called by the *will of God*
   to be an *apostle of Christ Jesus,*
   and our brother *Sosthenes,*

   GOD  (His Will)
   Christ Jesus
   Paul & Sosthenes

2. ²To the *church* of God which is at *Corinth,*
   to those *made holy* in *Christ Jesus,*
   to those *called out as saints*

   TO CORINTHIANS
   (Christ, you)

3. *together with all those who are called*
   by the *name of our Lord Jesus Christ,*
   in every meeting place *of them and of us.*

   TO ALL CHRISTIANS
   (Christ, they)

4. ³*Grace* to you and *peace*
   from *God our Father*
   and the *Lord Jesus Christ.*

   GRACE TO YOU
   From God our Father
   & Lord Jesus Christ

*The Prayer of Thanksgiving* (1:4-9)

5. [4]I give *thanks to God* always for you           GRACE TO YOU
   because of the *grace of God*                From God
   which was *given to you* in Christ Jesus,     In Christ

6.     [5]that in every way you were *enriched* in him
          in all *speech* and all *knowledge*
          [6]even as the *testimony to Christ* was *sustained* among you    CHRIST SUSTAINED
          [7]so you are *not lacking in any spiritual gift*,    Among You (now)

7.      as you wait for the revealing of *our Lord Jesus Christ*;
          [8]who will *sustain* you to the end,          LORD JESUS CHRIST
          guiltless in the day of *our Lord Jesus Christ*.    Will Sustain You (then)

8.     [9]*God is faithful*,                  GOD is faithful
       *by whom you were called*           Your Calling
       into the *fellowship* of his Son, *Jesus Christ our Lord*.   Christ Son/Lord

**Figure 1.0(1). 1 Corinthians 1:1-9**

## THE RHETORIC

In these opening verses references to the senders, the addressees, the greetings, the tradition, the initial thanksgiving prayer and the introduction to the entire epistle are woven tightly together into eight interlocking cameos. This particular rhetorical style with two sections (each composed using an A-B-B-A structure) appears in five other texts in this same letter.[1] Here, important themes run throughout the eight cameos.

## COMMENTARY

The simplest expression of the underlying structure of these eight cameos is demonstrated in figure 1.0(2).

Paul called by the *will of God*
     To the Corinthian saints
     To all those called by the name of Jesus Christ
*God is our Father*
- - - - - - - - - - - - - - - - - - - - - - - -
The *grace of God* to you
     Believers enriched in the present
     Believers sustained to the end
*God is faithful*

**Figure 1.0(2). The underlying structure of 1 Corinthians 1:1-9**

---

[1]See 3:5-9; 4:8-13; 4:17–5:6; 7:25-31; 15:51-58.

Initially it is clear that this passage says four things about the *nature* of God and these references appear at the beginning and at the end of each of the two halves of the passage. The list is as follows:

1. God has a will
4. God is our Father
5. God extends grace
8. God is faithful

These same eight cameos have eight things to say about *Jesus*. In order these are:

1. Christ Jesus calls *apostles*
2. Christ Jesus *makes the Corinthians holy*
3. All *believers are called by the name* of our Lord Jesus Christ
4. The Lord Jesus Christ *extends grace and peace*
5. *Grace* to them in Christ Jesus is a *source of thanksgiving*
6. *A testimony to/from Christ that was available to the Church*
7. Our Lord Jesus Christ is able to *sustain them guiltless*
8. Jesus Christ our Lord is *the Son (of God)* and he *creates a special fellowship*

Amazingly there are also eight things said about the believing community. Following the order of the text these are:

1. The Church has apostles and brothers/sisters
2. The Corinthians are "made holy" and called to be "saints"
3. All believers are called by the name of "our Lord Jesus Christ"
4. They are recipients of grace and peace
5. The grace they received is a source of thanksgiving
6. They are enriched by speech, knowledge and all spiritual gifts
7. They will be sustained guiltless to the end
8. They are called into the fellowship of God's Son

Noting these three lists of weighty theological statements, there are aspects of each of the eight cameos that deserve comment. We will repeat the text for easy reference.

| | | |
|---|---|---|
| 1. | [1:1]Paul, called by the *will of God* | GOD |
| | to be an *apostle of Christ Jesus,* | CHRIST |
| | and our brother *Sosthenes,* | APOSTLES (senders) |

As he opens the epistle, Paul is already defending his apostleship. That defense comes to full flower in 9:1-18. Here he reminds his readers that he did not choose his calling as an apostle, but he was *called by the will of God* to this ministry.

It is impossible to prove that the Sosthenes mentioned in this text is, or is not the Sosthenes who initially opposed Paul in Corinth (Acts 18:12-17). But there are good reasons to suppose that the two may be the same man. In Acts 18:17 Sosthenes is identified as the head of the synagogue in Corinth. Under his leadership the synagogue initiated a case in the Roman courts against Paul before Gallio, a famous Roman judge. Gallio dismissed the case, publicly humiliating the Jewish community which then took out its frustrations and ensuing anger on Sosthenes by beating him in front of the court for having led them into this public debacle. What happened next?

We are not told what happened to Sosthenes after his beating. But it is natural to assume that the evening of the beating, Sosthenes and his family were trying to recover from the day by dressing Sosthenes' physical and psychic wounds. They were isolated, humiliated, wounded and frightened. The Jews had beaten him and the Roman authorities had watched the violence without intervening. No one could expect Paul's new converts to side with the man who tried to harm their leader and their cause. But is it not like Paul to have visited Sosthenes on that occasion to express sympathy for the abuse that Sosthenes had sustained? The irony of such a visit could not have been missed by anyone. The purpose of Sosthenes' action was to harm Paul. That plan failed, and the harm intended for Paul ricocheted back onto Sosthenes. Overcoming evil with good was a formative part of Paul's theological and ethical DNA (Rom 12:19-21). In this very epistle Paul writes, "When reviled, we bless; when persecuted, we endure" (4:12). Had Paul made such a visit, Sosthenes would have been deeply moved. Did such a visit take place, and did it lead Sosthenes, in time, to follow Jesus the crucified Messiah? We do not know, but we can entertain this outcome as a possibility.

If he is the same man, having served as the head of the synagogue in Corinth, Sosthenes naturally would have known a great deal about the Jewish-Christian members of the Corinthian church and could have provided great help to Paul in the writing of this letter. Regardless of his identity, Sosthenes was most certainly known to the Corinthians, otherwise Paul would not have mentioned him by name. The two of them undoubtedly discussed what to include and what to omit in this critical epistle.

At the same time, by including Sosthenes as a joint sender of the letter, he is saying,

I know that I am a newcomer to your city. Please understand that I am not sitting here in Ephesus in grand isolation from the real world of Corinth and its society, dreaming up criticisms of your theology and ethics. Sosthenes agrees with everything I have to say to you. Keep that in mind as you read. We are together sending you this letter.

Paul could "field test" his letter simply by reading it to Sosthenes. In any case, Paul offers Sosthenes a high compliment by attaching his name to this famous letter as a "joint author." It is a very nice touch.

After naming the senders, Paul identifies the recipients of this letter [see fig. 1.0(3)].

2. ²To the *church* of God which is at *Corinth*,
   to those *made holy* in *Christ Jesus*,
   to those *called out as saints*

   TO CORINTHIANS
   (Christ, you)

3. *together with all those who are called*
   by the *name of our Lord Jesus Christ*,
   in every meeting place *of them and of us.*

   TO ALL CHRISTIANS
   (Christ, they)

**Figure 1.0(3). The receivers of 1 Corinthians (1:2)**

As observed in the introduction, Paul routinely identifies the recipients of his letters. The book of Romans was addressed to "God's beloved at Rome" (Rom 1:7). Galatians mentions "the churches of Galatia" (Gal 1:2), and Philippians tells of "the saints in Christ Jesus who are at Philippi" (Phil 1:2). But here in 1 Corinthians Paul describes two types of readers, the Corinthians *and all Christians everywhere.* The Corinthians are identified as "Those who were made holy" and who were "called out as saints [i.e., holy ones]" (1:2). They were getting drunk at Holy Communion and shouting insults at each other. One of them was sleeping with his mother-in-law. The prophets (preachers) were all talking at once in their worship services and some of the women were chatting and not listening to anyone. They had split into factions, and some thought that polished language was more important than historical realities like the cross. Others denied the resurrection. Yet Paul called them "saints." Remarkable! Clearly, for Paul, "a saint" meant a person who had received the Holy Spirit and not a person who had reached some undefined stratospheric level of piety. The troublesome Corinthians *were saints!*

Second, as noted, Paul includes the entire church among his readers. He appears to be doing more than merely reminding the Corinthians that they belong to a larger fellowship, although that is surely part of his intent. Nor is he primarily affirming his authority over all the church, and thereby building his case for the authenticity of his apostleship. Rather, he stresses that he is indeed writing this letter for all Christians everywhere. This helps explain the extensive use of polished rhetoric, and the meticulous construction of the five essays before us. From Paul's own words we can be confident that Paul means this epistle as a "general letter." How so?

Initially we see that the word "called" (*epi-kaloumenois*) used here is a *passive*. The BAGD *Greek-English Lexicon* affirms that this passive word is used when "someone's name is called over someone to designate the latter as the property of the former."[2] Isaiah 43:7 reads, "everyone who is called by my name, whom I created for my glory." Jeremiah 7:11 states, "Has this house, which is called by my name, become a den of robbers in your eyes?" Such language declares that God's name is called upon the things that belong to God, be they objects like temples, or people. They are no longer their own—they belong to the God who calls his name upon them. Many English translations have turned the passive tense of the key verb (in this text) into an active tense and read "who call upon the name" as though the Christians were doing the "calling." This latter is possible, but it loses the weight of the affirmation that all those "sanctified in Christ Jesus" now belong to the Son of God. God in Christ called them "into the fellowship of his Son" (1:9) and they are thereby a part of his very body of Christ (12:12-27). Later in the epistle, using the language of the institution of slavery (6:19-20), Paul writes, "You are not your own; you were bought with a price." Paul's readers belonged to God. Surely Paul intends his readers to understand that they belong to God as affirmed both in 6:19-20 and here in the opening verses of the epistle. "All those on whom is called the name of our Lord Jesus Christ" means all Christians everywhere. Furthermore, even if we disregard the passive tense of the verb *epikaloumenois*, Paul affirms that he is writing this book for the Corinthians *along with all Christians in every place*. Realizing the full scope of Paul's intended readership is critical for how we understand much of what Paul has to say throughout the epistle.

The fourth cameo states:

4. [3]*Grace* to you and *peace*     GRACE TO YOU
    from *God our Father*        From God our Father
    and the *Lord Jesus Christ.*    & Lord Jesus Christ

---

[2]BAGD, p. 294. In 2 Cor 1:22 Paul writes, "he has put his seal upon us and given us his Spirit in our hearts as a guarantee." Those who bear the seal of God belong to God.

"Peace to you" was a standard Jewish greeting. Greeks would expect "*chairein*" (Hail!), which sounds much like Paul's greeting of "*charis*" (grace).[3] By writing "Grace to you and peace," Paul is identifying with both "Jew and Greek." Paul desires intensely to unite Jewish and Gentile believers into one body and one temple and this yearning appears a number of times throughout the epistle. The crosscultural Greek/Jewish greeting encourages that journey of reconciliation. It also brings together two of the greatest words in Paul's theological vocabulary. Grace (Hebrew: *khesed*) has to do with covenant faithfulness that expresses itself in mighty acts in history to save. Peace (Hebrew: *shalom*) refers to a comprehensive reconciling peace that flows from the grace of God. It is through grace that deep peace is possible. God is "our Father" and the above mentioned grace and peace flow to us from the Father through the Lord Jesus Christ. After this introduction, Paul turns to his opening prayer of thanksgiving.

Paul's letters usually open with a thanksgiving prayer. To the Corinthians Paul writes:

5.  [4] I give *thanks to God* always for you          GRACE TO YOU
        because of the *grace of God*                         From God
        which was *given to you* in Christ Jesus,      In Christ

This is Paul at his diplomatic best. He cannot thank God for their "faith" (Rom 1:8), or for their "partnership in the Gospel" (Phil 1:5), or for their "faith . . . and . . . love" (Col 1:4), or for their "faith, . . . love . . . and hope" (1 Thess 1:3). So he offers thanks for *the grace given to them*. This is like a father addressing a "difficult child" at dinner and saying to him, "Johnny, every night I am deeply grateful to your mother who bathes you and dresses you in clean clothes before supper." This is not a compliment to Johnny. The Corinthians had received a great deal of grace. Their responses to that grace were deeply flawed. The most kindly thing Paul can honestly say to them is to remind them of the grace they have freely received. They have no grounds for boasting because all their spiritual heritage was a gift.

Cameos 6 and 7 are a carefully balanced pair [see fig. 1.0(4)].

---

[3] See Garland, *I Corinthians*, pp. 29-30; Thiselton, *First Epistle*, pp. 82-84.

6.  [5]that in every way you were *enriched* in him
     in all *speech* and all *knowledge*                    CHRIST SUSTAINED
     [6]as the *testimony of Christ* was *sustained* among you    Among You (past & present)
     [7]so you are *not lacking in any spiritual gift*,

7.  as you wait for the revealing of *our Lord Jesus Christ*;
     [8]who will *sustain* you to the end,                   LORD JESUS CHRIST
     guiltless in the day of *our Lord Jesus Christ*.        Will Sustain You (present & future)

---

**Figure 1.0(4). Cameos 6-7 (1 Cor 1:5-8)**

The Corinthians were proud of their "speech" (tongues), "knowledge" and "spiritual gifts" in general. Actually, they were quarreling over these matters. Paul does not deny their gifts or the importance of them. He will discuss this subject in detail in chapters 12 and 14.

The testimony they have heard is "of Christ" (NRSV) or it is testimony "to Christ" (RSV). The first means that they have heard some of the teachings of Jesus. The second would only indicate that they have been told about him. Both options are faithful to the original text. What matters for Paul's larger argument is that with these words he is invoking *the tradition* which they had received. He will do this at the opening of each of the five essays. Everything Paul says to them is built on the foundation of a *tradition which they had heard and received.*

Cameo 6 discusses the present while cameo 7 holds up the mirror of eternity. The key word *bebainoo* occurs in each of these stanzas. The RSV translates "confirmed" for the first and uses "sustained" for the second. The NRSV chooses "strengthened" for both texts which allows the English reader to more easily observe the connection between the two. The point is that the confirming/sustaining/strengthening that has already taken place in the present will continue until the Day of Judgment. Regardless of all the ethical and theological failings that Paul found in the church in Corinth, he was confident that the Corinthians would stand "guiltless in the day of our Lord Jesus Christ." O that the antagonists in church fights in every age might maintain this amazing confidence.

The final cameo in these opening verses (8) makes a concluding statement about the nature of God.

8.  [9]*God is faithful,*                              GOD is faithful
     *by whom you were called*                        Your calling
     into the *fellowship* of his Son, *Jesus Christ our Lord.*    Christ Son/Lord

The Corinthians may not be faithful—but God is! Furthermore, it is instructive to note that the word "to call" (*kaleo*) occurs three times in the opening lines and reappears here in cameo 8. Paul, Sosthenes, the Corinthians and all Christians everywhere were *called* into "the Church of God" (cameos 1-2) and into "the fellowship of his Son" (cameo 8).

Finally, the rare phrase "our Lord Jesus Christ" appears three times in this introduction along with the similar phrase "Jesus Christ our Lord" shown here. It ties the Corinthians to all believers in every place. Paul uses it once more in the following verse as he introduces the problem of their divisions. But then this four-word phrase disappears until the very end of the fifth essay where in 15:57 Paul affirms victory over death through "our Lord Jesus Christ." In spite of denials, divisions, ethical failings and theological lapses, Jesus is still "our Lord Jesus Christ." Paul uses this phrase as a golden thread at the beginning and at the end of the epistle, binding the letter together.

This densely packed introduction and thanksgiving is like a diamond that sheds light in many directions. To summarize it is to recite the full text. Having said very important things about God, Jesus and the church, Paul is ready to launch into the first essay, which focuses on *unity, the cross and the Spirit.*

# The Cross and Christian Unity

## 1 CORINTHIANS 1:10–4:16

*αυτοις δε κλητοις*
*Ἰουδαιοις τε και Ελλησιν*
*Χριστον θεου δυναμιν και θεου σοφιαν*
(1:24)

# The Problem

*Divisions, Baptism and the Cross*

1 CORINTHIANS 1:10-16

THIS FIRST ESSAY IS COMPOSED of four sections that are as follows:

*1.1. The Problem: Divisions, Baptism and the Cross (1:10-16)*
1.2.   The Wisdom and Power of God: The Cross (1:17–2:2)
1.3.   The Wisdom of God: Revealed Through the Spirit (2:3-16)
1.4. Christian Unity: Paul, Apollos and Cephas as One (3:1–4:16)

Having invoked *the tradition* in his introduction, Paul is ready to present the first problem he wants to discuss with them, which has to do with serious divisions in the church (note italics above). After naming the problem (1.1) he sets to work at once building a theological base out of which a solution to that problem can be found (1.2 and 1.3). He then returns to the problem in the light of that theology (1.4). The problem (1.1) is set out in figure 1.1(1).

**THE RHETORIC**
Using ring composition, Paul opens with three positive cameos that are then matched (in reverse order) with three negatives. At the end of the homily he adds an aside.

The center is a point of special emphasis. He urges them to unite, not fight.

1.  <sup>1:10</sup>I appeal to you, brethren,                    JESUS IS OUR LORD
        *by the name of our Lord Jesus Christ,*          Name—of Jesus

2.          that all of you *agree*                              DIVISIONS
            and that there be *no divisions* among you,

3.              but that you be *united* in the *same mind*
                and of the *same judgment.*                      MUST UNITE

4.          <sup>11</sup>For it has been reported to me, my brethren,
                by Chloe's people, that there is *quarreling* among you.  NOT FIGHT

5.      <sup>12</sup>What I mean is that each one of you says,
            "I am of Paul," or " I am of Apollos," or "I am of Cephas,"
            or "I am of Christ." <sup>13</sup>Is Christ divided?          DIVISIONS

6.  Was *Paul crucified* for you?                      JESUS DIED FOR YOU
    Or were you baptized in the name of Paul?    Name—of Paul?

----------------------------------------------------------------------------------

(aside 1:14-16)

<sup>14</sup>I am thankful that I baptized none of you except Crispus and Gaius; <sup>15</sup>lest any one should say that you were baptized in my name. <sup>16</sup>I did baptize also the household of Stephanas. Beyond that, I do not know whether I baptized anyone else.

**Figure 1.1(1). Divisions in the church: Paul, Apollos and Cephas as competitors (1 Cor 1:10-16)**

## COMMENTARY

Cameo 1 begins with "I appeal to you" (*parakaleo*). This verb is used to describe the father in the parable of the prodigal son as he goes out to reconcile his older son standing defiantly in the courtyard of the family home (Lk 15:28). It is a strong word that indicates a deep desire for reconciliation. Paul "entreats them" "in the name of our Lord Jesus Christ." They were baptized using this latter phrase or something close to it. Also, as noted, the full phrase "our Lord Jesus Christ" occurs four times at the beginning of chapter 1 and is not heard again until the conclusion of chapter 15. Its repetition is a strong call for unity.

The declaration "I appeal to you—in the name . . ." is Paul's strongest theological appeal. In cameo 2 he requests them to "say the same thing," that is, to agree, with no divisions (literally *skhisma* [schism: no splits]). Rather, he calls on them to "agree," literally "fit together" (*kat-artizo*). The language is that of a tentmaker or indeed, of a brass-maker. Pieces of canvas must "fit together" or the tent will leak. If the canvas "splits," the tent is worthless. Corinth was famous for its brass work (13:1-13). No one will buy a brass pot with a handle that does not fit tightly to the pot. Paul summons (cameo 3) his readers to be of the same "mind" and the same "purpose/intention."[1] People with differences can work together if they have the same purpose. Paul wants all of them to think along the same lines, and to have a united purpose.

He then turns from his intended goals for their life together, and faces them with the present reality by naming names (cameo 4). The family of Chloe must have been prominent and respected or Paul would not have revealed his source. The divisions within the church were serious. The word here translated "quarreling" is the Greek word *Eris,* who was "a goddess who excites to war."[2] In Greek mythology Eris's brother was Aris, the Greek god of war. Aris in turn was the equivalent to *Mars,* the Roman god of war.[3] In Greek the word *eris* was also used to depict "battle-strife."[4] With such language, Paul was not discussing a "little misunderstanding" but rather bitter quarreling and contention. There was a battle raging in Corinth. What was the root of it all?

In cameo 5, Paul identifies four parties in the church. Chrysostom argues that Paul is really talking about known leaders in the church in Corinth and their followers, but that Paul "makes his argument less severe, not mentioning by name the rude dividers of the Church, but concealing them, as behind a sort of masks [*sic*], with the names of the Apostles."[5] This is a thoughtful suggestion. To call the leaders of the various factions by name would have inflamed the situation and put Chloe into an impossible position. What then was Paul talking about?

Having lived for decades in multicultural Middle Eastern communities, I know that ethnic divisions run deep. As far as we know there was no successful "melting pot" ideology in the ancient world. The city of Corinth was destroyed in 146 B.C. by the Romans for having opposed them, and then in 44 B.C. it was reborn as a *Roman* colony to facilitate the movement of goods across the isthmus of Corinth and as a center of trade. As a commercial town composed of various ethnic communities it was thriving in the first century, and the three groups that would have naturally dominated the young Christian community would have been the Romans, the Greeks and the Jews.

Writing to a church in the largest Roman colony in the empire, Paul would

---

[1]BAGD, p. 163.

[2]LSJ, *Greek-English Lexicon*, p. 689.

[3]W. Bridgwater and S. Kurtz, eds., *The Columbia Encyclopedia*, 3rd ed. (New York: Columbia University Press, 1963), p. 102.

[4]LSJ, *Greek-English Lexicon*, p. 689.

[5]Chrysostom, *First Corinthians*, Hom. III, p. 11.

have triggered unnecessary hostility in the wider community if he had written, "In our new fellowship, Romans, Greeks and Jews are all equal." In Corinth the Romans were inevitably at the top of the pecking order. The town was in Greece, so the Greeks would have been second. As powerless foreigners the Jews would naturally have been at the bottom of that threesome. A rough equivalent might be an American military base in Germany. On the base, the Americans run everything. The Germans who work there would be second, and any Turkish guest workers would be third. Paul was a Roman citizen. Apollos was Greek and Paul refers to Peter as "Cephas," using his Jewish name. Romans would naturally prefer Roman leadership. Greeks wanted to listen to a native Greek speaker and Jews would naturally lean toward a Jewish leader, especially if he "was from Galilee or Judea" and thereby "from the home country." Their various ethnic loyalties were quite likely causing serious tension in the church and Paul may well have been referring to those loyalties. Bishr ibn al-Sari thinks Paul added his name to the list "to demonstrate that it was not necessary for anyone to call himself a follower of Paul."[6] What then of the fourth party?

A group in the church claimed "we are of Christ" and that phrase implies, "The rest of you are not 'of Christ.' We alone can claim that identification." Many churches have a small clique of people who consider themselves "the true believers." They are not sure of the salvation of their pastor, but they are praying for him! Self-righteousness is usually on display in such groups and dealing with them can be extremely difficult. Perhaps something of this same dynamic was present in Corinth and elsewhere. Paul continues,

| | |
|---|---|
| 6. Was *Paul crucified* for you? | JESUS DIED FOR YOU |
| Or were you *baptized in the name of Paul?* | Name—of Paul? |

Assuming the centrality of Christ, and denying that he seeks any party loyalty to himself, Paul rings "the big bells" by invoking baptism and the cross. Each is given special prominence. Their unity is anchored in these two realities. Who died for *us?* In whose name were *we* baptized? The shift from the singular to the plural is significant. Each is saying "I am of Paul," etc. But Paul asks, "Who was crucified for you [pl.]?" They are a community united around a cross and for Paul their baptism is profoundly related to that cross.

He then appears to have added an aside of the type that is outside of the rhetorical structure of the passage. This is called a *katacrusis* and is as follows:

---

[6]Bishr ibn al-Sari, *Pauline Epistles*, p. 52.

The "aside" (1:14-16) reads:

[14]I am thankful that I baptized none of you except Crispus and Gaius; [15]lest any one should say that you were baptized in my name. [16]I did baptize also the household of Stephanas. Beyond that, I do not know whether I baptized anyone else.

This fascinating "aside" mentions "Stephanas" who was the first convert in the province and whose name reappears at the very end of the epistle. He and his friends brought written messages to Paul in Ephesus and most probably carried the finished epistle back to Corinth.

This appears to be the way Paul writes when he is not following prophetic models. Second Corinthians is full of this kind of composition. Verses 14-15 make a statement. Verse 16 "dribbles on" indicating something that he forgot to mention in the first part. He baptized one household—perhaps others—he can't remember. After this very human aside, Paul is ready to discuss the central event that can bring them together—the cross.

The following high points are prominent in this brief homily.

1. Breaking into ethnic enclaves is unacceptable. Furthermore, loyalties to individuals is not an excuse for breaking the unity of the church. Their leaders are not adequate centers of primary loyalty.

2. No group in the church has the right to claim that they alone are loyal to Christ.

3. They are "called by the name of our Lord Jesus Christ" (1:2) and in that name they can find their unity (1:10).

4. Baptism and the cross also call them together.

5. The question is not "Who is *my* leader?" but rather, "Who died for *us*?"

With the problem of this first essay stated boldly, Paul turns to the cross in the shadow of which their divisions can be eclipsed (1:17–2:2).

# The Wisdom and Power of God

*The Cross*

I Corinthians 1:17–2:2

In the early centuries of the Christian church, as the Greek world became Christian, a group of scholars now called "the apologists" arose and took up the daunting task of relating the new Christian faith to their Greek intellectual heritage. Their task, as Andrew Walls the distinguished Scottish church historian has described it, was "to baptize their memories into Christ."[1] As the twenty-first century unfolds, Christian theologians of the global South are taking up this same important task.[2] Paul's hymn to the cross is a brilliant start to an early journey down that road. Only, as we will see, Paul managed to relate to both the Jewish intellectual past and to Greek history at the same time in the same passage.

Paul's majestic chapter on love in chapter 13 is widely acclaimed. The great hymn to the cross under study in this chapter is worthy of the same attention and praise. Initially we intend to observe the "ring composition" of the passage with its three sections and its balanced cameos.[3] Second, this passage needs to be compared with the third of the great servant songs of Isaiah (50:4-11) in order to hear the bells that were ringing in the minds of Paul's Jewish readers. Finally, we will examine how this hymn to the cross relates to Greek history and literature. Greek readers could also hear connec-

---

[1]Andrew Walls, quoted from a public lecture given at the Overseas Ministries Study Center, New Haven, Conn., November 11, 2009.
[2]Andrew Walls, "Eusebius Tries Again: Reconceiving the Study of Christian History," *International Bulletin of Missionary Research* 24 (July 2000): 105-11.
[3]For this section of this chapter see Kenneth E. Bailey, "Recovering the Poetic Structure of I Cor. i 17-ii 2," *Novum Testamentum* 17, no. 4 (1975): 265-96.

tions to their world. The hymn relates profoundly to Pericles' oration in praise of the fallen Athenians at the end of the first year of the Peloponnesian war. We will attempt to trace those ties as well. First then is the text itself with its parallel stanzas.

1.[1:17]For Christ did not *send* me to baptize     PAUL SENT
       but to *preach* the gospel,     Preach Gospel
       *not* with *wise words*,     Not Wise Words
       lest it be emptied of its power, the *cross of Christ*.     The Cross

2. [18]For the word of the cross, to *those being destroyed*, is folly,     Destroy
       but to *us* who are *being saved*     The Power
       it is the *power of God*. [19]For it is written,     of God
       "I will *destroy* the wisdom of the *wise men*,     Scripture: Destroy
       and the cleverness of the clever I will thwart."

3. [20]Where is the *one who is wise*?
       Where is the *scribe*?     JEWISH SCHOLAR
       Where is the *scholar* of this age?     Greek Scholar
       Has not *God made foolish* the wisdom of the *world*?

---

4. [21]For since, in the *wisdom of God*,     WISDOM OF GOD (past)
       the *world* did *not know God* through wisdom,     World Ignorant

5. it pleased *God* through the *folly of the kerygma*     KERYGMA
       to save *those* who *believe*.     Believers

6. [22]For *Jews* demand *signs*     JEWS
       and *Greeks* seek *wisdom*,     Greeks

7. [23]*but* we preach     WE PREACH
       *Christ crucified*,     The Cross

8. a *stumbling block* to *Jews*     JEWS
       and *folly* to *Gentiles*,     Greeks

9. [24]but to *those* who are *called*, both *Jews and Greeks*,     THOSE CALLED
       Christ the *power of God* and *wisdom of God*.     Christ: Power/Wisdom

10. [25]For the *foolishness of God* is *wiser* than *human wisdom*,     GOD WISE/STRONG (present)
       and the *weakness of God* is *stronger* than human strength     Humans Weak/Foolish
       [26](for example, consider *your call* brethren).

---

11.        For (there are) *not many wise (m.pl.)* according to the flesh,
                not many (are) *powerful*,                                    JEWISH SCHOLARS—FEW
                not many of *noble birth;*                                    Greek Scholars—Few
        [27]But, the *foolish things* (n.pl.) of the world God chose to *shame* the *wise people* [m.pl.],

[The weak things (n.pl.) in the world, God chose to shame the strong things (n.pl.).[28] The low/base, and
contemptible things in the world, God chose even the things (n.pl.) that are not, to make powerless the
things (n.pl.) that are,]

12.   [29]so that *all flesh* might *not boast* in the presence of God.        BOASTING
            [30]From him *you* are *in Christ Jesus*,                          The Wisdom—of God
            who became *wisdom for us* from God (that is, righteousness, sanctification and redemption)
        [31]therefore, it is written, "Let *him who boasts*, boast in the *Lord*."    Scripture: Boasting

13.[2:1]And *I came* to you brethren,                      I PAUL CAME
    *not* in *lofty words* or wisdom,                      Not Wise Words
    *proclaiming* to you the mystery *of God*.             Proclaiming
        [2]For I decided to know nothing among you except *Jesus Christ* and him *crucified*.    The Cross

---

**Figure 1.2(1). The wisdom and power of God: The cross (1 Cor 1:17–2:2)**

## The Rhetoric

This homily is about the inadequacy of *wise words* and *wise people* and the
resulting necessity of the *cross as the wisdom and power of God*. The hymn
contains three major sections that include a seven cameo ring composition
in the center. The preaching of the cross appears at the beginning, middle
and end of the homily. The six outer cameos produce three pairs. Each of
these six is composed of *four lines*. These three pairs are like three outer
envelopes around the center. Each of the seven cameos in the center is composed of *two lines*. The seven cameos form a prophetic rhetorical template.

The shift from four lines per cameo (on the outside) to two lines per cameo
(in the center) is a significant linguistic "tag" that separates the three sections.[4] This is not the only time Paul divides a larger homily into three parts.
On three occasions Paul organizes a larger homily into three sections. This
occurs in his discussion of the Lord's Supper which is as follows:

I.   Hunger, Drunkenness, Quarreling: Not the Lord's Supper (11:17-22)
II.  The Received Tradition: The Lord's Supper (11:23-26)
III. Examine Yourselves, Discern the Body: Then Celebrate (11:27-33)

A similar threefold division of a single homily appears in Paul's discussion
of love in chapter 13, which is divided into:

---

[4]On at least eight occasions in Is 40–66 there are homilies that are divided into three parts.
These include 43:14-15; 44:21-28; 45:14-19; 49:1-7; 56:1-8; 58:9-14; 61:1-7; 66:17-25.

I. Love and the Spiritual Gifts (13:1-3)
II.   Love Defined (13:4-7)
III. Love and the Spiritual Gifts (13:8-13)

In like manner, here the hymn to the cross is in three parts. References to the "preaching of the cross" brilliantly tie the three together. The three sections can be roughly summarized as follows:

I.   Wise words and wise people are inadequate [Needed: the cross] (1:17-20)
II.   The Power and wisdom of God in the Cross (1:21-26a)
III. Wise words and wise people are inadequate [Needed: the cross] (1:26b–2:2)

There are three "asides" that appear to be additions to the larger hymn. These will be examined with care as they appear.

## COMMENTARY

The beginning, the middle and the end of this glorious hymn (seen side by side) appear as follows:

The beginning:
1. a. ¹˸¹⁷For Christ did not *send* me to baptize     PAUL SENT
   b. but to *preach* the gospel,     Preach Gospel
   c. *not* with *wise words*,     Not Wise Words
   d. lest it be emptied of its power, the *cross of Christ*.     The Cross

---------------

The center:
7.          *but we preach*     WE PREACH
            *Christ crucified,*     The Cross

---------------

The end:
13. a. ²˸¹And *I came* to you brethren,     I PAUL CAME
    c. *not* in *lofty words* or wisdom,     Not Wise Words
    b. *proclaiming* to you the mystery *of God*.     Proclaiming
    d. ²For I decided to know nothing among you     The Cross
       except *Jesus Christ* and him *crucified*.

**Figure 1.2(2). Cameos 1, 7 and 13 (1 Cor 1:17–2:2)**

In the introductory chapter on prophetic rhetorical styles, we observed Isaiah's parable of the two buildings (Is 28:14-18). That homily, like the passage above, opens and closes with cameos of four lines and shifts to two-line cameos in the center. The beginning, center and end of Isaiah's homily are as follows:

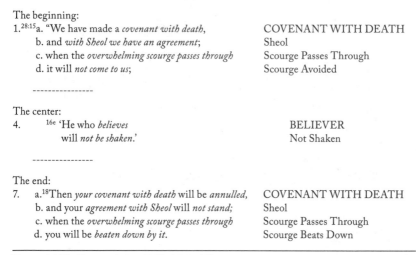

The beginning:

1.²⁸:¹⁵a. "We have made a *covenant with death*,          COVENANT WITH DEATH
    b. and *with Sheol we have an agreement*;              Sheol
    c. when the *overwhelming scourge passes through*      Scourge Passes Through
    d. it will *not come to us*;                           Scourge Avoided

    ----------------

The center:

4.      ¹⁶ᵉ 'He who *believes*                                    BELIEVER
        will *not be shaken.*'                               Not Shaken

    ----------------

The end:

7.      a.¹⁸Then *your covenant with death* will be *annulled*,   COVENANT WITH DEATH
        b. and your *agreement with Sheol* will *not stand*;      Sheol
        c. when the *overwhelming scourge passes through*         Scourge Passes Through
        d. you will be *beaten down by it*.                       Scourge Beats Down

**Figure 1.2(3). Cameos 1, 4 and 7 (Is 28:14-18)**

Clearly this rhetorical model was available to Paul and is exhibited in 1:17–2:2. In this Isaiah passage the four opening lines (cameo 1) are in the same order as the four matching lines at the end (cameo 7). Paul also opens and closes with four matching lines, but the order is not quite the same. Paul may have written this *hymn to the cross* some time before the composition of 1 Corinthians. As he incorporated it into his letter, he may have rearranged the order of ideas in his first cameo (1) to make a smooth transition from the subject of "baptism" (in the previous section) to that of "the cross." The original may well have been:

1.  a. ¹⁷For Christ *sent* me                              SENT
    b. *not* with *wise words*,                            Not Wise Words
    c. to *preach* the gospel,                             Preach Gospel
    d. lest it be emptied of its power, the *cross of Christ*.   The Cross

This is the order of phrases that appears in cameo 13 at the end of his hymn. In any case, the themes of *sent, no wise words, to preach* and *the cross* occur in the opening and the closing of the hymn. Here Paul declares that he is rejecting "lofty words and wisdom." But he makes this declaration using language that is constructed with great care following classical prophetic patterns. This is somewhat like the winner of the Miss Universe beauty pageant saying, "Physical beauty doesn't matter. What matters is having a beautiful spirit." When a *beautiful woman* makes such a statement, it has a powerful impact. Using *highly polished language*, Paul says, "Polished language is not the point!" The Corinthian setting for such a statement is also important.

Dio Chrysostom (born ca. A.D. 40) visited the city of Corinth and in his *Discourses* commented on his visit. He noted the "large numbers gathered at Corinth" and attributed this to the harbors, the prostitutes and to the fact that the city was situated at the crossroads of Greece. He noted that when the Isthmian Games were held, "everybody was at the Isthmus."[5] While there one could hear

> Crowds of wretched sophists around Poseidon's temple shouting and reviling one another, and their disciples, as they were called, fighting with one another, many writers reading aloud their stupid works, many poets reciting their poems while others applauded them, many jugglers showing their tricks, many fortune-tellers interpreting fortunes, lawyers innumerable perverting judgment, and peddlers not a few peddling whatever they happened to have.[6]

Paul wants to emphasize that he will not *under any circumstances* join the "carnival" described by Dio Chrysostom. He is not showing off his rhetorical skills and he has no desire to entertain his readers. In 2 Corinthians he writes, "For we are not, like so many, peddlers of God's word; but as men of sincerity, as commissioned by God, in the sight of God we speak in Christ" (2 Cor 2:17). None of this prevents him from presenting his message *as winsomely as he can.*

Paul is not providing an excuse for sloppy preaching; rather he is affirming that the preacher does not *create the meaning* in his/her mind, but reports God's *acts in history*, and the report of those acts should be *well composed.* Paul's hymn is so carefully composed that in the center (in cameo 7 and in the two lines that follow in cameo 8) each line has seven syllables, with an end rhyme (as we will note).

A further pair of important ideas emerges when cameos 1 and 13 are compared. In cameo 1 Paul is "sent" while in cameo 13 he says, "I came." God acts *to send*, and Paul responds by *coming*. The sovereignty of God in "sending" and the freedom of the human response in "coming" is presented in balanced lines. This same set of ideas will reappear in cameos 4 and 9 where they are applied to the *readers* who are "called" (God's act) and yet must "believe" (their act).

There remains the question as to what Paul means when he denies using "wise words" lest the cross be "emptied of its power." Paul proclaims saving events in history; he does not offer a beautifully formulated series of better

[5]Dio Chrysostom, *Discourses* 8.5, quoted in Jerome Murphy-O'Connor, *St. Paul's Corinth* (Collegeville, Minn.: Liturgical Press, 2002), p. 100.
[6]Ibid.

ideas than his philosophical competitors. What matters on the deepest level
for Paul is that God *acted in history to save*. His text reads like Isaiah, not like
Aristotle. If history is not proclaimed as the arena of revelation and salvation,
then the cross, for that speaker/writer, is "emptied of its power." This hymn is
an anti-Gnostic text and yet it is not anti-intellectual.

Anti-intellectualism has tried for centuries to find a home in the last
line of cameo 13, as if in Corinth Paul rejected all attempts at scholarship
and instead determined to present the gospel to his Jewish and Greek audiences by simply preaching "Jesus Christ and him crucified." The inadequacy of this understanding of the text will become clearer as we discuss
the Jewish and the Greek texts that stand behind this hymn. Keeping in
mind the above threefold affirmation of the preaching of the cross in cameos 1, 7 and 13, we turn to the second set of matching cameos (2 and 12)
set out in figure 1.2(4).

| | |
|---|---|
| 2. ¹:¹⁸For the word of the cross, to *those being destroyed*, is folly, | DESTRUCTION |
| but to *us* who are *being saved* | The *Power* |
| it is the *power of God*. | of God |
| ¹⁹For it is written "I will *destroy* the wisdom of the *wise men*, | SCRIPTURE: |
| and the cleverness of the clever I will thwart." | Destruction |
| | |
| 12.²⁹so that *all flesh* might *not boast* in the presence of God. | NO BOASTING |
| ³⁰From him *you* are *in Christ Jesus*, | The *Wisdom* |
| who became *wisdom for us* from God (that is, righteousness, | of God |
| sanctification and redemption) | |
| ³¹therefore, it is written, "Let *him who boasts*, | SCRIPTURE: |
| boast in the *Lord*." | Boasting |

**Figure 1.2(4). Cameos 2 and 12 (1 Cor 1:18-19, 29-31)**

Each of the above cameos opens with a *negative* (folly/boasting) which in
each instance is matched and reinforced at the end of the cameo with a *Scripture quotation*. The centers of these two cameos together affirm the two leading ideas in the hymn. The first focuses on *the power of God* and the second
describes *the wisdom of God*. The two cameos are carefully matched.

Paul knew that his message of a crucified Son of God was heard as weakness in Jewish scribal circles and as utter foolishness in the Greek academy.
Yet his confidence in its power (cameo 2) and wisdom (cameo 12) was un-
shakable. In cameo 12 (above) Paul is adamantly against boasting in the presence of God. Unfortunately, our traditional translations of cameos 10-11 give

the Corinthians reasons for *boasting to the high heavens*. For centuries we have read cameo 11 as a series of compliments to the Corinthians. We imagine that the Corinthian reader is led to understand that not many of the *Corinthians* were wise, powerful or nobly born, *and yet* God *used them* (above all others) to shame the wise and turn the strength of the powerful into weakness. Such compliments would be enough to swell the head of any member of the Corinthian congregation! How then can Paul claim to be writing these things "so that all flesh *might not boast* in the presence of God"? This question will be examined below with some care.

But why does Paul insist that no one can boast? The negative side of "boasting" for Paul was the attitude of "self-confidence which seeks glory before God and which relies upon itself."[7] The Roman could boast of the power of empire. The Greek could boast of the greatness of Greek civilization. The Jew could boast in the covenant, the patriarchs, the law and much more (Rom 9:4-5). But for Paul the power and wisdom *of the cross* made all such boasting meaningless. God chose to save by means of *weak things* (the incarnation and the cross) so that *no one could boast* in his presence (1:29).

The only legitimate "boasting" had to do with serving Christ in ways that went beyond what Christ commanded. In such a case, on the Day of Judgment, one would be able to "boast." To this topic Paul will return, but here he is affirming that earthly power is not a mirror image of the power of God. Granted, righteously executed earthly power was not for Paul inherently evil (Rom 13:1-7). The problem emerges when individuals, communities and nations begin subtly to see their power as an extension of the power of God. Then "boasting" emerges, and as that happens, disaster ensues. The broad sweep of history gives chilling witness to many such disasters.

We have translated the third line in cameo 12 as "who became wisdom for us from God (that is, righteousness, sanctification and redemption)." The words here translated "that is" are *te kai*. The best understanding of these two words, as they appear in this text, is to translate them "that is." The same two words appear in the center of the hymn (cameo 9) where Paul writes, "but to those who are called *te kai* Jews and Greeks." Who are "those who are called"? They are "Jews and Greeks." Both occurrences of *te kai* in this hymn introduce explanations of what has just been said.[8] Someone asks

---

[7]Rudolf Bultmann, "καυχαομαι" in *TDNT,* 3:648-649.
[8]F. Blass and A. Debrunner, *A Greek Grammar of the New Testament and Other Early Christian Lit-*

at a dinner party, "What is for dessert?" The host answers, "I can bring a bowl of fruit, *that is*, apples, oranges and bananas." In first-century Greek the words "that is" would be *te kai*.[9] The generic "bowl of fruit" is explained with the words "apples, oranges and bananas." What is the meaning of the affirmation "Christ Jesus who became wisdom for us from God"? The text is not clear. So Paul adds *te kai* and explains his meaning with three profound theological words that do not appear elsewhere in the entire hymn. These are "righteousness, sanctification and redemption." Through his grace flowing from the cross, God grants believers the status of acceptance in his presence which is *righteousness*.[10] Through faith and baptism they receive the Spirit that "makes holy" which is *sanctification*, and in the process are rescued from the power of sin through the cross of Christ which is *redemption*. The first word focuses on God, the second on the Holy Spirit and the third on the work of Christ. These three noble words clarify mightily what Paul means when he affirms "Christ Jesus who became wisdom for us from God."

The third pair of matching cameos (also using four lines per cameo) needs to be examined along with the extended aside that Paul adds to his hymn. The two cameos (with the aside) read:

3.[1:20] Where is the *one who is wise?*
 Where is the *scribe?*                         JEWISH SCHOLAR—(?)
 Where is the *scholar* of this age?            Greek Scholar—(?)
 Has not *God made foolish* the wisdom of the *world?*

-----------------------------------------------------------------------------------

11. For (there are) *not many wise people* [*m.pl.*] according to the flesh,
  not many (are) *powerful*,                     JEWISH SCHOLARS—FEW
  not many of *noble birth*;                     Greek Scholars—Few
   [27]But, the *foolish things* [n.pl.] of the world God chose to *shame* the *wise people* [m.pl.],

[the weak things (n.pl) in the world, God chose to shame the strong things (n.pl.),[28] the low/ base, and contemptible things in the world, God chose, even the things (n.pl.) that are not, to make powerless the things (n.pl.) that are,] (my translation)

**Figure 1.2(5). Cameos 3 and 11 (1 Cor 1:20, 26-28)**

---

*erature* (Chicago: University of Chicago Press, 1961), p. 230 (#444). Cf. Bailey, "Recovering the Poetic Structure of I Cor. i 17–ii 2," pp. 275-77.
[9]The words *te kai*, following Greek usage, appear in the Greek text just after the first word in the list that it introduces.
[10]It is *God* who grants *righteousness*. *Sanctification* comes through the *Holy Spirit*, and *redemption* is a result of the work of *Christ*. These three words have Trinitarian echoes.

Cameo 3 is constructed as follows:

a. Where is *the wise one*
b.　　　　The scribe
c.　　　　The scholar of this age
d. God has made wisdom *foolish*

The first line (a) is best read as a *general reference*. And the fourth line (d) looks backwards and negates the first line. The wisdom of the wise one (a) is made foolish *by God* (d). Three times in the middle of this hymn Paul specifically mentions "Jew and Greek." It is possible to see the center of this stanza as a fourth case of that same pairing. The "scribe" (b) is clearly a Jewish reference, while it is easy to see "the scholar of this age" (c) as referring to a Greek scholar.

Cameo 11 also has four lines which literally translated and summarized are as follows:

11. a. For not many *wise people* [masculine plural] according to the flesh
b.　　　　Not many powerful
c.　　　　Not many of noble birth
d. but God used foolish *things* [neuter plural] to shame *the wise people* (masculine plural).

Cameo 11 (like cameo 3) starts (a) with a general reference to "the wise people" (masculine plural). In the matching fourth line (d), God shames those same "wise people" using "foolish *things*" (neuter plural) as his agents. Cameos 3 and 11 are a closely matched pair. But we have a translation problem. Cameo 11a literally reads:

For not many wise [m.pl.] according to the flesh,

Many of our English versions have added three words (not in the Greek) and translated this line as:

For not many *of you were* wise according to the flesh

Two important decisions are encoded in those three extra words. Paul's original sentence has no verb "to be." Hebrew has a verb "to be" in the future and in the past tenses but none in the *present*. As in this text, Paul sometimes leaves out the verb "to be." Because Paul was a Hebrew-speaking Jew, when he omits the verb "to be," it is natural to assume that he is thinking in the *present tense*. Thus in the text before us it is appropriate to add "are" (present tense) rather than "were" (past tense) as happens in RSV and NRSV. The end result is as follows.

Paul wrote, "not many wise [m.pl.] according to the flesh," meaning: wise people are few in number. With a present tense assumed, we can translate this sentence literally to read, "There *are* not many wise people according to the flesh." Paul can be understood to be saying:

> Yes, the scribes like to think of themselves as a powerful intellectual guild. I lived in Jerusalem and I know them. But they are very few—do not be intimidated by them. On the Greek side, the philosophers of Athens like to think that they are the center of intellectual life for the entire world. But they also are very few. Trust me—I have just spent a serious block of time debating with them and I am not impressed. Do not be afraid of them.

For more than a millennium Middle Eastern translations have read this text, "not many wise according to the flesh."[11] As in cameo 3, so here in cameo 11 Paul starts with a generic statement. So if with Paul and the long tradition of Middle Eastern Semitic versions we keep this statement in the present tense we have only solved half of our problem.

The second half has to do with the addition of the two words "of you" which changes everything. When those two words (absent from the Greek text) are added, the sentence is no longer a *general reference* that means "there are few wise people" but rather becomes a *specific reference* that now means *"Among you Corinthians*, not many were wise." The reader is then led to understand that Paul is offering to *the Corinthians* the highest possible praise. Even though few of them were wise, or powerful or nobly born, yet God fashioned them into his instrument for shaming the wise and breaking the power of the strong. Such a compliment would have led the Corinthians to boast to the highest heavens! But this possibility for understanding the text is flatly denied in cameo 12 where Paul affirms clearly that God's goal is to make it *impossible* for *anyone* to *boast in the presence of God.*

Furthermore, did the Corinthians have any contacts either with Greek philosophical scholarship or with the Jewish academy represented by the scribes? Were the Christians of Corinth such outstanding examples of the faith that they were useful instruments in the hand of God to shame the wise and break the strength of the powerful with whom they had never engaged?

---

[11]Twenty-two of the Oriental versions chosen for this study maintain the present tense in this sentence. The only exception is the Bible Society (1993) version. The added phrase "among you" appears in: Syriac Peshitta; Vatican Arabic #13 (8th-9th cent); Mt Sinai 151 (867); Mt. Sinai Ar #73 (9th c.); Erpenius (1616); Paulist—Fakhoui (1964); New Jesuit (1969). The two Hebrew texts and the remaining 14 Arabic versions omit these words. See appendix II, plate A.

In what contexts did these theologically and ethically flawed Christians achieve great victories over the Greek and the Jewish worlds? Where was Rome's power broken by them?

Add to this the fact that some of the members of the church in Corinth were wealthy enough to host the entire church in their homes. Among them were Aquila and Priscilla who had a home in Corinth into which they welcomed Paul as a guest. In addition, they also had a home in Ephesus large enough to accommodate a "house church." It is also possible that they had a home in Rome. How would the leaders of the Corinthian church feel if Paul referred to *all of them* as "low born, despised in the world, even those who do not exist" (1:28)? Paul may be writing this letter while living with Aquila and Priscilla in Ephesus. Is he insulting his hosts? How can this possibly be what Paul means?

Finally, such an understanding cannot be correct because it cuts out the heart of the hymn. The solution to this part of the puzzle is simple. Paul is not talking about the Corinthians. Here in cameo 11 he is making a general statement that mirrors cameo 3. Paul's intent can be summarized as follows:

11. a.   There are not many wise (people) according to the flesh
    b.       not many are powerful   [like Jewish scribes]
    c.       not many of noble birth; [like Greek scholarly aristocrats]
    d.   But, the foolish things (neuter plural) God chose to shame the wise
             people (masculine pl.)

What is this all about? The scribes were a powerful guild in the Second Temple period and they were one of the three groups that composed the Sanhedrin. Regarding the scribes, Shaye Cohen writes, "A new type of authority figure emerged to replace the classical prophets; the *scribe*, whose authority derived . . . from his erudition in the sacred scriptures and traditions."[12] Saldarini summarizes Ben Sirach's views on the scribe[13] and writes, "The scribe is not simply a scholar or a teacher in the modern mold, but a high official, advisor to the governing class, and international ambassador and traveler."[14] But they were, so far as we know, few in number. Having lived for some time in Jerusalem, Paul understood all of this. What then about the Greeks?

The Greek intelligentsia was composed of noblemen. With their wealth

---

[12]Shaye J. D. Cohen, *From the Maccabees to the Mishnah* (Louisville: Westminster John Knox, 2006), p. 11 (italics his).

[13]*Ben Sirach* 38:24–39:11.

[14]Anthony J. Saldarini, "Scribes," in *The Anchor Bible Dictionary* (New York: Doubleday, 1992), 5:1014.

and slaves, they alone had the leisure necessary to cultivate the mind, and Aristotle waxes eloquent when he discusses the importance of "noble birth" for the scholarly guild.[15] They were also few in number. When understood in this manner, references to Jews and Greeks appear in the center of cameo 11. The fourth line shows that they were shamed, not by the Corinthians, but by "the *foolish things* [neuter plural] of the world." What things we ask?

Paul is talking about the *incarnation and the cross* (not the Corinthians). Here he seems to be sorely tempted to "stop preaching and start meddling." That is, he would love to offer specific details. But to do so would be very dangerous. A Roman court in Corinth (a Roman colony) had ruled in his favor and declared Christianity to be a sect of Judaism, and thereby a legal religion. At this point in his discussion Paul adds an astute aside. He writes,

[the weak things (n.pl.) in the world, God chose to shame the strong things (n.pl.), 28the low born, and contemptible things in the world, God chose, even the things (n.pl.) that are not, to make powerless the things (n.pl.) that are,]

Events in Bethlehem (a humble birth) and Jerusalem (death on a cross) possess wisdom and power that unmask the powerful as weak and the wise as foolish. The manger and the cross are here affirmed to be things that "are not" and it is *they* that make powerless "the things that are." Herod, Pilate and Caiaphas were gone—Jesus was not! The *cross* was the instrument in the hand of God to shame the powerful, *not the Corinthians!* This is the heart of the entire hymn. At the cross the world discovered that you cannot beat brokenness!

He means that the Greeks see Jesus as worthless because he was "low born." He is despised by Jews, Greeks and Romans because he died on a cross. But God used those despised events to set loose in human history a power and a wisdom that makes Rome appear weak and Athens look foolish. The risen Christ is alive and active through the Spirit across the Roman world and beyond. Paul's language is forthright but guarded. Each reader/listener must "fill in the blanks."

Paul could have caused great harm to the church in Corinth and endangered the lives of its members if he had written, "The cross (and the resurrection) make Rome look weak." Writing to the largest city in Greece, is he expected to say, "The Greek heritage of art, architecture, philosophy and democracy is foolishness when compared to the cross"? Rather he observes that "the things *that are not*" make "powerless *the things that are.*" He is not

---

[15]Aristotle, *The "Art" of Rhetoric* 1.3-5, trans. J. H. Freese (Cambridge, Mass.: Harvard University Press, 2006), p. 49.

subverting Rome and turning the world upside down—or is he?

If this extended "aside" is lifted out of the text, cameo 12 follows cameo 11 seamlessly, and the text would read:

(cameo 11)   But, the *foolish things* of the world God chose to shame the *wise people*, (. . .)

(cameo 12)   so that all flesh might not boast in the presence of God.

This flawless connection supports the idea that Paul's original hymn did not have the "aside" that appears between cameos 11 and 12.

The Corinthians, along with the rest of us, have no grounds for boasting. In any age the faithful can appropriately sing, "In the cross of Christ I glory, towering o're the wrecks of time."[16]

With this understanding of stanza 11, we have yet to deal with the dangling phrase in cameo 10c, "For consider *your call* brethren," that appears between stanzas 10 and 11.[17] That discussion needs to be a part of an examination of the seven cameos that form the center of the hymn. This brings us to figure 1.2(6).

| | | |
|---|---|---|
| 4. | [21]For since, in the *wisdom of God*, <br> the *world* did *not know God* through wisdom, | WISDOM OF GOD (past) <br> World Ignorant |
| 5. | it pleased *God* through the *folly of the kerygma* <br> to save *those* who *believe*. | KERYGMA <br> Believers |
| 6. | [22]For *Jews* demand *signs* <br> and *Greeks* seek *wisdom*, | JEWS <br> Greeks |
| 7. | [23]*but we preach* <br> *Christ crucified*, | WE PREACH <br> The Cross |
| 8. | a *stumbling block* to *Jews* <br> and *folly* to *Gentiles*, | JEWS <br> Greeks |
| 9. | [24]but to *those* who are *called*, both *Jews and Greeks*, <br> Christ the *power of God* and *wisdom of God*. | THOSE CALLED <br> Christ: Power/Wisdom |
| 10. | [25]For the *foolishness of God* is *wiser* than *human wisdom*, <br> and the *weakness of God* is *stronger* than human strength <br> [26](for example, consider *your call* brethren). | GOD WISE/STRONG (present) <br> Humans Weak/Foolish |

**Figure 1.2(6). Cameos 4-10 (1 Cor 1:21-26a)**

As noted above, here Paul shifts from four lines to two lines per cameo. This

---

[16]From a hymn titled "In the Cross of Christ I Glory" by John Bowring, 1849.

[17]See figure 1.2(1) at the beginning of this chapter.

shift marks these seven cameos as the center of a three-section hymn.

Before examining the seven cameos before us, it is possible to reflect on what can best be understood as a brief comment that closes this central section. Adding a contextualized reference to these seven cameos Paul writes, "For example, consider *your call* brethren" (emphasis mine). The topic of "calling" is important to Paul all through the epistle and each reference to it must be taken seriously. Usually the brief command to "consider your call" that appears in this line is attached to what follows. However, the only other reference in this hymn to any *call* occurs in cameo 9 *just before* this command and reads "but to those who are *called* both Jews and Greeks." There Paul was talking about a "call" in general. Now he applies this to his readers. In the light of all that he has said thus far in the hymn, Paul can be understood to mean,

> Each of you has come recently into faith in Jesus from Judaism or from Paganism. So, why did you believe? Consider *your call*! Why did you accept baptism? Were you attracted by "human wisdom" or by "human power"? Had we dazzled you with our philosophical acumen and the irresistible force of our logic? Were we a military force headed for victory and you wanted to join? What was the driving force behind *your call*—to what did you respond? Did you not see that the foolishness of God in sending his Son to earth as a babe is wiser than all the philosophers of Mars Hill? Did you not understand that the weakness of God in allowing his only Son to absorb ultimate evil and die on a cross—seen by many as utter foolishness on God's part—was stronger than human strength? It is stronger than Herod, Pilate, Caiaphas and all the legions of Rome! Yes, I know, that in the eyes of the world this story makes God look foolish and weak. But *consider your call*! Think about it! Your decision of faith, deep in your own hearts resonates with what I am trying to say!

Such an understanding of the text supports Paul's claim that he is writing to make certain that *no one can boast* in the presence of God! The Corinthians were guilty of considerable boasting on various levels, none of it noble. Love does not boast (13:4). With this understanding of Paul's command to "consider your call" Paul's emphasis on the power of the cross is confirmed rather than weakened. Cameos 4-10 must now be examined.

The two outer cameos presented here (4 and 10) are precisely balanced. The first (4) tells the reader that (in the past) the wisdom of God was not known through human wisdom. This idea is reinforced in cameo 10 with the affirmation that God at his most foolish is wiser than human wisdom at its peak. In addition,

God's greatest weakness is stronger than human power in its most powerful expression. Picture a man on a roof trying to pass a delicate glass, full of diamonds, to a man on the ground. The man on the roof slowly stretches down as far as he can. The man on the ground reaches up on his tiptoes straining to grasp the precious glass. The man on the ground fails—he cannot reach the diamonds; the distance is too great. In like manner Paul affirms (cameo 10) that God in his greatest weakness and in his most foolish moment is beyond what humans can reach even at the point of their greatest wisdom and strength. The seamless way that cameo 10 complements cameo 4 is so smooth that if cameos 5-9 were missing, the reader would not notice any interruption in the flow of the text.

Moving toward the center, in cameo 5 Paul affirms that God saves through the "folly of the *kerygma*" (the message). Then in cameo 9, that *kerygma* is defined as "Christ the power of God and wisdom of God." Furthermore, cameo 5 mentions "those who believe" while in cameo 9 there is reference to "those who are called."[18] God *calls*, and we must *believe*. We have already noted that in this homily Paul speaks of his own spiritual journey in the same way. In cameo 1 he mentions that he was "sent" while in cameo 13 he affirms, "I came." The first is God's call and the second is Paul's response. This same balancing of the sovereignty of God and the responsibility and freedom of the individual, Paul applies here to his readers.

Cameos 6 and 8 form an unmistakable set of parallels that focus on "Jew and Greek." Paul knew exactly what the two major ethnic (unbelieving) communities around him wanted to hear. As with Jesus, Paul's Jewish listeners wanted proof through miraculous signs. The Greeks wanted meaning created by syllogisms fashioned into an interconnected logical whole. Paul boldly affirmed that his message was Christ crucified, even though this was "a stumbling block to Jews and folly to Gentiles."

Paul's rhetorical skills come to an even finer polish in the center where the four lines in cameos 7 and 8 each have seven syllables and all four of them rhyme at the end. These are:

7.    1:23He-meis de ke-rus-so-men         η-μεις δε κη-ρυσ-σο-μεν
       Chris-ton es-tou-ro-men-on           Χρισ-τον εσ-ταυ-ρω-μεν-ον

8.     Iou-dai-ois men skan-da-lon          Ιου-δαι-οις μεν σκαν-δα-λον
       Eth-ne-sin de mo-ri-an               εθ-νε-σιν δε μω-ρι-αν

---

[18]In this case the two themes in cameo 5 are inverted in cameo 9. Together the two create an AB-BA parallel.

The creation of two lines with seven syllables per line was a well-known ancient Semitic poetic meter. Ephraim the Syrian used this meter extensively in the fourth century A.D. It is amazing to find this classical Semitic meter in a Greek text. In the hymn at large, Paul not only presents seven cameos which he matches in reverse, he also manages to state his climax in the center with seven syllables per line—and the lines rhyme at the end. But of course, he has no "lofty words" or "wise words" in this hymn!

As seen, these claims occur in the beginning (cameo 1) and at the end (cameo 13), while here in the center (cameos 5-9) we uncover astounding linguistic polish. By breaking into *a Semitic poetic meter* in the *Greek language* he strives mightily to gain the respect of both Jew and Greek and to bring them together at the cross.

With the ring composition of this hymn in mind, we turn to the artistic counterpoint that it employs. Not only does the material exhibit the balanced form just examined, but a "second rhetorical tune" appears in the same lines [see fig. 1.2(7)].

This rhetorical form can be called a "double ring composition." It can also be referred to as a theological "double-decker sandwich." The threefold repetition of "A" (the Cross) comprises the "three layers of bread." The cameos labeled "B" and "C" are the sandwich filling. As we will note, Isaiah 50:4-11 uses this same format. One of the features of both texts is that the "bread" in the middle is the "bottom" of the top half of the sandwich and at the same time it is the "top" of the lower half of the sandwich.[19] That is, the center cameo (A2) faces both ways.

Amazingly, in 1 Corinthians 1:17–2:2 two rhetorical structures appear in the same piece of literature. The reader can "hear" or "see" an outline that moves from 1-7 and then from 7-1 as in figure 1.2(1) (above). Or the reader can "see/hear" A-B-C-B-A, followed by a second round of the same A-B-C-B-A as set out in figure 1.2(7) below.

In this latter case Paul works with three ideas. These are:

(A) "the Cross"
(B) "people who believe the message vs. people who do not"
(C) the "opponents who fail"

---

[19]Paul uses the "double-decker sandwich" format in 1:17–2:2 and also in 7:17-24; 9:12b-18; 14:1-12. In each case there are slight modifications of the format presented above. Chapter 1:1-9 is also a modified form of this style.

| I PREACHING THE CROSS | II ACCEPTANCE AND REJECTION (the message: acceptance & rejection) | III OPPONENTS FAIL |
|---|---|---|
| A1. [1:17]I preach the *cross* of Christ | | |
| | B1.[18]The *word of the cross* Those being *destroyed* but [*de*] We who are *being saved* | |
| | | C1.[20]God made *foolish* (the wise) the *scribe* the *scholar* |
| | | C2.[21]The *world* does *not know* |
| | B2.[21-22]The folly of the *kerygma* *Those who believe* since [*epeide*] *Jews and Greeks* who *reject* | |
| A2.[23]We preach *Christ crucified* | | |
| | B3. [23]*Jews and Gentiles* who *reject* [24]but [*de*] Those who are *called* *Christ, the wisdom and power of God* | |
| | | C3.[25]Men are weak and *foolish* |
| | | C4.[26-27]God *shamed* (the wise) the *powerful* the *nobility* |
| | B4. [29]*Boasters* in God's presence but [*de*] *You are in Christ Jesus* *Christ who became wisdom* for us from God | |
| A3.[2:1-2]I proclaim *Christ crucified* | | |

**Figure 1.2(7). The counterpoint of the hymn (1 Cor 1:17–2:2)**

These three ideas are presented and then repeated backwards. Following this, the entire sequence is repeated. The end result is a double presentation of: A-B-C C-B-A as noted.[20] When these two rhetorical styles are contemplated, a literary "counterpoint" emerges. Two literary "tunes" are being "played" at the same time and some listeners will hear the first, some the sec-

---

[20]A2 in the center does not repeat and functions to join the two halves of the rhetorical structure.

ond, and yet others will be enriched by hearing the two at once. This second
"tune" is particularly important for first century Jewish readers/listeners because the same rhetorical device appears in Isaiah 50:5-11, which also discusses a unique person who suffers and whose suffering is significant for others. That hymn is:

1. (A)$^{50:5}$I was not rebellious,                        (-)
    I turned not backward.                        (-)          PERSECUTORS
      $^6$I gave my back to the smiters,          (+)          Torment the Servant
      and my cheeks to those who pulled out the beard.   (+)
   I hid not my face                                (-)
   from shame and spitting.                          (-)

2.    (B) $^7$For the Lord God helps me;                    SERVANT
      therefore I have not been confounded;          (Helped—Not Confounded)

3.     (C) therefore I have set my face              PARABLE OF
       like a flint,                               Flint

4.    (B) and I know that I shall not be put to shame;     SERVANT
      $^8$he who vindicates me is near.               (Vindicated—Not Shamed)

5. (A)$^{8b}$Who will contend with me?
   Let us stand up together.                         PERSECUTORS
   Who is my adversary?                              And the Servant
   Let him come near to me.

6.    (B) $^9$Behold, the Lord God helps me;                SERVANT
      who will declare me guilty?                     (Helped—Not Guilty)

7.     (C) $^{9b}$Behold, all of them will wear out like a garment;   PARABLE OF
       the moth will eat them up.                    Moth/Garment

8.    (B) $^{10}$The one among you who fears the Lord        SERVANT
      let him obey the voice of his servant.           (Obeyed)
       The one who walks in darkness
       and has no light
      let him trust in the name of the Lord
      and rely upon his God.

9.(A)$^{11}$Behold, all you who kindle a fire,
   who set brands alight!
   Walk by the light of your fire,                   PERSECUTORS
   and by the brands which you have kindled!          In Torment
   This shall you have from my hand:
   you shall lie down in torment.

**Figure 1.2(8). The third servant song (Is 50:5-11)**

The book of Isaiah includes four "servant songs." The fourth of them is the well-known "suffering servant song" of Isaiah 52:13–53:12. The above text is the third in this series of four and is the first that discusses the *suffering of the servant*. This third song is of particular interest for our attempt at understanding the Jewish background to Paul's hymn to the cross.

Initially, it is clear that the above Isaiah text follows the same double-decker sandwich style just seen in 1 Corinthians 1:17–2:2. Isaiah includes three dominant themes. These three clusters of ideas need to be traced using the same methodology we employed in the 1 Corinthians passage. The three themes are:

First, the *servant and his persecutors* appear three times (note the three sections marked "A"):

1 (A)　The persecutors torment the servant.

5 (A)　The persecutor is summoned to appear for a second confrontation.

9 (A)　The persecutors are themselves tormented by the fire they have kindled.

The progression of ideas through this series of three is clear. In cameo 1, the servant is the powerless victim of suffering. In cameo 5, the servant challenges the persecutor to "come near." In cameo 9 the persecutors self-destruct and end "in torment."

The second series of four cameos (marked B) focuses on *the servant and God*. In the order of the text, these four are as follows:

2 (B)　*God* helps the *servant*—he is not confounded.

4 (B)　The *servant* is vindicated (by *God*)—and not put to shame.

6 (B)　*God* helps the *servant*—no one can call him guilty.

8 (B)　Those in darkness who fear *God* must *obey his servant*.

Cameos 2, 4 and 6 are closely parallel. Cameos 2 and 6 are exceptionally close. In cameo 8 the identities of God and his servant are almost fused. The one who fears God is told to *obey God's servant*. Thus the four "B" cameos affirm that the *servant* is *helped, vindicated, helped* again and finally *obeyed*.

The third series (C) has two cameos, each of which is a metaphor/parable. These are examples of "encased parables" (as noted earlier).[21] The first of these two (C3) is a parable of the servant who is "like a flint." The second (C7) is a metaphor/parable describing the tormenters who will

---

[21]See Is 55:8-9.

wear out and be eaten by the moth, "like a garment." In short, three ideas dominate the song as a whole. Summarizing what is noted above, these are:

A. The servant willingly *suffers* from tormenters—and does not retaliate.
B. A series of *contrasts* are presented that *relate the servant to God.*
> God helps the servant and the servant is not confounded, shamed or declared guilty.
>
> Those who fear God are ordered to *obey the servant.*
C. The servant is *like flint* while the *opponents* are *like a moth-eaten garment.*

There are some contrasts between 1:17–2:2 and Isaiah 50:5-11. A major point of contrast is that Isaiah focuses on the *servant* and his *tormenters* who finally self-destruct. Paul has nothing to say about Jesus' opponents. Instead of focusing on Jesus and the high priests, Paul moves beyond the cross and reflects on those who believe/are called, verses Jews/Greeks who see the cross as foolish and weak and fail to believe.

A second point of divergence between the two texts is the skillful use of two encased parables in Isaiah (cameos 3 and 7). The first describes the servant (he is like flint) and the second talks about his opponents (who wear out and are like a moth-eaten garment). Having ignored the opponents Paul has no need for Isaiah's parables. He focuses on the greatest parable of all: a concrete historical event—the cross. In the centers of his two inversions (C1, 2, 3, 4) Paul focuses on how the wise in the world are *foolish, ignorant and weak* and how God *shamed them* and made them *foolish.*

A third point of divergence with Paul is that in Isaiah's homily, the final self-destruction of the opponents of the servant occurs at the *end* in cameo 9. The opponents of the cross are made foolish in the two *centers* of Paul's double-decker sandwich (C1, 2, 3, 4).

But there are also striking parallels between the two texts. First, each passage creates a double-decker sandwich. Second, each works with three themes. All three themes noted in Isaiah appear in 1 Corinthians and are in much the same order. Third, each text focuses on a single central figure who suffers and does not retaliate. Fourth, in each text opponents of the sufferer sustain critical losses. Fifth, in each account, those who believe in/follow the sufferer reap significant benefits. That is, in Paul's hymn the believer is promised "salvation" and in Isaiah, believers who *walk in darkness* are commanded to obey the voice of the servant and (assumedly) find themselves *in the light.*

Paul seems to be saying to his Jewish readers:

You know Isaiah's account of God's unique suffering servant who gives his back to the smiters. You will recall that the servant is vindicated while his tormenters "wear out like a garment" and "lie down in torment." The servant is victorious *through suffering*. The pattern of suffering seen in that unique servant of God reappears in the life of Jesus the crucified Messiah. But I do not want to focus on Jesus vs. Pilate and the high priest. Instead I urge you to reflect on how God was acting in history through the cross to demonstrate his wisdom and power. That wisdom shames human wisdom and for those who believe, it brings "wisdom for us from God (that is: righteousness, sanctification and redemption)." I know that a suffering Messiah is difficult for you to accept. I urge you to see how such a suffering leader was already envisioned and described by Isaiah the prophet. What I proclaim to you does not violate our Jewish tradition; rather it brings our tradition to its finest expression.

By building on Isaiah, Paul discusses the cross in a way that could communicate to Jewish readers/ listeners on a very deep level.

But Paul was not only writing for Jews, he was also concerned for his Greek readers/listeners who would not have had the background in the book of Isaiah to understand the above. Three times in the passage Paul specifically mentions "Jews and Greeks." To this list we can add the references to the powerful (Jewish) scribe and the nobly born (Greek) scholar. So, if Paul was indeed writing also for Greeks—what might they have heard?

The Greek world had a powerful tradition of heroes who died to save. That tradition is engagingly described in the Pulitzer Prize–winning book *Lincoln at Gettysburg* by Garry Wills.[22] In that volume Wills discusses Pericles, the famous fifth-century B.C. orator. We learn that in 430 B.C., at the end of the first year of the Peloponnesian war, on request, Pericles delivered a famous oration praising the Athenians who had died to save the city of Athens from Sparta. The oration was called an *epitaphios* (a speech over a tomb), and by law such a speech was to be delivered each year. Six of these ancient orations, dating from 431-332 B.C. have survived. The *epitaphios* of Pericles was the first and remains the most famous of the series. Wills argues that both speakers (Everett and Lincoln) at the dedication of the cemetery at Gettysburg, Pennsylvania, on November 19, 1863, were influenced by Pericles' funeral oration. On that occasion Everett, an eminent Greek scholar, delivered a long oration

---

[22]Garry Wills, *Lincoln at Gettysburg: The Words That Remade America* (New York: Simon & Schuster, 1992).

that was deliberately fashioned after the famous speech by Pericles whom he mentions by name. The point of Wills's book is that Lincoln was also influenced by Pericles, because America was in the middle of a period of Greek revival in art, literature, architecture and politics. But it was *Lincoln*, not Everett, who succeeded in doing for America what Pericles had done for Athens. *Lincoln* was the one who praised heroes who died to save and in the process helped to unite the country.

Wills ably describes the nature of Greek oratory and Pericles' use of it. Commenting on Pericles' speech, Wills writes,

> As the earliest known prose performance mandated by the democratic polis, it set the tone and style for most later public rhetoric. By the continuity of its themes and values, it established a sense of Athenian identity.[23]

It is my observation that much of what Wills says about Pericles (and Lincoln) fits Paul's presentation of Christ crucified. By an extraordinary coincidence Lincoln used 272 words in his famous Gettysburg Address (over the tombs of the American Civil War dead) and Paul's hymn on Christ crucified is composed of 273 words.

Consider the following. In his dialogue with Menexenus, Plato reflects on the Greek funeral oration tradition. He writes:

> O Menexenus! death in battle is certainly in many respects a noble thing. The dead man gets a fine and costly funeral, although he may have been poor, and an elaborate speech is made over him by a wise man who has long ago prepared what he has to say, although he who is praised may not have been good for much. The speakers praise him for what he has done and for what he has not done— that is the beauty of them—and they steal away our souls *with their embellished words*; . . . and they praise those who die in war, and all our ancestors who went before us; and they praise ourselves also who are still alive, until I feel quite elevated by their laudations, . . . and I become enchanted by them, and all in a moment I imagine myself to have become a greater and nobler and finer man than I was before. . . . This consciousness of dignity lasts me more than three days, and not until the fourth or fifth day do I come to my senses and know where I am; in the meantime I have been living in the Islands of the blest. Such is the art of our rhetoricians, and in such manner does the sound of their words keep ringing in my ears.[24]

---

[23]Ibid., p. 49.
[24]Plato, "Menexenus," in *The Dialogues of Plato*, trans. B. Jowett (New York: Random House, 1937), 2:775 (italics mine).

Plato also observes:

> noble words are a memorial and a crown of noble actions, which are given to the
> doers of them by the hearers. A word is needed which will duly praise the dead
> and gently admonish the living . . . to imitate their virtue.[25]

What kind of words are required? Plato gives a list that includes:

1. praise of their noble birth
2. praise of their nurture and education
3. praise for their noble actions that demonstrate them worthy of their education.[26]

Paul does not fulfill any of these expectations. Rather Paul specifically
mentions "low born." But there are many things in the *epitaphios* tradition that
Paul does incorporate into his hymn on the cross. Furthermore, rhetoric was
an important part of Greek art which had known characteristics. Wills is
again helpful.

Reflecting on these famous ancient Greek funeral orations, Wills observes
that they exhibit the characteristics of classic art which are:

compression
grasp of the essentials
balance
awareness of the deepest polarities in the situation

All of these characteristics appear in Paul's hymn to the cross. Indeed, Paul
went to the Greek world, including Athens, and his preaching of Jesus who
died to save could easily have been heard by Greeks through the filter of the
funeral orations. A careful examination of Pericles' oration and Paul's hymn
to Christ crucified reveals seven points of comparison and contrast.[27] These
are as follows:

1. Both speeches remember and reflect on the saving significance of the
death of a revered champion or champions.

> a. For Pericles, the champions are Athenian soldiers who died to save the city.
> Plato reinforces this idea when he writes, "In their life they rejoiced their own
> friends with their valor, and *they gave their death in exchange for the salvation of
> the living.*"[28]

---

[25]Ibid., p. 777.
[26]Ibid.
[27]Wills prints the entire oration by Pericles and also includes a shorter oration by Gorgias. Wills,
*Lincoln at Gettysburg*, pp. 249-59.
[28]Plato, "Menexenus," 2:777 (italics mine).

b. Paul affirms that it pleased God through the folly of Christ crucified to *save all who believe.*

The big difference between the two is that the Greek champions died in battle as war heroes.

Jesus died a criminal's death nailed to a cross. This looks like weakness, not strength. It is, at least in Greek eyes, a stupid waste. The Greek is prepared to hear about a noble hero who dies to save his people. But that hero does so by killing the enemies of the state, not by dying nailed to a cross like a runaway slave or a common criminal. It is easy to imagine the temptation before the Christian preachers of that age to reshape the proclamation of the saving effect of the death of Jesus by picturing him as a Greek hero like those acclaimed in the funeral orations.[29] Paul refused to do so. Bravely, he did not hide the nature of the death of Jesus the Messiah (Christ) nor did he reshape Jesus into a Greek champion. Boldly, Paul reminds his readers that among them he had one subject—*Christ crucified.*

2. *Compression*, as noted, was a characteristic of the Greek orations. Wills observes:

> The compactness is not merely a matter of length. There is a suppression of particulars . . . in the Greek orations. This restraint produces the aesthetic paradox that makes these works oddly moving despite their impersonal air. Restraint deepens passion by refusing to give it easy vent.[30]

The Greek orations were short in length and offered no widescreen details. There are no flashing swords, no tramping horses and no bleeding wounds. An oration by Gorgias, a younger contemporary of Plato, is about the same length as Paul's hymn. Paul also offers no details. He speaks of "the word of the cross" and "the Greeks seek wisdom." He writes, "the Jews demand signs." Using even more hidden language he tells of "the weak things in the world" and "the low/base, and contemptible things in the world." But there are no explanations. A part of us longs for those missing details. But the compressed essentials are there and the mind is powerfully stimulated by them.

3. Both texts offer *polarities* in the situation. The polarities that appear in the six extant Greek funeral orations include:

---

[29]In a revolutionary age, Jesus is presented as a revolutionary. In an age that turns "inclusivity" into an absolute, Jesus is proclaimed as the all-inclusive one. This is an old problem.
[30]Wills, *Lincoln at Gettysburg*, p. 53.

The one and the many
Light and dark
Mortal and immortal
Athenians and others
Word and deed
Teachers and taught
Age and youth
Male and female
Choice and determinism
Past and present
Life and death[31]

Similarly, Paul has numerous polarities. Some of the *epitaphioi* polarities reappear. These include:

Life and death—"those who are being destroyed,
those who are being saved"

The nobly born vs. the low born

Choice (I came) and determinism (I was sent)

New polarities unique to Paul's hymn include:

Wisdom vs. foolishness (the wisdom of God vs. the wisdom of men which is foolishness)

Power vs. weakness (the power of God vs. the power of men which is weakness)

Being vs. non-being (things that are not—bring to nothing the things that are)

Those who boast vs. those who are in Christ Jesus

Wise words vs. the word of the cross

4. The Greek orations always had some *advice* for the living. This element is muted in Paul. Paul's hymn has some direct admonitions such as "consider your call" and "let all flesh not boast in the presence of God." But the advice to the reader is more in the form of a pervasive call to accept the cross as the wisdom and power of God unto salvation.

5. There is the question of *language*. The Greek *epitaphioi* focus on *language* as the necessary (indeed legislated) addition to the brave deeds accomplished on a battlefield. The *language* adds otherwise absent meaning to the death of

---

[31]Ibid., pp. 56-57.

the champions. Here Paul *disagrees* deliberately and completely. When he is talking about the cross he is *not* adding a missing element to its significance and power. This background helps explain Paul's phrase "No wise words lest the cross be emptied of its power." The *event of the cross* creates its own power and meaning. Carefully composed speech is appropriate to reveal and mediate the power that is already there, but it does not add power to the cross that it does not already have.

Lincoln said, "The world will little note nor long remember what we say here, but it can never forget what they did here."[32] The President knew he had a good speech, but he also understood that the event of the battle of Gettysburg was what mattered. For Paul, against Pericles, the word of the cross (that is the event of the cross) was itself the power and wisdom of God.[33]

A further parallel between the two "orations" appears around the question of language. Pericles *opens* with a reference to his oratorical powers. He *concludes* by saying, "I have spoken the best words I could for the occasion, as the law required."[34] Paul appears to know the details of Pericles' speech because in contrast Paul *opens* with a *denial* that he comes "with wise words" (*en sophia logou*) to add to the cross and *concludes* with a disavowal of "lofty language" or wisdom. To be sure his readers note his rejection of Pericles' views on this topic, Paul, like Pericles, discusses this matter at the *beginning* and at the *end* of his hymn. At the opening and the closing of the hymn, Paul's total focus is on Christ crucified, an event in history.

6. The two texts reflect the same interplay between "I" and "we." As he begins his speech, Pericles uses the first person and talks of "I" do this and that. The admonitions in the center are addressed to all Athenians and he shifts to "we." In his final paragraph, Pericles returns to "I have spoken." Paul also has "I preach" at the beginning and at the end of his hymn. "We preach" appears in the center. It appears that Paul knew Pericles' oration very well indeed.

7. *Power* is an important aspect of Pericles' oration. The power he discusses is always the military, ethical and cultural power of the city of Athens. Paul discusses the power of God demonstrated in Christ crucified. The "power of this world" is seen as foolishness. This would not have been easy for Greeks to

---

[32]Ibid., p. 261.

[33]The father in the parable of the prodigal son runs down the road to find him and restore him to "life." This is the wisest and most powerful thing he could have done (cf. Kenneth Bailey, *The Cross and the Prodigal* [Downers Grove, Ill.: InterVarsity Press, 2005]).

[34]Pericles, quoted in Wills, *Lincoln at Gettysburg*, p. 256.

accept. But for Paul *God transformed* the weakness of the cross into strength and its foolishness into wisdom. This message Paul will proclaim boldly regardless of consequences.

These seven points of comparison and contrast oblige us to consider the possibility that (in addition to Isaiah) Paul had Pericles in mind as he composed his hymn on the cross.

This understanding of the text clarifies Paul's intent when he writes, "I decided to know nothing among you except Jesus Christ and him crucified." In the light of the possible connection to Pericles we can clarify Paul's purposes which include the following:

Paul does *not* intend any form of anti-intellectualism.

He does *not* mean that he is rejecting the method of appealing to the Greek mind through its own literary sources such as he pioneered in Athens.[35]

He does *not* mean a rejection of rhetoric with its careful attention to precision, balance, clarity and indeed beauty. (As noted, his call is not an excuse for sloppy sermon preparation.)

He *does* mean that the deeply imbedded presuppositions of Pericles with his famous *epitaphios must be rejected* in order to understand the mystery of the wisdom and power of God in Christ crucified.

What then can we conclude regarding Paul's method and message?

Four aspects of Paul's *methodology* can be identified.

1. Paul started with his theology of the cross that was built on events in history. He then discovered connections between those events and Isaiah's suffering servant song in Isaiah 50:5-11. The major themes and the rhetorical framework of that servant song were used by Paul as a foundation for his hymn to Christ crucified. With Isaiah's help he built a bridge to the Jewish world.

2. Paul then reflected on the rhetoric, history, literature and language of the Greek world and judged Pericles' oration to be a suitable point of entry for his theology of the cross into that Greek world. Paul was probably also aware of Plato's dialogue with *Menexenus*.

3. With Isaiah 50:5-11 as a foundation, Paul then shaped his hymn in the light of Pericles' funeral oration. Much stayed the same while the original founda-

---

[35]See Acts 17:22-34.

tion in Isaiah 50 remained visible. He adapted this hymn for reuse in a mixed Greek and Jewish environment. Deliberate comparisons and contrasts with the famous *epitaphios* of Pericles were included in the revision. Agreements and disagreements with Plato's *Dialogue with Menexenus* were also consciously made and some new ideas were added. The result was a brilliant hymn to Christ crucified that spoke simultaneously to Jews and Greeks.

4. He compromised *nothing*. Points of disagreement with the funeral oration tradition and with Jewish expectations of the messiah were boldly stated. Aspects of agreement were loud and clear. Paul did *not* make Jesus into an Athenian hero in order to gain a sympathetic hearing, but rather endured rejection and ridicule in order to remain loyal to Christ crucified. The result was a powerful Christian word to both Jew and Greek.

What then can be said regarding *theology*? The following summary may provide a starting point for reflection.

1. Paul affirms the centrality of the cross, and the necessity of its proclamation to all, regardless of their cultural and theological perspectives.

2. Paul's "word of the cross" is an event in history, not a good speech. This hymn is anti-Gnostic without being anti-intellectual.

3. There is a theology of suffering in the hymn. The cross is transformed *by God* from weakness to strength and from stupidity to wisdom. The new power and wisdom of God shames and overcomes the world. (This theology comes to its climax in chapter 15 with its discussion of the resurrection.)

4. The cross is God's instrument of wisdom and power—not the Corinthians. "All flesh," including the Corinthians, can only boast "in the Lord."

5. Jewish readers were encouraged to see the crucified messiah as a fulfillment of one of the rich theological streams in the book of Isaiah. Thoughtful Jewish readers could have "overheard" clear references to the third servant song of Isaiah and were challenged to see in the cross the fulfillment of that great classical vision of God's unique servant.

6. The Greek world was given the opportunity to continue to honor Pericles and the Greek heroes who died to save Athens. At the same time they were encouraged to offer loyalty to a new champion. Paul offered a new funeral oration in praise of a new hero who died in a new way to save a new people who, through that death, became the wisdom and power of God for all who believe.

7. Well-written rhetoric and unforgettable poetry were demonstrated to be honorable tools for the proclamation of the gospel.

8. Salvation is presented as a process. The believing community is "being saved" (cameo 2). The matching cameo (12) expands the nature of salvation by declaring, "From him (God) you are in Christ Jesus, who became wisdom for us from God" (that is, righteousness, sanctification and redemption).

9. This hymn had the power to heal ethnic divisions between Jew and Greek. Both Jews and Greeks were challenged to see Christ and his cross as the power and wisdom of God. Ethnic *differences* remained but ethnic *divisions* could evaporate. The party spirit that declared, "I am of Apollos" (Greek) and "I am of Cephas" (Jewish) was rendered meaningless. The not-so-subtle message was, "We do not have to break up into ethnic enclaves. There is space for all of us to bring the best of our cultural heritages into the body of Christ." Christian unity flows from Christ crucified. (The same message appears in Eph 2:11-22.)

10. In chapter 4:1 Paul describes himself and his colleagues as "stewards of the mysteries of God." While in Ephesus, composing this epistle, Paul was caring for all the churches, teaching daily in the hall of Tyrannus,[36] dealing with the silversmiths, escaping a mob in the arena and trying to earn a living sewing tents. In spite of those pressures, in this passage he fulfills brilliantly fulfills a part of this ministry.[37] He never allowed his "stewardship of the mysteries of God" to evaporate. This creative theological effort was at the heart of who he was and what he struggled mightily to accomplish.

11. Paul was "sent" and "he came." Jews and Greeks were "called" and they "believed." The sovereignty of God and the responsibility of the faithful are held in dynamic tension throughout the hymn.

After this ringing affirmation that God's power is demonstrated in the foolishness of the cross, Paul turns the theological coin over and talks about the "secret and hidden wisdom of God" (2:7). To that "other side of the coin" we now turn.

---

[36]Acts 19:8-10.

[37]In chapter 2:1 [figure 1.2(1)] Paul affirms that he is proclaiming "the mystery of God."

# The Wisdom of God

*Revealed Through the Spirit*

1 CORINTHIANS 2:3-16

I<small>N</small> REVIEW, THE OVERALL structure of Paul's first essay is as follows:

1.1 Divisions in the Church (1:10-16)
1.2 The Wisdom and Power of God: Revealed Through the Cross (1:17–2:2)
*1.3 The Wisdom of God: Revealed Through the Spirit (2:3-16)*
1.4 Christian Unity (3:1–4:16)

The italicized section C, before us, is composed of two homilies. These are

God's Wisdom: Hidden and then revealed through the Spirit (2:3-10a)
God's Wisdom: Revealed through God, his thoughts and his Spirit (2:10b-16)

Each of these will be examined in turn.

The first homily is displayed in figure 1.3(1).

## THE RHETORIC (THE APPROACH)

In the introductory chapter "Prophetic Homily Rhetorical Style and Its Interpretation" we saw that Isaiah 43:25–44:8 uses a biblical homily style I have called the "high jump format." A high jump is executed in four connected movements. First is the quick sprint toward the bar. Second is the arched jump. Third is the crossing of the bar and finally the arched descent on the far side of the bar (that is the reverse of the ascent). The climax of the entire effort is the crossing of the bar. Here for the first time Paul uses this precise format. First he presents a short series of cameos introducing the topic (the approach: 1-3). He begins his new subject with three cameos (the jump: 4-6) that come to a climax (crossing the bar: 7). The "jump" is then

1.  2:3And I was with you in weakness            PAUL:
        and in much fear and trembling,         Fear and Trembling
        4and my speech and my message           HIS MESSAGE:
        were not in plausible words of wisdom,  Spirit and Power
        but in demonstration of the Spirit and power,

2.  5that your faith might not rest
        in the wisdom of men                    YOUR FAITH
        but in the power of God.                In the Power of God

3.  6Yet wisdom we do impart among the mature,
        wisdom, not of this age,                FOR THE MATURE
        or of the rulers of this age,           Wisdom
        who are passing away.                   This Age Cannot Understand

4.  7But we speak *God's wisdom*        GOD'S WISDOM
        *hidden* in a *mystery*,        Hidden in a Mystery

5.      That which *God decreed*            GOD DECREED
            from the ages for *our glory*.  For Our Glory

6.          8That which *none* of the rulers         NOT UNDERSTOOD BY PEOPLE
                of this age *understood*;

7.              for if they had understood,
                    they would not have *crucified*     THE CROSS
                    the *Lord of glory*.

8.          9But, as it is written,
                "That which *eye has not seen*, nor *ear heard*,
                    nor the *heart of man conceived*,   NOT UNDERSTOOD BY PEOPLE

9.      that which *God prepared*           GOD PREPARED
            for *those who love him*,"       For Us Who Love Him

10. 10for *to us God* has *revealed*    GOD'S WISDOM
        *through the Spirit*.           Revealed Through the Spirit

---

**Figure 1.3(1). The wisdom of God: The Spirit (1 Cor 2:3-10a)**

matched with the "descent" that is the reverse of the jump (the descent: 8-10). This could also be called "a prophetic rhetorical template with an introduction." With some modifications Paul uses this high jump format a total of thirteen times in 1 Corinthians.[1] Once again, Paul is using a rhetorical style available to him out of his Jewish literary heritage.

---

[1]See 1 Cor 2:3-10; 3:1-19; 6:13-20; 9:1-12; 9:12b-18 (modified); 10:1-13; 10:23–11:1; 11:2-17; 12:31–14:1 (modified); 14:13-25; 15:21-34; 15:35-40 (modified).

## Commentary

Paul begins with "the approach," which is composed of four closely related cameos. The first of them has to do with his inner spiritual condition.

| | | |
|---|---|---|
| 1. | 2:3And I was with you in weakness and in much fear and trembling, | PAUL: Fear and Trembling |

As observed previously, this statement has often been read in an anti-intellectual fashion. The common assumption is that Paul tried "the intellectual approach" in Athens. There he delved into Greek philosophical sources and tried to relate the gospel to them. The experiment was a failure. He was not able to start a church. The fallout of that failure was that he left Athens depressed and headed for Corinth. On the way he decided on a shift in his methodology. Instead of trying to connect with pagan sources, he opted to give up on "the wisdom of men" and rely totally on "preaching Christ and his cross." His decision was blessed by God, and in Corinth he was able to found a church. Conclusion: In proclamation do not try to relate to the intellectual or spiritual heritage of the audience; just preach Christ.

Consciously or unconsciously, this is a widely held popular view. But is it accurate? As noted in section 1.2, "The Wisdom and Power of God: The Cross," Paul's hymn to the cross engaged both the Greek mind (by debating with Pericles) and the Jewish mind (by interacting with Is 50:5-11). With considerable theological and rhetorical skill he did both at the same time. This demonstrates that his presentation of the gospel in 1 Corinthians is steeped in Greek and Jewish scholarship. Related to this fact is the question, Did he fail in Athens?

The philosophical guild in Athens was the intellectual center of the entire Greco-Roman world. Leading Roman families often sent their children to Athens for advanced education. To have received a hearing in that bastion of Greek learning was a huge victory in itself. The intellectual center of the Islamic world is al-Azhar, in Cairo. That venerable university is more than a thousand years old and is revered from Indonesia to Morocco and beyond. A few years ago, His Grace George Carey, the Archbishop of Canterbury, was invited to address al-Azhar. All of us who were involved in ministry anywhere in the Islamic world were thrilled and electrified by the very fact of the invitation. Archbishop Carey and his presentation were well received, and Middle Eastern Christians were overjoyed. No, he did not "start a new church" in the shadow of al-Azhar university.

No one expected that he might. The event was judged by all to be a great success.

The fact that Paul was able to attract the attention of the philosophers of his day in Athens and was then *invited* to address them on Mars Hill was a stunning achievement. His speech set a direction for the church's witness to the Greek world that came to full flower with the Greek apologists of the third century. The Greek Orthodox Church emerged from that effort. Paul received a hearing, planted a seed, set a direction and moved on.

On many occasions in Christian history the gospel first took root among the poor and the disenfranchised. Yes indeed, Athens was the intellectual center of the Mediterranean world, but Corinth was the largest international commercial city in the eastern Mediterranean. The faith could move out across the region from Corinth in ways that would not have been possible from Athens. Paul must have understood this. If then discouragement over failure was *not* Paul's mood as he left Athens and approached Corinth, what did he mean when he wrote 2:3?

Initially Paul knew that Corinth was not Athens. Quoting Greek philosophical sources would mean nothing to Corinthian dock workers. Furthermore Paul approached every person and place "in weakness," not in power. This was central to the theology of mission in the early church. There was no attempt to establish a power base, raise an army and conquer territory as a first step to evangelization. The apostles were not Spanish conquistadors. Yes, Constantine conquered as much territory as he could and used his political and military power to advance what he understood to be "the gospel." In the seventh century Islam used that methodology as it burst on the Middle Eastern world with a conquering army. Charlemagne followed Constantine's lead. But Paul went to what is now Greece and Turkey in total weakness. For Paul "fear and trembling" meant that he went in humility, trusting in the grace of God, not in earthly power or in his own abilities or good works. In Philippians 2:12 Paul commands his readers to "work out your own salvation with *fear* and *trembling*." "Fear and trembling" was not a special psychological condition experienced by Paul uniquely on the road from Athens to Corinth; but it was for him the appropriate spiritual attitude for all Christians as they fulfilled their callings.

Paul continues by reminding his readers of his weakness and God's power [see fig. 1.3(2)].

2.   [4]and my speech and my message
      were not in plausible words of wisdom,                PAUL'S MESSAGE:
      but in demonstration of the Spirit and power,        Spirit and Power

3.   [5]that your faith might not rest
      in the wisdom of men                                 YOUR FAITH
      but in the power of God.                             In the Power of God

**Figure 1.3(2). Cameos 2-3 (1 Cor 2:4-5)**

Paul is here summarizing and repeating ideas he first presented in his hymn to the cross (1:17–2:2). As observed, "no plausible words of wisdom" did not mean ignoring contacts with Greek thought or the skillful use of polished rhetoric. Here, he adds to that picture by noting that his "speech and message" involved "demonstrations of the Spirit and power." Clearly the "charismatic gifts" were an important aspect of his presentation of the gospel. Some of the details of these Spirit-filled meetings are described in chapter 14, where he mentions revelation, knowledge, prophecy, teaching, edification, encouragement, consolation and mysteries in the Spirit. Along with these aspects of worship he also mentions speaking in tongues, interpretation of tongues, the working miracles and gifts of healing. The cold logic of the Sophists and the Epicureans was not the fabric of his presentation of the gospel, but instead his witness was full of "demonstrations of the Spirit and power." He wanted the Corinthians' faith to rest on the power of God and not on the wisdom of people.

Paul concludes his introduction by pointing to a different kind of wisdom that he imparts to the mature. He writes:

3.   [2:6]Yet wisdom we do impart among the mature,
      wisdom, not of this age,                             YOUR FAITH
      or of the rulers of this age,                        Wisdom
      who are passing away.                                This Age Cannot Understand

Neither the intellectuals nor the political rulers of the age had access to the wisdom Paul presents. They were passing away. What Paul has to say falls into the category of the wisdom of God that is anchored in saving events in history, that are permanent and *do not* pass away. The daring of this cameo is often overlooked. Paul was writing to a Roman colony that worshiped Caesar as God. Were their gods passing away? Caesar Augustus died in A.D. 14 and was quickly deified by the Roman Senate with the title "Divus Augustus." Honoring Divus Augustus was part of the imperial cult, and that cult had a huge temple facing the central square of Corinth.[2] The rebuilding of the city of Corinth had proceeded for almost a hundred years when Paul was writing. It is impossible to imagine that the imperial cult was without influence in Rome's largest colonial city. Paul's language is daring and electrifying. Having gained his readers' rapt attention, he proceeds to present this hidden wisdom of God now revealed through the Spirit. With the "approach" completed, Paul is ready to open his new topic with a "jump up to the bar." For ease of reference the entire prophetic rhetorical template with its seven cameos is repeated.

| | | |
|---|---|---|
| 4. | [7]But we speak *God's wisdom* / *hidden* in a *mystery*, | GOD'S WISDOM / Hidden in a Mystery |
| 5. | <u>That which</u> [*en*] *God decreed* / from the ages for *our glory*. | GOD DECREED / For Us |
| 6. | [8]<u>That which</u> [*en*] *none* of the rulers / of this age *understood*; | NOT UNDERSTOOD BY PEOPLE |
| 7. | for if they had understood, / they would not have *crucified* / the *Lord of glory*. | THE CROSS |
| 8. | [9]But, as it is written, / "<u>That which</u> [*a*] *eye has not seen*, nor *ear heard*, / nor the *heart of man conceived*, | NOT UNDERSTOOD BY PEOPLE |
| 9. | <u>that which</u> [*a*] *God prepared* / for *those who love him*," | GOD PREPARED / For Us |
| 10. | [10]for *to us God* has *revealed* / *through the Spirit*. | GOD'S WISDOM / Revealed Through the Spirit |

**Figure 1.3(3). God's wisdom: Hidden and revealed (1 Cor 2:7-10a)**

## RHETORIC

This particular rhetorical template contains a special feature. Four occurrences of the Greek relative pronoun (that which) are skillfully placed to introduce four balanced cameos. Reduced to its simplest expression the seven homilies are as follows:

---

[2]Jerome Murphy-O'Connor, *St. Paul's Corinth: Texts and Archaeology* (Collegeville, Minn.: Liturgical Press, 2002), p. 26.

1.    God's wisdom: Hidden in mystery
2.      *that which*: God decreed—for us
3.         *that which*: Rulers misunderstood
4.            The cross of the Lord of glory
5.         *that which*: no one understood
6.      *that which*: God prepared—for us
7.    God's (wisdom): Revealed through the Spirit

---

**Figure 1.3(4). Summary of homily (I Cor 2:7-10a)**

In the magnificent hymn on wisdom and the cross (1 Cor 1:17–2:2) examined earlier, Paul presents seven cameos which he then repeats backward. That hymn opens, centers and concludes on the preaching of the cross. Here Paul is again discussing *wisdom* and the *cross*. Except in this text he presents one series of seven cameos rather than two. The cross again appears at the center, tying this homily to 1:17–2:2. As before, the beginning, the middle and the end are profoundly related.

### COMMENTARY

The previous hymn discusses the cross and wisdom. Here *wisdom* is mentioned at the *beginning* (4), the *cross* is discussed in the *center* (7) and *wisdom* is implied at the *end* (10). Paul concludes, "To us God has revealed [his wisdom]." Also at the beginning, the middle and the end are three affirmations of deity. These are: *God* (4), the *Lord of glory* (7) and finally the *Spirit* (10). That is, this homily reflects stirrings of reflection on the Trinity. Paul is already thinking in Trinitarian ways. As we will see, this is followed in the next homily by a striking number of carefully constructed affirmations related to the Trinity.

In addition to this whiff of the Trinity, *God* appears in the first two cameos (4, 5) and again in the last two (9, 10). These four cameos tell us four things about God:

- God hides
- God decrees
- God prepares
- God reveals

In addition to this series there is a careful balancing of ideas in the paired cameos. The first (outer) pair is composed of 4 and 10, which reads:

| 4. | <sup></sup>2:7But we speak *God's wisdom hidden* in a *mystery*, | GOD'S WISDOM Hidden in a Mystery |
|---|---|---|

------------------------------

| 10. | <sup></sup>10for *to us God* has *revealed through the Spirit*. | GOD'S WISDOM Revealed Through the Spirit |
|---|---|---|

*Hiding* and *revealing* are matched. In the first (4) we read of how God *hid* his wisdom "in a mystery." The reader inevitably asks, What mystery is he talking about? Hints of an answer come in this homily and in the homily that follows. The center of this homily (cameo 7) is the cross, which is undoubtedly the heart of the mystery that Paul has in mind. Then in cameo 10 Paul speaks of God *revealing* that mystery *through the Spirit*. Again, the reader is stimulated to ask, What revelation does he have in mind? The answer appears in the center. Paul is discussing the revelation of God's mystery in the cross and in the person of the crucified one who was not merely a Galilean carpenter—but rather *the Lord of glory*.

"The Spirit of God" is known in the biblical tradition ever since the Spirit of God moved "over the waters" at creation (Gen 1:2). But who can understand the *cross* of "the Lord of glory"? Truly, this is a hidden mystery! Here the divinity of Christ, the wonder of his suffering and the mystery of glory revealed are all involved, and all three are deeply embedded in the mystery of the Trinity. This mystery continues in the second pair of cameos which are:

| 5. | <sup></sup>2:7bThat which *God decreed* from the ages for *our glory*. | GOD DECREED For Our Glory |
|---|---|---|

------------------------------

| 9. | <sup></sup>9bthat which *God prepared* for *those who love him*," | GOD PREPARED For Us Who Love Him |
|---|---|---|

There is measured progression through the four affirmations concerning the actions of God. God first *hides* (4) and then *decrees* (5). Having *decreed* (5) he must *prepare* (9). Finally comes the *revelation* (10). This is the movement of a lover who initially *hides* his intentions regarding his beloved. He then *decides* to win her. Next he must *prepare* what he is going to do to achieve his goal. Finally he *reveals* his intentions by proposing to her.

This pair of cameos describes the "decree" of God as being "from the ages." The incarnation and the cross are not unexpected interruptions in God's plan. They are not ghastly mistakes. They are not "plan Z" after all else has failed.

In Paul's mind, they are the result of God's eternal plan.

Comparison with Islam and rabbinic Judaism may be helpful. In Islamic thought the Qur'an is eternal in the mind of God. In the early Middle Ages a movement of Islamic scholars (called the *Mu'tazalin*) argued for a "created Qur'an." Their ideas were eventually rejected and they were killed. No, insists Islam, the Qur'an, like God himself, is eternal. In the same manner, rabbinic thought held the view that the Torah was uncreated. God used the Torah as a guidebook for the creation of the world. Paul had no concept of an eternal book, but he presents a God who possesses *eternal wisdom*, which was a hidden mystery "from the ages."

Furthermore, Islamic thought has always seen the cross as an event that could not have happened because God never allows his prophets to be overcome by their enemies. The prophets may struggle for a while, as did Muhammad at Mecca. But then the Prophet moved to Medina where he was vindicated by the acquisition of political and military power. That vindication continued as he won all his military battles. Both the Greek and the Jewish world had problems with the cross, which they saw as weak and foolish, as Paul admitted (1:22-23). But, no, Jesus was "delivered up according to the definite plan and foreknowledge of God" (Acts 2:23). And what was a part of the purpose of this amazing plan?

God decreed the cross from the ages (cameo 5) *"for our glory"* and prepared it (9) *"for those who love him."* The same balancing of the active and the passive noted in the opening and closing of the hymn to the cross in 1:17–2:2, recurs here. There, Paul writes "I was sent" and at the same time he affirms "I came." In this text (5) *God acts* "for our glory." In the balancing cameo (9) we find that this divine act was "for those who love him." God *acts*; believers *respond with love*. Their loving acceptance of the mystery is a critical component in the divine-human relationship.

The phrase *for our glory* is itself mysterious. Later Paul affirms that the faithful will "judge angels" (6:3). On the day of judgment believers will participate with God as members of the court and judge not only people but also angels! This may be part of what Paul has in mind in this text. But beyond that possibility is the fact that behind the Greek word *doxa* (glory) is the Hebrew word *kabod* (weight). In Middle Eastern culture, a "weighty" person (*rajul thaqil*) has to do with wisdom, balance, stability, reliability, sound judgment, patience, impartiality, nobility and the like. Latin has preserved these ideas and attached them to the word *gravitas*. Glory has to do with *gravitas*!

Every family, community and church desperately wants and needs such a person to guide them, comfort them and help them solve their problems. God's plan for all ages has to do with the cross and with the emergence on the other side of the cross of men and women who embody these qualities. Indeed glory (*gravitas*), for those who love God, flows from the cross of "the Lord of glory." This leads to the third pair of cameos with its center climax [see fig. 1.3(5)]:

| | | |
|---|---|---|
| 6. | [8]That which [*'en*] *none* of the rulers of this age *understood*; | NOT UNDERSTOOD BY PEOPLE |
| 7. | for if they had understood, they would not have *crucified* the *Lord of glory*. | THE CROSS |
| 8. | [9]But, as it is written, "That which [*'a*] *eye has not seen*, nor *ear heard*, nor the *heart of man conceived*, | NOT UNDERSTOOD BY PEOPLE |

Figure 1.3(5). Cameos 6-8 (1 Cor 2:8-9)

The content of cameos 6-8 is striking. Paul does not blame the Romans (Pilate) or the Jews (the high priest) for the crucifixion. Does this text contain echoes of "Father, forgive them; for they know not what they do" (Lk 23:34)? Quite likely. Paul could have dumped blame on either or both of these communities and their leaders. Again we sense that Paul is fully aware of his readership. This letter was primarily addressed to Greek and Jewish Christians living in a Roman colony. After all Paul was both a Roman and a Jew. He proclaimed the truth of the gospel without blaming his readers or their leaders. The text has no hint of anti-Semitism. The refusal to look backwards to the perpetrators of the cross in 1:17–2:2 is repeated here. The passion was the eternal plan of God "from all ages."

Indeed, the mystery of the crucifixion of the Lord of glory was so amazing that *no one* had "seen" or "heard" or even imagined it. Nor could they have dreamed that it could produce "glory" (*kabod, gravitas*, weight) in the hearts of those who love him.

It is no mistake that the Scripture quotation chosen by Paul for this homily (8-9) is a free rendition of Isaiah 52:15 which in turn is one of the opening verses of the suffering servant song of Isaiah 52:13–53:12. In Paul's mind that song was obviously an important key to understanding the mystery of "the Lord of glory" on a cross, which creates glory for those who love *God*, the *Lord of glory* and the *Spirit*.

## SUMMARY

This homily touches on many themes. Six of them can be summarized as follows:

1.  Here Paul continues to clarify and present his message. In Corinth he did not jettison his concern to build bridges for communicating the gospel to the Greeks and the Jews around him. Yet, as everywhere, he was sensitive to this new audience to which he came in weakness, not with worldly power.

2.  God hides, decrees, prepares and then reveals the mystery of the crucified Lord of glory. It is an eternal plan, not an accident of history.

3.  *God's* mystery is about *the Lord of glory*, and that mystery is now revealed through the *Spirit*. Paul is thinking in Trinitarian terms.

4.  As the eternal plan of God, the cross can produce glory, *doxa, kabod, gravitas* and weight for those who love God.

5.  Pilate (the Romans) and the high priest (the Jews) are not blamed for the cross. Pilate and the high priest did not understand what they were doing—indeed God's plan was beyond the understanding of anyone.

6.  The suffering servant of Isaiah stands behind the cross of Jesus. A quotation from the first is quoted to explain the second.

In the next homily Paul continues his discussion of the mystery once hidden and now revealed [see fig. 1.3(6)].

This carefully constructed, theologically dense passage has puzzled interpreters for centuries. These reflections will concentrate on illuminating its rhetorical structure and its unmistakable emphasis on the Trinity.

## RHETORIC

Like Isaiah 28:14-18, with great skill, a number of rhetorical features are here interwoven into a single homily.

Initially the homily is composed of five cameos linked by means of ring composition. Second, there is a balancing of *parable* (1) and *Scripture* (5). As previously observed, in prophetic rhetoric, the center of ring composition is often filled with a parable/metaphor, a nature miracle or a quotation from an earlier sacred tradition. The text before us opens and closes with mini-ring compositions (cameos 1 and 5). Each of these two cameos has an A-B-A structure. In the first (1) the center is filled with the "parable of the human person." While in the last (5) the center contains a quotation from Isaiah

| | |
|---|---|
| 1.[2:10b]For the *Spirit* searches all things, even the *deep things* of God. | SPIRIT/DEEP THINGS/OF GOD |
| [11]For what person knows a *man's thoughts* except the *spirit of the man* which is in him? | *Parable* of Man/Thoughts/Spirit |
| So no one knows the *thoughts* of God except the *Spirit of God*. | God/Thoughts/Spirit |
| | |
| 2. a.[12]And we, not the spirit of the world we receive, | WE RECEIVE |
| b. but the *Spirit* which is *from God*, | The Spirit from God |
| c. that we might understand *the things from God* | We Understand Things from God |
| d. *graced* upon us. | Graced upon Us |
| | |
| 3. [13]And this we impart | WE IMPART |
| not in teachings of human wisdom by words | Teachings of Spirit |
| but in teachings of spirit to spiritual people, | To Spiritual People |
| spiritual things interpreting. | |
| | |
| 4. a.[14]The natural person does not receive | NATURAL MAN—NOT RECEIVE |
| b. the *things* of the *Spirit* of *God*, | The Gifts of the Spirit |
| (for they are folly to him), | |
| c. and he is not able to understand them | He Cannot Understand Them |
| d. because they are spiritually discerned. | They Are Spiritually Discerned |
| | |
| 5. [15]The *Spiritual One* discerns all things, | |
| but is himself discerned by no one. | SPIRITUAL ONE DISCERNS ALL |
| [16]"For who has known the mind of *the Lord* | *Scripture* related to |
| so as to instruct him?" | Mind of the Lord (Yahweh) |
| But we have the *mind of Christ*. | Mind of Christ |

**Figure 1.3(6). The wisdom of God: Revealed through the Spirit (1 Cor 2:10b-16)**

40:13. Paul understands exactly what he is doing rhetorically. The climax of the homily as a whole appears in the center.

## COMMENTARY

Once again it seems appropriate to examine the matching cameos side by side, beginning with the first and the last of the five cameos [see fig. 1.3(7)].

Cameo 1 opens with "the Spirit searches all things." This is matched in the first line of cameo 5 where "the *Spiritual One* discerns all things." The parallel between the two adds weight to the idea that "the Spiritual One" referred to in cameo 5 is the Holy Spirit, and *not a spirit-filled believer*.[3] Indeed Paul is reflecting on the Trinity in both cameos. This is evident in the first cameo, which opens with:

---

[3]C. K. Barrett affirms this understanding of the text as an option, but then rejects it (see Barrett, *First Epistle*, p. 77).

2:10bFor the *Spirit* searches all things,
    even the *deep things* of God.

The phrase *deep things* is borrowed from popular Gnostic thought. Paul
uses this language to build a bridge from his thought world to the world of his
readers, but he is careful to see that the traffic flows from his mind to theirs.

1.10bFor the *Spirit* searches all things,
    even the *deep things* of God.                           SPIRIT SEARCHES ALL
        11For what person knows a *man's thoughts*               *Parable* of
            except the *spirit of the man* which is in him?      Man/Thoughts/Spirit
    So no one knows the *thoughts* of God                        God/Thoughts/Spirit
    except the *Spirit of God.*

---------------------------------------------------

5. 15The *Spiritual One* discerns all things,
    but is himself discerned by no one.                       SPIRITUAL ONE DISCERNS ALL
        16"For who has known the mind of *the Lord*               *Scripture* related to
            so as to instruct him?"                              Mind of the Lord (Yahweh)
    But we have the *mind of Christ.*                            Mind of Christ

**Figure 1.3(7). Cameos 1 and 5 (1 Cor 2:10b-11, 15-16)**

Without such bridges, communication is virtually impossible. What then
does Paul mean by "the deep things"? The simplest answer is that he is talking
about the Word of God that broke into human history in the person of Jesus
and his cross. This was the climax of the previous apostolic homily. The "deep
things of God" are not philosophical ideas withheld from common folk and
available only to the initiated few (Gnosticism), but rather the mystery of the
incarnation and the cross. Thus the subject of this opening statement is a
threefold way of talking about God who is: the *Spirit,* the *deep things* of God
(i.e., the Lord of glory), and *God.*

Continuing in cameo 1, Paul presents the first Christian parable on the
Trinity:

2:11For what person knows a *man's thoughts*
    except the *spirit of the man* which is in him?

This parable has three parts: the *man,* his *thoughts* and his *spirit.* I am a
person, and my name is Ken Bailey. I have thoughts. These thoughts are a
part of me, and in a deep sense they represent me. Because you are reading
this chapter, you are engaged with some of my thoughts. You cannot know
me without knowing my thoughts. My person and my thoughts are one,

and yet they are not identical. Also I have a spirit. My family and good friends know what my spirit is like and can describe it better than I can. Touch my spirit, and you have touched me. They are the same, and yet in some indefinable way they are not the same. All three of these realities— the person Ken Bailey; his thoughts, which are revealed through his words; and his spirit—function together even though it is possible to partially understand them in isolation from each other. Where did this wondrous combination of "three in one" come from? Are we not made in the image of God (Gen 1:27)?

In 2004 I was invited by the archbishop of Canterbury to join an international bridge-building conference of fifteen Muslim scholars and fifteen Christian scholars. We met for a week in Doha, the capital of the Sheikdom of Qatar in the Arabian Gulf. One evening an Egyptian Muslim scholar joined my Christian friend and me at dinner. During a lull in our conversation, she asked, "Gentlemen, can one of you explain the Christian doctrine of the Trinity to me? I have been trying to find an explanation that I can understand for twenty-five years and have failed. Can you help me?" After negotiating with my friend as to which of us would venture to answer this serious, friendly question, I offered a brief discussion of the text before us with its Pauline parable of the human person. I told my questioner that in the Qur'an one can read about "God," "the Word of God" and the "Spirit of God." The Islamic tradition has chosen not to reflect on how those three Quranic descriptions of the divine come together. That choice is their privilege, and I respect their freedom in that decision, I told her. But in the Christian tradition we also have *God*, his *Word* and his *Spirit*, and we have chosen to reflect on how these three form a unity. Greatly relieved the professor replied, "At last! Someone has given me an explanation of the Trinity that I can understand. I am so grateful." I quickly assured her that thanks were not due to me, but to St. Paul, who gave us the text (with its parable).

After this remarkable opening Paul continues,

> [11b]No one knows the *thoughts* of God
> except the *Spirit of God*.

Here the same trilogy reappears. The three elements are *God*, his *thoughts* and his *Spirit*. Paul confirms that his parable of the human person indeed refers to the mystery of the nature of God, who is three in one. The "thoughts" of God have to do with the Word of God, who became flesh in Jesus. In short,

this cameo contains three affirmations of the Trinity that include a parable.
What then of the matching cameo (5)?

| | |
|---|---|
| 5. [15]The *Spiritual One* discerns all things,<br>    but is himself discerned by no one.<br>        [16]"For who has known the mind of Yahweh<br>            so as to instruct him?"<br>    But we have the *mind of Christ*. | SPIRITUAL ONE DISCERNS ALL<br><br>*Scripture* related to<br>Mind of the Lord (Yahweh)<br>Mind of Christ |

As noted, "the Spiritual One" is best understood to refer to the Holy
Spirit (not a "spiritual" believer in Jesus). Indeed, the Holy Spirit "is discerned by no one." What is the nature of "God the Father"? Answers to
this question can be found in the Hebrew and in the Greek Scriptures.
What is "the mind of Christ"? The Gospels and the Epistles give a great
deal of information to help us answer that question. But what is the *nature*
of the Holy Spirit? We can see and experience the *work* of the Holy Spirit,
but do we know the *nature* of the Holy Spirit? That Spirit remains mysterious (Jn 3:5-8).

In cameo 5 Paul borrows from the Greek Old Testament (LXX) translation
of Isaiah 40:13 and affirms that the "mind of Yahweh" is also unknown. But
all is not lost—we have the "mind of Christ." The unknown "mind of God"
is now revealed through the "mind of Christ." The "spiritual one," the "mind
of Yahweh" and "the mind of Christ" come together. The unknown has become known. The mystery of the wisdom of God is unveiled—thanks to the
triune God.

Continuing an examination of the matched cameos in this homily, we turn
to cameos 2 and 4 which appear side by side in figure 1.3(8).

| | |
|---|---|
| 2a. [12]And we, not the spirit of the world we receive,<br>  b.  but the *Spirit* which is *from God*,<br>  c.  that we might understand *the things from God*<br>  d.  *graced* upon us. | WE RECEIVE<br>But by the Spirit from God<br>We Understand Things from God<br>Graced upon Us |
| ------------------------------------------- | ------------------------------------- |
| 4a. [14]The natural man does not receive<br>  b.  the *things* of the *Spirit* of *God*,<br>      (for they are folly to him),<br>  c.  and he is not able to understand them<br>  d.  because they are spiritually discerned. | NATURAL MAN—NOT RECEIVE<br>The Gifts of the Spirit<br><br>He Cannot Understand Them<br>They Are Spiritually Discerned |

**Figure 1.3(8). Cameos 2 and 4 (1 Cor 2:12, 14)**

Reflection on the Trinity continues. In cameo 2 Paul writes about the *Spirit* from *God*, who reveals *the things from God*. What things from God is he talking about? Granted, the text is mysterious, but it is possible to understand that those things from God refer to the gospel: the reality of God in Christ and the power and wisdom of the cross that is the subject under discussion from 1:17 up to this text. That gospel, that event with its message of "Christ crucified," is indeed "graced upon us."

Cameo 4 presents the same Trinity but with a negative application. "The things of the Spirit of God" are *not received* by the natural man. An extra phrase that reads "for they are folly to him" appears here. This phrase has no balancing line. It may be in the text because it echoes the center of the hymn in 1:17–2:2 where the cross is presented as "folly to Greeks." Not only is the cross folly, but the very idea of the Trinity and the incarnation are also folly to the Greek mind. Is Paul not speaking to the whole church, both then and now?

These two cameos are also matched in other ways. In Isaiah 28 we noted the parallels between the interior lines of one cameo to the interior lines of another. Here Paul uses that same style with admirable skill. The common elements in the four lines that appear in each cameo are

    a. Receive versus not receive
    b. The Spirit
    c. Understand versus not understand
    d. Graced (given) and discerned (understood)

Far greater minds than mine have nobly struggled to understand this passage. To unlock a few treasures may be the best that anyone can hope to accomplish. It is evident that in 2a Paul is describing himself and those around him as having received the Spirit from God. In 4a he discusses "the natural man" who is unable to understand the things of the Spirit of God. Paul and his friends do not receive "the Spirit of the world" (2a) and the "natural man" does not receive "the things of the Spirit of God" (4a-b). Paul and his companions are able to understand "the things from God" (2c) while the natural man "cannot understand them" (4c). Those spiritual realities are *given through grace* (2d); at the same time they must be *spiritually discerned* (4d).

In the first of these (2d) the believer is the *passive recipient* of grace. In the second (4d) the reader discovers that the recipient must play an active part in *accepting* the grace that proceeds from the Spirit. Logic and reasoning are not enough. There is a component in the gift of grace that equips the believer to understand the things of God. Paul moves in a world that cannot be reconciled to the worldview of the Enlightenment. We are back to the cross that the world sees as weak and foolish, but for those who are being saved—it is the power and wisdom of God.

The center of this homily (3) is as follows:

3.    2:13And this we *impart*                                WE IMPART
         not in teachings of human wisdom by words            Not Human Wisdom
         but in teachings of spirit to spiritual people,      But Spiritual Teachings
         spiritual things interpreting.                       To Spiritual People—Spiritually

In this climactic center Paul becomes "missional." It is not enough that people acquire "spirituality" and wallow in it. For Paul there *are* deep things of God (1, 5), and we (not the natural person) *receive* the things of the Spirit of God (2, 4), but also "we *impart*" these "teachings of the Spirit to spiritual people" (3). The phrase *human wisdom* occurs only here in the center, and it is contrasted with "teachings of spirit" that are presented to spiritual people.

Summarized and seen rhetorically these same five cameos are

1. The Spirit, God, his thoughts.
2. *We receive understanding* from the Spirit.
3. We *impart teachings* of spirit to spiritual people (not wise words).
4. *Natural man does not receive* the things of the Spirit.
5. The Spirit, God, the mind of Christ.

It is no accident that the "missional" component of the homily is in the climactic center. All of this is given for the purpose of *imparting* these revealed mysteries of the Spirit, through the Spirit to others (cameo 3).

This seems convoluted to our Western Greco-Roman minds. But any reader steeped in ring composition expects to hear a series of ideas that comes to a climax and then (with a difference) is repeated backwards. For such a mind, this homily is well-organized in a clear and convincing way.

Consistent logic is not enough. Paul is interested in imparting the *mind of Christ* that is the hidden *wisdom of God* revealed through the *Lord of glory* and *his cross.*

## SUMMARY

1. Paul discusses the Trinity six times in this homily (1a, 1b, 1c, 2, 4, 5). The human person is Paul's parable of the Trinity (1). The "natural man" (without the Spirit) cannot understand these mysteries.

Summarized, these appear as follows:

| | | SPIRIT | CHRIST | GOD |
|---|---|---|---|---|
| (1) | | The *Spirit* (searches all) | *Deep things* | of *God* |
| | | The Spirit (knows) | The thoughts | of man  (parable) |
| | | The *Spirit* (knows) | The *thoughts* | of *God* |
| (2) | | From the *Spirit* | *Things graced upon us* | from *God* |
| (4) | | The *Spirit* | The *things* | of *God* |
| (5) | | The *spiritual One* | The mind of *Christ* | Mind of *Yahweh* (Scripture) |

**Figure 1.3(9). Paul's discussion of the Trinity in cameos 1-5**

2. Human knowledge and wisdom (rationality) are not enough. "Teachings of Spirit" that go beyond human knowledge are necessary.

3. The *Spirit* (alone) is insufficient. The Corinthians thought the Spirit (pneumatology) was all they needed to understand God. Paul's response is, "No, through the Spirit you receive *God's gifts*, but not *God's thoughts/ mind*. For this *mind of God* the *mind of Christ* (Christology) is required."

4. Grace is "given" as a gift and yet that gift must be received (spiritually discerned) by the believer.

5. The mystery of the Trinity and the cross are folly to the natural man.

6. The believer is responsible to *receive, understand* and finally *impart* the mysteries of God to others.

Paul has now reached a critical moment in his first essay with the introduction of the missional element into the discussion. They are to "impart" all of this to others. Because of this mandate, Paul turns to a second discussion of Paul and Apollos, who are not competitors but rather coworkers in this weighty task of communicating the gospel to others (3). To that discussion we now turn.

# Christian Unity

*Paul, Apollos and Cephas as One*

I CORINTHIANS 3:1–4:16

PAUL IS NOW READY to present the fourth section of the first essay. The outline of the whole is

The Cross and Christian Unity (1:10–4:16)
1.  The Problem: Divisions, Baptism and the Cross (1:10-16)
2.  The Wisdom and Power of God: The Cross (1:17–2:2)
3.  The Wisdom of God: Revealed Through the Spirit (2:3-16)
4.  *Christian Unity: Paul, Apollos and Cephas as One* (3:1–4:16)

With two homilies on the wisdom of God (in the cross and through the Spirit) firmly in place as a foundation, Paul is ready to take a second look at how his readers *should* see Paul, Apollos and Cephas. This final section of the essay (4) has four homilies, along with a word of general admonition attached to a personal appeal. These are:

1. Paul and Apollos: It is *about you*! (3:1-4)            Paul and Apollos (You)
2.    The parable of the *field and the farmers* (3:5-9)            Parable—The Farmers
3.    The parable of the *builders and the building* (3:10-17)        Parable—The Building
4. Paul, Apollos, Cephas: It is *about Christ* (3:18–4:7)    Paul, Apollos and Cephas (Christ)
A concluding general admonition and personal appeal (4:8-16)

The two parables are encased within a frame that discusses Paul, Apollos, Cephas *and Christ*. Paul opens with the text found in 3:1-4 [see fig. 1.4(1)].

## RHETORIC

The reintroduction of "Paul and Apollos" includes three cameos that follow one another in a *straight-line sequence*. The thrust of these three cameos is

1. <sup>3:1</sup>But I, brethren, could *not address you* as spiritual,   NOT READY
   but as people *of the flesh*, as children in Christ.   Of the Flesh
      <sup>2</sup>I fed you milk, not solid food;   PARABLE OF
        for you were not ready for it;   Milk and Solid Food
   and even yet *you are not ready*,   NOT READY
   <sup>3</sup>for you are still *of the flesh*.   Of the Flesh

2. For while there is jealousy and strife among you,
   are you not of the flesh,   STRIFE MEANS
   and walking in the ways of mankind?   Of the Flesh

3. <sup>4</sup>For when one says, "I belong to Paul,"
   and another, "I belong to Apollos,"   DIVISION MEANS
   are you not merely humans?   Nonspiritual

**Figure 1.4(1). Paul and Apollos: It is all about you! (1 Cor 3:1-4)**

"Paul and Apollos: It is not about us; it is about you!" The first cameo is structured very much like the first cameo in the previous homily (2:10b-11) with parallel ideas at the beginning repeated at the end that together encase a brief parable in the center.

## COMMENTARY

Paul had just told them that "among the mature" he was able to present the "deep things of God." The Corinthians thought that they, above others, were profoundly ready for those deep things. But, alas, they did not yet qualify. In the opening of this letter Paul addressed his readers as "enriched in him [Christ] with all speech and all knowledge . . . not lacking in any spiritual gift" (1:5, 7). Has Paul so quickly changed his mind about his primary readers? Hardly. It is possible to see this shift from chapter 1:5-6 to chapter 3:1-3 in the light of God's giving of *the Spirit* on the one hand (chapter 1) and the Corinthians' failure to receive those gifts on the other hand (chapter 3). This distinction is already subtly affirmed in the opening of the letter. As noted, in that introduction Paul did not give thanks for the *Corinthians*, but rather for *the gifts of God given to them* (1:4). Their reception (and use) of those gifts was not mentioned. Because they failed to properly receive God's gifts, the "deep things" of God (like the cross) were yet beyond them. So he gave them "milk," not "solid food." Even with that nourishment they were "still of the flesh" and thereby not ready for the mysteries of God. What was Paul's measuring stick to make such a judgment? The text continues:

2. [3b]For while there is jealousy and strife among you,
   are you not of the flesh,
   and walking in the ways of ordinary human beings?

   STRIFE MEANS
   Of the Flesh/Ordinary Humans

3. [4]For when one says, "I belong to Paul,"
   and another, "I belong to Apollos,"
   are you not merely human beings?[1]

   DIVISION MEANS
   Ordinary Humans

The issue for Paul was not "You have not completed your introduction to theology, and so I can't give you an advanced course." A lack of intellectual acumen was not the problem. Their *jealousy* and *strife* were the issue. The word *jealousy* will reappear in Paul's classical definition of love in chapter 13.[2] Furthermore, the word for "children" in this text (*nepios*) also reappears in chapter 13. Here Paul begins to point out that his readers have failed to love.

In chapter 1 he noted that "strife" (*Aris:* a goddess of war) was active among them. Having lived and worked for decades (both as a student and as a professor) in academic institutions, I am intimately acquainted with the academy. Jealousy and strife have not disappeared from that subculture. And at the same time, when those qualities raise their ugly heads, very few connect them to the pursuit of truth. No one says, "Professor X is envious of professor Y, therefore professor X's courses are superficial." Paul accused his readers of being "babes in Christ" who could not understand the "solid food" of the "deep things of God" *because they were jealous and quarrelsome.* As children of the Enlightenment we have largely come to see the acquiring of truth as a head trip, and that a good mind and a willingness to work hard is all that is required to understand any form of truth, including theological truth. Paul disagrees. He was not willing to feed the Corinthians the "solid food" of theology because of broken relationships in their community. When he first preached to them, he had to give them milk to drink. At the time of writing, he was still obliged to do so. Granted, this entire epistle is "solid food," and he sent it to the Corinthians. This would indicate that a significant part of the congregation in Corinth was not caught up in their quarrels. Paul also told his readers that this letter was for the whole church. We can fondly hope that the church at large was not quarreling as badly as the Corinthians.

---

[1]My translation. Here and in the parallel line above it the Greek word *anthropoi* (men) appears.
[2]We will observe a number of the negatives listed in the center of chapter 13 will surface as we proceed.

The ancient Eastern churches did not have scholars or theologians, but rather "Fathers of the church." The assumption behind that language is: Only when we see the authenticity of your piety, and your commitment to the church, will we take your scholarship seriously.

The Corinthians thought that when they declared themselves to be "of Apollos" or "of Paul" that they were making complimentary statements *about their champions*. No, replies Paul, by creating these divisions you are saying nothing about us—you are *talking about yourselves*, and what you are saying is not flattering! Do not imagine that we are pleased! Your fights are *all about you*—not *about us*!

Paul is acting like a mother. He is feeding milk to the children.[3] The image is from Isaiah 28:9 which reads:

> Whom will he teach knowledge,
>> and to whom will he explain the message?
> Those who are weaned from the milk,
>> those taken from the breast?

The assumption of the text in Isaiah is, "You can't teach knowledge/the message to a young child." Paul's response is, "I have a young child in my arms. I have to become its mother and feed it milk." A few verses later at the end of this same section, Paul describes himself as their father (4:15). Both images should inform and shape our understanding of Paul and our view of Christian ministry in any age.

This opening of the final section of the essay has at least two major points. First is the affirmation that strife and jealousy impede any attempt to understand the truth of God. Those who do not love cannot penetrate the deep things of God. Second is the window into Paul's self-understanding. He is the mother (and later father) of the faithful.

After this introduction to this second discussion of "Paul and Apollos," Paul presents two parables that explain how they should see him and his colleagues. These two apostles are not leaders of competing factions in the church. Instead they are like farmers and builders. The first of these two parables is displayed in figure 1.4(2).

## RHETORIC

The passage is composed with simplicity, skill and rhetorical balance. Three

---

[3]Literally, "giving them milk to drink."

| | | | |
|---|---|---|---|
| 1a. | | [5]What then is Paul? | |
| b. | | What is Apollos?[4] | WE ARE SERVANTS |
| c. | | Servants through whom you believed, | Assigned by the Lord |
| d. | | as the Lord assigned to each. | |
| | | | |
| 2. | e. | [6]I planted, | WE FARM |
| | f. | Apollos watered, | God Gives Growth |
| | g. | but God gave the growth. | |
| | | | |
| 3. | e. | [7]So neither he who plants | |
| | f. | nor he who waters is anything, | WE ARE NOTHING |
| | g. | but God who gives the growth. | God Gives Growth |
| | | | |
| 4a. | | [8]The one who plants | WE ARE EQUAL SERVANTS |
| b. | | and he who waters are equal, | Workers for God |
| c. | | and each shall receive his wages according to his labor. | |
| d. | | [9]For we are fellow workers for God; | |

**Figure 1.4(2). The parable of God's field and the two farmers (1 Cor 3:5-9)**

features are prominent. First, Paul is dealing with a double set of seven (the perfect number). The seven ideas in 1-2 are matched (internally) line by line in 3-4. Second, the matching cameos use step parallelism. That is, the four ideas in 1 are matched in 4 and the three ideas in 2 are balanced in 3. Finally, overall, the four cameos themselves are presented to the reader using ring composition (A-B-B-A).

## COMMENTARY

The topic is "Who are Paul and Apollos?" In 1:10-16 the Corinthians saw them as leaders of opposing parties. Here Paul tells the Corinthians how they should see him and his coworkers. Paul does not discuss this subject apart from his understanding of the church. The agricultural image of planting and the resulting growth is from Isaiah. This theme appears in Isaiah a number of times. One of them is Isaiah 41:19, which reads:

---

[4]In stanza 1a and 1b I have chosen the text of the Armenian, Ethiopic and Syriac traditions (and the *Textus Receptus* along with some other early Greek texts) and have placed Paul before Apollos. With a great deal of strong early evidence, modern textual critics have understandably placed Apollos before Paul in these two lines. However the rhetorical form has never been considered (to my knowledge) as evidence for the text. Surely the tightness of the composition of these fourteen lines is strong evidence for the placing of Paul first in this text and thus restoring the order that appears, as noted, in the three Eastern language traditions. Apollos is mentioned at the end of 3:4. An early scribe may have been influenced by this and accidentally repeated Apollos first in verse 5.

I will put in the wilderness the *cedar*,
> the *acacia*, the *myrtle*, and the *olive*;
I will set in the desert the *cypress*,
> the *plane* and the *pine* together.

We note in passing that seven trees are mentioned in this verse. *God* as a farmer *plants* these trees in the wilderness and the desert. The same imagery reoccurs in Isaiah 44:3-4.

> For I will pour water on the thirsty land,
> and streams on the dry ground;
>> I will pour my Spirit upon your descendants,
>> and my blessing on your offspring.
> They shall spring up like grass amid waters,
> like willows by flowing streams.

Again, *God* is the *farmer* who in this case irrigates the dry ground. The outpouring of the Spirit is involved.

Isaiah 60:21 is even closer to the language of Paul. There the people are called

> The shoot of my planting,
> the work of my hands,
> that I may be glorified.

In this case God does the planting while at the same time observing the new shoots that result from that planting.

In the age of the Messiah the people will be comforted

> that they may be called oaks of righteousness,
> the planting of the LORD,
>> that he may be glorified. (Is 61:3)

Paul takes imagery available to him and uses it. God planted Israel (in a dry place) and Paul (for God) plants the church (among the Gentiles). In both cases the Spirit is involved. Yet, surely the parable of the sower (in Lk 8:4-8), which is prominent in the Synoptic Gospels, is also indirectly reflected here in Paul's parable of the farmer. Was Paul familiar with the parable of Jesus on this subject? Or is Paul reflecting the language of the church that in turn borrowed from Jesus? We do not know. Yet influence is likely, be it direct or indirect.

In this brief apostolic homily, Paul and Apollos are mentioned four times. Paul calls himself a *diakonos* (minister/servant). This same word is used for

Phoebe (Rom 16:1), for Timothy (1 Tim 4:6) and for other early church leaders. A careful comparison of the seven pairs of images/ideas in this parable of two farmers and "God's field" reveals the following:

1. Paul and Apollos are *servants* (not masters). Surely, this self-understanding reflects the person and language of the one who said, "I am among you as one who serves." In the case of Paul, as with Jesus, this is coupled with a leadership role.

2. Each of them has a *special ministry*. Paul plants, while Apollos waters. Not all callings are to the same task.

3. The ministry of each is an *assignment* primarily "from the Lord," not from the church. In Paul's case, a part of the church was involved. The Holy Spirit spoke to "the church at Antioch" telling them to "set apart" Barnabas and Saul for a special task. Jerusalem was not involved—only Antioch. If they had waited for Jerusalem to send them a directive to launch the mission to the Gentiles, how long might they have waited? Furthermore, the two men were not trying to advance their careers. The assignment from the Lord was all that mattered.

4. They were *equal partners*. From the information available to us, it is easy to see that Paul was clearly more prominent than Apollos. Yet Paul describes the two of them as equals.

5. Their separate *tasks were equal in value*. That is, evangelism and Christian education are of equal importance. It is easy for evangelists and educators to each judge their task to be more important than the other. Evangelists at times reflect an anti-intellectual stance and judge Christian education as a waste of time. Some types of Christian educators look condescendingly at evangelists as semi-intelligent, misguided enthusiasts. Paul does not allow for either of these attitudes. For him the two ministries were equally valid.

6. *God gives the growth*. That growth was not the result of skillful methods or good publicity. It was and is a gift of God. As he writes, Paul knows that some fields yield little. In Antioch of Pisidia, after initial success, Paul was driven out of the city (Acts 13:13-50). The mystery of the spiritual and numerical growth of the church is beyond human comprehension. Fifty years ago the *Makana Jesu* church in western Ethiopia had around fifty thousand members and an uncertain future. Today its people number more than four million. God gives the growth, and the Holy Spirit moves in centuries. In the text Paul does not take credit for his successes. Furthermore, God's action in giving the growth is here described with an imperfect verb. In Greek this

means a "past continuous action." Paul planted and Apollos watered. Those actions were events that happened in the past. But God *continuously* gives the growth. John Bengel notes that without the action of God to give the growth, "the grain from the first moment would be like a pebble."[5]

7. Paul describes himself and his colleague Apollos as "fellow workers *for God.*" Yes, they are servants of the church in every place, but on a deeper level they are God's workers. In Isaiah, God planted Israel. Paul is God's agent assigned to God's task, and he fulfills it for God by "planting the church."

8. They are *fellow workers*, not leaders of competing parties vying for influence and power.

9. Each worker receives *wages* "according to his *labor,*" not according to his or her production! A capitalistic world judges the value of everything on the basis of production. This attitude is deeply ingrained in Western society. Throughout history many faithful servants have labored and seen little fruit as judged by the world. God has a different measuring stick, and wages are on the basis of labor, not production. In this text Paul affirms that God is pleased with and will reward that labor, irrespective of the visible results.

Paul then shifts from the *farmer* to the *farm* and continues on to discuss the *building* and the *builders*. This deceptively simple statement may be the climax of this section of his essay. He writes in verse 9b,

> You are God's field,
> God's building.

The point of climax repeats the images (while reversing the order) of the call of Jeremiah whose task was "To build and to plant" (Jer 1:10). The same double image of builders and farmers appears in Isaiah's vision of the great day of "the anointed one" who will grant gladness to those who mourn so that they can become builders and "build up the ancient ruins" (Is 61:4). At the same time they are to become farmers and receive a "double portion" of land (Is 61:7).

But there is a difference. Jeremiah was the builder and the planter of the nation of Israel. The people were to build and plant, and by their efforts "raise up the former devastations" (Is 61:4) *in Israel.* It is profoundly true that in other places the reader is encouraged to join Paul in building and planting. But *in this text* Paul's reader is not the builders and planters—

---

[5]John A. Bengel, *Bengel's New Testament Commentary* (Grand Rapids: Kregel, 1981), 2:179.

rather they are "God's *field*, and God's *building." They are the land and the temple!* The struggling, newly born, deeply flawed congregations that he was founding were, in his eyes, the *restored land* and the *glorious temple* promised by the prophets. He was not de-Zionizing the tradition; rather he was *transforming it into a new form of Zionism* that needed no particular geography and no special building! All of this comes to a stunning climax at the end of the parable.

In his parable about farmers, Paul (as noted) echoes Jesus' parable about a farmer. Here, Paul creates a parable about builders, and the parable of the two builders told by Jesus (Lk 6:46-48) lingers in the background as we will see. At the same time both Jesus and Paul are part of a yet longer tradition regarding this image, and Isaiah is significant.

In Isaiah 28:14-18 the prophet announces the destruction of one building (Israel) and the promise of *a new foundation* of *precious stones* on which those who believe can build.[6] A second use of this image appears in the Dead Sea Scroll *The Community Rule* (VIII) which reads,

> In the Council of the Community there shall be twelve men and three Priests, perfectly versed in all that is revealed of the Law, whose works shall be truth, righteousness, justice, loving kindness, and humility. . . . When these are in Israel, the council of the Community shall be established in truth. It shall be an Everlasting Plantation, a House of Holiness for Israel. . . . It shall be that tried wall, that *precious corner-stone*, whose foundations shall neither rock nor sway in their place.[7]

This section of the *Community Rule* is important for the text before us. The "Council of the Community" was to be both "an everlasting plantation" and at the same time it was "that *precious corner-stone.*" Paul's focus on "plantings" and "foundations" appears here in this pre-Christian Jewish document. The Qumran community claimed these prophetic promises for the leadership of *their* community. Paul claims the same promises, but finds them fulfilled in a different way. The plantation for Paul is the church, "the precious cornerstone" is Jesus Christ, and on him God's new building (temple) is being built.

A second important early Jewish use of the image of the foundation relates

---

[6]For the rhetorical style of this text see figure 0.4 in the earlier discussion of prophetic homily rhetorical style.

[7]Geza Vermes, "The Community Rule," in *The Dead Sea Scrolls in English* (Baltimore: Penguin Books, 1973), p. 85.

to the second temple. The Mishnah records that when the Jewish authorities cleared the rubble on the temple mount to rebuild the sanctuary, they found an elevated stone in the middle of the old holy of holies. The text reads,

> After the ark was taken away a stone remained there from the time of the early prophets, and it was called *"Shetiyah."* It was higher than the ground by three fingerbreadths. On this he used to put [the fire-pan].[8]

As Danby confirms with a note, *shetiyah* means "foundation." This text is discussing the rebuilding of the second temple and the celebration of the Day of Atonement. According to this account, on that most sacred day of the year the high priest would take a fire pan (full of charcoal and incense), enter the holy of holies and place the pan on a raised stone in the center of the room. This ritual was a meaningful way to venerate that holy space. Paul must have known of this stone and that its name was "the foundation." In the text before us, Paul specifically mentions the temple. Surely, as Paul refers to Jesus Christ as "the foundation" of God's building—the *third temple*—he is thinking of this stone in the holy of holies of the *second temple* that was specifically named "the foundation." Jesus Christ is "the foundation" for the *third temple*.

From the point of view of historical order, between the affirmations of Qumran and Paul's two parables are two parables of Jesus. As noted, the first parable of Jesus is that of the sower, and the second is the parable of the two builders.[9] Is Paul conscious of the writings of the Qumran community? Has he heard these two parables of Jesus? We are obliged to guess, and allowed to suppose that he is aware of both of these earlier uses of "God's planting" and "God's building." Paul freely created the two parables before us. He could have fashioned parables out of other metaphors. Instead he chose images with both an ancient and a recent history in Jewish thought.

Thus, Jesus was not presented by Paul as "the foundation" in the way that Aristotle is a foundation under the theology of Thomas Aquinas. Rather, in the light of the above texts it is clear that Paul saw Jesus as the center of the holy of holies of the new temple he describes.

The text of the second parable is displayed in figure 1.4(3).

---

[8]*Mishnah, Mo'ed Yoma* 5:2 (*The Mishnah*, trans. H. Danby [Oxford: Oxford University Press, 1980, c. 1933], p. 167).
[9]For a discussion of the parable of the two builders in the light of this background, see Kenneth E. Bailey, *Jesus Through Middle Eastern Eyes* (Downers Grove, Ill.: IVP Academic, 2008), pp. 321-31.

1. [3:10]According to the commission of God given to me,
   like a skilled master builder
   I *laid* a *foundation*, and another is building upon it.
   Let each man take care how he builds upon it.          THE FOUNDATION
   [11]For *no other foundation* can any one lay            Is Jesus Christ
   than that which is laid, which is *Jesus Christ*.

2.    [12]Now if any one *builds* on "*the foundation*"          BUILT ON
      with gold, silver, precious stones,                  "The Foundation"
      wood, grass, stubble—                                Fireproof versus Flammable
      [13]each man's work will become manifest;

3.       for *the Day* will disclose it
         because it will be *revealed with fire*,              TESTED
         and the fire will test                               By Fire
         what sort of *work each one has done*.

4.    [14]If the work which any man has *built* on "*the foundation*" survives,
      he will receive a *reward*.
      [15]If any man's work *is burned up*,                    BUILT ON
      he will suffer *loss*,                                 "The Foundation"
      though *he will be saved*,                             Survived—Burned Up
      but only as through fire.

5.    a.[16]Do you not know *that you are God's temple*
         b. and that *God's Spirit dwells in you?*
            c.[17]If any one *destroys God's temple*,             THE TEMPLE
            c'. God will *destroy him*.                        Composed of You
         b'. For *God's temple is holy*
      a'. and *that temple you are.*

**Figure 1.4(3). The parable of God's building and the builders (1 Cor 3:10-17)**

## THE RHETORIC

Five cameos form yet another ring composition. The parable opens (cameo 1) with a discussion of "the foundation," which is "Jesus Christ." The matching cameo (5) presents "God's temple" that is already built on that foundation. In the second cameo (2) Paul addresses "anyone who builds" on that foundation, and focuses on two lists of building materials. There are three items in each list. Gold, silver and precious stones will withstand fire while wood, hay and straw will not. The matching cameo (4) reflects on the result of such a fire. One list survives, and the builder is rewarded. The second list of materials is destroyed, but not the builder. The climax is in the center (3) where Paul projects ahead to "the Day" when all things will be tested and revealed by fire.

Cameo 5 also exhibits ring composition. The three themes of (a) *temple*, (b) (Holy) *Spirit* and (c) *destroy* are presented and then repeated backwards.

## COMMENTARY

Paul now describes himself as a "master builder." A good master builder can exercise his or her authority by becoming a servant. In fact, that authority, when exercised through servanthood, is in a marvelous way profoundly attractive. For the destitute and dying poor of Calcutta, Mother Teresa became a servant in the most self-emptying way on the streets of that teeming city, and people from India and from around the world were drawn to line up behind her and help her. In like manner, Paul is both "master builder" and "servant."

As a master builder, Paul was laying a foundation for a building that we soon discover is the (new) temple. For him the only foundation possible was Jesus Christ. His fellow worker Apollos was building upon it, and from the previous parable it is clear that Paul was at ease with Apollos. But there were other would-be builders in Paul's readership. Hence the warning, "Let each man take care how he builds upon it." For this building no other foundation was possible. Neither Gnosticism nor Roman imperialism nor Epicureanism nor Stoicism nor the establishment of an independent Jewish state with the Zealots, nor a retreat into the desert with the Essenes were adequate in Paul's mind as a foundation for the third temple.

But the first cameo in this apostolic homily needs to be examined along with cameo 5, which is its matching cameo. These two cameos appear side by side in figure 1.4(4):

1.   [10]According to the commission of God given to me,
       like a skilled master builder
       I laid a *foundation*, and another is building upon it.
       Let each man take care how he builds upon it.          THE FOUNDATION
       [11]For *no other foundation* can any one lay           Is Jesus Christ
       than that which is laid, which is *Jesus Christ*.

       - - - - - - - - - - - - - - - - - - - - - - - - - -

5.   a.[16]Do you not know *that you are God's temple*
        b. and that *God's Spirit dwells in you?*
          c.[17]If any one *destroys God's temple*,
          c'. God will *destroy him*.                          THE TEMPLE
        b'. For *God's temple is holy*                         Composed of You
       a'. and *that temple* you are

**Figure 1.4(4). Cameos 1 and 5 (1 Cor 3:10-11, 16-17)**

One of the striking features of these two cameos is that in cameo 1 only the foundation was in place. Paul had laid the foundation and other builders were lining up to participate in the construction. The completed building was a long way off. But in the matching cameo 5, the reader discovers that the building is "God's temple," and that it is somewhat finished in that God's Spirit has already taken up residence in it. Then the readers were told, "you are that temple." When Paul wrote those words, the temple in Jerusalem was intact and the twice-daily sacrifices were offered without fail for the sins of the people. The high priest was in residence and the various rituals were observed. Jewish pilgrims flocked to Jerusalem from around the empire because God was present in his holy house. In a unique way it was there that God's presence (the *shekinah*) was found among his people.

With the temple in all of its glory still functioning in Jerusalem, Paul announced dramatically to his Jewish and Gentile readers that "you [pl.] are God's holy temple" and "God's Spirit dwells in you [pl.]." He is not talking exclusively to the Corinthians. Rather, as he affirms in 1:2, he is addressing "All those in every place upon whom is called the name of our Lord Jesus Christ." All Christians together were the third temple, and the second temple was thereby already obsolete. Comparisons with the Islamic world may be helpful.

Islam honors Mecca because the *Ka'ba*, the holy black stone, is in the central sanctuary of Mecca. Consequently, every mosque must be built facing Mecca, and the five prescribed daily prayers must be offered facing Mecca. In the Islamic worldview, it is in the *Ka'ba* that God is uniquely present among his people. Imagine a Muslim scholar, say, in France, writing to Muslims across Europe announcing, "The pilgrimage to Mecca is no longer necessary because you as a community are the new sacred sanctuary of Islam, and God now dwells uniquely in you. You are the new *Ka'ba*, and your community of faith now constitutes the dwelling place of God among his people."

Such an announcement would be stunning indeed! The readers would be electrified, and if they accepted this new view of the dwelling place of God, their lives could never be the same again. The proclaimer of this message would not be popular among Muslim leaders elsewhere. Yet such is the earth-shaking nature of what Paul writes to his readers in this passage.

This third temple was already "up and functioning" (cameo 5), but at the same time only its foundation was laid (cameo 1). A great deal of construction work lay ahead. Surely this imagery of the church is appropriate for any age. The church everywhere "is built" and functioning, and at the same time it is barely off of its foundations, with a great deal of construction yet to be completed. In connection with this announcement Paul presents his strongest argument for the unity of all believers who together are the new temple built on the foundation of Jesus Christ. In the center of cameo 5 lies a stern warning that,

If anyone destroys God's temple
God will destroy him. (3:17a)

Middle Easterners take their sacred spaces and their sacred buildings *very seriously*, and they always have. The book of Acts records the account of Paul in the temple during his final journey to Jerusalem. On that occasion a rumor circulated that Paul had introduced Gentiles into the temple precinct (Acts 21:28-30). That suspicion was enough to start a riot that almost ended his life. The rumor in the city was "he has defiled this holy place." It was holy because Israel's holy God was uniquely present in it. What would have happened if on that occasion Paul had announced to the crowd that there was a new temple under construction (full of Gentiles) where God was now dwelling among his people in a new way?

If the second temple was so very holy, what about the third temple? For Paul, protecting that third temple from damage was of great importance. In cameo 5, Paul affirms that God himself will destroy anyone who tries to destroy the third temple. Ergo, the Corinthians with their quarreling parties were engaged in activities that could damage the third temple and make them the enemies of God.

This brings us to the second "semantic envelope" along with the center climax. The three cameos can be seen in figure 1.4(5).

| | | |
|---|---|---|
| 2. | [12]Now if any one builds on "*the foundation*" with gold, silver, precious stones, wood, hay, straw— [13]each man's work will become manifest; | BUILT ON "The Foundation" Fireproof versus Flammable |
| 3. | for *the Day* will disclose it because it will be *revealed with fire*, and the fire will test what sort of *work each one has done*. | TESTED By Fire |
| 4. | [14]If the work which any man has built on "*the foundation*" survives, he will receive a *reward*. [15]If any man's work *is burned up*, he will suffer *loss*, though *he will be saved*, but only as through fire. | BUILT ON "The Foundation" Survived—Burned Up |

**Figure: 1.4(5). Cameos 2-4 (1 Cor 3:12-15)**

The end of cameo 2 and the first line of cameo 4 connect so smoothly that if cameo 3 were missing, no reader would notice the omission. In cameo 2 Paul continues to advise anyone who approaches with the intent of building on the foundation (which is Jesus Christ). Some will come with valuable building materials (gold, silver, precious stones) while others will bring poor quality supplies (wood, hay and straw). Most buildings in the ancient Middle East were constructed out of stone. Paul chooses colorful images for each of his two lists. The one builder comes with gold, silver and *precious stones*. Paul is borrowing imagery from Isaiah's parable of the two buildings (Is 28:14-18), which promises a "precious stone" for a new foundation. Both types of builders (bringing their differing building materials) will engage in construction. Then comes the test—which is "the Day."

In cameo 3 "the Day" (read: the Day of Judgment) will come like a great fire. Amos spoke of a fire that would "devour the strongholds of Jerusalem" (Amos 2:5). Corinth as a city had experienced such a fire. The city had resisted the Roman conquest, and in 146 B.C. was overrun and burned. Naturally the precious metals and gem stones survived that conflagration. It remained a ruin for just over a century and in 44 B.C., rebuilding began. When Paul arrived in Corinth in the early fifties of the first century, the initial stage of reconstruction was no doubt finished, but the commercial success of the city must have guaranteed considerable new construction. Paul's parable was thus created out of the fabric of life in Corinth at the time of writing.

Furthermore, dating back to the fourth century B.C., Corinth was famous for its work in bronze. Josephus records that the inner sanctuary of Herod's temple had nine gates whose doors were covered with plates of silver and gold. But one of them on the Eastern side "was of Corinthian brass, and greatly excelled those that were only covered over with silver and gold."[10] Corinthian brass was so stunning that it was judged to be more beautiful than gold or silver. The two doors of that particular gate were sixty feet high according to Josephus and it may be the "beautiful gate" that appears in Acts 3:2. In short, expensive building materials were associated with the city of Corinth.

Jerome Murphy-O'Connor suggests that many of the craftsmen may have escaped the destruction of the city in 146 B.C. and kept the crafts alive. Their descendants most likely returned to restart the guilds after the city was reborn. Corinthian bronze had a highly prized finish that looked like gold or silver. The craftsmen also worked in gold and silver. In any case, much new construction in Corinth was built on scorched earth because the city has been burned. The Corinthians also knew that precious metals and gemstones could survive such a fire.[11] Paul's images of precious metals and destructive fires

[10]F. Josephus, *The Wars of the Jews* 5.5.3 (Loeb Classical Library, Paragraph 201).
[11]Jerome Murphy-O'Connor, "Corinthian Bronze," in *St. Paul's Corinth: Texts and Archaeology*

would have been particularly powerful. And what is the anticipated result of the great "fire" on "the Day"?

Each person's work will be tested (3). There is no need to pass judgment on that work in the present. Some will fail to build on "the foundation." Others will indeed build on the only sure foundation, and yet do so with inferior materials. The latter will "suffer loss." It is painful to watch years of effort destroyed, especially when the destruction leaves behind it the verdict of "worthless." Paul encouraged his readers with the assurance that the builder "will be saved" even if his work is destroyed.

Paul is here dealing with divisions in the church at Corinth and the judgments that the various parties were making against one another. Such judgments *must be left* for "the Day," knowing that the work of some will survive and the work of others will perish. Paul's advice is, "Select the best building materials and build on the only foundation that will last. That is all that matters." Those who choose the wrong building materials will sustain painful losses—but their own lives will be saved.

This parable of God's building and the builders includes the following ideas:

1.  The church is God's field (the land) and God's building (the temple). The land of Israel and the temple in Jerusalem are thereby rendered obsolete.

2.  Paul is both a servant and the commissioned master-builder. He laid the foundation.

3.  Jesus Christ is the foundation of the new temple. (There is no other.)

4.  Some are building on that foundation. Others use materials that will last (gold, silver, precious stones). Some are using poor quality materials (wood, grass and stubble).

5.  On the day of judgment, fire will test the work of all. The work of some will last and the efforts of others will be burned up. But the builders will be saved in spite of it.

6.  The Corinthians are "off the hook." They do not need to pass judgment on shoddy efforts. The day of judgment will deal with that problem.

7.  The readers of Paul's letter are already God's holy temple, and the Holy Spirit is already present in that temple even though there is a great deal of building yet to be completed.

8.  God will destroy anyone who tries to tear down this third temple.

(Collegeville, Minn.: Liturgical Press, 2002), pp. 199-218.

Having presented these two parables Paul takes a final look at how his readers should see their leaders [see fig. 1:4(6)].

1. [18]Let no one deceive himself.
   If any one among you thinks he is wise in this age,
   let him become a fool that he may be wise.                    NO BOASTING
   [19]For the wisdom of this world is folly with God.           About Yourselves

2. For it is written,
   "He catches the wise in their craftiness"                     SCRIPTURE:
   [20]and again,                                                 No Boasting
   "The Lord knows                                                About Leaders
   that the thoughts of the wise are futile."
   [21]So let no one boast of men.

3. For all things are yours,
   [22]whether Paul or Apollos or Cephas                         PAUL—APOLLOS
   or the world or life or death                                 All Yours
   or the present or the future,
   all are yours;
   [23]and you are Christ's; and Christ is God's.

------------------------------------------------

4a. [4:1]This is how one should regard us,                       SEE US AS
    as servants of Christ                                        Servants and
    and stewards of the mysteries of God.                        Stewards
    [2]Moreover it is required of stewards                       Under
    that they be found faithful.                                 Judgment

4b. [3]To me it is trifling to be judged by you
    or by any human court.
    I do not even judge myself.                                  THE LORD
    [4]I am not aware of anything against myself,                Judges Me
    but I am not thereby acquitted.
    It is the Lord who judges me.

4c. [5]Therefore do not pronounce judgment before the time,
    before the Lord comes,                                       THE LORD
    who will bring to light the things now hidden in darkness    Judges and
    and will disclose the purposes/motives of people's hearts.   Commends All
    That every person receive his commendation from God.

------------------------------------------------

5. [6]I have applied all this to myself                          PAUL—APOLLOS
   and to Apollos for your benefit, brethren,                    All Yours

6. that you may learn by/in us
   not to go beyond that which is scripture,                     SCRIPTURE:
   that none of you may be puffed up                             No Getting Puffed Up
   in favor of one against another.                              About Leaders

7. [7]For who sees anything different in you?
   What have you that you did not receive?                       NO BOASTING
   Then, if you received it why do you boast                     About Yourselves
   as if you did not receive it?

---

**Figure 1.4(6). Paul, Apollos and Cephas: It is about Christ (1 Cor 3:18–4:7)**

## THE RHETORIC

This apostolic homily can be called a modified prophetic rhetorical template. It exhibits the traditional seven inverted cameos with a climax in the center. At the same time it is modified in that the center is extended and divided into three sub-cameos presented in a sequence as indicated in the formatting of figure 1.4(6) above.[12]

This type of three-stanza center appears five times in Isaiah 40–66. One clear case is Isaiah 44:18-20 [see fig. 1.4(7)].

| | | |
|---|---|---|
| 1. | [18]They know not, nor do they discern; | |
| | for he has shut their eyes so that they cannot see, | THEY CANNOT |
| | and their minds so that they cannot understand | Understand |
| | | |
| 2. | [19]No one considers, | THEY DO NOT |
| | nor is there knowledge or discernment to say, | Understand |
| | | |
| 3. | "Half of it | WOOD FOR |
| | I burned in the fire, | Heat |
| | | |
| 4. | I also baked bread on its coals, | WOOD FOR |
| | I roasted flesh and have eaten; | Cooking |
| | | |
| 5. | and shall I make the residue of it an abomination? | WOOD FOR |
| | Shall I fall down before a block of wood?" | Idols? |
| | | |
| 6. | [20]He feeds on ashes; | THEY DO NOT |
| | a deluded mind has led him astray, | Understand |
| | | |
| 7. | and he cannot deliver himself or say, | THEY CANNOT |
| | "Is there not a lie in my right hand?" | Understand |

**Figure 1.4(7). Isaiah 44:18-20**

Here Isaiah uses the prophetic rhetorical template of seven cameos. But the center is a series of three cameos that follow a straight-line sequence. Again, Paul uses a literary style available to him from the writing prophets.

Returning to 1 Corinthians 3:18–4:7, the first three cameos are carefully balanced with the last three. Cameo 5 is redundant but it is needed to balance cameo 3. The very center (4b) uses ring composition. This center is held together with a *matching of ideas* more than a *pairing of words*. This can be seen as follows in 4:3-4:

---

[12]This same feature occurs twice in the parable of the prodigal son (Lk 15:11-32). The two prophetic rhetorical templates have a climactic center cameo that is divided into two parts (see Kenneth E. Bailey, *Jacob and the Prodigal* [Downers Grove, Ill.: InterVarsity Press, 2003], pp. 96-97).

<sup>3</sup>Your judgment of me is trivial
   Any court judgment of me is trivial
     I do not judge myself
     <sup>4</sup>I know nothing against myself
   I am not acquitted (by a court)
  The Lord judges me

Immediately after the opening cameo (2) and just before the closing cameo (6), Paul quotes or invokes Scripture. This identical rhetorical feature occurs in the apostolic homily on the cross [1:17–2:2; see fig. 1.2(1)]. With these features in mind we turn to the text.

## COMMENTARY

Paul is once again attempting to heal the Corinthian divisions by reference to the hymn on the cross in 1:17–2:2. It is important to catch Paul's train of thought by means of his carefully crafted parallels as seen in cameos 1 and 7, which are as follows:

1.   <sup>3:18</sup>Let no one deceive himself.
     If any one among you thinks he is wise in this age,    NO BOASTING
     let him become a fool that he may be wise.    About Yourselves
     <sup>19</sup>For the wisdom of this world is folly with God.    (Look at yourselves)

   ------------------------------------------------

7.   <sup>4:7</sup>For who sees anything different in you?
     What have you that you did not receive?    NO BOASTING
     Then, if you received it why do you boast    About Yourselves
     as if you did not receive it?    (Others look at you)

Figure 1.4(8). Cameos 1 and 7 (1 Cor 3:18-19; 4:7)

In his introduction to the epistle, Paul complimented his readers by saying, "in every way you were enriched in him in all speech and all knowledge" (1:5). At least some of the Corinthians had "knowledge" and may have been considered "wise" in the wisdom of this age. Paul may be referring to the secret knowledge claimed by the Gnostics. But here he focuses on the wisdom of God revealed in a cross. Only by becoming fools (as judged by the world) could they become wise in the things of God. The "secret wisdom of God" revealed through the Spirit (2:10b-16) was also involved. Only the humble can acquire such wisdom. It is like learning a foreign language as an adult. To do so one must become "a fool" and accept to be easily surpassed by a small child. So it is with the wisdom of God. Only self-confessing fools qualify to take a

course in wisdom. Clearly the Corinthians were boasting about having enough
wisdom to choose Paul against Apollos. If they had had the wisdom of God
available to self-confessed fools (1), they would not have boasted about themselves (7). The word "boasting" will also reappear in the center of chapter 13.

The rejection of boasting continues in cameo 7 where Paul asks, "What
have you that you did not receive?" Life, breath, community, family, daily
bread, education, teachers, the gospel, the spiritual gifts—what did the Corinthian Christians have that they did not receive? All their named leaders
were gifts. Paul refuses to allow for the pitting of one apostolic leader against
another. This brings us to the second pair of cameos [see fig. 1.4(9)].

2.  [3:19b]For it is written,
     "He catches the wise in their craftiness"[13]    SCRIPTURE:
     [20]and again, "The Lord knows           No Boasting
     that the thoughts of the wise are futile."[14]  About Leaders
     So let no one boast of men.

6.  [4:6b]that you may learn by/through[15] us
     not to go beyond that which is scripture,   SCRIPTURE:
     that none of you may be puffed up       No Getting Puffed Up
     in favor of one against another.         About Leaders

**Figure 1.4(9). Cameos 2 and 6 (1 Cor 3:19b-20; 4:6b)**

Trying to reconcile Paul's Old Testament quotations with the Greek and
Hebrew originals is an arduous task. Yet at least some of Paul's reasons for
quoting these texts are obvious. God's wisdom is beyond anything that humankind can produce. For Paul Scripture was an authoritative source that
shed light on a discussion of the wisdom of people versus the wisdom of God.
The conclusion of the matter is: Therefore, "let no one boast of men." Let not
the Calvinist boast of Calvin or the Lutheran boast of Luther. Having completed advanced theological degrees in both Calvinistic and Lutheran institutions, I am convinced that each tradition has a great deal to teach the other.
Surely one can rejoice in one's own tradition and at the same time be open to
new insights out of another. The Corinthians were setting one teacher *against*
the other. The balancing cameo (6) is both amazing and complicated.

Paul writes (literally), "That in us you may learn the things not beyond that

---

[13]Job 5:13.
[14]Ps 94:11.
[15]The Greek preposition here is *en*. The RSV translates it "by" while NRSV offers "through." Both
are possible.

which is written." Thiselton presents a marvelous, extensive, fully documented discussion of this dense verse. He sets out and discusses seven interpretive options[16] and his thoughtful conclusion is,

> Most of all, he [Paul] urges *the sufficiency of the gospel of the cross interpreted within the framework of biblical tradition*, as against the misguided and indeed damaging effects of trying to *add* "wisdom" aspects or notions of being "people of the Spirit" without the cross.[17]

Cameos 2 and 6 both focus on Scripture. A proper understanding of Paul's intent surely includes the affirmation that church tradition, reason and experience are all valuable. But none of them must *ever* be allowed to "go beyond scripture" (4:6). This will prevent being "in favor of one [leader] against another." Christian history is strewn with wreckage caused by violations of Paul's directives in this matched pair of texts.

The third set of parallel cameos is displayed in figure 1.4(10).

| | | |
|---|---|---|
| 3. | 3:21bFor all things are yours, | |
| | 22whether Paul or Apollos or Cephas | PAUL—APOLLOS |
| | or the world or life or death | All Yours |
| | or the present or the future, all are yours; | |
| | 23and you are Christ's; and Christ is God's | |
| | | |
| 5. | 4:6I have applied all this to myself | PAUL—APOLLOS |
| | and to Apollos for your benefit, brethren, | All Yours |

Figure 1.4(10). Cameos 3 and 5 (1 Cor 3:21-23; 4:6)

The sweeping nature of what Paul is saying takes the reader's breath away. In cameo 3 Paul includes the full list that appeared in 1:12. Paul, Apollos, Cephas and Christ are mentioned. But here in cameo 3 being "of Paul" or "of Apollos" or "of Cephas" lose their preeminence because *all believers* are (literally) "of Christ" and Christ is "of God." The divisions in the church then and now pale in the bright light of such a comprehensive worldview. The rising movement of the text must not be missed. The three church leaders are mentioned first. Next comes "the world, or life or death or the present or the future." The text finally reaches its summit with "you are of Christ and Christ is of God." The view from that lofty height does not allow for quibbling over Paul, Apollos and Cephas. Instead, the reader is powerfully stimulated to re-

16Thiselton, *First Epistle*, pp. 352-56.
17Ibid., p. 356 (italics his).

flect deeply on what Paul intends when he writes "all things are yours" as the mind and spirit move up the high mountain to its summit. The Christian traditions out of Syriac, Coptic, Greek, Armenian, Latin, Arabic, German, French, English and Spanish as they are in harmony with Scripture and currently affirmed in Africa, Asia, Europe, South America and North America (and more)—are *all ours!*

In the matching cameo (5) Paul tells his readers that he has applied "all this" to himself and Apollos for their benefit. In the fourth century Chrysostom argued that Paul chose to omit the names of the contending Corinthian leaders and astutely mentions only himself and Apollos. Chrysostom writes, "if he had applied his argument in their persons, they would not have learnt all that they needed to learn, nor would have admitted the correction, being vexed at what was said."[18]

This brings us to the extended cameo that forms the climax of this apostolic homily [see fig. 1.4(11)].

| | | |
|---|---|---|
| 4a. | [4:1]This is how one should regard us, | SEE US AS |
| | as servants of Christ | Servants and |
| | and stewards of the mysteries of God. | Stewards |
| | [2]Moreover it is required of stewards | Under |
| | that they be found faithful. | Judgment |
| | | |
| 4b. | [3]And to me it is trifling to be judged by you | |
| | or by any human court. | |
| | I do not even judge myself. | THE LORD |
| | [4]I am not aware of anything against myself, | Judges Me |
| | but I am not thereby acquitted. | |
| | It is the Lord who judges me. | |
| | | |
| 4c. | [5]Therefore do not pronounce judgment before the time, | |
| | before the Lord comes, | THE LORD |
| | who will bring to light the things now hidden in darkness | Judges and |
| | and will disclose the purposes/motives of people's hearts. | Commends All |
| | That every person receive his commendation from God. | |

**Figure 1.4(11). Cameo 4a, b, c (1 Cor 4:1-5)**

This center forms an important point of emphasis not only for the homily but for this section of the essay. The Corinthians had seen their founders as leaders of competing and conflicting groups in the church. As noted, ethnicity may have been involved. In any case, after three closely argued chapters Paul at last tells his readers how they *should* see him and his leadership team.

---

[18]Chrysostom, *1 Corinthians*, p. 64.

The question of "judgment" runs through the three parts of this climax.

Within a few verses Paul uses four key words to define himself and his colleagues. Two of these were in the parable about farmers (3:5-9). The other two are in this text. Seen together the four are as follows:

| | |
|---|---|
| *diakonoi* assigned by the Lord | (*servants* assigned by the Lord) |
| *sunergoi* for God | (*fellow workers* for God) |
| *huperetai* of Christ | (*assistants* to Christ) |
| *oikonomoi* of the mysteries of God | (*stewards* of the mysteries of God) |

The first two make clear that they are *servants* "assigned by the Lord" and that they work *for God* (not the Corinthians). The third and fourth appear in the text before us. I have chosen to translate *huperetai* as "assistants." As a Greek word it was used for a physician's assistant, an adjutant and a priest's helper.[19] It was also the word for a synagogue official, and in the Gospels it is used for assistants in the temple in Jerusalem. In a detailed discussion of the synagogue in the early Christian centuries, Shemuel Safrai notes that *huperetes* was the Greek equivalent for the Hebrew word *hazzan*. He writes,

> The head of the synagogue had an adjutant the *hazzan*, undoubtedly the *huperetes* of Luke 4:20, who acted as executive officer in the practical details of running the synagogue. . . . The *hazzan* acted in fact as master of ceremonies throughout the whole liturgy.[20]

In Paul's mind Christ was the *head of the synagogue/church*, and the apostles were the *huperetai*.

In this text Paul asks his readers to look on the apostolic band as "*assistants* to Christ" and "*stewards* of the mysteries of God." In the parable about the farmers, Paul presented himself as a *servant*. But having been assigned by "the Lord" he and his colleagues were, on the deepest level, "*fellow workers* for God" rather than "*servants* of the Corinthians." In the first two out of the four words listed, *lowliness* is emphasized. Here, *leadership* is central.

In every place Paul was ready to serve the church gathered in that city. But he obeyed orders from a higher authority. In regard to his readers he was not a "quivering mass of availability." One of the illuminating texts in this regard is Mark 1:35-38. In that account Jesus withdraws early in the morning "to a lonely place" for prayer. Simon and others follow him, find him and say

---

[19]BAGD lists "servant, helper, assistant," p. 842.
[20]Shemuel Safrai, "The Synagogue," *The Jewish People in the First Century* (Philadelphia: Fortress, 1976), 2:935-36.

"Everyone is searching for you." Jesus replies, "Let us go on to the next towns, that I may preach there also; for that is why I came out." The people he served did not control his agenda—he did! Paul acts out this theology with clarity when in the book of Romans he writes, "But now, since I no longer have any room for work in these regions, . . . I go to Spain" (Rom 15:23-24). How could there be nothing left to do in Greece or Asia Minor? Were Christian communities established in all the towns and villages of the area? As "a servant of Christ" Paul was on his way. The people he served could not trump that higher obedience.

Paul also saw himself as a "steward of the mysteries of God." The inner core of his identity was not formed by *counseling* or *administration* or even by *preaching*. He was certainly engaged in first-century forms of those activities as he lived out his "anxiety for all the churches" (2 Cor 11:28). But out of the inner core of his identity he sensed responsibility for the "mysteries of God." This vision of Christian leadership is a noble standard for the church in every age.

This title of "steward of the *mysteries of God*" appears in this first essay, where he discusses the cross, the Trinity and the hidden mysteries now revealed through the Spirit. Then in essay five, he concludes with "behold, I tell you a *mystery*" (15:51). There the steward again fulfills his assigned task. This theme provides an *inclusio*, a thread that helps connect the end to the beginning and bind the letter together.

Yet Paul does not act out his servanthood and stewardship as a freelancer. By its very nature the apostolic band required some clear authority that could provide oversight and review. A steward is a steward *for someone*, and the servant cannot serve in a vacuum. He concludes this opening section of the cameo by saying, "moreover it is required of stewards that they be found faithful." Found by whom?

Two aspects of this statement are worthy of note. First, biblical languages (and modern Arabic) have no word for *honesty*. Honesty is a Roman concept, and the word has roots in Latin, Old French, Italian and Spanish. It has to do with commitment to an impersonal ideal. The biblical word is *faithful*, which requires *a person to whom one is faithful*. A servant is *faithful to his or her master*. Paul was faithful to "our Lord Jesus Christ" (as stated repeatedly in the opening chapter). One day the master will say, "Give an account of your stewardship."

Second, Paul does not say the steward must be "successful" but rather "faithful." A parallel to this text is the parable of the talents in Luke 19:12-27, where a master gives large sums of money to his servants and leaves. On his return he calls them in that he might know "how much business they had transacted."[21] The first *was* successful, but the master congratulates him on his faithfulness, not on his success. The first is clearly more important than the second.

The second cameo (4b) in this compound center reads:

4b.       [3]And to me it is trifling to be judged by you
                or by any human court.
                    I do not even judge myself.                    THE LORD
                        [4]I am not aware of anything against myself,   Judges Me
                but I am not thereby acquitted.
            It is the Lord who judges me.

Paul displays a deep sense of spiritual and psychological balance. No one judges him—neither his readers nor any human court, nor even himself. The Corinthian efforts to put him under their microscope and tear him to pieces will not influence him. They can pass any judgment they like—it will not affect him. His personal worth is not related to how they feel about him. At the same time when Paul is under personal attack, he does not dissolve in a barrage of self-criticism. Yet, he is not acquitted—the Lord will judge him!

In cameo 4c Paul continues on the same subject.

4c.       [5]Therefore do not pronounce judgment before the time,
                before the Lord comes,                              THE LORD
                who will bring to light the things now hidden in darkness   Judges and
                and will disclose the purposes/motives of people's hearts.   Commends All
                That every person receive his commendation from God.

The Corinthians had assumed the right to subject their leaders to scrutiny and then divide up into competing groups on the basis of their conclusions. Paul knew that the key to all of this was the inner motive of those involved. It was time for acceptance, not judgment. The Lord, in his good time, would bring to light the motives of hearts now hidden in darkness. Then and only then every person, not just Paul, Apollos and Cephas, but *everyone* will receive "their commendation from God." Case closed.[22]

If Paul's admonitions are followed, the party spirit that was dividing the church would evaporate, and the Corinthians could recover health as a part of the one body of Christ.

[21]Cf. Bailey, *Jesus Through Middle Eastern Eyes*, pp. 397-403.
[22]Paul is discussing "jealousy and strife," not the sexual misconduct of 5:1-2, where judgment is
    required.

This homily includes the following themes.

1. The wisdom of God is beyond the wisdom of this age.

2. One must "become a fool" to acquire such wisdom.

3. Boasting before God is not acceptable, because all we have comes to us as gifts.

4. Boasting about various leaders is meaningless.

5. The Christian must never go beyond Scripture.

6. All Christian leaders belong to all Christians, and all Christians belong to Christ in God.

7. Authentic Christian leaders are servants of Christ and stewards of the mysteries of God.

8. The Lord alone can judge others, because he alone knows the secrets of the heart.

9. Paul accepts the judgment of the Lord, but not the judgment of the Corinthians.

10. Lowliness is always an essential part of authentic Christian leadership.

Paul concludes this opening essay with some final reflections [see fig. 1.4(12)].

## THE RHETORIC

Paul is winding down as he brings his first essay to an end. He again uses seven cameos to express his concluding thoughts and his personal appeal. Paul opens with three cameos of comparison between the Corinthians and the apostles (1-3). To this he adds three cameos that describe the world within which the apostles carry out their mission (4-6). There is a climax in the center of each half of the homily. In the center of the first (2) he offers the parable of the Roman spectacle. This creates an encased parable. The center of the second half describes the apostles' responses to their suffering.

At the same time the two sets of three cameos interlock. Cameo 2 (Paul's suffering) becomes the beginning (4) and the end (6) of the next section and thus locks the two sets of cameos together. Cameo 2 presents a picture of brutalized, ragged captives at the end of a Roman victory parade. The picture is filled out in 4 and 6. This method of interlocking occurs also in Isaiah 48:1-11 and Isaiah 55:6-9.

In the last cameo (7) Paul asserts his authority as their "father" with the right to "admonish" them. The final line is his personal appeal. Some type of personal appeal concludes each of the five essays. It is a form of literary signature. With it he is "signing off" on this first topic.

1.   [8]Already you are filled, already rich!
     Without us you have become kings!          YOU AND WE
     And would that you did rule,
     so that we might rule with you!

2.         [9]For I think that God has exhibited us apostles last,
           like men sentenced to death;            THE PARABLE OF
           because we have become a spectacle      God's Spectacle
           to the world, to angels and to men.     (the apostles' condition)

3.   [10]We are fools for Christ's sake,
     but you are wise in Christ.
     We are weak, but you are strong.            WE AND YOU
     You are held in honor, but we in dishonor.

     -------------------------------             -----------------

4.   [11]To the present hour we hunger and thirst,
     we are ill-clad and buffeted and homeless,   OUR CONDITION
     [12]and we labor, working with our own hands.

5.         When reviled, we bless;
           when persecuted, we endure.             OUR RESPONSE
           [13]when slandered, we try to conciliate;   To Our Condition

6.   we have become as the scapegoats of the world,
     the offscouring of all things until now.     OUR CONDITION

     -------------------------------             -----------------

7.   [14]I do not write this to make you ashamed,
     but to admonish you as my beloved children.  CONCLUDING
     [15]For though you have countless guides in Christ,   Personal Appeal
     you do not have many fathers.
     For I became your father in Jesus Christ through the gospel.

     [16]I urge you, then, be imitators of me.

**Figure 1.4(12). Christian unity: Paul, Apollos and Cephas—concluding remarks (1 Cor 4:8-16)**

## COMMENTARY

The first three cameos in this homily are seen in figure 1.4(13).

Paul opened this first essay (1:4-9) with gentle compliments telling them that they were enriched in Christ in "all speech and all knowledge" and "not

1. <sup>8</sup>Already you are filled, already rich!
   Without us you have become kings!  YOU AND WE
   And would that you did rule,
   so that we might rule with you!

2. <sup>9</sup>For I think that God has exhibited us apostles last,
   like men sentenced to death;  THE PARABLE OF
   because we have become a spectacle  God's Spectacle
   to the world, to angels and to men.  (the apostles' condition)

3. <sup>10</sup>We are fools for Christ's sake,
   but you are wise in Christ.
   We are weak, but you are strong.  WE AND YOU
   You are held in honor, but we in dishonor.

**Figure 1.4(13). Cameos 1-3 (1 Cor 4:8-10)**

lacking in any spiritual gift." In the center of the essay he started to open a can of worms related to their failures and flatly told them that they were still "children" and were thus only able to digest milk. Now at the end he pulls out all the stops and speaks to them harshly with irony and sarcasm.

Cameo 1 concentrates on the Corinthians while in cameo 3 the emphasis tilts in the direction of Paul and his colleagues. The Corinthians think they have become kings (without kingdoms) and they imagine themselves to be wise, strong and held in honor. They believe Paul and his friends are weak, foolish and dishonored. Paul is not amused by their preposterous views.

Then dramatically his ironic mood shifts as he exposes some deep pain. This pain appears as he tells the parable of the Roman spectacle in cameo 2. He becomes calm and reflective as he contemplates the idea that God is leading a great triumph with the world and the angelic hosts watching. After a major military victory Roman generals were given a grand parade through the streets of Rome. The conqueror rode in a chariot near the front followed by priests and notables. The victorious army marched behind them. Then came wagons loaded with captured booty. At the very end were captives in chains who, at the conclusion of the parade route, would be killed in a public sacrifice to the Roman gods. Paul wonders if God has formed such a parade and has placed the apostles at the end under sentence of death. What is amazing about this parable of the Roman triumph is its similarity to the crucifixion of Jesus. Jesus was also in a (Roman) parade that ended with his death in a public place.

On July 18, 1944, the German martyr Dietrich Bonhoeffer wrote a letter from prison to a friend. In it he said,

"Christians stand by God in God's suffering," and that distinguishes Christians from pagans. "Could you not keep awake with me one hour?" Jesus asks in Gethsemane. This is the reversal of everything a religious person expects from God. Human beings are called to suffer with God's own suffering caused by the godless world.[23]

Later in the same letter Bonhoeffer continues, "Being swept into the messianic suffering of God in Jesus Christ happens in the most varied ways in the New Testament."[24] In Philippians 3:10 Paul writes, "that I may know him, and the power of his resurrection, *and may share his sufferings, becoming like him in his death,* that if possible I may attain the resurrection from the dead." Was this what Paul was thinking about as he wrote the parable of the Roman triumph?

As noted, the center of this first essay focuses on the power and wisdom of the cross (1:17–2:2). As Paul concludes his discussion of this topic, his mind returns to the theme of the cross with hints of his own participation in the suffering of Christ.

This is an often neglected Pauline cry of dereliction. If this is God's triumphal parade, why are the apostles at the end anticipating death? "My God, my God—why . . . ?" Like Jesus, Paul is perhaps not expressing his studied conclusions but rather his deepest feelings. This is how *he feels,* and surprisingly, he is not ashamed to expose those feelings to his readers. Perhaps this is because such feelings connected him to the suffering of Jesus.

In the second set of three cameos Paul moves beyond the Corinthians and looks back over his ministry at large [see fig. 1.4(14)].

```
4.  ¹¹To the present hour we hunger and thirst,
        we are ill-clad and buffeted and homeless,      OUR CONDITION
    ¹²and we labor, working with our own hands.

5.      When reviled, we bless;
            when persecuted, we endure.                 OUR RESPONSE
        ¹³when slandered, we try to conciliate;         To Our Condition

6.  we have become as the scapegoats of the world,
        the offscouring of all things until now.        OUR CONDITION
```

**Figure 1.4(14). Cameos 4-6 (1 Cor 4:11-13)**

---

[23]Dietrich Bonhoeffer, *Meditations on the Cross* (Louisville: Westminster John Knox, 1996), p. 60.
[24]Ibid.

Paul contemplates his apostolic band and sees a small group of traveling preachers who are hungry, thirsty, poorly dressed, wounded and homeless. To top it off, they have to pay their own way. Paul appears to be borrowing vocabulary from a list in Isaiah 58:7. In that text God speaks, telling the people

> Is not this the fast that I choose: . . .
> Is it not to share your bread with the hungry,
> and bring the homeless poor into your house;
> when you see the naked, to cover him.

Paul's Greek word for "ill clad" (v. 11) also means "half-naked." The Hebrew phrase in the above text for "homeless poor" is *'anawim marudeem* which includes the idea of the *wandering*, homeless poor. Isaiah's text describes the apostles. For decades Paul had no permanent address, no place to call his own. Three out of the five descriptive words Paul selects appear in Isaiah's list. Paul's choice of words also links cameo 4 to the great "self-emptying" passage in Philippians 2:6-8. Here, to a lesser degree, we see the self-emptying of Paul.

Comparisons with the passion of Jesus are again compelling. John's Gospel records that on Easter evening Jesus appeared to the disciples in a locked room where they were hiding in fear. He showed them his hands and his side and said to them, "As the Father has sent me, even so I send you." In the text before us, a few sentences after this devastating description of his ministry, Paul writes "be imitators of me." I spent forty years in ministry in four different countries of the Middle East and survived seven wars with many life-threatening dangers. But I was rarely seriously hungry or thirsty. I tried to dress simply, but I was never "half-naked." I was never beaten, nor was I ever homeless, and I was not obliged to pay my own way. Had I been called on to walk in Paul's shoes, how would I have responded? Who is able for these things? Both the conversation with Jesus on Easter evening and the concluding remarks in this first essay are stunning challenges to all who choose to travel the narrow way. Even more amazing is the manner in which Paul responded to this litany of hardships.

When insulted, he blessed. When persecuted, he endured. When slandered, he sought reconciliation. In traditional Middle Eastern culture (and elsewhere), retaliation is considered one of the marks of an honorable self-respecting person. Aristotle agreed, and made "great-heartedness" (megalopsukhia) the highest virtue.[25] He then defined that virtue to include an *unwillingness* to endure insult. Cultures East and West endorse this view. For centuries the Islamic world has granted the right and indeed affirmed the duty of taking revenge to preserve honor. Islam has traditionally criticized Christianity for its failure to endorse the exercise of that right. Paul's responses to insult, persecution and slander were not approved or applauded in the culture of which he was a part. For the Jewish community, "An eye for an eye and a tooth for a tooth" was still a sacred law to be observed. But the "mind of Christ" and his sacrificial life pointed Paul in a radically new direction. That new narrow way, here on display, links Paul's earlier discussion of the cross to his personal life. This is how he takes up his cross and follows Jesus.

Paul then offers two final descriptions of his condition (cameo 6). The NRSV translates the first "We have become like the rubbish of the world." The word is *peri-katharma*, which was used to describe the dust and dirt that is thrown out at the end of a round of house cleaning. BAGD describes this word as "that which is removed as a result of a thorough cleansing, i.e., dirt, refuse. . . . Purification results from this activity."[26]

The second word, *peri-psema*, also has to do with scrapings, cleaning and purifying.

Regarding this text, William Orr and James Walther write,

> [Paul] knew what physical deprivation meant. . . . His reward was often insult, persecution and slander; but Paul responded according to the irenic admonition of Jesus. The end result of all this was that *the dirt scoured from the world* was poured upon him and his apostolic co-laborers. They then acted as cleansing agents, taking to themselves hate, malice, and bitterness; and by absorbing this without violent or vengeful response, they took away those evils. Thus in a particular way they were carrying on the work of Christ.[27]

Paul wrote to the Colossians, "Now I rejoice in my sufferings for your sake, and in my flesh I complete what is lacking in Christ's afflictions for the sake of his body, that is, the church." He continues and mentions "the mystery hidden for ages and generations and now made manifest to his saints" (Col 1:24, 26).

---

[25] Aristotle, *Ethica Nicomachea* 1107b.22, 1123a.34.
[26] BAGD, p. 647.
[27] Orr/Walther, *I Corinthians*, p. 192 (italics theirs).

As seen above, Paul brings this essay to its conclusion with a stunning homily composed of seven remarkable cameos. Only the final personal appeal remains [see fig. 1.4(15)].

7.  <sup>14</sup>I do not write this to make you ashamed,                 CONCLUDING
      but to admonish you as my beloved children.                        Personal Appeal
    <sup>15</sup>For though you might have ten thousand guardians in Christ,[28]
      you do not have many fathers.
      For I became your father in Jesus Christ through the gospel.

<sup>16</sup>I urge you, then, be imitators of me.

---

**Figure 1.4(15). Cameo 7 (1 Cor 4:14-16)**

As noted earlier, Paul was acting *like a mother* and feeding milk to a young child (the Corinthians). Now he presents himself as their *father*. The "guardian" in Greek culture was a well-known figure with a great deal of responsibility for forming the character of the child. But the father was naturally more important.

Paul's use of the metaphor "father" is significant. Behind him is Hosea 11:1-9 and the parable of the prodigal son in Luke 15:11-32. When these three texts are compared, six themes appear in all three, and one theme surfaces in two of the three. The list is as follows:

1. A father and his children appear in each.

2. The father is insulted and badly treated by his wayward children.

3. The father tries to reconcile/conciliate and calls his children beloved.

4. The father admonishes the wayward children.

5. The father goes beyond what is normally expected of a human father.

6. The father directly or indirectly presents himself as a model for his children to emulate.

7. Compassion is mentioned specifically (Hosea, Jesus).

It is certain that Paul knew the book of Hosea. The comparisons between Paul's use of the metaphor "father" and the parable of the prodigal son make it possible that Paul (directly or indirectly) knew something of that parable. Thus three of the parables of Jesus can be seen to share theological and ethical content with this section of Paul's first essay.

---

[28]NRSV.

In conclusion, the following aspects of Paul's concluding remarks can be noted.

1. Arrogance is irritating. The Corinthians saw themselves as rich, powerful and wise. Paul spares nothing as he points out their flawed self-image.

2. Paul openly admits that he becomes discouraged and makes no attempt to hide his feelings. At times he feels (like Jesus?) he is on the way to his death. In the final essay Paul affirms "I die every day" (15:31).

3. Yet, Paul accepts being a "fool for Christ's sake."

4. His lifestyle involves great hardship.

5. When cursed, persecuted and slandered, he responds with love.

6. He absorbs evil, and in the process that evil dies.

7. He is their father in the gospel and writes to admonish, not to shame, his "children."

The final personal appeal "be imitators of me" is not an ego trip for Paul. Students of a rabbi were expected to live with the rabbi. They could learn from him in two ways. His teachings provided one method of learning. Watching him live in observance of the law provided the other. How did he keep the sabbath? What about ceremonial purity? Which food stuffs did he subject to the tithe? Observing the rabbi's lifestyle was an indispensable part of the learning process. Paul would naturally assume this teaching method—but what a litany of suffering! As noted earlier, this final admonition needs to be placed beside the admonition of Jesus in the upper room on Easter night when he showed the fearful disciples his hands and his side and said, "As the Father has sent me, even so I send you" (Jn 20:21).

We will observe similar signature conclusions at the ends of each of the other four essays.

This brings us to the second essay.

# Sex

*Men and Women in the Human Family*

ܐܘ ܠܐ ܝܕܥܝܢ ܐܢܬܘܢ
ܕܦܓܪܟܘܢ ܗܝܟܠܐ ܗܘ
ܕܪܘܚܐ ܕܩܘܕܫܐ ܕܥܡܪܐ ܒܟܘܢ
(6:19)

# Immorality and the Church

1 CORINTHIANS 4:17–5:6A

PAUL IS NOW READY TO begin his second essay, which focuses on sexual practice and its theological foundation. The essay comprises four sections and one extended aside. The outline of the overall essay is as follows:

2.1. Immorality and the Church (4:17–6:8)
2.2. (Three Road Blocks: Leaven, Immorality and the Law Courts [5:6b–6:8])
2.3. Theology of Sexual Practice: Kingdom Ethics (6:9-12)
2.4. Theology of Sexual Practice: Joining the Body (6:13-20)
2.5. Sexual Practice in Harmony with the Gospel (7:1-40)

In each of the five essays, Paul opens with a call to *remember* the *tradition*. This is followed (as always) with a presentation of the problem under consideration. The new topic is sexual immorality.

Reference to the tradition (4:17) requires careful scrutiny. The text reads:

1. ¹⁷For this reason I sent to you Timothy,          THE TRADITION
   my beloved and faithful child in the Lord:
   to remind you of my ways in Christ Jesus,
   as I teach them everywhere in every church.

Many commentators have assumed that 4:17-21 is a conclusion to what precedes, and that Paul's discussion of sexual practice begins in 5:1. It is also possible to read 4:17 (cameo 1) as the opening of the essay on the topic of sexual practice that follows. The phrase "For this reason I sent to you" (4:17) is thus best seen as looking *forward* rather than *backwards*. This question is significant and deserves careful attention. A number of points can be made.

A clear break in the text between 4:16 and 4:17 has been observed for more than a thousand years. Writing an Arabic language commentary on

1 Corinthians in Damascus in A.D. 867, Ibn al-Sari of the Syrian Orthodox church placed his first chapter division between verses 16 and 17.[1] Key aspects of the text support Ibn al-Sari's view.

1. The two verses 16 and 17 (when read side by side) give the reader two occurrences in a row of the idea expressed by the English word *therefore*. Namely:

> [16]I urge you, *therefore* [*oun*], be imitators of me.
> [17]*Therefore* [*dia touto*], I sent to you Timothy, to remind you of my ways in Christ as I teach them everywhere in every church.

Both the RSV and the NRSV soften this problem by translating the first "therefore" (*oun*) as "then." But it is difficult to argue that Paul is summarizing his previous argument twice in a row with two similar phrases one after another. Rather, the first "therefore" is a word Paul often uses to summarize a previous discussion (cf. 10:31; 11:20; 14:23; 14:26; 15:11; 16:11; 16:18). This leaves the second phrase (*dia touto*) as an introduction to what follows.

2. The phrase "to remind you" (v. 17) clearly opens a new discussion in two of the following essays (1 Cor 11:2; 15:1), so why not here as well?

3. What Paul "teaches everywhere in every church" is the church tradition. Such a reference *begins each* of the five essays. This has been widely recognized in essays three, four and five. So why should a reference to these traditions be left here as a *conclusion* to the first essay?

4. To my knowledge, no ancient Middle Eastern paragraph system divided the text at 1 Corinthians 5:1. However, there is widespread early evidence for a break at the end of verse 4:15. Codex Vaticanus made such a break (adding the admonition "imitate me" of verse 16 to the new paragraph). The ancient paragraph divisions of the northern Coptic tradition and those of the classical Armenian tradition do the same.[2] The ancient liturgy of St. James, followed by the Syrian Orthodox Church, and also the liturgy of the Greek Melkite Church of the Middle East break at the end of verse 16 and read 4:17–5:5 as a single passage.[3] As noted, Ibn al-Sari

[1]Bishr ibn al-Sari, *Pauline Epistles*, p. 59. Harvey Staal chose to vowel this name as Ibn al-Sirri (which never occurs as a name). The much preferred voweling is the well-known name Ibn al-Sari. Outside of any direct quotation, the correct voweling will appear.
[2]G. Horner, *The Coptic Version of the New Testament in the Northern Dialect* (1898, 1905; reprint, Osnabruck: Otto Zeller, 1969), 3:138-39. For the classical Armenian I have examined Codex 212 of the Armenian Patriarchal Library, Antelias, Lebanon (dated 1293), folio 220 r.
[3]Philoxenius Yusif, Metropolitan of Mardin, *Muqaddes Ayrillirin Fihriste* (Turkish and Syriac) (Mardin: Hikmet Basımevi, 1954), p. 87; *Kitab al Risa'il* (Arabic) (Schwair, Lebanon: Monastery of St. John, 1813), p. 167.

placed a chapter division in the text at this point.[4]

5. In 4:17-19 Paul discusses Timothy's impending visit and his own. This topic indirectly reappears in 5:3 in reference to the judgment of the immoral man. Paul seems to be saying, "Some think I am not coming [4:18] but I am *indeed* coming [4:19]; as a matter of fact, although I am absent in body consider me already present in spirit [5:3]."

The references to the visits of Paul and Timothy thus support the inclusion of 4:17-21 with what follows.

6. In 4:18 Paul refers to some who are "arrogant" (*ephusiothesan*). In 5:2, using the same word, he becomes more pointed with the remark, "and you are arrogant!" That is, 4:18 joins 5:2 on the subject of "arrogance."

7. In 4:20 Paul refers to "the kingdom of God." This phrase occurs only nine times in Paul. Six of the nine are specific references to people *not* entering the kingdom of God. Setting aside the verse under discussion, four out of these five negative references (6:9, 10; Gal 5:21; Eph 5:5) specifically mention sexual immorality as one of the reasons for exclusion from the kingdom. The overwhelming weight of evidence is that when Paul is talking about sin and the kingdom of God, he is thinking of lists of sins that include sexual immorality. Here Paul specifically makes that connection (6:9, 10).

8. An examination of Paul's use of *dia touto* (for this reason) leads to the conclusion that this phrase always looks forward *in some sense*. Often it introduces a new thought with little or no reference to what has come before (cf. Rom 15:9; 1 Cor 11:30; 2 Cor 4:1; 12:10; Eph 1:15; Col 1:9; 2 Thess 2:11). At other times the phrase builds on a previous discussion and moves on to introduce a new idea (cf. Rom 1:26; 4:16; 5:12; 13:6; 1 Cor 11:10; 2 Cor 4:1; 7:13; Eph 5:17; 6:13; 1 Thess 3:5, 7). In most of these cases modern editors (RSV and others) have *dia touto* introduce a new paragraph. Schultz argues that in 1 Corinthians 4:17 *dia touto* points forward.[5] I suggest a translation of, "For this reason I sent to you Timothy . . . to remind you of my ways in Christ Jesus as I teach them everywhere." The reason for Timothy's visit is to remind them of Paul's ways in Christ.

9. There is a shift in tone between 4:14-16 (in the previous essay) and 4:17-21 (in the current essay). In verses 14-16 Paul speaks very gently. He wants

[4]Harvey Staal, ed. and trans., *Codex Sinai Arabic 151: Pauline Epistles, Part II*, in *Studies and Documents of the University of Utah* (Salt Lake City: University of Utah Press, 1969), 15:121.
[5]Anselm Schultz, *Nachfolgen und Nachakmen*, SANT, 6 (Munich: Lösel, 1962), pp. 309-10. (as noted in Conzelmann, *1 Corinthians*, p. 92 nn. 15, 20).

only to *admonish* his beloved children not to make them *ashamed*. But in verses 17-21 he is threatening the *arrogant* with a *rod!* C. K. Barrett has noted this dramatic shift of tone and writes,

> At verse 14 Paul began to moderate his tone towards his readers; he did not wish to humiliate them, only to see that they were soundly instructed in Christian principles. When however he recalls the actual . . . state of the Corinthian church he feels obliged to end his paragraph on a firmer note.[6]

It is easy to see the threat of beating with a rod as related to the new discussion of incest rather than as part of the previous discussion on the cross that concluded with a "gentle admonition."

10. If 4:14-21 is indeed one paragraph, then what is there in these verses that triggers Paul's sudden anger? When verses 14-16 end the previous discussion and verses 17-21 are read as the opening volley of the new topic, the answer to this question is obvious. In the first text (vv. 14-16) Paul, the "father" of the Corinthian believers, wants to deal gently with his wayward children. In the second (vv. 17-21) he is angry about their gross immorality. But without that break in the text there is no apparent reason for Paul's intense flare-up of anger.

Why then, we naturally ask, have commentators and editors placed the break in subject matter at 5:1 for so long? There are at least three possible reasons as to why this has happened.

1. First is the visit. In 4:18-21 Paul *is* talking about his coming visit. Chapter 5 discusses incest. They seem unrelated. But this reference to the coming visit is indirectly mentioned in 5:3. Paul's visit is an introduction to his discussion of the case of incest. His point is, "I am coming, and you had better get this matter taken care of, or on my arrival I will have to use a rod (4:18-21)! Do not await my return, but consider me already present in spirit and proceed (5:3-5)."

2. The discussion of "I am coming!" moves naturally into the directive "Here is the problem (5:1-2), and you must deal with it before I arrive (5:2b-6)." But if this connection is not noted, it is easy to see 5:1 as a major division.

3. Finally, there is the matter of the tradition. When the translator does not observe that in the other four essays Paul refers to the tradition at the *opening* of a new essay, making a chapter division in 5:1 becomes an option.

In conclusion, there are numerous reasons for seeing 4:17-21 as an introduction to the topic of immorality and not as a dangling personal aside. Like each of the other four, the second essay opens with a reference to *the tradition*. As

---

[6]Barrett, *First Epistle*, p. 117.

with other essays, this reference is attached to a call to *remember*.

After invoking the tradition Paul states the problem boldly and gives a firm directive to the Corinthian church regarding what they must do. Once again Paul composes an apostolic homily with seven cameos. The text is displayed in figure 2.1(1).

1.  [4:17]For this reason I sent to you Timothy,
    my beloved and faithful child in the Lord:
    to remind you of my ways in Christ Jesus,
    as I teach them everywhere in every church.

    THE TRADITION

    --------------------------------------------------------------------------

2.  [18]Some are arrogant, as if I were not coming to you.
    [19]But I will come to you soon, if the Lord wills,
    and I will find out not the talk of these arrogant people but their power.
    [20]For the kingdom of God does not consist of talk but power.

    ARROGANCE
    And Power

3.  [21]What do you want?
    Shall I come to you with a rod,
    or with love in a spirit of gentleness?

    A ROD
    Or Gentleness?

4.  [5:1]Everyone has reported that there is immorality among you,
    and of a kind that is not found even among the Gentiles;
    for a man has [conjugal relations with] his father's wife.
    [2]And you are arrogant!
    Ought you not rather to mourn?

    ARROGANCE
    And Immorality

    ----------------------------------                    -------------------

5.  Let him be removed from among you,
    the one who has done this.
        [3]For I, absent in body
            yet, present in spirit,
    I have already judged, as present,
    the one who has done this.

    HIM—REMOVE
    My Body
    My Spirit
    Him—Judge

6.  [4]In the name of the Lord Jesus Christ.
    When you are assembled,
    and my spirit is present,
    with the power of our Lord Jesus,

    NAME OF JESUS
    Your "body"
    My Spirit
    Power of Jesus

7.  [5]surrender this to Satan
    for the destruction of the flesh,
    that his spirit may be saved
    in the day of the Lord.
    [6a]Your boasting is not good.[7]

    HIM—REMOVE
    His Flesh
    His Spirit
    Day of the Lord

**Figure 2.1(1). The problem: Immorality, arrogance and what must be done (1 Cor 4:17–5:6a)**

---

[7] My translation. To highlight the parallels within and between cameos, I have been obliged to translate literally.

## THE RHETORIC

The structure of this apostolic homily is similar to the homily that precedes it in 4:8-16. The one structural difference is that in the previous homily the stand-alone cameo is at the end. Here it is in the beginning. Otherwise the two homilies have the same structure.

Again there are seven cameos. The first affirms the tradition. The other six are divided into two sets of three cameos, each of which has an A-B-A format.[8] The first set presents the problem: Incest! The second commands a response: Remove the offender! In 4:8-16 the concluding cameo looks *back* over *the entire essay* from 1:10–4:13. In this homily cameo 1 looks *forward* over *the entire second essay* that stretches from 4:18–7:40.

## COMMENTARY

As noted Paul opens with an invocation of the tradition.

1.  [4:17]For this reason I sent to you Timothy,[9]           THE TRADITION
    my beloved and faithful child in the Lord:
    To remind you of my ways in Christ Jesus,
    as I teach them everywhere in every church.

At the beginning of the first essay Paul wrote about "the testimony of/to Christ" that "*was confirmed*" among the Corinthians (1:6). Here the tradition is referred to as "my ways in Christ Jesus as I teach them everywhere," which were *not confirmed* (as he will quickly point out). What he has to say about sexual morality and its theological foundation is not something he is dreaming up for the occasion. His views on this new topic are known to all the churches. Previously he taught all of this to *them*. On his recent visit, Timothy repeated his views, and thus they cannot plead ignorance. Paul wants, once again, to set the record straight.

He then sets off a bomb [see fig. 2.1(2)].

After the invocation of the tradition, the pace quickens and the pitch rises. He begins by writing bluntly "some are arrogant." In cameo 4 he becomes more pointed by saying, "you are arrogant!" He is very angry! The word *arrogant* is another key word that appears in the definition of love in 13:4-7.

It appears that some in Corinth assumed that Paul would not return. In cameo 2 he affirms that he intends to come soon—and they will therefore have to deal with him. He has not faded out of the picture.

---

[8]This format is also used in 7:26-31.
[9]My translation.

2.  [4:18]Some are *arrogant*, as if I were not coming to you.            ARROGANCE
    [19]But I will come to you soon, if the Lord wills,               And Power
       and I will find out not the talk of these *arrogant* people but their power.
    [20]For the kingdom of God does not consist of talk but power.

3.     [21]What do you want?                                          I COME WITH
       Shall I come to you with a rod,                                A Rod?
       or with love in a spirit of gentleness?                       Or Gentleness?

4.  [5:1]Everyone[10] has reported that there is immorality among you,
       and of a kind that is not found even among the Gentiles;       ARROGANCE
       for a man has (is living with) his father's wife.             And Immorality
    [2]And you are *arrogant*!
       Ought you not rather to mourn?

**Figure 2.1(2). Cameos 2-4 (1 Cor 4:18–5:2)**

He then raises the question of "talk" (the use of language) and the reality of "power." The first essay discussed "talk" (beautiful language/the wisdom of this world) and "power" (the power of the cross and of the Spirit). The power of the cross overcomes the wisdom and power of the world. "The power of the Spirit" gives the ability to understand mysteries, to heal, to prophesy and to speak in tongues. On arrival Paul will want to discuss these things with them.

In 2 Corinthians 10:4-5 Paul offers an important clue to what he means by "power." He writes, "For the weapons of our warfare are not worldly but have divine power to destroy strongholds. We destroy arguments and every proud obstacle to the knowledge of God, and take every thought captive to obey Christ." Paul was able to "hold his own" while debating the philosophers in Athens, and he can certainly manage with the Corinthians who are proud of their sexual freedom to commit incest. The issues are not turf problems. Very serious matters are on the table and Paul is fully prepared to defend his views.

In cameo 3 he offers them a choice. He can come in "gentleness" or "with a rod," and they must choose between the two. Their choice will be made by how they deal with the man sleeping with his father's wife.

Paul begins his confrontation with the Corinthians over the case of incest with the key word *olos* that can be translated "actually it is reported" or "everyone has reported."[11] The RSV, NRSV and NIV have chosen "It is actually re-

---

[10]My translation.
[11]BAGD, p. 565.

ported." This carries the nuance of "I am sorry to have to say this, but *it is actually reported* that . . ." The second translation option of "everyone has reported" means "I am hearing this from all my sources." These English versions show that many in the Western world take the first view. But how have Middle Eastern Christians read this text?

Out of the twenty-three Semitic versions gathered for this study, both the Hebrew and eighteen of the Arabic versions read some form of "Everyone has reported" or "It is known for a fact."[12] Three of these translations have some form of "It is commonly known," and one lists simply "It is known."

The winner for more than a thousand years is "Everyone has reported." This option fits Paul's cultural context. The Corinthians had reported some things to him in writing (7:1), and he had heard about other things orally "from Chloe's people" (1:11). No doubt Stephanas (16:17) and Sosthenes (1:1) had their own "grapevines." But Paul does not reveal his sources. Such a disclosure would have given the Corinthians a chance to immediately shift the subject from the case of incest to the question, Who ratted on us? Paul protects his sources by saying, "The cat is out of the bag, *everyone has reported* . . ." That is, "Don't try to identify the person who gave me this information and then get angry at him or her. *I am getting this disgusting news from everyone!*"

The key word *immorality*, which appears in cameo 4, is a general term for all forms of unacceptable sexual behavior. The Mishnah legislates stoning for a man who has sexual relations with "his mother, his father's wife, his daughter-in-law, a male, or a beast."[13] Roman law also forbade incest. One of the aspects of this particular case that appears to anger Paul the most is that some in the congregation are "boasting" about this matter. Apparently they understood "freedom in Christ" to mean "anything goes!" "No!" thunders Paul— you should be in mourning!

The first trilogy of cameos (1-3) focuses on the problem. The second trilogy (5-7) gives attention to what the Corinthians have to do about it [see fig. 2.1(3)].

---

[12]These include Mt. Sinai 155 (9th cent.); Mt. Sinai 73 (9th cent.); Mt. Sinai 310 (10th cent.); Erpenius (1616); London Pollyglott (1657); Propagandist (1671); London Pollyglot rev. (1717); Shwair (1813); Martyn (1826); Shidiac (1851); Bustani-Van Dyck (1865); Jesuit (1880); Yusif Dawud (1899); Fakhouri (1964); New Jesuit (1969); Bible Society Arabic (1993); Hebrew (1817); Jerusalem (Bible Society). For the original texts, see appendix II, plate B.

[13]Mishnah, *Sanhedrin* 7:4 (Danby, p. 391).

| | | |
|---|---|---|
| 5. | 2bLet him be removed from among you, | |
| | the one who has done this. | HIM—REMOVE |
| | 3For I, absent in body | My Body (absent) |
| | yet, present in spirit, | My Spirit (present) |
| | I have already judged, as present, | Him—Judge |
| | the one who has done this. | |
| | | |
| 6. | 4In the name of the Lord Jesus Christ. | NAME OF JESUS |
| | When you are assembled, | Your "body" |
| | and my spirit is present, | My Spirit (present) |
| | with the power of our Lord Jesus, | Power of Jesus |
| | | |
| 7. | 5surrender this to Satan | HIM—REMOVE |
| | for the destruction of the flesh, | His Flesh |
| | that his spirit may be saved | His Spirit |
| | in the day of the Lord. | Day of the Lord |
| | 6Your boasting is not good. | |

**Figure 2.1(3). Cameos 5-7 (1 Cor 5:2-6)**

These three cameos are also inverted. The *removal of the offender* is the subject of the two outer stanzas (5, 7). In the center (6) the *authority for this action* is discussed. They are to act in the name and with the power of *our Lord Jesus*. The center of each of the three cameos touches on the themes of "body and spirit." The body and spirit of Paul appear in cameo 5 while the body and spirit of the offender are mentioned in cameo 7. The body of Christ ("when you are assembled") is subtly introduced into the climax (6). In 6:13-20 Paul argues that sexuality for the Christian is related to the doctrine of the church. Here, he is already reflecting that theological stance.

Paul is asking the congregation to take responsibility for its own life. He is also astutely avoiding a trap. Some in the congregation are at least contemplating (and perhaps urging) leaving this mess for Paul to sort out when he arrives. That way the congregation can avoid the painful and distasteful task of making a decision. Furthermore, whatever Paul decides, they can then blame *him*. "He said this," "He failed to do that," "If only he had . . ." The discussion can last for months and the damage for years. Regardless of what he says or does, some will blame him. Paul is too intelligent to be caught is such a bind. In short he says,

> You have to make a decision and carry it out. Don't wait for me. You must take
> responsibility for this problem. You want my opinion? Fine—I will give it to
> you. Don't stone him (a Jewish solution) and don't report him to the authorities

for trial and punishment (a Roman solution). Throw him out of the church! Furthermore, this action must be taken by you as a community. Do not delegate the decision to your leaders. You must assemble *as the church* and "surrender this . . . to Satan." The shock may lead him to repentance. It is your only hope for him and for yourselves.

On whose authority is this to be done? They are told to act "in the name of the Lord Jesus Christ" (v. 4a) and in the "power of our Lord Jesus" (v. 4d). Yes, there will be suffering involved for all. But "to us who are being saved" the cross is "the power of God" (1:18). That same cross is also the wisdom of God. Out of that power and wisdom, demonstrated in a cross, they are to act. Literally, Paul writes "surrender *this . . .* to Satan." This is a Middle Eastern way of talking. In English we usually translate it "surrender this *man*," but the word *man* is missing. When Paul writes, "surrender this . . . to Satan," the readers can add whatever adjective they want. It can be "this *idiot*" or "this *fool*" or something stronger. This same style of speech appears in the parable of the pounds in Luke 19:14. In that story a group of citizens who hate the nobleman send an emissary (presumably to Rome) to say, "We do not want *this . . .* to rule over us." Western translations again add the word *man* and offer, "We do not want this *man* to rule over us." Abraham Lincoln's enemies called him a "baboon," a "hairy ape" and "a gorilla." Both Jesus and Paul invite their listeners/readers to add the adjectives of their choices.

The meaning of cameo 7 is elusive. Anthony Thiselton has a full discussion of the many questions and options.[14] He writes, "there emerges a further strand to the issue which is relevant equally to Corinth and for today: *in certain cases law ministers to trust and to freedom*: it does not oppose freedom."[15] Gordon Fee's discussion is also extensive and helpful.[16] He comments on the fact that we live in a world where the church tolerates every kind of sin because (of course) we cannot be "judgmental." Fee then offers four astute general comments. These are (1) the entire church was told to participate. The problem was affecting all of them. (2) Discipline was intended to be "remedial, not judgmental." That is, the goal was the salvation of the sinner. (3) That discipline was important because the sin contaminated all of them. (4) In our day the man could simply have gone to another church that might too quickly accept him. Fee reflects on Paul's day where

---

[14]Thiselton, *First Epistle*, pp. 384-400.
[15]Ibid., p. 387 (italics his).
[16]Fee, *First Epistle*, pp. 196-214.

"exclusion could be a genuinely redemptive action."[17]

Yet after nearly two thousand years of study and discussion this text remains partially elusive. Paul's goal is trying to heal the church and save the man. To accomplish this purpose the church must "draw a line." "Everything goes" and "whatever society accepts has to be acceptable to us" is not good enough.

At the very end of the homily he tells them bluntly, "Your boasting is not good." As we will observe, boasting features in chapter 13 as a failure of love.

To summarize this first homily (in this essay), five points can be made

1. The church has a tradition; it is known and it is important.

2. Some are arrogantly affirming total freedom in sexual practice. Paul tells them to mourn.

3. They must come together in a public meeting and throw this man out of the church.

4. This action has the possibility of redeeming the sinner and restoring the church.

5. They are to act in the name and power of our Lord Jesus Christ.

Paul then turns to three roadblocks needing removal before he can lay a theological foundation for sexual practice that is in harmony with the gospel. It is possible to see these three roadblocks as profoundly relevant to the topic. To them we now turn.

---

[17]Ibid., pp. 213-14.

# Three Roadblocks

*Leaven, Immorality and the Law Courts*

1 CORINTHIANS 5:6B–6:8

IN THE PREVIOUS SECTION of the essay (2.1) Paul cut the Gordian knot. He told the Corinthians to remove the offender from the fellowship of the church. Here he discusses head-on three aspects of this case of incest that must be dealt with. These are not "asides" in the sense of "irrelevant topics" that interrupt the flow of Paul's argument. If Paul fails to discuss them, for the remainder of the essay the readers will mentally be saying "Yes, but . . ." and dismiss his argument. In brief these three are as follows:

1. You must consider the health of the church at large.
2. I wrote to you about dealings with evil people in the church, not in the world.
3. Do not dump this problem on the courts.

The text of the first of these roadblocks is displayed in figure 2.2(1).

Do you not know,

1. [6b]"A little *leaven* ferments all the dough"?
   [7]Cleanse out the *old leaven*                           OLD LEAVEN
   that you may be *new dough*, as you really are *unleavened*.   New Dough

2.    For *Christ*, our *paschal lamb*,                        CHRIST/LAMB
      has been *sacrificed*.                                   Sacrificed
      [8]Let us, therefore, *celebrate the feast*,             Feast

3.    not with the *old leaven*,
      the leaven of *malice* and *evil*,                       OLD LEAVEN
      but with the *unleavened bread* of sincerity and truth.  Unleavened Bread

Figure 2.2(1). The first roadblock: "This is a private matter" (1 Cor 5:6b-8)

## THE RHETORIC

The rhetorical style is simple and well known. There are three cameos. The first and the third are a pair. While the center contains the encased parable of the Passover lamb.

## COMMENTARY

The first roadblock is the pervasive attitude that says, "This is a personal matter. We should not be involved." This view has great staying power. Today it has been expressed with the statement, "God is not interested in what happens in the bedroom." A similar tension between the sin of one person and its effect on the community is discussed in *Midrash Rabbah, Leviticus* that reads,

> It is said, *Shall one man sin, and wilt Thou be wroth with all the congregation?* (Num. xvi, 22). R. Simeon b. Yohai taught: This may be compared to the case of men on a ship, one of whom took a borer and began boring beneath his own place. His fellow travelers said to him: "What are you doing?" Said he to them: "What does that matter to you, am I not boring under my own place?" Said they: "Because the water will come up and flood the ship for us all."[1]

The actions of an individual can profoundly affect the community, especially if that community is together in one ship! What was the reality of the situation in Corinth?

Many reconstructions of the case of incest in Paul's day have been suggested. One likely option is that of a family in which the mother died. The father then married a younger women. There was an adult son living in the home who was probably closer in age to the new wife than the father. A physical relationship developed between the son and the young wife. Some in the congregation arrogantly asserted that this was no more than an expression of their new freedom in Christ. After all—were they not expected to "love one another"? Were they not living under grace rather than law? But Paul knew that if there were no boundaries for sexual behavior, any form of social bonding as a community would be impossible. If the man who was sleeping with his stepmother attended church, those present would be traumatized by his presence. Every man and woman in the congregation would wonder, *Who is next? What is he thinking about? If we sit behind him,* his presence will distract us from the worship. *If we sit in front of him*—is he looking at my wife?

Members will avoid meetings when they know he will be present. This is

---

[1]*Midrash Rabbah, Leviticus* 1-19, trans. J. Israelstam (London: Soncino Press 1983), p. 55.

not a case of "negative attitudes should change." If incest is accepted, what about polygamy with its inevitable demeaning of women? Pederasty and bestiality will no longer be unthinkable. Yes, they are "under grace" and no longer "under the law," but what does that mean?

Paul chose the image of leaven in the dough (cameo 1). By means of that metaphor he was able to formulate one of the great New Testament parables for the atonement (cameo 2). Christ is "our Passover lamb." Only here do we find this metaphor for the atonement. No doubt, Paul used it often, and it is worthy of much reflection.

The case of incest was not a private matter. The sexual conduct of each member added to or detracted from the ability of the congregation to gather around the Eucharistic table in "sincerity and truth" (cameo 3).

The second "roadblock" is displayed below:

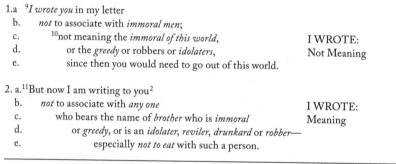

1.a     ⁹*I wrote you* in my letter
  b.     *not* to associate with *immoral men*;
  c.     ¹⁰not meaning the *immoral of this world*,      I WROTE:
  d.     or the *greedy* or robbers or *idolaters*,      Not Meaning
  e.     since then you would need to go out of this world.

2. a.¹¹But now I am writing to you² 
  b.     *not* to associate with *any one*      I WROTE:
  c.     who bears the name of *brother* who is *immoral*      Meaning
  d.     or *greedy*, or is an *idolater, reviler, drunkard* or *robber*—
  e.     especially *not to eat* with such a person.

Figure 2.2(2). The second roadblock: The church and the world (1 Cor 5:9-11)

### THE RHETORIC

In this double cameo Paul uses step parallelism such as appears in Isaiah 28:14-18. The first four lines in 1 clearly match the first four lines in 2. The two final lines (1e, 2e) do not match in content but are parallel in that each is a conclusion.

### COMMENTARY

Trying to sort out the timing and the content of Paul's various letters to the Corinthians is beyond the scope of this study. But clearly there was a "previous letter" and the Corinthians seem to have misunderstood part of it. Paul knew that some were currently saying, "In his last letter Paul told us to separate ourselves from all gross sinners. If I follow Paul's directive, I won't be able to go to work!" Paul is trying to correct that misunderstanding.

Christians do not need to avoid contact with all "immoral people." The list is instructive. In the world we will find immoral and greedy people along with robbers and idolaters. This is an open-ended list of sins. The word *immoral* covers a wide range of rejected sexual practices. The "greedy" are not just the people who eat too much but also those engaged in "conspicuous consumption." For many in our day this has become a virtue and even a consuming passion. Robbers do not all come in the night. Some of them steal while seated at computers in office buildings. Idols are created, then and now, out of many things. Idol worshipers are alive and well in our day.

While living in the world, contact with such types is unavoidable. Important to this topic is the fact that the word translated "associate with" is a rare compound word (*sun-ana-mignumi*) that has to do with mixing up together, joining, fusing and blending.[3] In the work-a-day secular/pagan world, then and now, such "mixing up together" is inevitable. Paul has no objection. When I mix with people in the office or shop who have no faith, the identity of my Christian community is not threatened. But "mixing up together" as the body of Christ, for Paul, was a very different matter. In a modern world that worships at the altar of inclusivity and sees all forms of inclusion as a "justice issue," Paul's admonition is deeply challenging.

The greedy and revilers are on the same list with idolaters and robbers. The admonition "not to eat" is best understood as referring to the celebration of the Eucharist, in that such celebrations were full meals. In short, Paul is saying that mixing with sinners in the pagan world is not the same as mixing with them in the body of Christ and at the Eucharist. The very identity of the church is at stake in the latter.

The third roadblock has to do with the courts [see fig. 2.2(3)].

## THE RHETORIC

This last section is composed of seven cameos. The first six are inverted. An extra cameo (7) appears at the end as a conclusion. Twice Paul has shown flexibility in the composition of apostolic homilies with seven cameos. There is a point of turning in cameo 5 and the concluding cameo is internally partially inverted.

---

[3]LSJ, *Greek-English Lexicon*, p. 1659; G. W. H. Lampe, *A Patristic Greek Lexicon* (Oxford: Clarendon, 1961), p. 1300.

1.[5:12]For what do I have to do with *judging outsiders?*
    Is it not those *inside the church* whom you are to *judge?*    YOU JUDGE
   [13]*God judges* those *outside.*
    "Drive out the *wicked person* from among you."

2.   [6:1]Does he presume, one of you, when he has a complaint against a *brother,*
    to go to law before the unrighteous instead of *to the saints?*    NOT COURTS

3.    [2]Do you not know that *the saints* will judge the *world?*    NOT KNOW?
    And if the world is to be judged by you,    Eternity
    are you unworthy to try *trivialities?*

4.    [3]Do you not know that *we are to judge angels?*    NOT KNOW?
    How much more then *everyday cases?*    Eternity

5.   [4]Therefore, if you have everyday cases,    NOT COURTS
    *why* do you lay them before those *despised by the church?*

6. [5]I say this to your *shame.*
   Is there not among you anyone *wise*    YOU JUDGE
   who is able to decide between members of the *brotherhood,*
   [6]but brother goes to *law* against brother, and this *before unbelievers.*

7.[7]Actually, it is utter defeat to you
   that you have cases against one another.
    Why not *rather suffer wrong?*    SUFFER WRONG
    Why not rather *be defrauded?*    Don't Wrong Others
   [8]But *you wrong* and *defraud,*
   even your own brothers.

**Figure 2.2(3). Roadblock three: The courts can settle this (1 Cor 5:12–6:8)**

## COMMENTARY

It appears that someone in the community had gone to the courts regarding this case of incest, or at least was threatening to do so. It could have been the trapped girl, her angry brother or perhaps her humiliated husband. Perhaps members of the church had opted to raise a case. Paul begins this apostolic homily with a full head of steam. Once again we will look at each of the pairs of ideas in the six-stanza ring composition. The outer pair is displayed in figure 2.2(4).

1.[5:12]For what do I have to do with *judging outsiders?*
    Is it not those *inside the church* whom you are to *judge?*    YOU JUDGE
   [13]*God judges* those *outside.*
    "Drive out the *wicked person* from among you."

------------------------------------------------

6. [6:5]I say this to your *shame.*
   Is there not among you any *one wise*    YOU JUDGE
   who is able to decide between members of the *brotherhood,*
   [6]but brother goes to *law* against brother, and this *before unbelievers.*

**Figure 2.2(4). Cameos 1 and 6 (1 Cor 5:12-13; 6:5-6)**

Paul opens his discussion of the courts by telling his readers to forget those "outside." God will take care of them. It is interesting that he does not say, "Leave them to the courts." Human courts in any age can be a frail instrument, a broken reed. The final arbitrator of justice for Paul is God. The Corinthians are responsible for those "inside the church." He then repeats his command to drive the wicked person out.

The matching stanza (6) is a polite way to say, "Shame on you!" In his gentle conclusion to the first essay (4:14) Paul specifically affirmed that he was not writing to make them ashamed. Now he is deliberately doing so. Dividing up into competing groups is one thing; condoning incest with arrogance is something else. Paul is direct and blunt as he in effect says, "You must come together, pass judgment and dismiss this person from your fellowship."

In the matching cameo (6) Paul raises the question of "wisdom." The Corinthians were proud of how "wise" they had become. In the opening of the letter he did not tell them they were "wise" but rather confirmed that they were "enriched in him with all speech and all knowledge." Then in the hymn to the cross he located the wisdom of God in the cross and quoted God saying, "I will destroy the wisdom of the wise" (1:19). At the end of the first essay his sarcasm was evident when he wrote, "We are fools for Christ's sake, but you are wise in Christ" (4:10). Now Paul nails them to the wall by asking, "Is there not among you any one wise?" The unspoken words that he leaves out are, "By going to the courts you are demonstrating in public that all of you are fools and thereby obliged to go to the courts to find a wise man to judge between you!" Are the unbelievers wiser than the believers in regard to this matter?

As Paul shames his readers and accuses them of asking the courts to wash the church's dirty laundry in public, he is surely recalling the court case in Corinth in which he was the accused. The synagogue in Corinth tried to attack Paul by bringing a case against him before Gallio, the proconsul for the year (Acts 18:12). Gallio threw out the case and the *Corinthian synagogue* was publicly humiliated. "Did you learn nothing?" Paul asks indirectly. The current case will be much worse! The Roman court will throw the book at the man and the whole town will despise the church in the process. Having watched the fiasco of the previous case where Paul was involved, is the *Corinthian church* going to make the same mistake made by the synagogue? Unbelievable!

Paul's sense of public shame in a honor-shame culture would naturally have been very strong. If the context was a dispute over land registration, that would be one thing. But when they were dealing with a man sleeping with his father's wife—a public trial would be too horrible to contemplate. "For heavens sake," Paul seems to be shouting, "are you trying to bring *disgrace on the gospel itself*? Don't flaunt this case of incest! Furthermore don't ignore it and don't hide it—deal with it!"

These two matching cameos are so carefully constructed that if the four cameos in the center were missing and the reader was left with only cameos 1 and 6, no one would notice the omissions. The four-cameo center is found in figure 2.2(5).

2. [1]Does he presume, one of you, when he has a complaint against a *brother*,
   to go to law before the unrighteous                         NOT COURTS
   instead of *to the saints?*

3.        [2]Do you not know that *the saints* will judge the *world?*        NOT KNOW?
          And if the world is to be judged by you,                           Eternity
          are you incompetent to try small claims?[4]

4.        [3]Do you not know that *we* are to *judge angels?*        NOT KNOW?
          How much more then matters pertaining to this life!        Eternity

5. [4]Therefore, if you have such cases,                        NOT COURTS
   *why* do you lay them before those
   who have no standing in *the church?*[5]

---

**Figure 2.2(5). Cameos 2-5 (1 Cor 6:1-4)**

## THE RHETORIC

The rhetorical structure is clear and simple. The outer envelope asks the question, Why do you go to the courts rather than the church? Each of cameos 3 and 4 say, "You will 'sit on the bench' in the next world! Can't you manage to do so in this world?" The connections between cameos 2 and 5 are so strong, and if 3 and 4 were missing, the reader would not observe any break in the flow of the passage.

## COMMENTARY

Fee rightly points out that Paul is discussing cases where one Christian is going to court against another Christian. He is not arguing against the courts in general. With Thiselton I have opted to translate *elakhiston* as "small" cases,

---

[4]This is the translation chosen by Thiselton, *First Epistle*, p. 430.
[5]NRSV.

rather than the RSV "trivial" cases.[6] When compared to "judging the world" they are indeed "small."

We can be confident that Paul does not intend to imply hostility toward the Roman officials. The court in Corinth did well by him. They are simply not a part of the company of the saints and are thereby not qualified to judge cases that relate to the faith commitments of Christians.

Precisely what is behind Paul's affirmation that "the saints will judge the world," and its parallel "we are to judge angels" is debatable.[7] Fee notes that this is "a common motif from Jewish apocalyptic eschatology."[8] What is clear is that Paul is again *holding up the mirror of eternity*. He did this already in his parable of the builder (3:10-17). In that text "the Day," with its fire of judgment, was at the center of an apostolic homily. In regard to the question of using the local courts to settle this particular church dispute over incest, Paul is saying:

> You think you can't handle this very difficult problem of incest in the congregation. Look at yourselves and at this problem in the light of eternity. On *the Day*, you will participate with the Lord in his judgment of all things, including fallen angels. In the light of that perspective there is no question about your ability to deal with this case of incest. Take courage, be bold, you *can do* what must be done.

In 1:5 Paul (perhaps sarcastically) congratulates the Corinthians on their knowledge. In 4:10 (certainly sarcastically) he tells them, "You are wise in Christ." They are now challenged with, "Is there not among you *any one wise?*"

The climax has to do with the matter of eternity in cameos 3 and 4, but the practical fallout appears in cameo 7 [see fig. 2.2(6)].

7.  6:7Actually, it is utter defeat to you
    that you have cases against one another.
    Why not *rather suffer wrong?*                SUFFER WRONG
    Why not rather *be defrauded?*               Don't Wrong Others
    8But *you wrong* and *defraud,*
    even your own brothers.

**Figure 2.2(6). Cameo 7 (1 Cor 6:7-8)**

[6]Thiselton, *First Epistle*, pp. 430-31.
[7]Fee, *First Epistle*, pp. 233-34; see also Dan 7:22; Wisdom of Solomon 3:8; Jubilees 24:29; Enoch 38:5, 95:3.
[8]Fee, *First Epistle*, p. 233.

Paul is pointing out that when they leave *such matters* to the courts they have already lost. Regardless of what the courts decide, they are the losers. Contentious court cases take on a life of their own. People are drawn into them and at times act against "the angels of their better natures."[9] Paul seems to know that at least some of them have track records of turning to the courts. He tells them, "you wrong and defraud, even your own brothers." Dealing with the incestuous man through the courts will neither redeem him nor heal the church.

Paul has now cleared away the brush. In summary, he has told his readers:

1. This is not a private matter. It affects the entire community. A case of incest in your midst is like yeast in bread dough.

2. Christ is our Passover lamb. Your celebrations of the Eucharist must be characterized by sincerity and truth.

3. In the world, you rub shoulders with gross sinners. Life in the church is a different matter.

4. Don't dump this problem on the courts. You have quite enough wisdom to deal with this as a community. Take responsibility for yourselves; consider the perspective of eternity and act. Remember, you will assist the Lord on the day of judgment.

Paul is now ready to lay a theological foundation for sexual practice, which he does in the following sections of this essay.

---

[9]A quotation from Abraham Lincoln's first inaugural address, March 1861.

# Theology of Sexual Practice

*Kingdom Ethics*

I CORINTHIANS 6:9-12

CHAPTER 6:9-20 HAS BEEN DESCRIBED as "somewhat disjointed and obscure." Reason for this has been found in "the unfinished spontaneous nature of these passages."[1]

Yet it is possible to see this text as a finely constructed literary whole that includes two apostolic homilies.[2] The first of these two homilies (6:9-12) has seven cameos [see fig. 2.3(1)].

## RHETORIC

This homily showcases a combination of features that have already appeared in the epistle. There are seven cameos, composed in three sections. The first section comprises four cameos using a simple ring composition with an A-B-B-A structure. This is followed by a second section that employs two cameos linked by step parallelism. The final cameo stands alone and provides a summary/conclusion to the homily. The last homily in the first essay (4:8-16) also had seven cameos, divided into three sections, with a concluding cameo.

---

[1]Jean Hering, *The First Epistle of Saint Paul to the Corinthians*, trans. A. W. Heathcote and P. J. Allcock (London: Epworth, 1962), p. 47.
[2]This chapter is a revision of Kenneth E. Bailey, "Paul's Theological Foundation for Human Sexuality: I Cor. 6:9-20 in the Light of Rhetorical Criticism," *Theological Review* 3, no. 1 (1980): 27-41.

1.<sup>6:9</sup>Do you not know that the *unrighteous*            THE UNRIGHTEOUS
    will not *inherit the kingdom of God?*            Not Inherit the Kingdom

2.    Do not be deceived;
        neither the immoral,
        nor idolaters,
        nor adulterers,            FIVE SINS
        nor catamites,            (sexual)
        nor sodomites,

3.      <sup>10</sup>nor thieves,
        nor the greedy
        nor drunkards,            FIVE SINS
        nor revilers,            (nonsexual)
        nor robbers

4.    will *inherit the kingdom of God.*            Not Inherit the Kingdom
  <sup>11</sup>And such were *some of you.*            LIKE SOME OF YOU

--------------------------------

5.<sup>11b</sup>But you were washed,
    but you were made holy [sanctified],
      but you were justified

6. in the name of the Lord Jesus Christ
    and in the Spirit
      of our God.

--------------------------------

7. <sup>12</sup>"All things are lawful for me,"
    but all things are not helpful.
  "All things are lawful for me,"
    but I will not be enslaved by anything.

---

**Figure 2.3(1). Kingdom ethics (1 Cor 6:9-12)**

## COMMENTARY

This homily opens with four cameos. Cameos 1 and 4 are clearly a pair. Examined together they read:

1. a.   <sup>6:9</sup>Do you not know that the *unrighteous*            THE UNRIGHTEOUS
   b.      will not *inherit the kingdom of God?*            Not Inherit the Kingdom
----------------------------------------------
4. b.  <sup>10b-11a</sup>will (not) *inherit the kingdom of God.*            Not Inherit the Kingdom
   a.   And such were *some of you.*            LIKE SOME OF YOU

The double use of the phrase *inherit the kingdom* occurs just before and just after the list of ten sins. Paul rarely mentions the kingdom of God. In all of his letters, only here does such a reference occur twice in a single text. The expressions "*inheriting* the kingdom" and "*inheriting* eternal life" are well known in the Gospels (Mt 19:29; 25:34; Mk 10:17; Lk 10:25; 18:18). The double use of the phrase "inherit the kingdom of God" binds (1a) "the unrighteous" to (4a) "such were some of you." Corinth was a "tough town," famous for its debauchery. Paul was a brilliant scholar. At the same time, he was able to "dumb down" his presentations of the gospel and could appeal to the uneducated, tough, immoral flotsam of Corinth. Working as a poorly dressed, itinerant tentmaker would have thrown him in with the tradespeople of the city. He gained a following—but his followers inevitably brought problems with them into their new life in Christ. The phrase "such *were* some of you" indicates that among Paul's readers were those who had been healed from the sins on his list. The ten sins can be seen as two sets of five. This in itself can be traced elsewhere.

In Colossians 3:5, 8, Paul sets out two lists of sins with five sins in each. The first is directly, or indirectly connected to sexual sins and is as follows:

| Paul's List | Paul's Categories |
| --- | --- |
| immorality | a catchall category for sexual sins |
| impurity | strong overtones of sexual misconduct |
| passion | sexual in nature (1 Cor 7:9) |
| evil desire | primarily related to "desires of the flesh" (Rom 1:24; 6:12; 13:14; Gal 5:6, 24; 1 Thess 4:5) |
| covetousness | faintly related to sexual sins. Coveting the neighbor's wife is proscribed in the Ten Commandments (Ex 20:17) |

Paul's second list in Colossians 3:8 also contains five sins.

| | |
| --- | --- |
| anger | nonsexual |
| wrath | nonsexual |
| malice | nonsexual |
| slander | nonsexual |
| foul talk | nonsexual |

This same pattern appears here in 2 and 3. The sexual sins are

| Paul's List | Paul's Categories |
| --- | --- |
| immoral | all forms of sexual sins—particularly heterosexual sins |
| idolaters | sacred prostitution was a part of the Corinthian world |
| adulterers | heterosexual sins (married) |
| catamites | the passive partner in a homosexual relationship |
| sodomites | the active partner in a homosexual relationship |

Both heterosexual and homosexual sins are condemned.[3] There is no indication that one is considered more heinous than the other. Idolatrous worship in Corinth involved sacred prostitution with the priestesses of Aphrodite/Venus, and thus idolatry in Corinth involved fornication.[4] This means that, like Colossians 3:5, 8, Paul begins his list of ten vices with five that relate to sexual misconduct.

These two similar Pauline lists of ten sins (five sexual and five nonsexual) are striking. Number ten is music playing in the background, and that number carries overtones of the Decalogue. Later in the epistle Paul will again use the number ten in a significant way (9:19-27). This is in harmony with the extensive use of seven, the perfect number. The word *catamites* is unique to this passage, and *sodomites* occurs only in one other text (1 Tim 1:10). In short, after affirming that the unrighteous will not inherit the kingdom, Paul gives a list of ten sins that relate to the problems he is discussing in this letter.

The reason for his special emphasis on sexual sins is obvious. In 5:1-5 Paul opened the case of incest that had erupted in the church. Then, in 5:6-8 he related this problem to the health of the Christian community as a whole and to the sacrifice of Christ. He issued a call to continue relations with such people *in the world* but not *in the church*, and told his readers that this issue should not be dumped on the public courts. Now, in 6:9 he starts to lay a theological foundation for sexual morality. Why then the second half of the list?

The second set of five sins is composed of:

- thieves
- greedy
- drunkards
- revilers
- robbers

At first glance these five seem to be a traditional list without any unifying emphasis. But here also Paul appears to have created a special list out of concern for the moral lapses of the Corinthians. Two points of overlap are visible. The first is the fact that Paul has just accused his readers of "defrauding" one

[3]Thiselton, *First Epistle*, pp. 440-55; Robert Gagnon, *The Bible and Homosexual Practice* (Nashville: Abingdon, 2001), pp. 303-32.
[4]John A. Bengel, *Bengel's New Testament Commentary* (Grand Rapids: Kregel, 1981), 2:195; Bailey, "Paul's Theological Foundation for Human Sexuality: I Cor. 6:9-20 in the Light of Rhetorical Criticism," *The Theological Review* (Beirut) 3 (1980): 27-41.

another in the courts. Defrauding is a form of stealing. Paul opens his list of nonsexual sins with "thieves" and ends the same list with "robbers."[5] The center of this short list includes "greedy, drunkards and revilers." As we will see, in 11:17-34 Paul discusses irregularities that occur in the Corinthian celebrations of the Eucharist. Some are *greedy* and stuff themselves, leaving others hungry. They were already quarreling (1:11-12) and thus when they got *drunk* at the Eucharistic meals, they quite likely hurled a few *insults* at their enemies in opposing parties. Paul has already written, "When reviled, we bless" (4:12). It is thus possible to see the Corinthian communal meals as a wild scene where some were indeed "greedy, drunkards and revilers."

Behind this list of ten sins lie aspects of three problems in the Corinthian church: stealing and their misuse of the courts, their sexual misconduct, and irregularities at their Eucharistic meals.

Paul then calmly reminds them that such behavior was part of their *past.* That is, among them were those who had been healed from these sins, both sexual and nonsexual. The healing power of the gospel had been at work and had already demonstrated its life-changing influence. He recalls for them the source of their new life in the present. The second part of this apostolic homily reads:

> 5. a. [11]But [*alla*] you were *washed,*[6]
>    b. but [*alla*] you were *made holy* [sanctified],
>    c. but [*alla*] you were *justified*
>
> 6. a. in the name of the Lord *Jesus Christ*
>    b. and in the *Spirit*
>    c. of our *God*

The first three lines in cameo 5 open with *alla* (but). The threefold repetition of *alla* (but) is striking. The six lines interrelate through the use of step parallelism. *Washing* (5a) refers to *baptism,* which for Paul (Rom 6:3) was "in the *name of the Lord Jesus Christ*" (6a). The phrase "you were *made holy*" (5b) matches "in the [*Holy*] *Spirit*" (6b). Finally, *justification* (5c) for Paul (Rom 8:33) is an act of *God* (6c). Orr and Walther define the two key terms succinctly when they write, "To be sanctified means to be consecrated in God's service and enrolled in His family. To be justified means to be forgiven of sins

---

[5]John 10:1, 8 pairs "thieves and robbers" together (but one of the two Greek words is different).

[6]The verb is an aorist middle. Thiselton argues that this is a "middle of personal interest," and he translates it "you were washed clean" (Thiselton, *First Epistle,* p. 453).

and accepted as righteous."[7] The order of the verbs denies a theological sche-
matizing of justification, then sanctification.

Yet one more overtone of a Trinitarian formula appears in the last three
lines with the mention of the Lord *Jesus Christ*, the *Spirit* and *God*. Paul invoked the Trinity in his discussion of the secret mystery of God revealed to
him (2:7-10a; 10b-16). Here the Trinity is at the heart of new life in Christ.

With this new status in the presence of God in mind, Paul turns to debate
the reasons the Corinthians (it seems) were giving to justify their behavior.

7.   [12]"All things are lawful for me,"
        but all things are not helpful.

     "All things are lawful for me,"
        but I will not be enslaved by anything.

Hering has already identified these four lines as a strophe constructed
"somewhat according to the rules of Hebrew poetry." He adds, "The parallelism of its members is clear."[8] It is generally accepted that Paul is quoting the
Corinthian libertines. These same four lines reappear with slight changes in
10:23, and the lead phrase "all things are lawful to me" must surely be a quote
from the mouths of the Corinthians. It has often been suggested that Paul
endorses the phrase (with qualifications), and thus it may well be his own
phrase originally used to oppose Jewish legalism. Out of context, some Greek
Christians used it to justify their libertinism. How can Paul reply? Again Orr
and Walther offer a suggestive analysis of the problem. They write,

> What is to be done when recipients of the gospel, upon realizing that they have
> been invited into God's home with full privileges, as it were, start wrecking the
> furniture, befouling the floors, and even tearing the building apart?[9]

The problem is complicated by the fact that the Corinthians were not
merely reflecting a carryover of their pre-Christian lifestyle, but as Conzelmann puts it, were "provided with an active/speculative justification" of their
action with the cry, "all things are lawful for me."[10]

What is Paul to do? One simple answer would have been to return them to
a rigorous enforcement of the law with its punishments. But to do so would be
to deny the gospel. Instead, Paul takes their point and then affirms that all

---

[7]Orr/Walther, *I Corinthians*, p. 201.
[8]Hering, *First Epistle of Saint Paul to the Corinthians* (London: Epworth, 1962), p. 45.
[9]Orr/Walther, *I Corinthians*, p. 202.
[10]Conzelmann, *1 Corinthians*, p. 108.

things are not "helpful." Robertson and Plummer explain this as meaning, "Christian freedom must be limited by regard for others."[11] The law is not a means of salvation, and it has been summarized as "the law of Christ." In this new form it is still in force to prevent "the collapse of society and the ruin of men's lives."[12] Paul is perhaps rephrasing his earlier statement, "All things are yours . . . and you are Christ's" (3:21, 23). A similar discussion in 10:23 indicates that the community's health is an important concern. Orr and Walther succinctly observe, "When one loves God, *all things are permissible;* but when one loves God, one loves what He loves. This means love for all others, for they are loved by God; and conduct will be regulated by this love."[13]

In the second response to "all things are lawful," Paul utilizes a play on words in Greek. The word *existin* (lawful) has *exousia* (authority) as its root. Paul then uses the verb *exousiazo* (to be enslaved) in his response. Robertson and Plummer catch this in English by aptly paraphrasing, "I can make free with all things, but I will not let any thing make free with me."[14] Freedom cannot be allowed to cancel itself. Emancipation from enslavement is clearly implied, a subject to which Paul returns later in the essay.

To summarize, in this seven-stanza cameo Paul affirms:

1.  Some of the Corinthians had previously engaged in sexual and nonsexual sins that were incompatible with the kingdom of God. From these sins they had been healed. These sins are listed.

2.  The three persons of the Trinity are mentioned along with something of their function in the reformation of new believers.

3.  All things are indeed lawful, but a Christian must avoid anything that does not build up the community and reject anything that enslaves.

The second half of Paul's theological foundation for sexual ethics is presented in 6:13-20.

---

[11]Robertson/Plummer, *First Epistle*, p. 146.
[12]Ibid.
[13]Orr/Walther, *I Corinthians*, p. 202.
[14]Robertson/Plummer, *First Epistle*, pp. 122-23.

# Theology of Sexual Practice

*Joining the Body*

I CORINTHIANS 6:13-20

THIS HOMILY PRESENTS the second half of Paul's theological foundation for sexual ethics (6:13-20). He offers his views in a marvelously structured apostolic homily with ten cameos. The text is displayed in figure 2.4(1).

## THE RHETORIC
This profound apostolic homily is composed of ten cameos organized around the high jump format. The high jumper begins with a short sprint (1-2). This is followed by the jump (2-5); then comes the crossing of the bar (6), concluding with the descent on the far side (7-10).

As marked on figure 2.4(1), each of the four lines in cameo 1 is matched in cameo 2 following the step-parallelism pattern. Then comes a brilliantly executed example of ring composition. The center climax is an encased Scripture quotation. There is a clear turning point just past the center in cameo 7. Cameo 2 looks both ways. At the same time the discussion of the *resurrection* in cameo 2 balances the affirmation of the *cross* in cameo 10.

1.a[13]"*Food* is meant for the *stomach*,          FOOD for STOMACH
 b. and the *stomach for food*"                      God Will Destroy Food
 c. and *God both this*                               God Will Destroy Stomach
 d. and *that* will *destroy*.

2a.  The *body* is *not for prostitution*, but *for the Lord*,
 b. and the *Lord for the body*.                     BODY for THE LORD
 c.[14]And *God raised* the *Lord*,                   God Raised: the Lord
 d. and *will raise us up* by his power.              God Will Raise: Us

3.     [15]*Do you not know*
            that *our bodies*                          OUR BODIES
            are *members* of *Christ?*                 In Christ

4.     So *taking away* the *members* of *Christ*        SIN AGAINST
       shall I make them *members* of a *prostitute?*    Christ
       May it never be!

5.          [16]Do you not know that the one *joining a prostitute*    ONE BODY
            becomes *one body with her?*                               With Prostitute

6.          For, it is *written*,                                     SCRIPTURE
            "*The two shall become one flesh.*"                        Two—One Flesh

7.          [17]But the one *joining* to the *Lord*              ONE SPIRIT
            becomes *one spirit with him.*                       With the Lord

8.          [18]Flee from prostitution.
            Every other *sin* which a man commits is *outside his body;*
            but the immoral man sins against *his own body.*    SIN AGAINST
                                                                 His Body

9.     [19]*Do you not know*
            that *your body*                            YOUR BODY
            is a *sanctuary* of the *Holy Spirit* within you,   Of Holy Spirit
            which you have *from God?*                   From God

10. You are not your own;                    CROSS
    [20]you were *bought with* a price.        With Body
    So *glorify God* in *your body.*           Glorify God

---

**Figure 2.4(1). Theology of sexual practice: Joining the body (1 Cor 6:13-20)**


## COMMENTARY

Here Paul builds a foundation for Christian sexual practice on the *cross*, the *resurrection*, the *trinity* and the doctrine of the *church*.

Similar cases of homilies that use the high jump format *with a Scripture quotation in the center* appear in 9:1-12a, 14:13-24 and 15:21-28.[1] The first two cameos of this homily are in figure 2.4(2).

1.  a. [13]Food is meant for the stomach
    b.  and the stomach for food,
    c.  and God both this
    d.  and that will destroy.

2.  a.  But body is not for sexual immorality but for the Lord,
    b.  and the Lord for the body;
    c.  [14]and God raised the Lord
    d.  and will raise us by his power.

---

**Figure 2.4(2). Cameos 1-2 (1 Cor 6:13-14)**

---

The parallels between these two stanzas are strong, and critical for Paul's argument. The parallels can be summarized and seen as follows:

| **Food** | **Sex** |
|---|---|
| Food is for the stomach | The body is for the Lord |
| The stomach is for food | The Lord is for the body |
| God—destroys stomach | God—raised the Lord |
| God—destroys food | God—will raise us (our bodies) |

Each line has its matching line. This step-parallelism is as old as Isaiah 55:10-11. Apparently the Corinthians were arguing that food and sex were parallel. It is possible that the first two lines of stanza 1 are quoted from their argument. *They say,* "Food is meant for the stomach and the stomach for food," meaning that both are destined for destruction. Sexual appetites, they seem to have argued, were in the same category because the body dies and the soul is immortal. The Gnostic/Stoic rejection of the body is clearly behind such thinking. Paul had another view.

Using carefully chosen words, Paul wrote: God *raised the Lord* (that is, his body) and he will *raise us* (that is, our bodies). There is a balancing of terms that makes *us* = our *bodies*. In explaining Paul, Rudolf Bultmann has written, "man does not *have* a *soma* [body]; he *is* a *soma* [body]."[2] The resurrection of the Lord assures the resurrection of the body for the believers, and

---

[1]Old Testament examples of an introduction attached to ring composition appear in Is 44:13-17 and Is 43:25–44:5. See above prelude, "Prophetic Homily Rhetorical Style and Its Interpretation."

[2]Rudolf Bultmann, *Theology of the New Testament* (London: SCM Press, 1952), p. 194.

the future resurrection of our bodies is determinative for how we behave sexually in this life.

James Moffat observes that Paul does not attack sexual immorality as a menace to public health or as a case of psychological unfairness to one of the partners, but as "a sin that strikes at the roots of the personality which is to flower into a risen life."[3] In short, if I take my body with me beyond death, then any permanent damage that I inflict on it in this life has eternal significance. Paul is objecting to the *dehumanizing* of sex that takes place when it is turned into a form of entertainment and made parallel to food. Paul is rejecting the view that says "I feel hungry—I eat. I feel sexual desire—I engage in sex."

The alignment of Paul's phrases is extremely precise. When the first lines of each stanza are put together this is evident. They read:

1a.   Food is meant *for the stomach*
2a.   The body is not for prostitution, but *for the Lord*

Paul seems to be saying, the Christian must understand that if his or her body is *for* the Lord, it cannot be *for* prostitution at the same time. If this is part of Paul's intention, we could conclude that marriage is also incompatible with a commitment of the body *for the Lord*. But in cameos 5-7 Paul clearly does not come to that conclusion. There he is careful to point out that he is *not* forbidding Christian marriage. More of this later.

Paul continues in 2b by writing, "and the Lord for the body." This has the unmistakable ring of double meanings. The term *body* certainly means the individual body of the believer, but also carries overtones of the community body, the church. The Lord is for *the body*, and *the body* is both of these. In this text one meaning seems to shade into another.

The crucial comparisons are between *the stomach* that is to be destroyed and *the body* that is to be raised. The advice given is: Do not damage the body with immorality because the body goes with you beyond death—it will be raised. Foods and stomachs are impermanent while bodies are permanent. Human sexuality, he affirms, is part of the inner core of the whole person called *the body*, and that body will be raised. Furthermore, that whole person (the body) will be affected negatively by immorality.

This raises a problem. In 15:43 Paul affirms that the Spirit-formulated body will be raised in "glory" and "in power." We are encouraged to believe

---

[3]Moffatt, *First Epistle*, p. 69.

from this language that in the resurrection the broken physical body of a dying cancer patient will be replaced with a Spirit-formulated body that is whole. Is Paul contradicting himself? Or is he discussing mysteries that are beyond both him and us? One beam of biblical light on this issue is the fact that Jesus' resurrection body was most certainly a new glorious body. Yet he had scars on his hands and in his side. Paul seems to be saying "Don't scar up *your own body*—it goes with you!"

Cameo 2 is not only related thematically to cameo 1, it is also the leading cameo for a larger statement of five cameos that come to a climax in a classical biblical text. The argument then repeats backwards in a near-perfect example of ring composition. This can be seen in figure 2.4(1) above.

The various pairs of balanced cameos deserve careful scrutiny. Cameos 2 and 10 are the outer envelope in the ring composition. Seen together they appear in figure 2.4(3).

| **Cameo 2 (resurrection)** | **Cameo 10 (the cross)** |
|---|---|
| [13b]The *body* is not for prostitution but for the Lord, and the Lord for the body; [14]and God *raised the Lord* and will *raise us up* by his power. | [19b]You are not your own; [20]*you were bought with a price.* So glorify God in your *body.* |

Figure 2.4(3). Cameos 2 and 10 (1 Cor 6:13b-14, 19b-20)

Cameo 2 tells of the body that will be raised and affirms the importance of that *resurrection* for sexual ethics. Sexual conduct has to do with *the body*, and it will be raised. Cameo 10 concludes the discussion by reference to the price paid on *the cross* and its significance for "your [pl.] body [sing.]." The "body" that "belongs to the Lord" is central to each cameo. In the first, the body is affirmed to be "for the Lord," and in the second the reader is reminded that "You are not your own" (that is: You belong to the Lord). The theme of "cross and resurrection" form a complementary pair.

An option for a slave in the first century was for him/her to slowly build up funds in an account in a local temple until her own price in the slave market was accumulated. He would then be "bought with a price" from his master by the priests of the temple and would formally become that god's slave. Actually, he would be a free man. Adolf Deissmann writes,

A Christian slave of Corinth going up the path to the Acrocorinthus, . . . would see towards the north-west the snowy peak of Parnassus rising clearer and clearer before him, and everyone knew that within the circuit of that commanding summit lay the shrines at which Apollo or Serapis or Aschlepius the

Healer *bought slaves with a price, for freedom.* Then in the evening assembly was read the letter lately received from Ephesus, and straightway the new Healer was present in spirit with His worshippers giving them freedom from another slavery, *redeeming with a price* the bondmen of sin and the law.[4]

Büchsel feels that "the details of sacral manumission need hardly be applied."[5] Conzelmann argues that Deissmann over-pressed his findings into a full theory of redemption.[6] But Paul identifies Jesus with the Passover lamb only once (5:7). In making that identification Paul was not creating "a full theory of redemption." Instead, he was unveiling an important aspect of the mystery of the atonement. The same can be said for the image of the manumission of the slave. The Corinthian slave believer was not set free from bondage to sin and death by saving his copper coins one after another for thirty years. Rather, God in Christ died on a cross to set him free. Here and elsewhere (1 Cor 7:23; Gal 3:13; 4:5) the text affirms that God paid a price for the believer and redeemed him or her. That price was the cross.

Turning to the final phrase in cameo 10, there is another possible Old Testament echo. Apart from 5:1-10, the only other case of incest in the Bible is in Amos where the prophet reports, "A man and his father go in to the same maiden" (Amos 2:7). Each account describes the problem in the same way. It is not a case of "a man and his son do so-and-so," but in both texts we are told that "a man and his father do so-and-so." It seems clear that the Amos passage is in Paul's mind. Starting with this assumption, Amos affirms a case of incest and then laments, "so that my holy name is profaned." The sin was certainly against the woman and against the father, but on another level it was a sin against God, whose holy name was thereby profaned. Amos uses the Hebrew word חלל (to profane). Change the Hebrew hard ח to a soft ה with a slight change in pronunciation or the slightest erasure and you have the word הלל (to praise).[7] Amos says, "Your sexual practice has become a חלל (profaning) of the

---

[4]Adolf Deissmann, *Light from the Ancient East* (Grand Rapids: Baker, 1987), p. 329.

[5]F. Büchsel, "αγοραζω, εξαγοραζω," in *TDNT*, 1:124-25.

[6]Conzelmann, *1 Corinthians*, p. 113.

[7]This shift from the written soft ה (h) to the hard ח (ch) is very easy in the Hebrew script of the Talmuds. This is also the case in the script of the Isaiah scroll of the Dead Sea Scrolls (see F. M. Cross, David N. Freedman and James A. Sanders, eds., *Scrolls from Qumran Cave I: The Great Isaiah Scroll From Photographs by John C. Trever* [Jerusalem: Albright Institute and the Shrine of the Book, 1972]). Also the change from the soft ה to the hard ח was easy in the Hebrew script of the time of Amos (see the Lachish Ostraca of the early sixth century B.C. and other ancient Hebrew scripts in James B. Pritchard, ed., *The Ancient Near East: An Anthology of Texts and Pictures* [Princeton: Princeton University Press, 1958], plates 80-82).

name of God." He seems to infer, "It should have been a הלל (an offering of praise) to a holy God." Only those with a Jewish background would have caught this play on words. Yet it is possible that such a nuance was in Paul's mind as he wrote.

There is an important double meaning to the word "body" that was known to all of Paul's readers. The "body" meant the physical body and also refered to the "body/church." The Corinthians are told to glorify God in your (pl.) body (sing.). The phrase "your [pl.] body [sing.]" has in cameo 9 just been defined as a sanctuary of the Holy Spirit. Their corporate body (the church) is the place where they are to glorify God. No doubt the individual body of the believer is a key aspect of Paul's focus here in cameo 10, but the communal body of Christ is unmistakably also intended. Defile the human body through sexual immorality and you defile the sanctuary which is the body of Christ. Because "you [pl.] were bought with a price" such defilement was abhorrent in the extreme.

Finally, in each cameo God is active *for the sake of the body*. In cameo 2d he "will raise us up," and in cameo 10 God in Christ buys them "with a price."

In summary, in Paul's mind the resurrection and the cross provide the larger theological framework within which human sexual practice is to find its appropriate forms of expression. Because of the *resurrection* the believer knows that her or his body will be raised and her or his sexual practice involves that body. Because of the *cross*, he or she is bought with a price and expected to use the physical body in a way that glorifies God, which brings us to the next pair of stanzas.

| Cameo 3 | Cameo 9 |
|---|---|
| [15]Do you not know | [19]Do you not know |
| that *our* bodies | that *your* [pl.] body [sing.] |
| are members of Christ | is a sanctuary of the Holy Spirit within you |
| | which you have from God? |

The familiar diatribe formula "Do you not know" is repeated twice. In the second line the words are identical except for the shift from "our" to "your." This shift is consistent with cameos 2 and 10. That is, Paul begins this rhetorical structure with a plural (cameo 2) "raise *us* up" and ends with a singular (cameo 10) "*your* body." *My* individual physical body is related to *our body* the church.

Returning to cameos 3 and 9, the third line can be seen to carry the theological weight of the two cameos. Here Paul uses complementary images. In the first (3) he tells his readers that they are *members of Christ*. In the balancing cameo (9) he affirms that the *"Holy Spirit* within" them is "from *God."* They are a *naos*, a *sanctuary* of the Holy Spirit. These spatial images are diagrammed in figure 2.4(4). See figure 2.4(5) for the two images combined.

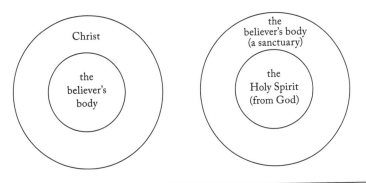

Figure 2.4(4). The spatial images of 1 Corinthians 6:15, 19

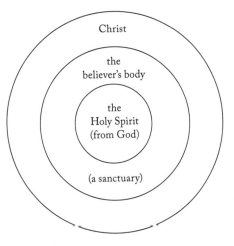

Figure 2.4(5). The combined spatial images of 1 Corinthians 6:15, 19

As early as chapter 2.3[8] we noted the Trinity was at work in purification. Now the Trinity appears again. The believer is *in Christ* and at the same time is a sanctuary of the *Holy Spirit* from *God.*

In the first pair of cameos (2 and 10) the reader is asked to formulate an understanding of sexual ethics within the theological framework of the *cross* and the *resurrection.* Here a second theological frame appears. This time it is

---

[8]Figure 2.3(1), cameos 5-6 (1 Cor 6:11).

the *Trinity*. Within the body is the *Holy Spirit* (from *God*) and that same body is *in Christ*. This is a pointed rejection of Epicurean and Stoic thought where the Spirit (of God) unites only with the soul while the body is part of the brutes.

Again, the phrase "your [pl.] body" in cameo 9 carries the overtones of body/church. This double meaning attached to "the body" becomes a significant part of the second half of this homily. In cameo 3 there is reference to "bodies" and to "members" of Christ. The reference is to individual bodies (united in Christ). But in cameo 9 the language shifts to "your [pl.] body [sing.]." Paul is not merely interested in the personal/bodily health and destiny of the individual, but also in the health of the *whole body of Christ*. This point was already affirmed in 1 Corinthians 5, where Paul expressed anxiety over how libertinism was damaging the health of the corporate body of Christ. In the two outer envelopes Paul sets sexual ethics into three great frames of reference. The first has to do with the *cross and the resurrection*. The second is the *Trinity*, and the third relates to the *church*.

The eschatology of the passage is also worthy of note.[9] Inheriting the kingdom is in the *future*. The unrighteous "*will not* inherit the kingdom," and God "*will* raise us up by his power." As regards the *present*, even now our bodies "are members of Christ." The *past* is important because in that past "God raised the Lord" and in the *past* believers were "bought with a price." So the believer *is* already united with the body of the risen Lord *in the present* even though "inheritance of the kingdom" and "the resurrection" are *in the future*.

In the center of the homily Paul turns from the great positives of the cross, the resurrection, the Trinity and the body of Christ to a strong set of negatives:

| Cameo 4 | Cameo 8 |
|---|---|
| [15b]So taking away the members of Christ | [18]Flee from prostitution! |
| Shall I make them members of a prostitute? | Every other sin *is* . . . outside his body |
| May it never be! | but the immoral man sins against his own body. |

Each of these passionately stated cameos contains an emphatic negative imperative. The first (4) is the familiar *me genoito* (may it never be) common in Romans. This is Paul's negative assertion against something that for him is blatantly impossible. The imperative of cameo 8 may well have an Old Tes-

---

[9]E. Schweizer, "Dying and Rising with Christ," *New Testament Studies* 14 (1967-1968): 6-8.

tament image behind it. Paul may be calling on his readers to imitate Joseph. When faced with the temptation to sexual immorality with Potiphar's wife, Joseph *ran* out of the house (Gen 39:7-12). Paul commands the Corinthians to *flee* from the sacred prostitutes who roam the city.[10] At the very end of the hymn to love Paul will tell them to "run after love" (14:1). They are to *run away* from the prostitutes, turn around, and *run after* the love of God.

In cameo 4 Paul focuses on the individual. He may be using his language imprecisely, but in light of the remarkable precision of expression in the rest of the structure it is doubtful. He affirms, "So taking away the members [pl.] of Christ shall I [sing.] make them members [pl.] of a prostitute?" Paul is making a statement about the inherent nature of sexual relations that is in total harmony with the Old Testament Scripture he is about to quote. For Paul, in sexual intercourse the *whole body*, that is *the whole person* becomes one flesh with the sexual partner.

Furthermore, Paul describes a wrenching process. The verb he uses is *airo*, which ordinarily means "take up" but here means "take away" and can carry the overtones of "take away by force." It was the cry of the high priests who before Pilate shouted, "Away with him" (Jn 19:15). The believer's body/self is joined to the body of Christ (cameo 3). Now that same body/self cannot be joined to another body (the prostitute) unless it is first *wrenched*, torn, taken away by force from Christ. The horror that Paul feels at this prospect evokes the cry, "May it never be!"

Cameo 8 is problematic. Drunkenness, suicide and gluttony are also sins against one's own body. This particular *crux* is handled by various commentators in various ways. Conzelmann remarks that this argument is "of course formulated *ad hoc*," and that for the moment Paul is only discussing this single case of offenses against the body.[11] Conzelmann then gently chides Paul for showing a lack of concern for the prostitute and for "taking his cue from a Jewish saying which describes fornication as the direst of sins (Prov 6:25ff)."[12] Moule suggests that the troubling phrase "every sin which a man commits is outside his body" is a Corinthian libertine slogan which Paul contradicts.[13] Barrett considers C. F. D. Moule's view, finds it attractive, but prefers to see

[10]F. F. Bruce, *1 and 2 Corinthians* (London: Oliphants, 1971), p. 65.
[11]Conzelmann, *1 Corinthians*, p. 112.
[12]Ibid.
[13]C. F. D. Moule, *An Idiom-Book of New Testament Greek* (Cambridge, Mass.: Cambridge University Press, 1968), pp. 196-97.

Paul as writing "rather loosely."[14] Barrett quotes John Calvin with approval where Calvin writes, "My explanation is that he does not completely deny that there are other sins, which also bring dishonor and disgrace upon our bodies, but that he is simply saying that these other sins do not leave anything like the same filthy stain on our bodies as fornication does."[15]

By contrast Dean Alford starts with the idea of "*from* without" and argues that the language is very precise and that drunkenness and gluttony are introduced *from without*, unlike fornication which comes from desire *within*.[16] A fourth alternative is yet possible. As Conzelmann affirms: "the 'body' differs from the 'belly' in that 'the body' is destined for resurrection."[17] Drunkenness, gluttony, suicide are against the physical part of a person that is to be destroyed by death. Fornication damages the self that is destined for resurrection. Fornication for Paul is thus unique among sins in that it is indeed "against *the body*." Hering catches this when he writes, "Has he [Paul] forgotten gluttony, drunkenness, suicide? No doubt for reasons we have mentioned he attributes to 'porneia,' a destructive quality with metaphysical repercussions."[18]

Other sins do not necessarily take the believer by force away from the body of Christ and join him or her to a new body. In Paul's view fornication does. As such it is singled out.

Paul's remarkable discussion breaks new ground. On the one hand, Paul cannot merely read the seventh commandment to them. They could counter that this is strictly a commercial arrangement. Especially if the person involved was unmarried, no covenant with another person would be broken. That is, they would not (in such a case) be "committing adultery." On the other hand, Paul cannot allow for the Gnostic view that the body is evil and doomed to pass away. Rather than speaking in general terms Paul's language is again precise.[19] The one sin that profoundly affects the *body* (now a part of Christ, destined to be resurrected) is the tearing of it away from the body of Christ and the joining of it to a prostitute. Within this pair of bold negatives (4, 8) he comes to the climax of his discussion [see fig. 2.4(6)].

---

[14]Barrett, *First Epistle*, p. 150.

[15]John Calvin, *The First Epistle of Paul to the Corinthians*, trans. J. W. Frazier, ed. David W. Torrance and T. F. Torrance (Grand Rapids: Eerdmans, 1960), pp. 131-32.

[16]Dean Alford, *The Greek Testament* (New York: Lee, Shephard & Dillingham, 1872), 2:518.

[17]Conzelmann, *1 Corinthians*, p. 111.

[18]Jean Hering, *The First Epistle of Saint Paul to the Corinthians*, trans. A. W. Heathcote and P. J. Allcock (London: Epworth, 1962), p. 46.

[19]Against Calvin, *First Epistle of Paul to the Corinthians*, p. 131.

5.       [16]Do you not know that the one joining a prostitute
         becomes *one body with her?*

6.              For it is written,
                "The *two* shall become *one flesh.*"

7.       [17]But the one joining to the Lord
         becomes *one spirit with him.*

---

**Figure 2.4(6). Cameos 5-7 (1 Cor 6:16-17)**

No doubt the libertines at Corinth argued that fornication with prostitutes did not constitute any significant union with the woman involved. There was no love, and no ongoing relationship. Paul affirms in cameos 5 and 6 that *any* act of sexual intercourse necessarily creates a new unity. D. S. Bailey commends Paul's "profound and realistic treatment of coitus." Bailey writes regarding this passage,

> Here his [Paul's] thought apparently owes nothing to any antecedent notions, and displays a psychological insight into human sexuality which is altogether exceptional by first-century standards. The Apostle denies that coitus is, as the Corinthians would have it, merely a detached and (as it were) peripheral function . . . of the genital organs. On the contrary, he insists that it is an act which, by reason of its very nature, engages and expresses the whole personality in such a way as to constitute a unique mode of self-disclosure and self-commitment.[20]

By comparing cameo 5 and cameo 7 Paul sees uniting with a prostitute as incompatible to joining with the Lord and becoming "one *spirit* with him." In this latter phrase we expect Paul to say that we become "one *body* with him." Paul's carefully chosen phrases are remarkably crafted. If he had affirmed that the believer becomes "one *body*" with the Lord, then joining with *any* sexual partner and joining with the Lord would be completely parallel. In such a case there would be no room for Christian marriage. This would have pushed Paul over the edge into joining his ascetic (Gnostic) enemies by condemning all marriage as violating the unity of the believer with the body of Christ. Paul emphatically disagrees and thus, in chapter 7, he is able to affirm a place for sanctified marriage. As Conzelmann notes, "'One spirit with him' explains what is the nature of this one body."[21]

In ring composition there is often a turning point just past the center; such

---

[20]D. S. Bailey, *The Man-Woman Relation in Christian Thought* (London: Longmans, 1959), pp. 9-10.
[21]Conzelmann, *1 Corinthians*, p. 112.

a device is used in this homily. The turning point is in stanza 7. With the word *but* the argument shifts dramatically, and the theme of becoming *one spirit* with the Lord is introduced.

This same compatibility between marriage and the giving of the whole person to God is again affirmed when the connection between the center and the outside of this ring composition is noted.

The climax in ring composition is usually the center. In this case a Scripture quotation (Gen 2:24) appears in that climactic center. In addition, the theme of the "two becoming one" that appears in the quoted Scripture is repeated (with different nuances) three times (in cameos 5-7).[22]

The summary of the beginning, the center and the end of the structure appears in figure 2.4(7).

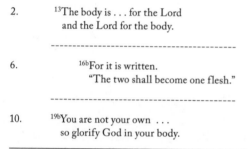

2.            [13]The body is . . . for the Lord
               and the Lord for the body.

6.                [16b]For it is written.
                  "The two shall become one flesh."

10.           [19b]You are not your own . . .
              so glorify God in your body.

**Figure 2.4(7). The beginning, the center and the end of 1 Corinthians 6:13-20**

In Paul's mind, affirming that the "body is . . . for the Lord" (2) and the glorifying of "God in your body" (10) is fully compatible with a man and a woman becoming "one flesh" (6).

In summary, this remarkable passage can be seen as a carefully written piece of Pauline theological rhetoric that uses a variety of ancient prophetic styles. Words are selected with care and placed in parallel phrases following well-established Hebrew patterns.

The foundation of a new sexual ethic is not grounded in abstract philosophical principles. There is no discussion of social responsibility for the potential newborn child or the possibility of disease. Inheriting property and complications in family life are not mentioned. Libertinism is rejected in the light of the cross, the resurrection, the participation in the body of Christ and

---

[22]In an earlier essay on this text I traced a connection between this passage and Eph 2:11-22; 5:22-33. Cf. Kenneth E. Bailey, "Paul's Theological Foundation for Human Sexuality: I Cor. 6:9-20 in the Light of Rhetorical Criticism," *The Theological Review* 3 (1980): 27-41.

the Trinity. Sexual immorality is seen as a forcible separation from Christ and as a forming of new unions destructive to the body/church.

The discussion is tied to the end of all things. The believer *is* part of the body of Christ and he or she *shall* be raised. Flesh and blood will not inherit the kingdom of God, but believers are cleansed, justified and sanctified.

The law is not fashioned into a club and used to administer a beating, but the loyalties of a new relationship and a new identity are set forth. The passage is Paul's foundation for Christian sexual ethics. When his style is observed the passage no longer appears "somewhat disjointed and obscure."[23] Rather it surfaces as a carefully ordered theological and ethical statement of Paul's views.

Paul first exposed the problem (chap. 2.1), and then removed three roadblocks to finding a solution (chap. 2.2). Next came a theological foundation for human sexuality (chaps. 2.3-2.4). He is now ready to discuss patterns of sexual practice that are in harmony with those foundations (chap. 2.5).

---

[23]Hering, *First Epistle of Saint Paul to the Corinthians*, p. 47.

# Sexual Practice in Harmony
# with the Gospel

By WAY OF REVIEW, the bare bones of this second essay are:

2.1.  Immorality and the Church (4:17–5:6a)

2.2.  (Three Roadblocks: Leaven, Immorality and the Law Courts) (5:6b–6:8)

2.3.  Theology of Sexual Practice: Kingdom Ethics (6:9-12)

2.4.  Theology of Sexual Practice: Joining the Body (6:13-20)

2.5.  *Sexual Practice in Harmony with the Gospel (7:1-40)*

This final section of the second essay (2.5) covers a series of topics. These can be divided into nine subsections, which are:

a. Equality in Conjugal Rights (7:1-5)

b. Widows/Widowers (7:6-9)

c. Believers and Unbelievers: Marriage, Separation and Divorce (7:10-16)

d. Jew and Greek, Slave and Free: Remain in Your Calling (7:17-24)

e. The Unmarried and the Impending Distress (7:25-31)

f. *Marriage and Anxieties* (7:32-35)

g. A Man and "His Virgin" (7:36-38)

h. In Case of Death (7:39-40)

i. Paul's Concluding Personal Appeal (7:40)

Each of these subsections merits examination. Paul opens with a discussion of equality and conjugal rights.

## A. EQUALITY IN CONJUGAL RIGHTS (7:1-5)

1.  [1]And concerning the matters about which you wrote.
    *"Is it well for a man not to touch a woman?"*

| | | |
|---|---|---|
| 2. | [2]Now because of *immorality*, | MARITAL RELATIONS |
| | each *man* should *have* [relations with] *his own wife* | Important (temptation) |
| | and each *woman* should have [relations with] *her own husband.* | |

| | | |
|---|---|---|
| 3. | [3]The *husband* should give to his *wife* her [conjugal] *rights*, | GIVE |
| | and likewise the *wife* to her *husband.* | Rights |

| | | |
|---|---|---|
| 4. | [4]For the *wife does not rule* over *her own body*, | HUSBAND |
| | but the husband does; | Rules Wife |

| | | |
|---|---|---|
| 5. | likewise the *husband does not rule* over *his own body*, | WIFE |
| | but the *wife does.* | Rules Husband |

| | | |
|---|---|---|
| 6. | [5]Do *not refuse* one another | GIVE |
| | except by *agreement* for a season, | Rights |
| | that you may *devote* yourselves to *prayer;* | |

| | | |
|---|---|---|
| 7. | but then *come together* again, | MARITAL RELATIONS |
| | *lest Satan tempt* you through *lack of self-control.* | Important (self-control) |

**Figure 2.5(1). Equality in conjugal rights (1 Cor 7:1-5)**

### THE RHETORIC

Paul again uses the high jump format observed in 1 Corinthians 6:13-20. There are seven cameos. The first stands alone and is followed by six inverted cameos with which it forms a single unit. As in the previous homily, the opening cameo determines the direction for the six that follow. The climactic center balances the rights of each partner in Christian marriage.

### COMMENTARY

Thiselton begins his extensive reflections on this chapter by writing, "Modern literature on these verses is vast in range and quantity."[1] Our focus is on biblical rhetoric and Eastern culture when it illuminates the text. The first of seven cameos says:

1.  [1]And concerning the matters about which you wrote:
    *"Is it well for a man not to touch a woman?"*

---

[1]Thiselton, *First Epistle*, p. 487. Thiselton presents a detailed and well-documented discussion of a wide range of themes that appear in this chapter (cf. ibid., pp. 484-605).

Many commentators, too numerous to note, have long assumed that this cameo is a hinge or turning point in Paul's letter.[2] Up to this point in the epistle, goes the argument, Paul was answering questions that came to him orally. From this point on he deals with problems sent to him in writing. But there is another option. It is possible to understand that when Paul mentions "the matters about which you wrote," he means "the matters [regarding sexual practice and food offered to idols] about which you wrote." His reference to a letter received from Corinth appears in the center of his carefully constructed, intense essay regarding sexual practice. The Corinthians *wrote to him* about things such as:

- Is it well for a man not to touch a woman?

- What about widowers and widows?

- What about divorce?

- What should a believer do who is married to an unbeliever?

- What about single people?

- Can we remarry after a spouse dies?

- Can we eat food offered to idols?

They *did not* write to him saying:

- We have broken up along ethnic lines (Greeks with Apollos, Jews with Cephas, etc.).

- We have a case of incest in the congregation. Some insist this is a private matter. Others say leave it to the courts. What do you think?

- Some trivialize casual sex with prostitutes. They argue that we are now under grace, not under law.

The Corinthians probably hoped that Paul would not find out about this latter list of deeply divisive (and embarrassing) problems related to sexual practice. We can almost hear the buzz of private conversations, behind closed doors in Corinth. They were likely saying things such as,

> We *can't* write to Paul about incest and sleeping with prostitutes. Besides, if we do commit such problems to writing, and send them as a letter—the letter could circulate across the church. If that happens, what would the other churches think of us? No self-respecting community hangs its dirty laundry in

---

[2]This verse is discussed briefly in the introduction above.

the front garden. No, no—we will ask him about things like divorce, remarriage and marriage to unbelievers—you know—the kinds of topics that can be discussed comfortably in public meetings. We must preserve our personal and community honor. We all know the proverb, "The olive oil merchant never says, 'My oil is rancid!'" Besides, if we remain silent, perhaps these "unfortunate incidents" will fade and the problems connected to them will go away. There are court cases threatening. It is better to claim ignorance. We must not make mistakes!

The Corinthian attempt to hide embarrassing topics and go public on carefully selected "safe" aspects of sexual practice did not succeed. Paul found out anyway. He seems to know that there was a cover-up in process and therefore (as noted) he introduces his discussion of incest by saying, "Everyone has reported . . ." That is, I am hearing about these hidden matters from everyone. Most likely this is why Paul chose to discuss the problems of incest and sleeping with prostitutes *before* he turned to "the things about which you wrote." By publicly affirming that he had received their sanitized list of questions, he is subtly and very politely saying, "Don't try this stunt again. As you can see from what I have just written—I find out everything anyway!"

In this connection a key aside appears at the end of 11:34, where Paul writes, "About the other things I will give directions when I come." Some of the problems that the Corinthians presented to Paul were not significant for the wider church. It was Paul who decided to discuss those questions in person with the Corinthians. In this epistle he will give guidance on the issues that are critical for the *entire church*. In short, their letter included the topics he discusses from 7:1–11:34.

Most probably they did not tell him about drunkenness at the celebration of the Eucharist. But, other than that, the rest of the issues discussed in chapters 7–11 are much less embarrassing and were no doubt reported to Paul in writing. He incorporated that letter into *his* five-essay outline. The letter did *not create* that outline.

Turning to the opening of Paul's first cameo on the topic of sexual practice in harmony with the gospel, the text can be read as *a statement of Paul's views*, or as a *question put to Paul by the church in Corinth*. Perhaps not recognizing that there is an alternative, for centuries the church (East and West) has seen it as Paul's statement. This understanding of the text hears Paul affirming, "It is good for a man not to touch a woman." Or, simply put, even for married couples, Paul seems to prefer celibacy. Is this what he means?

Nothing in the construction of the Greek sentence in question determines whether what Paul wrote is a question or a statement. In good Semitic fashion, the sentence does not have a verb "to be." The twenty-three Syriac, Arabic and Hebrew versions assembled for this study offer two options. The majority of them present a statement.[3] At the same time, two ninth-century Arabic versions list this sentence as a question.[4] One of them, Sinai 155, was translated from Greek.[5] Awareness of the possibility of this sentence being a question goes back for more than a thousand years.

Returning to the West, Thiselton reads it as a *statement*, but sees it as a *quotation from the Corinthians' letter to Paul*, not an affirmation of Paul's views.[6] Orr and Walther prefer to see it as a *question* put to Paul by the Corinthians. They translate these two lines as

> With reference to the matters about which you wrote:
> is it good for a man not to have sexual relations with a woman?[7]

After reviewing the options, Orr and Walther write, "It seems best to understand that the Corinthians have raised the question of the ascetic life."[8] Having dealt with the *libertines*, Paul turns to address the *ascetics*. The libertines are insisting "anything goes." The ascetics reply, "The body is evil. Thus, true spirituality means: Even if you are married, marital relations should be avoided." Paul speaks to Christian married couples who apparently have chosen to deny the validity of any sexual relations in their marriages. His reply is a luminous affirmation of mutuality in married sexual practice.

Paul presents his views in the six-cameo ring-composition homily set out above in figure 2.5(1). Each pair of cameos in that homily deserves attention. The opening and the closing of the homily (cameos 2 and 7) appear in figure 2.5(2).

---

[3]Syr. Pesh.; Vat. Ar. 13 (8th-9th cent.); Sin. Ar. 151 (867); Sin. Ar. 310; Martyn (1826); Yusif Dawud (1899); Heb. (1817), Heb. Jer.

[4]Mt. Sinai 155; Mt. Sinai 73. For the full evidence from the Oriental versions, see appendix II, plate D.

[5]Margaret D. Gibson, *An Arabic Version of the Epistles of St Paul to the Romans, Corinthians, Galatians*, Studia Sinaitica 11 (London: Cambridge University Press, 1894), p. 7. The second (Mt. Sinai No. 73) is also from the 9th century and its linguistic origin has yet to be identified.

[6]Thiselton, *First Epistle*, p. 497. See also Moffat, *First Epistle*, p. 75.

[7]Orr/Walther, *I Corinthians*, p. 205.

[8]Ibid., pp. 205-6.

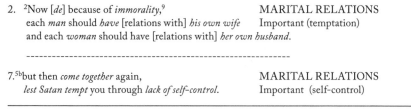

2.  ²Now [*de*] because of *immorality,*⁹          MARITAL RELATIONS
    each *man* should *have* [relations with] *his own wife*          Important (temptation)
    and each *woman* should have [relations with] *her own husband.*

    ----------------------------------------------------------------

7.  ⁵ᵇbut then *come together* again,          MARITAL RELATIONS
    *lest Satan tempt* you through *lack of self-control.*          Important (self-control)

**Figure 2.5(2). Cameos 2 and 7 (1 Cor 7:2, 5b)**

If cameo 1 is a question, then cameo 2 is *not* a sharp contrast to cameo 1.
Paul is not saying, "Sexual relations are to be avoided (cameo 1) *but*—in the
light of temptation—I can make allowances" (cameo 2). Rather he is saying,
"You have asked a question (1), let us discuss the matter." The verb "to have"
both here and in 1 Corinthians 5:1 means "to have sexual relations with." In
cameo 2 the reason Paul gives for mandating physical relations in marriage is
"because of *porneias* [immorality]." In the parallel cameo (7) Paul urges the
couple to come together lest Satan tempt them through *lack of self control.* In
these two outer cameos sex in marriage is therefore seen as acceptable because
of potential sin or lack of self-control.¹⁰

The second pair of cameos (3 and 6) is set out in figure 2.5(3):

3.  ³The *husband* should give to his *wife* her (conjugal) *rights,*          GIVE
    and likewise the *wife* to her *husband.*          Rights

    ----------------------------------------------------------------

6.  ⁵Do *not refuse* one another          GIVE
    except by *agreement* for a season,          Rights
    that you may *devote* yourselves to *prayer;*

**Figure 2.5(3). Cameos 3 and 6 (1 Cor 7:3, 5a)**

In the outer pair of cameos, marital relations were presented as a stopgap
for immorality (2) and as a crutch for those without adequate self-control (7).
There, the subject of sex in marriage is colored with a negative brush. But in
cameos 3 and 6 a positive attitude toward sex in marriage emerges. The marital relationship is now presented as a positive "right" that each partner is expected to *give as a gift* to the other. The husband and the wife are equal in this
regard. Neither partner is to demand those rights, rather each is to *give gifts* to
the other. Gifts given in love are always seen by the giver as valuable, other-

---

⁹BAGD identifies "(*de*) very freq. as a transitional particle pure and simple, without any contrast intended, *now, then,*" p. 171.
¹⁰This is one of the rare places in the New Testament where monogamy is assumed.

wise they would not be given. Furthermore, by definition, a gift is always offered as a result of free choice. If it is coerced, it is not a gift.

Yes, grants Paul, it is appropriate for the couple to withdraw from one another for special times of prayer—as long as that spiritual discipline does not lead to a permanent separation. This affirms that a life of deep spirituality accompanied by times for solitude and prayer is possible for the married, not only for the unmarried.

The climax, as usually occurs with ring composition, appears in the center with the two stunning parallel cameos in figure 2.5(4).

| 4. | ⁴For the *wife does not rule* over *her own body*, but the husband does; | HUSBAND Rules Wife |
|---|---|---|
| 5. | likewise the *husband does not rule* over *his own body*, but the *wife does*. | WIFE Rules Husband |

**Figure 2.5(4) Cameos 4-5 (1 Cor 7:4)**

Equality between the wife and the husband in Christian marriage is here presented in unforgettable terms. Each partner in a marriage has authority over the body of the other. No sexual games are possible in this kind of marriage. There can be no power plays such as, "Give me what I want, and I will sleep with you." No form of abuse is even thinkable. *Each* partner can say to the other, "I give gifts, and I have rights, and I have authority over your body." The granting of these gifts, rights and powers to each partner (on an equal basis) is truly amazing to discover in a first-century document!

The ten-volume *Midrash Rabbah* is a collection of interpretations of the Torah from the known sayings of the great rabbis of the first to the third centuries and beyond. Volume 1 on Genesis, while interpreting Genesis 20:8-18, discusses what to do when either spouse in a marriage refuses conjugal rights to the other. The text (with its notes) reads,

> If a woman revolts against her husband [Note: by refusing conjugal rights] *seven denarii* are deducted from her settlement [Note: at death or in case of divorce] weekly. And why *seven denarii?* Because of the seven labors which a woman owes to her husband: grinding corn, baking, laundering, cooking, suckling her child, preparing his bed, and working in wool: hence seven. Conversely, if a man revolts against his wife [Note: By refusing conjugal rights], her settlement is increased by three *denarii* per week. Why three? Because he owes her food, raiment, and marital privileges: hence three.

The text goes on to explain why the penalty for withholding conjugal rights is higher for women than for men.[11] A reason is found in Delilah's deception of Samson in Judges 16:16 which is quoted as saying, "That his soul was vexed unto death, but her soul was not vexed." The notes explain that the man suffers more than the woman from sexual privations, and so the woman's fine is greater. The logic of this text is revealing. The woman "owes" her husband more services and because of that she is penalized more if she walks out. She works harder so she must be penalized more! He also suffers more when intimacies are withheld than she does. Of course, men wrote the text. In a patriarchal society, it is not surprising to find this kind of bias in favor of the male. Paul could have reflected such views. He did not do so.

With knowledge of the common cultural attitudes exhibited in the above Midrash, Paul's affirmation of equality between male and female in regard to the intimacies of marriage is nothing less than amazing. In the light of Paul's directives in this text, it is easy to understand why Greek women of high standing were attracted to his preaching (Acts 17:4, 12).

To conclude, in this homily Paul deals with the ascetics who were convinced that spirituality and sexual practice were incompatible. He denies that division, and in the process establishes a timeless charter for sexual mutuality in Christian marriage. Sexual relations are not just a stopgap to prevent sin but are a positive right and gift that each freely gives to the other, and each has authority over the body of the other. Paul now turns to a discussion of various aspects of sexual practice that are in harmony with the gospel.

## B. WIDOWS/WIDOWERS (7:6-9)

First there is the question of widows and widowers. Including an introduction, Paul presents the following four cameos:

1. [6]I say this by way of concession, not of command,     I WISH ALL
   [7]and I wish that all were as I myself am.     Remain as I Am

2. But each has his own special spiritual gift from God,     GIFT OF CELIBACY
   one of one kind and one of another.     A Charismata

3. [8]To the widowers [*agamois* (de-married)] and widows I say     I WISH THE DE-MARRIED
   that it is well for them to remain as I am.     Remain as I Am

4.     [9]But if they cannot exercise control, they should marry.     NO SUCH GIFT
   For it is better to marry than to burn.     Get Married

**Figure 2.5(5). Widows and widowers (1 Cor 7:6-9)**

---

[11]The denarius was a day's wages for a working man. The woman has *seven days' pay* deducted *every week*!

## THE RHETORIC

These four cameos on widows and widowers appear in a simple A-B-A-B format.

## COMMENTARY

Paul starts with the familiar phrase "I say this." As in 4:17, he looks forward, not backwards. Cameo 1 is clear. Unlike the case of incest and the topic of sleeping with prostitutes, the question of the remarriage of widowers and widows has no definitive answer. Paul recommends his pattern of life, but does not insist on it. This raises the question: What pattern is he talking about?

Orr and Walther make a strong case that Paul was a widower.[12] They write, "Jewish leaders holding the position attributed to Paul in the New Testament ordinarily were married."[13] But Paul is clearly traveling without a wife (9:5). Apparently his wife had died. Greek has a word for "widowers" (*kheros*), but that word does not appear in the New Testament time period when Koine Greek was in use.[14] Later in this passage when Paul discusses the "unmarried," (7:25) he uses the traditional Greek word for "virgin" (*parthenos*). In the present text he discusses "*a-gamois* and widows." The natural way to read the text is to see these two words as a pair and understand that Paul is writing about "widowers and widows." Orr and Walther translate *a-gamois* literally as "de-married" and explain that in this passage it means "widowers."[15] Paul uses this word three times in this chapter. All of them can best be understood as meaning, "once married, now not married."

As Paul will affirm a few verses later, at this point in his ministry he is convinced that the end of all things is near. Widows and widowers are urged to think twice before getting remarried. This text affirms that one of the spiritual gifts (*kharisma*) is the ability to live a moral life and remain single (7:7). Paul's advice is that anyone who does not have that spiritual gift, and whose urges are strong, should marry.

After this brief discussion of widows and widowers, Paul turns to more complicated problems.

---

[12]Orr/Walther, *I Corinthians*, pp. 209-10; see also Fee, *First Epistle*, pp. 287-88.

[13]Orr/Walther, *I Corinthians*, p. 209.

[14]Fee, *First Epistle*, pp. 287-88; LSJ, *Greek-English Lexicon*, p. 1990.

[15]Ibn al-Sari (A.D. 867) translated *a-gamos* as "al-lathin laysa lahum nisa'" (those who have no wives). Vatican Arabic 13, folio 107v. gives the same translation. This language does not assume "unmarried virgins."

## C. BELIEVERS AND UNBELIEVERS: MARRIAGE, SEPARATION AND DIVORCE (7:10-16)

For these connected concerns he composes yet another seven-cameo homily that is figure 2.5(6).

1.¹⁰*To the* [believing] *married* I give charge, not I but the Lord,
   that the wife should not separate from her husband     SEPARATION (?)
   ¹¹but if she does, let her remain single [*a-gamos*]     Reconciliation
   or else be reconciled to her husband,     Divorce
   and that the husband should not divorce his wife.

---------------------------------------------------------------

2.¹²*To the rest* I say, not the Lord,
   that if any brother has a wife who is an unbeliever,     UNBELIEVING WIFE
   and she consents to live with him,     If Congenial
   he should not divorce her.     Stay Together

3.¹³If any woman has a husband who is an unbeliever,     UNBELIEVING HUSBAND
   and he consents to live with her,     If Congenial
   she should not divorce him.     Stay Together

4.    ¹⁴For the unbelieving husband
     is made holy through/in the wife,     UNBELIEVER
     and the unbelieving wife     Made Holy
     is made holy through/in her husband.

5.    Otherwise, your children would be unclean,     CHILDREN
     but as it is they are holy.     Holy

6.¹⁵But if the unbelieving partner
   desires to separate, let it be,     UNBELIEVING SPOUSE
   in such a case the brother or sister is not bound.     Desires It—Then Separate
   For God has called us to peace.     The Goal—Peace

7. ¹⁶For how do you know, wife,
   if you will keep your husband?     CAN YOU
   For how do you know, husband,     Keep Your Spouse?
   if you will keep your wife?

**Figure 2.5(6). Believers and unbelievers: Marriage, separation and divorce (1 Cor 7:10-16)**

### THE RHETORIC

Again Paul composes a seven-cameo apostolic homily. As in three of the previous homilies, the passage opens with a freestanding cameo. The six cameos that follow are formatted into three pairs. But in this case Paul opts for "variation on a theme." Rather than A-B-C-C-B-A such as appeared in 7:1-5, here the three pairs are presented on the page with an A-A, B-B, C-C structure. The perfect number seven surfaces, but each of the pairs is side by side with a climax in the center. A point of turning appears in the first line of cameo 6.

## Commentary

The homily opens:

1. ¹⁰*To the* [believing] *married* I give charge, not I but the Lord,
   that the wife should not separate from her husband   SEPARATION (?)
   but if she does, let her remain single [*a-gamos*]   Reconciliation
   or else be reconciled to her husband,   Divorce
   and that the husband should not divorce his wife.

Paul is discussing the marriage of two Christians. He clearly has access to the teachings of Jesus on this subject (Mt 5:31-32; Mk 10:11-12; Lk 16:18). This cameo presents an ideal toward which every married couple should strive. This is a directive, not a law. The soldier in training on the firing range asks the sergeant, "Where am I to fire?" The sergeant replies, "Shoot at the bull's-eye!" The sergeant's answer is a command, and the soldier will do his best, but will not be court-martialed if he fails.

The new element in this apostolic homily is the important phrase, "God has called us to peace." It is possible to see the component of "peace" as applying to the entire homily. The text of the first pair of cameos in the set of six is seen in figure 2.5(7).

2. ¹²*To the rest* I say, not the Lord,
   that if any brother has a wife who is an unbeliever,   UNBELIEVING WIFE
   and she consents to live with him,   If Congenial
   he should not divorce her.   Stay Together

3. ¹³If any woman has a husband who is an unbeliever,   UNBELIEVING HUSBAND
   and he consents to live with her,   If Congenial
   she should not divorce him.   Stay Together

**Figure 2.5(7). Cameos 2-3 (1 Cor 7:12-13)**

Some members of the church were arguing that the unbelieving spouse must be shut out of the social fellowship of the church through divorce to protect the purity of the "body." Paul does not agree. He affirms a mutuality between husband and wife. His views on this topic apply equally to the wife as to the husband. The reason for his insistence that such couples can and should stay married is presented in figure 2.5(8).

| 4. | [14]For the unbelieving husband<br>    is made holy through/in the wife,<br>    and the unbelieving wife<br>    is made holy through/in her husband.[16] | UNBELIEVER<br>Made Holy |
|----|---|---|
| 5. | Otherwise, your children would be unclean,<br>    but as it is they are holy. | CHILDREN<br>Holy |

**Figure 2.5(8). Cameos 4-5 (1 Cor 7:14)**

## THE RHETORIC

Cameo 4 demonstrates a "counterpoint" in its construction, where two rhetorical styles are woven together in the same four lines. These are:

(1) If the reader focuses on the three themes of *holiness, unbelieving* and *believing*, following the word order of the Greek text, two cameos of step parallelism emerge.

Made holy
    Unbelieving
        Believing
Made holy
    Unbelieving
        Believing

(2) If the focus is on *husband* and *wife*, we can see ring composition:

Husband
    Wife
    Wife
Husband

This sophisticated use of Hebrew poetic devices indicates the care with which this cameo (along with the entire homily) is composed.[17]

## COMMENTARY

Throughout the Old Testament discussion of "clean and unclean" there is the assumption that the unclean defiles the clean. In the temple Isaiah finds himself near to the *holy* and declares that he is *unclean* (Is 6:1-5) and

---

[16]My translation. This awkward English reflects the word order of the Greek sentence.

[17]Fee sees chiasm in 1 Cor 7:12-14, however he is obliged to leave out much of the language in the three verses to do so (see Fee, *First Epistle*, p. 299 n. 14).

thereby should not approach the holy. The Mishnah tractate *Tohoroth* (Cleanness) is conclusive evidence for this attitude among the rabbis.[18] In the ministry of Jesus this is reversed. Mark 5:21-43 tells the double story of Jesus and the woman with a flow of blood, and his raising of Jairus's daughter. In both cases Jesus touches or is touched by the "unclean." But he is not defiled. Rather he brings health to the sick and resurrection to the dead. Furthermore, to be made "clean" and to be made "holy" overlap on a very deep level. To discuss one is to invoke the other. In cameo 5 the children are not unclean but are holy. This is because (cameo 4) the unbeliever does *not defile the believer*. Indeed the opposite is true. The *believer* makes the unbeliever *clean/holy*, as did Jesus in the two Gospel stories noted above.

This startling text raises a significant question. Paul has just discussed the fact that in marriage the two "become one flesh." If this is true, then what happens to one partner in the union will influence the other partner. If an antibiotic is injected into one arm, the medicine enters the entire body. Thus if the two become "one flesh" and one member believes and is baptized, the Holy Spirit enters into that person and through him or her to the other and the two of them, *in some sense*, become "holy."

What then does "holiness" in this context mean? Orr and Walther offer one option. They refer to this as "a kind of 'uxorial sanctification'" (sanctification through the wife) and write: "The close contact [of marriage] produces a corporal unity between the two so that the unbelieving member actually is made holy by the faith of the believer. This is an astounding doctrine!"[19] Now for the third time an "astounding doctrine" has appeared in the epistle. The metaphor of Jesus as the Passover lamb occurs only here in all the writings of Paul (5:7-8). The second is the amazing equality between the wife and husband in marital intimacy that we just examined (7:1-5). Now comes a third startling affirmation.

Put bluntly, Paul appears to be saying, "There are two ways to be saved. One is to believe and be baptized. The other is to marry a Christian!" Is this what he intends? Orr and Walther say "yes," while admitting that this view of justification is counter to everything else that Paul has to say on the subject. There is another alternative.

A helpful discussion of this text is presented by Gordon Fee, who argues

---

[18]Mishnah, *Tohoroth* (Danby, pp. 714-32).
[19]Orr/Walther, *I Corinthians*, p. 213.

for a parallel between the use of the word "made holy" in this text and in Romans 11:16 where Paul writes,

> If the dough offered as first fruits is holy,
>     so is the whole lump;
> and if the root is holy,
>     so are the branches

Paul is discussing his fellow Jews, whom he describes as "rejected" and "broken off." They have "stumbled," but not "fallen." He wants to "save some of them," and *at the same time* all of them are "holy." Those few who believe are the "first fruits" that sanctify, make holy, the "whole lump." Fee writes, "The 'consecration' of the part, in the sense of 'setting it apart' for God, 'sanctifies' the whole." Although in unbelief, the Israel of Paul's day belonged "to God in this special sense."[20] Fee argues that this special understanding of *holy* is the key to the text in cameo 4.

This interpretation is supported by Paul's reference to the children, who are presumably too young to make decisions of faith. Yet they are in a special relationship with God because the believing parent is "holy" and has made the other parent "holy." Together the two "holy" parents have "holy" children. In *this special sense* these children are like "unbelieving" Israel in Paul's day. For Paul, Israel was both "broken off" *and* "sanctified" by the first fruits. In like manner the unbelieving spouse, and the children, are in a special relationship with God through the believing spouse. Fee writes, "from Paul's perspective, as long as the marriage is maintained the potential for their realizing salvation remains."[21] Referring to both the unbelieving spouse and the children, Fee concludes, "Thus in both cases Paul is setting forth a high view of the grace of God at work through the believer towards members of his/her own household (cf. 1 Pet. 3:1), and for him that constitutes grounds enough for maintaining the marriage."[22] Thiselton comments on the ethos of the home created by the believing partner. He writes, "The spouse's example, witness, prayer, and living out of the gospel make the spouse and the children *in this sense* **holy**."[23] The final pair of cameos in this homily reads:

---

[20]Fee, *First Epistle*, pp. 300-302.
[21]Ibid., p. 300.
[22]Ibid., p. 302.
[23]Thiselton, *First Epistle*, p. 530 (italics and bold print his).

6. [15]But if the unbelieving partner
   desires to separate, let it be,                                    UNBELIEVING SPOUSE
   in such a case the brother or sister is not bound.                 Desires It—Then Separate
   For God has called us to peace.                                    The Goal—Peace

7. [16]For how do you know, wife,
   if you will keep your husband?                                     CAN YOU
   For how do you know, husband,                                      Keep Your Spouse?
   if you will keep your wife?

---

**Figure 2.5(9). Cameos 6-7 (1 Cor 7:15-16)**

Jesus never faced the problem of a pagan married couple, where one member becomes a Christian. Paul's directive necessarily moves beyond what Jesus had to say on the subject of marriage. If the unbelieving partner does not want to live with the believing wife or husband, they can separate and the believer can remarry: he or she is not bound. *The goal is peace.*

The final cameo (7) turns on the understanding of the many-sided Greek word *sozo*. Is Paul talking about "saving the husband/wife" (that is: bringing him or her to faith) or about "keeping the marriage"? Paul's language is ambiguous. He could mean one or the other or both. However, *God in Christ* brings salvation to those who believe. *The wife* cannot save her husband nor does she make him *holy*. God is the actor in these great mysteries. Thus, I prefer to read it as referring to the *keeping (saving) of the marriage*. In his extended reflections on this entire passage Thiselton notes that the text is "a notorious crux of interpretation."[24]

Whatever conclusions one draws from a study of this extremely complicated passage, it is my hope that noting the carefully composed rhetoric of the homily will prove helpful. This brings us to the missional asides in the fourth section of the discussion.

---

[24]Ibid., pp. 525-43.

## D. JEW AND GREEK, SLAVE AND FREE:
## REMAIN IN YOUR CALLING (7:17-24)

The text of this section is displayed in figure 2.5(10).

1.　　[17]To each as the Lord assigned,
　　　　and to each as God has called—let him walk.　　FOLLOW
　　　　This is my directive in all the churches.　　Your Calling

2.　　　[18]Was any one at the time of his call circumcised?

　　　　Let him not seek to remove the marks of circumcision.
3.　　　Was any one at the time of his call uncircumcised?　　JEW (is nothing)
　　　　Let him not seek circumcision.　　Greek (is nothing)

4.　　　[19]For circumcision is nothing
　　　　and uncircumcision is nothing,
　　　　but keeping the commandments of God.

5.　[20]Every one in the calling　　REMAIN IN
　　　　in/to which he was called should remain.　　Your Calling

6.　　[21]Were you called [while] a slave?
　　　　Do not be disturbed over it.　　CALLED—SLAVE
　　　　But if you can gain your freedom,　　Gain Freedom
　　　　avail yourself of the opportunity.

7.　　[22]For the person in the Lord called a slave　　CALLED SLAVE
　　　　is a freedman of the Lord.　　Free in the Lord
　　　　Likewise he who was called free　　CALLED FREE
　　　　is a slave of Christ.[25]　　Slave of Christ

8.　　[23]You were bought with a price;　　SET FREE
　　　　do not become slaves of men.　　Stay Free

9. [24]Every one, in that which he was called, brethren,　　REMAIN IN
　　　　let him remain with God.　　Your Calling—with God

**Figure 2.5(10). Jew and Greek, slave and free: Remain in your calling (1 Cor 7:17-24)**

### THE RHETORIC

Paul constructs yet another double-decker sandwich homily. In this case cameos 1, 5 and 9 are the bread and 2-4 and 6-8 are the "meat, cheese and tomatoes" that complete the sandwich. This double-decker homily style is of great antiquity, in that it appears in Isaiah 50:5b-11.[26] A second case of Isaiah's use

[25]My translation.
[26]This is examined above under the discussion of the hymn to the cross in 1 Cor 1:17–2:2.

of this rhetorical style appears in 51:1-3, seen in figure 2.5(11).

| | | | |
|---|---|---|---|
| 1. | [1]"Hearken to me, you who pursue deliverance, <br> you who seek the LORD; | YOU WHO SEEK <br> The Lord | |
| 2. | look to the rock from which you were hewn, <br> and to the cistern from which you were taken out. | | ABRAHAM THE ROCK <br> Sarah the Cistern |
| 3. | [2]Look to Abraham your father <br> and to Sarah who bore you; | LOOK TO <br> Abraham and Sarah | |
| 4. | for when he was but one I called him, <br> and I blessed him and made him many. | | ABRAHAM IS CALLED <br> Abraham Is Blessed |
| 5. | [3]For the LORD will comfort Zion; <br> he will comfort all her waste places, | THE LORD <br> Comforts Zion | |
| 6. | and will make her wilderness like Eden, <br> her desert like the garden of the LORD; | | PARABLE OF <br> Eden |
| 7. | joy and gladness will be found in her, <br> thanksgiving and the voice of song. | ZION <br> Rejoices | |

Figure 2.5(11). Isaiah 51:1-3

This Isaiah text contains seven cameos and exhibits the double-decker sandwich style. The outer frame is composed of 1, 5 and 7. Those three cameos standing alone make perfect sense. Figure 2.5(12) displays them together.

1. [1]"Hearken to me, you who pursue deliverance,        YOU WHO SEEK
   you who *seek the LORD;*                              The Lord

   ------------------

5. [3a]*For the LORD* will *comfort Zion;*               THE LORD
   he will *comfort* all her waste places,               Comforts Zion

   ------------------
7. [3c]*joy and gladness* will be found in her,          ZION
   thanksgiving and the voice of song.                   Rejoices

Figure 2.5(12). Isaiah 51:1, 3

If this were the entire homily, no reader would sense anything missing. There is even a chain-link connection between the three cameos. Cameo 1 ends with "seek the LORD," which is matched with "For the LORD will comfort Zion" in the opening line of cameo 5. Likewise, "comfort" in the second line of 5 matches "joy and gladness" that opens cameo 7. One could even suggest that Isaiah may have first composed these three interlocking cameos and then decided to strengthen his case by introducing specific references to God's past actions in history to save. For the top half of the sandwich he added references to Abraham and Sarah (God's care for his covenant people), and for the bottom half he reached back to Eden in order to recall God's past grace for all humankind. The precision with which such a simple yet profound homily was composed is striking. This double-decker sandwich style appears no less than eight times in 1 Corinthians.[27]

## COMMENTARY

Initially the placing of the discussion of Jew-Gentile and slave-free in the middle of this chapter on Christian patterns of sexuality appears puzzling. Why is this particular discussion placed in *this text?* The answer to this question may lie in Galatians 3:28, where Paul writes, "In Christ . . . there is neither *Jew nor Greek*, there is neither *slave nor free*, there is no *male and female*; for you are all one in Christ Jesus." In 7:1-16 Paul discusses male and female. This may have triggered his mind to continue and finish the above trilogy by adding the other two topics.

At the same time, in verses 10-16 he discusses "Christians married to non-Christians." He was probably referring to Greek Christians and their unbelieving fellow Greeks. But there was also a social-theological divide between *Christian* and *Jew*, and the social-economic separation between *slave* and *free*. From this point of view it is perfectly natural to expect Paul (while discussing points of friction in marriages) to include a few brief remarks on these two latter types of divisions.

Turning to the details of this homily we will look first at the three cameos (the three slices of bread) that provide structure for the homily. Second, the subject of "circumcised and uncircumcised" presented in cameos 2-4 will need examination. Finally we will reflect on "slave and free" in cameos 6-8.

First is the outer frame of the homily.

As in Isaiah 51:1-3 so here in 7:17-24, the three slices of bread that hold the double-decker sandwich together are closely related and seen together are as follows:

---

[27]1 Cor 1:1-9; 1:17–2:2 (the "Counterpoint"); 7:17-24; 25-31; 9:12b-18; 14:1-12; 12b-36; 15:35-50.

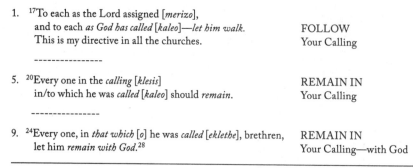

1.  <sup>17</sup>To each as the Lord assigned [*merizo*],
    and to each *as God has called* [*kaleo*]—*let him walk.*          FOLLOW
    This is my directive in all the churches.                           Your Calling

    ----------------

5.  <sup>20</sup>Every one in the *calling* [*klesis*]                  REMAIN IN
    in/to which he was *called* [*kaleo*] should *remain.*             Your Calling

    ----------------

9.  <sup>24</sup>Every one, in *that which* [*o*] he was *called* [*eklethe*], brethren,   REMAIN IN
    let him *remain with God.*<sup>28</sup>                             Your Calling—with God

**Figure 2.5(13). 1 Cor 7:17, 20, 24**

The themes of "walking in" the *calling* and "remaining in" the *calling* unite the three cameos. Like Isaiah, Paul adds illustrative material in between these cameos in order to complete the sandwich. The filler in the top has to do with Jew and Greek while the filler in the bottom relates to slave and free.

Finally, the central slice of bread for the sandwich is a single cameo (5) that has a double function. It forms the bottom of the top half of the sandwich. At the same time it creates the top of the lower half of the sandwich. That is, it looks both ways. Sometimes Paul repeats this center (see 1:1-9; 7:25-31; 14:1-12). Five times (as here) the center is a single cameo that closes the first half and opens the second half (see 1:17–2:2; 7:17-25; 9:12b-18; 14:26-36; 15:35-50). Allowing for the double use of the center, each half has five cameos.

The Greek verb *kaleo* (to call) is prominent in this epistle. Paul uses words with this root seven times in the first chapter alone.<sup>29</sup> The feminine noun *klesis* (calling) appears in the New Testament eleven times.<sup>30</sup> Leaving aside the current text, the other ten uses of this word unambiguously refer to the call of God in Jesus Christ. As used by non-Christian writers this word *can mean* "station in life."<sup>31</sup> Some English language translators have chosen this latter option and read the first line in cameo 5 (v. 20) as "Every one should remain in the *state* in which he was called" (RSV). The RSV then translated the relative pronoun "in which" (*o*) in cameo 9 (v. 24) as meaning "whatever *state*" and thus cameo 9 reads, "So, brethren, in *whatever state* each was called, there let him remain with God." This leads the reader to understand that Paul is

---

<sup>28</sup>My translation, following the Greek word order to exhibit the parallels in the passage.
<sup>29</sup>1 Cor 1:1, 2a, 2b, 2c, 9, 24, 26.
<sup>30</sup>Rom 11:29; 1 Cor 1:26; 7:20; Eph 1:18; 4:1,4: Phil 3:14; 2 Thess 1:11; 2 Tim 1:9; Heb 3:1; 2 Pet 1:10.
<sup>31</sup>BAGD, p. 436.

urging slaves to remain in slavery. This possibility needs to be examined on a number of levels, some of which we will discuss later. Here it is important to clarify the word "calling."

1. Beginning with the Peshitta Syriac (4th century) and moving on through twelve of the early Arabic versions from the ninth to the nineteenth centuries[32] and concluding with the 1817 Hebrew, the two texts in 1 Corinthians 7:20, 24, translate some form of "in the *calling* to which you were *called*, remain with God." These versions all refer to "the call of God" and not to a socioeconomic position in life.

Starting with Erpenius (1616) and moving on to the Propagandist (1671) and including four twentieth-century Arabic versions, the translation *fe al-hal* (in the condition) is introduced. These six versions read some form of "in *the condition* in which you were called, there remain with God."[33] Thus, in the Oriental versions this reference to "the condition" is a latecomer that I have not found anywhere before the seventeenth century. For more than a thousand years, Middle Eastern Semitic-speaking Christians read this text as a discussion of a "calling before God," not of a pre-conversion socioeconomic status.

2. If all other occurrences of the feminine noun *call* in the New Testament refer to "the call of God" and not to a person's state or condition in life, then surely the clear preference is to read verses 20 and 24 as also referring to *God's call*.

3. In this homily Paul affirms, "You were bought with a price; do not become slaves of men." How, in the same text, can he on one hand tell his readers to avoid slavery like the plague, and on the other hand urge slaves to remain in slavery?

4. In cameo 6 Paul states, "If you can gain your freedom, avail yourself of the opportunity." Granted, the language is ambiguous and can be read as "even though you have the possibility of becoming free, remain a slave."[34] But in the light of Paul's unambiguous directive "Do not become slaves to men," the first of these options is to be preferred.

5. In this homily *called* is attached to *assigned* (cameo 1). In 3:5 Paul declares

---

[32]Vat. Ar. 13 (8th-9th cent.); Mt. Sinai 151 (867); Mt. Sinai (9th cent.); Mt. Sinai 310 (10th cent.); London Polyglot (1657); London Polyglot rev. (1717); Shwair (1813); Shidiac (1851); Bustani-Van Dyck (1860); Bustani-Van Dyck (1865); Jesuit (1880).

[33]Erpenius (1616); Propagandist (1671); Martyn (1826); New Jesuit (1969); Yusif Dawud (1899); Fakhouri (1964); Bible Society Arabic (1993). See appendix II, plate E.

[34]See Thiselton, *First Epistle*, pp. 552-65; and Fee, *First Epistle*, pp. 308-22.

that God "assigned" special tasks to him and to Apollos. In Romans 11:29 the "gifts and the call of God" are connected. Furthermore, for Paul, faith and obedience are so intimately connected that he can write about "the obedience of faith" (a genitive of apposition; see Rom 1:5; 16:26). Faith is something you do. The call of God is not merely a new state of being in Christ but carries with it the necessity of a lifestyle of obedience.

6. The relative pronoun "in which" in cameo 9 is attached to "calling," and there is no mention of any state or condition. There is a similar relative pronoun in the parallel cameo (5) that is also attached to the word *called*.

7. If Paul wanted all believers to remain in their pre-Christian socioeconomic state or condition, then he should have remained a rabbinic teacher in Jerusalem. In his parable of the farmer Paul defined himself and Apollos as "Servants through whom you believed, as *the Lord assigned to each*." Paul was *assigned* the task of "planter" and Apollos was *assigned* the responsibility of watering the new plants (3:5-9). For both of them these were new tasks that did not represent their pre-conversion social positions. In like manner Paul certainly knew that Peter was a fisherman on the Sea of Galilee before he was called by Jesus. Is Paul here telling Peter, Andrew, James and John that when Jesus called them to follow him, Jesus should have added, "Stay in your boats, and continue fishing the lake"? Before his vision on the road to Damascus, Paul was a Jerusalem-based rising star in the rabbinic world, with the confidence of the high-priestly class. He left that social setting and became a Christian theologian and traveling evangelist. Is Paul telling his readers, "This change in direction was fine *for me*—but don't imitate me—it is not an acceptable pattern *for you*." Three chapters earlier Paul wrote, "I urge you, then, be imitators of me" (1 Cor 4:16). Is he now reversing himself and telling them to ignore his pattern of discipleship and remain in their pre-conversion socioeconomic position in the community?

A new trend in many American seminaries is the second-career student. Such students launch careers and after some years sense a call to full-time ministry. To respond to such a call, these individuals set aside "the state in which they were called" in order to fulfill their obedience. Are all of these students/pastors violating Paul's mandate? Certainly not. Like Peter they heard the call "follow me," and that call led them to change from one profession to another. Had Peter been told by Jesus to "stay in your boat" he could have worked out his new commitments to Jesus as Messiah while remaining a fisherman, but he was never asked to do so.

Jewish Christian, Gentile Christian, free disciple, slave believer—the special circumstances in life of each of Paul's readers created unique opportunities for discipleship. All were *called* and all received gifts and assignments from the Lord.

Second is the question of Jew and Gentile. Having examined three cameos that make up the outer frame of the homily (cameos 1, 5, 9) we must now consider the inner content of the top half of the sandwich, which has to do with *circumcised and uncircumcised* [see fig. 2.5(14)].

1.  [17]To each as the Lord assigned,
    and to each as God has called—let him walk.        FOLLOW
    This is my directive in all the churches.              Your Calling

2.      [18]Was any one at the time of his call circumcised?
        Let him not seek to remove the marks of circumcision.

3.      Was any one at the time of his call uncircumcised?      JEW (is nothing)
        Let him not seek circumcision.                              Greek (is nothing)

4.      [19]For circumcision is nothing
        and uncircumcision is nothing,
        but keeping the commandments of God.

5.  [20]Every one in the calling              REMAIN IN
    to which he was called should remain.         Your Calling

Figure 2.5(14). The circumcised and the uncircumcised (1 Cor 7:17-20)

It is utterly astounding to read these words from a first-century Jewish scholar. The sign of the covenant was circumcision. Here that commandment of God is set aside (having been replaced by baptism).

Paul is talking about *the calling/assignment of God* and telling the entire church that there is no special cultural identity required for discipleship in the kingdom of God. The Jew does not have to become a pig-eating Gentile. The Gentile does not have to be circumcised and join the Jewish-Christian branch of the church. There is no sacred culture and no sacred language. Paul is writing in Greek, not in Hebrew. He tells his readers that regardless of their ethnic origins (Jewish or Greek) there is an "assignment," a "calling" from the Lord tailored to who they are that does not require becoming someone else. From Constantine onward, the times and places where this vision of Paul has not been honored are legion.

At the same time, everyone has an ethnic heritage that is relevant. Paul is saying, "God has a calling for you that will be shaped by your own unique cultural identity—be it Jewish or Gentile, slave or free." Paul himself was a prime example of what he was talking about.

Paul urges his readers to set aside the law (by ignoring circumcision), and in the next breath tells them that what matters is "keeping the commandments of God." What commandments? At least he is referring to the commandment to love one another, which he will expound fully in chapter 13. Surely he also is referring to the assignment (commandment?) that the Lord gives to each disciple. As the Corinthians will read later, the hand (an honorable part of the body) cannot say to the foot (an unclean part of the body), "We have no need of you." Neither part of the church (Jewish or Gentile) could be denigrated as inferior, and neither could assert superiority. Both Jew and Greek could participate fully in their new missional life. The leopard did not have to change its spots. A new age had dawned.

Third is the question of *slave and free*.

Cameo 5 closes the first half of the homily while at the same time it opens the second half. The inner content of the second half of the sandwich focuses on the topic of slavery and the predicament faced by the Christian slave. The full text of that second half is displayed in figure 2.5(15).

| | | |
|---|---|---|
| 5. | [20]Every one in the calling [*klesis*] | REMAIN IN |
| | in/to which he was called [*eklethe*] should remain. | Your Calling |
| | | |
| 6. | [21]Were you called (while) a slave? | |
| | Do not be disturbed over it. | |
| | But if you can gain your freedom, | GAIN FREEDOM |
| | avail yourself of the opportunity. | |
| | | |
| 7. | [22]For the person in the Lord called a slave | SLAVE |
| | is a freedman of the Lord. | Free |
| | Likewise he who was called free | Free |
| | is a slave of Christ. | SLAVE |
| | | |
| 8. | [23]You were bought with a price; | |
| | do not become slaves of men. | STAY FREE |
| | | |
| 9. | [24]Every one, in that to which he was *called*, brethren, | REMAIN IN |
| | in that let him remain with God. | Your Calling—with God |

**Figure 2.5(15). Cameos 5-9 (1 Cor 7:20-24)**

## RHETORIC

The ring composition of the five cameos in figure 2.5(15) is clear and the parallels strong. The climax in the center affirms that they are all "slaves" and all "freed men" in the Lord.

## COMMENTARY

In the opening of this chapter we reflected on Paul's use of the word "call." Before proceeding we need to pause to briefly examine Paul's attitude toward slavery. Four times in the New Testament slaves/servants are told to obey their masters (Eph 6:5; 1 Tim 6:1-2; Tit 2:9; 1 Pet 2:18). Paul's dealing with slavery can be easily misunderstood. The church under Stalin in Russia had very few *public* options. Having lived most of my adult life as a part of the Arabic-speaking Christian community in the Middle East, I know that they also have a limited number of *public* options. For more than a millennium they have lived out their faithfulness in the midst of a sea of Islam. Public criticism of the Islamic social, political and economic foundations of the state has never been a possibility for them.

In the first century, preaching in the catacombs by the light of an oil lamp was one thing. There they could speak freely. Circulating a *written document* was something else; into whose hands might it fall? Russian Christians under Stalin had one *public* option—obey the state. Any other option was suicide. Any book or paper written and published by Christians in Russia during that period carried with it special risks. Paul could not, *in writing*, attack the institution of slavery and survive. The best option for a slave in that society was to obey the master. Failure to do so would have brought on crucifixion. In this critical passage Paul pushes the envelope as far as he can. In effect he says:

> If you are caught in slavery, try to get free. If you are free—do not become a slave. Yet, if you are caught in this (horrible) institution you can yet find and carry out an *assignment*. You can exercise your *gifts* and respond to your *call*. If you are a slave do not look wistfully at me with my freedom and the privileges of Roman citizenship and say, "Of course the Lord can use *him*. But I am a slave—*I can do nothing!*" Don't forget *your* calling, and *never imagine that there is no calling for you because you are a slave.*

My family and I lived through ten years of the Lebanese civil war that raged from 1975 to 1991 and during that war many things were not possible. Many plans failed, many dreams died, and many friends were killed.

Yet, every step downward into the abyss created new possibilities for faithfulness and ministry. The army had collapsed, the police were gone from the streets, the electricity was off and there was little water in the water mains. Phones did not work, traffic lights were dark, garbage was not collected and 150 private armies controlled the broken fragments of the city.

During those perilous days anonymous bombers detonated a sack of dynamite at the main entrance of the Greek Catholic cathedral down the street from the seminary in Beirut where I was teaching. The morning after the bombing we contacted the resident priest. At his invitation we shut down the seminary for a day and *en masse* walked over to the cathedral. With a cumulative total of about five hundred hours of hard work, we managed to sweep and shovel the debris out of the sanctuary, seal up the doors and windows with plywood, dispose of the wreckage and move the unbroken pews into the basement so that the congregation had a place to assemble for worship. As we carried out these tasks, we were watched intently by a silent crowd of thousands. There were no classes at the seminary. That is, we did not teach any theology that day—or did we?

As noted, the focus of these five cameos is a valiant attempt to convince the reader that the believer's civil status (be it slave or free) is an arena within which God can call a believer to ministry. God's gifts and call are not limited to any single culture or social status. Paul tells the Corinthians that for each of them *there is a calling/assignment.* Paul does not endorse slavery or tell people to remain slaves. It is an evil system, *yet* the call of God can be heard and obeyed within it.

Cameo 6 tells the slave to strive to gain freedom if possible. Cameo 7 (the climax of the five cameos) affirms, We are all slaves and all free. How is this possible? Cameo 8 provides the answer: "You were bought with a price." In chapter 6, Paul saw the cross as a light shining in the darkness to guide confused Corinthians through the swamp of sexual confusion (6:20). In cameo 8 he finds the cross (cameo 8) central to the formation of a new identity that frees the slave and enthralls the free.

Having dealt with *Jew and Greek*, and *slave and free* in Christ, Paul is ready to return to *male and female* in Christ. He opens with the "not yet married" [see fig. 2.5(16)].

## E. THE UNMARRIED AND THE IMPENDING DISTRESS (7:25-31)

1.    [25]Now concerning the *virgins [parthenoi]*,      THE VIRGINS
   I have no command of the Lord,      An Introduction
   but I give my opinion as one who by the Lord's mercy is trustworthy.

   ----------------------------------------------------

2.    [26]I think that in view of the *impending distress*      TROUBLE IS
   it is well for a person to remain as he is.      Threatening

3.      [27]Are you *bound* to a wife?
         Do not seek to be *free*.
        Are you *free* from a wife?      REMAIN AS
         Do not seek *marriage*.      You Are
        [28]But if you *marry*,
         you do *not sin*.
        And if a girl [virgin] marries
         she does not sin.

4.    Yet those who marry will have *worldly troubles*,      TROUBLE IS
   and I would spare you that.      Threatening

   ----------------------------------------------------

5.    [29]I mean, brethren, the *appointed time*      TIME IS
   has *grown very short*; from now on,      Short

6.      let those who have *wives*
         live as though they had *none*,
        [30]and those who *mourn*
         as though they were *not mourning*,      FAMILY
        and those who rejoice      Social Occasions
         as though they were *not rejoicing*,      Economic Activity
        and those who buy      All Impermanent
         as though they did *not enjoy possessions*,[35]
        [31]and those who *deal with the world*
         as though they had *no dealings with it*.

7.    For the *form of this world*      FORM OF WORLD
   is *passing away*.      Passing Away

**Figure 2.5(16). The unmarried and the impending distress (1 Cor 7:25-31)**

### THE RHETORIC

Paul fashions a unified homily composed of seven cameos. A single cameo introduces the subject of the homily. While the following six cameos present the details. Those six in turn form another double-decker sandwich.

---

[35]My translation.

The second half of the sandwich relates closely to the first and yet moves beyond it. The first says, "Things are tough." The second echoes, "The time is short." The outer frames of the two halves could stand alone with little change. The homily is so exquisitely composed that it moves beyond rhetoric to poetry. Moffat calls the passage "a lyrical outburst."[36]

## COMMENTARY

The structure of the six cameos mirrors the style of the introduction to the epistle (1:1-9). With very slight change the four cameos that form the framework of the homily, when seen alone, are displayed in figure 2.5(17).

| | | |
|---|---|---|
| 2. | [26]I think that in view of the *impending distress* it is well for a person to remain as he is. | TROUBLE IS<br>Threatening |
| 4. | [28c]Those who marry will have *worldly troubles*, and I would spare you that. | TROUBLE IS<br>Threatening |
| | ------------------------------------------------ | |
| 5. | [29]I mean, brethren, the *appointed time* has *grown very short*; from now on [know that], | TIME IS<br>Short |
| 7. | [31b]The *form of this world* is *passing away*. | THIS WORLD<br>Passing Away |

Figure 2.5(17). Cameos 2, 4-5 and 7 (1 Cor 7:26, 28c, 29, 31b)

Cameos 2 and 4 tell of the distress/troubles that are "impending." Cameos 5 and 7 affirm "the time is short." The four cameos interlock smoothly. They present the reality of life in the world (as Paul sees it). In cameos 3 and 6 Paul presents his directives on how they should live in the light of the exterior world. He has eight lines in the external frames and nine sets of Hebrew parallelisms in the two centers. The first half of this poem (cameos 2-4) focuses exclusively on the subject of marriage. The second half of the sandwich (cameos 5-7) broadens to include five topics. These are

- marriage

- mourning (a death?)

- rejoicing (a wedding? a birth?)

---

[36]Moffat, *First Epistle*, p. 93.

- buying and enjoying possessions

- dealing with the world (commerce)

The first three in this list are life-changing, unforgettable moments in the life of any family or community. The last two would have had special meaning in Corinth. The city was a crossroads for commercial traffic north and south as well as east and west. There were more goods available in Corinth than anywhere else in Greece. The opportunities for shopping were the best available, and Corinth was a wealthy city. Paul speaks of "those who buy" as not *katekho*. This word had to do with "holding fast to something."[37] When used in connection with property it carried the nuance of "enjoying possessions . . . especially of property."[38] Robertson and Plummer note, "Earthly goods are a trust, not a possession."[39] Paul's referring here to the attachments that form between people and the things they buy. The fifth category Paul mentions is on the subject of relations with the outside world. To "do business" in Corinth merchants needed to "deal with the world," and that world stretched from Brittany to Syria and from the northern tribes to the limits of habitation in North Africa.

Paul expected the imminent end of all things. We now look back over almost two thousand years since he recorded those perceptions. Yet his advice regarding the de-absolutizing of this wide-ranging list of human experiences and endeavors is as timely as ever. Marriage, death, birth, possessions and livelihood are all transitory. Remembering this reality can add a priceless component to our outlook on all of life. Borrowing from 1 Corinthians 15, the words of the African American spiritual "Steal Away to Jesus" affirm,

> The trumpet sounds within-a my soul
> I ain't got long to stay here.

The *last* "trumpet will sound" at the end of history (15:52), but should it not also sound today "within-a my soul"?

## F. MARRIAGE AND ANXIETIES (7:32-35)

Paul is not finished with the topic of Christian marriage. He concludes section 2.5 with three final questions (7:32-40). The first of these is displayed in figure 2.5(18).

---

[37]BAGD, p. 423.

[38]LSJ, *Greek-English Lexicon*, p. 926.

[39]Robertson/Plummer, *First Epistle*, p. 156.

1. [32]I want you to be free from anxieties.      FREE FROM ANXIETIES

2.     Now the de-married [*agamos*] man        DEMARRIED MAN
      is anxious about the affairs of the Lord,     Free for the Lord
      how to please the Lord;

3.        [33]but the married man          MARRIED MAN
         is anxious about worldly affairs,      Busy with Wife
         how to please his wife, [34]and he is divided.

4.     The de-married [*agamos*] woman and the virgin [*parthenos*]
      are anxious about the affairs of the Lord,    DEMARRIED WOMAN
      how to be consecrated in body and spirit;    Free for the Lord

5.        but the married woman
         is anxious about worldly affairs,       MARRIED WOMAN
         how to please her husband.          Busy with Husband

6. [35]I say this for your own benefit,
    not to throw a noose upon you,
    but to promote good order [*euskhenon*]     SECURING UNDIVIDED LOYALTY
    and to secure your undivided devotion to the Lord.

**Figure 2.5(18). Marriage and anxieties (1 Cor 7:32-35)**

## RHETORIC

In between an introduction and a conclusion, Paul presents four cameos that exhibit an A-B-A-B structure[40] found also in 7:6-9.

## COMMENTARY

Regarding these verses (and the verses that follow), Jerome Murphy-O'Connor writes, "This is probably the most difficult and controverted section of the Letter. There are many different interpretations, and none of them is immune to objections."[41] The problem is that Paul knew and worked with Priscilla and Aquila who hosted a church in their home. Together they taught Apollos (Acts 18:26). From what we know, their marriage did not hamper their effectiveness in ministry. Demas began well (Col 4:14; Philem 24) but then went "the way of the world" (2 Tim 4:10). The assumption is that he was single. Being single did not prevent him from failing. If the spouse is not committed to the things of God, then the marriage *can* be a huge hindrance to "devotion to the Lord." Paul's thoughts on this subject can perhaps be best read as a warning, not

---

[40]This same A-B-A-B structure appears in Is 43:3-4.

[41]Murphy-O'Connor, *1 Corinthians*, p. 71.

as a ruling. The root of the term *good order* reappears in the definition of love in chapter 13.

## G. A MAN AND "HIS VIRGIN" (7:36-38)

Paul concludes with two brief sections having to do with "his virgin" and "in case of death." The first has to do with a person and "his virgin" [see fig. 2.5(19)].

1.   [36]If any one thinks that he is not behaving properly towards his virgin,
  > if his passions are strong,
  >> and if it has to be, let him do what he wants;
  >> he does not sin, let them marry.

2.   [37]But whoever is firmly established in his heart,
  > being under no necessity but having his desire under control,
  >> and has determined this in his heart,
  >> to keep her as his virgin, he will do well.

3.   [38]So that he who marries [gives in marriage?] his virgin does well;
  > and he who refrains from marrying [giving in marriage?] will do better.

---

**Figure 2.5(19). A man and "his virgin" (1 Cor 7:36-38)**

Using ten lines, Paul composed three cameos. Orr and Walther offer a succinct summary of the options for understanding this puzzling passage. The text can be discussing

  1. a young man and his fiancée
  2. a father and his virgin daughter
  3. some kind of a "spiritual marriage"
  4. a levirate marriage[42]

Because we do not know the precise situation to which Paul was writing, it is difficult to choose among these four alternatives. As T. W. Manson somewhere said about the parable of the unjust steward (Lk 16:1-8), "The literature is voluminous and unrewarding."

## H. IN CASE OF DEATH (7:39-40A)

Paul's final admonition has to do with the death of one partner in a marriage. He composes seven lines that form three cameos [see fig. 2.5(20)].

---

[42]Orr/Walther, *I Corinthians*, p. 223.

10.    ³⁹A wife is bound [*dedetai*] to her husband
       as long as he lives.

11.    If the husband dies,
       she is free to be married to whom she wishes,
       only in the Lord.

12.    ⁴⁰But in my judgment she is happier
       if she remains as she is.

---

**Figure 2.5(20). In case of death (1 Cor 7:39-40a)**

Paul ends this subsection where he began. It is good to stay single, but marriage "in the Lord" is approved.

## I. PAUL'S CONCLUDING PERSONAL APPEAL (7:40B)

13.    ⁴⁰ᵇI think that I have the Spirit of God.

Paul concludes his first essay by saying, "I urge you, then, be imitators of me." That personal appeal does not fit this discussion of sexual practice. He therefore reshapes his appeal by telling his readers that he senses the Spirit of the Lord guiding him in what he is writing. The admonition is still personal, but now fits the nature of the topics discussed in the essay. With this "signature conclusion" the second essay comes to an end.

The third essay poses a new question, which is: *How should a Christian live in a non-Christian world?* To this new topic we now turn.

# Christian and Pagan

*Freedom and Responsibility*

1 CORINTHIANS 8:1–11:1

ואם ככה תחטאו לאחיכם-
למשיח אתם תחטאים
(8:21)

# Food Offered to Idols

*Freedom and Responsibility*

I Corinthians 8:1-13

Pᴀᴜʟ's ᴛʜɪʀᴅ ᴇssᴀʏ covers 8:1–11:1. Its outline is as follows:

The overall essay focuses on the question of how Christians are to live out their lives in a pagan world. Are they to accommodate to that world, and if so—to what extent? Are they to blend in or stand apart? The question of food offered to idols offered Paul a concrete case study for a discussion of this critical concern.

Paul's reference to *the tradition*, with which he begins each essay, appears here as well. In this case he presents what is probably an early Christian confession about God as Father and Jesus as Lord (1 Cor 8:6). He then moves on to set out *the ethical problem* in focus throughout this essay. In the process he introduces the theme of "freedom and responsibility." This triggers his mind to reflect on his personal freedom and responsibility (section 3.2). In the center of the essay he again builds a *theological foundation* for a solution to the problem under discussion.[1] This foundation takes the form

---

[1] Murphy-O'Connor has noted the A-B-A pattern of the material. See Murphy-O'Connor, *1 Corinthians*, p. 77.

of three patterns of life for Christians living in a non-Christian world. Sometimes they can *identify fully* with that world (chap. 3.3). At other times they can *identify partially* (chap. 3.4), and finally there are times when they must *stand totally apart* (chap. 3.5). Murphy-O'Connor rightly sees Paul's reflections in the center of this and other essays as the deepening of "our understanding of the principles underlying his more practical discussions."[2] At the end of the essay Paul returns to a *concluding discussion* of food offered to idols (chap. 3.6). Once again he "signs off" on the essay with a personal appeal as he writes, "Be imitators of me, as I am of Christ" (11:1). With the overall outline of Paul's third essay in mind, we turn to his first discussion of food offered to idols in 8:1-13.

## FOOD OFFERED TO IDOLS: FREEDOM AND RESPONSIBILITY (1 COR 8:1-13)

This opening homily is composed of nine cameos that fall under four headings.

### A. Knowledge, Love and God

1. [1]Now concerning idol food.[3] We *know*       WE KNOW
      "all of us have *knowledge*."              Knowledge
         "*Knowledge*" puffs up but *love* builds up.      Love

2. [2]If any one imagines that he *knows* something,     HE KNOWS
      he does not yet *know* as he ought to *know*.       Not Yet Knows
        [3]But if one *loves God*, one is *known by him*.     Love

---------

### B. Knowledge, Idols and God

3. [4]Hence, as to the idol food,              KNOWLEDGE
     *we know* that "an idol has no real existence,"     No Idols
      and "*there is no God but one*."           And One God
   [5]For although there may be so-called gods in heaven or on earth—
     as indeed there are many "gods" and many "lords,"

4. [6]yet for us there is *one God, the Father*,     ONE GOD—FATHER
       from whom are all things            Creation
         and we are his;               We Are His
     and *one Lord, Jesus Christ*,       ONE LORD—JESUS CHRIST
       by whose hand are all things       Creation
       and we are by his hand.[4]         We Are by His Hand

----------

---

[2]Ibid.

[3]Paul uses the Greek word "idol food" (*eidolo-thutos*) rather than the usual word "devoted food" (*hiero-thutos*). See LSJ, *A Greek-English Lexicon*, p. 483 and p. 821.

[4]Here I am following a strong New Testament translation tradition in Hebrew, Syriac and Arabic.

**C. Knowledge, the Weak and God**

5. [7]However, not all possess this knowledge.                           KNOWLEDGE & IDOLS
    But some, through being hitherto accustomed to idols,   Weak in Conscience
    eat food as really offered to an idol;                               Defiled
    and their conscience, being weak, is defiled.

6.  [8]Food will not commend us to God.
    We are no worse off if we do not eat,                        GOD and FOOD
    and no better off if we do.                                  The Weak—Stumble
    [9]Only take care lest this liberty of yours                 Freedom and Responsibility
    becomes a stumbling-block to the weak.

7. [10]For if any one sees you, a man of knowledge,
    reclining in an idol's temple,                               KNOWLEDGE and IDOLS
    if his conscience is weak,                                   The Weak in Conscience
    might he not be encouraged                                   Freedom and Responsibility
    to eat food offered to idols?

----------

**D. Knowledge, Your/My Brother and Christ**

8. [11]And so by *your knowledge*                               Your Knowledge
    this *weak* man is *destroyed*,                                 Weak—Destroyed
        *the brother* for whom Christ died.                            The Brother/Sister
    [12]Thus, sinning against *your brethren*                      Your Brothers/Sisters
    and *wounding* their conscience when it is *weak*,             Weak—Wounded
    *you sin against Christ.*                                    Your Sin—Against Christ

9. [13]Therefore, if food is a cause
    of my brother's stumbling,                                   MY BROTHER STUMBLES
    I will never eat meat,                                       I Do Not Eat
    lest I cause my brother to stumble.

---

**Figure 3.1(1). Food offered to idols: Freedom and responsibility (1 Cor 8:1-13)**

## THE RHETORIC

The nine cameos (in their four sections) are set out in a straight-line progression. Section A has three sets of loosely formulated step parallelisms. In section B, the center of cameo 3 is an affirmation of faith. That center ("there is no God but one") is picked up by Paul, repeated and expanded in cameo 4. The six lines of cameo 4 form three pairs of step parallelism. Section C is composed of three inverted cameos, and section D uses two.

The "weak person" is defined in the last section D as "a brother," then "your brother" and finally "my brother." Using a straight-line sequence, the homily climaxes at the end with the affirmation that irresponsible treatment of the brother/sister is a sin against Christ. The church as the body of Christ is presupposed. The theme of "love" begins and ends the homily.

## COMMENTARY

A clear and powerful progression of thought moves through the homily. The four sections can be summarized as follows:

A. *Knowledge, love and God.* Love is more important than knowledge. Love builds, while knowledge creates pride. It is not what we know that matters, but who knows us! If we love God, God "knows" us.

B. *Knowledge, idols and God.* We *know* that idols have no existence. There is only one God who has created all things through one Lord.

C. *Knowledge, your brother/sister and God.* The weak person may think that idols are real, and such a person's conscience is defiled if he or she sees you eating meat offered to idols.

D. *Knowledge, your brother/sister and Christ.* This weak person is your sister or brother, and causing him or her to stumble is a failure to love and thereby a sin against Christ.

Each of these four deserves some reflection. Section A reads:

| | |
|---|---|
| 1. ¹Now concerning idol food.⁵ We *know* | WE KNOW |
| "all of us have *knowledge*." | Knowledge |
| "*Knowledge*" puffs up but *love* builds up. | Love |
| | |
| 2. ²If any one imagines that he *knows* something, | HE KNOWS |
| he does not yet *know* as he ought to *know*. | Not Know |
| ³But if one *loves God*, one is *known by him*. | Love |

Figure 3.1(2). Section A: Knowledge, love and God (1 Cor 8:1-3)

## SECTION A. CAMEO 1

This topic was extremely sensitive. At the Jerusalem Council (Acts 15:1-35) the apostles agreed to request Gentile believers to abstain from "what has been sacrificed to idols" (*eidolo-thuton*: Acts 15:29). For a Jew such food was strictly prohibited. Some Gentile believers inevitably thought this requirement was unnecessary. If idols did not exist, then why the restriction? Most of the meat available was first offered to one of the many idols and then sold in the market. In the ancient city of Corinth the central market was virtually surrounded by pagan temples, and the great archaic temple almost overshadowed the meat market.⁶

---

⁵Paul uses the Greek word "idol food" (*eidolo-thutos*) rather than the usual word "devoted food" (*hiero-thutos*). See LSJ, *A Greek-English Lexicon*, p. 483 and p. 821.
⁶Jerome Murphy-O'Connor, *St. Paul's Corinth: Text and Archaeology* (Collegeville, Minn.: Liturgical Press, 2002), p. 26.

A Greek pagan by the name of Pausanias traveled across Greece in the mid-second century and wrote *Description of Greece*, which has survived. Discussing the central *agora* (market square) of Corinth, Pausanias mentions temples and statues for Dionysus, Artemis, Baccheaus, Fortune, Poseidon, Apollo, Aphrodite, Hermes, Zeus, Zeus of the Underworld, Zeus Most High and the Muses.[7] Two general markets hugged the wall of the great archaic pagan temple and a fish and meat market was across a narrow street. On the west side of the agora was a huge temple dedicated to the imperial cult. All of this was within 150 yards of the center of the town. The sacrifices were the property of the priests of the various temples and what the priests could not eat, they sold. During the numerous feasts there was an inevitable glut in the meat market, and the price would drop accordingly. For many of the poor of the city (which certainly included at least some of the Christians) that was probably the only time they could afford to eat meat. Furthermore, if a person didn't ask the butcher, he or she would not know whether a particular piece of meat had been offered to an idol or not. None of the idols existed anyway, so why not enjoy some rarely affordable beef or lamb?

In the context of a city like Corinth all of this made perfect sense. But if reported in Jerusalem, such a practice would sound like a trashing of the Jerusalem agreement. Paul could have simply issued a ruling such as, "Barnabas and I agreed with the apostles in Jerusalem on this matter and I insist that our agreement be honored. No Christian is allowed to eat meat offered to idols, and that's final!"

Instead of issuing a new law, Paul asks his readers to reflect on "knowledge" and "love." In the six lines of cameos 1-2 [see fig. 3.1(2)], the words *knowledge* and *knowing* appear seven times with at least one occurrence in each line. The words *know* and *love* occur together twice. The last line in cameo 1 reads, "*knowledge* puffs up but *love* builds up" and cameo 2c affirms, "But if one *loves God*, one is *known* by him."

The two key words *knowledge* and *love* reappear in the hymn to love in 13:4. Once again, Paul is quietly building up a list of negatives that appear when love is absent. In the process, he describes the inner workings of "knowledge" on the one hand and "love" on the other. Knowledge, by its very nature, can easily create pride and arrogance. The one who has large amounts of knowledge can easily look down on those less informed.

In my hearing, the famous Lesslie Newbigin publicly described Western

---

[7]Ibid., pp. 24-25.

biblical scholarship as "cannibalistic." "Each generation," he told us, "the children eat their parents."[8] A true scholar must be rigorous, scientific, objective and thoroughgoing. If love does not contribute to those interests, then *love* can be set aside. *Knowledge* is all we need. Or is it?

By contrast, "love" *builds up* rather than tearing down. Paul had already presented himself and his colleague Apollos as "master builders." He urged everyone to *build* the new temple on the foundation of Jesus Christ, using the highest quality building materials. The Corinthians who *knew* that idols did not exist were in grave danger of using that knowledge in a way that would tear down what Paul, with great effort, had built up. The issue of food offered to idols could easily split the church in Corinth and elsewhere into Jewish-background believers and Gentile-background believers. Inscribed on the seal of the United Presbyterian Church of North America (1857-1957) was the inscription "The Truth of God—Forbearance in Love." Paul continues this discussion in the second cameo.

## SECTION A. CAMEO 2

Those who focus on how much they know do not yet know as they "ought to know." The key to knowledge of God is: Does the seeker after knowledge about God, love God? Such love for God opens channels of knowledge rather than closing them because that person is in a special sense "known by God."

The longing to be known is a deep inner yearning within every soul. A loving spouse knows a great deal about the beloved marriage partner. The same self-revelation takes place between dear friends. Yet we are strangers in a strange land. Each of us has an intimate personal history that is known only to us. To tell it to others is not the same as experiencing the events described. How can I take you, gentle reader, through my experiences of surviving seven Middle Eastern wars? Can you understand what it means to be a stranger in your native land after decades of absence?

For Paul, the person who "imagines that he knows something" (about God) is headed in the wrong direction. Rather the one who opens his or her mind and heart to "love God" will be known by God and thereby be able to understand. Paul is again starting a discussion of love that will come to its most complete expression in chapter 13, where the reader discovers that only at the end of all things "shall I know even as I am known" (13:12 KJV).

---

[8]Lesslie Newbigin, public lecture, Crouther Hall, Selly Oak Colleges, Birmingham, England, October 1990.

Speaking for God, Amos told the people of Israel "Only you have I known of all the families of the earth" (Amos 3:2). Paul affirms, "But if one loves God, one is known by him." The term *to know* is biblical language for the marital relationship and the linking of "to love" and "to know" reaches into the heart language of intimacy. God's love is always there searching for the faithful. The act of accepting that love opens the flow of love from God to the believer. The father in the parable of the prodigal son loved his son from the beginning, but only as the son accepted *being loved* did that love become a life-changing force in the son's life (Lk 15:11-32). Paul tells his readers that the one who loves God is "known by him."

We live in an unprecedented age of information technology. In our day more knowledge is floating around in cyberspace than can be imagined by anyone. How much of it is linked to love, and how much of it is stunted and perverted by its isolation from love? Paul's readers thought they had knowledge. Some of them did not have the love that was the key to the very knowledge they sought. Section B continues this discussion.

| | |
|---|---|
| 3. ⁴Hence, as to the idol food, | KNOWLEDGE |
|     *we know* that "an idol has no real existence," | No Idols |
|       and *"there is no God but one."* | And One God |
|    ⁵For although there may be so called gods in heaven or on earth— | |
|    as indeed there are many "gods" and many "lords," | |
| | |
| 4. ⁶yet for us there is *one God, the Father,* | ONE GOD—FATHER |
|     from whom are all things | Creation |
|       and we are his; | We Are His |
|     and *one Lord, Jesus Christ,* | ONE LORD—JESUS CHRIST |
|       by his hand are all things | Creation |
|       and we are by his hand. | Through Him We Exist |

**Figure 3.1(3). Section B: Knowledge, idols and God (1 Cor 8:4-6)**

## Section B. Cameo 3

Cameo 3 begins with what the Corinthians may have written to Paul. Indeed, idols do not exist. There is no Zeus in the heavens, no Athena on the earth and no Poseidon in the sea. The four outer lines in cameo 3 form a frame around the central confession of faith: "There is no God but one." This affirmation stems from the Jewish confession of faith in Deuteronomy 6:4, which reads, "Hear, O Israel: The Lord our God is one Lord." It is also very close to the Muslim affirmation of faith: "There is no God but God." In Islam all five daily prayers repeat *sura* 117 from the Qur'an that opens "God is one."

Significantly, this prayer uses the Hebrew word for "one" (*ahad*) rather than the Arabic *wahad*. The three Abrahamic faiths are united in this affirmation. But Paul continues with some elaboration.

## SECTION B. CAMEO 4

In cameo 4a Paul presents yet another startling theological affirmation. There is one God who is named "the Father." The nature of that Father is suggested in Hosea 11 and most perfectly revealed in the parable of the prodigal son (Lk 15:11-32). No other definition is biblically legitimate.

The one God and Father has created all things, and "we are his." The Greek text of this cameo has no verb "to be." This absence of the verb "to be" in the present tense is a characteristic of Hebrew, Syriac, Aramaic and Arabic. Paul may be quoting an early Hebrew/Aramaic creedal formulation, and thereby leaves out the present tense verb "to be." Or he may have composed this affirmation of faith. We cannot know. Had the Corinthians written it, the verb "to be" would appear in the text.

With this in mind, it is important to observe how Eastern Christians across the centuries translated this Greek cameo back into Semitic languages. The translation of cameos 3-4 was made after consulting the twenty-three Syriac, Arabic and Hebrew texts selected for this study. This exercise has led to the awareness of a possible link to the Hebrew text of Psalm 95:3-5, which is displayed in figure 3.1(4).

| | |
|---|---|
| 1.a. [3]For the LORD is a great God, | THE LORD |
| b. And a great *King above all gods*. | Above All Gods |
| | |
| 2.a. [4]By *his hand* [*biyado*] are the *depths* of the *earth*;[9] | IN HIS HAND—the Earth |
| b. the heights of the *mountains are his* [*lo*] also. | The Mountains Are His (*lo*) |
| c. [5]The *sea is his* [lo], for *he made it*; | The Sea Is His (*lo*) |
| d. for *his hands* [*biyado*] formed the *dry land*. | HIS HANDS—the Land |

**Figure 3.1(4). Psalm 95:3-5**

Numerous features in this psalm are prominent in the confession of faith we are examining. In particular we can note:

1. The psalm text opens with an affirmation of the greatness and power of *Yahweh* over "all gods."
(In like manner Paul notes the "many 'gods' and many 'lords'" who are nothing

---

[9]The Hebrew "b" that appears in the text indicates agency in creation. The phrase "for he made it" strengthens this translation option.

when compared to the one God and one Lord that Paul and his readers confess.)

2. In the psalm there is a strong emphasis on creation. *Yahweh* has created the depths of the earth, the heights of the mountains, the sea and the dry land. (In the Corinthian passage Paul focuses on one God "from whom are all things" and one Lord "through/by whom are all things.")

3. In the psalm God acquires rights. All that he has created belongs to him. The Hebrew phrase for ownership is *lo* which literally reads "for him." (This precise grammatical construction "for him" [*lo*] is also used in Syriac and Arabic to indicate ownership. Furthermore in four of the Arabic versions examined, along with one of the two Hebrew versions the same *lo* "for him" appears.)

4. In the psalm the creation is the work of the "hands of God." The earth and the mountains are created "by *his hands*" and thereby belong to him. "*His hands* formed the dry ground." In the imagery of the psalm, God creates (like a craftsman) *by using his hands*.

(In twelve of the Semitic versions of the 1 Corinthians text examined, the two phrases "*through whom* are all things" and "*through whom* we exist" are translated using the Semitic "b," which is a letter attached to the fronts of words. One of its primary meanings is "instrumental," indicating "by means of."[10] In English this translates as "*by him* are all things" and "*by him* we exist." Four of the remaining texts examined intensify the sense of "by him" by translating these two lines as "*by his hands* are all things" and "we are *by his hands*." The Sinai Arabic no. 310 reads this latter phrase as "and one lord Jesus Christ who has everything *in his grip*, and we are *by him* and *in his hands*." This latter translation greatly intensifies the image of God's hands at work in creation.)

In short, from the fourth/fifth century Peshitta Syriac to the modern Hebrew Bible five oriental versions have translated the text before us as "by his hands are all things" and "we are by his hands."[11]

The four points of contact noted between Paul's language and Psalm 95:3-5 make it possible to see that Paul is using the words and images of Psalm 95:3-5 as a window to shed light on the new reality of "one God, the Father" and "one Lord Jesus Christ," who together are "one God." That one God replaces and abolishes all of the so-called gods and lords that stare down at the Corinthians every time they go to the markets in the town square. Yahweh of the psalmist is

---

[10]William Holliday, *A Concise Hebrew and Aramaic Lexicon of the Old Testament* (Grand Rapids: Eerdmans, 1971), p. 32.

[11]These include: Peshitta Syriac; Sinai Arabic 151; Sinai Arabic 310; Euripides Arabic; The Modern Hebrew. See appendix II, plate F.

the God of this creed, and he is above all so-called gods. He creates everything "by his hands" and all created things are *lo* (for him). The world is his.

Here, for the first time, Paul discusses the preexistence of Christ. When he wrote 1 Corinthians, the composition of Philippians 2:5-11 and Colossians 1:15-20 were in the future. We have noted a number of startling new beginnings in this letter. This sudden out-of-the-blue affirmation of the Lord Jesus Christ as God's agent in creation needs to be added to the list.

John understood Jesus as the *divine Word* who was from the beginning and who was God's agent in creation. John 1:3 reads, "all things were made through him." For John it was the *creative Word* that became flesh and dwelled among us (Jn 1:14). The author of Hebrews tells of a Son "through whom also he created the world" (Heb 1:2). In harmony with these references, in 1 Corinthians 8:6, the one Lord Jesus Christ is the agent of creation "by whose hand are all things." If the echoes of Psalm 95:3-5, heard and repeated in the Syriac, Arabic and Hebrew translations of the text, are taken seriously, then this early creed allows us to overhear echoes of Jesus as the *hands of God* that God used at creation to fashion the world.

The pagan citizens of a Roman colony affirmed "Caesar is Lord [*kurios*]." The fabric of social life in such a city was built on that confession. The large temple to the cult of the empire that stood in the center of the town reinforced that belief. When Paul writes, "for us there is . . . one Lord, Jesus Christ," he was quietly denying the cult of the empire. It was a courageous statement.

Section C of this homily (cameos 5-7) looks at *knowledge, God* and the *weak* [see fig. 3.1(5)].

5. [7]However, not all possess this knowledge.      KNOWLEDGE AND IDOLS
   But some, through being hitherto accustomed to idols, Weak in Conscience
   eat food as really offered to an idol;      Defiled
   and their conscience, being weak, is defiled.

6.   [8]Food will not commend us to God.
   We are no worse off if we do not eat,       GOD AND FOOD
   and no better off if we do.          The Weak—Stumble
   [9]Only take care lest this liberty of yours   Freedom and Responsibility
   becomes a stumbling-block to the weak.

7.[10]For if any one sees you, a man of knowledge,
   reclining in an idol's temple,       KNOWLEDGE AND IDOLS
   if his conscience is weak,        The Weak in Conscience
   might he not be encouraged       Freedom and Responsibility
   to eat food offered to idols?

**Figure 3.1(5). Section C: Knowledge, the weak and God (1 Cor 8:7-10)**

## SECTION C. CAMEO 5

At the beginning of this discussion (8:3) Paul called on his readers to factor love into knowledge. In cameo 5 he proceeds to apply his own principle. It was my privilege across thirty years in Egypt and Lebanon to teach future Christian leaders from the South Sudan who were often the first of their respective families to become Christian. Having a casual chat with one of my Sudanese students, one day I asked him about his father and his father's view of the world. "My father worships the red snake as a god. He keeps one in our grass-roofed one-room home," came the answer. In such a world, dealing with believers whose extended families still worshiped the red snake would take finely tuned pastoral skills. Make one wrong move and you could be killed either by the snake or by its owner.

Paul's context is easy to reconstruct. Temples served meals where the meat on offer had been sacrificed to one of the gods. Even in private homes, extended family social occasions would involve meals where the "main course" was meat offered to idols. Such meat was perhaps the only meat the family could afford. Paul presents the problem in cameo 5. What about the people who were still frightened by the ever-present temples with their statues of "the gods"? If they ate meat offered to them, were they not *ingesting the god into their very lives?* "Isn't that what happens at the celebration of the Holy Supper?" they could have asked. Or perhaps the "god" they no longer worshiped would make them sick if they ate "his meat" while refusing to worship him? The "strong" in the community were likely insisting "these gods do not exist. This meat is 'food for the stomach,' and nothing more needs to be said." But, what about the "weak"?

In cameo 3 Paul grants the validity of this argument as it was made by these "strong" believers. Idols do not exist. But here in cameo 5, as an act of love, Paul urges his readers to refrain from opening the way back to idol worship for those who do not yet *emotionally feel* what their heads are telling them. As G. G. Findlay has written, "Knowledge operating alone makes it an engine of destruction."[12]

With the passage of time, this text has produced a special kind of fallout. For example, someone whose conscience is as strong as a brick barn tries to bully the congregation of which he is a part into enforcing a particular dress code on the women of the church. Remembering this text, members of the congregation say, "Well, we must go along with him be-

---

[12]Findlay, *First Epistle*, p. 839.

cause he has a conscience on this matter and we must not offend his conscience." Paul's advice does not apply. This contemporary illustration is not a case of a *weak conscience* embedded in the heart of a new Christian who is easily lead astray. It is a case of a person with a *strong conscience* who wants to force his ethical choices on others. On the other hand there are those who walk their own path ignoring the havoc their choices will wreak in the body of Christ.

## SECTION C. CAMEO 6

In cameo 6, Paul (the ex-Pharisee) makes the remarkable statement that *God does not care what we eat*. "Food will not commend us to God," he writes. Paul was familiar with the food laws and must have kept them until he became a Christian. In the previous chapter (7:19) he told his readers that circumcision was not important. Now he (like Jesus before him [Mt 15:10-20]) jettisons the centuries of discussion and application of the food laws. Paul is thus in concurrence with a direction already set by Jesus, and what Paul writes here ties him once more to the Jesus tradition.

Paul continues, "We are no worse off if we do not eat." That is, it would have been easy for those who ate idol meat to boldly affirm, "There are no idols, so there is no problem! We the strong can eat this meat. Doing so proves the strength of our faith." Those same people would naturally have looked down on the "weak" who were not strong enough to eat this good, cheap food. No, replies Paul, the one who chooses to refrain is not worse off (i.e., weak in faith) and you who eat this meat are not better off (i.e., strong in faith). The issue has to do with love. You the "strong" can become a stumbling block for the "weak." Love must influence how you use your knowledge.

## SECTION C. CAMEO 7

In cameo 7 Paul becomes more pointed. What if one of the faithful sees *you* reclining in a pagan temple eating food offered to idols? You eat this food knowing that the idols do not exist. Someone else might fall back into idolatry by observing, and following your actions.

8. [11]And so by *your knowledge*               Your Knowledge
    this *weak* man is *destroyed*,               Weak—Destroyed
      *the brother* for whom Christ died.               The Brother
     [12]Thus, sinning against *your brethren*               Your Brothers
    and *wounding* their conscience when it is *weak*,               Weak—Wounded
*you sin against Christ.*               Your Sin—Against Christ

9. [13]Therefore, if food is a cause
    of my brother's stumbling,               MY BROTHER STUMBLES
I will never eat meat,               I Do Not Eat
    lest I cause my brother to stumble.

---

**Figure 3.1(6). Section D: Knowledge, your/my brother and Christ (1 Cor 8:11-13)**

## SECTION D. CAMEO 8

The six lines of cameo 8 are constructed using ring composition. The climax appears in the center with the affirmation of the brother as being one *for whom Christ died*. This theme was already introduced in the first essay, where Paul told his readers that through the cross we are "being saved" (1:18). His preaching of the cross was effective to "save those who believe" (1:21) and their "redemption" flowed from the cross (1:30). Later in chapter 15 Paul will quote an early Christian creed that affirms "Christ died for our sins."

In the very center of cameo 8 Paul also shifts from singular to plural. The sin against the individual is a sin against the community that is made up of "your brothers/sisters." The cutting edges of their consciences can be dulled by the exercise of loveless knowledge.

Furthermore, sin against the brother or sister is sin against Christ because the church is the body of Christ. Paul is here anticipating what he will say in chapter 12. The failure to love others in the debate over "food offered to idols" is not a little disagreement on a minor point of ethics. It is a *sin against Christ*, whose love was so great that he died to save.

## SECTION D. CAMEO 9

The conclusion of the matter (cameo 9) is that if eating the meat available in the market causes my brother or sister to stumble, I will place self-imposed limits on my actions and become a vegetarian.

Paul sets limits on his personal freedom for the sake of the gospel. If the gospel ministry requires it, he will forgo eating meat. For Paul the same self-limitation applies to accepting a salary and to marriage. To that personal vignette we now turn.

# Paul's Personal Freedom and Responsibility

1 CORINTHIANS 9:1-18

In the previous section (8:1-13) Paul presses home two points in his discussion of food offered to idols: (1) You know idols do not exist. Therefore, you have the *freedom and right* to eat idol food. (2) Your *responsibility* to love other believers may require you to set that right aside.

In this section Paul applies these two rules to his own life. He presents his case in two apostolic homilies which together form a whole. The first says, "Here are my rights/freedoms." The second says, "I have set aside those rights/freedoms for the sake of the gospel." Each homily exhibits a carefully constructed rhetorical style. The first is displayed in figure 3.2(1).

## THE RHETORIC
The two apostolic homilies mentioned above are a pair. At the same time each of them stands alone. Figure 3.2(1) is a prophetic rhetorical template of seven cameos with two additional cameos placed at the beginning as an introduction.[1] This is another case of the high jump format. There is a short run (cameos 1-2) followed by the jump (cameos 3-5). Then comes the crossing of the bar (cameo 6) and finally the descent on the far side (cameos 7-9). The homily that follows is a modification of this same high jump format.

The opening short run is a brief defense of Paul's apostleship. The seven-cameo ring composition that follows is his defense of his right (as an apostle) to receive financial support. In this first homily he introduces some

---

[1]Paul has already presented two homilies using this format (see 1 Cor 2:3-10a; 6:13-20).

1. ⁹:¹Am I not free?                                MY IDENTITY
   Am I not an apostle?
   Have I not seen Jesus our Lord?
   Are not you my workmanship in the Lord?

2. ²If to others I am not an apostle,
   at least I am to you;
   for the seal of my apostleship,
   you are, in the Lord.²

3. ³This is my defense to those who would examine me.      *MY RIGHTS*
   ⁴Do we not have *the right* to our *food and drink?*
   ⁵Do we not have the *right* to be accompanied by a believing *wife*,³
   as the *other apostles* and the brothers of the Lord and Cephas?
   ⁶Or is it only Barnabas and I who have no right to refrain from working for a living?

4.    ⁷Who serves as a *soldier* at his own expense?       SOLDIER
      Who *plants a vineyard* without getting any of its fruit?   Vinedresser
      Who *tends a flock* without getting some of the milk?   Shepherd

5.    ⁸Do I say this on human authority?
      Does not the *law* say the same?
      ⁹For it is written in the *law of Moses*,            TORAH
                                                           Of Moses

6.    "You shall *not muzzle* an *ox*                       SCRIPTURE
      when it is treading out the *grain*."                The OX

7.    Is it for oxen that *God is concerned?*
      ¹⁰Does he not speak especially for our sake?⁴         TORAH
      It was *written* for *our sake*,                     Of God

8.    for the *plowman* should plow in hope                PLOWMAN
      and the *thresher* thresh in hope of a share in the crop.   Thresher

9. ¹¹If we have sown spiritual things among you,
   is it too much if we reap your material benefits?       *MY RIGHTS*
   ¹²If others share *this rightful claim* upon you,
   Do not we still more?

**Figure 3.2(1). Paul's identity and his freedoms/rights (1 Cor 9:1-12a)**

²My translation. This is an attempt to keep the lines in the original Greek cameo intact.
³The Greek text literally reads "a sister wife." That is, a wife who is "a sister," meaning "a believer."
⁴My translation.

extraordinary features. Earlier I noted that in Isaiah 40–66 the center of a ring composition is usually filled with one of three things. These are:

(1) a parable/metaphor,
(2) a reference to an earlier sacred tradition or Scripture, and
(3) a nature miracle.

This text has no nature miracle, but Paul uses the other two types of center climaxes with great skill and presents them together *in the same homily*. This is rare and may be unique. The outer frame affirms:

3. We have the right to food, drink and a believing wife.

----------------------------------------------------------------

9. We have the right to be paid.

Inside this outer frame Paul introduces not one but five parables/metaphors. The result is seen in the following figure.

We have the right to food, drink and a believing wife.
 parable of the soldier
 parable of the vinedresser
 parable of the shepherd
 parable of the plowman
 parable of the thresher
We have the right to be paid.

**Figure 3.2(2). Five parables/metaphors (1 Cor 9:4-11)**

Paul then divides the list of parables into two halves and adds two general references to the Torah which he again divides, placing a direct Scripture quote in the very center. Summarized, the end result is seen in figure 3.2(3).

1. We have the right to food, drink and a believing wife.
2.  The parables of the *soldier*, the *vinedresser*, the *shepherd*
3.   The Torah of Moses
4.    "You shall not muzzle an ox . . ."
5.   The Torah of God
6.  The parables of the *plowman* and the *thresher*
7. We have the right to be paid.

**Figure 3.2(3). Summary of 1 Cor 9:4-11**

The idea of presenting a list of metaphors, splitting them and adding new material in the middle occurs in Isaiah 44:1-5 [see fig. 3.2(4)].

| | | |
|---|---|---|
| 3. | [1]But now hear, *O Jacob my servant*, | JACOB MY SERVANT |
| | *Israel* whom I have *chosen!* | Israel My Chosen |
| | [2]Thus says the LORD who made you, | (The Lord made you) |
| | who formed you from the womb and will help you: | |
| | Fear not, *O Jacob my servant*, | |
| | Jeshu'run whom I have *chosen*. | |
| | | |
| 4. | [3]For I will pour *water* on the *thirsty land*, | PARABLES OF |
| | and *streams* on the *dry ground;* | Water and Streams |
| | | |
| 5. | I will pour *my Spirit* upon your descendants, | MY SPIRIT |
| | and *my blessing* on your offspring. | My Blessing |
| | | |
| 6. | [4]They shall spring up *like grass amid waters*, | PARABLES OF |
| | like *willows by flowing streams*. | Water and Streams |
| | | |
| 7. | [5]This one will say, "I am the LORD's," | JACOB—YOUR NAME |
| | another will call himself by the *name of Jacob*, | Israel—Your Name |
| | and another will write on his hand, "The LORD's," | (You are the Lord's) |
| | and surname himself by the *name of Israel*. | |

**Figure 3.2(4). Isaiah 44:1-5**

References to *Jacob* and *Israel* form the outer envelope of this brief homily (cameos 1, 7). Isaiah then compiles a series of four images relating to water. These are:

- water on thirsty land
- streams on dry ground
- grass amid waters
- willows by flowing streams

Isaiah (like Paul) divides this list of four images, and places his climax in the center, which is,

5. I will pour my Spirit upon your descendants,
   And my blessing on your offspring.

Paul has this model in his literary past. The homily before us goes beyond it with the addition of a carefully designed center. The only other passage I have found that begins to compare to this text in sophistication of rhetorical design is the parable of the compassionate employer in Luke 12:37-38.[5] In this latter case the parable starts with two lines which are then repeated with

---

[5]Kenneth Bailey, *Jesus Through Middle Eastern Eyes* (Downers Grove, Ill.: IVP Academic, 2008), pp. 365-77.

a pair of extra lines added to the center. The sandwich is then completed with the addition of three new lines—again in the middle. Figure 3.2(5) shows the result.

| | |
|---|---|
| 1. [37]*Blessed* are those *slaves* | SLAVES—blessed |
| 2.　　who on *coming,* the *master finds* awake. | MASTER—comes/finds |
| 3.　　　　*Amen,* I say to you, he *will gird himself* | MASTER—prepares |
| 4.　　　　　　and cause *them to recline* [to eat], | SERVANTS—serves |
| 5.　　　　and *come to them* and *serve them.* | MASTER—serves |
| 6.　　[38]*If* (in the second or third watch),[6] he *comes* and *finds* thus, | MASTER—comes/finds |
| 7.　*blessed* are those *slaves.*[7] | SLAVE—blessed |

**Figure 3.2(5). Luke 12:37-38**

As in Luke 12:37-38 (and Is 44:1-5), here Paul builds up a layered sandwich with distinct kinds of sandwich filling. He takes five parables, two references to Torah and a Scripture quotation, and out of them creates a complex center, all of which is framed with an outer envelope on the subject of his rights. The homily thus created exhibits both encased parables, encased references to the Torah and an encased Old Testament quote. The result is a masterpiece of rhetorical art. The topic is thereby marked out by Paul as being extremely important.

## COMMENTARY

Paul begins with a spirited defense of his apostleship (cameos 1-2). The Corinthians were asserting their freedom by eating meat offered to idols and apparently attacking Paul as a man controlled by rules. "No," he answers, "I am a free man."

Furthermore, those who claimed "I am of Cephas" may have insisted that Paul was not a true apostle because he was not a witness to the resurrection. Paul here affirms that he had indeed "seen the Lord." For Paul the occasion of his witness to the resurrection was an historical event as concrete as any resurrection appearance, or perhaps as any interaction with Jesus during his earthly ministry (Acts 1:21-22).

These things are strange to us in the West. Not so in the contemporary Middle East. Over the last two decades literally thousands of Middle Easterners have had encounters with Jesus both in their dreams and during their

---

[6]The phrase in parenthesis may be a comment added to an earlier composition.
[7]My translation. I have followed the order of the phrases in the Greek text.

waking hours. Within the last year I have met two Christian leaders, one a Turk and the other a Sudanese, both of whom came to faith in Jesus through personal encounters with him. One of them was on a pilgrimage when Jesus appeared to him in the middle of the day. The other was awakened by Jesus in the night on three occasions. In the case of this second witness, two of his brothers, a sister and his mother have also been drawn to faith in Jesus through living encounters with him. These dear people, like Paul, do not have to fight through a post-Enlightenment worldview in order to accept the validity of their conversations with Jesus, who has appeared to them and called their names. They point to the spiritual journey of Paul and his initial encounter with Jesus in the middle of the day. Paul had no doubts regarding the one to whom he was talking. "Have I not seen Jesus our Lord?" he asks.

To be an apostle, witnessing the resurrection was not enough. Paul himself affirms that on one occasion more than five hundred people saw Jesus alive after the crucifixion (15:6). They were not all apostles. Paul had witnessed the resurrection, and *in addition* he had received a call from Jesus to preach the gospel. He insists that the success of his ministry in Corinth is proof of his calling as a preacher. His readers had come to faith through his "planting" of the seeds of faith. The Lord who called him had blessed his preaching ministry and to this *they were witnesses*.

Paul then presents his case for his right to receive financial assistance (cameos 3-9). Four of the parables he creates are agricultural in nature. The first on the list is a military image (cameo 4). Many of the people who settled the reconstructed city of Corinth were veterans of the Roman army. Paul could quickly catch the attention of the descendants of such residents by starting with a military illustration. The air they breathed was inevitably permeated by military history and language. Veterans, farmers, the Torah (of Moses and of God) and finally the lowly ox are all invoked by Paul to make a very strong case.

These agricultural images are in harmony with Amos's vision of "the day" of the Lord (Amos 9:14) where farmers will plant vineyards and gardens and benefit from their fruit. Paul understands the new day to have dawned (10:11), and paraphrases Amos 9:12 as he begins this epistle (1:2).

As observed, there was no doubt friction between Paul and the Corinthians because he worked with his hands. For most Jewish believers this would not have been a problem. Granted, Ben Sirach looked down on all craftsmen

and traders, but the rabbis did not.[8] The rabbis supported themselves financially, often through some trade or skill. Indeed, they were *required* to do so.
No one was allowed to "dig with the crown." The Torah was thought of as a
"golden crown" and no one was permitted to use it as "a spade" (that is, use it
to make money). The teacher of Torah could not receive any material benefit
from his students except food and housing.[9] Hillel, who lived one generation
before Jesus, is quoted as having said, "He that makes worldly use of the
crown shall perish."[10] Paul fit into that rabbinic mold. On the other hand, for
Christians with a Greek background things were different. Intellectuals were
expected to be financially independent. Only with the leisure that comes
from such independence was it possible to cultivate the mind. How could
Greeks accept the intellectual and spiritual leadership of a tentmaker? This
is not totally foreign to many modern cultures East and West. Is the local
priest/pastor respected when he insists on supporting himself as a garage
mechanic? The congregation tries to pay him and he replies, "I prefer to fix
cars!"

In the cameo about the ox (6), the RSV and NRSV translate, "Does he not
speak *entirely* (*pantos*) for our sake?" (emphasis added). This reading means
that God cares nothing about the ox. However the word *pantos* can also mean
"especially."[11] This would allow the text to mean: Yes, God cares for the ox,
but he is *especially* concerned for us.[12] From cameo 9 it is evident that the
Corinthians were supporting other traveling preachers. Paul thus had the
right to expect the same financial assistance.

Paul's readers know what is coming. In spite of his freedom (and right) to
receive financial assistance, he was not paid by the Corinthians. So why this
carefully constructed, lavishly illustrated defense of a right he has set aside?
The second homily provides the answer [see fig. 3.2(6)].

In the first of these two homilies, Paul defends his rights. Here he explains why he has not claimed them. The rhetorical structure is again
imaginative.

---

[8] *Ben Sirach* 38:24-34.

[9] Shemuel Safrai, "Education and the Study of the Torah," in *The Jewish People in the First Century* (Philadelphia: Fortress, 1976), 2:966.

[10] Mishnah, *'Abot* 1:17 (Danby, p. 447). This was repeated by R. Ishmael in *'Abot* 4:5 (Danby, p.
453).

[11] LSJ, *Greek-English Lexicon*, p. 1301.

[12] The majority of the Arabic versions of the last one thousand years have preferred this latter
translation. They often use *bil-ahray*, meaning "more specifically."

1.  ¹²ᵇNevertheless, we have *not made use of this right*,     *NOT USING MY RIGHTS*
    but we endure anything
    rather than put an obstacle in the way of the gospel of Christ.

2.       ¹³Do you not know that those who are *employed* in the *temple service*
         get their *food* from the *temple*,
         and those who *serve at the altar*              TEMPLE
         *share* in the sacrificial *offerings?*         (OT)

3.       ¹⁴In the same way, the *Lord commanded*¹³
         that those who *proclaim* the *gospel*          LORD'S COMMAND
         should get their *living* by the *gospel*.      (NT)

4.  ¹⁵But I have *not made use* of any of these *rights*,
    nor am I writing to secure such provision.       *NOT USING MY RIGHTS*

5.       For I would rather die                       GROUND FOR
         than have any one deprive me                 Boasting
         of my *ground for boasting*.

6.       ¹⁶For if I *preach the gospel*,
         that gives me *no ground for boasting*.         NECESSITY
         For *necessity* is laid upon me.
         Woe is me if I preach not the gospel!

7.            ¹⁷For if I do *this* [i.e., surrender rights]
              of my own will,                            IF OF MY WILL
              I have my reward;                          I Have—Reward

8.            but if not of my own will,
              I am entrusted with a *commission*.      COMMISSION

9.       ¹⁸*Where then* is my *ground for reward*? Just this:
              that in my preaching                    GROUND FOR
              I make the gospel free of charge,        REWARD

10.  not making *full use of my right*                *NOT USING MY RIGHTS*
     in the gospel.

---

**Figure 3.2(6). Paul's freedom to set aside his rights (1 Cor 9:12b-18)**

## THE RHETORIC

The double-decker sandwich format observed in 7:17-24 appears again here. Paul states "I am not using my rights" three times (cameos 1, 4, 10) and then introduces explanatory blocks of material between the three. As in 7:17-24, the explanatory material in the first half is in a straight-line series of two cameos. The first (cameo 2) is a reference to the Old Testament tradition,

---

¹³See Lk 10:7.

which is followed by an invocation of the Jesus tradition (cameo 3). The encased tradition is used as a literary device in both Isaiah and in 1 Corinthians. Paul used this style in the previous homily. Here he is encasing *both* an old and a *new* tradition side by side. The latter part of the double-decker sandwich uses the prophetic rhetorical template of seven inverted cameos.

## COMMENTARY

Paul makes reference both to the temple and its compensated staff, and to "the Lord's command." By placing these two references side by side in this structure, Paul presents them as equals. This is significant for any reflection on the development of the canon in the early church. Even at this early stage (A.D. 55) Paul is granting the sayings of our Lord the same level of authority he affirms for the Old Testament tradition.

The overall flow of ideas in the seven final cameos are summarized in figure 3.2(7).

4.  Not using rights (to be paid)
5.      My ground for boasting (refusing pay)
6.          No reward for duty
7.              Going beyond the call of duty has rewards
8.          No reward for duty
9.      My ground for reward (refusing pay)
10. Not using rights (to be paid)

Figure 3.2(7). Summary of 1 Cor 9:15-18

As observed previously, Paul uses the word *boasting* in a negative and in a positive sense. Negatively, boasting means bragging before God because of one's heritage or accomplishments. In Ephesians 2:8-9 Paul reminds his readers that they are saved by grace—"not because of works, lest any man should *boast*." That negative sense also appears in 1:29, where Paul insists that God chose "what is low and despised in the world, . . . so that no human being might *boast* in the presence of God" (see also 3:21; 4:7; 5:6).

By contrast, Paul uses the word *boasting* positively when he is discussing the willingness to go beyond the call of duty so that on the day of judgment the believer may be able to say, "I did more than what was required of me." Paul writes, "For what is our hope or joy or crown of *boasting* before our Lord Jesus at his coming? Is it not you?" (1 Thess 2:19). To the Philippians he talks about "Holding fast the word of life, so that in the day of Christ I may *boast* that I did not run in vain or labor in vain" (Phil 2:16). This positive meaning for boasting is what Paul is discussing.[14]

For Paul, preaching the gospel was a *necessity* (cameo 6), indeed it was a *commission* (cameo 8). It was what he *had to* do, and thereby it provided no ground for boasting and no reward. "No thanks for duty" was his assumed standard. But if Paul surrendered his rights to receive financial support from the church, he would have gone *beyond the call of duty* and thereby have established a ground for *boasting*, which in turn merited a *reward*. This positive sense of *boasting* and the topic of *reward* were closely linked in his mind, which is why they are paired in cameos 5 and 9.

The relationship of the center (cameo 7) to the outside (cameos 4 and 10) is crucial. The word *this* in cameo 7 does *not* refer to *the phrase immediately before it* but looks back to cameo 4 and ahead to cameo 10. As often happens in ring composition, the center (cameo 7) relates to the beginning (cameo 4) and to the end (cameo 10). Attempting to relate the word "this" in cameo 7 to the cameo immediately before it (cameo 6) throws the homily into confusion. Paul does *this* (i.e., surrenders his rights [cameos 4, 10]) in order to receive his reward (cameo 7). Once this feature of Paul's style is identified the passage is clear.

To put it another way, the preaching of the gospel is a "necessity" (cameo 6), it is a "commission" (cameo 8) and thus not of Paul's own will. He must do it, and when he does God owes him nothing. But sewing tents for a living is *not* a part of what he is obliged to do. It is not a "necessity" (cameo 6) or a part of his "commission" (cameo 8), therefore he can expect a reward (cameo 7).

At the same time on occasion Paul does accept financial aid, not only for the "poor in Jerusalem" but also for himself (Phil 4:14-18). Travel costs appear to be in a special category for Paul as we shall see in chapter 16. Paul's working principle seems to be: I will not accept financial assistance for serving you, but you can help me serve others. Perhaps the key phrase is the question "Am I not free?"

If Paul accepts financial assistance from the Corinthians, they will have considerable control over him. If he only accepts help in reaching out to others, they will have a much harder time telling him what to do. Paul is here not only making "the gospel free of charge" for the benefit of the Corinthians. He is also maintaining his own freedom to obey the promptings of the Spirit to go where he is called. This is one of the critical freedoms built into an authentic theology of mission.

---

[14]Boasting will appear again in Paul's discussion of love in 1 Cor 13.

Paul maintains the freedom to *choose the path of his servanthood.* Jesus did not contact the high priest and ask permission to go up to Jerusalem to die for the sins of the world. If he had asked, the answer would have been "No!" In like manner Paul did not allow the Corinthians to control the direction of his mission to the Gentiles. "Am I not free?" he asks at the beginning of this two-homily discussion. Having established the fact of his freedom, he discusses how that freedom plays out in his ministry. To that discussion we now turn.

# Freedom in Mission

## *Full Identification*

I CORINTHIANS 9:19-27

PAUL HAS NOW COME TO the center of his third essay, which is on the subject of how a Christian can live in a pagan society. "Freedom and responsibility" continue to be the overall focus. The outline of the essay as a whole is as follows:

1. Food Offered to Idols: Freedom and Responsibility (8:1-13)
2. Paul's Personal Freedom and Responsibility (9:1-18)
3. *Freedom in Mission: Full Identification (9:19-27)*
4. Old Covenant Sacraments and Idolatry: Partial Identification (10:1-13)
5. New Covenant Sacraments and Idolatry: No Identification (10:14-22)
6. Food Offered to Idols: Freedom and Responsibility (A Final Word) (10:23–11:1)

The homily before us (italicized above) is the first of three that form the center of this essay. The question Christians in every age must ask is: How far should we go in identifying with the culture around us? Paul replies: The question of food offered to idols is important but it can be solved relatively easily. The answer is, "Sometimes yes and sometimes no, depending on how much you know and who is watching. But the issue touches on deep theological concerns that merit discussion."

Looking at the big picture of a Christian in a non-Christian world, Paul offers three options.

- Total identification    (all things to all people)    [consider OT and NT law]
- Partial identification    (some things to some people)    [consider OT sacraments]
- No identification    (nothing to anybody)    [consider NT sacraments]

It is easy to look at one of these homilies and overlook the other two. The phrase "all things to all people" is often quoted in isolation, but in this text it is part of a trilogy. Each of the three patterns noted requires careful reflection. Paul opens with a discussion of "total identification."

As a new Christian community the Corinthians were swimming in a pagan world. "By Jove" as an oath survived in the English language for more than a thousand years after Jove died. A favorite team wins a football game and the people "thank their lucky stars." The language is pure paganism. If these traces of the gods have survived into the modern age, what was it like to live the Christian life surrounded by active self-conscious paganism? To the extent that postmodern secularism has recreated paganism, this problem is also our problem. The first of the three options is "total identification"—that is, almost total [see fig. 3.3(1)].

## THE RHETORIC

Two topics present themselves in this homily: *cultural identification* with others (seen in the light of the law [Torah]), and the need for *discipline*. They are related. In cameos 1-6 Paul enunciates a radical call for *identification*. Then in cameos 7-12 he discusses the tremendous energy such identification requires. The discipline demanded, argues Paul, is like that of a runner and a boxer. These parables from the world of athletics appear in the second section (cameos 7-12).

As in the previous text, Paul again uses ring composition (in each half), only in this case he composes with six cameos rather than seven.

The first half of the homily climaxes in the center (cameos 3-4) where there is a discussion of the law. We also notice that the six cameos are composed of two matching sets of ten lines (with one extra line). The double use of ten lines is most likely an allusion to the Decalogue. The phrase "but under the law of Christ" is outside of these ten pairs of lines, and has no match. It may be a "footnote" added by Paul to correct a possible misunderstanding of the text.[1]

In the first half (cameos 1-6) Paul engages in counterpoint. If the reader focuses on the *six cameos*, it is at once clear that they interrelate using the inverted parallelism of ring composition. But at the same time, much like

---

[1] In our discussion of 1 Cor 1:17–2:2 we noted "extra material" that was most likely added after the original hymn was composed. It is possible that the same is true here.

1.   [19]For though I am *free from all* people,[2]
     I have made myself a *slave to all*,                ALL PEOPLE
     that I might *win* the *more*.

2.        [20]I became *to the Jews*
          as a *Jew*,                                     JEW
          that I might *win Jews*;

3.             to *those under the law*
               I became as *one under the* law—          LAW
               though *not being* myself *under the law*—  (Jew)
               that I might win *those under the law*.

4.        [21]To *those outside the law*
          I became as *one outside the law*—
          *not being without* the *law of God*            NO LAW
          (but under the law of Christ)                   (Gentile)
          that I might *win those outside the law*.

5.        [22]I became *to the weak*
          as one *weak*,                                  WEAK
          that I might *win the weak*.                     (Gentile)

6.   To *all people*
     *I have become all* things,                          ALL PEOPLE
     that I might by all means *save some*.

- - - - - - - - - - - - - - - - - - - - - - - - - - - - - - - - - - - - - - - - -

7.   [23]I do it all for the sake of the *gospel*,        THE GOSPEL
     that a *partner of it* I may become.[3]              Become A Partner (Teammate?)

8.        [24]Do you not know that in a race all the *runners* compete,   PARABLE OF
          but only one receives the prize?                The Runner
          So run that you may obtain it.

9.             [25]Every athlete exercises self-control   DISCIPLINE
               in all things.

10.            They do it to receive a perishable wreath, THE PRIZE
               but we an imperishable.

11.       [26]Hence, *I do not run aimlessly*,            PARABLES OF
          I do not *box as one beating the air;*          The Runner
          [27]but I pommel my body and subdue it,         The Boxer

12.  lest after *preaching* to others                    PREACHING
     I myself should be *disqualified*.                   Not Disqualified

**Figure 3.3(1). All things to all people (1 Cor 9:19-27)**

---

[2]Here and in cameo 12 the Greek text reads "men."
[3]My literal translation of the Greek.

Isaiah 28:14-18, each pair of cameos exhibits step parallelism.[4] That is, the three lines in 1a, b, c, match the three lines in 6a, b, c and so forth. Ring composition and step parallelism are like two tunes being played at the same time. The learned Jewish reader/listener would hear both of them.

## COMMENTARY

I have heard speakers and read scholarly essays where the speaker/writer says something like, "We all know that Paul said, 'To the Jews I became a Jew and to the Gentiles I became a Gentile.'" The difficulty is that Paul never made such a claim. The structure of the text expects that he say this, but he does not do so. Reduced to its briefest outline the six cameos are as follows:

1. I became a slave to all people.
2.    I became a *Jew.*
3.       For Jews I lived under the Torah.
4.       For Gentiles I lived outside the Torah.
5.    I became *weak.*
6. I became all things to all people.

In cameos 1 and 6 Paul talks about identifying with "all people." In the middle (cameos 3, 4) he talks about living like a Jew (for Jews) and living like a Gentile (for Gentiles). Each cameo has its match! This is a ring-composition homily. The reader fully expects cameos 2 and 5 to also be a pair. In cameo 2 Paul says "I became a Jew," thus the readers anticipates "I became a Gentile" in cameo 5. But to our surprise—the pattern is broken. Paul does not write, "To the Gentiles, I became a Gentile." Why not? The answer is simple—he is a Jew, *he cannot become a Gentile!* Even in the homily where he is specifically saying "To all people I have become all things," he affirms limits.

After spending forty-seven years in the Arab world, and after acquiring the ability to lecture in four kinds of Arabic, I never said to my Arabic-speaking friends, "We Arabs." Knowing where that un-crossable line is drawn is a critical piece of acquired awareness. As regards *lifestyle* Paul can live as "one under the Torah" (cameo 3), and he can live as "one not under the Torah" (cameo 4). But in regard to his *identity*, he knows that *he cannot become a Gentile,* and he plays no games with his readers. Only when we are deeply rooted in our own culture can we risk reaching out across a cultural chasm to people on the other

---

[4]See the above prelude, "Prophetic Homily Rhetorical Style and Its Interpretation," figure 0.4, p. 34.

side. A bridge must be securely anchored at each end. Only then can the bridge be completed and only then is travel across that bridge possible.

Paul will do *whatever he can* to cross cultural lines in the name of Christ. He will even make himself a slave. But he is realistic about his limits. Each matching pair of cameos is worthy of brief reflection.

### CAMEOS 1 AND 6

Paul is "free from all people" (cameo 1). By working as a tentmaker he finances himself. In rejecting patronage he assures that no one controls the direction or focus of his ministry. At the same time, in order to "win the more" he is willing to become a *slave to all*. Enormous skill is required to maintain that delicate balancing act between freedom and slavery. He wants by all means to save some (cameo 6) and he will strive mightily to achieve that goal.

### CAMEOS 2 AND 5

In cameo 2 Paul declares his method with his fellow Jews. He becomes a Jew. In the synagogue and in the Jerusalem temple he openly and sincerely presented himself as a faithful Jew. In the matching stanza (cameo 5) Paul does not claim to have become a Gentile, but says, "I became to the weak as one weak."

Leaders usually want to appear strong. They are often willing to serve the weak, as long as they are seen by the public as strong. From a position of strength they will reach out to those in need. In contrast Paul deliberately *becomes weak* to "win the weak." His mission from below informs everything he does. As a Roman citizen he could have claimed status and privilege. A profound theology of mission is affirmed in these simple words.

The incarnation itself was an act of "becoming as one weak." Paul explores the incarnation with his famous words about Jesus, "who, though he was in the form of God, did not count equality with God a thing to be grasped, but emptied himself, taking the form of a slave" (Phil 2:6). In John's Gospel, at a well in Samaria, Jesus emptied himself to the extent that he needed the help of a simple, immoral, foreign woman (Jn 4:7). As he sent his disciples out two by two, he carefully instructed them to travel with almost nothing. They were to take "no staff, nor bag, nor bread, nor money" (Lk 9:3). In short, they were to go in weakness and poverty, and to travel *in need of those they sought to serve.* Following his Lord, Paul went to the world in great weakness, which he describes dramatically in 2 Corinthians 11:23-29. That catalog of powerlessness ends with "Who is weak, and I am not weak? Who is made to fall, and I am not on fire with indignation?" (*puromai*).[5]

Earlier in this essay Paul affirmed his compassion for "the weak" over against "the strong" (8:7-13). In the next essay we will see him defending the hungry and humiliated who "have nothing" (11:21-22).

D. T. Niles of Sri Lanka wrote, "To serve from a position of power is not true service but beneficence." He continues:

> One of the features of the life of the Christian community in the lands of Asia is the number of institutions of service which belong to this community. We run schools, hospitals, orphanages, agricultural farms, etc. But what we do not adequately realize is that these institutions are not only avenues of Christian service but are also sources of secular strength. Because of them, we can offer patronage, control employment, and sometimes make money. The result is that the rest of the community learn to look on the Church with jealousy, sometimes with fear, and sometimes even with suspicion. . . . The only way to build love between two people or two groups of people is to be so related to each other as to stand in need of each other. The Christian community must serve. It must also be in a position where it needs to be served.[6]

Paul understood that the only way to "win the weak" was to join them in their weakness. Easter evening Jesus tells the disciples, "As the Father has sent me, even so I send you" (Jn 20:21).

In this connection Paul's style of mission was in harmony with the message he preached. He was proclaiming the God who entered history beginning with a lowly birth and ending on a cross (1:17–2:2). The world judged such events to be foolishness and weakness. Paul's missional approach in every place was to reflect that worldly weakness. The pattern put in place by Constantine was for the Christian empire to conquer territory and then citizens of the empire could proclaim the gospel to the defeated peoples. The army comes in overpowering strength and in its shadow preachers proclaim the gospel of the one who came in total weakness. Paul's theology of mission had no place for such a pattern.[7] With his team of evangelists he moved among the people ill-clad, buffeted and homeless (4:11). His message and his missional approach were harmonious.

---

[5]My translation. See also 2 Cor 4:7-11; 6:3-10.
[6]D. T. Niles, *This Jesus . . . Whereof We Are Witnesses* (Philadelphia: Westminster Press, 1965), pp. 24-25.
[7]This pattern repeats with Charlemagne and with the Spanish conquistadores.

## CAMEOS 3 AND 4

While among the Jews, Paul kept the regulations of the Torah (cameo 3). He became "as those under the Torah" in order to "win those under the Torah." The four lines in cameo 3 are parallel to four of the lines in cameo 4. To those "outside of the Torah" (read "Gentiles") Paul becomes *as* "one outside the Torah." Is Paul therefore living in an antinomian world where anything goes? Certainly not. There is a fifth line in cameo 4. Paul is "under the law of Christ." The "mind of Christ" guides him (2:16).

In the following two homilies Paul will discuss Old Testament *and* New Testament sacraments. In like manner, here he refers to the "Torah" *and* "the law of Christ." The "law of Christ" is parallel with "the Torah." Paul is thereby again affirming the authority of the Jesus tradition and placing it on the same level with the Torah of Moses.

In spite of the limitations of his Jewish birth, culture, language and race, Paul strains mightily to cross cultural barriers that he might by all means "save some." A great deal is required, and a great deal is at stake in this process. This brings us to the second half of this homily [see fig. 3.3(2)].

7. ²³I do it all for the sake of the *gospel*,
   that a *partner of it* I may become.
   
   THE GOSPEL
   Become a Partner (Teammate?)

8. ²⁴Do you not know that in a race all the *runners* compete,
   but only one receives the prize?
   So run that you may obtain it.
   
   PARABLE OF
   The Runner

9. ²⁵Every athlete exercises self-control
   in all things.
   
   DISCIPLINE

10. They do it to receive a perishable wreath,
    but we an imperishable.
    
    THE PRIZE

11. ²⁶Hence, *I do not run aimlessly*,
    I do not *box as one beating the air;*
    ²⁷but I pommel my body and subdue it,
    
    PARABLES OF
    The Runner
    The Boxer

12. lest after *preaching* to others
    I myself should be *disqualified.*
    
    PREACHING
    Not Disqualified

Figure 3.3(2). Teamwork, discipline and the prize (1 Cor 9:23-27)

## THE RHETORIC

Paul presents his ideas using six inverted cameos. As in the previous homily, he invokes more than a single metaphor. Here he mentions "runners" and "boxers." The runner appears twice. As always in ring composition, the climax is in the center. In this case the center includes a summary (cameo 9) and a conclusion (cameo 10).

This is a clear case of where Paul's ring composition is confusing to modern readers. We anticipate example one, then example two, and at the end—a conclusion. That is, we expect:

| First Parable: (Runner) | [24]Do you not know that in a race all the *runners* compete, but only one receives the prize? So run that you may obtain it. [26]Hence, *I do not run aimlessly.* |
|---|---|
| Second Parable: (Boxer) | I do not *box as one beating the air*; [27]but I pommel my body and subdue it. |
| Conclusion: | [25](Indeed) every athlete exercises self-control in all things. They do it to receive a perishable wreath, but we an imperishable. |

Such an order of presentation has a niche in the back of our minds. But Paul confuses the modern mind by placing his climax in the center and then adding to it a second parable.

## COMMENTARY

The Isthmian Games were held in Corinth every two years. Spectators and athletes were housed in tents. Paul and his tent-making colleagues Priscilla and Aquila could easily find customers in the city of Corinth. Furthermore, the town was inevitably full of sports enthusiasts. In the previous homily, Paul utilized the military world of the soldier and his pay to make his point (9:7). In a sports crazy environment Paul turned to the world of athletics to find metaphors that could communicate his message.

The outside pair of cameos (7, 12) are displayed in figure 3.3(3).

| 7. | [23]I do it all for the sake of the *gospel*, that a *partner of it* I may become. | THE GOSPEL Become a Partner (Teammate?) |
|---|---|---|
| 12. | [27b]lest after *preaching* to others I myself should be *disqualified.* | PREACHING Not Disqualified |

Figure 3.3(3). Cameos 7 and 12 (1 Cor 9:23, 27b)

The RSV translates the second line in cameo 7 as "that I may share in its blessings." The word *blessing* does not appear in the Greek text, which I have translated literally.[8] Paul does not argue that he "must become all things to all people" so that the gospel *can receive a hearing and be accepted*. For him, God, through the gospel, was already at work across cultural lines and he wanted to become *its partner*. The gospel train was moving and he could jump on or get left behind. This wonderful language describes a gospel out of control that has its own energy and is on the move. No one can chain it down (2 Tim 2:9).

That same sense of wonder and excitement is currently felt by people all over the world as they observe the continuing rapid expansion of the gospel in Asia, Africa and South America. We, like Paul, have two choices: Join that movement or be left behind by it.

The key word *partner* (*sugkoinonos*) is a general expression that refers to a variety of relationships including that of a business partner.[9] In light of the fact that this text is permeated with sports images, it may be that there are overtones of the word "teammate." This is reinforced by the matching stanza (cameo 12), which talks about being "disqualified." Paul wants to remain a part of the team and not be disqualified from it. If he can't keep up, he will be dropped. Each of the two lines in these two cameos match as follows:

7.   a. For the sake of *the gospel*
        b. becoming a *"teammate"* (*sug-koinonos*) "a joint-partner"

12.  a. *Preaching (the gospel) to others*
        b. not being *disqualified (from the team)*

The second pair of cameos is 8 and 11 [see fig. 3.3(4)].

| | | |
|---|---|---|
| 8. | [9:24]Do you not know that in a race all the *runners* compete, but only one receives the prize? So run that you may obtain it. | PARABLE OF<br>The Runner |
| | - - - - - - - - - - - - - - - - - - - - - - - - - - - - - - - - - | |
| 11. | [26]Hence, *I do not run aimlessly*, I do not *box as one beating the air*; [27]but I pommel my body and subdue it, | PARABLES OF<br>The Runner<br>The Boxer |

**Figure 3.3(4). Cameos 8 and 11 (1 Cor 9:24, 26-27a)**

---

[8]See the Arabic and Syriac versions.
[9]BAGD, p. 774.

In our day the entire world is aware of the intense discipline required for
Olympic athletes. With the Isthmian Games sponsored by the city of Corinth,
the citizens of that city could not help being fully aware of the time commitments and energy required to compete in those games.[10] Paul builds on that
awareness and tells his readers that the same level of discipline is required to
cross cultural lines in the name of Christ. He does "jog" but not "aimlessly."
He is constantly in training and has a goal like the professional competitors in
the games.

Paul's use of the image of boxing is significant. He does not box an enemy.
Nor does he box the air. He boxes himself. If he fails to do this, he risks being
thrown off of the team (being disqualified). This language was used in later
centuries to justify extreme asceticism. Those who sought a higher level of
spiritual life were expected to "beat their bodies" in order to achieve that
goal.[11] But this text is the second half of a single topic. Paul is not talking
about ascetic disciplines, he is discussing the high commitment required if
one is to successfully cross cultural barriers in the name of Christ. He is discussing *mission*! Gulian Lansing, a Presbyterian missionary to Egypt, wrote in
1864, "I would rather transverse Africa from Cairo to the Cape of Good
Hope, than undertake a second time to master the Arabic language."[12]

The Corinthian correspondence is particularly full of Paul's descriptions of
his suffering. In 2 Corinthians 4:7-12 he informs his readers, "We are afflicted in every way, but not crushed; perplexed, but not driven to despair;
persecuted, but not forsaken; struck down, but not destroyed." In 2 Corinthians 6:3-10 he speaks of being, "in afflictions, hardships, calamities, beatings,
imprisonments, tumults, labors, watching, hunger." Finally, in 2 Corinthians
11:23-29 he records, "Five times I have received at the hands of the Jews the
forty lashes less one. Three times I have been beaten with rods; once I was
stoned. Three times I have been shipwrecked; a night and a day I have been
adrift at sea." What level of discipline is required to endure four beatings of
thirty-nine lashes on the back for preaching Christ and then continue preaching, knowing that your next sermon may result in a fifth beating? In this
epistle he wrote, "I worked harder than any of them" (15:10), and to the Colossians he says, "I toil, striving with all the energy which he mightily inspires
within me" (Col 1:29).

---

[10]For original texts on the Isthmian games see Jerome Murphy-O'Connor, *St. Paul's Corinth:
Texts and Archaeology* (Collegeville, Minn.: Liturgical Press, 2002), pp. 12-15, 100, 104-5.
[11]Thiselton, *First Epistle*, p. 712.
[12]Gulian Lansing, *Egypt's Princes* (Philadelphia: William S. Rentoul, 1865), p. 8.

Paul was a student of Gamaliel in Jerusalem and may have been raised there. In Acts 22:3 Paul affirms that he was "brought up (*anatethrammenos*) in this city at the feet of Gamaliel." This same word (*anatrepho*) describes Moses as being "brought up" by Pharaoh's daughter (Acts 7:21). F. F. Bruce writes, "He would have entered the school of Gamaliel at some point in his 'teens, but his parents saw to it that even his earlier boyhood was spent under wholesome influences in Jerusalem."[13]

If Paul grew up in Jerusalem as a conservative Jew, where did he learn his Greek? We have no definitive answer. Bornkamm has suggested that Paul "decided to become a Jewish missionary to the Gentiles along the lines taken by Jewish orthodoxy, and had launched his Jewish mission before becoming a Christian."[14] To do this he would naturally have been obliged to learn more Greek than was necessary to live in Jerusalem. Another option is to note that after his conversion and his trip to Jerusalem, he went "into the regions of Syria and Cilicia" (Gal 1:21). He stayed there for ten years or more. Did he take up a serious study of Greek at that time? We do not know. Aramaic and Hebrew would have been his native languages, and fluency in oral and written Greek would have required great personal discipline. All his life, in one way or another, Paul had to "beat his body" in order to cross cultural lines and fulfill his calling as an apostle to the Gentiles. He warns his readers that the task of "all things to all people" takes enormous energy. He is discussing the cost of *crosscultural, incarnational mission*. As they prepared for the Isthmian Games, athletes in Corinth submitted their bodies to intense discipline. Paul "pummeled his body" in order to be a faithful witness to the gospel.

Paul's climax appears in the center where he writes:

9.      25Every athlete exercises self-control          DISCIPLINE
        in all things.

10.     They do it to receive a perishable wreath,      THE PRIZE
        but we an imperishable.

Having spent forty years of my life trying to cross cultural lines into the world of the "forgotten faithful" who are the millions of Arabic-speaking Christians of the Middle East, I can witness to the profound truth of what Paul is affirming. Language, culture, history, art, literature, politics, world-view, music, civil unrest and war—all must be experienced, comprehended

[13]F. F. Bruce, *Paul: Apostle of the Heart Set Free* (Grand Rapids: Eerdmans, 1977), p. 43.
[14]Günther Bornkamm, *Paul* (New York: Harper & Row, 1971), p. 12.

and embraced if one is to effectively enter into another culture.

Short bursts of exertion are not enough. Self-control in all things is required. The athlete at the Isthmian Games received the reward of a crown of pine (or celery). No gold medals were available! How long would the pine or celery last? Plutarch discussed this matter when he wrote,

> The noble man holds his hardships to be his greatest antagonist, and with them he is ever wont to battle day and night, not to win a sprig of celery, as so many goats might do, nor for a bit of wild olive or of pine, but to win happiness and virtue throughout all the days of his life.[15]

Paul's goals reached out beyond this life. He was after an imperishable crown. Furthermore he was not focused on "happiness and virtue" for himself. His goal was to "spread the fragrance of the knowledge of him (Christ) everywhere" (2 Cor 2:14). Following New Testament usage, Paul is here best understood as talking about *a crown of righteousness*, a *crown of glory* or a *crown of life*.[16]

So much for "all things to all people." Paul is ready to discuss "some things to some people."

---

[15]Plutarch, quoted in Murphy-O'Connor, *St. Paul's Corinth*, p. 101.
[16]Thiselton, *First Epistle*, p. 714.

# Old Covenant Sacraments and Idolatry

*Partial Identification*

I CORINTHIANS 10:1-13

$P$AUL'S NEXT HOMILY is displayed in figure 3.4(1).

In the previous homily he affirmed the need for Christians to identify fully with the world around them. They were to be "all things to all people," and through the use of metaphors from the world of sports Paul challenged his readers to commit the energy and accept the discipline required for such identification.

In this homily he discusses problems created by that identification. One can identify with other cultures in regard to food, clothing, music, patterns of social interaction and the like. Such points of identification are relatively easy. The crux of the matter comes when one considers the *sacraments* of others. Throughout 1 Corinthians the issues related to Jew and Greek are either at the center of the discussion or awaiting attention at its edges. What about Jewish and Greek sacraments?

Knowing that the two are different, Paul dedicates a full homily to each. The homily under discussion in this chapter looks at sacraments from the Jewish past. We will look first at the rhetoric of the homily and then at its theological and ethical content.

## THE RHETORIC

The rhetorical form of this homily is a favorite for Paul. It consists of a number of cameos in a straight-line sequence that form an introduction followed by finely crafted ring composition, often composed of seven cameos. With

0.   10:1I want you to know, brethren,

1.      that *our fathers* were all under the *cloud*,                    BAPTISM
            and all *passed through the sea*,
         2and all were *baptized* into *Moses* in the *cloud*
            and *in the sea*,

2.      3and all ate the same *spiritual food*                           EUCHARIST
         4and all drank the same *spiritual drink*.
         For they drank from the *spiritual Rock* which followed them,
            and the *Rock* was *Christ*.

3.      5Yet with most of them *God was not pleased;*                   THEY WERE
         for they were *overthrown* in the wilderness.                   Overthrown

4.       6Now these things are *warnings for us*,                        WARNING
            not to desire *evil as they did*.                            For Us

5.          7Do not be *idolaters* as some of them were;
               as it is written,
               "The people sat down to eat and drink                    IDOLATRY
               and rose up to play."

6.          8We must not indulge in *immorality*
               as some of them did,                                     IMMORALITY
               and twenty-three thousand fell in a single day.

7.          9We must not put the *Lord to the test*,
               as some of them did                                      TESTING GOD
               and were destroyed by serpents;

8.          10nor *grumble*
               as some of them did,                                     GRUMBLING
               and were destroyed by the Destroyer.

9.       11Now these things happened *to them as a warning*,            INSTRUCTION
            but they were written down *for our instruction*,           For Us
            upon whom the end of the ages has come.

10.  12Therefore let any one who thinks that he stands       ANY ONE TAKE HEED
         take heed lest he fall.                                        Lest He Fall

-----------------------------

11. 13(*No temptation* has overtaken you that is not common to man. God is faithful, and he will
not let you be *tempted beyond your strength*, but with the *temptation* will also provide the way of
escape, that you may be able to *endure* it.)

**Figure 3.4(1). Old covenant sacraments and idolatry: Partial identification (1 Cor 10:1-13)**

freedom for modification Paul uses this particular form nine times.[1] This is another instance of the *high jump format*. The jumper begins with a quick sprint, then comes the jump, followed by the climax (the passage over the bar) and finally the completion of the jump in the descent on the far side. Often Paul's rhetorical high jumps are composed of a two-cameo opening approach followed by a seven-cameo jump over the bar that we have called the prophetic rhetorical template. The homilies comprising 9:1-12a and 9:12b-18 (just examined) are prime examples of this style. The homily now under study [see fig. 3.4(1)] follows the high jump style, but with variations.

In the two introductory cameos Paul turns to the story of the exodus, where he discovers theological roots for Christian baptism and the Lord's Supper. The center of the ring composition that follows is expanded to include four ethical issues that erupted in the story of the exodus. That four-cameo center is then encased by a pair of cameos that have to do with warning and instruction. A second outer envelope speaks of being "overthrown" and "falling." A pastoral aside appears at the end of the homily as a kind of footnote.

### COMMENTARY

The text of the introduction is displayed in figure 3.4(2).

0.  [10:1]I want you to know, brethren,

1.  that *our fathers* were all under the *cloud*,        BAPTISM
    and all *passed through the sea*,
    [2]and all were *baptized* into *Moses* in the *cloud*
    and *in the sea*,

2.  [3]and all ate the same *spiritual food*        EUCHARIST
    [4]and all drank the same *spiritual drink*.
    For they drank from the *spiritual Rock* which followed them,
    and the *Rock* was *Christ*.

---

**Figure 3.4(2). Cameos 1-2 (1 Cor 10:1-4)**

This homily is addressed to the "brethren," which represents all believers, male and female, regardless of their ethnic background. Paul does not say, "Those of you with a Hebrew background can look back to their fathers who were all under the cloud." Instead he writes about "our fathers." Is Paul forgetting that many of his readers do not have a Hebrew heritage? Surely not.

---

[1] 1 Cor 2:3-10a; 6:13-20; 9:1-12a; 12b-18; 11:2-16; 13:1–14:1 (with significant modification); 14:13-25; 15:21-28; 15:35-50 (with modification).

Such insensitivity would have been deeply insulting to his readers. I know of
one case in the Middle East where an expatriot Anglican congregation was
made up of Christians from a dozen nations. Perhaps 20 percent of them
were English. Yet on the English "Memorial Day" the English vicar covered
the altar with a Union Jack as is sometimes done in an Anglican cathedral in
England. Non-English members of the congregation were highly offended.
Is Paul making the same mistake? Up to this point in the letter he has shown
sensitivity to the differences between Jews and Greeks. How can he use such
language in a letter for all Christians to read? Clearly, for Paul the Greeks
were still Greeks with their own language, history and culture, yet as they
joined the body of Christ they were transformed into building blocks for a
new temple. As this happened they became descendants of Abraham and
members of the household of God. As such they could rightly think of Old
Testament history as *their history*, the story of the exodus as *their story* and the
people involved in it as *their fathers*. This self-understanding on the part of
Paul's readers was apparently so widely appropriated that Paul did not need
to explain it or defend it. Everyone understood that those who crossed
through the Red Sea were the fathers (and mothers) of all believers. Built on
this shared identity, Paul proceeds to reflect on sacraments old and new.

Were Christian baptism and the Lord's Supper brand-new rituals created
by Jesus and the apostles, and administered by Paul and his friends? Or did
these sacraments have deep roots in the sacred (Hebrew) traditions of the
past, and did all believers share those roots? Paul found such roots both for
baptism and for the Lord's Supper. The faithful who experienced the exodus
were in the *cloud* and in the *sea*. That was their *baptism*. They ate divinely
provided food and drank the water of life that flowed out of *the rock*. By means
of allegory, Paul identifies the rock as *foreshadowing Christ*. Paul is, in effect,
saying to his readers,

> The gospel that I preach is in continuity with the identity-forming experiences
> of the faithful during the exodus. The Jewish believer and the Gentile who
> joins the "Israel of God" can see the sacrament of baptism and the celebration
> of the Lord's Supper as more perfect expressions of what the faithful have al-
> ready known and experienced for centuries.[2]

Paul is finding ways to "baptize their memories into Christ." As noted,

---

[2]In our day, some Christian thinkers are struggling with the possibility of finding links between
the gospel and the sacred past of Islam.

Andrew Walls has used this language to describe the crucial task in any age that is before every ethnic community that comes newly into the Christian faith.[3]

But were these sacraments in themselves enough? The pivotal issue became, How did the Hebrew people *respond* to those great saving events? In the eight inverted cameos that follow, Paul makes clear that their ethical responses were inadequate and indeed angered God [see fig. 3.4(3)].

| | | |
|---|---|---|
| 3. | [5]Yet with most of them *God was not pleased;* <br> for they were *overthrown* in the wilderness. | THEY WERE <br> Overthrown |
| 4. | [6]Now these things are *warnings for us,* <br> not to desire *evil as they did.* | WARNING <br> For Us |
| 5. | [7]Do not be *idolaters* as some of them were; <br> as it is written, <br> "The people sat down to eat and drink <br> and rose up to play." | IDOLATRY |
| 6. | [8]We must not indulge in *immorality* <br> as some of them did, <br> and twenty-three thousand fell in a single day. | IMMORALITY |
| 7. | [9]We must not put the *Lord to the test,* <br> as some of them did <br> and were destroyed by serpents; | TESTING GOD |
| 8. | [10]nor *grumble* <br> as some of them did, <br> and were destroyed by the Destroyer. | GRUMBLING |
| 9. | [11]Now these things happened *to them as a warning,* <br> but they were written down *for our instruction,* <br> upon whom the end of the ages has come. | INSTRUCTION <br> For Us |
| 10. | [12]Therefore let any one who thinks that he stands <br> take heed lest he fall. | ANY ONE TAKE HEED <br> Lest He Fall |

**Figure 3.4(3). Cameos 3-10 (1 Cor 10:5-12)**

The "outer envelope" of this series of eight inverted cameos says:

| | | |
|---|---|---|
| 3. | [5]Yet with most of them *God was not pleased;* <br> for they were *overthrown* in the wilderness. | THEY WERE <br> Overthrown |
| 10. | [12]Therefore let any one who thinks that he stands <br> take heed lest *he fall.* | ANY ONE TAKE HEED <br> Lest He Fall |

[3]From a lecture delivered in my hearing by Professor Walls at the Overseas Ministries Study Center in New Haven, Connecticut, October 2009.

Participation in these great sacramental events was not enough to please God. The Hebrews were "overthrown" (passive). God overthrew them. In the balancing cameo (10) Paul warns his readers that the one who *thinks* that he *stands* must "take heed lest *he fall*" (active). God *overthrows*, and *they fall*. This same balancing of the active and passive occurred twice in 1:17–2:2.

Why were the Hebrews overthrown? The answer begins to evolve in the second pair of balanced cameos (4, 9).

| | | |
|---|---|---|
| 4. | [6]Now these things are *warnings for us*, <br> not to desire *evil as they did.* | WARNING <br> For Us |
| 9. | [11]Now these things happened *to them as a warning*, <br> but they were written down *for our instruction*, <br> upon whom the end of the ages has come. | INSTRUCTION <br> For Us |

**Figure 3.4(4). Cameos 4 and 9 (1 Cor 10:6, 11)**

Paul argues that God overthrew the Hebrews in the wilderness as a *warning for them*, and the event was recorded in a text as *instruction for us*, upon whom "the end of the ages has come." Islam brings these two concerns together and teaches that the task of Muhammad, the prophet of Islam, was to provide guidance and warning. For Islam God is unknown, and the Qur'an reveals the *will* of God (guidance), not his *nature*. In addition, the Qur'an provides *warnings* that if God's will is not obeyed, there will be serious consequences. In contrast, Paul does not point to a divine law but rather to God's *rescue in history* through the sea and to his gifts in the wilderness. He then notes the inappropriate responses of the people to those gifts of grace. This is exactly where Paul finds the Corinthians. They too have received much grace but their responses have been inadequate.

The climax of the homily is: Why was God "not pleased"? The answer appears in the four-cameo center (5-8) of the ring composition [see fig. 3.4(5)].

The four ethical issues that Paul chose from the story of the Exodus are significant. All four of them were problems in Corinth. Paul's list was not simply a catalog of the sins of ancient Israel; they were also Corinthian moral lapses. These were:

*1. Idolatry.* Paul quotes Exodus 32:6, where the people fashioned a golden calf and offered burned offerings to it. They created an idol and worshiped it. They then "sat down to eat and drink and rose up to play." The Hebrew word "play" (*tsakheq*) often has erotic implications. In Genesis 26:8 Abimelech, king of the Philistines, saw "Isaac fondling (*mitsakheq*) Rebekah his

| | | |
|---|---|---|
| 5. | [7]Do not be *idolaters*<br>as some of them were; as it is written,<br>"The people sat down to eat and drink<br>and rose up to play." | IDOLATRY |
| 6. | [8]We must not indulge in *immorality*<br>as some of them did,<br>and twenty-three thousand fell in a single day. | IMMORALITY |
| 7. | [9]We must not put the *Lord to the test*,<br>as some of them did<br>and were destroyed by serpents; | TESTING GOD |
| 8. | [10]nor *grumble*<br>as some of them did,<br>and were destroyed by the Destroyer. | GRUMBLING |

**Figure 3.4(5). Cameos 5-8 (1 Cor 10:7-10)**

wife." Abimelech then got angry because Isaac had claimed that Rebekah was his sister. The same word is critical in the earlier story of Isaac and Ishmael as children. In Genesis 21:9 Sarah saw Ishmael "playing" (the Greek Old Testament [LXX] and the commentaries of the rabbis include "with her son Isaac"). As a consequence, Sarah became angry and insisted that Hagar and her son be sent away. The "playing" (*tsakheq*) apparently involved more than innocent children's games.[4] Rabbi Akiba (A.D. 40-135) argued that the Exodus story "refers solely to idolatrous worship, since it is said, and the people sat down to eat and drink and they arose to play (Exod 32:6)."[5] But a contemporary of Akiba, R. Eliezer b. R. Yose, the Galilean, added, "Playing stated here (in Exod 32:6) refers only to fornication, as it is said, The Hebrew servant whom you have brought among us came into me to play with me (Gen 39:17)."[6] In cameo 5 the Greek word for play is *piazo*. In discussing *piazo* Bertram writes, "As in Gen 26:8 (cf. 39:14, 17) צחק (play) has an erotic sense, so צחק can denote both idolatry and also the cultic licentiousness often associated with it."[7] The reader is expected to keep this larger scene in mind when he or she reads that God was angry because "The people sat down to eat and drink and rose up to *play*." Paul seems to be invoking these connotations of sexual license because the second item of

---

[4]The same word occurs in the account of Joseph's troubles with Potiphar's wife (Gen 39:7-18).
[5]Tosefta, *Sotah* 6:6 (Jacob Neusner, translator, *Tosefta*, vol. III [New York: KTAV, 1979], p. 172).
[6]Ibid.
[7]G. Bertram, "παιζω," in *TDNT*, 5:629-30.

ethical failure he mentions is "immorality." The Corinthians were having trouble with both issues.

**2. Immorality.** Paul reminds his readers that the Hebrews were at fault in this regard (as were the Corinthians).

**3. Putting the Lord to the test.** This story appears in Numbers 21:4-9, where the people were "testing the Lord" and also "grumbling." Paul appears to be recalling one error (putting the Lord to the test) and at the same time looking forward to the next item on his list (grumbling). In his hymn on the cross (1:17–2:2) Paul mentions "the Jews demand signs." This statement is not pointed in the direction of the Corinthians, yet it is an example of trying to "put the Lord to the test."

**4. Grumbling.** The theme of grumbling against God and against Moses runs all through the story of the exodus. The various Corinthian parties mentioned in 1:10-13 and again in 3:21 certainly engaged in a great deal of grumbling. Their attacks on Paul's leadership and on the authenticity of his apostleship were expressions of the same moral failure.

It is worth noting that "grumbling" is included in the list with "idol worship" and "immorality." Paul gives no hint that some of the items on his list were more serious than other items. In contemporary churches that I have known, there is often a great deal of grumbling. Would that those involved realized the list on which they place themselves as they do so.

In Paul's day some apparently thought that as long as the sacraments were celebrated, idol worship could be tolerated. In this homily Paul reminds them of the tradition of the fathers who participated in the sacraments, and yet fell into idolatry, immorality and other evils *and were destroyed*. The sacraments were *not* enough. God was angry at their ethical failures, and the episode was recorded as a "warning for us." Israel was guilty of these things, and so were the Corinthians.

The sacraments of ancient Israel were a treasure to remember and celebrate in their renewed form in the church. In the present, Paul's readers were invited to *identify* with ancient Israel and its sacraments. But they were to *avoid* the ethical failings that occurred during the exodus in spite of those great sacraments. Word and sacrament had to be kept together. There were patterns of response appropriate to those sacraments.

As Paul wrote he was sensitive to his readers. Some of them could have asked themselves, "If God overthrew the Hebrews in the wilderness for things like 'putting the Lord to the test' and 'grumbling,' what hope is there for us?" By this point in the epistle Paul's compassion for "the weak" was already expressed. Apparently not wanting to cause despair among his readers, after this warning (10:7-10), Paul introduced an extended aside to encourage them. He wrote,

> 11. (*No temptation* has overtaken you that is not common to humankind. God is faithful, and he will not let you be *tempted beyond your strength*, but with the *temptation* will also provide the way of escape, that you may be able to *endure* it.)

This comment is outside the parallelisms of the homily that precedes it. A similar footnote appears in 1:16. That earlier footnote also occurs at the end of a homily. Findlay notes that Paul "ascribes to God not the origination, but the *control* of temptation."[8] Findlay also observes that the Corinthians had to deal with "both the allurements of idolatry and the persecution which its abandonment entailed."[9] A special burden of temptation is keenly felt by anyone in any age who leaves one faith commitment and embraces another. The conclusion of the matter is that "Shut in a *cul de sac*, a man despairs; but let him see a door open for his exit, and he will struggle on with his load."[10] Paul assures his readers that God provides such an exit. This may be a pastoral footnote, or it could be a marginal note left by some early preacher that has been copied into the text. With no textual evidence for this latter option, it is preferable to assume that it is a pastoral footnote by Paul.

As he offers this pastoral note Paul repeats the profound theological affirmation with which he began the letter (1:9), namely, *pistos ho theos* (God is faithful). In both texts there is again no verb "to be." Paul is thinking in Hebrew and writing in Greek. Only in these two texts does Paul use this precise phrase.[11] John tells us that "God is love." Paul's affirmation that "God is faithful" is equally important. "Faithful to what?" we ask. He is faithful to fulfill his covenantal promises. In Paul's mind God freely chooses to be both *loving* and *faithful*, and that choice fulfills rather than limits his sovereignty.

After advising his readers that as they contemplate their Hebrew past, their appropriate stance is "partial identification," Paul has a third approach to engagement with the surrounding culture. This third option is "nothing to anyone."

To that third option we now turn.

---

[8]Findlay, *First Epistle*, p. 862.
[9]Ibid.
[10]Ibid.
[11]See 1 Thess 5:24 "the one who called you is faithful"; 2 Thess 3:3 reads, "The Lord (is) faithful."

# New Covenant Sacraments and Idolatry

*No Identification*

1 CORINTHIANS 10:14-22

THIS IS THE THIRD HOMILY in Paul's trilogy on identification with culture.

Paul first told his readers to accommodate to everyone and become "all things to all people." He then reflected on the *Hebrew sacramental past*, and his advice was "some things to some people." That is, Christian sacraments have continuity with the Hebrew experience of the exodus. But their ethical responses to those experiences were inadequate. Now Paul turns to the *Gentile sacramental past* that surrounded all of his readers. He warns,

> In a private home or in a temple-owned restaurant, eating meat offered to idols is not necessarily a problem. Joining in pagan/Gentile worship is *very* different! *Have nothing to do with it.* In this case my judgment is—*no identification is possible!* Our loyalty to Christ translates into "nothing for anyone."

## THE RHETORIC

Paul again uses the prophetic rhetorical template of seven inverted cameos with the climax in the center. This homily is constructed with care. The seven cameos are in place, and the parallels strong and clear. The center climax introduces the "demons."

The detailed construction of the prophetic homily observed previously in Isaiah 28:9-14 not only presented seven inverted cameos, it also used step parallelism to relate the paired cameos to each other.[1] In like manner, here in

---

[1]See "Prelude: Prophetic Homily Rhetorical Style and Its Interpretation," figure 0.4.

1. <sup>10:14</sup>Therefore, my beloved,
    *flee* from the *worship of idols.*                FLEE FROM
    <sup>15</sup>I speak as to sensible people;                 The Idols
    judge for yourselves what I say.


2.  a. <sup>16</sup>The *cup of blessing* which we bless,       THE CUP—Communion
    b.    is it not communion *in the blood of Christ?*    The Blood of Christ
    c.  The *bread which we break,*                 THE BREAD—Communion
    d.    is it not communion *in the body of Christ?*   The Body of Christ
       <sup>17</sup>Because there is *one loaf,* we the many are *one body,*
       for we *all partake of the same loaf.*


3.       <sup>18</sup>Look at *Israel according to the flesh;*
    a.  are not *those who eat* the *sacrifices*          COMMUNION
    b.  in communion with *the altar?*                With the Altar


4.         <sup>19</sup>What do I say then?
          That *food sacrificed to idols is anything,*       SACRIFICE
          or that an *idol is anything?*              To Idols Is
          <sup>20</sup>No, but what the Gentiles sacrifice is to *demons,*   SACRIFICE
          *not to God* do they *sacrifice.*            To Demons


5.  a.  I do *not want you* to be                 COMMUNION
    b.  in communion *with demons.*              With Demons


6.  a. <sup>21</sup>You *cannot drink the cup of the Lord*        THE CUP
    b.    and the *cup of demons.*               Of the Lord & Demons?
    c.  You *cannot partake of the table of the Lord*     THE TABLE
    d.    and the *table of demons.*             Of the Lord & Demons?


7. <sup>22</sup>Shall we provoke the *Lord to jealousy?*        DO NOT ANGER
    Are we *stronger than he?*                The Lord!

---

**Figure 3.5(1). New covenant sacraments and idolatry: No identification (1 Cor 10:14-22)**


10:14-22, Paul presents four lines in cameo 2 which he matches with four lines in cameo 6 using step parallelism. The two lines in cameo 3 are also carefully paired with the two lines of cameo 5. There is an extra sentence in the last two lines of cameo 2 that is not matched in cameo 6.

## COMMENTARY

It is necessary to examine the matching cameos as pairs to discern Paul's intent.

The outer pair can be seen in figure 3.5(2).

1. [14]Therefore, my beloved,
    *flee* from the *worship of idols.*          FLEE FROM
   [15]I speak as to sensible people;            The Idols
    judge for yourselves what I say.
-----------------------------------------------------------------------
7. [22]Shall we provoke the *Lord to jealousy?*     DO NOT ANGER
    Are we *stronger than he?*                   The Lord!

**Figure 3.5(2). Cameos 1 and 7 (1 Cor 10:14-15, 22)**

At first glance these two cameos seem to have little in common. Cameo 7 is not parallel to cameo 1, nor does cameo 7 repeat or contradict cameo 1. Yet on reflection the second flows seamlessly from the first. Paul is saying, "You are sensible people who can easily understand that if you, as worshipers of God, start to worship idols [cameo 1], God will be angry. Are you powerful enough to deal with his jealous wrath [cameo 7]?" If the rest of the homily (cameos 2-6) were removed, no reader would note the omission. The members of the Corinthian church with a Jewish background knew full well that when Israel worshiped idols, God allowed the Assyrians and the Babylonians to conquer them, destroy their cities and take them captive into exile. Do the Christians of Corinth want a sequel to that painful history? If they are "sensible people" (cameo 1) they will know exactly how God will respond to any worship of idols (cameo 7).

Cameo 1 includes the cry "flee from the worship of idols." Earlier they were ordered to *flee (pheugete) from prostitution* (6:18). The two cries are related in that idol worship in Corinth involved sacred prostitution. Standing on a street corner and chatting with one of the professional temple prostitutes was not a good idea. They were to run away. In like manner, mixing casually with idol worshipers as they gathered in the outer court of a pagan temple was a bad idea. The Corinthians needed to run away.

In the next rhetorical envelope the plot thickens [see fig. 3.5(3)].

2. a. [16]The *cup of blessing* which we bless,          THE CUP—Communion
   b.    is it not communion *in the blood of Christ?*    The Blood of Christ
   c. The *bread which we break,*                        THE BREAD—Communion
   d.    is it not communion *in the body of Christ?*     The Body of Christ
      [17]Because there is *one loaf,* we the many are *one body,*
      for we *all partake of the same loaf.*
-----------------------------------------------------------------------
6. a. [21]You *cannot drink the cup of the Lord*          THE CUP
   b.    and the *cup of demons.*                          Of the Lord & Demons?
   c. You *cannot partake of the table of the Lord*        THE TABLE
   d.    and the *table of demons.*                        Of the Lord & Demons?

**Figure 3.5(3). Cameos 2 and 6 (1 Cor 10:16-17, 21)**

With Jerome Murphy-O'Connor and G. G. Findlay I have translated the Greek word *koinonia* as "communion" rather than "partnership."[2] The word *partnership* has an organizational and even a commercial flavor. *Communion* brings the language into the sphere of the holy.

With these two cameos, Paul shows the impossibility of being both "in communion with the Lord" in the Eucharist and joining "in communion with demons" through idol worship. These are not two country clubs where membership in both would not be a problem. Paul is affirming that idol worship involves a deep sacramental participation with demons, and that the Corinthians can drink the "cup of the Lord" or "the cup of demons" *but not both*!

"Communion in the *body* of Christ" unites us *both* to Christ and to the church that is his body. Paul wants to ensure that his readers catch this double meaning. To do this he adds a footnote interpreting the theological significance of the "one loaf." We are all "one body, for we all partake of the same loaf."

In cameo 2 he speaks of "the cup" and "the bread," while in the parallel cameo (6) he writes of "the cup" and "the table." I am convinced that this language is influenced by Psalm 23. In that Psalm David affirms "he [God] brings me back" (Ps 23:3).[3] This language projects the image of a lost sheep and a good shepherd who finds him and "brings him back" to the village. Death (deep darkness) and sin (evil) surface in verse 4a, but in spite of them the psalmist has no fear (Ps 23:4b). How is this possible? The answer appears in the following line, which reads, "for thou [God] art with me." This affirmation resonates with the name "Emmanuel" (God is with us). The psalmist continues as he declares, "He [God] prepares *a table* before me" and "*my cup* overflows." This banquet comes at great cost because it is spread "in the presence of my enemies" (Ps 23:5), and those enemies will not take kindly to the mercy/grace (*khesed*) that is extended to me (Ps 23:6). Paul has apparently reflected deeply on Psalm 23 in the light of the life and sacrificial ministry of Jesus, the good Shepherd (Lk 15:4-7).[4] The result is that when discussing the Eucharist, Paul easily and naturally speaks of "the cup" and the "table."

The climactic center is displayed in figure 3.5(4).

---

[2]Findlay, *First Epistle*, pp. 863-64; Murphy-O'Connor, *1 Corinthians*, p. 97.

[3]This is my literal translation of the Hebrew *yashubib nefshi*. The Arabic versions consistently use this language. Traditional English reads "he restores my soul" (NRSV).

[4]We recall that Luke was a traveling companion of Paul. Cf. Kenneth E. Bailey, "The Parable of the Lost Sheep (15:4-7)," in *Finding the Lost: Cultural Keys to Luke 15* (St. Louis: Concordia, 1992), pp. 63-92.

| 3. | | [18]Look at *Israel according to the flesh;* | |
|----|----|----|----|
| | a. | are not *those who eat* the *sacrifices* | COMMUNION |
| | b. | in communion with *the altar?* | With the Altar |

| 4. | [19]What do I say then? | |
|----|----|----|
| | That *food sacrificed to idols is anything,* | SACRIFICE |
| | or that an *idol is anything?* | To Idols Is |
| | [20]No, but what the Gentiles sacrifice is to *demons,* | SACRIFICE |
| | *not to God* do they *sacrifice.* | To Demons |

| 5. | a. | I do *not want you* to be | COMMUNION |
|----|----|----|----|
| | b. | in communion *with demons.* | With Demons |

**Figure 3.5(4). Cameos 3-5 (1 Cor 10:18-20)**

These three cameos open with the imperative "Look at Israel according to the flesh,"[5] which the KJV translates as "Behold Israel after the flesh."[6] Following this important phrase in verse 18 there are five other key words that require reflection and translation. The six are:

| 1. *ton Israel kata sarka* | "Israel according to the flesh" (v. 18) |
|----|----|
| 2. *ta ethne* | "Gentiles" (v. 20)[7] |
| 3. *apistos* | "unbelievers" (v. 27) |
| 4. *Judaiois* | "Jews" (v. 32) |
| 5. *Ellenes* | "Greeks" (v. 32) |
| 6. *te ekklesia tou theou* | "the church of God" (v. 32) |

These key words will not unlock all their secrets, and thus no explanation of them is fully satisfying. But we must try to make our way through the maze. A partial understanding of them could be:

1. *ton Israel kata sarka* "Israel according to the flesh" (v. 18)

If there is an "Israel according to the flesh" in Paul's mind, there must also be an "Israel according to the Spirit." This other Israel surfaces in Galatians 6:16, where Paul refers to "the Israel of God." In Romans 9:3 he writes of "my brethren, my kinsmen *kata sarka* (according to the flesh)," using the same words. In Romans Paul continues to reflect on Abraham's descendants "ac-

---

[5]My translation.

[6]The RSV reads "Consider the practice of Israel." All of the twenty-two Hebrew, Syriac and Arabic versions consulted for this study translate this text with some form of "Israel according to the flesh." These stretch from the fifth to the twentieth centuries (see appendix II, plate G).

[7]The phrase *ta ethne* may be an ancient gloss. There is strong evidence for it and it is included [within brackets] in *The Greek New Testament*, ed. Kurt Aland et al. (New York: United Bible Societies, 1966), and appears in both the RSV and the NRSV.

cording to the promise," and how Hosea promised that "those who were not my people I will call 'my people'" (Rom 9:25). In Ephesians 2:11-22 Paul deals with this same subject [see fig. 3.5(5)].

1.  [11]Remember . . . then you the *Gentiles in the flesh*     IN THE FLESH
       the ones called *uncircumcised*                          Gentiles (uncircumcised)

2.     by those called *circumcised*                            IN THE FLESH
          which is made *in the flesh* by hands                 Jews (circumcised)

3.  [12]a. that you were once *separated from Christ*           SEPARATED FROM CHRIST
        b.   *alienated* from the *citizenship of Israel*       Alienated from Israel
        c. *strangers* to the *covenants of promise*            Strangers to the Promise

4.     a. having *no hope*                                      NO HOPE
       b. and without God *in the world.*                       In the World

5.        [13]a. But now *in Christ Jesus* you who were *once afar off*
             b. have been *bought near* in the *blood of Christ.*     FAR OFF/Near

6.           [14]a. For *he is our peace*                       OUR PEACE
                b. Who has made *the two one*                   Hostility Ends
                c. and has *destroyed the dividing wall* of *hostility in his body,*

7.                 [15]*abolishing* the *law of commandments and ordinances*
                      in order that of the *two* he might *create in himself one new humanity*

8.              a. so *making peace*                            PEACE
                [16]b. reconciling *the two in one* body to God *through the cross*
                c. bringing the *hostility to an end in it.*    Hostility Ends

9.           [17]a. And he came and preached *peace* to *you who were far off*
                b. and *peace* to *those who were near;*        FAR OFF/Near

10.  [18]a. for through *him* we both have *access*            ACCESS
        b.   *in one Spirit* to the *Father.*                   In the Spirit

11.  [19]a. So then you are *no longer strangers* and sojourners
        b. but *fellow citizens* with the saints                FELLOW CITIZENS
        c. and *members of the household of God,*               Members of House of God

12. [20]built upon the foundation of the *apostles and prophets*
(Jesus Christ himself being the chief cornerstone [21]in whom the whole structure is joined together)
       and grows into a *holy temple in the Lord,*             IN THE LORD

13.[22]into which you are also built
       for a *dwelling place of God in the Spirit.*            IN THE SPIRIT

**Figure 3.5(5). Jews and Gentiles become one in the cross (Eph 2:11-22)**

This magnificent apostolic homily uses the rhetorical style observed in 1:17–2:2, with its seven cameos that are then matched in reverse order. Here the "Gentiles in the flesh," once alienated from "citizenship of Israel" (cameo 3) have become "fellow citizens with the saints and members of the household of God" (cameo 11), which is also called "one new humanity." This is accomplished through "the blood of the cross." The overlap between this Ephesian text and the Corinthian text before us is extensive. Together the two texts show that through the cross of Christ a new reality is born in which Jewish and Gentile believers share equal "citizenship" in "the household of God."

In 1 Corinthians, when Paul writes "Israel according to the flesh," he is including the pious Jews who were twice daily celebrating the sacrifices in the Jerusalem temple. They were "in communion" with the altar.

2. *ta ethne* "Gentiles" (v. 20)

This second key word is translated by the RSV as "pagans." The Syriac Peshitta uses the word "*hanif*," which can mean either "pagan" or "Gentile." The two Hebrew versions consulted use the standard Hebrew word for Gentiles (*goyim*). Ten of the Arabic translations from the ninth to the nineteenth centuries read "Gentiles," while three list "pagans." The dominant word used across the centuries is "Gentiles."[8] In 12:2 Paul writes, "back when you were *ethne* (Gentiles)" you did so-and-so. So what are they now? Paul could not bring himself to say, "I became a Gentile." Can he expect Gentiles to become Jews? Certainly not. They are not circumcised, and Paul has insisted that "circumcision is nothing" (7:19). So who are they now?

The word *ethne* (Gentiles) is the Greek form of "the nations," the *goyim* who were enemies of Israel throughout the Old Testament. Paul could have written "the idol worshipers sacrifice to demons." Instead he declared that "the Gentiles" make such sacrifices. Having just found ethical faults in the *Hebrew* past, he now points out *Gentile* failings. They also, like Israel, were guilty of worshiping idols.

What are the implications of the language that appears here and in Ephesians 2? Assuming that Paul is speaking precisely, we can understand him to mean,

> As regards believers in Jesus, the Jew remains culturally Jewish, the Greek is still a Greek, the Roman maintains a Roman identify, and all three are an inti-

---

[8]See appendix II, plate G.

mate part of the new humanity that is the "household of God." The "blood of the cross" creates a new unity that reaches beyond these ethnic and linguistic particularities (Eph 2:11-22). "I am of Cephas" and "I am of Apollos" will no longer do! In Christ the old Jewish—Gentile divisions are gone.

Thus Paul can criticize "the Gentiles" who worship idols, and not intend any slurs against Christians with a Gentile origin, even as he is not expressing negative feelings against Jewish believers when he criticizes the ethical failures of their Hebrew ancestors during the exodus.

3. *apistos* "unbelievers" (v. 27)

This word appears in the final homily of this essay where Paul discusses being invited to banquets by "unbelievers." Why did Paul introduce this new word? I am not sure. Perhaps he chose a culturally neutral word because those unbelievers were most likely friends and often family members of the believing Christians. In a city like Corinth the unbeliever could be Greek, Jewish, Roman, Egyptian, Syrian and so on. A large commercial city such as Corinth included all of those cultures and more.

4-5. *Ioudaios* "Jews" and *Hellenas* "Greeks" (v. 32)

These two categories are easy to identify. They both refer to the two ethnic communities of Jews and Greeks who do not belong to the "church of God."

6. *te ekklesia tou theou* "the church of God" (v. 32)

This title refers to the community of believers to whom Paul was writing. Made up of people with a range of ethnic backgrounds, they were the "new humanity." Each shared with the ethnic identity of his or her heritage, and on a deeper level each was an equal member of the new "household of God," which is not mentioned but seems to be assumed. Paul's ethnic identity was Pharisaic Judaism, as he proudly affirms (Phil 3:4-5). He also participated in the "new humanity" in which he was a central figure. With these suggested understandings of these words, we return to the three central cameos of the homily.

In the climactic center (cameo 4) Paul reaffirms what he said earlier. Sacrifices to idols are nothing, and idols are nothing. Isaiah already covered this ground in Isaiah 44:14-17, where he pointed out the total stupidity of idol worshipers and makers who cut down a tree, use part of it to warm themselves, part to cook with and the last part they make into an idol to which they pray, "Deliver me, for thou art my god!" What could be more ridiculous? In the same vein, Paul affirms that the sculptured stone images in the temples were pieces of stone, no more. Killing an animal in front of such stones was as meaningless as killing that same animal in front of a large rock a pasture.

So much for the exterior world. But what about the unseen world in the mind and in society? "There is a demonic component to what happens in their *worship*," argues Paul. It is what goes on in the minds and hearts of people, individually and communally, that matters. They are invoking demons. "The demons are real. Do not worship them," he thunders! Joining in such worship is "communion" with demons, and as such it is a betrayal of Christ. Today Christians all across the Global South face such problems, and Paul's advice is extraordinarily profound and sensitive.

Paul has presented three aspects of the subject of identification. These can be summarized as:

- First homily: "All things to all people." Share with others in their cultural setting without losing your own identity. That way you can "join the movement of the gospel" and commend it to others.

- Second homily: "Some things to some people." The sacraments of the exodus are to be remembered and honored, but the Hebrews failed in their ethical responses to those sacraments. They fell into idolatry and other sins and were destroyed, and their story is a warning for us.

- Third homily: "Nothing to anyone." The worship of idols is "communion" with *demons*. As such it is incompatible with the union with the body of Christ made possible in the Eucharist.

Having clarified these three options for "identification" Paul concludes this essay with a final word about "meat offered to idols." To that closing section of this essay we now turn.

# Food Offered to Idols

*Freedom and Responsibility (A Final Word)*

1 Corinthians 10:23–11:1

The text of Paul's final homily in this third essay is displayed in figure 3.6(1).

Paul opened this essay with a discussion of food offered to idols, and following the pattern he established in the first two essays, he now returns to the same topic for a concluding word on the subject. He is not confused and the material is not a jumble. Rather, in a measured, balanced way, he returns to the opening homily of this essay, and in the light of what he has written throughout the essay, completes the discussion.

## THE RHETORIC

Once again Paul uses the prophetic rhetorical template of seven inverted cameos with a climax in the center. Cameo 1 is the summary principle and cameo 7 applies that principle in a broad, all-inclusive manner. Cameos 2 and 6 focus on "Think of others and eat or do not eat—to the glory of God." The next pair of cameos (3 and 5) continues with *"Eat what you are served* in private homes and give thanks for it." The climactic center focuses on the special occasions in which love requires that they *not eat* (cameo 4).

The material tells the reader:

Eat
Eat
  Do Not Eat
Eat
Eat

1. [10:23]*"All* things are *lawful,"*                    THE SUMMARY PRINCIPLE:
   but *all things* are *not helpful.*                   Seek What Helps and Builds
   *"All* things are *lawful,"*                          Seek the Advantage of the Other
   but *not all* things *build up.*
   [24]Do not seek your own advantage
   but that of the other.[1]

2.      [25]*Eat* whatever *is sold* in the meat market
        without raising any question on the *ground of conscience.*
        [26]For "the earth is the Lord's,                EAT
        and everything in it."                           All Is the Lord's

3.      [27]If any one of the unbelievers invites you to dinner
        and you are disposed to go,                      EAT
        *eat whatever is set before you*                 All Offered to You
        without raising any question on the *ground of conscience.*

4.          [28]But if some one says to you,
            "This has been offered in sacrifice,"         DO NOT
            then out of consideration for the man who informed you,   EAT
            and for conscience' sake—
            [29]I mean his conscience, not yours—do not eat it.

5.          For why should my liberty
            be determined by another man's scruples?      EAT
            [30]If I partake with *thankfulness,*          and Give Thanks
            why am I denounced because of that for which *I give thanks?*

6.          [31]So, whether you eat or drink,
            or whatever you do,                            EAT
            do *all* to the *glory of God.*                In All—Glorify God

7.  [32]Give *no offense to Jews* or to *Greeks*          APPLICATION OF PRINCIPLE:
    or to the *church of God,*                            Offense Does Not Build Up
    [33]Indeed I try to *please all people* in everything  I Try to Please All
    not seeking my own advantage,                         Not Your Advantage
    but that of many, *that they may be saved.*           But Others'—for Salvation

    - - - - - - - - - - - - - - - - - - - - - - - - - -          - - - - - - - - - -

8.  [11:1]*Be imitators of me, as I am of Christ.*         A PERSONAL APPEAL

---

**Figure 3.6(1). Food offered to idols: A second look (1 Cor 10:23–11:1)**

---

[1]NRSV

This order confuses the modern reader. We are accustomed to:

On the *one hand*:
(1) Think of others and try to be helpful. (7) Don't offend people. (2) Eat (or don't eat) the meat you buy in the market for it is the Lord's. (6) Do so to the glory of God. (3) At a meal in a pagan's home eat whatever they serve you. (5) You are a free person, give thanks and *eat*.

*But* on the *other hand*:
(4) If someone whispers to you "This is idol meat, I am sure you would want to know," then *do not eat* (out of respect for his or her conscience, not your conscience).

Paul composes using the familiar ring composition style of the writing prophets—assuming his readers can follow him. The climax appears in cameo 4, and that center relates to the beginning and the end. The homily closes with Paul's signature personal appeal (cameo 8), which repeats and expands the concluding appeal at the end of his first essay.

## COMMENTARY

Following the pattern established previously, we will examine the matched pairs of cameos, starting with the outside. The first and the last of the seven cameos in this homily are seen in figure 3.6(2).

| | | |
|---|---|---|
| 1. | 10:23"*All* things are *lawful*,"<br>but *all things* are *not helpful*.<br>"*All* things are *lawful*,"<br>but *not all* things *build up*.<br>24Do not seek your own advantage<br>but that of the other. | THE SUMMARY PRINCIPLE:<br>Seek What Helps and Builds<br>Seek the Advantage of the Other |
| 7. | 32Give *no offense to Jews* or to *Greeks*<br>or to the *church of God*,<br>33Indeed I try to *please all people* in everything<br>not seeking my own advantage,<br>but that of many, *that they may be saved*. | APPLICATION OF PRINCIPLE:<br>Offense Does Not Build Up<br>I Try to Please All<br>Not Your Advantage<br>But Others'—for Salvation |

**Figure 3.6(2). Cameos 1 and 7 (1 Cor 10:23-24, 32-33)**

Cameos 1 and 7 both conclude with the strong statement, "Seek not your own advantage—but that of the other(s)." This unmistakably ties them together. The key to the discussion is not, "I want my rights!" but rather, "What will build up the community?" Once again, if cameos 2-6 were missing, no reader would notice their absence. The ideas in cameo 1 connect with cameo 7 in a seamless fashion.

Had the good Samaritan of the parable of Jesus (Lk 10:25-28) sought his own good, he would have continued riding down the hill. But unlike the priest and the Levite who "passed by on the other side," the Samaritan served the best interests of the unknown wounded man at the side of the road.

In 10:24, the RSV translated *heteros* as "neighbor," and added the word "good," which produced the reading "the good of his neighbor." Is it "the other" or "the neighbor," and is there a difference? There can be.

The phrase "Love your neighbor as your self" is a quote from Leviticus 19:18. The biblical setting of this quote reads,

> You shall not hate *your brother* in your heart, but you shall reason with *your neighbor*, lest you bear sin because of him. You shall not take vengeance or bear any grudge against the *sons of your own people*, but you shall love *your neighbor* as yourself: I am the LORD. (Lev 19:17-18, emphasis added)

In this text the "neighbor" is "your brother" and one of "the sons of your own people." But a few verses later in Leviticus 19:34 the text continues, "The *stranger who sojourns with you* shall be to you as the native among you, and *you shall love him as yourself;* for you were strangers in the land of Egypt: I am the LORD your God" (emphasis added). Jesus and the lawyer questioning him had these two options open to them in the dialogue recorded in Luke 10:25-28. When the lawyer asked Jesus, "Who is my neighbor?" he may have been seeking advice regarding which option to choose. Jesus had a radical option not in the text. Beyond "the son of your own house" and "the stranger living among you" is a third category, namely, "the stranger who does not live among you." Jesus opened up space for this third option when he created the famous parable of the good Samaritan. The Samaritan *became a neighbor* and reached out to an unidentified man in need. For Jesus the *Samaritan* was the neighbor, and he chose to serve the outsider not knowing where he lived. What then of Paul?

Paul, like Jesus, was concerned for others. Paul emphasized this sense of "otherness" by choosing the word *heteros*. The RSV translated this word as "neighbor" in 1 Corinthians 10:24, but the NRSV restored the more accurate translation of "the other." How then has this text been read across the centuries in the Middle East?

The fifth-century Syriac Peshitta uses the word *hbr* (friend, companion).

But across more than a millennium the Arabic versions used in this study are divided. Six of them have "friend," one reads "neighbor" and the remaining twelve translate "the other." The oldest of this latter group of version is the Mt. Sinai Arabic no. 155 (ninth century), and the most recent is the Bible Society Arabic Bible of 1993. The Hebrew translation of 1817 has "the other," while the modern Hebrew reads "friend/companion." Granting that both options have been used in the Middle Eastern versions, it is clear that the dominant understanding of this word across more than twelve hundred years has been "the other."[2] Paul is best understood to be urging his readers to reach out to the one who is different. The person in mind is someone who may have a different native tongue, or who remembers a different history or prioritizes different values in a different order. Paul created a multicultural church, and he urges his readers to care for the interests of "the other" (believer or nonbeliever), setting aside their own interests.

The opening lines of each of these two cameos are related in a special way. Cameo 1 sets out *general principles* while cameo 7 offers *applications of those principles*. We can almost hear the conversation between Paul and his readers. It is as if they are engaged in the following dialogue:

*Paul*  As a general principle (cameo 1) I can say, "All things are lawful to me, but they are not all *helpful*. Nor do all things *build up*."

*Paul's readers*  Can you give us a general sense as to how to apply these two principles?

*Paul*  Yes, I can (cameo 7). Let us look at the two parts of what I have just said.

1. Regarding being *helpful*, don't offend Jews, Greeks or the church of God. You gain nothing by offending people. It makes them angry, and they become entrenched in their opposing views. Giving offense is simply not helpful.

2. As for *building up*, when you do not *offend* you have the opportunity to *commend* your message of salvation, and in the process build up the community at large. You need to also build up the believing community internally. Work to build up, not tear down.

[2]See appendix II, plate H.

The first key word in cameo 1, *sumphero* (helpful), includes the idea of "bringing together."[3] It was also used to describe the carrying of something heavy as in "bear along with." That meaning includes the nuance of "bear suffering with" and "be in harmony with."[4] In secular speech it was used for two people coming together in marriage.[5]

The second phrase returns to the topic of "building up." We have already seen Paul's extensive use of the image of "building up" throughout the epistle. This word picture was particularly prominent in his parable of the master builder, which included the right foundation, the building of the holy temple, the need for good materials and the fire that will test the results (3:10-16). Here Paul wants to encourage the builders and discourage the wreckers.

In cameo 7 Paul sets a high standard. He is engaged in evangelism and his *theological goal* is clear. But his *method* is also clear. The standard is: Give no offense to Jews, Greeks or to the church. For him there will be no public attacks on the faith of others. Critical analysis, yes, attacks—no! While writing to *Christians* he does not hide the fact that the gods of the "the Gentiles" do not exist and that their worship brings them into fellowship with *demons*. As noted, archaeology has identified Greek shrines in Corinth dedicated to the worship of twelve different gods.[6] But there is no attack on any of these idols, their sacred books, their temples or their priests. When lecturing on Mars Hill (Acts 17:22-31) Paul found common ground between his message and respected Greek authors. In Paul's ministry, tolerance, open-mindedness and respect *flowed together with* critical analysis and non-apologetic evangelism. To update Paul's directive into the twenty-first century we could say, "Give no offense to Jews or to Muslims or to the church of God. Do not seek your own advantage, but theirs—*and* at the appropriate time, in a respectful and culturally sensitive way, bear witness to the Christian story without apology." This directive is clear, yet Paul leaves the reader with a further question.

In the second essay Paul boldly instructed the Corinthians to dismiss the incestuous man. In this third essay he directs them to give "no offense to the church of God." How can these two texts be reconciled? Was he not potentially offending at least a part of the church by urging the dismissal of the

---

[3]BAGD, p. 780.
[4]LSJ, *A Greek-English Lexicon*, pp. 1686-87.
[5]M. & M., p. 586.
[6]Jerome Murphy-O'Connor, "Corinth," in *ABD*, 1:1137-38.

offender? Surely he was. But a surgeon does not offend a patient by cutting out a deadly tumor. The operation may be painful and the recovery slow, but for the health of the body, such a procedure is necessary. In the case of the Corinthian church Paul's surgery offered the only hope for healing. It may be possible to combine these two texts by suggesting that what Paul means is, "Strive to avoid offending the conscience of anyone, and at the same time, maintain ethical standards within the body of Christ, even if that effort may require discipline in order to protect the spiritual health of the community and save the offender."

The second semantic envelope in this homily (cameos 2, 6) is also remarkable. The two matching cameos are seen together in figure 3.6(3).

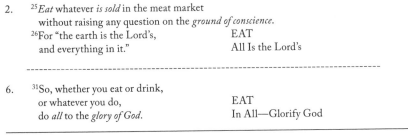

2.  $^{25}$*Eat* whatever *is sold* in the meat market
    without raising any question on the *ground of conscience.*
    $^{26}$For "the earth is the Lord's,              EAT
    and everything in it."                    All Is the Lord's

----------------------------------------------------------------------

6.  $^{31}$So, whether you eat or drink,
    or whatever you do,                       EAT
    do *all* to the *glory of God.*           In All—Glorify God

**Figure 3.6(3). Cameos 2 and 6 (1 Cor 10:25-26, 31)**

These two cameos unite around the topic of "eating and the divine." Cameo 2 tells the reader: All meat sold in the marketplace belongs to God, not to the idols, because the entire earth is the Lord's. This affirmation must have been hugely liberating for Paul's readers. Imagine a new Greek Christian entering the meat market in Corinth with great inner turmoil and wondering, "If this meat was offered to Asclepius the god of health, it must belong to him. And if I buy it and eat it, will Asclepius make me sick because I no longer worship him?" "No," answers Paul—"it all belongs to the one Lord who created all things" (cameo 2). Such fears are groundless. So if you eat it or do not eat it—give all glory to God alone (cameo 6) and do not be afraid.

This brings us to the three central cameos [see fig. 3.6(4)].

Paul begins cameo 3 by answering a second assumed question. The first was, "Can we buy idol meat and eat it in the privacy of our own homes?" Paul's answer was, "Yes, by all means. It all belongs to God anyway" (cameo 2), and "Don't forget to offer him the glory" (cameo 6). Paul now turns to answer the

3.      27If any one of the unbelievers invites you to dinner
          and you are disposed to go,                                    EAT
          *eat whatever is set before you*                               All Offered to You
          without raising any question on the *ground of conscience.*

4.              28But if some one says to you,
                  "This has been offered in sacrifice,"                  DO NOT
                     then out of consideration for the man who informed you,   EAT
                     and for conscience' sake—
                  29I mean his conscience, not yours—do not eat it.

5.      For why should my liberty
          be determined by another man's scruples?                      EAT
          30If I partake with *thankfulness,*                            and Give Thanks
          why am I denounced because of that for which *I give thanks?*

**Figure 3.6(4). Cameos 3-5 (1 Cor 10:27-30)**

question, "What about idol meat that is served to us when we are *guests in the home* of a *pagan?*" Paul replies, "Of course. Go ahead and eat! Don't let your conscience bother you" (cameo 3).

In the matching cameo (cameo 5) Paul expands this directive and applies it to himself. In effect he tells his readers, "I am a free man! I eat such meat and I thank God for it! If others make a different choice, that does not limit my freedom." Cameo 5 matches and completes what Paul says in cameo 3.

As is common the climax of the homily appears in the center (cameo 4), where love is prominent. Paul indirectly tells his readers, "Your rights and your freedom are not the only components in this discussion. What about love?" We do not know if the informant whispering in the ear of the Christian guest is the unbelieving host showing consideration to his guest, or a fellow Christian who happens to be present at the banquet. In either case, what should the Christian guest do when he or she is *specifically informed at the banquet* about the pagan origins of the meat?

To paraphrase Paul's directive he seems to be telling his readers,

> If you are invited to a meal in an unbeliever's home and someone quietly informs you that the meat is "idol food," out of your love for the informant, who is trying to be sensitive to what he thinks are your feelings, don't eat the meat. Your freedom should be tempered by love.

In the opening homily (8:1-13) of essay three, Paul asked that *knowledge* and *love* be kept together. At the close of the essay he urges the uniting of *freedom* and *love*. Paul is again subtly preparing the reader for the hymn to love that will appear in chapter 13.

The uniting of freedom and sensitivity/love here in cameo 4 is connected to cameo 1 at the beginning and cameo 7 at the end. Summarizing Paul's opening cameo he insists that "all things are lawful, but all are not helpful or upbuilding." Why is this? Because freedom must be marinated with love (cameo 4). At the end of the homily in cameo 7 Paul teaches: Give offense to no one, seek their advantage, not your own—that they may be saved. This reflects the love admonished in the center cameo.

The larger question is not, what does freedom assure me (cameos 3, 5)? But rather, what does love require of me (cameo 4)? For Paul's readers who were accustomed to ring composition, this climactic call for sensitivity/love was unambiguous and compelling.

As noted earlier, for many contemporary readers the order is confusing. We are conditioned to listening to a presentation that offers:

On the one hand:
At home (2) and at private banquets (3) give thanks, *eat what you like* (5) and give glory to God (6).

But, (*alla*) on the other hand:
If someone tells you, "This is idol meat," for *his sake* do not eat the meat (4).

This sequence is so deeply ingrained in the English-speaking world that the RSV placed parentheses around cameo 4 as if it were an aside. Its position in the center as the climax of the homily is thereby obscured.[7] But once Paul's use of the prophetic rhetorical template is identified, the center climax shines brightly with appropriate splendor.

This is how a Christian can live in a non-Christian society. As noted, Paul's theme song throughout the essay is "Freedom and Responsibility." That responsibility (cameo 4) takes on the color of love and sensitivity.

In summary, Paul has earlier discussed

1. What about idol meat served in temple-operated restaurants? Paul's answer is, It is acceptable if you really understand that the idols do not exist and as long as there is no one present who is still deeply unsettled about these so-called gods.

2. What about eating and drinking in an idol worship service? Paul's answer was, "Never! Such eating is participation in the worship of demons."

---

[7]Fortunately the NRSV corrected this error.

In this text Paul considers two further questions. These are:

3. Can I buy this idol meat in the market and eat it at home? Paul replies by saying, "Eat whatever is sold in the meat market" (cameo 2). The idols do not exist and the meat itself belongs to God—not to the idols. The whole earth is his.

4. What about a dinner party in the home of one of my unbelieving friends? Paul responds using language that is almost a direct quote from what Jesus told the seventy disciples when he sent them out two by two. Both Jesus (Lk 10:8) and Paul say, "Eat whatever is set before you" (cameo 3). But if someone tells you, "This is idol meat," out of love for the informant—don't eat.

Paul's near direct quote from Jesus opens the possibility of a relationship between Jesus' sending out of the seventy (Lk 10:1-12) and Paul's mission to the Gentiles.[8] Paul also traveled light, entered each community in weakness and seems to have followed the other instructions Jesus gave to the seventy.

Genesis 10 lists seventy Gentile nations and the book of *Jubilees* 44:34 (composed in Hebrew about 150 b.c.) also mentions the seventy nations. Regarding Luke 10:1 Marshall writes, "Although the content of the sayings is related to mission in Palestine, it is possible that Luke regarded this mission as prefiguring the church's mission to the Gentiles."[9] Thus, Jesus' sending out of the seventy disciples echoes a concern for people beyond Israel.

After his profound reflections on how a Christian can live out his or her life in the midst of a pagan world, Paul concludes the essay with his signature ending (cameo 8). The Corinthians are not to imitate him in everything, but insofar as he imitates Christ they can confidently take his life as a model.

It is not an accident that this essay appears in the center of the five essays that make up the epistle. How to live out the Christian life in a pagan world was (and is) a vital question for Christians in every age. The center of Romans discusses "Christian and Jew" (Rom 9–11). Here in 1 Corinthians the center is "Christian and Pagan." The two essays are a pair, and their placement in each case is deliberate.

Having discussed "men and women in the human family" in the second essay, Paul now opens a matching topic for the fourth essay. This new topic is "men and women in the church." To that essay we now turn.

---

[8]Barnabas, Paul's first traveling companion, was identified by some early authors to be one of the seventy. See Jon Daniels, "Barnabas," in *ABD*, 1:611. Did Barnabas tell Paul about Jesus' instructions to the seventy? Did Paul learn it from the apostles?
[9]I. Howard Marshall, *The Gospel of Luke* (Exeter, U.K.: Paternoster, 1978), p. 413.

# Worship

*Men and Women in the Church*

1 CORINTHIANS 11:2–14:40

المحبّة لا تسقط أبدا
(13:8)

# Men and Women Leading in Worship

*Prophets and How They Dress*

1 CORINTHIANS 11:2-16

LEAVING ASIDE THE INTRODUCTION (1:1-9) and final remarks, 1 Corinthians is composed of five essays. By way of review, these are:

1. The Cross and Christian Unity (1:10–4:16)
2. Sex: Men and Women in the Human Family (4:17–7:40)
3. Christian and Pagan: Freedom and Responsibility (8:1–11:1)
4. *Worship: Men and Women in the Church (11:2–14:40)*
5. The Resurrection (15)

In each essay thus far examined, Paul deals with a single problem and the larger reality that it invokes. The crisis discussed here in essay four has to do with various aspects of worship, with special emphasis on the place of men and women both as leaders and as worshipers. The outline of this essay is:

WORSHIP: Men and Women in the Church (11:2–14:40)
4.1 Men and Women *Leading in Worship*: Prophets and How They Dress (11:2-16)
4.2    Order in Worship: *Sacrament*—The Lord's Supper (11:17-34)
4.3        Gifts and the Nature of the Body (12:1-30)
4.4            The Hymn to Love (12:31–14:1)
4.5        Spiritual Gifts and the Upbuilding of the Body (14:1-25)
4.6    Order in Worship: *Word*—Prophets and Speakers in Tongues (14:26-33)
4.7 Women and Men *Worshiping*: No Chatting in Church (14:3b-40)

Of the five essays that make up the epistle, this is the most extensive. The other essays are composed of four to six sections while this essay boasts of seven. The seven sections follow the pattern of the prophetic rhetorical template already seen in various forms. Ring composition brings the essay to its climax with the famous hymn to love in the center. Like a river of pure water, the discussion of love (chapter 13) is placed in the center to nourish and cleanse the various aspects of worship presented in the six homilies that surround it. As in the other essays, Paul begins with a reference to the tradition. Here he opens with,

> [11:2]I praise you because you remember me in everything      THE TRADITION
> and maintain the traditions as I have delivered them to you.

In 1:4-9 Paul began the epistle as a whole with a word of thanks for the grace given to the Corinthians and for their "speech" and "knowledge." He then began at once to voice his displeasure over their quarreling. Likewise, here Paul opens with a strong word of *praise* for their having remembered him and for their preservation of "the traditions."[1] After a few verses he bluntly tells them that he cannot praise them (11:17-22). The initial compliments are followed by a list of their failings.

The key word *deliver* has an important rabbinic history. It is the second part of the rabbinic formula for passing on the sacred tradition of the community. One of the oldest tractates (chapters) of the Mishnah is called *'Abot* (The Fathers).[2] That venerable collection of the sayings of the early rabbis begins with, "Moses *received* the Torah at Sinai and *delivered* it to Joshua, Joshua to the elders, and the elders to the prophets, and the prophets to the men of the great synagogue."[3] The two key words are *received* (*qbl*) and *delivered* (*msr*). These words are the backbone of the formula used in the rabbinic world for the passing on of the traditions from one generation to another. This activity was extremely important for Judaism of the time. The material preserved through this method produced The Mishnah, The Babylonian and Jerusalem Talmuds, the Tosefta and finally the Midrash Rabbah. Together these sets comprise more than eighty volumes. Here Paul writes of the "traditions" he has "deliv-

---

[1]English versions have often softened "praise" into "commend." The Syriac, Arabic and Hebrew versions of the past sixteen hundred years have consistently maintained the word *praise*.

[2]The Mishnah is a compilation of the sayings of 148 named Jewish rabbis from around 50 B.C. up to A.D. 200. Edited by Judah the Prince about A.D. 200, it is the earliest collection of such sayings.

[3]Mishnah, *'Abot* 1:1 (my translation).

ered" to the Corinthians. A few verses later, as he focuses on the Lord's Supper, Paul uses the full formula for the passing on of tradition. He writes, "I *received* from the Lord what I *delivered* to you." In 15:3 Paul will affirm, "For I *delivered* to you as of first importance what I also *received*."

The text before us is the earliest reference we have to the formal passing on of a fixed *Christian tradition*. Jesus was crucified around A.D. 30, and Paul wrote 1 Corinthians in A.D. 54 or 55.[4] From what Paul writes in this text, it is clear that during the twenty-five-year period from A.D. 30-55 the Christian community was steadily collecting and organizing a body of traditions that were recognizable as such and judged worthy to be passed from one generation to another. They included (at least) the Jesus tradition, early creedal formulations, the words of institution of the Lord's Supper and probably some hymns (Phil 2:5-11?).

Paul did not *create a movement*, he *joined one*! He praises the Corinthians for remembering and maintaining the *Christian traditions* that he first *received* and then passed on to them. A reference to the traditions is the way Paul opens each of the five essays, and thereby becomes his marker for the beginning of a new topic.

After this reference to the tradition, Paul presents the first of seven homilies focused on "Worship: Men and Women in Worship." The text of this opening homily is displayed in figure 4.1(1).

Within the larger question of the place of women in the New Testament this passage is of critical importance. Across church history, various voices have found regimental colors or even battle cries in these verses. One quickly thinks of:

- "The head of woman is man."
- "Any woman who prays . . . with her head unveiled, dishonors her head."
- "Man was not made for woman but woman for man."

In its blunt form, the interpretation of these phrases is often summarized in the following manner:

This passage tells women that
(1) they are to live under male authority,
(2) keep their heads covered in public, and
(3) understand that they were created to serve men!

---

[4]Robert Jewett, *Dating Paul's Life* (London: SCM Press, 1979).

1. [11:3]Now [*de*] I want you to understand that          A THEOLOGICAL
   the head [origin] of every man is Christ,               Principle
   the head [origin] of woman is man,
   the head [origin] of Christ is God.

2. [4]Any man who prays or prophesies                      CHURCH PRACTICE
      with his head covered                                (and its reason)
         dishonors his head,
   [5]and any woman who prays or prophesies
      with her head unveiled
         dishonors her head—

3.        for it is the same as if her head were shaved,   EXAMPLE—WOMEN
          [6]for if a woman [prophet] will not veil herself,   (shaved = dishonor/disgrace)
          then let her cut off her hair;
          but if it is disgraceful for a woman to be shorn or shaved
          then let her wear a veil.

4.          [7]For a man ought not to cover the head,       MEN—NOT COVER
            since he is the image and glory of God;         (Gen 1:27)
            and woman is the glory of man.

5.            [8]For man is not from [*ek*] woman,          MAN—Not From Woman
              but [*alla*] woman is from [*ek*] man.        Woman from Man (Gen 2:21)

6.              [9]For man was not created because of [*dia*] woman,
                but woman because of [*dia*] the man.       DEPENDENCE (Gen 2:18)

7.                [10]Because of [*dia*] this
                  the woman should have authority on the head,
                  because of [*dia*] the angels.            AUTHORITY

8.              [11]More specifically [*plen*] woman is not independent of man
                nor man independent of woman in the Lord;   DEPENDENCE

9.            [12]for as the woman is from [*ek*] the man,  WOMAN—From Man and
              so also the man is [born] through [*dia*] the woman.   Through Woman
              And all things are from [*ek*] God.           (Gen 1:27)

10.         [13]Judge among yourselves:                     WOMEN—VEILED
            is it proper for a woman to pray to God unveiled?

11.       [14]Does not nature itself teach you             EXAMPLE—MEN
          that for a man to wear long hair                  (long hair = dishonor)
          it is dishonor to him,                            EXAMPLE—WOMEN
          [15]but if a woman has long hair,                 (long hair = glory)
          it is her glory?
          For her hair is given to her for a covering.

12. [16]If anyone is disposed to be contentious
    we recognize no other practice,                         CHURCH PRACTICE
    nor do the churches of God.

---

**Figure 4.1(1). Men and women leading in worship: Prophets and how they should dress
(1 Cor 11:3-16)**

Such a reading of the text is of great antiquity and has dominated large parts of church life for centuries. But does it represent what Paul intends? As elsewhere, this dense and mysterious passage does not reveal all its secrets to anyone. No interpretation can satisfy every reader. Yet, some things can be understood and some errors corrected. I will do my best.[5]

## THE RHETORIC

Two levels of rhetorical style are at work in this text. First is the connection between this homily and the seventh homily in this essay. As noted above, essay four is composed of seven inverted homilies with a climax in the center. Paul assumes that his readers understand what he is doing. In this opening homily Paul discusses the *male and female prophets*. In the seventh homily he will return to these same *male and female prophets*, some of whom are all talking at once. Some women had stopped listening and started chatting. Perhaps they did not know enough Greek. More of this later.

Internally, this homily is a further case of the high jump style already observed. Like a high jump, this homily has four parts:

The approach (cameo 1)
The jump (cameos 2-6)
The climax [crossing the bar] (cameo 7)
The fall to the pad on the far side (cameos 8-12)

Cameo 1 is an introduction. The opening presentation of Paul's case comprises cameos 2-6. Cameo 7, in the center, forms the climax. The remaining five cameos (8-12) are carefully paired with cameos 2-6. The church's practice opens and closes the ring composition that forms the bulk of the homily. Cameo 2 has six lines of carefully constructed step parallelism, such was observed in 8:6. As with the hymn to the cross in 1:17–2:2, so here Paul has longer cameos on the outside and a series of seven shorter cameos in the center. The seven-cameo center forms a perfect prophetic rhetorical template (cameos 4-10).

## COMMENTARY

The general problem is unmistakable. The Corinthian church had both male

---

[5]The literature on this passage is enormous. Thiselton lists more than eighty recent articles on these verses alone. His extended discussion is profound and thorough, and is highly recommended to anyone seeking a technical presentation of the current debate. See Thiselton, *First Epistle*, pp. 799-848.

and female prophets and both genders were participating in worship leadership. Paul tells his readers that the men who "pray and prophesy" are to *uncover* their heads, and that the women who "pray and prophesy" must *cover* their heads. It is easy to read cameo 1 and focus exclusively on the problem of head coverings. From the outset, it is clear that the issue is gender *distinctions*, not gender *subordination*.

The women and the men are doing the same things. They are both praying and prophesying. *Praying* can refer to private devotions, but the act of *prophesying* is a public function carried out in front of other people. It is impossible to prophesy meaningfully in the seclusion of one's closet. Paul is talking about men and women who are leading public worship. This provides a clue to understand the rest of the homily as it unfolds.

It appears that the women prophets had understood Paul's phrase "all things are lawful to me"[6] as meaning "Women do not need to cover their heads when prophesying in front of the worshiping congregation." But as the women prophets exercised this right, problems emerged. Some members of the congregation had a Jewish background, and others came to faith in Jesus from a Roman or Greek background. What then were the problems?

For the Christians with a Jewish background their tradition affirmed that self-respecting women cover their heads in public.[7] The Mishnah rules that women should be divorced if they uncovered their heads in public.[8] A woman's hair was to be seen only by her husband and the family. (The Amish community of North America is a contemporary Western example of this ancient practice.) In conservative Islamic countries today, the public head covering of a woman signals to all that she is a respectable woman who has a family that cares, and anyone who harasses her will face consequences.[9] It is a form of protection for her.

As regards the Greco-Roman world and the city of Corinth, Dio Chrysostomus (b. A.D. 40) describes Corinth toward the end of the first century. He observes that "large numbers gathered at Corinth on account of the harbors and the *hetaerae* [sacred prostitutes]."[10] In museums in Greece I have exam-

---

[6]Paul had apparently endorsed this principle (see 6:12; 10:23).

[7]Lightfoot, *First Corinthians*, pp. 231-41.

[8]Mishnah, *Ketubbot* 6:6 (Danby, p. 255).

[9]Thiselton, *First Epistle*, p. 801.

[10]Dio Chrysostom, *Discourses* 8:5-10, quoted in Jerome Murphy-O'Connor, *St. Paul's Corinth: Texts and Archaeology* (Collegeville, Minn.: Liturgical Press, 2002), p. 100.

ined the statues of women, and most of them have their heads covered. Some do not, but it is impossible to know which of these were statues of women at home, where their heads could be uncovered. In any case, most of the female statues of the early centuries present women with covered heads. We can assume that prostitutes did not cover their heads. Even if bare-headed women prophets would not have disturbed Greek Christians, it would still have been a serious concern for Jewish Christians. The outcry would have been: "What is this! Are these women advertising their charms? How are we expected to concentrate on worship with this going on?"

It is understandable that Paul felt the need to discuss the issue of the prophets and their "clerical garb." He does not put women down. He had a record on these matters. From the book of Acts we know that Greek women of high standing were attracted to the preaching of Paul (Acts 16:14; 17:4, 12, 34). Such women would not have been attracted to a movement that did not treat them as equals. The church in Philippi met in the house of Lydia, a seller of purple cloth. The fact that Paul visited her (most likely with the magistrates) on his way out of town indicates that she was the leader of the church (Acts 16:35-40). One of the two ports for the city of Corinth was Cenchrea. The church there was led by Phoebe (Rom 16:1-2), who is called a deacon (not deaconess) and a *prostatis* (leader). While in Corinth Paul lived with Aquila and Priscilla (Acts 18:1-4). Priscilla was a "professor of theology," who, with her husband, taught the famous Apollos (Acts 18:26). Living with this prominent Christian couple for eighteen months, and having them as personal friends, it is impossible to imagine Paul writing a letter to the Corinthians that would demean Priscilla. For more than a year he had *eaten at her table*. It is quite possible that Priscilla was one of the women prophets under discussion in this homily.

What then does the text infer regarding men and women, and how they presented themselves to lead in worship? The men (it seems) led in worship with heads uncovered! In the heady flush of freedom from the law, the women began to follow suit. Some in the church were upset and the issue was put to Paul in writing (7:1). The easy answer would have been, "Let the women refrain from praying and prophesying when you meet in worship." Instead, Paul affirms the rightness of having *both* male and female leadership in public worship. He then solves the problem by telling the women leaders to cover their heads *while leading in worship*. The men are to conduct worship with heads uncovered. What is his argument?

Paul begins with an introductory theological affirmation which is:

1.[11:3]Now [de] I want you to understand that      A THEOLOGICAL
     the head [origin] of every man is Christ,      Principle
     the head [origin] of woman is man,
     the head [origin] of Christ is God.

The Greek word *kefale* (head) has three meanings.[11] These are:

1. the cranium (as in "My *head* hurts")
2. in authority over (as in "Ms. Jones is the *head* of this company")
3. source of (as in "The *head* waters of the Nile flow from Lake Victoria")

The Jewish new year is celebrated as *Rosh Hashanah*, "the *head* of the year." The first day of the year is not "in authority over" the rest of the year. Rather, the year "flows from" that first day. In the Old Testament "The fear of the Lord is the *head* [*rosh*] of wisdom" (Ps 111:10). English language translations usually read, "The fear of the Lord is the *beginning* of wisdom."

In this introductory cameo, the first meaning does not fit. Traditionally many Christians have chosen the second option and read *kefale* (head) in this text as meaning, "authority over." But it is fully possible to select the third meaning of *kefale* and read "origin of." In this case the text would mean:

- "The origin of every man is Christ" (i.e., Christ is the agent of God in creation. In 8:6 Paul affirms that Jesus Christ is the one "through whom are all things.")

- "The origin of woman is man" (i.e., Genesis 2:21-23). Woman [ishah] is "taken out of man [ish]."

- "The origin of Christ is God" (i.e., the Christ is "the Messiah" and the origin of the Messiah is God). In the language of later centuries, "The Son proceeds from the Father." Christ comes *from God*. This is like "The *origin* of wisdom is the fear of the Lord" (Ps 111:10).

Just as wisdom has its origin in the fear of the Lord, even so the phrase "the origin of Christ is God" can be seen as an affirmation of the divine source from which Jesus has come and thus an affirmation of his divinity.

This raises the question of the order of creation. Much popular understanding of the second account of creation (Gen 2:4-25) notes that man was created first and woman second, and concludes that "created first" means "of first impor-

---

[11]For an extended discussion of this word see Thiselton, *First Epistle*, pp. 812-22.

tance." The difficulty with this conclusion is that the creation stories begin with the lesser forms of life and move on to the more advanced forms. If created earlier equals more important, then animals are more important than people, the plants are more important than the animals and the primitive earth "without form and void" is the most important of all! In spite of this obvious sequence in the creation story, traditional views of the creation account have affirmed men as more important than women because men were created first. Paul's readers were probably quoting Genesis 2:4-25, and thereby Paul starts from their vantage point in the hope of moving them forward to his own views.

We also notice that Christ is mentioned twice in this opening cameo. The only other mention of Christ is near the center, with a single reference to the interdependence of women and men "in the Lord" (cameo 8). It seems that Paul wants to introduce this homily with a strong christological affirmation. The origin of man (and indirectly of woman) is Christ, who is from God. With that banner flying, Paul proceeds to reflect on the problem.

As in earlier cases of ring composition, the various pairs of cameos that Paul offers to his readers will be examined, starting from the outside. The first two cameos and the matching final two are seen in figure 4.1(2).

2.   ⁴Any man who prays or prophesies                    CHURCH PRACTICE
        with his head covered                            (and its reason)
            dishonors his head,
        ⁵and any woman who prays or prophesies
        with her head unveiled
            dishonors her head—

3.           for it is the same as if her head were shaved,          EXAMPLE—WOMEN
             ⁶for if a woman [prophet] will not veil herself,        (shaved = dishonor/disgrace)
             then let her cut off her hair;
             but if it is disgraceful for a woman to be shorn or shaved
             then let her wear a veil.

-----------------------------------------------------------------------------------------

11.          ¹⁴Does not nature itself teach you                      EXAMPLE—MEN
             that for a man to wear long hair                        (long hair = dishonor)
             it is dishonor to him,                                  EXAMPLE—WOMEN
             ¹⁵but if a woman has long hair,                         (long hair = glory)
             it is her glory?
             For her hair is given to her for a covering.

12.  ¹⁶If anyone is disposed to be contentious
        we recognize no other practice,            CHURCH PRACTICE
        nor do the churches of God.

**Figure 4.1(2). Cameos 2-3 and 11-12 (1 Cor 11:4-6, 14-16)**

In the mid-seventeenth century John Lightfoot wrote,

> It was the custom of the Jews that they prayed not, unless first their head [*sic*] were veiled, and that for this reason; that by this rite they might show themselves reverent, and ashamed before God, and unworthy with an open face to behold him.[12]

Lightfoot presents a series of rabbinic texts to document this statement. With this as the Jewish standard, why did Paul think that a man leading in worship with his head covered *dishonored* Christ? Aware of the long discussion on this question, I can but offer my own view. In the Middle East the servant is expected to cover his head in the presence of his master. In regard to servants this view is universally understood and applied across the region. But Jesus called his disciples "friends" not "servants/slaves" (Jn 15:12-17). The servant/slave does not know what his master is doing. But Jesus revealed to his disciples "all that I have heard from my father" (Jn 15:15). Yet the close relationship between Jesus and his disciples reaches even deeper levels.

Earlier in John's Gospel Jesus affirms:

> I am the good shepherd.
> The good shepherd lays down his life for the sheep. (Jn 10:11)

Three verses later the same two lines are quoted with new material in the center. The resulting sandwich reads:

> *I am the good shepherd*;
> I know my own and my own knows me,
> as the Father knows me and I know the Father;
> *and I lay down my life for the sheep.* (Jn 10:14)

This new material affirms an amazing depth of intimacy between Jesus and his Father and between Jesus and his flock, *because of the cross*.[13] That is, the description of the intimacy between the Father and the Son, and the linked intimacy between the Son and his flock, is placed in an envelope that tells of the good shepherd's action in dying for the sheep. Paul's views are in harmony with this theology.

For Paul righteousness as applied to the believing community (Rom 3:21-31; 5:1-2) had to do with granting an undeserved status of acceptance that a king or Lord gives to an unworthy servant. Once that status is granted, such

---

[12]Lightfoot, *1 Corinthians*, pp. 229-30.

[13]The biblical word *to know* is the word used for the marital relationship. It implies intimate personal knowledge.

servants can stand "with unveiled faces" before the king. In 2 Corinthians 3:12-18 Paul describes how Moses had to veil his face, "but when a man turns to the Lord the veil is removed. . . . And we all, with unveiled face, beholding the glory of the Lord, are being changed into his likeness from one degree of glory to another" (vv. 16, 18).

Putting this together, the Lord (the *kurios*) accepts his slaves/servants as friends, affirming that they are no longer merely servants (John). That same Lord grants those servants the unearned title of "righteous," and removes the veil over their faces by dying on the cross (Paul). As this happens, can those servants respond by assuming shame and again veil their faces? And if they do, are they not *dishonoring* that Lord? The prodigal, in the parable of the prodigal son, accepts the father's costly love. He accepts to be found (Lk 15:20-24) and is given the father's best robe to wear. Can the prodigal then cast that robe aside and appear at the banquet that evening dressed in his rags? If he did, would he not *dishonor* his father? So much for the men. What then can be said about the women?

We cannot be sure, but it is possible to assume that for Paul this also applied to the women—*in the worshiping congregation*. But the prophets who *participated in worship leadership* had a special responsibility. If a female prophet led in worship (in that Jewish-Roman culture) with her head bare, all eyes would be on her (unlike the women seated in the congregation). Her bared head would be seen by some as inappropriate exposure. The Babylonian Talmud records a saying of Rabbi Shesheth (third to fourth century) that reads, "A woman's hair is a sexual incitement, as it says, *Thy hair is as a flock of goats* [Song 4:1]."[14] Such attitudes are of great antiquity and they persist across the Middle East, in conservative areas, to this day.

Furthermore, shifting to the second account of creation, her human "origin" was the man (Gen 2:21-23). It is possible (with the RSV) to read "her head" (cameo 2) as meaning "her husband." Understood in this manner, said husband would be acutely embarrassed by having his wife, with head uncovered, leading the congregation in worship. He would be in the position of a modern husband watching his clergy wife leading in worship wearing a dress that is too tight and too low-cut.

Paul could easily have said, "As regards the women leading in worship, the subject is too complicated. They had better stay seated in the congregation." Instead his directive is,

---

[14]Babylonian Talmud, *Berakot* 14a.

Women prophets, carry on! The church needs your prophetic ministry. But please, I beg you, cover your heads when you prophesy so that the congregation will not be distracted away from your prophetic word. Your message is what matters, and that is what we want the people to hear and remember.

Paul follows up on this directive by telling his readers in cameo 3:

Women prophets, if you don't like this suggestion—there is a second alternative. Cut it all off and the problem is solved. If you are not comfortable doing so, please consider my first proposal.

Cameo 11 matches the haircut solution offered in cameo 3. Surely, observing the intended connection between 3 and 11 is the key to understanding cameo 11. Paul is continuing the discussion of "cutting it all off" (cameo 3) and reminding his readers (in cameo 11) that women are expected to have long hair. When men grow long hair, they dishonor themselves (in that culture).[15] But not so women. For women, their hair is their glory. Don't cut it off, he pleads—that would make them look like men. His solution is simple: Cover the hair (not the face) when leading in worship. That pretty hair can be exposed at the appropriate time to the appropriate people and the problem is solved, simply and honorably.

Finally in cameo 12 Paul closes the directive he presented in cameo 2 by telling his readers that the pattern of male prophets (with uncovered heads) and female prophets (with heads covered) is the worship leadership dress code followed by *all the churches* and is the only pattern he can commend. He seems to plead, "Please do not fight over a problem that has an easy solution."

The third envelope of two matching cameos includes cameo 4 and cameo 10 [see fig. 4.1(3)].

| 4. | [7]For a man ought not to cover the head, since he is the image and glory of God; and woman is the glory of man. | MEN—NOT COVER Gen 1:27 |
|----|----|----|
| 10. | [13]Judge among yourselves: is it proper for a woman to pray to God unveiled? | WOMEN—VEILED |

**Figure 4.1(3). Cameos 4 and 10 (1 Cor 11:7, 13)**

[15]John of Damascus (d. 750) visited Constantinople and was shocked at what he saw. "Women went about with uncovered heads and unveiled their limbs in a provocative and deliberately sensuous way. Young men grew effeminate and let their hair grow long" (quoted in William Dalrymple, *From the Holy Mountain* [New York: Henry Holt, 1997], p. 37; see also Kenneth E. Bailey, *Jesus Through Middle Eastern Eyes* [Downers Grove, Ill.: IVP Academic, 2008], pp. 248-49).

These two cameos need a "Guide for the Perplexed." I understand a part of what Paul is saying, but in the midst of much disagreement and confusion in the current literature, I do not see an uncluttered path forward for cameo 4 as a whole. The following, however, is clear to me:

1. Paul starts with theological data from the second story of creation that appears in Genesis 2:21-23 probably because at least some of his readers were using that text to marginalize women. He then introduces ideas from Genesis 1:26-27, where God created male and female *together* and *both* were made *in the image of God*. Paul asserts that the man was in the image of God, but he does not say that the woman was "in the image of man." Such a statement would violate Genesis 1:26 where "humankind" (Hebrew: *adam*) is in the image and likeness of God. Paul assumes that the women (of course) are also in the image of God as Genesis 1:26 affirms.

2. "Woman is the glory of man" *can mean* "woman is the glory of human-kind." She was created as the final climax of the creation story. God started with light. He continued as he created water, land, plants, birds, animals, man and finally woman. As noted, the process was on an ascending scale that mentions the creation of the man (in passing) and reaches its peak with the creation of a woman who is the "glory of man[kind]." When the worshipers look at a man leading worship (with no head covering) they could appropriately think, *How great is our God who created a human being*. But when they look at a woman leading in worship (without a head covering) they could think, *How great is this climax of creation*. Rather than contemplating *the Creator*, they could (?) mentally turn to reflect on *the creation*. By uncovering her hair (in that culture) she draws special attention to her gender.

3. Paul is clearly still working on his proposed solution. He tells them, "Men, (while leading in worship) don't cover your heads. Women, (while leading in worship) cover your heads."

Beyond these three aspects of the text there is mystery that I have yet to understand.

The matching cameo 10 is straightforward (and becomes more so in the light of cameos 5-9). The central focus in 4 is *"Men should not cover their heads."* This is matched here in cameo 10 with the assumption *"Women should cover their heads."* The two together make up Paul's proposed solution. Do the Corinthians really think that it is in the interest of the church, living in a Jewish and Roman/Greek context, to have women leading worship with uncovered heads? Surely not! This brings us to the five-cameo center of the homily [see fig. 4.1(4)].

5.  8For man is not from [*ek*] woman,                    MAN—Not from Woman
    but [*alla*] woman is from [*ek*] man.               Woman from Man (Gen 2:21)

6.      9For man was not created because of [*dia*] woman,    DEPENDENCE
        but woman because of [*dia*] the man.                Gen 2:18

7.          10Because of [*dia*] this
            the woman should have authority on the head,        AUTHORITY
            because of [*dia*] the angels.

8.      11More specifically [*plen*], woman is not independent of man
        nor man independent of woman in the Lord;           DEPENDENCE

9.  12for as the woman is from [*ek*] the man,             WOMAN—From Man and
    so also the man is [born] through [*dia*] the woman.  Through Woman
    And all things are from [*ek*] God.                    (Gen 1:27)

**Figure 4.1(4). Cameos 5-9 (1 Cor 11:8-12)**

The center climax of the homily is cameo 7, examined below.

Cameos 5 and 9 are so carefully matched that if cameos 6-8 were missing, no one would notice their absence [see fig. 4.1(5)].

5.  8For man is not from [*ek*] woman,                    MAN—Not from Woman
    but [*alla*] woman is from [*ek*] man.               Woman from Man (Gen 2:21)

-------------------------------------------------------------------------------

9.  12for as the woman is from [*ek*] the man,             WOMAN—From Man and
    so also the man is [born] through [*dia*] the woman.  Through Woman
    And all things are from [*ek*] God.                    (Gen 1:27)

**Figure 4.1(5). Cameos 5 and 9 (1 Cor 11:8, 12)**

This precise matching of separated cameos is a sure sign of an author highly skilled in the use of ring composition. Paul opens cameo 9 by repeating what he said in cameo 5 and continues by noting the interdependence of male and female. The chain-link logic used here is strong. Apparently some in the church thought the woman was inferior because she was taken out of the side of Adam (Gen 2:21-23). Paul counters by saying to his male readers,

It is true that the woman was created *from the man* (4), but where did you come from? Your mother came before you and you were taken *out of her body* (8), so what are we arguing about? The female came *out of the body of the male*, and every male (since Adam) has come *out of the body of a female*. The conclusion of the matter is "all things (both male and female) *come from God*" (Gen 1:27).

Paul knows that his readers are fully aware of the second account of creation in Genesis 2:21-23. Affirming that text, Paul deftly introduces theological data from the first story recorded in Genesis 1:26-28. Then in the three center cameos he clinches his argument [see fig. 4.1(6)].

| | | |
|---|---|---|
| 6. | ⁹For man was not created because of [*dia*] woman, | DEPENDENCE |
| | but woman because of [*dia*] the man. | Gen. 2:18 |
| | | |
| 7. | ¹⁰Because of [*dia*] this | |
| | the woman should have authority on the head, | AUTHORITY |
| | because of [*dia*] the angels. | |
| | | |
| 8. | ¹¹More specifically [*plen*], woman is not independent of man | |
| | nor man independent of woman in the Lord; | DEPENDENCE |

**Figure 4.1(6). Cameos 6-8 (1 Cor 11:9-11)**

The first key to these seven lines is the Greek preposition *dia* which appears four times in a row. All four are in the same case and should be read together. The translator can render this preposition as "for" or as "because of." For centuries we have used "for" in the first two cases of *dia* but have translated the last two as "because of." Many translations thus give us some form of:

6.    ⁹For man was not created *for* [*dia*] woman
      but woman *for* [*dia*] man

7.    ¹⁰*because of* [*dia*] this
      the woman should have authority on the head
      *because of* [*dia*] the angels.

This translation has had great influence in shaping both female and male understanding of the place of women in the Christian scheme of things. Why do we have women? God has created them, the argument goes, *for men*, that is, to serve men. In the contemporary scene I have read entire books (written by women) that take this translation as a touchstone for understanding the "proper" biblical place for Christian women in the family, the church and in society.

The difficulty with this view is that it is built on a *particular translation* of the text, not on *the text itself*. This interpretation translates the Greek preposition *dia* as "for" (in the first two lines) and immediately reads the same word as "because of" (in the second two lines). This view rightly confirms that *dia* in this text *can be translated* "because of." But, what happens if "because of" is selected as a translation for *all four* occurrences of the preposition *dia*? Choosing this option, the text reads:

6.    ⁹for the man was not created *because of* the woman
    but the woman *because of* the man.

7.    ¹⁰*Because of* this
    the woman should have authority on the head
    *because of* the angels.

Now cameo 6 refers to the Genesis story of Adam and Eve (Gen 2:18). It was not *Eve* who was lonely, unable to manage and needed help. Instead, it was *Adam* who could not manage alone. Eve was then created as an *'ezera*. The Hebrew word *'ezer* is often used for God when God comes to help or save Israel. It appears in the name *el-'ezer* (which in Greek becomes Lazarus), that is, "the one whom God helps/saves." The word *'ezer* does not refer to a lowly assistant but to a powerful figure who comes to help/save someone who is in trouble.

Seen in this light, our understanding of the text and of Paul's view of women are transformed. Women, for Paul, are not created "for men," that is, for their bed and board. Rather women, as descendants of Eve, are placed by God in the human scene as the strong who come to help/save the needy (the men). In this reading of the text, Paul the Middle Eastern male chauvinist disappears. In its place Paul emerges as a compassionate figure who boldly affirms the equality and mutual interdependency of men and women in the new covenant. I would submit that this is the heart of what Paul has to say in the five cameos that make up the center of this homily. This reading of the text helps explain why Greek women of high standing were attracted to Paul's message and why they joined the movement he represented.

Cameos 6 and 8 are often presented as contrasts, whereas they should be seen as two aspects of a single theme. Cameo 8 is introduced with the Greek word *plen* which can mean "more specifically" or "in any case." BAGD explains this word as "breaking off a discussion and emphasizing what is important."[16] *Alla*, the common Greek word for a contrast, appears (introducing a contrast) in the second line of cameo 5. Here at the opening of cameo 8, *plen* draws attention to "what is important" in the previous discussion. Thus Paul is saying

Women (like Eve) were created because the men (like Adam) needed help (6).

---

[16]BAGD, p. 669. Cf. LSJ, *A Greek-English Lexicon*, p. 1419.

More specifically [*plen*] what I mean is, *in the Lord* men and women are mutually interdependent (8).

The same affirmation of the interdependency of male and female appeared in Paul's discussion of *Christian marriage* (7:2-5). Here, interdependence is broadened to apply to men and women in Christ in their life together *in the church*.

Finally, how are we to understand "authority on the head" and "because of the angels" that appear in cameo 7? Initially, the first line of cameo 7 reads "because of *this*," and the word *this* refers back to the creation story where the woman was created to help/save the struggling lonely man. The woman was the hero of the story up to that point. Remembering her noble origins, Paul affirms that she should "have *exousia* [authority] on the head." Adam was *El-'ezer*, that is, he was Lazarus, "the one whom God helped." And how did God help him? By sending an *'ezra* (a helper: i.e., Eve), and for this reason the woman should have a sign of authority on her head when she prophesies before the worshiping congregation. When Queen Elizabeth II wears a crown, that crown is a symbol of her authority. For Paul the same assumption applied to the women prophets who led the congregation in worship. He intended for them to see the head covering as a visible symbol of their authority to proclaim a prophetic word to the congregation.

Morna Hooker of Cambridge University has argued that the background of this text is rabbinic and that in those circles "to some extent authority for the created order had devolved upon [the angels], and we should therefore expect angels to be concerned with seeing that the ordering of things established at creation is maintained."[17] The head covering for women prophets was a sign of their *exousia* (authority) in the community as they joined with the men in leading the worship of the faithful.

In this connection Midrash Genesis Rabbah discusses the very first sabbath at the end of the six days of creation. The text reads: "When the sun set on the night of the Sabbath, the light continued to function, whereupon all began praising, as it is written, *under the whole heaven they sing praises to Him* (Job XXXVII, 3)."[18]

Adam and Eve may have joined in, but the angels were the primary singers in that outpouring of praise "under the whole heaven." Paul had already af-

---

[17]Morna D. Hooker, "Authority on her Head: An examination of I Cor. XI.10," *New Testament Studies* 10 (1963-1964): 412

[18]Midrash Rabbah Genesis, 1.12.6 (London: Soncino Press, 1983), p. 92.

firmed that the angels were watching the activities of the apostles (4:9). So here, the angels present at creation were still on duty, observing the life of the church, and eager to praise God for his *new* creation.

But there may be even more taking place in the seven lines that make up the climax of this homily. Paul's hymn to the cross (1:17–2:2) involved thirteen cameos (with three extra notes). In that homily's center there is remarkable poetical artistry. The same special attention to the center appears to be at work here as well. The seven lines not only fall into the three cameos we have just examined. They also make sense when seen as a mini-prophetic rhetorical template [see fig. 4.1(7)].

| | |
|---|---|
| 1. For man was not *created* because of [*dia*] woman, | Man Not Because of Woman |
| 2.   but woman because of [*dia*] the man. | Woman Because of Man |
| 3.     Because of [*dia*] this (the creation) | Because of (Creation) |
| 4.        the woman should have *authority* on the head, | Woman—Authority |
| 5.      because of [*dia*] the angels. | Because of (Creation) |
| 6.   More specifically, woman is not independent of man | Woman Not Independent |
| 7. nor man independent of woman *in the Lord*; | Man Not Independent of Woman |

**Figure 4.1(7). Cameos 6-8 (1 Cor 11:9-11)**

This carefully written set of seven lines exhibits counterpoint. The seven lines fall into three cameos (6-8) that fit into the overall composition of the homily. At the same time the lines follow the prophetic rhetorical template seen above. The third line "because of *this*" means, "because of the great event of creation witnessed and praised by the angels." With this understanding of line 3 the reader is prepared to contemplate and understand the angels that appear in line 5. The climax in the center affirms women in worship leadership and gives them a sign of their authority.

To summarize, the rabbis argued that creation was such an astounding event that there must have been an audience to praise God for this wondrous accomplishment. Who was there to do it? Answer: the angels witnessed creation and sang praises to God. Even so, Paul seems to be referring to the presence of those same angels around the new creation of God—the church, the new temple. They were there for the same reason—to praise God for this wonderful event. (In this connection, each of the seven churches in the book of Revelation had an angel watching over it [Rev 2–3].) Furthermore, a part of this new creation is the restoration of the equality and mutual interdependence between men and women in Christ (presented in this text). Thus Paul says to the people in Corinth (and to the whole church):

Let the men and the women continue to pray and prophesy—only ladies, please, be reasonable! Cover your heads as you do so! Don't send the wrong signal to the worshipers, male and female. Do not distract them with your beautiful hair. If you don't like my solution, I have an alternative. Cut it all off (cameo 2). Appearing bald will solve the problem. If you would rather not go that route, then why not give my suggestion a try? Covering your heads when you lead in worship is not a putdown. Eve helped Adam in his weakness and need. Male and female need each other. Let the head covering be a sign for female prophets of their authority to exercise their prophetic gifts in leadership along with the male prophets. Do it *because of the angels*. The angels praised God at the first creation. Let them praise the wondrous fact of your restored status in the new creation, and let the image of God in which you were created shine forth through your prophetic word. This way you will preserve your rightful leadership role and will not distract or upset the congregation in the process.

You must know that a woman's hair, exposed in public, is seen as a come-on in sections of the society in which you live. I am not asking you to cover your heads every time you leave home. My suggestion only applies when you are *leading in worship* and all eyes are on you. I am asking for sensitivity to your cultural setting. Love for harmony in the church must be a key part of how you exercise your new freedom.

How then might this directive regarding dress for worship leaders be lived out in the twenty-first century? We are not living in first-century Corinth. Yet important theological principles are affirmed in the text. To men and to women in any age, I hear Paul saying:

> Men and women have gifts that they share together, and prophecy is among them (Acts 2:17-18). Those with these gifts should participate together in the leadership of worship. When doing so, do not dress in a manner that leads to misunderstanding or in any way detracts from the task of bringing the faithful into the presence of God. Both women and men are created in the image of God. Let the focus be on God, not on yourselves. In the Lord you are equal and mutually interdependent. Let the angels rejoice once again.

In conclusion, we can here see a finely tuned theological discussion on the place of men and women in Christian leadership that needs to have some ancient barnacles scraped from its surface so that its original intent can shine forth with grace and power.

But this was not the only problem in Corinth related to worship. Their celebrations of Holy Communion were a disaster. To that topic we now turn.

# Order in Worship

*Sacrament—The Lord's Supper*

1 Corinthians 11:17-34

In 11:17-34 Paul delivers a three-part homily on the Lord's Supper. The full text is displayed in figure 4.2(1).

### A. Hunger, Drunkenness, Quarreling: Not the Lord's Supper (11:17-22)

1. [17]But in the following instructions I do *not praise you*,
   because it is *not* for the *better*                    NO PRAISE
   but for the *worse when you assemble.*                   You Assemble

2. [18]For, in the first place,
   when you *assemble as a church,*                         CHURCH
   I hear that there are *divisions* among you;             Divisions

3. and I partly believe it,
   [19]for there must be *quarreling* among you             QUARRELING
   in order that those who are genuine among you may be recognized.

4. [20]Therefore when you *assemble*                        ASSEMBLE
   it is *not the Lord's supper* that you eat.              Not the Lord's Supper

5. [21]For in eating, each one goes ahead with his own meal,
   and *one is hungry* and *another is drunk.*             HUNGRY and DRUNK
   [22]What! Do you not have houses to eat and drink in?

6. Or do you despise *the church of God*                    CHURCH
   and *humiliate* those who have nothing?                  Humiliation

7. What shall I say to you?
   *Shall I praise you* in this?                            NO PRAISE
   *I will not praise you.*                                 For You

### B. The Received Tradition: The Lord's Supper (11:23-26)

| | | |
|---|---|---|
| 1. | [23]For I *received* from the Lord<br>what I also *delivered* to you, | PAUL RECEIVED<br>and Delivered |
| 2. | "The Lord Jesus<br>on the night when he was betrayed, | JESUS<br>the Night Betrayed |
| 3. | took bread, [24]and when he had given thanks,<br>he broke it, and said, | TOOK BREAD<br>Broke and Said: |
| 4. | 'This is my body which is for you.<br>Do this in remembrance of me.' | MY BODY<br>Remembrance |
| 5. | [25]In the same way also the cup<br>after supper saying, | TOOK CUP<br>Saying: |
| 6. | 'This cup is the new covenant in my blood.<br>Do this, as often as you drink it, in remembrance of me.' | MY BLOOD<br>Remembrance |
| 7. | [26]For as often as you eat this bread<br>and drink this cup,<br>you proclaim the Lord's death until he come." | BREAD & CUP<br>Proclamation<br>Till He Come |

--------------------------------------------------------------------------

### C. Examine/Judge Yourselves and Discern the Body (11:27-34)

| | | |
|---|---|---|
| 1. | [27]Whoever, therefore, *eats the bread*<br>or *drinks the cup* of the Lord in an *unworthy manner*<br>will be guilty of *profaning the body and blood of the Lord.* | EAT<br>Guilty |
| 2. | [28]Let a man *examine himself,*<br>and so eat of the bread and drink of the cup. | EXAMINE<br>Self |
| 3. | [29]For any one who eats and drinks<br>without *discerning the body*<br>eats and drinks *judgment upon himself.* | JUDGMENT<br>On Self |
| 4. | [30]That is why many of you are weak and ill,<br>and some have died. | WEAK/ILL<br>Dead |
| 5. | [31]But if we *judge ourselves,*<br>we should not be judged. | JUDGE<br>Self |
| 6. | [32]But when we are *judged* by the Lord, we are chastened<br>so that we may not be *judged* along with the world. | JUDGED<br>By the Lord |
| 7. | [33]So then, my brethren, when you come together to eat,<br>wait for one another—<br>[34a]if anyone is *hungry,* let him eat at home—<br>*lest you come together to be condemned.* | EAT<br>Condemned |

--------------------------------------------------------------------------

8. [34b]About the other things I will give directions when I come. *(Private Corinthian Matters)*

---

**Figure 4.2(1). Worship irregularities and the Lord's Supper (1 Cor 11:17-34)**

## THE RHETORIC

Paul's creative artistry is again on display. If we were arranging the components of this homily we would present all of the *negatives* and then turn to the *positives*. Our text would be ordered like this:

> 1. (-) Your so-called celebrations of the Lord's Supper are ghastly exhibitions of divisions, drunkenness and humiliation of the poor.
>
> 2. (-) These actions, and your failures to judge yourselves have left you sick and dying.
>
> 3. (+) You need to remember and emulate the Holy Eucharistic meal that I *received* from the Lord and *delivered* unto you which is: "The Lord on the night in which he was betrayed, etc."

Using ring composition, Paul prefers an A-B-A outline that affirms

> Your Eucharistic celebrations are a disaster—full of drunkenness and quarreling.
> 　Here is the tradition I passed on to you.
> Your Eucharistic celebrations are a disaster—be self-critical and reform yourselves!

In Isaiah, as observed, the climactic center of a homily was sometimes composed of a reference to an earlier sacred tradition.[1] Seven times Paul places an *Old Testament text* at the center of a homily.[2] Following this pattern, on six occasions he places an *early church tradition* in the middle of his discussion.[3] This text on the Eucharist is one of them. Yet the style of the overall homily is unique.

Each of the three sections that make up this homily has seven cameos [see fig. 4.2(1)]. The first (A) is a classic example of the prophetic rhetorical template. Then the "words of institution" (B) can be seen to roughly fall into seven cameos that exhibit a somewhat straight-line sequence.[4] The concluding section (C) again has seven cameos, but with a modified inversion pattern. The climax of *the overall homily* is the "words of institution" (B). The climaxes of A and C appear at their centers. The text will be repeated for easy reference in each section.

---

[1] Is 43:16-19; 51:1-3; 65:20-23.
[2] 1 Cor 6:13-20; 9:1-12a; 9:12b-15; 10:1-13; 14:13-25; 15:24-28; 15:42-50.
[3] 1 Cor 1:17–2:2; 2:7-10; 11:17-34; 14:37-40; 15:1-11; 15:12-20.
[4] The text exhibits some step parallelism, but the straight-line sequence appears to dominate.

## COMMENTARY

The homily opens with:

1. ¹⁷But in the following instructions I do *not praise you*,
   because it is *not* for the *better*
   but for the *worse when you assemble*.

   NO PRAISE
   You Assemble

2. ¹⁸For, in the first place,
   when you *assemble as a church*,
   I hear that there are *divisions* among you;

   CHURCH
   Divisions

3. and I partly believe it,
   ¹⁹for there must be *quarreling* among you
   in order that those who are genuine among you may be recognized.

   QUARRELING

4. ²⁰Therefore when you *assemble*
   it is *not the Lord's supper* that you eat.

   ASSEMBLE
   Not the Lord's Supper

5. ²¹For in eating, each one goes ahead with his own meal,
   and *one is hungry* and *another is drunk*.
   ²²What! Do you not have houses to eat and drink in?

   HUNGRY and DRUNK

6. Or do you despise *the church of God*
   and *humiliate* those who have nothing?

   CHURCH
   Humiliation

7. What shall I say to you?
   *Shall I praise you* in this?
   *I will not praise you.*

   NO PRAISE
   For You

**Figure 4.2(2). Section A (1 Cor 11:17-22)**

The traditional style of connecting the beginning, the middle and the end appears in section A [see fig. 4.2(3)]. These three cameos provide the framework around which the homily is built. Summarized, they are:

1. ¹⁷I will not *praise* you
   when you *assemble*

   ----------------------

4. ²⁰When you *assemble*
   You do *not* eat the *Lord's Supper*

   ----------------------

7. ²²ᶜShall I *praise* you for this?
   I will *not praise you.*

**Figure 4.2(3). Cameos 1, 4, 7 (1 Cor 11:17, 20, 22)**

These three cameos are so closely linked that standing alone they make perfect sense. He cannot praise them (cameos 1, 7) because their celebrations of the Eucharist are "not the Lord's Supper" (cameo 4). The other four cameos fill in the frame created by these three.

Cameos 2 and 6 focus on the church. There are divisions (cameo 2). But these divisions are not the party divisions mentioned in 1:10-16. The problems are deeper and more threatening. By their actions they are "despising the church of God" and "humiliating those who have nothing" (cameo 6). This is strong language. As Murphy-O'Connor has written, "The unity of the church is something more than physical juxtaposition in a determined space. . . . Their behavior, in addition to humiliating the 'have-nots,' shows that they hold true community in contempt (v. 22)."[5] Paul exposes the fact that they have broken up into the satisfied rich and the hungry poor, with no awareness of what it means to be "the church of God." The very sacrament that was intended to help create and sustain their oneness had become one more drinking party where some were stuffed and drunk, and others were hungry (cameo 5) and humiliated (cameo 6).

Jesus told a story the church has titled "Lazarus and the Rich Man" (Lk 16:19-31). In that parable a poor beggar named Lazarus languishes without help outside the gate of a rich man. They both die, and Lazarus finds himself beside Abraham at a banquet (in heaven) while the rich man awakes in the fires of Hades. As the story unfolds, the reader discovers that Lazarus's deepest anguish on earth was not related to his *sores* or his *hunger*, but rather to the *psychic pain* of knowing that the desperately needed help was just a few yards away, and yet unavailable. Each day a sumptuous banquet was spread and devoured by the rich man and his friends, while Lazarus lay *alone* in the street. In heaven he was *comforted* (Lk 16:25). At last he was among Abraham and the angels, who loved and honored him.[6] His agony was over.

The destitute Christians of Corinth were obliged to suffer even greater anguish. Unlike Lazarus, they were invited to be *among the diners*, but by the time they got off of work and arrived at the house church (in the evening), the food was gone and some of the rich were already drunk (cameo 5). The idle rich had arrived early and eaten all the available fare.

The worst part of it all was that many were indifferent to the problem. The poor and the rich were theoretically eating from the same table, and that was

---

[5]Murphy-O'Connor, *1 Corinthians*, p. 111.
[6]See Kenneth E. Bailey, *Jesus Through Middle Eastern Eyes* (Downers Grove, Ill.: IVP Academic, 2008), pp. 378-96.

good. But being the "holy temple" and "the body of Christ" meant (and means) that the community was expected to be transparent with the pain of each known to all. When that did not happen and the rich lived in ignorance of the suffering they were inflicting on the poor, the consequences were dire. The major purpose of the gathering (the Eucharist) was thereby destroyed. "It is not the Lord's supper that you eat" writes Paul in the center climax of this first section (cameo 4). Going through the motions was not enough. Paul appreciated the whistleblowers who reported these things to him. He was also happy that they were arguing about it. Such disagreements indicated that at least *some* of the worshipers were horrified at what was taking place (cameo 3).

Following this stiff public rebuke Paul recites the sacred tradition that he had "received" and then "delivered" to them when he was among them [see fig. 4.2(4)].

| | | |
|---|---|---|
| 1. | [23]For I *received* from the Lord<br>what I also *delivered* to you, | PAUL RECEIVED<br>and Delivered |
| 2. | "The Lord Jesus<br>on the night when he was betrayed, | JESUS<br>The Night Betrayed |
| 3. | took bread, [24]and when he had given thanks,<br>he broke it, and said, | TOOK BREAD<br>broke and said: |
| 4. | 'This is my body which is for you.<br>Do this in remembrance of me.' | MY BODY<br>Remembrance |
| 5. | [25]In the same way also the cup,<br>after supper, saying, saying: | TOOK CUP |
| 6. | 'This cup is the new covenant in my blood.<br>Do this, as often as you drink it,<br>in remembrance of me.' | MY BLOOD<br>remembrance |
| 7. | [26]For as often as you eat this bread<br>and drink this cup,<br>you proclaim the Lord's death until he come." | BREAD & CUP<br>Proclamation<br>Till He Come |

**Figure 4.2(4). Section B (1 Cor 11:23-26)**

Paul affirms that this tradition was "received from the Lord" (cameo 1). There is no need to assume that Paul must have had a personal vision of Jesus in which Jesus dictated these words to him. For Paul "the community" was Christ's body" (1 Cor 6:15; 8:12; 12:12).[7] Having received this tradition from

---

[7]Murphy-O'Connor, *1 Corinthians*, p. 112.

the "body of Christ" (and from eyewitnesses who were present), he had received it from the Lord.

The six cameos that comprise the remainder of the words of institution of the Eucharist have probably received more attention in Christian literature over the centuries than any other text. Hundreds of thousands of words have been printed in an attempt to press as far as possible into the mysteries of these words sacred to all Christians. Thiselton offers fifty-one pages of profound scholarly discussion on this homily (11:17-34) and with it an extensive bibliography of articles.[8] Jeremias's monograph, *The Eucharistic Words of Jesus*, is a masterful study of the various relevant texts.[9] With deep gratitude for the above scholarship one remembers the advice of the Preacher in Ecclesiastes, who wrote, "God is in heaven, and you upon the earth; therefore let your words be few" (Eccles 5:2).

The beauty of a diamond is related to the fact that it has many facets which shed light in many directions. Any attempt to force that light in one direction is to destroy the diamond. The mystery of the presence of Christ in the Eucharist is beyond any of our attempts, however heroic, at explaining it. I have joyfully received the Eucharist from the hands of many celebrants on five continents. These include Latin Catholics, Greek Catholics, Antiochian Orthodox, Coptic Orthodox, Armenian Orthodox, Armenian Evangelicals, Coptic Evangelicals, Anglicans, Lutherans, Presbyterians, Methodists, Episcopalians, Baptists, Pentecostals and others. As one of my dear Roman Catholic friends has said, "The will to exclusivity is dying." Each can hold firmly to his or her own sacred tradition and be blessed by "the other" who with us is a part of the body of Christ.

Judas was present at the inaugural Eucharist. John tells us that during the meal Jesus broke off a piece of bread, dipped it into the common dish and offered it to Judas (Jn 13:26). This is a traditional Middle Eastern act of kindness often used by one person to express deep friendship to another. The piece of dipped bread is usually offered with the accompanying phrase, "Eat this for my sake." Jesus extended this friendship ritual to Judas, who refused it and then withdrew from the table. John reports ominously "and it was night" (Jn 13:30); indeed it was! In spite of everything, Jesus singled out Judas and extended to him a profound demonstration of costly love. Judas preferred his chosen path of deception and death.

---

[8]Thiselton, *First Epistle*, pp. 848-99.
[9]Joachim Jeremias, *The Eucharistic Words of Jesus* (New York: Scribner's, 1966).

Middle Eastern hospitality is legendary. In the Bible it extends from Abraham's welcome of the three visitors (Gen 18:1-15) to the Last Supper and beyond. The idea that in any Middle Eastern setting a family might have a hungry guest present and eat in front of the guest without including him or her in the meal is unthinkable. To say or imply "We will only feed you after you are adopted into our family" is unimaginable for the host and the guest. In spite of all the stumbling blocks, I have been the recipient of luminous grace at the "table of the Lord" on numerous unforgettable occasions. But that is another story.

Again, Murphy-O'Connor perhaps speaks for many when he writes,

> For Paul, . . . authentic remembrance is concerned with the past only insofar as it is constitutive of the present and a summons to the future. What he desires to evoke is the active remembrance of total commitment to Christ which makes the past real in the present, thus releasing a power capable of shaping the future.[10]

This brings us to the third section of the homily [see fig. 4.2(5)].

1  27Whoever, therefore, *eats the bread*
    or *drinks the cup* of the Lord in an *unworthy manner*    EAT
    will be guilty of *profaning the body and blood of the Lord.*    Guilty

2.    28Let a man *examine himself,*    EXAMINE
    and so eat of the bread and drink of the cup.    Self

3.    29For any one who eats and drinks
    without *discerning the body*    JUDGMENT
    eats and drinks *judgment upon himself.*    On Self

4.    30That is why many of you are weak and ill,    WEAK/ILL
    and some have died.    Dead

5.    31But if we *judge ourselves,*    JUDGE
    we should not be judged.    Self

6.    32But when we are *judged* by the Lord, we are chastened    JUDGED
    so that we may not be *judged* along with the world.    By the Lord

7.  33So then, my brethren, when you come together to eat,
    wait for one another—    EAT
    34aif anyone is *hungry*, let him eat at home—    Condemned
    *lest you come together to be condemned.*

------------------------------------------------------

8.34bAbout the other things I will give directions when I come. *(Private Corinthian Matters)*

**Figure 4.2(5). Section C (1 Cor 11:27-34)**

[10]Murphy-O'Connor, *1 Corinthians*, p. 112.

Again the opening (cameo 1) and the closing (cameo 7) of this section of the homily are linked with the center (cameo 4). Seen together they appear in figure 4.2(6).

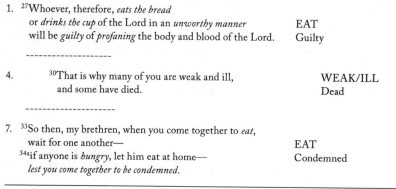

1.  <sup>27</sup>Whoever, therefore, *eats the bread*
       or *drinks the cup* of the Lord in an *unworthy manner*    EAT
       will be *guilty* of *profaning* the body and blood of the Lord.   Guilty

4.     <sup>30</sup>That is why many of you are weak and ill,    WEAK/ILL
        and some have died.    Dead

7.  <sup>33</sup>So then, my brethren, when you come together to *eat*,
       wait for one another—
      <sup>34a</sup>if anyone is *hungry*, let him eat at home—    EAT
      *lest you come together to be condemned.*    Condemned

**Figure 4.2(6). Cameos 1, 4, 7 (1 Cor 11:27, 30, 33-34)**

## RHETORIC

If the four remaining cameos of section C were absent, the Corinthian readers would not have noticed any omission. These three cameos provide the framework, and cameos 2-3 and 5-6 fill in the details. But in this case these four cameos form a straight-line sequence.

## COMMENTARY

This text has also undergone intense scrutiny. In cameo 1 the question is: What is the "unworthy manner"? The key lies in the comparisons between sections A (11:17-22) and C (11:27-34). In section A the Corinthians had broken up into quarreling groups. Rich people came early, ate all the food and got drunk. The poor (who had to work) came later, found nothing to eat, remained hungry and were humiliated by being left out. The "church of God" (the entire Christian community) was "despised" in the process. This outrageous activity was clearly the "unworthy manner" that Paul was talking about. When this happened, the Corinthians were "guilty of profaning the body and blood of the Lord." This was more than "disrespect for the elements," although that was no doubt a part of what Paul was saying. Rather, such outrageous behavior was criminal activity against "the body" of Christ, that is, against the community that was his body.

The important Greek word in cameo 1 is *enokhos* (guilty). The RSV appropriately translated this word "guilty of profaning." Middle Eastern versions over the last thousand years and more have used a series of very strong words for *enokhos* (guilty). Some read *shajab* (destroy) or *shajib* (destroyer). "Guilty against" appears along with "criminal in regard to." *Khati'a ila* (sin against) is used both in Arabic and in Hebrew. All of these versions recognize that something dark and sinister is taking place.

The gross sin recalled is not related to the particulars of worship style. Nor does it focus on an exacting description of the presence of Christ in the elements. It has to do with hunger and drunkenness that "despises the church" and "humiliates those who have nothing" (cameo 6, sec. A). More of this later.

The serious negative results of this activity are described in the center climax. Some are sick and others have died (C-4). On the physical side, overeating and drunkenness can contribute to ill health. But Paul, mysterious as ever, suggests that the broken nature of their fellowship negatively affected both their spiritual and their physical health.

Paul's recommendation for the insensitive rich appears at the end in cameo 7. If they want sumptuous meals—let them eat at home. When they come together for the sacramental meal, they should not start eating until everyone has arrived. Only then, as an authentic gathering of the church of God, could they eat together and be renewed physically and spiritually.

The four cameos remaining (2-3, 5-6) form a straight-line sequence [see fig. 4.2(7)].

| | | |
|---|---|---|
| 2. | [28]Let a man *examine himself,* <br> and so eat of the bread and drink of the cup. | EXAMINE <br> Self |
| 3. | [29]For any one who eats and drinks <br> without *discerning the body* <br> eats and drinks *judgment upon himself.* | JUDGMENT <br> On Self |
| 5. | [31]But if we *judge ourselves,* <br> we should not be judged. | JUDGE <br> Self |
| 6. | [32]But when we are *judged* by the Lord, we are chastened <br> so that we may not be *judged* along with the world. | JUDGED <br> By the Lord |

Figure 4.2(7). Cameos 2-3 and 5-6 (1 Cor 11:28-29, 31-32)

Standing alone this sequence makes good sense. Each cameo is connected to what precedes and to what follows like the links of a chain. "Eating and drinking" closes cameo 2 and opens cameo 3. Cameo 3 closes with self-judgment and that same theme opens cameo 5. In turn cameo 5 closes with a divine passive that refers to the judgment of the Lord, and that topic begins cameo 6. The first two have to do with judging ourselves, while the second two include the Lord's judgment upon us. The precision with which the whole is constructed is amazing.

Cameos 2 and 3 (along with cameo 1) have caused a great deal of agonized introspection across the church throughout the centuries. In the light of the broken nature of the fellowship that Paul is addressing, "examine yourself" is related to "discerning the body." This surely means: "Remember that you enter into this gathering as a part of the body of Christ that has come together for healing, restoration, proclamation and empowerment." Paul's readers were asked to remember that this is not one more Greek drinking party. It is not merely a social occasion to pass the time with select friends. There is no audience watching a performance. Leaders and led are all participants. They have come together as the body of Christ to remember the saving events that created them as a body and to proclaim that salvation to the world.

Each worshiper is intimately connected with the other worshipers, and the struggles, joys, fears and failures of all are known and shared. All come as sinners in need of grace, and in that shared awareness there is openness to receive needed healing. The only believer who is unworthy to receive the Holy Communion is the person who thinks that he/she is worthy to receive it.

Cameo 5 is a divine passive. "We should not *be judged*" means "God will not judge us." This theme is continued in cameo 6, where the judgment of the Lord protects us from being judged along with the world.

Attached to this homily is a personal note from Paul to the Corinthians (cameo 8), which reads, "About the other things I will give directions when I come." The Corinthians had written to him about many things. But their oral and written questions did not determine Paul's outline. He had his own agenda, and he chose topics of importance *for the entire church* (1:2). Topics that reflected special Corinthian problems he would discuss with them privately.

Having dealt with the issue of men and women in worship leadership (see chap. 4.1) and the disastrous Corinthian Eucharistic celebrations (chap. 4.2), Paul was ready to open a third area of confusion in the church's worship, that of the nature and exercise of spiritual gifts. To that topic we now turn.

# Gifts and the Nature of the Body

I Corinthians 12:1-30

In this homily, 12:1-30, Paul discusses the third problem related to worship covered in this essay [see fig. 4.3(1)]. In review, the three are:

1. Male and female prophets leading in worship and how they should dress (11:2-16).
2. Gross irregularities at the celebration of the Eucharist (11:17-34).
3. *The spiritual gifts and the nature of the body (12:1-30).*

**The Rhetoric**

This homily on spiritual gifts is the longest in the epistle. This is primarily due to the extended *parable of the human body* that forms its center. With its nineteen cameos, the overall homily is another example of the high jump format. Four cameos compose the introduction (cameos 1-4) which is followed by the topic of "many gifts" (cameo 5). Paul then turns to "the body of Christ" using four short cameos. The parable of the human body is composed of five cameos (10-14). A second discussion of "the body of Christ" (cameos 15-17) appears followed by a second discussion of "many gifts" (cameos 18-19). The outline is simple and can be summarized as follows:

| | |
|---|---|
| 1-4 | Introduction |
| 5 | Many Gifts |
| 6-9 | The Body of Christ |
| 10-14 | The Parable of the Human Body |
| 15-17 | The Body of Christ |
| 18-19 | Many Gifts |

The text of this third discussion is shown in figure 4.3(1).

1.   ¹²:¹Now concerning *spiritual gifts*, brethren,          *INTRODUCTION*
     I do not want you to be ignorant.                         Ignorance Unacceptable

2.   ²You know that when you were *Gentiles*,
     you were led astray to *dumb idols*,                      Emotion not Enough
     *however* you may have been *moved*.

3.   ³Therefore I want you to understand
     that *no one* speaking by the *Spirit of God*
     ever says, *"Jesus be cursed!"*                           Jesus Is Honored as Lord
     and no one can say, *"Jesus is Lord,"*
     except by the *Holy Spirit*.

4.   ⁴Now there are *varieties of gifts*,
        and the same *Spirit;*
     ⁵and there are *varieties of ministries*,                One Spirit
        and the same *Lord*,                                  One Lord
     ⁶and there are varieties of *energizings*,¹              One God
        and the same *God who energizes* them all in everyone.

------------------------------------------------------------------------------------

5a.  ⁷To each is given the *manifestation of the Spirit*      *A. MANY GIFTS*
        for the *common good*.                                Spiritual Gifts—For the Common
                                                              Good

 b.     ⁸To one is given through the Spirit a word of *wisdom*,
           to another a *word of knowledge* according to the same Spirit,
        ⁹to another *faith* by the same Spirit,
           to another *gifts of healing* by the one Spirit,
        ¹⁰to another the *working of miracles*,               GIFTS
           to another *prophecy*,
           to another the ability to *distinguish between spirits*,
           to another various *kinds of tongues*,
           to another the *interpretation of tongues*.

 c.  ¹¹All these are *inspired by* one and the *same Spirit*,
       who apportions *to each one individually as he wills*.  Spiritual Gifts—For the Individual

------------------------------------------------------------------------------------

6.   ¹²For just as the *body is one*                          *B. THE BODY OF CHRIST*
        and has *many members*,                               One Body—Many Members

7.      and all the *members of the body*,
        though many, are *one body*,                          CHRIST
        so it is with *Christ*.                               (one and many)

8.   ¹³For by *one Spirit* we were *all baptized* into *one body*—
        *Jews or Greeks, slaves or free*—                     SPIRIT
        and all given to *drink of one Spirit*.               (one and many)

9.   ¹⁴For the body does *not* consist of *one member*
        but of *many*.                                        One Body—Many Members

------------------------------------------------------------------------------------

¹My translation. I have created an English word trying to catch the play on words in the Greek text.

| | | |
|---|---|---|
| 10a. | [15]If the *foot* should say,<br>　"Because I am *not a hand,*<br>　I do *not belong* to the body,"<br>　that would *not make it any less* a part of the *body.* | *C. THE PHYSICAL BODY*<br>(a parable) |
| b. | [16]And if the *ear* should say,<br>　"Because I am *not an eye,*<br>　I do *not belong* to the body,"<br>　that would not make it any less a part of the *body.* | I DO NOT<br>Belong |
| 11. | [17]If the whole body were an *eye,*<br>　*where* would be the *hearing?*<br>　If the whole body were an *ear,*<br>　W*here* would be the sense of smell? | ALL ARE<br>Needed |
| 12. | [18]But as it is, *God arranged the organs in the body,*<br>　each one of them as *he chose.*<br>　[19]If all were a single organ,<br>　where would the body be?<br>　[20]But as it is, there are *many parts,*<br>　yet *one body.* | GOD ARRANGES<br>God Chooses |
| 13. | [21]The *eye* cannot say *to the hand,*<br>　"I have *no need of you,"*<br>　nor again the *head to the feet,*<br>　"I have *no need of you."* | ALL ARE<br>Needed |
| 14a. | [22]On the contrary, the *parts of the body*<br>　which seem to be *weaker*<br>　are *indispensable,* | |
| b. | [23]And those *parts of the body*<br>　which we think *less honorable*<br>　we invest with *greater honor,* | I AM<br>Inferior |
| c. | and our *unpresentable parts*<br>　are treated with *greater modesty,*<br>　[24]which our presentable parts do not require. | |
| d. | But God has so *adjusted the body,*<br>　to the *inferior part,*<br>　giving the *greater honor* | |

----------------------------------------------------------------------

| | | |
|---|---|---|
| 15. | [25]that there may be *no discord* in the body,<br>but that the members may have the same care for one another. | *B. THE BODY OF CHRIST* |
| 16. | [26]If *one* member *suffers,*<br>　*all suffer together;*<br>　if *one* member is *honored,*<br>　*all rejoice together.* | |
| 17. | [27]For you are the body of Christ<br>　and individually members of it. | |

----------------------------------------------------------------------

18.²⁸God has appointed in the church                    *A. A VARIETY OF GIFTS*
    first apostles,
      second prophets,
        third teachers,
          then workers of miracles,
            then gifts in healing,
              helpers,
                administrators,
                  speakers in various kinds of tongues.

19.²⁹Are all apostles?
  Are all prophets?
  Are all teachers?
    Do all work miracles?
     ³⁰Do all possess gifts of healing?
      Do all speak in tongues?
      Do all interpret?

**Figure 4.3(1). Gifts and the nature of the body (1 Cor 12:1-30)**

The placing of a parable or metaphor in the center of a homily often occurs in the prophecy of Isaiah. Three short cases of this style (Is 53:3-8a) appear one after another in a section of the famous servant song of Isaiah 52:13–53:12.

The text of Isaiah 53:3-8a is displayed in figure 4.3(2).

1. ⁵³:³He was despised            DESPISED
  and rejected by others;        By Others

2.   a man of sorrows,              ACQUAINTED WITH
  and acquainted with grief;    Sorrow/Grief

3.   and *as one from whom others hide* their faces    PARABLE of a PERSON
  he was despised, and we esteemed him not.    Despised/Esteemed Not

4. ⁴Surely he has borne our griefs      HAS BORNE OUR
  and carried our sorrows;        Griefs/Sorrows

5. Yet we esteemed him stricken,    ESTEEMED NOT
  smitten by God, and afflicted.  Smitten by God

6. ⁵And [*wa*] he was wounded for our transgressions,    HE SUFFERED
  he was bruised for our iniquities;    For Us
  upon him was the chastisement that made us whole,
  and with his stripes we are healed.

7. ⁶All we *like sheep* have gone astray;    PARABLE OF THE
  we have turned every one to his own way;    Lost Sheep

8. and the Lord has laid on him      HE SUFFERED
  the iniquity of us all.          For Us

| 9. | [7]He was oppressed, and he was afflicted, | HE WAS OPPRESSED |
|---|---|---|
| 10. | yet he opened not his mouth; | He was Silent |
| 11. | *like a lamb* that is led to the slaughter,<br>and *like a sheep* that before its shearers is dumb, | PARABLE OF THE<br>Suffering Lamb/Sheep |
| 12. | so he opened not his mouth. | He Was Silent |
| 13. | [8]By oppression and judgment he was taken away. | HE WAS OPPRESSED |

Figure 4.3(2). The suffering servant (Is 53:3-8a)

Each of the three parts of figure 4.3(2) climaxes with a concrete image. The first is the *parable of the man no one can look at*. The second affirms that *we are like sheep*. In the third the suffering servant *is like a sheep*. That means—he is like us!

Isaiah 40–66 contains fifteen other occurrences of parables/metaphors placed in the centers of ring compositions.[2] This style also appears in Luke's Gospel.[3] Here in chapter 12, Paul's artistic skills are again on display. Not only does he place a parable in the center but he expands that center into a full-blown ring composition with five cameos, most of which have multiple parts.[4] Paul's method can be described as "wheels within wheels."

## COMMENTARY

Four cameos make up the introduction [see fig. 4.3(3)].

In his introduction to the epistle (1:5-7), Paul praised his readers for their knowledge and their spiritual gifts. Now he is ready to focus on their *lack of knowledge* and their *misunderstandings of the gifts*. Again, the gentle touch is first followed by reproof and correction.

Paul is talking about the *pneumatikon*, the *"spiritual* gifts." The English language has taken the word *gifts* and secularized it to mean "natural abilities." North American public schools have special courses for "gifted students." There

---

[2]See Is 42:1-4; 44:18-20; 48:17-22; 49:1-7; 50:5-8a; 50:8b-11; 51:4-7; 55:8-9; 58:2-9; 58:9c-14; 63:12b-14; 64:4-9; 65:20b-23; 66:1-6; 66:10-14. For the formatting of the above see www.shenango.org/Bailey.Isaiah.htm.

[3]See Lk 7:36-50; 11:9-13; 18:18-30. See Kenneth E. Bailey, *Jesus Through Middle Eastern Eyes* (Downers Grove, Ill.: IVP Academic, 2008), p. 240; *Poet and Peasant: A Literary Cultural Approach to the Parables in Luke* (Grand Rapids: Eerdmans, 1976), p. 135; *Through Peasant Eyes* (Grand Rapids: Eerdmans, 1983), pp. 157-58.

[4]Ezekiel 36:16-36 is comparable to 1 Cor 12 in length and complexity. However the Ezekiel text does not have an extended metaphor/parable in the center.

1.  ¹Now concerning *spiritual gifts*, brethren,
    I do not want you to be ignorant.                          *INTRODUCTION*

2.  ²You know that when you were *Gentiles*,
    you were led astray to *dumb idols*,
    *however* you may have been *moved*.

3.  ³Therefore I want you to understand
    that *no one* speaking by the *Spirit of God*
    ever says, "*Jesus be cursed!*"
    and no one can say, "*Jesus is Lord*,"
    except by the *Holy Spirit*.

4.  ⁴Now there are *varieties of gifts*,
    and the same *Spirit;*
    ⁵and there are *varieties of ministries*,                   SPIRIT
    and the same *Lord*,                                        LORD
    ⁶and there are varieties of *energizings*                   GOD
    and the same *God who energizes* them all in everyone.⁵

**Figure 4.3(3). Cameos 1-4 (1 Cor 12:1-6)**

graduate degrees in this subject and parents press to have their children classified as among the "gifted." This has nothing to do with the Spirit of God. The secularization of this important biblical word has come home to roost, and in the life of the church many voices are raised urging people to "use their gifts" for the kingdom of God. The intent of this language is to urge people to use their time, education, experience and natural abilities to serve others. All of this is highly commendable, but is not focused on what Paul is discussing in this text.

In contrast, Paul is reflecting on the unique gifts of the Holy Spirit that come to those who believe and are baptized in the name of Christ. They are *spiritual gifts*, not *natural abilities*. They are "manifestations of the Spirit" (12:7), not native intelligence or education. Every believer is invited by Paul to reflect on, "How can I build up the body of Christ by using the spiritual gifts and energy given to me *through the Holy Spirit* who filled my life when I believed and was baptized?" Chapter 12 is devoted to this subject.

Cameo 2 reads:

²You know that when you were *Gentiles*,
you were led astray to *dumb idols*,
*however* you may have been *moved*.

---

⁵My translation. I have attempted to reflect the Greek text by creating an English word.

Paul uses the striking phrase "when you were *ethne* [Gentiles]" and expresses amazement that they had followed idols that could not talk! How
ridiculous! Not only that, but they were *deeply moved* in their worship of these
mute leaders. The centuries-old test of "it feels right" is not an accurate measure of truth, insists Paul. Deep emotion alone is not an adequate guide for the
divine pilgrimage.

Furthermore, Paul did not write "back when you were *unbelievers.*" Instead
he said, "back when you were *Gentiles.*" Had they become Jews? Obviously
not, because he had just told them, "For neither circumcision counts for anything nor uncircumcision, but keeping the commandments of God" (7:19). At
the same time, in 10:1 he wrote, "*our fathers* were all under the cloud." As argued earlier, surely with this language he was addressing both Jewish and
Gentile readers. The whole church was now part of the community of God
that could speak of ancient Israel as "our fathers." Yet, as seen in our earlier
discussion (9:19-23), Paul was careful not to say, "To the Gentiles I became a
Gentile." No one was expected to cast aside any ethnic identity when he/she
came to faith in Christ, but rather to purify and enrich it.

Paul was writing in Greek, not Hebrew, and he never dropped the slightest
hint that Greek was inadequate to explain the mysteries of God. In the process Paul abandoned the very idea of a sacred language and thereby jettisoned
commitment to any sacred culture. What then does Paul mean when he
writes, "when you were Gentiles"?

One easy way to dismiss this problem is to translate *ethne* as "heathen"
(rsv). But the kjv reads "ye were Gentiles" and the Vulgate translated *Scitis
quoniam cum Gentes essetis.* The two Hebrew versions of the New Testament
consulted use the word *goyim* (Gentiles) and the Peshitta Syriac has *hanefo*
(Gentiles). The twenty Arabic versions, which stretch from the ninth to the
twentieth centuries, are divided. Four early versions use some form of the
word *wathaniyin* (idolaters).[6] But eight versions examined read *umam*
(Gentiles).[7]

Two early Arabic versions simply omitted the phrase. One of these, the earliest of all extant Arabic versions (Vat. Ar. 13 [8th-9th cent.]) reads, "You were
led to the idols." The other (Mt. Sinai 155 [9th cent.]) translates, "You know
that you, indeed you, to the idols that do not speak or raise their voice, were

---

[6]These include Mt. Sinai 151 (867); Mt. Sinai 310 (10th cent.); Erpenius (1616); Propagandist
(1671).

[7]Mt. Sinai 73; London Polyglot (1657); Shidiac (1851); Bustani-Van Dyck (1851); Bustani-Van
Dyck (1845-1860); Jesuit (1880). See appendix II, plate K.

dragged and led" (my translation). These two versions are of great interest. Perhaps the translators omitted the phrase "when you were Gentiles" out of fear lest
their readers think the apostle was trying to turn the Corinthians (and others)
into Jews. For if they were no longer Gentiles, what else could they be?

What did Paul intend when he used the word *ethne* (Gentiles) in this text?
In Paul's day a Greek attracted to Judaism had two choices. A male Greek
could become a Jew through Jewish baptism, circumcision and the rejection of
his Greek culture. Or, he could remain a Greek as a "God fearer" and figura-
tively sit at the back of the synagogue. Such a person would naturally remain
an outsider to the Jewish community. Paul, however, could not accept either
option. For him, Jews and Greeks had become one in Christ. Yet each could
maintain his/her own language and ethnic identity. To categorize baptized
Greeks as Gentiles involved the huge risk of drawing an indelible line between them and us. The book of *Jubilees*, written in Hebrew about 150 B.C.,
has some extremely harsh things to say about the Gentiles. It records an imaginative blessing Abraham supposedly used to bless Jacob. Much of this "blessing" is in the form of advice, a part of which reads:

> Separate yourself from the Gentiles,
> and do not eat with them,
> and do not perform deeds like theirs,
> and do not become associates of theirs.
> Because their deeds are defiled,
> and all of their ways are contaminated, and despicable, and abominable.[8]

Paul had already told the Galatians (literally translated) that in Christ,
"There is neither Jew nor Greek, there is no slave nor free, there is neither male
and female; for you are all one in Christ Jesus" (Gal 3:28). Acts 6:1-6 describes
a disagreement between Christians with Jewish names and Christians with
Greek names. The two groups are described as "Hellenists" and "Hebrews."
(The word *Gentile* is avoided.) Early in 1 Corinthians Paul took pains to describe the cross in ways that both Jews and Greeks could understand (1:17–2:2).
There seems to be a studied avoidance of the word *Gentile* when speaking
about Greeks who had believed and been baptized.[9] They were "members of
the household of faith" (Eph 2:19) and, in this very homily, will be called

---

[8]O. S. Wintermute, trans., *Jubilees* 22:16, in *The Old Testament Pseudepigrapha*, ed. James H.
Charlesworth (New York: Doubleday, 1985), 2:98.
[9]Col 1:27 speaks of the proclamation of the gospel among the Gentiles. It does not call those
who believe "Gentiles."

members of the "body of Christ" (12:27). They were called into "the fellowship of his Son" (1:9). As such they were built into the new temple and God's Spirit was already present among them (3:16-17). Paul wrote to the Ephesians, "you who once were far off have been brought near in the blood of Christ" (Eph 2:13). One can almost hear Paul saying to his Greek readers,

> Once we called you "Gentiles," and with that word we shut you out. We drew a line that you could not cross because you were born on the other side of it. You could become "God fearers" and remain outsiders. You could even become proselytes and still not be trusted by many. No more! I have accepted your language as a sacred language that can express the deep things of God. We are one family, and all of you are my brothers and sisters. Each of us can keep his or her ethnic skin and on that level of identity we will be different. But we can and have created a new identity in Christ that unites us on a level that is deeper than our ethnicity. Together we share that new identity. We Jews refuse to think of you as "Gentiles."

Paul had just written, "Give no offense to Jews or to Greeks or to the church of God" (1 Cor 10:32). The very "church of God" about which he speaks was composed largly of Jews and Greeks, and yet they were more than what those identity markers signified. They had a new and deeper identity as "the church of God," "the holy temple" and "the body of Christ."

Peter thought through the same issue, and borrowing language from Hosea 1:10–2:1, he wrote, "Once you were no people but now you are God's people; once you had not received mercy but now you have received mercy" (1 Pet 2:10).[10] This topic peeks out at the reader throughout 1 Corinthians. Paul's non-Jewish listeners were once "Gentiles," but that community-dividing word no longer applied to Greeks who had become a part of "the fellowship of his Son" (1 Cor 1:9).

The third cameo in the introduction has troubled interpreters for centuries. Thoughtful and extended reflections are available in the major commentaries. Just as Paul's readers were led astray by their emotions in their idol-worshiping days, even so, if Pneumatology replaces or even trumps Christology they can also be led astray by their emotions in their new faith. If what I *feel* is not controlled by what I *know of Christ*, I am intellectually and spiritually adrift and able to attribute horrible things to the prompting of the Spirit. The Spirit of *God* "never says 'Jesus be cursed!'"[11]

---

[10]This text is built on Hos 2:1, 23 where the prophet gathers his family together and adopts his illegitimate children.

[11]Both some idol worshipers and some Jews may have voiced this curse, claiming to be inspired by the Spirit to do so.

During the 1950s C. S. Lewis carried on an extended correspondence in classical Latin with Dom Calabrie of Italy. On one occasion Lewis was on the eve of a visit to Ireland and wrote Dom Calabria, "There [in Ireland] indeed both yours and ours 'know not by what Spirit they are led.' They take lack of charity for zeal and mutual ignorance for orthodoxy."[12]

What does it mean to confess "Jesus is Lord"? Marianne M. Thompson offers a thoughtful definition: "To confess that Jesus is Lord is not to confess that in him we have found a way to God, but that in him God has embodied a way to us."[13] At the same time, the confession "Jesus is Lord" for Paul was not a rationally provable concept. Logic cannot force the mind to that affirmation. The empire said "Caesar is *Kurios* [Lord]." Anyone who affirmed "Jesus is Lord" was also saying, "Caesar is *not* Lord," and such a claim was dangerous. The Gnostics were safe. They were only interested in the inner life of the soul and its access to salvation through secret knowledge. But Christians who wanted the kingdom of God to come *on earth* (Mt 6:10) were thereby challenging the cult of the empire. Only the Holy Spirit could move the heart, mind and will to the dangerous and mysterious affirmation "Jesus is Lord." There was no other way. Paul continues his introduction with a fourth cameo which reads:

· 4.　⁴Now there are *varieties of gifts*,
　　　　and the same *Spirit;*
　　　⁵and there are *varieties of ministries*,　　　　　Spirit
　　　　and the same *Lord,*　　　　　　　　　　　　Lord
　　　⁶and there are varieties of *energizings*　　　　　God
　　　　and the same *God who energizes* them all in everyone.[14]

---

**Figure 4.3(4). Cameo 4 (1 Cor 12:4-6)**

---

This cameo looks both ways. It concludes the introduction composed of cameos 1-4 and at the same time opens the door to the discussion of spiritual gifts and the body of Christ that follows. In cameo 4 Paul again invokes the Trinity. If I am going to complete any task, I need three things. I need the necessary tools, a specific assignment and adequate energy to complete the job. Give me a broom, assign me the task of sweeping a particular room,

---

[12]C. S. Lewis, *Letters: C. S. Lewis and Don Giovanni Calabria* (Ann Arbor, Mich.: Servant Books, 1988), p. 83.

[13]Marianne M. Thompson, "Jesus Is Lord: How the Earliest Christian Confession Informs Our Proclamation in a Pluralistic Age," published privately, 2002, p. 13.

[14]My translation. I have created an English word trying to catch the play on words in the Greek.

and if I have the energy to do what you say, I can sweep the room. The first need is for the necessary *gift* (the broom). The second is the *designated task* (the assignment). The third is the *energematon* (energizing) with which he *energon* (energizes) us (that is, the energy needed to complete the task). These three aspects of the Christian life and ministry Paul identifies with the three persons of the Trinity. *The Spirit* gives us the "spiritual gifts," which naturally flow from the Holy Spirit. Paul's readers already know that *the Lord* assigns a *task* to each believer (3:5). Finally, *God* provides the energy necessary to complete that task. *God energon* (energizes) us to carry out the appointed ministry. In a few verses Paul will repeat the fact that God's grace made him who he was, and through that grace he "worked harder than any of them" (15:10).[15] The reference to the Trinity in this text complements the extended references to the Trinity that appear in 2:6-16.

In Hebrew, as in other Semitic languages, the word *spirit* is almost always feminine. In Greek the word *pneuma* (spirit) is neuter in gender. But New Testament authors were often thinking in Hebrew as they wrote in Greek. Thinking of the Holy Spirit in feminine terms thus has a serious biblical foundation. If humans were created as *male* and *female* "in the image of God" (Gen 1:27), then to think long thoughts about God in both feminine and masculine terms is biblically based. This idea is as old as the prophet Isaiah, who likened God to a "mighty man" (Is 42:13) and in the same passage compared God to a "woman in travail" (Is 42:14).

Paul now presents a list of some of the spiritual gifts under discussion. He includes:

| | | |
|---|---|---|
| 5a. | [7]To each is given the *manifestation of the Spirit* for the *common good.* | SPIRIT<br>For the Common Good |
| b. | [8]To one is given through the Spirit a word of *wisdom,*<br>    to another a *word of knowledge* according to the same Spirit,<br>    [9]to another *faith* by the same Spirit,<br>    to another *gifts of healing* by the one Spirit,<br>    [10]to another the *working of miracles,*<br>    to another *prophecy,*<br>    to another the ability to *distinguish between spirits,*<br>    to another various *kinds of tongues,*<br>    to another the *interpretation of tongues.* | <br><br><br><br>GIFTS |
| c. | [11]All these are *inspired by* one and the *same Spirit,*<br>    who apportions *to each one individually as he wills.* | SPIRIT<br>For the Individual |

**Figure 4.3(5). Cameo 5 (1 Cor 12:7-11)**

---

[15]Paul uses the same play on words in Col 1:29.

Paul presents a partial list of the spiritual gifts. As he does so he introduces and concludes the list with two important references to the Holy Spirit. These two bookends seen side by side are:

5a. [12:7]To each is given the *manifestation of the Spirit*    SPIRIT
    for the *common good.*    Common Good

---------------------------------------------------------

 c.  [11]All these are *inspired by* one and the *same Spirit*,    SPIRIT
    who apportions *to each one individually as he wills.*  Individually Given

The various spiritual gifts are not given to help the believer focus on personal spiritual enrichment. They are for the *sumpheron* (the common good). *Sumpheron* is the noun form of the verb *sumpero*, which Paul uses in 6:12 to describe things that are "helpful." All things are lawful for Paul, but "not all things *sumpherei* " (contribute to the common good). Here Paul is discussing how the manifestations of the Spirit are specifically given for that same common good. The Spirit blows where it wills (Jn 3:8). We are refreshed by its breeze, but cannot control its direction.

At the same time these spiritual gifts are apportioned to each person individually—*as God chooses.* Each believer is important and each must be willing to receive the gift(s) offered. Yet no one can *select* a desired gift. Nor does the community have the right to insist on a particular gift as a requirement for full acceptance. God chooses gift(s) for each believer, and each gift is to be received, honored and used.

The gifts listed (cameo 5b) fall easily into two categories. The first can be called *non-dramatic gifts* and the second *dramatic gifts.* Paul begins with the non-dramatic gift of "wisdom." The Corinthians were confident in their "knowledge" (1:5). Paul prefers to start with "wisdom" (the very subject he discussed in the opening of his first essay [1:17–2:2]). The reader is expected to remember that "wisdom" is a serious topic and that the *wisdom of God* was displayed on a cross. Paul is not discussing rhetorical or philosophical wisdom, but rather the wisdom that comes as a gift of God. Some of the Greeks understood a part of this God-given wisdom.

Aeschylus, the Greek tragic poet (525-456 B.C.) wrote, "God, whose law it is that he who learns must suffer, and even in our sleep pain that cannot forget, falls drop by drop upon the heart, and in our own, despite, against our will, comes wisdom to us by the awful grace of God."[16] For Aeschylus "wis-

---

[16]Aeschylus, quoted in Edith Hamilton, *The Greek Way to Western Civilization* (New York: Mentor Books, 1924), p. 44.

dom" was much more than "acquired knowledge." The *wisdom* of the wise is not necessarily attached to education. Some of the wisest people I have known are barely literate Middle Eastern peasants.

Paul's second word—*gnosis*—was another core gnostic-Corinthian term. Across the centuries there have been biblical commentators and dogmatic theologians who have confessed that aspects of their *knowledge* come to them as gifts that reach beyond acquired information.

*Faith* in the New Testament is composed of intellectual assent, a response in obedience and a daily walk of trust, come what may. Many are gifted in one or more of these three aspects of faith.

All belief requires some faith. But some are gifted with "great faith."

After this list of three gifts, Paul turns to what can be called *dramatic gifts*. Gifts of *healing* are given at times to doctors and also to simple people of faith. In areas of our world traditionally closed to the gospel, astounding *miracles* are taking place that cannot be forced into a post-Enlightenment worldview. On listening to the telling of such stories, the question becomes: Are we deists or theists? For the deist, God does not act in history. For the theist, he does. *Prophecy* is at least preaching at its best. Many have experienced it to be more; it cannot be less. The ability to *distinguish between spirits* is an intuition (gift) known in the charismatic community. The text describes no generic form of "tongues." Paul's experience included "various kinds of tongues." Did he consider singing in the Spirit as one of the forms of speaking in tongues? Having heard both speaking in tongues and singing in the Spirit, I am inclined to think that he did. The *interpretation of tongues*, as it is currently experienced in charismatic churches and fellowships around the globe, includes interpretation by the one who speaks in tongues, or by a second person.

Is this list suggestive or inclusive? It cannot be inclusive because at the end of chapter 12 other gifts are mentioned. Furthermore, Paul has already described the ability to live a celibate life as a spiritual gift (7:7). It is possible to infer from the same text that Paul considered sacramental marriage to be a spiritual gift. Some Christians sense that their natural abilities have been enhanced by a gift of the Spirit. Is the ability to maintain faith in the midst of great suffering a spiritual gift? What of the fortitude to respond in a Christlike manner to "the slings and arrows of outrageous fortune"?[17] Is this related to the spiritual gifts? The questions go on and on.

---

[17]William Shakespeare, *Hamlet*, act 3, scene 1, line 47.

Regardless of how we read the particulars of this list, for Paul none of them should be separated from the introduction and conclusion that he places around the list. They are gifts *of the Spirit*, not natural abilities with which we are born, nor skills which come with hard work and hard knocks. They are given to *individuals* and intended *for the common good*. All of them are inspired by the same Spirit, and God (through the Spirit) freely distributes those gifts *as he chooses*.

Paul then introduces his first discussion of the body of Christ [see fig. 4.3(6)].

| | | |
|---|---|---|
| 6. | [12]For just as the *body is one* and has *many members*, | **B. THE BODY OF CHRIST** <br> One Body—Many Members |
| 7. | and all the *members of the body*, though many, are *one body*, so it is with *Christ*. | **CHRIST** <br> (one and many) |
| 8. | [13]For by *one Spirit* we were *all baptized* into *one body*— *Jews or Greeks, slaves or free*— and all given to *drink of one Spirit*. | **SPIRIT** <br> (one and many) |
| 9. | [14]For the body does *not* consist of *one member* but of *many*. | One Body—Many Members |

**Figure 4.3(6). Cameos 6-9 (1 Cor 12:12-14)**

In his discussion of sexual practice Paul reflected on "the body," meaning the human body. At times the words "the body" meant the body of Christ, the church (6:12-20). Here Paul returns to the same image and relates it to the topic of the spiritual gifts and their function in the church. The congregation is composed of many people, and they are different, yet they are one in the body of Christ.[18]

In cameo 8 two metaphors appear. First, Paul reminds his readers that they were all baptized into one body. In the sacrament of baptism the recipient *passively* accepts being baptized. Someone does the baptizing; and the water is external to the person being baptized. But Paul continues with a second metaphor. He affirms that all are "given to drink of one Spirit." When offered a glass of water, I must take hold of the glass, raise it to my lips and drink. When I drink, the water enters my mouth and becomes part of my body. Set-

---

[18]Paul mentions "Jews or Greeks, slaves or free" but makes no mention of "male or female" such as appears in Gal 3:28. However, the four categories of people he does mention are all either male or female, and so both genders are inevitably included.

ting aside the long debate as to whether this text is discussing one or two baptisms, we can note the active and the passive. It is not enough that I am baptized. That decision was made by my parents when I was a baby. But I am responsible, on a daily basis, to "drink of one Spirit." By choosing the metaphor of "drinking," Paul affirms that the Christian needs the constant infusion of the Spirit as badly as a physical body needs water.

In this text Paul does not offer advice on how this infusion is to take place. Yet the reader is inevitably stimulated to reflect on this important question. Gordon Fee writes, "Such expressive metaphors (immersion in the Spirit and drinking to the fill of the Spirit), it needs to be added, do imply a much greater experiential and visible manifest reception of the Spirit than many have tended to experience in subsequent church history."[19]

Having affirmed that all Christians are members of the one body of Christ through the infusion of the one Spirit, Paul presses on to the extended parable in the center of the homily. The carefully constructed text, composed of cameos 10-14, is displayed in figure 4.3(7).

### THE RHETORIC

Paul composed this remarkable parable using ring composition with the following outline:

10.    I do not belong.
11.       All are needed.
12.          God arranges as he chooses.
13.       All are needed.
14.    I am inferior.

The climax in the center affirms that God arranges the parts of the body *as he chooses*. Assuming Middle Eastern traditional culture, if the parts of the body were free to choose their own functions, every part of the body would be an eye, a right hand or a head, and the body would die.

Paul imagines the human body as a community. Every part of the body is personified while the foot, the ear, the eye and the head become actors in a drama and each of them gives a speech. The first two (the foot and the ear) may be soliloquies. The last two (the eye and the head) address other members of the body. Some of them are on stage and give speeches, while others are off stage, yet called to mind. The parable is another example of Paul's creative artistry.

---

[19]Fee, *First Epistle*, p. 605.

10a.   ¹⁵If the *foot* should say,                    C. *THE PHYSICAL BODY*
     "Because I am *not a hand,*                    (a parable)
     I do *not belong* to the body,"
   that would *not make it any less* a part of the *body.*

b.   ¹⁶And if the *ear* should say,
     "Because I am *not an eye,*                    I DO NOT
     I do *not belong* to the body,"                Belong
   that would not make it any less a part of the *body.*

11.   ¹⁷If the whole body were an *eye,*
     *where* would be the *hearing?*                ALL ARE
   If the whole body were an *ear,*                    Needed
     W*here* would be the sense of smell?

12.   ¹⁸But as it is, *God arranged the organs in the body,*
     each one of them as *he chose.*
     ¹⁹If all were a single organ,                GOD ARRANGES
     where would the body be?                     God Chooses
     ²⁰But as it is, there are *many parts,*      One—Many
     yet *one body.*

13.   ²¹The *eye* cannot say *to the hand,*
     "I have *no need of you,*"                    ALL ARE
   nor again the *head to the feet,*                    Needed
     "I have *no need of you.*"

14a.   ²²On the contrary, the *parts of the body*
   which seem to be *weaker*
   are *indispensable,*

b.   ²³And those *parts of the body*                    I AM
   which we think *less honorable*                Inferior
   we invest with *greater honor,*

c.   and our *unpresentable parts*
   are treated with *greater modesty,*
   ²⁴which our presentable parts do not require.

d.   But God has so *adjusted the body,*
   to the *inferior part,*
   giving the *greater honor*

---

**Figure 4.3(7). Parable of the physical body (1 Cor 12:15-24)**

## COMMENTARY

Paul begins his mini-drama (cameo 10a) with the lowly foot. The text reads:

| | | |
|---|---|---|
| 10a. | ¹⁵If the *foot* should say, | C. THE PHYSICAL BODY |
| | "Because I am *not a hand*, | (a parable) |
| | I do *not belong* to the body," | |
| | that would *not make it any less* a part of the *body*. | |
| b. | ¹⁶And if the *ear* should say, | |
| | "Because I am *not an eye*, | I DO NOT |
| | I do *not belong* to the body," | Belong |
| | that would not make it any less a part of the *body*. | |

**Figure 4.3(8). Cameo 10 (1 Cor 12:15-16)**

In Middle Eastern traditional culture feet, and all shoes, are considered to be unspeakably unclean. The left hand is also unclean, but less so than the foot. The right hand is fully honorable. These attitudes are of great antiquity and have persisted up to the present. God asked Moses to remove his shoes because he was on holy ground (Ex 3:5). Unclean shoes must not touch holy ground. Ancient Israel hated Edom, and the psalmist offered the insult of insults to Edom when he wrote, "upon Edom I cast my shoe" (Ps 60:8; 108:9). John the Baptist affirmed his lowliness in comparison to Jesus by stating that he was not worthy to untie Jesus' sandals (Mk 1:7). Jesus referred to Judas's betrayal by saying, "He who ate my bread has lifted up his heel against me" (Jn 13:18).[20] The rabbis determined that a new shoe became unclean the moment it was lifted off the shoemaker's anvil and first touched the floor. Sacred books must never touch the floor, and the sole of a person's shoe must never be visible to others at home or in any public place. Dalits (untouchables) in India often *feel* that they are worthless. They are not worthless, but that is how they feel. When Saddam Hussein's statue was pulled to the ground in Baghdad in 2003, many of the Iraqis present beat on the statue with their shoes. In February 2011 Egyptians in Madan al-Tahrir, in Cairo, Egypt, held up their shoes as a sign of their total rejection of then President Hosni Mubarak. Ethiopian Orthodox Christians remove their shoes outside the door of the church as they enter. Across the Arabic-speaking Middle East the very words *foot* and *shoes* are "four-letter words." A speaker must apologize to an audience before pronouncing them.

It is not by accident that Paul opens his parable with a speech given by the

---

[20]To show the sole of the foot to anyone at any time is an intended insult across the Middle East.

*unclean foot.* The foot is saying, "I am inferior and worthless. Therefore I do not belong." The ear looks at the eye and gives a similar speech. The ear is a noble part of the body but not as honored in Middle Eastern culture as the eye. Paul's point is: What the foot and the ear *think* about themselves is irrelevant. Their *feelings of worthlessness* that lead them to give such speeches have nothing to do with their importance to the body. Such feelings need to be ignored because they do not reflect the truth. Only someone who is not a "foot" or an "ear" can evaluate their worth, and the foot and the ear need to accept that affirming judgment, ignoring how they feel about themselves.

Paul may have in mind some old Christian slave with no family, health or commercial value. To such a person Paul is saying, "The world may judge you as worthless, but in this new community we are all one body. Indeed we are the body of Christ and each part is of *inestimable value.* Everyone participates, each serves and all belong."

Cameo 11 says,

11.      <sup>17</sup>If the whole body were an *eye,*
               *where* would be the *hearing?*              ALL ARE
           If the whole body were an *ear,*                Needed
               *where* would be the sense of smell?

Figure 4.3(9). Cameo 11 (1 Cor 12:17)

Each part of the body has a unique function that gives it worth. In a capitalistic society the corporate model is extremely powerful and tends to dominate the way the church thinks of itself. I cannot help but wonder what would happen if the contemporary Western church took Paul's model seriously? We pay "the hand" far more than "the foot" because the hand produces more! Ergo: it must be worth more. Paul does not agree.

The climax in the center reads,

12.      <sup>18</sup>But as it is, *God arranged the organs in the body,*
               each one of them as *he chose.*
           <sup>19</sup>If all were a single organ,              GOD ARRANGES
               where would the body be?                  God Chooses
           <sup>20</sup>But as it is, there are *many parts,*
               yet *one body.*

Figure 4.3(10). Cameo 12 (1 Cor 12:18-20)

If the organs chose their own functions, the result would be a disaster. God arranges the organs as *he chooses*. The Spirit gives spiritual gifts. Each believer is invited to receive the offered gifts and serve the body through their use rather than rank the worth of the gifts and complain by asking, "Why am I an unclean foot and not an honorable right hand? It's not fair!" The body needs all of its parts. God arranges those parts into one body. It is not by accident that cameo 12 is in the climactic center of the parable.[21]

Cameo 13 continues:

| 13. | [21]The *eye* cannot say *to the hand*, | |
|---|---|---|
| | "I have *no need of you*," | ALL ARE |
| | nor again the *head to the feet*, | Needed |
| | "I have *no need of you*." | |

**Figure 4.3(11). Cameo 13 (1 Cor 12:21)**

The emphasis is on the problem of self-sufficiency. This cameo can be understood to reach beyond the status of individual Christians and apply also to congregations. By the time Paul was writing, Christian congregations had sprung up in a wide variety of places around the eastern Mediterranean. Those communities needed each other. As the church grew and spread, in a very few years there were Greek, Latin, Jewish, Syrian and Coptic expressions of the church, each with their own language and culture. The strong tendency then and now was and is for each tradition to become self-sufficient and say to the rest of the Christian world, "We do not need you! We have our own language, liturgy, history, theology, tradition and culture. All we need we find within ourselves." For at least sixteen hundred years Christians have been talking this way to each other forgetting that the mystery of the nature of the church is beyond any of our definitions of it. If 1 Corinthians was written to "all those in every place on whom is called the name of our Lord Jesus Christ" (1:2), then *all of us together* are "the body of Christ" and "the holy temple." That single body was created by God, and when it is healthy the various parts work together harmoniously. Any disruption of that harmony is a sign of illness. God's Spirit is not promised

---

[21]The Midrash Rabbah, *Genesis* has an interesting account of a discussion between the mouth and the stomach shortly after death. The mouth says to the stomach, "All that I have robbed and taken with violence, I have put into thee." Three days later the stomach bursts open and replies, "Here is all that thou didst rob and take with violence." (Midrash Rabba, *Genesis* [London: Soncino, 1983], 2:995.) The account is attributed to Rabbi Bar Kappara, a 2nd/3rd century Palestinian rabbi. Paul's parable is not a quarrel but rather affirmations of mutual dependency.

uniquely to us in our divergent organizational structures, but in our faithfulness to the one body of Christ. The sin condemned is not pride but self-sufficiency. The deepest problem is not, "I am better than you" but rather, "I don't need you." Archbishop Desmond Tutu has said, "A self-sufficient human being is subhuman. . . . God has made us so that we will need each other."[22] No church is an island.

Paul's parable comes to an amazing conclusion in cameo 14. The text (literally translated) is seen in figure 4.3(12).

| | | |
|---|---|---|
| 14a. | [22]On the contrary, the *parts of the body*<br>    which seem to be *weaker*<br>    are *indispensable,* | |
| b. | [23]And those *parts of the body*<br>    which we think *less honorable*<br>    we invest with *greater honor,* | I AM<br>Inferior |
| c. | and our *unpresentable parts*<br>    are treated with *greater modesty,*<br>    [24]which our presentable parts do not require. | |
| d. | But God has so *adjusted the body,*<br>    to the *inferior part,*<br>    giving the *greater honor* | |

**Figure 4.3(12). Cameo 14 (1 Cor 12:22-24)**

A quick glance at this four-part cameo reveals that it is discussing the "unmentionable" genitals. Cameo 14a looks backwards and forward. But the last three parts of cameo 14 refer to the organs of reproduction. The language is very polite but also unmistakable. Why does the parable conclude with this special emphasis? The simple answer is that the body needs to reproduce itself. Paul is discussing the importance of evangelism.

This extraordinary emphasis at the conclusion of the parable shines light on at least seven overlapping aspects of Paul's understanding of evangelism. These are:

1. Evangelism is primarily *a very private affair.* One person enters into the sacred space of another person's inner life. Public meetings are important. Yes, Paul affirms in Romans 10:17 that faith comes through hearing the preaching. But here Paul turns that coin over and speaks of the private nature of heart-to-heart communication.

2. Evangelism involves *deep personal relations.* Only when authentic trust is

[22]Quoted in Eliza Griswold, *The Tenth Parallel: Dispatches from the Fault Line Between Christiantiy and Islam* (New York: Farrar, Straus & Giroux, 2010), p. vii.

built between two people can the deep things of God be appropriately discussed and communicated from heart to heart.

3. Evangelism is intended to be *sacred and honorable*. There must be no manipulation, scare tactics or intellectual or spiritual violence.

4. Long-term commitments are assumed. Love does not win and then dump the beloved. If I break with the past and come to faith in Jesus as Lord—what will happen to me? Authentic proclamation of the gospel is deeply aware of long-term responsibilities that accompany the communication of the gospel.

5. Personal advantage must never be involved. Authentic faith cannot be bought or sold. There can be no "pay me X and I will offer you Y." In the gospel, faith has its rewards but those rewards are offered to those who do not seek them. They are not bait placed on a hook to snare unsuspecting fish. Peter was called to catch fish *alive* (Lk 5:10) and not kill them in the process.

6. Evangelism must *always be motivated by love*, not by a will to power. The goal of evangelism is not a successful "membership drive" so that an organization can prosper. Its purpose is to demonstrate the deepest forms of love to people in their brokenness and to make it possible for the lost to be found and for the wounded to find healing.

7. The fact that Paul repeats this theme four times in a row is surely indicative of its importance.

The ring composition of the parable is now complete, but the question remains: Is there any connection between the beginning, the end and the center of the parable (as often occurs in ring composition)? In the center Paul affirms that *God* arranges the body as *he chooses*. This center does indeed relate to the beginning and the end of the parable, but perhaps the center is a summary of all five cameos. And there is more.

As observed earlier in the epistle, Paul (thinking in Hebrew) occasionally omits the verb "to be" in the present tense. The center of cameo 12 is such an occasion. The Greek text behind the English phrase "where would the body be" has no verb "to be." The Greek reads, "Where the body?" Two-thirds of the twenty-three Arabic, Syriac and Hebrew texts examined for this book maintain this linguistic feature along with its meaning.[23] The assumption behind this phrase is, "The body would disappear?" "Where is Billy?" translates into Semitic languages as, "Where Billy?" In short: Billy is lost. If the

---

[23]These texts do not add a future-tense verb "to be." Grammatically they could have done so. See appendix II, plate L.

body cannot reproduce—it will die and what it represents will be irretrievably lost. So it is with the church.

With his parable complete, Paul continues with a second discussion of "the body of Christ" (cameos 15-17) that matches the first discussion of the same topic (cameos 6-9). This second section is displayed in figure 4.3(13).

15.  ²⁵that there may be *no discord* in the body,
      but that the members may have the same care for one another.

16.  ²⁶If *one* member *suffers*,
        *all suffer together*;
     if *one* member is *honored*,
        *all rejoice together*.

17.  ²⁷For you are the body of Christ
        and individually members of it.

**Figure 4.3(13). The body of Christ (1 Cor 12:25-27)**

The opening and closing of this section expands and reinforces ideas presented in the earlier matching section (cameos 6-9). In cameo 17 the language is bold and strong. "You [pl.] are the body of Christ." Paul is not writing to an individual but to "all those in every place on whom is called the name of our Lord Jesus Christ (1:2)." Realizing the full scope of Paul's intended readership makes all the difference in this text.

This section has two critical additions to the previous discussion of the body of Christ. The first introduces the subject of *discord* that appears repeatedly in the letter. A healthy body maintains balance and harmony. Discord in the body is a disease.

The second new element has to do with suffering and honor. This text is in harmony with Romans 12:15 that admonishes "Rejoice with those who rejoice, weep with those who weep." To always be able to suffer/weep with those who weep requires enormous stores of energy. When living among those who suffer, compassion fatigue is a major problem. Without the presence of the Holy Spirit, this task is impossible. Paul does not ask his readers to "listen attentively" to those who suffer. Instead, his directive is that they should share the pain of the sufferer. A professional counselor may choose to remain objective and hold pain at a distance. In the body of Christ such professional objectivity is not sought. Instead, "all suffer together." Who is able for these things? And there is a further problem.

It is *relatively* easy for the whole body to join with the member that is suffering. Many times parts of the body of Christ isolate themselves from other parts that are suffering. Yet the privilege of sharing the suffering of others has its own quiet rewards. The second half of Paul's command is more difficult.

The word *honored* is *doksazetai* (literally: clothed in splendor). The wrist receives a gold bracelet that the foot does not acquire. The head receives a crown, not the hand. The finger receives a diamond ring; the leg does not. Your book is published, and my rejected manuscript sits on the shelf. I am then invited to attend a party honoring you for the release of your new book! Your classes are full of students. Some of my courses are canceled due to lack of enrollment. At the end of the term you are honored as the teacher of the year, and we "all rejoice together." Or do we? This only happens if I am one body with you so that when your heart rejoices, my feet begin to dance!

The final section of the homily returns (as expected) to a second discussion of the variety of gifts [see fig. 4.3(14)].

18.[28]God has appointed in the church
    first apostles,
      second prophets,
        third teachers,
          then workers of miracles,
            then gifts in healing,
              helpers,
                administrators,
                  speakers in various kinds of tongues.

19.[29]Are all apostles?
    Are all prophets?
      Are all teachers?
        Do all work miracles?
          [30]Do all possess gifts of healing?
            Do all speak in tongues?
            Do all interpret?

**Figure 4.3(14). A variety of gifts (1 Cor 12:28-30)**

The emphasis is again on "God has appointed." Paul is not discussing elected church officers or natural abilities, but spiritual gifts. Jesus chose the apostles, and in John's Gospel Jesus tells the disciples, "You did not choose me, but I chose you and appointed you that you should go and bear fruit and that your fruit should abide" (Jn 15:16).

James Dunn has translated *antilempseis* as "helpful deeds," and he prefers "giving council" for *kuberneseis*. The latter word was used for the helmsman

who steered a ship and has overtones of "directing the community."[24] Dunn
also points out that both of these words "refer to functions, actions, rather
than to people." Both words are in the plural. He writes, "The charismata
therefore are the concrete deeds of helpfulness, the actual giving of guidance
on different occasions."[25] *Charisma* in other words is *not a latent power or ability* which may be sometimes displayed and sometimes not. *Only the actual deed
or word is the charisma.*[26] There are no "rights" in this list, only gifts; no privi-
leges, only responsibilities.

Paul concludes this extended homily with the phrase, "And [*de*] earnestly
seek the higher gifts." This phrase is a conclusion to the preceding homily and
an introduction to the homily on love that follows. It is best translated as a
continuation rather than as a contrast, as will be seen in our discussion of
chapter 13.

[24]James G. D. Dunn, *Jesus and the Spirit* (Philadelphia: Westminster Press, 1975), p. 252.
[25]Ibid., p. 253.
[26]Ibid. (italics his).

# The Hymn to Love

1 Corinthians 12:31–14:1

In many churches the "love chapter" is read only at weddings. Naturally, it is fully appropriate for wedding ceremonies and is a matchless guide for Christian marriage, but Paul clearly intended this *hymn to love* [see fig. 4.4(1)] to be a model for all of life. In this fourth essay (chapters 11–14) he places a discussion of love at the center of six homilies that focus on Christian worship. He thereby commends love as a source of healing for the various problems set out in the essay.[1] Before savoring the delights of the text, a brief introduction may be helpful.

The verb Paul uses for *love* is *agapao*. The Greek language of his day had two primary words for love. The first was *eros*, which had to do with passionate love, either religious or sexual. The second was *phileo*, which was used to describe love between friends and the kind of love that is shared in a healthy family. But neither of these words was adequate for what Paul and the other writers of the New Testament wanted to describe. Moving to a higher level of love they wanted and selected a new word, the term *agapao*.

In the Greek Old Testament *agape*, as a noun, appears only in the Song of Songs. It is rare in classical Greek, and when used it has to do with "inclining toward" something. Paul and his friends selected this word that had no clear footprint in the Greek language, and filled it with new meaning. Five things can be said about *agape* as it appears in the New Testament generally and in this text in particular.

---

[1]The theme of "love" has appeared directly or indirectly in many places thus far in the epistle. Prominent among them are 1 Cor 1:10-16; 2:9; 3:3; 4:14; 8:1, 11-12; 10:24, 28-29, 32-33; 12:26. Personal freedom and knowledge must be tempered by love.

1.    [12:31]And continue in zeal for the highest spiritual *gifts* [*Charismata*].
      And in addition, I will give directions for a journey over a mountain pass [*huperbolen hodon*].

--------------------------------------------------------------------------------

2.    [13:1]If I speak in the *tongues* of men                    LOVE AND
          and of angels,                                          Tongues
      but *have not love*,                                        Prophecy
      I am banging brass or a clanging cymbal.                    Knowledge

3.        [2]And if I have *prophetic powers*
      and understand all *mysteries* and all *knowledge*,

--------------------------------------------------------------------------------

4.    and if I have all *faith*                    **LOVE AND THE**
          so as to remove mountains,               **Spiritual Gifts**
      but *have not love*,
      I am nothing.

5.        [3]And if I dole out all my possessions,              LOVE AND
      and if I surrender my body so *that I may boast*,         Faith
      but *have not love*,                                      Hope
      I gain nothing.

--------------------------------------------------------------------------------

6.    [4]Love is *patient*.              **LOVE DEFINED**        LOVE AND
          Kind is love:                 **Positively**          Knowledge
                                                                ??
7.        not jealous,                                          ??
          not boastful,
          [5]not arrogant,
          not rude,
8.          *not seeking what is for itself*,    **LOVE DEFINED**
9.        not quick to anger,                    **Negatively**
          not recording wrongs,[2]
            [6]not rejoicing in unrighteousness
          but rejoicing in community when truth prevails,

                                                                LOVE AND
10.   [7]covers all, believes all,        **LOVE DEFINED**      Faith
      hopes all, *patiently endures all*.  **Positively**       Hope

--------------------------------------------------------------------------------

_____

[2]My translation.

| | | |
|---|---|---|
| 11. | [8]Love never falls.<br>As for *prophecy*, it will be *discarded*;<br>as for *tongues*, they will cease;<br>as for *knowledge*, it will be *discarded*. | LOVE AND<br>Prophecy<br>Tongues<br>Knowledge<br>(- Three Discarded) |

12.  [9]For our knowledge is *imperfect*
      and our prophecy is *imperfect*.
      [10]But when the *perfect comes*,
      the *imperfect* will be *discarded*.

                                         - Imperfect
                                         + Perfect

13.  [11]When I was a child,                           PARABLE
      I *spoke* like a child,   **LOVE AND THE**   Child and
      I *thought* like a child,   **Spiritual Gifts**   Man
      I *reasoned* like a child.                      (Maturation
      When I became a man                   and Discard)
      I *discarded* my childish ways.

14.  [12]For now we see in a *mirror dimly*,       - Imperfect
      then *face to face*.                          + Perfect
      Now my knowledge is *imperfect*,
      then I shall *know* fully as I am *fully known*.

15.  [13]And thus there abides          LOVE AND:
      *faith, hope and love*,            Faith
      these three;                        Hope
      but the *highest* of these is *love*.   (+ Three Abide)

---

16.[14:1] Run after love    **ZEAL FOR THE *SPIRITUAL* GIFTS** (Strive for Love)
      and continue in zeal for the *spiritual* gifts (*pneumatika*)

---

**Figure 4.4(1). The hymn to love (1 Cor 12:31–14:1)**

First, it is *universal*. This is a love that reaches out to everyone. Jesus' parable of the good Samaritan in Luke 10:25-37 is a primary example. Within this form of love there is "neither Jew nor Greek, there is neither slave nor free, there is neither male and female; for you are all one in Christ Jesus" (Gal 3:28). Even the enemy is to be loved (Mt 5:44). The German Christian martyr Dietrich Bonhoeffer discusses this latter text and writes, "By our enemies Jesus means those who are quite intractable and utterly unresponsive to our love, who forgive us nothing when we forgive them all, who requite our love with hatred and our service with derision."[3]

Bonhoeffer's point is that the enemy is not the person who is softened by love and becomes a friend. Instead he or she is the person who refuses the of-

---

[3]Dietrich Bonhoeffer, *The Cost of Discipleship* (London: SCM Press, 1954), p. 127.

fered love and remains stubbornly opposed to the one extending the love.

Second, *agape* (love) is the new "royal law," which directs all believers to love God and one's neighbor. As early as 7:19 Paul wrote that circumcision was nothing, and what mattered was "keeping the commandments of God." Certainly at the top of that mysterious list was the commandment to love. In 9:21 Paul referred to "the law of Christ." At the end of this essay, in 14:37, he urges his readers to accept the "commandment of the Lord." That commandment is to love God and one other. All of these references look to the "royal law" of love.

Third, the model for this love is the life of Christ. They are to love one another, "as I have loved you" (Jn 15:12).

Fourth, as shown in this hymn, love is the indispensable ingredient for each of the gifts. Without love none of them is of any value. At the same time, by the end of the hymn, love stands on its own and becomes the highest of all the gifts. The Corinthians had many gifts (1:7), but they were critically lacking in love. That omission left every other gift deeply flawed.

Fifth, the source of this love is the indwelling Spirit of God that makes possible the flow of the love of Christ into the life of the believer. Without that Spirit, this *agape* love is impossible. "We love because he first loved us" (1 Jn 4:19). We love God and *then* our neighbor.

With these general characteristics in mind the interpreter must first decide where the hymn opens and where it closes. This cannot be determined without observing the "wheels within wheels," which come to a climax in this homily.

## THE RHETORIC

The outer wheel is the entire essay. The homily on love appears in the center of an essay (chaps. 11–14) composed of seven sections. By way of review, these are:

1. Men and Women Leading in Worship: Prophets and How They Dress (11:2-16)
2.    Order in Worship: *Sacrament*—The Lord's Supper (11:17-34)
3.      Gifts and the Nature of the Body (12:1-30)
4.        *The Hymn to Love* (12:31–14:1)
5.      Spiritual Gifts and the Upbuilding of the Body (14:1-25)
6.    Order in Worship: *Word*—Prophets and Speakers in Tongues (14:26-33a)
7. Women and Men Worshiping: No Chatting in Church (14:33b-36)

Within this larger seven-part prophetic rhetorical template the hymn to love participates in a second ring composition, which is as follows:

1. The *spiritual gifts* (12:1-31)
2.      Love and the *spiritual gifts* (13:1-3)
3.          Love defined (13:4-7)
4.      Love and the *spiritual gifts* (13:8-13)
5. *The spiritual gifts* (14:1-25)

This ring composition highlights the fact that the hymn to love (chap. 13) is integrally woven together with what precedes and with what follows. The *spiritual gifts* are the threads that do this weaving. Within this second ring is yet a third ring composed of seven distinct parts. Summarized, this is:

1. Continue in zeal for *the higher gifts* and I will show the way (12:31)
2.      **Love and the spiritual gifts (13:1-3)**
3.          **Love defined positively (13:4a)**
4.             **Love defined negatively (13:4b-6)**
5.          **Love defined positively (13:7)**
6.      **Love and the spiritual gifts (13:8-13)**[4]
7. Continue in zeal for *the gifts* and run after love (14:1)

These seven sections create yet another example of the prophetic rhetorical template. Paul's definitions of love in 13:4-7 are the *center* of the *center* of the *center* of the essay.

## COMMENTARY

Reflection on this homily must begin by examining its outer frame. The problem is that for a very long time 12:31 and 14:1 have been partially or entirely separated from chapter 13, and some reflection on the connections that tie those two verses to the hymn to love is essential.[5] We begin with 12:31, a verse that raises some important questions. These include:

1. Do the two sentences in verse 12:31 form a single connected idea, or should they be divided? Some versions and commentators have divided them, placing the first sentence at the end of chapter 12 and the second at the beginning of chapter 13. These versions stretch from the Latin Vulgate to the RSV. Others see the two sentences as a unit. The fifth-century Syriac Peshitta reads, "But if you are searching for the greater gifts, I will show you a more excellent way."[6] Bishr ibn al-Sari endorsed this reading and translated 12:31

---

[4]Note the bold print in figure 4.4(1) above.

[5]*Codex Vaticanus* and the Latin Vulgate add 12:31a to chapter 13.

[6]Peshitta, Lamsa.

as, "If you are earnestly seeking the greatest gifts, then I will also guide you to the superior way."[7] Bishr then comments,

> He [Paul] demonstrated here that they were wrangling, seeking the praise of men. He says, "If you desire the superior gifts, then why do you not prize that which is better and more beneficial and good for yourselves. It is this matter which I point out to you." He means love.[8]

Both the original Arabic text and the comment by Bishr ibn al-Sari join the two phrases in 12:31 into a single unified sentence. Other early Arabic versions reinforce the connection between the two sentences in 12:31 by repeating the term *more excellent* in the translation. This results in some form of "If you desire the *more excellent* gifts, then I will show you a *more excellent* way" (italics added).[9] Granted, this is an interpretive translation in that Paul uses two different words. At the same time, the two words are both related to height. The first of them urges the readers to be zealous for the *higher* gifts. The second points to the *high road* over a *mountain pass*. By uniting the two sentences Bishr Ibn al-Sari is emphasizing an aspect of the text that is indeed present in it. In modern times both the Jerusalem Bible and the French *Segond* Version (1962) do the same. I am convinced that they should be read together.

2. A second decision that needs to be made has to do with grammar. Do we read the verb *zeloute* as an imperative and translate it as, "Continue in zeal for the higher gifts"? Or should the verb be seen as an indicative and read, "*you are zealous* for the higher gifts, and in *addition* [*eti*][10] I will show you . . ." This latter option is reflected in the Syriac Peshitta, which translates "you are searching for" and in the tenth-century Sinai Arabic Gospels 310 that reads, "In that you have been zealous and envious for the greater gifts, I will show you the more excellent way." The traditional reading of the text as an imperative appears to be the better option because two imperatives conclude the homily in the matching verse at the end (14:1).[11]

3. The third question has to do with placement. Should we see these two sentences exclusively as a conclusion to chapter 12? Or, as is common in this epistle, did Paul compose a hinge verse? Specifically, did he intend the reader

---

[7]Bishr ibn al-Sari, *Sinai Arabic 151* (867) (English text), p. 79.
[8]Ibid., n. 27.
[9]Gibson, Mt. Sinai (9th cent.); Erpenius (1616); Propagandist (1671); Yusif Dawud (1899) among others.
[10]BAGD, p. 316.
[11]See appendix II, plate M.

to see 12:31 as the conclusion to chapter 12 and *at the same time* as an introduction to chapter 13? A similar hinge appears in 15:58 and joins chapter 15 to chapter 16. Seeing 12:31 as a hinge verse between the two chapters appears to be the best option because verse 31 does indeed conclude chapter 12 and at the same time it provides an important introduction to chapter 13.[12] Accordingly 12:31 needs to be examined and compared to 14:1.

These two verses are tied together with a number of threads. First are the texts themselves. When placed together these two verses say,

1. [12:31]And [de] *continue in zeal* for the higher spiritual gifts [*kharismata*].

    And in addition, I will give directions for a journey over a mountain pass.

--------------------------------------------------------------------------------

16. [14:1]Run after love,

    and *continue in zeal* for the spiritual gifts [*pneumatika*]

The traditional understanding of these two cameos is reflected in the RSV which reads,

1. [12:31]But earnestly desire the higher gifts.

    And I will show you a still more excellent way.

--------------------------------------------------------------------

16.[14:1]Make love your aim,

    and earnestly desire the spiritual gifts.

The understanding of the text that lies behind this translation is of great antiquity. The popular assumptions that have grown out of this reading are:

> The Corinthians had been arguing and fighting over the spiritual gifts. Paul mentions "higher gifts" and then says, "I will show something still better—the way of love. Set aside the *entire list* of these troublesome spiritual gifts; all that really matters is the still more excellent way—the way of love."

Supporting this view, in the Kittel article on *huperbole*, Gerhard Delling writes, "In an adjectival use [of υπερβολη] 1 C. 12:31b calls the mode of Christian life described in 13:1-7 one which 'far surpasses' ('a much superior way') the life controlled by charismata, 12:28-30."[13]

But this view is flawed. The difficulty is that at the end of the hymn to love, Paul appears to reverse himself and tell his readers "continue in zeal for the spiritual gifts—especially that you may prophesy" (14:1). That is, on the

---

[12]In like manner 14:1 concludes chap. 13 and introduces chap. 14.

[13]Gerhard Delling, "υπερβαλλω, υπερβαλλοντως, υπερβολη," in *TDNT,* 8:521.

one hand, in 12:31 Paul seems to tell his readers to set aside all these *divisive gifts*. On the other hand, in 14:1 he *reintroduces spiritual gifts with a flair!* This apparent disjointedness leads some to see "rough connectives" and even to suggest that the hymn to love is probably out of place. Should it not come at the end of chapter 14? In that way the two discussions on gifts (chaps. 12, 14) would be together. Paul would then be saying "Here are the spiritual gifts [chaps. 12, 14]. But I can point you to something *far better than all of them*: The way of love [chap. 13]." Are chapters 12-14 confused, or out of order, and what is the relationship between 12:31 and 14:1? What can be said?

1. Initially we observe that the word *de* opens cameo 1. This Greek particle translates the Hebrew *wa* which is a common connective. It can better be read as "and" rather than "but." Paul is not offering a sharp contrast; instead he is presenting two lists of gifts. The first list, made up of "tongues, prophecy and knowledge" is a selection of important gifts that are needed by the church, and Christians should continue in zeal regarding them. The second list is composed of "the higher gifts" (faith, hope and love) which are *more important* than those noted in the first list. In the hymn to love Paul argues that both lists are significant, but the second list is *permanent* while the first is *transitory*. The verb *zeloute* as a present imperative (continue in zeal for) appears in each of the two verses under consideration (12:31 and 14:1). The word *zealot* comes from this verb. Paul's readers are to be *zealous* in their engagement with *each list* even though the first will "pass away" while the second will "abide." Noting the double use of the verb *zeloute* (continue in zeal for) encourages the reader to see 12:31 and 14:1 as the "bookends" that hold the hymn together.

2. A second thread that ties these two verses together is the fact that 12:31 refers to the *kharismata* (spiritual *gifts*) while 14:1 speaks of the *pneumatika* (*spiritual* gifts). The first emphasizes that all is because of *grace* (*kharis*). These gifts are not rewards for faithful service; they are *gifts*. The second focuses on the fact that they are not natural abilities or material possessions, but *spiritual* gifts. The two words form a complementary pair that also frames the hymn.

3. A more important consideration turns on the translation of the second sentence in 12:31b that has often been understood to mean "I will show you a more excellent way." The word for "I will show you" means "I will describe a journey." It does not explain the *road* but rather the *journey* on that road. What kind of a journey? Here the key phrase *kath huperbolen hodon* (along a *huperbo-*

*len* road) has usually been translated "a more excellent way." But this translation has difficulties.

The word *huperbolen* produced the English word *hyperbole*, which like the Greek word is ethically neutral. In Greek, this word has to do with some form of excess, good or bad. It is a compound word made up of *huper* (over) and *ballo* (to throw). The root meaning has to do with "overshooting" and "throwing beyond."[14] Paul is the only New Testament author to use this word, and he does so (as a verb and as a noun) a total of twelve times. As a verb, Paul writes positively about "the transcendent power" (2 Cor 4:7), the "eternal weight of glory" (2 Cor 4:17) and the "abundance of revelation" (2 Cor 12:7). Negatively he uses this verb to refer to being "utterly crushed" (2 Cor 1:8) and being "sinful beyond measure" (Rom 7:13). As a noun (used as a kind of adjective) he writes positively about "immeasurable greatness" (Eph 1:19), "immeasurable riches of his grace" (Eph 2:7), "surpassing splendor" (2 Cor 3:10), "surpassing grace" (2 Cor 9:14) and "surpassing knowledge" (Eph 3:19). Negatively he remembers, "I violently tried to destroy [the church]" (Gal 1:13). In each of these cases something, *positive or negative*, is being *intensified*. But in the case of a "way," you can start with "a crooked way," add *huperbole* and have "a *very* crooked way." Or, you can begin with "a straight way," attach *huperbole* to the sentence and describe "an *extremely* straight way." But you cannot make sense out of "an extremely way." As noted, *huperbole* is morally neutral as is the word *way*. In summary, following Paul's usage, grace is good and thus he can add *huperbole* to grace and speak of "abundant grace." But how are we to understand an "extremely way" in 12:31?

Needing some kind of a positive, translators have traditionally turned the "way" into an "excellent way" and read *huperbole hodon* as "a more excellent way." But there is another option. *Huperbole* can also refer to "a mountain pass." This language describes a way that goes up, over and beyond other ways; *the high road* (not the *low road*) is the *huperbole hodon*.[15] This meaning for *huperbole* is found in Diodorus Siculus's *Historicus* (19:73), Xenophon's *Anabasis* (3.5.18; 4.1.21; 4.4.18), Strabo (7.1.5) and elsewhere.[16] This raises a further question.

If Paul, as suggested, is comparing the way of love to a stiff climb over a mountain pass, we would expect him to build on that image with other ap-

---

[14]BAGD, p. 840.
[15]Ibid. This option was overlooked by BAGD, p. 840.
[16]LSJ *Lexicon*, p. 1861.

propriate phrases and metaphors, and indeed he does so. There are six occasions in this homily where Paul's language echoes or compements a mountain-pass journey. These are:

a. The *higher gifts* (12:31). These will be defined as faith, hope and love.

b. The journey *over a pass* (12:31). This is the way of love.

c. Faith that *removes mountains* (13:2). If you remove them you don't have to climb them.

d. Love *never falls* [not fails] (13:8). Mountain climbing involves the risk of falling. Love does not fall.

e. The *highest* of these is love (13:13). The image Paul began with in 12:31 now reappears.

f. *Run after love* (14:1). The journey over the mountain pass is hard because it is uphill and you are to run in spite of the hills.

James Moffat caught much of this understanding of the text, which he translated, "And yet I will go on to show you a still higher path."[17] Mountain climbing is strenuous, exacting and dangerous. The road is uphill. It requires planning, training, energy, discipline, commitment, a huge investment of time and the setting of long-term goals. It is also exciting, compelling, fulfilling, rewarding and exhilarating; the view from the top, on a clear day, is thrilling beyond measure. The higher we climb, the more painful the fall. All of this applies to the journey (way) of love.

4. Athletics joins these two verses. In 12:31 Paul discusses mountain climbing. In 14:1 he urges his readers to "run after love," and Corinth was a town committed to sports. Mountain climbing was not a recognized sport, but running was, and climbing mountains is good training for runners. Both activities require strong legs. Sadly, both of these concrete images have been turned into abstractions in the English translation tradition.

5. One final observation can be made regarding the opening (12:31) and closing (14:1) of the hymn to love. In 12:7 Paul records that each believer "is given" (passive) "the manifestation of the Spirit." Furthermore, God distributes the gifts "as he wills" (12:11). In addition, God "has appointed in the church . . ." (12:28). No one can demand a particular gift or despise God's selections for his people. At the same time a gift must be *received* for it to accomplish its purpose. If I send a $100 check to a friend, and on arrival the friend

[17]Moffat, *First Epistle*, p. 191.

burns it, the gift is not "received" and thereby does not achieve its purpose. God, through the Spirit, distributes spiritual gifts, but the believer must receive and use the gifts or they become inert and worthless. As observed, 12:31 is best understood to mean "continue in zeal." Orr and Walther allow the present imperative its full significance. Readers are urged to *continue*, doing what they are *already doing*.[18] God acts to give, and they respond by receiving and using the gifts. Paul is again dealing with his readers in a gentle manner.

Before launching into the hymn itself, it is important to note one further "tune" that is being played as the homily unfolds. This has to do with the aforementioned set of comparisons between the two lists of gifts. The *important (yet temporary) gifts* are:

- Tongues
- Prophecy
- Knowledge

The *highest (permanent) gifts* in Paul's thinking are:

- Faith
- Hope
- Love

Two out of the three sections of the hymn begin and end with these two lists [see fig. 4.4(2)]. (The center section includes only one half of the double list.)

**1. Love and the spiritual gifts (13:1-3)**
Opens with tongues, prophecy and knowledge
Closes with faith, hope and love

**2. Love defined (13:4-7)**
(Opens with an indirect reference to knowledge)
Closes with faith, hope and love

**3. Love and the spiritual gifts (13:8-13)**
Opens with tongues, prophecy and knowledge (temporary)
Ends with faith, hope and love (permanent)

**Figure 4.4(2). The two lists of gifts in 1 Cor 13**

Rhetorical and ethical melodies are played together harmoniously in this literary masterpiece. This brings us to the first discussion of love and the gifts.

---

[18]Orr/Walther, *I Corinthians*, p. 288.

## LOVE AND THE SPIRITUAL GIFTS (1 COR 13:1-3)

Each of the four cameos in this section of the hymn deserves reflection. Paul opens with,

| | | |
|---|---|---|
| 2. [13:1]If I speak in the *tongues* of men and of angels, | LOVE AND | |
| | Tongues | |
| but *have not love*, | Prophecy | |
| I am banging brass or a clanging cymbal. | Knowledge | |

Before it was destroyed by the Romans in 146 B.C., the old city of Corinth was famous across the Roman Empire for its brass and bronze work and for its fine craftsmanship in precious metals. Beginning in 44 B.C., while the city was being rebuilt, the brass-making trade almost certainly resumed. In any case, the fame of the earlier Corinthian brass was legendary. Many wealthy Romans collected "Corinthian bronzes." After examining all the evidence available, Jerome Murphy-O'Connor writes, "Since so much bronze working was carried on in the center of the city, it seems likely that there must have been many other installations in outlying areas. Trade in bronze must be considered to have made a significant contribution to the commerce of Roman Corinth."[19]

Murphy-O'Connor also presents evidence that casting was involved, particularly in the making of large items such as statues. But more common household pieces would naturally have been fashioned by hammering the soft brass. In Aleppo, Syria, a large brass-makers' market is still functioning in the center of the city. There, along both sides of a narrow street, one can visit rows of small shops, each about two meters by three meters in size. Seated in the street, each craftsman makes and sells his own products. While lecturing in Aleppo in the 1980s, I was interested in visiting this famous market and initially was obliged to ask for directions as I trudged eagerly down a narrow pedestrian street in the old city. But as soon as I approached from a distance of about half a kilometer, I only needed to follow the racket! On arrival I found myself in the middle of more than two hundred craftsmen hammering slabs of copper or brass into cooking pots, drinking vessels, cheese-making ladles and the like. Even though all of this craftsmanship was taking place in the open air, the noise was deafening. To talk to any of the skilled workmen I was obliged to bend down, place my lips within two inches

---

[19]Jerome Murphy-O'Conner, *St. Paul's Corinth: Texts and Archeology* (Collegeville, Minn.: Liturgical Press, 2002), p. 218.

of the artisan's ear and shout at the top of my voice. The noise levels were ear-splitting.

As tentmakers, Paul, Aquila and Priscilla would have needed to be present in the marketplace in order to pursue their trade and contact customers. Enduring the high-pitched racket of banging brass would have been a common experience for all Corinthians every time they entered the market. In the opening of his discussion of love and the spiritual gifts, Paul invokes this powerful image. Their gift of tongues had to do with the language of humans, not angels. The angels spoke a different tongue, as Paul affirms. But if he managed to "speak in the tongues of men" and if beyond that could even talk to the angels, but *without love*, his words would be as meaningless as the roar of banging brass in the market. Some in Corinth were proud of their spiritual gifts and disdainful of their fellow Christians. They were "enriched with all speech" (1:5) yet at the same time they were quarreling (1:11)! This lack of love reduced their much-prized speaking in tongues to the level of the deafening, high-pitched roar in the brass market.

Cameo 3 introduces three gifts, which are:

3.   ²And if I have *prophetic powers*
        and understand all *mysteries* and all *knowledge*,

In cameos 2, 4 and 5 Paul establishes a four-line pattern:

If this is true
and this is true
and there is no love,
then this will result.

With this pattern established, the reader expects cameo 3 to say something like:

And if I have prophetic powers
and understand all mysteries
and have no love,
my prophesying is worthless.

It is pointless to speculate as to why in cameo 3 Paul broke the pattern he used in each of the other three cameos in this series. Perhaps the answer is as simple as lack of space on the page. What matters is that cameo 3 includes *prophetic powers*, *knowledge* and *mysteries*. By mentioning *prophecy* and *knowledge* immediately after a cameo on *tongues*, cameos 2 and 3 together include the same list of prophecy, tongues and knowledge that appears in cameo 11. As it stands, cameo 3 affirms that without love, all *prophecy*, an understanding of all *mysteries* and the acquisition of all *knowledge* together are worthless. "I am *nothing*" is a deeper self-abrogation than "I am *banging brass*."

*Prophecy* is at least preaching, but it is better understood as Spirit-inspired preaching, and if love does not shine through that preaching—it is worthless. Earlier in the epistle Paul defined himself and his friend Apollos as "stewards of the *mysteries* of God" (4:1). Here he affirms that if he penetrates *all mysteries* (Christian and pagan) without love, he is nothing. In regard to *knowledge*, it is far too common that arrogance accompanies the acquisition of knowledge. Paul's longstanding equation of "knowledge without love equals nothing" is a countercultural voice in any age. A pervasive perception in significant areas in the academy is that knowledge has no necessary connection to love.

Furthermore, *knowledge* (*gnosis*) was a key word in the Gnostic worldview. According to that system of thought, humankind was saved through the acquisition of secret knowledge that set the devotees apart from ordinary human beings. They needed no savior, only knowledge, and God did not act in history to save. Paul signals that if a person acquires *all knowledge* and has no love he or she *is nothing*.

Having discussed *tongues*, *prophecy* and *knowledge* (without love), Paul now turns to *faith* and *hope* (without *love*). Cameo 4 reads:

| 4. | [2b]and if I have all *faith* | LOVE AND THE |
|---|---|---|
|  | so as to remove mountains, | Spiritual Gifts |
|  | but *have not love*, |  |
|  | I am nothing. |  |

In 12:9 faith is listed as one of the spiritual gifts. Clearly, great faith is there presupposed. The image of faith that can move mountains is from Jesus (Mt 17:20; 21:21). Paul is again writing personally. If he reaches the level of faith described by Jesus and in the process despises those of lesser faith, he *is nothing*. An author may publish books and articles, record lectures and publish plays, but if she/he does not exhibit love for others in the process, he/she *is nothing*. After faith comes *hope*.

| 5. | [3]And if I dole out all my possessions, | LOVE AND |
|---|---|---|
|  | and if I surrender my body so *that I may boast*, | Faith |
|  | but *have not love*, | Hope |
|  | I gain nothing. |  |

This cameo begins with a powerful image. The key word in the first line of cameo 5 is *psomiso* (if I dole out). The picture is of someone who is very generous and, a little bit at a time, gives away everything he or she possesses in the hope that there will be a reward. Is Paul echoing the story of the rich ruler who approached Jesus hoping to earn his salvation through good works, and asked, "Good teacher, what shall I do to inherit eternal life?" (Lk 18:18). Jesus told him, "Sell all that you have and distribute to the poor" (Lk 18:22). The ruler failed to obey. By contrast, here Paul reflects on a person who obeys this command of Jesus. What will happen to him/her? We cannot proceed to the answer without sorting out a textual problem that occurs in cameo 5.

We are accustomed to reading cameo 5b as "if I surrender my body so *that it may burn.*" But the finest Greek texts read "that I may boast." Which text is the best and what is Paul saying?

The oldest and most reliable early Greek texts read *kaukhesomai* (that I may boast), while *early translations* of 1 Corinthians into Latin, Syriac and Armenian along with many patristic writers opt for *kauthesomai* (that I may burn). The difference is one letter. The first has a χ in its center and the second uses a θ.[20] Bruce Metzger calls the evidence for the first "both early and weighty."[21] In short, when looking at the early Greek copies, "that I may boast" is the preferred choice. Where then did the familiar "that I may burn" come from and what is at issue?

At the time Paul was writing, no Christian had been burned alive for his or her faith. Yet the story of the three young men who were thrown into the fire in Daniel 3:1-25 was well known (among Jews). Then in A.D. 64 (ten years after Paul wrote 1 Corinthians), Rome burned. Seeking a scapegoat, Nero blamed the Christians and began the first Roman persecution of the church. On one brutal occasion, Nero smeared a group of Christians with pitch, crucified them and set them on fire as torches "to light the Emperor's races in the Vatican Circus."[22] After that scene of spectacular horror the Christian community would inevitably have been seared with the memory of the martyrs who had been burned to death for their faith. After A.D. 64 it is fully understandable that some scribe copied καυθησωμαι (that I may be burned) rather than καυχησωμαι (that I may boast). Such an error would eas-

---

[20]For a thorough discussion of the textual problem see Bruce Metzger, *A Textual Commentary on the Greek New Testament* (New York: United Bible Societies, 1971), pp. 563-64.

[21]Ibid., p. 563.

[22]Miriam Griffin, "Nero," in *ABD*, 4:1078 (see Tacitus, *Annals* 15:44; Suetonius, *Nero* 16.2).

ily have become popular, and Christian readers would naturally have preferred the new reading. It called to mind the recent martyrs, and generally speaking it was and is more attractive to think of Paul offering his body to be "burned" than to contemplate his interest in "boasting." But which word did he actually write?

The first problem is that the very phrase "that I might burn" is never translated the way it is written, even by those who prefer this reading of the text. "That *I* might burn" is always changed (without textual evidence) into some form of "that *it* might burn" to have the translation make sense (KJV, RSV, NIV). When faced with the word *burn* in the text the translator naturally feels the pressure to let Paul offer "it" (his body that he has just mentioned) to the fires.

But if we choose the reading "that *I* might *boast*" no shift of person is needed. Paul is talking about *his own* boasting. Furthermore, the concluding line in this cameo is not "I am nothing," such as occurs in cameo 4. Rather Paul writes, "I *gain* nothing." Gain what and when? Paul was describing his hope to be able to boast on the Day of Judgment. Whatever does this mean?

As noted earlier, for Paul "boasting" carried two meanings. The first was *negative* and had to do with boasting about one's spiritual achievements or credentials. As early as 1:29-30 Paul discusses how God used weak things to shame the strong, "so that no human might boast in the presence of God." The second meaning is *positive* and relates to serving the Lord in a way that reaches *beyond the call of duty.* Paul had also discussed this positive aspect of boasting with the Corinthians. In 9:15-16 he wrote, "For I would rather die than have any one deprive me of *my ground for boasting.* For if I preach the gospel, that gives me no *ground for boasting.* For necessity is laid upon me." His point is that he is *obliged* to preach the gospel in order to fulfill his commission. But he is *not obliged* to refuse financial support for doing so. If therefore he preaches and is not paid, on the Day of Judgment he will be able to say to the Lord, "Lord, I did more than you commissioned me to do! Everywhere I went I supported myself financially." This same positive aspect of boasting appears in 1 Thessalonians 2:19, where Paul writes, "For what is our hope or joy or crown of *boasting before our Lord Jesus at his coming?* Is it not you?" In Philippians 2:16 as well he urges his readers to hold fast to the word of life, "so that in the day of Christ I may *boast* that I did not run in vain or labor in vain." For Paul this positive type of *boasting* has to do with *the Day of Judgment* at the end of all things.

Add to this the directive that Paul gives in Romans when he writes, "Present your bodies as a living sacrifice, holy and acceptable to God" (Rom 12:1). In like manner here in 13:3 Paul appears to be saying,

> If I dole out my possessions until all are gone, and if I surrender my body [as a living sacrifice] in decades of self-emptying witness and service in the fond hope that on the day of the Lord, I will be able to boast of having done more than was asked of me, *and have no love*—it is all in vain. On that last great day there will be no reward for me! *I will gain nothing!*

Offering gifts to those in need has special problems connected to it. Without self-awareness and sensitivity to the dynamics involved, such offerings can stimulate pride in the giver and humiliation in the receiver. It is possible to give gifts out of our needs which are at times unrelated to the felt needs of the very people the gifts are intended to help. It is easy to send money to build church buildings for Christians in central Africa. But what if it is too hot inside those buildings, and people would rather worship outside under a large tree? Such a gift would reflect failure in authentic love. If there is *no authentic love* for the receiver, writes Paul, all giving of both resources and of self is, for the givers, in vain. Discerning love is a necessary ingredient for everything.

Seen in this light the earliest Greek texts can be allowed to trump some of the early fathers and early translations, and the text read appropriately, "that I may boast" (NRSV).[23] Paul is talking about hope, his hope to receive a reward on the Day of Judgment. Indeed, in cameos 1-2 he discussed *tongues, prophecy* and *knowledge*, and in cameos 4-5 he writes about *faith, hope* and *love*. If *faith* and *hope* are not soaked in *love* they are worthless. Paul is now ready to define this crucial component called "love."

## LOVE DEFINED (1 COR 13:4-7)

Paul's readers know what *eros* (passion) is all about, and they understand *phileo* (to be a friend). But what is this *agape* (love) that Christians constantly discuss? Paul offers positive definitions, then negatives, and finally a second list of positives [see fig. 4.4(3)].

---

[23]Both the Nestle and the Bible Society Greek New Testaments have chosen this reading. See Kurt Aland, *The Greek New Testament* (New York: United Bible Societies, 1968), and Eberhard Nestle, ed., *Novum Testamentum Graece* (Stuttgart: Deutsche Bibelstiftung, 1979).

| | | | |
|---|---|---|---|
| 6. | [4]Love is *patient.* Kind is love: | LOVE DEFINED Positively | LOVE AND Knowledge ?? |
| 7. | not jealous, not boastful, [5]not arrogant, not rude, | | ?? |
| 8. | *not seeking what is for itself,* | LOVE DEFINED | |
| 9. | not quick to anger, not keeping records of wrongs, [6]not rejoicing in unrighteousness but rejoicing in community when truth prevails, | Negatively | |
| 10. | [7]covers all, believes all, hopes all, *patiently endures all.* | LOVE DEFINED Positively | LOVE AND Faith, Hope |

**Figure 4.4(3). Love defined (1 Cor 13:4-7)**

## THE RHETORIC

The rhetoric of this section of the homily is simple and straightforward. The positives open and close the section. The negatives appear in the center, and that center is split with the single line: "not seeking what is for itself." This line reflects the opening and the closing of the entire homily.

## COMMENTARY

The five cameos include fifteen definitions of love each of which is worthy of note, but first a few general comments may be helpful.

In cameo 1 the readers are told to "continue in zeal [*zeloute*] for the highest spiritual *gifts.*" By the end of the homily (cameo 16) those same readers are told to "continue in zeal [*zeloute*] for the *spiritual* gifts." As seen in an early chapter, in Isaiah 28:14-18 the prophet relates the center of his ring composition to the opening and closing phrases of the homily. This same feature appears here as we compare cameos 1, 8 and 16. In the very center (cameo 8) the text affirms that love does "not *zetei* [seek] what is for its self." With strong overlap in meaning, there may be an intended play on words between *zeloute* (continue in zeal for) and *zetei* (seek). They are to continue in *zeal for the gifts* (12:31; 14:1) remembering that they are "for the common good" (12:7), and knowing that *love does not seek* [*zetei*] *what is for itself* (13:5).

Paul deliberately placed the negative definitions of love in the center (cameos 7-9). He could have recorded the *positives* in the middle and left the *negatives* at the beginning and the end of this second section.[24] Why then did he center the negatives? His reason for doing so is fairly evident. The list of eight negatives *describes his readers.*[25] Many of these negatives appear throughout the first twelve chapters. In this homily the list is brought together and completed.

The opening section (cameos 2-5) is personal. Paul reflects on his own pilgrimage in regard to the greater and the lesser gifts and the critical component of love. In the center (cameos 6-10), however, love itself *becomes a person* and walks on stage.[26] Love embodies some primary virtues and rejects a list of vices. Paul's ethical model is Jesus his Messiah and Lord.

A second striking feature of this personification of love is the fact that the list of attributes begins and ends with the two great New Testament words for *patience.* Cameo 6a tells the reader that "Love acts patiently [*makro-thumei*]." *Makro* (far away) is combined with *thumos* (anger). The person who has *makro-thumos* is the person who is able to "put anger far away." As Horst points out, with this word the Greek Bible translates the Hebrew "to delay wrath."[27] This is the patience of the powerful who have the clout to retaliate but choose to refrain.

This kind of patience is illustrated by David at Engedi when Saul pursued him with three thousand men intending to kill him. David was hiding in a cave with his men. Unaware of David's presence in the cave, Saul entered the same cave to relieve himself. David managed to sneak up behind Saul and cut off a piece of the king's robe rather than kill him. Saul then left the cave, and David followed him out into the open, waving the severed piece of robe in his hand and calling out to the king that he, David, could have killed him. Saul wept and confessed "you have repaid me good, whereas I have repaid you evil" (1 Sam 24:17). David demonstrated *makrothumia* (patience) as he set aside his anger. Two chapters later Saul was again pursuing David, this time into the wilderness of Ziph. With Abishai, one of his men, David penetrated Saul's camp in the middle of the night and stood over the sleeping king. Abishai requested permission to kill the king. David refused and instead took Saul's spear and water jug, and left. In the morning, from across the valley, David

---

[24]Granted, the last line in cameo 9 presents a transition to the positive and speaks of love "rejoicing in community when truth prevails."

[25]See 1 Cor 3:3; 4:6, 7; 5:6, 9-12; 8:1; 12:7; 14:12.

[26]In the parable of the human body (12:15-25) the various parts of the body enter the drama and begin talking. Here *love* becomes an actor on stage with a "speaking part."

[27]J. Horst, "μακροθυμια," in *TDNT,* 4:376.

called to Saul and his men waving the spear and jug. Again, David acted with
*makrothumia*. American history has an example of *makrothumia* in President
Abraham Lincoln (at the end of the Civil War) when a Northern victory was
assured and many wanted to punish the South for the "rebellion." The occasion was March 4, 1865, when Lincoln delivered his second inaugural speech
and said, "With malice towards none; with charity for all; with firmness in
the right, as God gives us to see the right, let us . . . do all which may achieve
and cherish a just, and a lasting peace, among ourselves, and with all nations."
Lincoln exhibited *makrothumia*. The English language does not have a precise
word for this vital character trait. Arabic does; it is the word *halim*. This form
of patience characterizes the person who has the power to demolish the enemy,
but out of love (patience) chooses not to do so.

Moving ahead to the end of Paul's list of definitions of love (cameo 10d) we
are told that love *panta hupomenei* (patiently endures) all things. Again Paul
uses a compound word. In this case the term he chooses is *hupo-meno*. *Hupo*
has to do with "under" and *meno* means "to remain." As a compound, this
word describes "The affliction under which one remains steadfast."[28] If *makrothumia* is the patience of the powerful, *hupomene* is the *patience of the weak*
who unflinchingly endure suffering. The example of Mary standing silently
at the foot of the cross is a matchless demonstration for every Christian of this
crucial form of patient love. Mary can do nothing to change the horrible
events taking place around her. Her only choice is to exercise *hupomene* and at
great cost remain rather than depart that scene of suffering. Jesus himself is
the supreme example of the same virtue.

*Makrothumia* (cameo 6a) and *hupomene* (cameo 10d) create the perfect set
of bookends within which Paul presents the other characteristics of love.

The second introductory positive word for love (cameo 6b) is *khresteuomai*
(to be kind).[29] In the fourth century, Chrysostom explained that such people
work to extinguish the flame of anger and "by soothing and comforting, do
they cure the sore and heal the wound of passion."[30]

Paul then turns to describe love using eight negatives. He opens with
(cameo 7a) "not jealous" (*zeloi*). The positive aspects of this word which appear
at the beginning and at the end of the homily have already been observed.
Here its negative side surfaces. Paul had already criticized the Corinthians

---

[28]BAGD, p. 846.
[29]This word, as a verb, occurs only here in all of Greek literature. Paul may have created it.
[30]Chrysostom, *First Corinthians*, 33.1, p. 195.

(3:3) for their "jealousy and strife." In 2:26 he reminded his readers that in the body of Christ, "if one member is honored, all rejoice together." Yes, they can rejoice together if the green eye of jealousy is overcome. When it is not, the honor given to one member of the body triggers the cancer of jealousy that can destroy the body.

I recall a witty story I heard in Beirut, Lebanon, describing the difference between a Lebanese capitalist and a Syrian socialist. A Lebanese notices a man driving by in a brand new Mercedes and says, "Ah—some day I will own a car like that!" In the next block a Syrian observes the same man driving by and says, "One day we are going to drag that dog out of his car, thrash him and force him to walk with the rest of us!" Both men are fueled by jealousy. In the first case jealousy creates envy while in the second envy produces resentment of another's achievement. Love does not fall prey to either of these instincts.

Regarding "love is . . . not *boastful*" (cameo 7b), Barcley writes, "True love will always be far more impressed with its own unworthiness than its own merit."[31] Boasting is a two-sided coin. On one hand the person does not like him/herself and feels compelled to regale others with stories of personal success, hoping to be liked, admired and accepted. Or one can boast about "our group" or "my brilliant son" in an attempt to assert superiority. On the other hand, boasting about others is often a form of flattery that attempts to manipulate. Perhaps you will enjoy the wonderful things I am telling you about yourself, and this will help me influence you. Love does not need to boast about itself and makes no attempt to control the other through flattery.

Paul continues with, "love is . . . not *arrogant*" (cameo 7c). Someone has said that an "expert" is the person who has all the answers and has stopped listening. He/she is also the person who cannot absorb someone else's data. The root of the Greek verb has to do with inflating something. The KJV translates this as "is not puffed up." This form of failure to love is closely related to the boasting just mentioned. Secure in their own identity, be it acclaimed or ignored, those who love have no need to be exalted. Both the translations of "arrogant" (RSV) and "proud" (NRSV) are helpful. In 1 Corinthians 4:6, 18 and 19 Paul uses this word to describe the enthusiasts for one party against another, and as a criticism of the libertines who are proud of the man who is sleeping with his father's wife. Arrogance appears in both accounts.

Neither is love *rude* (cameo 7d). The Greek word used here is *askhemonei*

---

[31]William Barclay, *1 Corinthians* (Philadelphia: Westminster Press, 1975), p. 121.

(without good order). Hays insists that "shameful behavior" is involved, not just "rudeness," in that as a noun this word is used by Paul to describe the shameful acts of male homosexuals mentioned in Romans 1:27.[32] This same word appears in 7:36, where it has to do with acting in a proper fashion toward a virgin. "Without good order" also relates to personal appearance. The guest who attends a wedding banquet without a wedding garment (Mt 22:11-12) could be described as *askhemonos*. The flippant comment, "I don't care how I look" is not a mark of humility but a lack of love. Others are obliged to look at the person who doesn't care, and thereby he or she is inflicting psychic pain on them. For love's sake I will dress in a manner that signals my love and respect for those around me. My freedom to dress as I choose must always be conditioned by my love for others. Love is concerned for the other (not the self) in all matters related to personal appearance and lifestyle.

The climax in the center says love does not seek "*what is for itself*" (cameo 8). This virtue is yet another case of where one item on Paul's list (here, self-seeking) is closely related to an earlier text in the epistle. Paul has just told his readers not to seek their own good (10:24) but to seek the advantage of many (10:33). The ego is not the center of the life of the lover who knows that the world does not revolve around him or her.

Furthermore, authentic justice means that I care about your rights, not merely my own. In his book *The Open Secret*, Lesslie Newbigin writes,

> If we acknowledge the God of the Bible, we are committed to struggle for justice in society. Justice means giving to each his due. Our problem (as seen in the light of the gospel) is that each of us overestimates what is due to him as compared with what is due to his neighbor. Consequently, justice cannot be done, for everyone will judge in his own favor. Justice is done only when each one acknowledges a judge with authority over him, in relation to whose judgment he must relativize his own. . . . A just society can flourish only when its members acknowledge the justice of God, which is the justice manifested and enacted in the cross. If I do not acknowledge a justice which judges the justice for which I fight, I am an agent, not of justice, but of lawless tyranny.[33]

"Love seeketh not its own" (KJV).

Love is not *irritable*, writes Paul (cameo 9a). Barrett translates this phrase

---

[32]Hays, *First Corinthians*, p. 226.
[33]Lesslie Newbigin, *The Open Secret* (Grand Rapids: Eerdmans, 1978), pp. 124-25.

"love is not touchy."[34] A modern colloquial expression describes this aspect of love by saying, "Love has a long fuse." Love knows that "a soft answer turns away wrath" (Prov 15:1). The experienced diplomat knows that to lose one's self-control is to lose the ability to influence a discussion. But the lover has a different motive. He or she is willing to absorb hostility out of love for the other, knowing that by absorbing it, that hostility can fade away.

Love "keeps no record of wrongs" (cameo 9b, NIV). The term used here is from the world of accounting. Love allows the hurts of the past to fade away. Of all Paul's admonitions in this list, this directive is perhaps the most difficult. When we are deeply hurt, the pain of those wounds remains for a very long time—is it forever? When the wrongs suffered are serious but relatively limited, as time passes, the hurt can fade. In such a case Paul's admonition applies with relative ease. An Egyptian Arabic proverb says,

> Your friend will swallow gravel for you (*Habibak bi-yibla'lak al-zalat*).
> Your enemy maximizes your mistakes (*'Aduuak bi-yukattirlak al-ghalat*).

Love can absorb evil, as seen in the previous paragraph. Here we see that love manages to erase the ledger of wrongs suffered which the mind, un-prompted, all too readily recalls. But when deep wounds are inflicted, the problem is greatly complicated.

Paul's advice is extremely puzzling in the light of his own suffering. Earlier in the epistle (4:9-13) he recorded a list of wrongs he had suffered, along with a report on how he responded to that suffering. "When reviled we bless, when persecuted, we endure," he reports. In 2 Corinthians 6:4-10 and again in 11:23-29 the catalogs of his sufferings are long and sobering. Paul had not forgotten any of those painful events, and the list was readily available in his mind for instant recall. The second list concludes with, "Who is weak, and I am not weak? Who is made to fall, and I am not indignant?" (2 Cor 11:29). He does not recite the list to demonstrate his strength but his weakness, and to declare his sympathy for and empathy with all who are "made to fall." Yet the wrongs *were remembered*. How are we to reconcile these lists with Paul's affirmation that love "keeps no record of wrongs"? As a survivor of seven Middle Eastern wars, stretching from 1942 to 1995, suffering and injustice surrounded our family for decades, and some of that suffering reached into the depths of our own lives. Thus, for me this concern opens deep questions.

Yes, Paul had lists and remembered them. But he did not quote them to

---

[34]Barrett, *First Epistle*, p. 303.

brag about how much he had suffered or to "even the score." At the end of the third essay he did not write, "I can never forget how those Jews stoned me and left me for dead." Nor does he say, "I was ridiculed mercilessly in public on Mars Hill by those arrogant Greeks." Instead he gently advises, "Give no offense to Jews or to Greeks" (10:32-33). His suffering did not dictate how he would respond to his persecutors. But recognizing this, the question remains—why are the lists still fresh in his mind? How can we reconcile his description of love that *forgets* and his recorded *remembrances* of suffering? What and how should we remember?

The twentieth century opened with the Armenian Genocide, which began in the 1890s and continued through the First World War. The Armenians suffered both genocide and ethnic cleansing. Today the pressure to remember what happened is intensified by the stubborn denial of the Turkish government that anything out of the ordinary (in time of war) took place.[35] The ethnic cleansing of Palestine from 1947 to 1949 involved the ruthless driving out of approximately 50 percent of the settled Palestinian population of the Holy Land. The Israeli historian Ilan Pappi documents the fact that somewhere between eight hundred thousand to one million people were driven from their homes from November 1947 to January 1949.[36] In the process 537 towns and villages were first "purified" by violence, which meant that the people who had lived there for centuries were either killed or expelled, and the buildings (mostly) destroyed. As with the Turkish government, from the very beginning this ethnic cleansing was and is denied by the Israeli government. The same type of tragedy has played itself out in the South Sudan where, from 1955 to the present, millions have died due to violence and war-instigated starvation. As in Turkey and Israel, Sudanese acts of ethnic cleansing (bordering on genocide) are flatly denied by the Sudanese government.

Going further back in history, the nineteenth century witnessed brutal atrocities against native peoples in North America and Australia. Christian, Jewish and Muslim hands are not clean. None of us can claim the moral high ground. Yet the sins of all must be exposed and named for what they are. The question becomes: Does Paul's directive to "keep no account of wrongs" apply to such appalling suffering? Should these things be forgotten?

---

[35]Peter Balakian, *The Burning Tigris: The Armenian Genocide and America's Response* (New York: HarperCollins, 2003).
[36]Ilan Pappi, *The Ethnic Cleansing of Palestine* (Oxford: Oneworld, 2008), pp. 86-198.

Elie Wiesel, the Nobel Peace Prize winner, wrote a book titled *Night*.[37] In that famous volume he describes his suffering and survival in the Auschwitz and Buchenwald concentration camps in 1944-1945. On one occasion he was badly beaten by his supervisor in a slave labor factory. When the beating was finally over, a young French girl came over to him, wiped his face and told him, "Keep your anger, your hate, for another day, for later. The day will come but not now. . . . Wait. Clench your teeth and wait."[38]

The French girl's call to remember evil reflects great courage, discipline and a noble cry for justice. Along with that cry is the recent stunning work of Miroslav Volf titled *The End of Memory: Remembering Rightly in a Violent World*.[39] The book is his answer to the question, "So what is the relationship between remembering well and redeeming the past?"[40] To remember is not good enough; we must "remember well." Every page of this volume offers profound reflections on the subject of suffering and human memories of it. No quick summary is possible.

Volf, a Yugoslavian, was imprisoned and brutally interrogated for months by the communist security forces. This book is his Christian response to those experiences. One paragraph is particularly poignant and applicable to our subject. Volf writes:

> By opening ourselves to God's love through faith, our bodies and souls become sanctified spaces, God's "temples," as the Apostle Paul puts it (1 Corinthians 6:19). The flame of God's presence, which gives us new identity, then burns in us inextinguishably. Though like buildings devastated by wind and flood, our bodies and souls may become ravaged, yet we continue to be God's temple—at times a temple in ruins, but sacred space nonetheless. Absolutely nothing defines a Christian more than the abiding flame of God's presence, and that flame bathes in a warm glow everything we do or suffer.[41]

In his final chapter Volf writes, "Being in God frees our lives from the tyranny the unalterable past exercises with the iron fist of time's irreversibility. God does not take away our past; God gives it back to us—fragments gathered, stories reconfigured, selves truly redeemed, people forever reconciled."[42]

---

[37]Elie Wiesel, *Night*, trans. Marion Wiesel (New York: Hill & Wang, 2006).
[38]Ibid., p. 53.
[39]Miroslav Volf, *The End of Memory* (Grand Rapids: Eerdmans, 2006).
[40]Ibid., p. 42.
[41]Ibid., p. 79.
[42]Ibid., p. 201.

He concludes the final chapter by saying,

> We will not "forget" so as to be able to rejoice; we will rejoice and therefore let
> those memories slip out of our minds! The reason for our non-remembrance of
> wrongs will be the same as its cause: Our minds will be rapt in the goodness of
> God and in the goodness of God's new world, and the memories of wrongs will
> wither away like plants without water.[43]

Perhaps this is part of what Paul means when he says, "[love] keeps no account
of wrongs." Memories of his suffering did not constantly return uninvited to
the screen of his mind in the form of nightmares or mind-numbing daytime
recollections. They were there, but they did not control his present or his
future.

At the same time, however, they were not buried, festering and unconsciously influencing all that he did and said. The pus had gone from the
wounds. Yes, he could recall those memories when he needed to record them
for others to read, but they never returned uninvited in the waking hours of
the night. He kept no account of wrong. Volf did not simply remember, he
"remembered well." The need is to be "set free from the tyranny the unalterable past exercises with the iron fist of time's irreversibility." Having worked
for decades among Middle Eastern peoples (Jewish, Christian and Muslim)
who have endured such wounds, unanswered questions remain, and I cannot
say more. I dare not say less.

Paul concludes his list of negatives by writing, love does "not rejoice in
unrighteousness but rejoices in community when truth prevails" (cameos 9c,
d). Usually rumor is much more exciting than fact—except for the lover. Authentic love rejoices to find that reported evil is not true.

In the foreground Paul is certainly referring to the arrogance of the Corinthians who were rejoicing rather than mourning over the person sleeping with
his father's wife (5:1-5). But the broader scene that Paul invokes deals with
deeper issues. A modern way to express this admonition is to say, "Love does
not find violence entertaining."

The ancient Romans staged their gladiatorial battles in the Coliseum, and
the modern world has its violent movies. Both are violations of the love of
God that is revealed in its fullness in the cross and resurrection of Jesus.

There is a pornography of sex. There is also a pornography of violence
whose rush is like heroin. The more of it you take, the greater the dose needed

---

[43]Ibid., p. 214.

to achieve the same high. Nothing compares in pure stimulation to the horrible excitement of war. Even when violence breaks in upon us against our will, love is never attracted to or entertained by that violence. Woe to those who are hooked on their own adrenaline!

The early church directive was that Christians should not attend the various violent spectacles in the Roman amphitheaters. Violence for those Christians was not entertaining, but they understood its magnetic soul-destroying power. In his *Confessions*, Augustine describes his friend Alypius who was against the gladiatorial games but allowed himself to be dragged there by his companions. For a while Alypius managed to look away from the violence. Then

> Upon the fall of one in the fight, a mighty cry from the whole audience stirring him strongly, he, (was) overcome by curiosity, . . . and that mighty clamor was raised, which entered through his ears, and unlocked his eyes, to make way for the striking and beating down of his soul. . . . For (as soon as) he saw that blood he therewith imbibed a sort of savageness; nor did he turn away, but fixed his eye, drinking in madness unconsciously, and was delighted with the guilty context, and drunken with the bloody pastime. Nor was he now the same as he came in, but was one of the throng . . . and a true companion of those who had brought him thither. . . . He looked, shouted, was excited, carried away with the madness which would stimulate him to return.[44]

Philippians 4:8 offers a profound "TV guide." The text reads,

> Finally, brothers and sisters, whatever is true, whatever is honorable, whatever is just, whatever is pure, whatever is lovely, whatever is gracious, if there is any excellence, if there is anything worthy of praise, think about these things.

Films that fit these categories make wonderful viewing.

The dark visceral thrill that sweeps through a nation when that nation goes to war is horrifying to observe at close range. Because of television, the country becomes a vast audience viewing "gladiatorial combat." Love does not rejoice at wrong. Instead, it rejoices to find that the enemy is not composed of monsters but rather, like ourselves, is a collection of misguided human beings. This discovery sobers us and reminds us that we too know not what we do.

After this telling list of negatives, Paul returns to the positive aspects of love as he pens his four concluding definitions.

---

[44]Augustine, *Confessions* 6.8, quoted in Whitney Oates, ed., *Basic Writings of Saint Augustine* (New York: Random House, 1948), 1:82.

The list begins with "love . . . covers all things" (cameo 10a). The NIV reads love "always protects." The verb *stego* has a number of nuances. Its root has to do with covering something. As noted, Thiselton rightly complains "Most English translations, especially NRSV and often NIV, simply abstract the conceptual content of the metaphor from its forceful emotive imagery."[45] It is good not to make that mistake here. The verb *stego* was used in connection with keeping a fluid in or out.[46] That is, *stego* meant "it doesn't leak" and was related to waterproofing. The noun form of this word (*stegos*) meant "roof." A good roof protects the people in the house by keeping water out. The same was said about a good ship. In both cases water was kept out. Those who prefer this meaning of the verb translate the text before us as "love covers all" or "love protects all."

The same verb was used for keeping fluid *in a container*; that is, it described a pot that could hold water. As brass manufacturers, the Corinthian metal workers would have been careful to make pitchers, bowls and drinking cups that did not leak. In making a bowl, if the craftsman hammered in one place a little too long, or cut the metal too deeply in the process of decorating the exterior of the bowl, or attached the spout onto a pitcher carelessly, the vessel would leak and be worthless. Orr and Walther chose this meaning and translated, "It [love] keeps all confidences."[47]

Because you love me you will *cover me*, and thereby protect me from exterior harm (the first meaning). You are also *trustworthy*. I can share the secrets of my heart with you knowing that you will not "leak" those secrets to anyone because of your love for me (the second meaning).

But there is also a third meaning. The KJV, RSV and NRSV use the traditional reading of "bears all things." Although this is not a dominant meaning in Greek literature, it fits well in 1 Thessalonians 3:1, 5 and is a candidate for Paul's intention here in 3:7. The difficulty with this understanding of *stego* for verse 7 is that it overlaps significantly with the fourth item in Paul's list of "all things." Namely, what is the difference between "bears all" and "endures all"? A distinction is possible. I *bear* the weight of my heavy suitcase as I pick it up, and I *endure* the struggle to carry it to the car. Yet the two words are very close. In his Kittel article, Wilhelm Kasch argues that in such a short list Paul would not have chosen two words that meant much the same

---

[45]Thiselton, *First Epistle*, p. 1053.
[46]LSJ, *Greek-English Lexicon*, p. 1626.
[47]Orr/Walther, *I Corinthians*, p. 289.

thing. He prefers "covers all," which he feels shares meaning with "keep silent about all things." He also argues that these meanings are appropriate for 9:12 rather than "bears all."[48] That is, while serving in Corinth, Paul (out of love) "kept silent" about his right to be paid by the Corinthians for his ministry among them.

In conclusion, we remember that Jesus told his disciples, "You are the salt of the earth." Salt both preserves and flavors. The reader is not obliged to choose between those two aspects of the nature of salt. They are both relevant to Jesus' intent, and the reader can be enriched by both of them. The same may be true here. All three of the above are authentic to the meaning of love and to the text. Perhaps a combination of "keeps all confidences" and "covers all" is the best choice.[49]

Paul continues with "believes all" (cameo 10b). Yet again the apostle tantalizes the reader with a scarcity of information. Thiselton chooses to translate this phrase "never loses faith." What does Paul intend? One aspect is certain. Love never confirms a liar's lies with the naive response, "I believe you." It is possible to see two of these four positive aspects of love as directed toward humans and two focusing on God in the following manner:

10. a. Covers all    (primarily with humans)
    b.    Believes all    (primarily with God)
    c.    Hopes all    (primarily with God)
    d. Patiently endures all  (primarily with humans)

Briefly stated, Paul is writing from the point of view of the believer. "Covers all" (cameo 10a) has to do with the lover reaching out to protect the beloved. In cameo 10b and c Paul is describing love active (primarily) in relationship to God. In like manner the fourth characteristic in this list (cameo 10d) returns to focus (primarily) on people and their need to endure the suffering inflicted by others (or by natural disasters, accidents or illness).

More fully explored, love believes all of God's revelation of himself through nature, the prophetic word and the person of Jesus. Failure to do so can be called "unbelief." But on a deeper level it is a failure to respond to the love of God offered through Jesus Christ. The attitude that says "I believe that God

---

[48]Wilhelm Kasch, "στεγω," in *TDNT*, 7:587.

[49]Three of the oriental versions translate "covers all" (Martyn [1826]; Bustani-VD [MSS]; New Jesuit [1969]). The older Arabic versions are divided between "endures all" and "is patient with all." See appendix II, plate N.

exists, but I cannot accept that he is involved in history" would be judged by Paul as a failure to love the one who acted with costly love in history to save.

The same is true with "hope" (cameo 10c). Granted, the human lover both *believes in* and *hopes for* all good things for the beloved. But hope is more than that. For Paul, hope is centered in Jesus Christ crucified and risen from the dead. In the next essay Paul will tell his readers that if Christ is not raised, they are *without hope* and are "of all people most to be pitied" (15:19). Christian hope is profoundly focused on victory over sin and death that is brought to its climax by/in/through the resurrection. It is far more than, "I hope my son will do well in business" or, "I hope my friend will recover his health." It includes, "Christ in you the hope of glory" (Col 1:27).

The first section in the hymn to love concluded (cameos 4-5) with "faith, hope and love." This second section (cameo 10) concludes the same way, as will the third (cameo 15). Does the middle section open with echoes of "tongues, prophecy and knowledge" like the first section? Not really. We can only note 8:1 where "knowledge puffs up, but love builds up." This aspect of love is echoed here in cameo 7b with the affirmation "(love is) not boastful (puffed up)."

As observed previously, the final item in this list is *hupo-menei* (cameo 10d). This is the patience of the *powerless* who can do little or nothing to alleviate their own suffering or that of others, but have the courage to "remain under" and endure with dignity the affliction that comes their way. This same word (without the attached preposition) appears at the end of the hymn as Paul talks about three things that will abide (*menei*).

With these positive and negative definitions of love before the reader, Paul turns to a second discussion of "love and the spiritual gifts" [see fig. 4.4(4)].

## THE RHETORIC

This final section of the homily is composed of five cameos. The first (11) presents the temporary nature of prophecy, tongues and knowledge that *will be discarded* (or cease). The matching cameo (15) tells of faith, hope and love that will *abide*. The themes of "imperfect versus perfect" make up cameo 12 and those themes are matched in cameo 14 with its contrasts between "seeing dimly" versus "face to face," and "imperfect knowledge" versus "fully known." The climax in the center is a brief encased parable, the parable of the child and the man.

Paul chooses ring composition again as a literary method. The text reads:

| | | |
|---|---|---|
| 11. | ⁸Love never falls.<br>As for *prophecy*, it will be *discarded*;<br>as for *tongues*, they will cease;<br>as for *knowledge*, it will be *discarded*. | LOVE AND<br>Prophecy<br>Tongues<br>Knowledge<br>(- Three Discarded) |
| 12. | ⁹For our knowledge is *imperfect*<br>and our prophecy is *imperfect*.<br>¹⁰But when the *perfect comes*,<br>the *imperfect* will be *discarded*. | - Imperfect<br>+ Perfect |
| 13. | ¹¹When I was a child,<br>I *spoke* like a child,<br>I *thought* like a child,<br>I *reasoned* like a child.<br>When I became a man<br>I *discarded* my childish ways. | PARABLE<br>Child and<br>Man<br>(Maturation<br>and Discard) |
| 14. | ¹²For now we see in a *mirror dimly*,<br>then *face to face*.<br>Now my knowledge is *imperfect*,<br>then I shall *know* fully as I am *fully known*. | - Imperfect<br>+ Perfect |
| 15. | ¹³And thus there abides<br>*faith, hope and love*,<br>these three;<br>but the *highest* of these is *love*. | LOVE AND<br>Faith<br>Hope<br>(+ Three Abide) |

**Figure 4.4(4). Love and the spiritual gifts (1 Cor 13:8-13)**

## COMMENTARY

In the first cameo (11a) of this set of five Paul tells his readers, "Love never falls." Oriental versions have preserved this concrete image and consistently translated the text literally.[50] In the days before dynamite, bulldozers and backhoes, most Mediterranean mountain "roads" were narrow paths. Falling was an ever real possibility. Strabo (9.4.1) describes the road from Athens to Corinth by saying, "The road approaches so close to the rocks that in many places it passes along the edge of precipices, because the mountain situated above them is both lofty and impracticable for roads."[51]

---

[50]Among those that include this translation are Peshitta Syriac (4th-5th cent.); Mt. Sinai 151 (867); Mt. Sinai 155 (9th cent.); Mt. Sinai 310 (10th cent.); Erpenius (1616); Propagandist (1671); Bustani-Van Dyck (1865); Hebrew (1817). See appendix II, plate N.

[51]Strabo, quoted in Murphy-O'Conner, *St. Paul's Corinth*, p. 60.

Paul had walked that road. Regardless of danger along "the mountain pass," love does not fall. Paul's model was surely the life of Christ. He was the one whose love never "fell down," even while nailed to a cross.

However, *prophecy* and *knowledge* will be discarded and *tongues* will cease (11b, c, d). These gifts are important for the life of the church *now*. But in the light of eternity, they are *impermanent*. All those books, articles, plays and recorded lectures will not last. Why so?

Cameo 12 provides the answer. The value of these things must be judged in the light of eternity. Paul holds up that light and asks his readers to take a second look at the *tongues, prophecy* and *knowledge* about which they are quarreling. Our knowledge and our prophecy are imperfect; and when the perfect comes the imperfect will be discarded. The Arabic-speaking peoples of the Middle East have a proverb for nearly every occasion. A pious person is expected to wash his/her hands before praying. But if one is traveling in the desert with no water available, the worshiper is allowed to use sand and go through the motions of washing the hands. The proverb says, *In hadar al-ma, batula al-tayammum* (When water is available, the sand-washing stops). When you have access to the real thing, the substitute is discarded. All our knowledge is the sand. When the Lord comes, or we meet him at death (awaiting the final resurrection), our partial knowledge (the sand) will be discarded in the light of his perfect knowledge (the water).

Yet another parable appears in the center (cameo 13). By way of review, frequently the center of ring composition relates to the beginning and the end of the inverted set of cameos. The opening, center and closing of this set of cameos are as follows.

> Opening: *Tongues, prophecy and knowledge* (discarded).
>     Center: I was a *child* and I became a *man*.
> Closing: *Faith, hope and love* (abiding).

Paul is not talking about when he was a boy. The word for "child" that appears here is *nepios,* and in 3:1 Paul used that word to describe the (adult) Corinthians. He could not feed them "solid food" because they were still *nepioi* (children). Here, Paul creates a parable about himself, perhaps in order to soften his criticism of them. When *he* was a *nepios* (child) he confesses, his speech (he spoke like a child), his disposition and aim (he thought like a child) and his mental activity (he reasoned like a child) were childlike.[52] Paul

---

[52]Findlay, *First Epistle*, p. 900.

is best understood here as meaning "back when I was a new Christian, I was guilty of some of your errors." What did he do during that first decade of his life in Christ? He was fiercely engaged in debates over *tongues, prophecy* and *knowledge,* all of which are impermanent. Now that he is a "man"—that is, now that he has matured in faith—he knows that the gifts that matter are those that last. *Faith, hope* and *love* are the center of his attention. The parable in the middle of this section focuses and clarifies the intent of the set of five cameos.

Paul's skillful use of metaphors also appears in cameo 14. The mirrors of the ancient world were made of brass. The famous Corinthian brass workers must have fashioned them, and a brass mirror could be easily etched. When someone ordered a mirror, the artist would naturally offer to etch the face (or back) of the mirror along the lines of the customer's interests. Discovering that the buyer worshiped Poseidon (for instance), the brass worker would obligingly lightly etch the face of Poseidon (and perhaps other gods) on the mirror. Then, upon rising in the morning and looking into the mirror you would have the pleasure of "seeing yourself among the gods." A nice touch for those so inclined. On one of the coins minted at Corinth, Aphrodite is depicted standing in the center of the Acrocorinth gazing at herself in a polished brass shield functioning as a mirror. Buy a mirror with Aphrodite sketched on it and a person could join her image on the polished surface. But alas, the mirror soon tarnished and the mind games quickly grew old. The person was not *really* among the gods, and they did not talk to him or her. Indeed "now we see through a mirror dimly" but then "face to face." On that great day the mirror will fall from the believer's hand and he/she will be face to face with the risen Savior. This means that "knowledge is imperfect." But in that glorious future "I shall know fully as I am fully known." Now God's knowledge *of me* is complete. Then my knowledge *of him* will also be complete.[53]

Paul has now directly or indirectly invoked brass objects three times in chapter 13:

1. The banging brass and the clanging cymbal (v. 1)

2. The brass vessel that does not leak (v. 7)

3. The brass mirror that quickly tarnishes (v. 12)

Taken from brass making, these images can be added to the allusions to mountains and mountain climbing. Corinth had mountains visible to the

---

[53] At last I will have a definitive solution to the Synoptic problem!

north and to the south, and brass making was a major industry in the city. Paul knew well how to contextualize his message.

The final cameo (15) in this third section affirms that *faith, hope* and *love* are permanent and will not be discarded like *prophecy, tongues and knowledge* (cameo 11). Earlier, Paul listed faith as one of the spiritual gifts (12:9). He also told his readers that "no one can say 'Jesus is Lord' except by the Holy Spirit" (12:3). That is, faith is also a gift of the Holy Spirit. Furthermore, love is not just the indispensable component that brings meaning and value to all the gifts, it is also the very nature of God. "We love because he first loved us" wrote John (1 Jn 4:19). Paul wrote to the Romans, "God shows his love for us in that while we were yet sinners, Christ died for us" (Rom 5:8). It is that God-like love that comes to the believer as a spiritual gift. Listed with the other two permanent gifts, Paul must surely mean that hope is likewise a gift of the Spirit. This leaves us with a further mystery.

Love lasts forever. But when "belief" becomes "sight," in what sense does belief remain? Perhaps the answer is in the awareness that for Paul faith was also obedience. I *truly* believe what I act upon. In Romans 1:5 Paul writes about "the obedience *of* faith." He means "the obedience *which is* faith," because faith includes something you do. Paul concludes the epistle with the same expression (Rom 16:26). Perhaps he means that faith as obedience remains forever.

The mystery deepens when we consider hope. When hope is fulfilled, for what does it hope? Findlay writes, "Faith and Hope are elements of the perfect and permanent state; new objects of trust and desire will come into sight in the widening visions of the life eternal."[54] Thiselton is again helpful when he concludes, "In one sense faith and hope abide also, but in forms in which faith becomes assimilated into sight, and hope absorbed into the perfect, forever in the form in which Christ and the cross has revealed it."[55] Try as we may—an element of mystery remains.

The final cameo (16), which closes the hymn, reads:

Run after love,
and continue in zeal for the *spiritual* gifts (*pneumatika*).

Having affirmed love to be the *highest* of all, Paul concludes the hymn by urging his readers to "run after love." The verb is *diokete* (run after), which also

---

[54]Findlay, *First Epistle*, p. 901.
[55]Thiselton, *First Epistle*, p. 1074.

means "hasten after, pursue, seek after, strive for."

Paul has now invoked the image of "running" five times. These are as follows:

| Run away from prostitutes | 6:18 |
| Run away from idol worship | 10:14 |
| Run after the prize | 9:24 |
| Run (like Paul) with a goal in mind | 9:26 |
| Run after love | 14:1 |

Knowing that Corinth sponsored the biennial Isthmian Games, Paul was quick to use athletic imagery to communicate his message. This final reference to running (here in 14:1) brings the list of five to an appropriate climax.

At the same time, the command to "run after love" may echo the mountain-climbing image with which the hymn opens (12:31). Mountain climbing is a strenuous activity that requires great energy. In like manner, the journey of love requires joyful and unending exertion—like running—even uphill in the mountains.

There may also be a play on words at work here. The Isthmus of Corinth had a stone roadway across it built by Periander (625-585 B.C.) and called the *diolkos*. Although the road was only 3.4 miles, a ridge of low mountains barred the way from one side of the isthmus to the other. Because of the narrowness of the road the *diolkos* only allowed for traffic one direction at a time. Small ships (up to ten tons) were placed on carts and moved by oxen across the isthmus. Goods had to be unloaded from incoming ships at one end and reloaded onto outgoing ships at the other end. A great deal of backbreaking labor was necessarily involved in the process. Various attempts, from Nero onward, to dig a canal failed (until A.D. 1893) due to the elevation of the ridge. To move goods and ships across the *diolkos* (the stone road), a great many people were obliged to *diokousi* (urge on, carry forward) to get the job done.[56] Some of the Corinthian (Christian) slaves and free workmen may have been involved in this gigantic daily effort. "Daily, many work on the *diolkos* (roadway), up over the ridge and back to the sea on the far side," implies Paul, "so how about *diokomen* (we urge on) the great task of traveling along the mountain-pass journey of love."

Paul concludes with the directive to "continue in zeal for the *pneumatika* (spiritual gifts)" (16b). He opened the hymn by urging them to continue in

---

[56]LSJ, *Greek-English Lexicon*, p. 440.

zeal for the *highest gifts* (which remain). We know that these are faith, hope and love. As he closes the homily he presses them to demonstrate zeal for *the spiritual gifts* (that pass away), especially prophecy. This second list, although temporary, is still important for the life of the church, and it leads naturally to the next homily.

This matchless hymn to love has moved the hearts and directed the wills of millions of Christians around the globe for nearly 2,000 years. It seems appropriate to listen to at least one voice out of that great throng that no one can number. On February 2, 1984, during the height of the Lebanese civil war, a fourteen-year-old boy from the village of Bahamdun (Lebanon) wrote the following reflection from a relative's home in Ashrafiyya, Beirut.

> I can still hear the sound of thundering guns telling me that somewhere nearby people are dying.
>
> Ever since we left the village I feel as though something has been shattered inside me. We have lost everything. Our house was burned. My books were torn to pieces. Our furniture was stolen. But what is more important is that the soft nights and the fresh mornings in the village are gone and with them I have lost my roots and have become "like grass blown by the wind," as the Psalmist put it.
>
> Time is no longer the unending chain of hours and minutes, marked by the hands on the huge clock at the entrance to my grandfather's house in the village. The big clock, with its rhythmic sound, that kept track of every heartbeat throughout the house, is broken. And time on it is standing still. For me, time used to be the time of sleeping and of waking up and of working in the fields—the time of life. But now time has left me. It belongs to the one who stands behind the thundering gun. It is the time of death.
>
> One night early in September our village was shelled and we fled. We hid in a cave near our small brook waiting for the mad night to subside. But the guns did not stop so we fled again through the valley until we reached Beirut.
>
> We thought we had escaped, but the dark night caught up with us in all its madness. Am I living through a nightmare? Has time really stood still ever since the big clock was broken on the wall of my grandfathers' house in the village?
>
> One day someone came and told us that our house in the village (my grandfather's house), was looted and burned. The young men burned it after emptying it together. My anguish grew into hatred. Hatred is strange for it takes many forms. For me it is like a boil. It took root within me and sowed the seeds of death in my heart. It grew and spread like a boil with nothing but pus inside.

I woke up at the sound of the big guns and asked myself, "How can a young man stand behind a gun and fire all those rockets around us?" I thought of that young man and to me he acquired the face of that other young man who looted and burned my grandfather's house.

Then in the midst of the sound of thundering guns, from the depths of my despair and pain, I finally understood. "If I speak with the tongues of men and of angels and have not love," I am but sounding brass like the empty shell cases of the big guns. Love alone can bear the burden of the living for it bears all things. It bears this young man who is standing behind the gun, and that other young man who burned my grandfather's house.

We carry our dead with us like open wounds. All of us have such wounds. Life is different. Life is the realm of love which overcomes death. I pray that the living Lord may reign in our lives, and not our dead.

—Hanna Haddad[57]

---

[57]The text of this reflection was read at morning prayers at the Near East School of Theology in Beirut, Lebanon, in March 1984 by Miss Hanna Haddad. I acquired the text from her and have shortened it slightly.

# Spiritual Gifts and the Upbuilding of the Body

I Corinthians 14:1-25

Paul includes two homilies (14:1-12, 13-25) in this section of the larger essay.[1] Figure 4.5(1) displays the text of the first of the two.

1.  [14:1] *Seek* the *spiritual gifts,*          SEEK GIFTS
       especially that you may *prophesy.*       Especially Prophecy

2.      a. [2]For one who *speaks in a tongue*     TONGUES
        b. *speaks* not to men but *to God;*      To God
        c. for no one understands him,            Mysteries
        d. but he *utters mysteries in the Spirit.*

3.            a. [3]On the other hand, he who *prophesies*     PROPHECY
              b. *speaks to men*                               To People
              c. *for their upbuilding*                        Upbuilding
              d. and *encouragement* and *consolation.*

4.      a. [4]He who speaks in a *tongue*          TONGUES
        b. builds up *himself,*                    Build up Self

5.            a. but he who *prophesies*           PROPHECY
              b. builds up *the church.*           Build up Church

6.  [5]Now I want you *all to speak in tongues,*     SEEK GIFTS
       but *even more to prophesy.*                  Especially Prophecy
       A *prophesier* is *greater* than a *tongues speaker,*
       unless *someone interprets,* so the *church may be built up.*[2]

---

[1]This style of composing a homily in two parts appears in 1 Cor 1:1-9; 4:17–5:6; 7:17-24; 14:1-12; 15:21-34; 15:35-50.
[2]My translation.

7.  ⁶Now, brethren, if *I come* to you speaking *in tongues,*
    *how shall I benefit* you                                  I—BENEFIT
    unless I bring you some *revelation or knowledge*   The Church
    or *prophecy or teaching?*

8.        a. ⁷If even lifeless instruments, such as the *flute* or *harp,*   PARABLE OF
             b. do not give *distinct notes,*                                flute
                c. *how* will anyone *know* what is *played?*                harp
          a. ⁸And if the *bugle*                                            bugle
             b. gives an *indistinct sound,*
                c. who will *get ready* for *battle?*

9.           ⁹So with yourselves; if you in a tongue
          utter speech that is *not intelligible,*                          NOT CLEAR
          how will anyone know what is said?                                To the Church
          For you will be speaking into the air.

10.       ¹⁰There are doubtless many *different languages* in the world,
          and none is without meaning;                                     PARABLE OF
          ¹¹but if I do *not know* the meaning of *the language,*          foreign
          I shall be a *foreigner* to the speaker                          language
          and the speaker a foreigner to *me.*

11.   ¹²So with yourselves;
          since you are *eager for spirituality,*                          YOU—BUILD UP
          in the *building up of the church*                               The Church
          seek to *excel.*

**Figure 4.5(1). Spiritual gifts and the upbuilding of the body: The insiders (1 Cor 14:1-12)**

## THE RHETORIC

The opening line (cameo 1) functions both as a conclusion to the previous homily (12:31–14:1) and as the introduction to the current passage. This connecting of two texts (within a homily or between homilies) with a hinge attached to what precedes and what follows is a stylistic device Paul uses a number of times in this epistle.[3]

The first half of 14:1-12 opens (cameo 1) and closes (cameo 6) with the admonition to pursue the spiritual gifts in general and the gift of prophecy in particular. In the middle (cameos 2-5) Paul presents an A-B, A-B set of comparisons between tongues and prophecy. This same style was used in 7:32-40 and will appear again in 14:26-36.[4] Here, in the first half, the four lines of cameo 2 balance the four lines of cameo 3, using step parallelism [as shown in

---

[3]See 1 Cor 3:5-17; 7:17-24; 9:12-18; 14:26-36; 15:36-50; 15:51-58.
[4]See also Kenneth E. Bailey, "The Parable of the Pharisee and the Tax Collector," in *Jesus Through Middle Eastern Eyes* (Downers Grove, Ill.: IVP Academic, 2008), p. 344.

fig. 4.5(1)]. The same is true of the two lines in cameo 4 that balance the two lines in cameo 5.

The second half of this homily uses a five-cameo inversion. The striking feature of this second half is a list of four parables composed of flute, harp, bugle and foreign languages. This cluster of parables functions as the center of cameos 7-11, while at the same time Paul divides the list and places a more focused climax in the very center (cameo 9). The dramatic use of a series of parables occurs elsewhere in the epistle.[5] At the same time, cameo 8 contains six lines of matching step parallelism.

Finally, in the middle of the first half of the homily (cameo 3) Paul presents a list of positive benefits that result from prophesying. These are upbuilding, encouragement and consolation. Additionally, the opening (cameo 7) and closing (cameo 11) of the second half of the homily repeat and enlarge this list. Cameo 7 reports *revelation, knowledge, prophecy* and *teaching*. Cameo 11 repeats the theme of *building up*. This feature of selecting ideas from the center of one section and using them at the beginning and at the end of the following section is particularly prominent in Isaiah 56:6-11, where this rhetorical device occurs twice in a row.[6] The homily exhibits a sophisticated use of multiple prophetic rhetorical patterns.

## COMMENTARY

Paul now returns to his discussion of the spiritual gifts that he began in chapter 12. His focus in this homily is the *superiority of prophecy over tongues*. Each half is worthy of brief reflection.

The outer frame of the first half (cameos 1, 6) is displayed in figure 4.5(2).

1.  [14:1]*Seek* the *spiritual gifts,*          SEEK GIFTS
    especially that you may *prophesy.*        Especially Prophecy
    -------------------------------------------------------------------
6.  [5]Now I want you *all to speak in tongues,*   SEEK GIFTS
    but *even more to prophesy.*                Especially Prophecy
    A *prophesier* is *greater* than a *tongues speaker,*
    unless *someone interprets,* so the *church may be built up.*

---

**Figure 4.5(2). Cameos 1 and 6 (1 Cor 14:1, 5)**

---

[5]See 1 Cor 3:10-17 (modified); 9:1-12; 12:1-31 (cameos 10-14); 15:35-42 (in this case the list is not divided).
[6]See Kenneth E. Bailey, *Through Peasant Eyes* (Grand Rapids: Eerdmans, 1983), p. xviii.

As often observed, if cameos 2-4 were missing the reader would not notice their absence. Ideas flow smoothly from cameos 1 to 6. This strengthens their function as a set of bookends for the six cameos. As before, Paul affirms the preeminence of prophecy over tongues. Even though tongues and prophecy are temporary (13:8), they are important for the life of the church in the present, and Paul affirms significance for each. But there is a problem.

Cameo 1 is clear. Paul is especially eager that they prophesy. Cameo 6, however, seems to "muddy the water" by introducing two new aspects of the relationship between tongues and prophecy. In 12:7-10 Paul wrote that the gifts were "given" (by the Spirit) and in verse 11 the Spirit apportions to each one "as he wills." Through the Spirit, *God makes the decision* about which gifts he will give to each individual. The congregation is to accept and respect God's choices. This view is reinforced by Paul in his extended parable about the "body." The foot cannot look at the hand and decide that it is not a part of the body. Applying Paul's parable, *God arranges* the organs of the body, and *God decides* what gifts to give to each member of the congregation. All of this is straightforward.

But suddenly in cameo 6 Paul writes, "Now I want you all to speak in tongues," as though tongues were a special gift that everyone should possess, and those who do not have this particular gift should seek it. Is Paul contradicting what he wrote in chapter 12? Should the eye be dissatisfied until it is able to see?

A parable may be helpful. Imagine a secondary school where basketball gradually becomes more and more important in the life of the institution. The school has a championship team, and halfway through the season it has not lost a game. Everyone in the school is thinking, talking and dreaming about *basketball*. With its undefeated team, this particular sport becomes all-consuming. Every other activity, including the academic program of the school, is pushed aside by a passion for basketball. Something has to be done. Finally the headmaster (principal) of the school calls an assembly and says, "I am glad that we have a good team, and it is wonderful that we are undefeated. Your support of our great team is commendable. Please do not misunderstand me. I am not against basketball. In fact—*I hope you all learn to play basketball!* But right now—we must remember the importance of our academic program and get back to studying!"

Paul's position vis-à-vis the Corinthians was similar to that of the principal in the high school. It appears that Paul's readers were enthusiasts for the gift of speaking in tongues which was a dramatic gift that easily marked the recipients as blessed by the Holy Spirit. On the positive side, Paul affirms that this spiritual gift is indeed from God, and that those who have this gift are talking to God. Furthermore, the tongues speaker is personally built up. But, on the negative side, the community is *not built up*. Ah—yes—when there is someone to interpret, the church *can be built up* (cameo 6). Paul does not dismiss the validity of this gift, nor does he tell the tongues speakers to be silent. Furthermore, he leaves the door open for the upbuilding of the church through an interpreter, while at the same time he affirms the greater importance of prophecy in the life of the congregation.

The meaning of the four cameos in the center is also unmistakable [see fig. 4.5(3)].

| | | |
|---|---|---|
| 2. | a. ²For one who *speaks in a tongue* | TONGUES |
| | b. *speaks* not to men but *to God;* | To God |
| | c. for no one understands him, | Mysteries |
| | d. but he *utters mysteries* in the *Spirit.* | |
| | | |
| 3. | a. ³On the other hand, he who *prophesies* | PROPHECY |
| | b. *speaks to men* | To People |
| | c. *for their upbuilding* | Upbuilding |
| | d. and *encouragement* and *consolation.* | |
| | | |
| 4. | a. ⁴He who speaks in a *tongue* | TONGUES |
| | b. builds up *himself,* | Build up Self |
| | | |
| 5. | a. but he who *prophesies* | PROPHECY |
| | b. builds up *the church.* | Build up Church |

**Figure 4.5(3). Cameos 2-5 (1 Cor 14:2-4)**

*The tongues speaker* addresses *God* (cameo 2) and builds up *himself* (cameo 4). The one who *prophesies* speaks to *people* (cameo 3) and benefits the *church* (cameo 5). From prophecy the church receives "upbuilding and encouragement and consolation."

The Greek word *oikodome* (upbuilding) has the double meaning of "building *as a process*" and "building *as an edifice*" that results from the hard work of the builders.[7] English has the same double meaning for the word *building*. We can say, "*Building* the house took two years, and fortunately when the storm struck the *building* was not damaged." In the first incidence the word *building* means "the work of construction," while in the second case it refers to "the

---

[7]BAGD, pp. 558-59.

completed edifice." As noted earlier, Paul lived for eighteen months in the thriving commercial city of Corinth where significant construction work can be assumed. Using that aspect of life in Corinth, he created his parable of the foundation and the master builder seen in 3:10-17. The metaphor of "building" is also prominent in this homily. It is used four times in the first half and once in the second half. Each half concludes on the note of "building up the church." The RSV translation of this word as "edify" is formally correct and smoother in English, but it does not trigger the connection between the parable of the master builder and this homily. Furthermore, in current use the word *edify* does not preserve the concrete metaphor (edifice) out of which it was formed. In chapter 3 Paul was the master builder. Here the focus is on the *Corinthians* who must continue the task of *building the church*. Perhaps Paul wanted the sound of the stone cutters' hammers that probably rang across the city to remind them of their calling to *build up the church*.

Again, Paul affirms the acceptability of including speaking in tongues in their corporate worship (if there is an interpreter). Yet, tongues remain secondary to prophecy.

The second section (14:6-12) offers the reader five inverted cameos. The outer envelope is displayed in figure 4.5(4).

| | | |
|---|---|---|
| 7. | [6]Now, brethren, if *I come* to you speaking *in tongues,* | |
| | *how shall I benefit* you | I—BENEFIT |
| | unless I bring you some *revelation or knowledge* | The Church |
| | or *prophecy or teaching?* | |
| | - - - - - - - - - - - - - - - - - - - - - - - - - - - - | |
| 11. | [12]So with yourselves; | |
| | since you are *eager for spirituality,* | YOU—BUILD UP |
| | in the *building up of the church* | The Church |
| | seek to *excel.*[8] | |

**Figure 4.5(4). Cameos 7 and 11 (1 Cor 14:6, 12)**

In this case it is not *key words* that unite the two cameos, but *parallel ideas*. In cameo 7 Paul presents *himself* as an example while in cameo 11 he pointedly affirms that he expects *them* to do what he has done, which is *build up the church!* They are not spectators seated comfortably in the stands watching an athletic event. They are fellow runners in a relay race. They are stone masons building a temple. He has laid the foundation on which they must build. If cameos 8-10 were missing the text would move smoothly from cameo 7 to

---

[8]My translation.

cameo 11. Paul confirms (cameo 11) that they are "eager for spirituality," and authentic spirituality is deeply committed to "building up the church." How is that to be accomplished? They are expected to bring (cameo 7) some *revelation* or *knowledge* or *prophecy* or *teaching*.

G. G. Findlay notes, "In the four *he* (or) clauses, the second pair matches the first; revelation comes through the prophet, knowledge through the teacher."[9] Seeing this pairing, it is obvious that the four items mentioned are not a jumble of synonyms. The church needs both *new insights* into the nature of the faith (which means *revelation* that comes through the *prophet*), and in addition the congregation needs to receive the *knowledge* already available and the *teacher* is the key person in this regard.

Furthermore, this list provides an interlock between the two sections. This can be seen as follows:

* Cameo 3 focuses on *upbuilding, encouragement* and *consolation*. (These are needed in a suffering church.)

* Cameo 7 focuses on *revelation, knowledge, prophecy* and *teaching*. (These have to do with a deeper *understanding of the faith*.)

Both lists present needs that tongues cannot provide (unless there is an interpreter).

The center of the ring composition includes cameos 8-10 [see fig. 4.5(5)].

8.      a. [7]If even lifeless instruments, such as the *flute* or *harp*,   PARABLE OF
            b. do not give *distinct notes*,                                  flute
                c. *how* will anyone *know* what is *played?*                 harp
            a. [8]And if the *bugle*                                          bugle
                b. gives an *indistinct sound*,
                    c. who will *get ready* for *battle?*

9.          [9]So with yourselves; if you in a tongue
            utter speech that is *not intelligible*,                          NOT UNDERSTOOD
            how will anyone know what is said?                                To the Church
            For you will be speaking into the air.

10.     [10]There are doubtless many *different languages* in the world,
            and none is without meaning;                                      PARABLE OF
            [11]but if I do *not know* the meaning of *the language*,          foreign
            I shall be a *foreigner* to the speaker                           language
            and the speaker a foreigner to *me*.

**Figure 4.5(5). Cameos 8-10 (1 Cor 14:7-11)**

[9]Findlay, *First Epistle*, p. 903. (Following the United Bible Society text, the verse has four cases of η εν.)

The split list of parables in cameos 8 and 10 is fascinating. The flute and the harp are instruments that invoke tranquility and soothe the troubled soul. The harp in particular needs "distinct notes" if the listener is to be moved by the performance.[10] Prophecy (a part of preaching) must be able to do this. But with his selection of the image of the bugle, Paul shifts to a very different type of metaphor. The trumpet/bugle calls the troops to prepare for conflict and directs them in the midst of battle. Prophecy must also be prepared to offer leadership in the struggle against "principalities and powers." As Findlay has written, "How disastrous, at the critical moment, to doubt whether the trumpet sounds Advance or Retreat!"[11] Many of the families that settled in reconstructed Corinth were headed by retired soldiers. The step parallelism of the cameo reinforces the contrast between the sounds of peace and the sounds of war.

The matching cameo on foreign languages in cameo 10 emphasizes that "speaking in tongues" is more than simply "speaking a foreign language." The Christian with the gift of speaking in tongues is *compared to* (not identified with) a stranger who is talking in a foreign language. Paul knew Hebrew, Aramaic and Greek. More than 90 percent of the stone inscriptions that have survived from the Corinth of Paul's day are in Latin.[12] The workforce of an international commercial city such as Corinth must have spoken a cacophony of languages. Communication problems created by this multiplicity of languages surface at the end of chapter 14. Paul's point is that (unknown) foreign languages divide people; they do not unite them. The person who hears someone speaking a foreign language immediately knows that the speaker is not "one of us."

The center (cameo 9) is a strong affirmation regarding the weakness of tongues. The speaker is not talking to the church but rather is "speaking into the air." This blunt assessment of what the tongues speakers were doing is the negative climax of the five cameos. The balancing positive affirmations appear at the opening (cameo 7) and the closing (cameo 11) of the ring composition, where the emphasis is on building up the church.

Finally, the beginning and the end of the overall homily are tied together. Their zeal in "seeking *(zeteite)* the spiritual gifts" (cameo 1) must be matched

---

[10]Amos twice uses the image of a trumpet/bugle (see Amos 2:2; 3:6).

[11]Findlay, *First Epistle*, p. 904.

[12]Jerome Murphy-O'Connor, *St. Paul's Corinth* (Collegeville, Minn.: Liturgical Press, 2002), p. 8.

with a willingness to "seek (*zeteite*) to excel in building up the church" (cameo 11). The spiritual gifts should have united them in the common task of building up the church. Sadly, for the Corinthians, those gifts were instead dividing them.

The two-part homily discussed here focuses mainly on *the internal upbuilding of the church*. Paul adds to this important discussion a second homily on tongues and prophecy as it relates to the *foreigner, the unbeliever* and *the outsider*. To this second homily we now turn [see fig. 4.5(6) on page 395].

## SPIRITUAL GIFTS AND THE UPBUILDING OF THE CHURCH: INQUIRERS/UNBELIEVERS (1 COR 14:13-25)

### THE RHETORIC

This homily repeats the high jump form common to the epistle which involves:

| | | |
|---|---|---|
| 1. The approach | (introduction) | (cameos 1-2) |
| 2. The jump | (the opening argument) | (cameos 3-5) |
| 3. The crossing of the bar | (the climax) | (cameo 6) |
| 4. The balancing arc of descent | (the completion of the argument) | (cameos 7-9) |

This rhetorical style appears eight times in 1 Corinthians and is clearly one of Paul's favorite rhetorical devices.[13] The homily in 9:1-12 has the identical arrangement of cameos. After the introduction (1-2) Paul presents yet another prophetic rhetorical template of seven stanzas with a climax in the center. Seven times (including this text) Paul places an Old Testament quotation in the climactic center of a ring composition.[14] This is one of his trademarks.

---

[13]See 1 Cor 2:3-10; 3:1-17; 6:13-20; 7:1-5; 9:1-12; 10:1-13; 14:13-25; 15:21-34.
[14]See 1 Cor 6:13-20; 9:1-12; 10:1-13; 14:13-25; 15:21-28; 15:42-50. To this list we can add 1 Cor 15:1-11, where the center contains a quotation from the fixed apostolic tradition. It can be called the beginning of a New Testament Scripture.

1. [14:13]Therefore, he who *speaks in a tongue*
   should pray for the power to interpret.
   [14]For if I pray in a tongue, my spirit prays
   but my *mind is unfruitful.* [15]What am I to do?

   WITH TONGUES
   Mind Unfruitful

2. I will *pray with the spirit*
   and I will *pray with the mind* also;
   I will *sing with the spirit*
   and I will *sing with the mind* also.

   PRAY/SING WITH
   Spirit and Mind

   ----------------              ------------------------

3. [16]Otherwise, if you bless with the spirit,
   *how* can any one in the position of *an inquirer*[15]
   *say* the *"Amen"* to your thanksgiving
   when he does not know what you are saying?
   [17]For you may give thanks well enough,
   but the *other man is not built up.*

   FOR INQUIRERS
   Tongues:
   Incomprehensible
   Ineffective
   Do Not Build Up

4. [18]I thank God that I speak in tongues more than you all;
   [19]yet, *in church* I would rather speak five *words with my mind,*
   in order *to instruct others,*
   than ten thousand words in a tongue.

   IN CHURCH:
   No tongues
   Rather: Instruction

5. [20]Brethren, do not be children in your *thinking*;
   be babes in evil,
   but in *thinking be mature.*

   THINK
   Mature

6. [21]*In the law* it is written,
   "By men of strange tongues
   and by the lips of foreigners
   I will speak to this people,
   and even then they will not listen to me,
   says the Lord."

   SCRIPTURE

7. [22]Thus, *tongues* serve as a *sign,*
   not for *believers* but for *unbelievers*
   while *prophecy is not a sign*
   for *unbelievers* but for *believers.*

   TONGUES
   Prophecy

8. [23]If, therefore, *the whole church assembles*
   and *all* speak in *tongues,*
   and an *inquirer or unbeliever enters,*
   will he not say that you are *mad?*

   IN CHURCH:
   Unbeliever enters
   Tongues = mad

9. [24]But if *all prophesy,*
   and an *unbeliever or inquirer* enters,
   he is *convicted* by all,
   he is *called to account* by all,
   [25]the secrets of his heart are disclosed;
   and so, *falling on his face,*
   he will *worship God*
   and declare, *"God is really among you!"*

   FOR UNBEL./INQUIRER
   Prophesy:
   Conviction
   Self Revelation
   Surrender
   Worship
   Witness

**Figure 4.5(6). Spiritual gifts and the upbuilding of the church (1 Cor 14:13-25)**

[15]For the Greek word *idiotes* I have chosen the NIV (margin) translation of "inquirer."

## COMMENTARY

This homily (14:13-25) is full of difficulties. The literature is extensive and the disagreements many. As always, Thiselton, Fee and others offer commendable extended discussions of these matters. Our limited focus is to look at Paul's rhetorical style in order to see what light it sheds on his intent. The two-cameo introduction is displayed in figure 4.5(7).

1. ¹⁴˸¹³Therefore, he who *speaks in a tongue*
         should pray for the power to interpret.          WITH TONGUES
      ¹⁴For if I pray in a tongue, my spirit prays        Mind Unfruitful
      but my *mind is unfruitful.* ¹⁵What am I to do?

2.    I will *pray with the spirit*
      and I will *pray with the mind* also;              PRAY/SING WITH
      I will *sing with the spirit*                       Spirit and Mind
      and I will *sing with the mind* also.

**Figure 4.5(7). Cameos 1-2 (1 Cor 14:13-15)**

Both speaking in tongues and the importance of communication are still on Paul's mind. He does not dismiss tongues, he only limits their usefulness. Although Paul sees the primary use of tongues as a private form of devotion, throughout this chapter he never fails to affirm tongues speaking as a legitimate aspect of public worship (if interpretation is available). After an opening reference to "the one who" (third person) Paul shifts attention to himself. His private devotional life included praying and singing "with the mind" along with praying and singing "with the spirit." Obviously the forms of devotion that Paul describes as being "with the spirit" had no engagement of the mind. His mind, on such occasions, was "unfruitful." Theodoret of Cyr (d. c. 466) comments on this verse and writes, "The *fruit* of the speaker is found in the profit of the hearer."[16] Many speakers (political, academic and religious) strive to serve their own interests. Not so Paul. He has just stated his goals, which are to *build up, console* and *teach* his listeners (14:3, 6). He will use both the spirit and the mind in his pursuit of these objectives.

It has been my personal privilege to worship with charismatics engaged in singing in the spirit. I found it to be an exquisite sound, and the occasion was a rich worship experience for me, as I am sure it was for those around me who were exercising this gift. It is no wonder that Paul keeps insisting on the valid-

---

[16]Theodoret of Cyr, *Commentary on the First Epistle to the Corinthians,* quoted in Findlay, *First Epistle,* p. 907.

ity of praying and singing "with the spirit" along with praying and singing "with the mind." This introduction shows that, for Paul, both were important even though worshiping "with the mind" was for him more important. Remembering this dual focus is significant for the rest of the homily.

After this introduction Paul presents his case using a prophetic rhetorical template of seven inverted stanzas with a climax in the center. The outer envelope of the template is constructed of cameos 3 and 9 which are displayed in figure 4.5(8).

3.  [16]Otherwise, if you bless with the spirit,
       *how* can any one in the position of *an inquirer*     FOR INQUIRERS
       *say* the *"Amen"* to your thanksgiving     Tongues:
       when he does not know what you are saying?     Incomprehensible
       [17]For you may give thanks well enough,     Ineffective
       but the *other man is not built up.*     Do Not Built Up

---

9.  [24]But if *all prophesy*,
       and an *unbeliever or inquirer* enters,     FOR UNBELIEVER/INQUIRER
       he is *convicted* by all,     Prophesy
       he is *called to account* by all,     Conviction
       [25]the secrets of his heart are disclosed;     Self Revelation
       and so, *falling on his face,*     Surrender
       he will *worship God*     Worship
       and declare, *"God is really among you!"*     Witness

**Figure 4.5(8). Cameos 3 and 9 (1 Cor 14:16-17, 24-25)**

Four words are central to an understanding of the seven cameos in this prophetic rhetorical template. These are:

- Foreigner (*heteros*)
- Unbeliever (*apistos*)
- Believer (*pistos*)
- Inquirer (*idiotes*)

The "foreigner" (*heteros*) appears only in the quotation from Isaiah 28 (cameo 6). In this text it refers to someone who speaks an unknown language and is a part of a foreign culture. The "unbeliever" could be an unbelieving Greek or a non-Christian Jew. The third word, *believer*, refers to a confessing Christian. The fourth word, however, is problematic. The *idiotes* could be a believer who had not received any of the spiritual gifts. It could also be a person who was "ignorant." BAGD suggests, "The *idiotes* are neither similar to the *apistoi* (unbelievers), nor are they full-fledged Christians; obviously they stand between the two groups as a kind of proselytes or catechumens; perhaps *inquirer*."[17] This group of worshipers knows enough of what is happening around them in Christian worship that they want to say "amen." The Hebrew-Aramaic word *amen* was common in Jewish worship, but unknown among the Greeks. The *idiotes* knew this word and were happy to participate in Christian worship through its use. Paul as much as says, "You are not giving these poor people a chance to say *amen*. When you speak in tongues (with no interpreter) they have no idea what is being said and thus cannot participate." Two lines later Paul writes, "The other man (meaning the *idiotes*) is not built up." Clearly the *idiotes* has attended the service of worship for that specific purpose. Following BAGD and the margin of the NIV, *inquirer* seems to strike the right balance.

Cameo 9 offers a conclusive contrast. Here Paul presents his most complete picture of what he expects from authentic Christian worship. If all prophesy, both the unbeliever and the inquirer can understand and participate in what is happening around them. The intended outcome of worship is impressive. It includes five movements:[18]

1. "He is convicted by all" (by the prophetic word, not by the worshipers). The Holy Spirit moves in the interior world of the feelings and thoughts bringing conviction of sin and confession of truth.

2. "Called to account by all" (that is, by all of the proclamation). The prophetic word reviews the worshiper's commitments and actions, pressing the worshiper to take responsibility for them.

3. "The secrets of his heart are disclosed" (the inner life is exposed). The prophetic word is not feel-good preaching. It penetrates to and exposes the dark corners of the worshiper's mind and heart. Fee writes, "No wonder the Corinthians preferred tongues; it not only gave them a sense of being more truly 'spiritual' but it was safer!"[19]

4. "Falling on his face, he will worship God" (he surrenders to and worships God). A modern equivalent might be, "He falls on his knees."[20]

5. He will declare, "God is really among you" (he will witness to his faith). For both Jew and Greek, a god "lived" in his or her temple or "house." If you

---

[17]BAGD, p. 370.
[18]Gordon Fee helpfully describes four stages in *First Epistle*, pp. 686-87. It is possible to see five distinct movements.
[19]Ibid., p. 687.
[20]Thiselton, *First Epistle*, p. 1129.

wanted therefore to draw close to God you needed to go to his or her house. Paul had told his readers "you are God's temple and . . . God's Spirit dwells in you [pl.]" (3:16). In public worship, when prophetic witness achieves its purpose, the unbeliever and the inquirer discover this astounding reality to be true and vocalize this confession.[21]

Worshipers did not attend to be entertained. They were participants in a great unfolding drama. *They* were the actors. With no distinction between clergy and laity, there was space and expectation that everyone could participate in worship according to their (spiritual) gifts.

The second envelope of this homily is composed of cameos 4 and 8, which are seen together in figure 4.5(9).

| | | |
|---|---|---|
| 4. | [18]I thank God that I speak in tongues more than you all; | IN CHURCH: |
| | [19]yet, *in church* I would rather speak five *words with my mind*, in order *to instruct others*, | No tongues Rather: Instruction |
| | than ten thousand words in a tongue. | |
| | ---------------------------------------------------------------------------- | |
| 8. | [23]If, therefore, *the whole church assembles* | |
| | and *all* speak in *tongues*, | IN CHURCH: |
| | and an *inquirer or unbeliever enters*, | Unbeliever enters |
| | will he not say that you are *mad*? | Tongues = mad |

**Figure 4.5(9). Cameos 4 and 8 (1 Cor 14:18-19, 23)**

These two cameos are so closely intertwined that the ideas flow effortlessly from the first to the second. If cameos 5-7 were missing, no reader would detect their absence. Paul had the gift of speaking in tongues (cameo 4) and he used it more than any of them, but not in church. The listener was more important than the speaker. Paul's concern is: what benefit will the listener receive? The reader knows that for Paul, when there is someone to interpret, speaking in tongues in worship is acceptable. The key to cameo 8 is "if . . . *all* speak in tongues." That is, if there is no prophetic voice raised and the only language spoken in the service is that of the speakers in tongues, the result will be disastrous. The inquirer will stop his inquiry and the unbeliever will join him in concluding that this is one more mystery-religion cult with its irrational gibberish. Paul's mandate is: Some speaking in tongues (with interpretation) is fine, but *the prophetic voice must dominate!*

The three center cameos also need to be examined together [see fig. 4.5(10)].

---

[21]In Is 45:14 the Egyptians, the Ethiopians and the Sabeans make a similar confession.

5.   $^{20}$Brethren, do not be children in your *thinking*;
      be babes in evil,                                    THINK
      but in *thinking be mature*.                         Mature

6.       $^{21}$*In the law* it is written,
          "By men of strange tongues
           and by the lips of foreigners                   SCRIPTURE
           I will speak to this people,
           and even then they will not listen to me,
           says the Lord."

7.   $^{22}$Thus, *tongues* serve as a *sign*,
      not for *believers* but for *unbelievers*            TONGUES
      while *prophecy* is *not a sign*                     Prophecy
      for *unbelievers* but for *believers*.

**Figure 4.5(10). Cameos 5-7 (1 Cor 14:20-22)**

Paul once again places a Scripture quotation in the center of a ring-composition homily. But in this instance, Paul has quoted the center of an Old Testament ring composition and placed it in the center of his new ring composition. The Isaiah text is displayed in figure 4.5(11).

This six-cameo prophetic homily has obviously been on Paul's mind at various times during the composition of 1 Corinthians. In a number of places (note the italics), his interests overlap with this homily from Isaiah. The following is noteworthy:

1. Isaiah's cameo 1 begins with a focus on the *teaching of knowledge* and the task of *explaining the message*. These themes have been prominent throughout chapter 14, as Paul repeatedly insists on the preeminence of prophecy over speaking in tongues. In 14:19 (cameo 4) he is eager to "instruct others."

2. At the end of Isaiah's first cameo the image of breastfeeding occurs. Already in 3:1-2 Paul was talking about feeding milk (not solid food) to babes. This theme reappears in 14:20 (cameo 5), where he urges his readers to be *mature*, not as children or *babies*.

3. Paul quotes from the center of the Isaiah homily with its references to "men of strange tongues." He abbreviates Isaiah's text, but is careful to quote from both parts of the center. Paul selects the beginning of Isaiah's cameo 3 and the end of Isaiah's cameo 4.

4. Isaiah uses the image of "falling" and applies it to wayward Israel who will *fall backwards*. Paul concludes his homily with the same image, but he reverses it. The one who accepts the new prophetic message will *fall on his face*, worshiping God and declaring faith in him.

1. ²⁸·⁹"Whom will he teach *knowledge*,
    And to whom will he *explain the message?*      TO WHOM THE MESSAGE?
    Those who are *weaned from the milk*,      To Babes?
    Those taken *from the breast?*

2.     ¹⁰For it is precept upon precept
    Precept upon precept,      PRECEPT ON PRECEPT
    Line upon line, line upon line,      Line on Line
    Here a little, there a little."      Here/There a Little

3.     ¹¹*Nay, but by men of strange lips*      VIA ALIEN LANG.
    *And with an alien tongue*      The Lord Speaks
    *The Lord will speak to his people,*      To His People

4.     ¹²To whom he has said,
    "This is rest;      THIS IS REST
    Give rest to the weary;      This Is Repose
    And this is repose";      They Will Not Hear
    *Yet they would not hear,*

5.     ¹³Therefore the word of the Lord will be to them
    Precept upon precept,      PRECEPT ON PRECEPT
    Precept upon precept,      Line on Line
    Line upon line, line upon line,      Here/There a Little
    Here a little, there a little

6.     That they may go,
    *and fall backwards*,      THEY GO/FALL BACK
    and be broken,      Broken, Snared, Taken
    and snared, and taken.

---

**Figure 4.5(11). The Lord and his people: Isaiah, Israel and the alien tongue (Is 28:9-13)**

5. Isaiah is criticizing disobedient Israel who refuses to listen to the prophetic message. Paul began his ministry in Corinth among his own people. He "argued in the synagogue every sabbath" (Acts 18:4). He was "occupied with preaching, testifying to the Jews that the Christ was Jesus" (Acts 18:5). This went on for months. It was a case of "line upon line, precept on precept, here a little, there a little" (Is 28:10, 13). Some believed, while others rejected his message and tried to pressure the Roman courts to prosecute him under Roman law (Acts 18:12-17). In Paul's mind the Corinthian Jews who rejected him were like Israel of old that rejected the prophets' message. Hence Paul's quote from Isaiah 28:11-12.

In one way or another, five of the six cameos in Isaiah's prophetic homily are reflected in Paul's letter to the Corinthians (and to the whole church).

With these relationships between Isaiah 28:9-13 and 1 Corinthians 14:16-25 in mind, we need to briefly look at cameo 7. The Assyrian language spoken by invading soldiers was God's way of talking to his deaf, childish people, who refused to realize that God was trying to communicate with them. Paul asserts that tongues speaking is a "sign for unbelievers." In what way? A hundred years ago Plummer suggested that Paul knew ancient Israel was chastised by its refusal to listen to the prophets. In like manner Paul understands speaking in tongues to be a chastisement in his day against those who refused to believe *his* message.[22] Tongues speaking was a negative sign of judgment in both accounts. All commentators on 1 Corinthians have struggled with this verse.[23] With fear and trembling I offer the following.

Chrysostom wrote, "Tongues are a sign to unbelievers not for their instruction, as prophecy is for both believers and unbelievers, but to astonish them."[24] Picture the following scene: An inquirer and an unbeliever attend a worship service of the Christian assembly in Corinth. The prophets give their messages. Old Testament texts are presented as fulfilled in the life and ministry of Jesus. The cross and the resurrection are discussed. "Precept on precept" are presented. The unbeliever is still not convinced. It is all quite rational, even though delivered with passion. The inquirer has heard various religious enthusiasts present their views and said inquirer is still not convinced. Then one of the prophets finishes his remarks and suddenly, out of nowhere, a speaker in tongues starts praying. When the speaker is finished, a third party translates the prayer. The tongues speaker was not raging out of control. He or she waited until the prophet was finished and only then began his or her Spirit-filled, incomprehensible prayer language. The unbeliever is startled and amazed. He has never heard anything like this in his life. There was no emotional build up with song, dance, drums, sacrifice and exciting music to work the crowd into a frenzy. The strange yet attractive incomprehensible words seemingly came out of nowhere. Then, also mysteriously, a second person translates those words into rational speech. Something is going on that the unbeliever cannot explain. Perhaps—just perhaps—God is present and speaking to this gathering of Christians in this private home. Has the divine touched earth, asks the unbeliever? The *inquirer* is accustomed to such things.

---

[22]Robertson/Plummer, *First Epistle*, pp. 316-17.

[23]Thiselton, *First Epistle*, pp. 1120-26; Fee, *First Epistle*, pp. 679-85; Kistemaker, *1 Corinthians*, pp. 500-502; Hays, *First Corinthians*, pp. 238-40.

[24]Chrysostom, *1 Corinthians* 36.2, quoted in *1-2 Corinthians*, ed. Gerald Bray, Ancient Christian Commentary on Scripture (Downers Grove, Ill.: InterVarsity Press, 1999), 7:142.

This is not a sign for him. He is eager to focus on the message of the prophets, respond with his *amen* and reflect on what it means for his life. The *believers* are deepened in their faith by those same prophetic messages. But for *unbelievers* this strange Spirit-filled language is indeed a sign pointing to a divine reality beyond the veil. As Paul affirmed, tongues are a "sign for unbelievers," while prophecy is a "sign for believers." Perhaps, after all is said and done, Chrysostom provides the key to this centuries-old puzzle.

Having established guidelines for prophecy and tongues among baptized Christians (14:1-12), along with inquirers and unbelievers who may attend their worship (14:13-27), Paul turns to a new form of "disorder in worship" that requires a further homily.

# Order in Worship

*Word—Prophets and Speakers in Tongues*

1 CORINTHIANS 14:26-33

PAUL'S SECOND DISCUSSION on the topic of *order in worship* is brief. It takes its place in the seven sections of the larger essay as follows:

WORSHIP: Men and Women in the Church (11:2–14:40)
1. Men and Women Leading in Worship: Prophets and How They Dress (11:2-16)
2. Order in Worship: *Sacrament*—The Lord's Supper (11:17-34)
3. Gifts and the Nature of the Body (12:1-30)
4. The Hymn to Love (12:31–14:1)
5. Spiritual Gifts and the Upbuilding of the Body (14:1-25)
6. *Order in Worship: Word—Prophets and Speakers in Tongues (14:26-33)*
7. Women and Men Worshiping: No Chatting in Church (14:33b-40)

We have now arrived at section 6 (italicized above). Corinthian worship involved both *word* and *sacrament*. They had problems with each aspect of worship. When they celebrated the sacrament of the *Lord's Supper*, some were hungry and others drunk. Paul discussed these problems in chapter 11:17-34. Here in 14:26-33 he is ready to deal with the other side of the coin and talk about disorder in the *preaching* and *praying*. The text is displayed in figure 4.6(1).

## THE RHETORIC
The rhetorical style used here includes *introduction* + A-B, A-B + *conclusion*. This pattern appears a total of five times in 1 Corinthians.[1] The final cameo

---

[1]See 1 Cor 7:6-8 (modified); 7:32-35; 14:1-5; 14:26-33; 15:51-58 (modified).

(6) in this homily functions in both directions. It is the conclusion to what proceeds and an introduction to what follows. This feature is also common in 1 Corinthians.[2]

| | | | |
|---|---|---|---|
| 1. | | [14:26]What then, brethren? When you come together, each one has a *hymn*, a *lesson*, a *revelation*, a *tongue*, or an *interpretation*. Let *all things* be done *for upbuilding*. | ORDER<br>For Upbuilding |
| 2. | A. | [27]If any speak in a *tongue*, let there be only *two or at most three*, and *each in turn;* and let one interpret. | TONGUE?<br>Two or Three |
| 3. | B. | [28]But if there is no one to interpret, let each of them *keep silent in church* and speak to himself and to God. | SILENCE<br>(When Needed) |
| 4. | A. | [29]Let *two* or *three prophets* speak, and let the *others weigh* what is said. | PROPHETS?<br>Two or Three |
| 5. | B. | [30]If a revelation is made to another sitting by, *let the first be silent.* [31]For you can all prophesy one by one, so that all may learn and all be encouraged; [32]and the spirits of prophets are subject to prophets. | SILENCE<br>(When Needed) |
| 6. | | [33]For God is *not a God of confusion* but of peace, as in *all the churches* of the saints. | ORDER AS<br>In All the Churches |

**Figure 4.6(1). Word—Order in worship (1 Cor 14:26-33)**

## COMMENTARY

Cameo 1 offers a further window into early church worship. Everyone participated. There were no spectators. Five types of worship involvement are listed. These include a hymn (*psalmon*), teaching (*didakhen*), revelation (*apokalupsin*), tongue (*glossan*), and interpretation (*hermeneian*). The first involved singing, the second and third are related to prophecy and the last two have to do with speaking in tongues. Paul affirms that all three elements have their place in worship. With no history of Christian hymns, it seems that they composed their own. With no seminaries to train clergy (other than the apostles and their traveling companions), they relied on prophets and teachers in the congregation. To this was added speaking in tongues and the

---

[2]See 1 Cor 3:17; 7:17 (5); 6:13-20; 9:12b-18 (4); 14:26-33; 15:35-50.

necessary interpreters of tongues. People apparently attended worship thinking about what they were going to *contribute*, not about what they were going
to *receive*.

The services were, it seems, becoming counterproductively long. Paul starts
with the tongues speakers, and limits them to two or three with one interpreter (cameos 2-3). Clearly the tongues speakers could control the use of their
gift. They were able to "wait their turn." If there was no interpreter, they were
to "keep silent in church." The speaker in a tongue could exercise this gift silently speaking "to himself and to God."

The parallel admonitions for the prophets are most interesting. They too
were limited to two or three, followed by a break for reflection. The following
aspects of Paul's remarks are noteworthy.

1. The prophets were composed of men and women. Assuming an awareness of Paul's essay divisions, the readers would have been fully conscious of
11:4-5, where the prophets included both genders.[3] This admonition must
be kept in mind in any consideration of 14:34-36 (examined below), which
is often quoted or studied in isolation from chapter 11 with its women
prophets.

2. The prophets are politely told, "Two or three at a time is appropriate."
This introduces some order into the process of prophesying. At the same
time there is some ambiguity in the text. Apparently those present (men
and women) were free to receive the gift of prophecy, and all were free to
"prophesy one by one." What then is the meaning of "two or three prophets"? Are cameo 4 and cameo 5 at odds? It is possible to understand that
Paul means "two or three" prophets followed by reflections on what has
been said. Two or three more can then prophesy. This relates to the following consideration.

3. After each set of prophets have their say, "the others" are to "weigh what
is said." *Diakrino* translates as "pass judgment on, deliberate over, render a
decision regarding."[4] It appears that after brief remarks by up to three prophets, they were to break into a general discussion regarding what had been
said. It sounds like an informal setting with presenters and responders. Bishr
ibn al-Sari, in his ninth-century study of 1 Corinthians, comments on these
respondents by saying, "The ones who have been given the gift of distin-

---

[3]On the day of Pentecost Peter quoted from the prophecy of Joel. That quote affirms that the
menservants and maidservants will receive the Spirit and *prophesy* (Acts 2:18).
[4]BAGD, p. 185.

guishing the spirits should distinguish and examine what they are saying."[5] This is a thoughtful suggestion. In 12:10 Paul mentions those who have the "ability to distinguish between spirits." Those with this gift would naturally participate in the post-homily discussion. Each set of brief homilies was immediately subject to *public* comment as a part of worship. There is much here to ponder.

4. If a seated worshiper senses an inspiration of the Spirit, the speaker is to "be silent."

5. The prophet who is on his or her feet is reminded that the prophets must *be subject* to the spirits of prophets and, when necessary, *be silent*. This language is used to give direction to the prophets, and it reappears in the following discussion of women worshipers. First, the "tongues speakers" were, in certain circumstances, to be silent. Now the prophets are instructed to be silent when others want to speak.

6. Paul writes, "you can all prophesy one by one." In harmony with everything he writes about the variety of gifts in chapter 12, the word *all* seems to mean "all those with the gift of prophecy." The text (12:29) indicates that all are not prophets.

7. The goal of the exercise of prophecy was that all may *manthemeno* (learn)[6] and be *paraklontai*, that is, be comforted/reconciled/encouraged. The Greek word *parakaleo* describes the father who leaves the banquet hall and empties himself as he goes down and out to reconcile his older son in the parable of the prodigal son (Lk 15:28). It is a strong word and Paul uses it twenty-three times in the Corinthian correspondence alone. The worshipers who come with their pain should find *comfort*. Those who are estranged should see open doors for *reconciliation*, and the depressed should find *encouragement*. Paul's language includes all of these nuances.

These directives are intended to bring order both to the tongues speakers and to the prophets, because "God is not a God of confusion but of peace." The Greek word *akatastasia*, here translated "confusion," is a strong word that carries the meaning of "unruliness" and "insurrection."[7] Between the lines we can overhear the fact that the problems in Corinth related to their *ministry of the word* were as profound as the irregularities at *Holy Communion*. The striking combination of both structure and freedom, exuber-

---

[5]Bishr ibn al-Sari, *Pauline Epistles*, p. 84 n. 27.
[6]This word carries the meaning of learning through instruction or obedience. BAGD, p. 490.
[7]BAGD, p. 30.

ance and order, speaking and quietly listening is impressive, and the text leaves much to ponder.

Paul concludes the essay on worship with the widely debated comments on women (and men) in worship. To that discussion we now turn.

# Women and Men Worshiping

*No Chatting in Church*

THE FIRST SECTION in this essay on worship affirmed both women and
men in their roles as prophets (11:2-16). Paul suggested that they dress differently to avoid misunderstanding and carry on praying and prophesying. At
the end of the essay on worship (14:33-36) he returns to the same question of
women and men in worship. In the opening text (section 4.1) he focused on
*the worship leadership* (male and female). Now as he concludes the essay on
worship (section 4.7) he looks at a special problem that has to do with *the
worshipers*, both female and male. It is important to see this concluding discussion as part of the overall essay, the outline of which is as follows:

WORSHIP: Men and Women in the Church (11:2–14:40)
4.1 Men and Women Leading in Worship: Prophets and How They Dress (11:2-16)
4.2  Order in Worship: *Sacrament*—The Lord's Supper (11:17-34)
4.3   Gifts and the Nature of the Body (12:1-30)
4.4    The Hymn to Love (12:31–14:1)
4.5   Spiritual Gifts and the Upbuilding of the Body (14:1-25)
4.6  Order in Worship: *Word*—Prophets and Speakers in Tongues (14:26-33a)
*4.7 Women and Men Worshiping: No Chatting in Church (14:33b-36)*
   *(Concluding Summary and Personal Appeal [14:37-40])*

Chapters 4.1 and 4.7 (italicized) form a pair. Chapter 4.1 focuses on men
and women *leading worship*, while 4.7 looks at women and men *as worshipers*.
At the same time the four verses in chapter 4.7 are also related to the homily
that precedes it. In chapter 4.6 Paul told both the *tongues speakers* and the
*prophets* to *be silent* when others were talking. Each could participate in turn.

He offers the same advice to those women who were chatting during the worship service.

This fourth essay, as with the three previous essays, concludes with a personal appeal. In this instance, the personal appeal (14:37-40) includes a summary of the essay. Both the discussion of "the chatting women" and the summary of the essay warrant reflection. Homily 4.7(1) falls into the following five cameos.

1.  14:33God is *not a God of confusion* but of peace.          ORDER NECESSARY
        As in *all the churches* of the saints,                       As in All the Churches

2.       34the *wives should keep silence* in the churches.
           For they are *not permitted to chat*,                      WIVES—NO CHATTING
           but should be *subordinated*,                              During the Worship
           even as the *Torah* says.

3.            35If there is anything they desire to know,             QUESTIONS
                let them *ask their husbands at home*.                 At Home

4.          For it is *shameful*                                       WIVES—NO CHATTING
              for a *wife to chat in church*.                          During the Worship

5.   36Did the *word of God originate with you*,                      ORDER NECESSARY
        or are you the only ones it has reached?                      As in All the Churches

---

**Figure 4.7(1). Women and men worshiping: No chatting in church (1 Cor 14:33b-36)**

## THE RHETORIC

Five inverted cameos appear in this brief homily and in the conclusion that follows it. The two opening lines (on confusion and peace) close the previous homily and open the ring composition before us. The double link is not as smooth as in Paul's previous use of this rhetorical device but it still functions to make a connection between the two passages.

The climax in the center (cameo 3) indicates that Paul is not discussing all Christian women but rather married women whose husbands are believers in regular attendance at worship. In the center Paul offers a solution to this problem.

## COMMENTARY

On the surface, this short homily appears to be in direct conflict with what Paul wrote in the beginning of the essay concerning the right of women to prophesy in the congregation (11:2-16). While resident in Corinth, Paul lived with Aquila and Priscilla. Priscilla (with her husband) taught Apollos, the well-known preacher from Alexandria. Luke, Paul's companion and colleague, recorded this for the church to read and ponder. Luke also recorded Peter's sermon at Pentecost (Acts 2:17-18), where "God declares, . . . your sons *and your daughters* shall prophesy." The quote from Joel 2:28-32 continues with "yes, and on my menservants and *my maidservants* in those days / I will pour out my Spirit; and they shall prophesy" (italics added).

Not only will the sons and daughters of the house prophesy, but the menservants and maidservants will step out of their places in the social order and join the sons and daughters in prophesying. In addition, Luke recorded the Song of Mary (Lk 1:46-56) and by so doing affirmed Mary as a teacher of theology and social ethics for the entire church for as long as his Gospel is read. Women of some means were a part of the band of disciples that traveled with Jesus and the apostles (Lk 8:1-3). Among those women was Joanna the wife of Chuza, Herod's steward. This wealthy, high-class woman helped fund Jesus and his traveling band. She also *joined them* and was present among the women at the resurrection (Lk 24:10).

Luke records that on that singular occasion the angel at the empty tomb told the women, "Remember how *he told you*, while he was still in Galilee, that the Son of man must be delivered into the hands of sinful men, and be crucified, and on the third day rise" (Lk 24:6-7, italics added). The incident here described was either Luke 9:18 or Luke 9:43-45. In both cases Jesus was addressing "his disciples," and Joanna was among them. This confirms that she was one of "the disciples."[1] In Cenchreae (the eastern harbor of Corinth), Phoebe was the *deacon* (the word is masculine, not feminine). She was not just "one who served"; she held the office of "deacon." Elsewhere in the New Testament the word *diakonos* is usually translated "minister." Phoebe was clearly a leader, and most likely *the* leader (minister) of the infant church in that harbor town near Corinth. Mary, the mother of Jesus, was last mentioned in Acts 1:14 as a pious woman meeting in prayer with the apostles, the women and the brothers of Jesus.[2] The extent of her leadership role in the early church cannot be established historically, but to assume that she had no voice is unthinkable. The text of 1 Timothy 5:1-2 can be translated "Do not rebuke *an elder* but exhort him as you would a father; treat younger men like brothers, *women el-*

[1]Richard Bauckham, "On the Road with Jesus and His Disciples," in *Gospel Women: Studies of the Named Women in the Gospels* (Grand Rapids: Eerdmans, 2002), pp. 110-21.
[2]The synodical letter of the Council of Ephesus (A.D. 431) places Mary in Ephesus and claims that she lived, died and was buried there.

*ders* like mothers, younger women like sisters, in all purity" (italics added).[3] Is Paul in the text before us (14:33-36) overthrowing all of this? Writing to the Corinthian church, where Priscilla housed and fed him for eighteen months, is he insulting her by telling her to be silent in church? How can we understand this text?

Anthony Thiselton offers a thorough discussion of the extensive debate concerning this passage. With a detailed analysis and a specialized bibliography, he represents fairly the major views set forth in the current literature. For those eager to follow the details of the debate, Thiselton's eighteen pages are a superb guide.[4] I can but offer a few comments.

This passage balances the overall essay on worship which opens in 11:2 and concludes with 14:40. As observed (with this passage included) seven sections form a prophetic rhetorical template with a climax in the center. The hymn to love in 12:31–14:1 is strategically placed in the middle to function as a healing flow of *agape* (love) into the various problems discussed in the essay. If 14:33-36 is omitted, an abrupt hole is created in the set of seven carefully balanced sections. If it were missing, the reader would anticipate some other discussion regarding women and men in worship to balance Paul's opening discussion in 11:2-16.

Ben Witherington has astutely written, "It should be recognized that what an individual says to correct an error cannot be taken as a full or definitive statement of his views on a particular subject."[5] This truism was observed when Paul wrote, "I want all of you to speak in tongues" (14:5). As he recorded those words he was trying to correct an error. He was not contradicting his earlier affirmation that God gives the spiritual gifts as *he chooses*, not as the believers choose (12:11).

The key to the passage before us can perhaps be found in the composition of the church in Corinth.

Corinth was the largest city in Greece and inevitably the most diverse. Manufacturing was extensive and the workforce large. With commerce flowing north, south, east and west and with goods (and small ships) to haul across the six-kilometer (3.5 mile) stone road (*diolkos*) that spanned the isthmus of Corinth, a great deal of slave labor was required. The biennial Isthmian

---

[3]See Leonard Swidler, *Biblical Affirmations of Women* (Philadelphia: Westminster Press, 1979), p. 315.

[4]Thiselton, *First Epistle*, pp. 1146-62.

[5]Ben Witherington, *Women in the Earliest Churches* (Cambridge: Cambridge University Press, 1988), p. 25.

Games would have brought in a further influx of internationals. Greek was their only common language. For the lower classes, enough Greek to function on the job would have been vital. But what about women at home? Whether the families involved were slaves, traders, day laborers or skilled craftsmen, the languages spoken at home would have been numerous.

Added to this was the problem of accent. Often when a public speaker is functioning in a second language, even when the speaker is fluent, there can be great difficulty in communication due to accent. When a speaker's words and phrases are not understood, a low buzz can break out as listeners ask each other, "What did she say? What was that word?"

The short attention span for simple people (like modern television addicts) was most certainly another problem. From 1957-1962 it was my privilege to be part of a team of Egyptian Christians engaged in teaching simple villagers in the south of Egypt how to read their own language (Arabic). The women, through no fault of their own, had a special problem. Due to the limited nature of their social contacts, their attention span, so I discovered, was about fifteen-seconds. For this reason, occasionally, I was obliged to teach no more than three women at a time. I broke the material I was presenting into fifteen-second segments, and in class I would call the first woman by name and talk to her for fifteen seconds. During those fifteen seconds the other two women were not listening. Instead they were chatting among themselves, or to grandma in the next room, or to the neighbor twelve feet away seated across the village alley, or to one of the children playing at their feet. After presenting my fifteen seconds to the first woman, I would call the second woman by name and deliver the same fifteen seconds of information to her. During this second recitation the first woman's attention was elsewhere, as was the mind of the third woman. I would repeat the process for the third woman and then start over with the second fifteen-second segment. The women were intelligent, committed and interested. In fact they were the volunteer supervisors of the classes we had organized across the village. Having never focused their minds for an extended period of time on any topic, their attention span was naturally short. Understanding this, I was happy to meet them where they were rather than expect them to fit into my acquired pattern of speaking and listening. Large groups of simple, uneducated women presented special challenges.

Ancient cultures often developed a classical language and a colloquial language. I am personally acquainted with this reality in Arabic, Syriac and modern Greek. The way people such as Paul and Apollos spoke formally in church was not necessarily the way Greek speakers talked to one another on the street and in private homes. We know Paul's written style, and Luke tells us that Apollos was "an eloquent man" (Acts 18:24). A very small percentage of people were literate across the Mediterranean world of the first century; I have read estimates as low as 10 percent. Naturally, we have no record of how people spoke because even personal letters were the work of that 10 percent who wrote in *literary* Koine Greek.

The first four verses of Luke's Gospel are a single polished sentence of thirty-nine words. I am sure that the wives of illiterate dock workers in Corinth, listening in their second (or third) language, would not have been able to comprehend that sentence. A few Greek words, enough to buy food in the market, were likely the limit of their Greek vocabulary. I worked for decades with Westerners who served in the Middle East and who studied hard to acquire "courtesy and survival Arabic" and found themselves *totally lost* in an Arabic language worship service. Yes, the authors of the New Testament were not trying to imitate the classical Greek authors. They wrote in *Koine*—but yet!

I have preached in village churches in Egypt where the women were seated on one side of the church and the men on the other. There was a wooden partition about six feet high separating the two sections. I preached in simple *colloquial* Arabic, but the women were often illiterate and the preacher was expected to preach for at least an hour—and we had problems. The women quickly passed the limit of their attention span. The children were seated with them and chatting inevitably broke out among the women. The chatting would at times become so loud that no one could hear the preacher. (These villages had no electricity and no sound amplification.) One of the senior elders would stand up and in a desperate voice shout, "Let the women be silent in the church!" and we would proceed. After about ten minutes the scene would repeat. I was encouraged by the fact that John Chrysostom of Antioch experienced the same problem.

Preaching in the cathedral of Antioch in the latter part of the fourth century, stenographers recorded the following words from Chrysostom:

> Text—And if they [the women] will learn anything let them ask their husbands at home. Chrysostom: Then indeed the women, from such teaching keep silence; but now there is apt to be great noise among them, much clamor and talking, and nowhere so much as in this place [the cathedral]. They may all be seen here talking more than in the market, or at the bath. For, as if they came

hither for recreation, they are all engaged in conversing upon unprofitable subjects. Thus all is confusion, and they seem not to understand, that unless they are quiet, they cannot learn anything that is useful. For when our discourse [sermon] strains against the talking, and no one minds what is said, what good can it do to them?[6]

If this was the scene in the cathedral of the great city of Antioch in the fourth century, what can we imagine in Corinth in the days of Paul? Paul had just affirmed that the Corinthians were getting drunk at the Lord's Supper and that the prophets and tongues speakers were all talking at once! It seems that some of the women gave up and started chatting. Who could blame them? Yet all needed to work together to create the required "decency and order" necessary for meaningful worship.

The women are consequently called on to "be subordinated," but to whom? Clearly Paul means "be subordinated to the worship leadership," and the reader knows that the leadership includes men and women prophets. Also relevant is the fact that 14:26-36 lists three groups of people who were disturbing worship. These are:

1. The (male and female) *prophets* are told:

- Don't all talk at once.

- *Be silent* in church.

2. The (male and female) *speakers in tongues* are told:

- If there is no interpreter,

- *be silent* in church.

3. *Married women* with Christian husbands (who attend) are told:

- Don't ask questions during the worship and don't chat.

- Ask your husbands at home and *be silent* in church.

Each of these groups is told to be silent when it disturbs worship. Paul is not telling the female prophets discussed in chapter 11 to stop prophesying!

But there is a further reality at play. Middle Eastern society is predominantly an oral culture. I experienced this for seventeen years in Egypt, seventeen years in Syria and Lebanon, and for ten years in Israel and Palestine. People process information by talking more than by sitting quietly and re-

---

[6]Chrysostom, "Homily IX [I Timothy ii. 11-15]," in *Nicene and Post-Nicene Fathers* (Grand Rapids: Eerdmans, 1979), 13:435.

PAUL THROUGH MEDITERRANEAN EYES

flecting. This can be observed at many levels of society. A university professor will have the attention of the class and turn to write something on the blackboard. The moment he or she pauses to write, the entire class breaks out talking. They are not inattentive or rude, they are simply turning to a fellow student and chatting about the subject. This social style is particularly prominent at meetings of women. Taking advantage of any pause, women will often begin talking out loud—sometimes to themselves. They are simply verbalizing the information they have heard in order to better absorb and retain it.

Multiple factors must be considered. Attention-span problems, limited knowledge of Greek, accent issues, language levels of Greek in use, lack of amplification for the speakers, along with chatting as a methodology for learning are all involved. The women slip into the list along with the tongues speakers and prophets. All three categories, when worship is disrupted, are asked by Paul to "keep silent in church." Paul is saying, "Women, please stop chatting so you can listen to the women (and men) who are trying to bring you a prophetic word but cannot do so when no one can hear them."

Paul is very polite. Unlike Chrysostom, he does not say, "You women chat more in church during the sermon than you do in the marketplace or at the baths!" Some of the women (probably seated in linguistic groups) are no doubt asking their neighbors about the meaning of this or that word in Greek. Paul picks up on these legitimate questions and in effect says,

> I know your Greek is limited. But your husbands have learned a bit more Greek than you have managed to absorb. They have to in order to function on the job. You have not had this chance and it is not your fault. But things have gotten out of hand on a number of levels. Please be helpful and put your questions to your husbands after you return home. I have just told the speakers when to be quiet. This is a situation in which you also need to listen quietly even if you can't follow what is said.

Another problem in this text is the English word *shame*. Western cultures are no longer primarily honor-shame cultures. In the West the word *shame* is preserved for serious matters. Across the Middle East, without exception, honor and shame are primary categories. Every noble person is expected to act honorably and avoid all things shameful. As categories that permeate every aspect of life, the concept of shame can be used for casual occurrences. Consider the following conversation between a husband and wife.

"Dear, you saw your friend yesterday, you don't need to visit her today."

"No, I must go. She has caught a cold. I have to visit her. Shame on me if I don't."

Paul does not say, "This is illegal." Nor does he label their chatting "immoral." Rather it is "shameful" (in the sense indicated in the husband-wife dialogue). The cultural equivalent in English might be the Victorian sense of "improper." *Ladies* do not chat during worship. It is "not done."

Paul's concluding note is best understood to be looking back over 14:26-36. They did not formulate the word of God, and it has reached others (cameo 10). Other churches have managed to listen to tongues speakers, give prophets their turn and sit quietly even when they could not understand everything that was said. Paul challenges the Corinthians to do the same. A concern for decency and order also appears at the end of the summary that concludes the essay.

## CONCLUDING SUMMARY OF "MEN AND WOMEN IN CHURCH" (1 COR 14:37-40)

Paul's summary of his fourth essay, which covers 11:2–14:40, is displayed in figure 4.7(2).

6    37If anyone thinks that he is a *prophet*, [chap. 11]    PROPHECY (Order Needed)

7.      or *spiritual*, [chap. 12]      GIFTS (Order Needed)

8.      he should acknowledge that what I am writing to you
   is a *command of the Lord*. [chap. 13]    THE COMMAND
   38If any one does not recognize this,    To Love
   he is not recognized.

9.    39So, my brethren,
   earnestly *desire to prophesy*, [14:1-12]    GIFTS
   and do *not forbid speaking in tongues;* [14:13-25]    Prophecy & Tongues

10.   40but *all things* should be done    ALL THINGS IN ORDER
   in *decency and in order*. [14:26-33]    (in Order)

**Figure 4.7(2). Summary of "Men and Women in Church" (1 Cor 14:37-40)**

### RHETORIC

Using ring composition Paul concludes his essay on worship by looking back over the essay and summarizing many of its main points. Drunkenness at the Lord's Supper is omitted. A reference to chapter 13 is the climax of the summary.

## COMMENTARY

Paul concluded the third essay (on Christians living in a pagan world: 10:32-33) with a summary. For a second time, he follows that same pattern.

The "command of the Lord" in the center of the summary is the royal command of love defined in chapter 13. If one reads this summary as a this-after-that sequence, then the "command of the Lord" is defined by the previous verses and becomes the command to the women to be silent in church. Sadly, for centuries this text has been fashioned into a club with which to keep women from the full use of their spiritual gifts in the leadership of worship in the church. The command Paul is invoking is the highest of all, the command to love. The many worship problems discussed in this great essay that stretches from 11:2–14:40 can only be adequately solved by the love that Paul so brilliantly defines in chapter 13.

Paul's summary also includes his customary personal appeal. The phrase *imitate me* does not fit. Nor does "I have the Spirit of the Lord." But "What I am writing to you is a command of the Lord" serves him well as a closing plea.

The great chapter on the resurrection now awaits us.

# Resurrection

*Faith, Christ and Victory*

1 CORINTHIANS 15:1-58

*Thanks be to God*
*who gives us the victory*
*through our Lord Jesus Christ*
(15:57)

# Resurrection

*The Message and the Validity of Faith*

I CORINTHIANS 15:1-20

THIS FINAL ESSAY COMPLETES the circle of five essays that make up the epistle. These are:

1. The Cross and Christian Unity (1:10–4:16)
2.   Sex: Men and Women in the Human Family (4:17–7:40)
3.     Christian and Pagan: Freedom and Responsibility (8:1–11:1)
4.   Men and Women in Worship (11:2–14:40)
5. *Resurrection: Faith, Christ and Victory (15:1-58)*

Having discussed the cross at some length in the first essay, Paul is now ready to reaffirm the cross and move on to an extensive discussion of the resurrection.

His presentation of the resurrection (15:1-58) is also carefully structured and falls into the following five sections:

1. Resurrection: The Message and the Validity of Faith  (vv. 1-20)
2.   Resurrection: Adam and Christ               (vv. 21-28)
3.     Resurrection and Ethics                  (vv. 29-34)
4.   Resurrection: Adam and Christ               (vv. 35-50)
5. Resurrection: Victory[1]                   (vv. 51-58)

The first section of this fifth essay is composed of two homilies. The first focuses on the message of the resurrection, and the second deals with the validity of faith.

---

[1]The outline suggested here is nearly identical to the outline proposed by N. T. Wright, *Resurrection*, p. 312.

## RESURRECTION: THE MESSAGE (1 COR 15:1-11)

The text of the first homily is displayed in figure 5.1(1).

1. ¹⁵:¹Now I would remind you, brethren, of *the gospel*      I PREACHED
   which *I preached* to you, which *you received,*      You Received

2.     in which you *stand,*      (!)
       ²by which you are *saved,*      (!)      GRACE RECEIVED
       *if you hold it fast*—      (?)      In Vain?
       *unless you believed in vain.*      (?)

3.     ³For *I delivered* to you as of first importance      AN APOSTLE
       *what I also received,*      Delivers Tradition

4.     a. *"Christ died for our sins,*
         in accordance with the *scriptures,"*      THE CROSS
       b.   ⁴*"he was buried,"*

5.     c. *"he was raised on the third day*      RESURRECTION
         in accordance with the scriptures,"      First
       d.   ⁵*"he appeared to Cephas,*      Appearances
         then to *the twelve."*

6.     ⁶Then he appeared to more than
       *five hundred brethren* at one time,      LATER
       most of whom are still alive,      Appearances
       though some have fallen asleep.

7.     ⁷Then he appeared to *James,*
       then to all the apostles.      LATER
       ⁸Last of all, as to one untimely born,      Appearances
       he *appeared also to me.*

8.     ⁹For I am the *least of the apostles,*      AN APOSTLE
       *unfit* to be called an *apostle,*      Unfit Persecutor
       because I persecuted the church of God.

9. ¹⁰But by the *grace of God,*
       I am what I am,
       and *his grace* toward me was *not in vain.*      GRACE RECEIVED
       Rather, *I worked harder than any of them,*      Not in Vain
         though it was *not I,*
       but the *grace of God* which was in me.

10. ¹¹Whether then it was I or they,      WE PREACHED
    so *we preached* and so *you believed.*      You Believed

---

**Figure 5.1(1). Resurrection: The Message (1 Cor 15:1-11)**

### THE RHETORIC

Paul presents a homily composed of seven semantic units with an extended center. If the extended center is read as a single unit, the overall homily falls into the prophetic rhetorical template of seven inverted cameos, which occurs frequently in this epistle.[2] Seven times in this letter Paul creates an extended center in the middle of a ring composition.[3] Of particular interest is 10:5-12, which also includes an extended center composed of four cameos.

Within this homily there is an early Christian creed with four affirmations. I have identified these with the letters a, b, c and d. The four divide into two cameos. Together Paul lists six occasions in which followers of Jesus were witnesses to the resurrection. These include:

- Cephas

- The Twelve

- Five hundred brethren

- James

- All the apostles

- Paul

By the time he composed this epistle, Paul had quarreled with Peter (Cephas) in person and in writing (Gal 2:11-14). Here Paul lists Cephas (Peter) as the first witness to the resurrection and himself as the last. It is a nice touch. Paul opened this letter by observing divisions in the church, where one insisted, "I belong to Paul" and another declared, "I belong to Cephas" (1:12-13). This text reverses the order and presents Cephas and Paul standing together as witnesses to the resurrected Jesus.

Furthermore, this list of six has a built-in *expectation* that grows out of Paul's use of step parallelism. The creed that Paul recited (cameos 4, 5) uses six phrases presented in step parallelism. He appears to repeat that simple pattern with a surprise at the end. This is as follows:

---

[2]I have opted to format the center as four cameos to facilitate a discussion of its parts.
[3]See 3:18–4:7; 6:9-11; 7:17-20; 7:25-31 (two examples); 10:5-12; 13:4-7; 15:35-42. If we included the cases of A-B, A-B centers, and the collections of metaphors that occasionally appear, the list would be longer.

Cephas
  The Twelve
    The five hundred

James
  The apostles
    "The six hundred"?
    (No! Rather the text presents: The miscarriage baby—Paul!)

The first three occasions reflect a build up of Cephas, the Twelve, then the five hundred. Accustomed to Paul's use of step parallelism, and noting the step parallelism in the creed (cameos 4-5), the reader naturally expects the second list to unfold with James, the apostles, and finally some grand number.[4] Such is not the case. Instead of an eye-popping conclusion, Paul finishes with a baby born by a miscarriage—namely, himself.

## COMMENTARY

As in each of the four previous essays, Paul begins by recalling the tradition. In this final essay the tradition becomes the center of an entire homily. Actually as the epistle unfolds it is possible to discern a progression that is gathering steam through the five references to the tradition:

- Essay 1. There is a brief reference to "The *testimony to Christ* was confirmed among you" (1:6).

- Essay 2. There is a concise reference to "*My ways* in Christ Jesus as I teach *everywhere in every church*" (4:17).

- Essay 3. The reference to the tradition is in the form of a short early creed: "Yet for us there is one God, the Father . . . and one Lord, Jesus Christ . . ." (8:6).

- Essay 4. The tradition is invoked and then quoted in the words of institution: "I commend you because you *remember me in everything and maintain the traditions* even as I have delivered them to you" (11:2). To this are added *the words of institution* (11:23-26).

- Essay 5. This concluding essay opens with further references to the tradition. Paul begins with, "Now I would remind you, brethren, in what terms *I preached to you the gospel, which you received* . . ." (15:1-2). He continues by

---

[4]See 1 Cor 6:11; 7:12-13; 8:1-3a; 8:6; 11:4-5; 13:2b-3; 15:13, 14, 16-17. Each of these texts presents two sets of three.

quoting the formula, "For *I delivered to you* as of first importance *what I also received.*" He then quotes a second early Christian creed (15:3-5).

This gradual expansion of the discussion of "the tradition" is striking. Paul's quiet voice calling his readers to honor the received tradition gradually grows louder as he proceeds.

Paul's "lapel touch" is again evident. The Corinthians were introducing various self-destructive ethical practices and identity-damaging theological stances that were not in harmony with that received tradition. He wanted to call them back to the fixed tradition that gave the church its identity, an identity that in the early fifties of the first century had already taken a recognizable shape. Again, Paul did not start a movement, he joined one. His method was to compliment his readers for their steadfastness in remembering and keeping the tradition, and at the same time slowly present larger and larger sections of that tradition. In essay five, the tradition is the climactic center of the opening homily.

As with previous cases of ring composition, we will look at the series of envelopes Paul places around his center climax, and then examine the center itself. His first (outer) envelope is cameo 1 and cameo 10 [see fig. 5.1(2)].

| | | |
|---|---|---|
| 1. | ¹Now I would remind you, brethren, of *the gospel* which *I preached* to you, which *you received,* | I PREACHED<br>You Received |
| 10. | ¹¹Whether then it was I or they, so *we preached* and so *you believed.* | WE PREACHED<br>You Believed |

**Figure 5.1(2). Cameos 1 and 10 (1 Cor 15:1a, b, 11)**

Paul preached "the gospel" (cameo 1) as did the other apostles (cameo 10). He affirms that his preaching was in harmony with the proclamation of the other apostles and that the Corinthians had heard the same gospel from all of them. This reference to the unity of the apostolic preaching is a theme that ties this final essay to the first essay. These two essays are not only linked through the cross and the resurrection, but also through the unity of the apostolic preaching. The divisions the Corinthians had created were ridiculous (1:10-16). They could not pit "I am of Paul" against "I am of Cephas," because all of the apostles preached the *same gospel*; indeed "we preached and so you believed." In the middle (between 1 and 10) Paul describes himself as unfit to be an apostle, even while working harder than any of them.

But what matters in this outer envelope is that his readers both *received* the gospel (cameo 1) and at the same time *believed* it (cameo 10). The word *receive* was the first half of the rabbinic formula for passing on the fixed tradition. It is a good word and an important word. The tradition needs to be received before it can be passed on. But a deeper level of commitment is affirmed through the use of the word *believed*. I can receive a report and deliver it to others without making a commitment to its content. Paul opens with the first word (cameo 1) and closes with the second (cameo 10). They believed!

The second rhetorical envelope brings together cameos 2 and 9, which also need to be examined as two parts of a whole [see fig. 5.1(3)].

| | | | |
|---|---|---|---|
| 2. | in which you *stand*, | (!) | |
| | ²by which you are *saved*, | (!) | GRACE RECEIVED |
| | *if you hold it fast—* | (?) | In Vain? |
| | *unless you believed in vain.* | (?) | |

---

| | | |
|---|---|---|
| 9. | ¹⁰But by the *grace of God*, | |
| | *I am what I am,* | |
| | and *his grace* toward me was *not in vain.* | GRACE RECEIVED |
| | Rather, *I worked harder than any of them,* | Not in Vain |
| | though it was *not I,* | |
| | but the *grace of God* which was in me. | |

Figure 5.1(3). Cameos 2 and 9 (1 Cor 15:1c-2, 10)

Salvation for Paul had a past, a present and a future. In this text he affirms salvation in the present. They are able to *stand* because of the gospel, and they *are saved* by it. He does not say that they "*were* saved" but they "*are* saved," and thus they (and he) can work out their salvation "with fear and trembling" (Phil 2:12; 1 Cor 2:3) in the midst of the demands and pressures of daily discipleship.

The question "Did they believe in vain?" is of deep concern. That concern is raised in cameo 2 and answered in cameo 9, where Paul reflects on his *response* to the grace given to him. The *grace of God* forms the beginning and the end of cameo 9, and at the end Paul declares that God's grace was *in him*. In the interior pair of matching lines, Paul first affirms, "I am what I am" and then adds, "But it was not I, but the grace of God which was in me." His deepest identity was not formed by being "of the people of Israel" or "under the law blameless" (Phil 3:5-6). He was who he was because of "the grace of God," which was in him.

That grace, he affirms, "*was not in vain.*" The words *in vain* (*kenoo* and *kenos*) have to do with being "empty" and "without effect."[5] Paul's confidence was rooted in his awareness that God's grace was a dynamic force in his life. "I worked harder than any of them," he affirms. He had gone beyond and above the call of duty (9:1-18). Faith that is "in vain" is the faith that does not trigger a response of obedience. Indeed, faith does include intellectual assent to a particular vision of reality, but it is also *something we do.*

The woman in Luke 7:36-50 never speaks. Throughout the story she is quiet. Yet at the end of the narrative Jesus tells her, "Your faith has saved you." Her dramatic actions reflected and demonstrated her deep faith. The outcome of faith is "the obedience of faith" (Rom 1:5; 16:26). Paul's confidence was not grounded in his successes but in his faithful obedience.

The third "folder" (cameos 3 and 8) is best examined along with the climactic center. These six cameos are displayed in figure 5.1(4).

| | | |
|---|---|---|
| 3. | [3]For *I delivered* to you as of first importance *what I also received,* | AN APOSTLE<br>Delivers Tradition |
| 4. | a. "*Christ died for our sins,*<br>    in accordance with the *scriptures,*"<br>b.    [4]"he was *buried,*" | HE DIED<br>He Was Buried |
| 5. | c. "he was *raised on the third day*<br>    in accordance with the scriptures,"<br>d.    [5]"he *appeared* to *Cephas,*<br>    then to *the twelve.*" | HE WAS RAISED<br>He Appeared to Cephas<br>And the Twelve |
| 6. | [6]Then he appeared to more than<br>*five hundred brethren* at one time,<br>most of whom are still alive,<br>though some have fallen asleep. | 500 SAW HIM<br>Some Still Alive |
| 7. | [7]Then he appeared to *James,*<br>then to all the apostles.<br>[8]Last of all, as to one untimely born,<br>he *appeared also to me.* | JAMES SAW HIM<br>Plus Apostles<br>Plus Paul |
| 8. | [9]For I am the *least of the apostles,*<br>*unfit* to be called an *apostle,*<br>because I persecuted the church of God. | AN APOSTLE<br>Unfit Persecutor |

**Figure 5.1(4). Cameos 3-8 (1 Cor 15:3-9)**

[5]BAGD, p. 427.

Cameos 3 and 8 have to do with apostleship. An apostle was "one sent" (with a message). Paul ably fulfilled the primary sacred task of an apostle. He *delivered* what he had *received* (cameo 3). At the same time he felt himself to be the least of all of the apostles because he "persecuted the church of God" (cameo 8).

This confession that he was "unfit to be called an apostle" comes on the heels of his aggressive defense of his apostleship in 9:1-12, where he wrote, almost defiantly, "Am I not an apostle? Have I not seen Jesus our Lord?" Paul is like a man who pounds the table with his fist shouting, "These are my rights," and then takes a deep breath, leans back and quietly adds, "But I am unworthy of them." His deep faith and innocent transparency emerge as he writes, and through these lenses we discover his humility.

The four-stanza center forms the climax of the homily. The first two cameos are best understood as an early Christian creed. In cameo 4 Paul opens with the Greek word *hoti* which can be read to mean "that" (introducing indirect speech) or as a set of quotation marks (introducing direct speech).[6] In English it is easy to see the difference between the two following sentences:

I said that I will finish this manuscript.
I said, "I will finish this manuscript."

The reader can easily spot the difference between these two sentences thanks to the quotation marks. But first-century Greek had no quotation marks. In Koine Greek, the above two sentences would appear exactly the same on paper. The result is that when faced with the word *hoti* in a New Testament text, the translator has to decide between indirect and direct speech. In the text before us the word *hoti* appears four times in a row. It is grammatically and historically legitimate to read these four as four quotations from the tradition that Paul received, which he here passes on to the Corinthians. They describe two events and fall into four sentences that together include six phrases. The six phrases exhibit the following step parallelism:

1. The event:          "*Christ died* for our sins
2. Its sacred roots:       in accordance with the scriptures."
3. Its historical proof:    "He was *buried*."

4. The event:          "He was *raised on the third day*
5. Its sacred roots:       in accordance with the scriptures,"
6. Its historical proof:    "he *appeared* to Cephas, then to the twelve."

---

[6]BAGD, pp. 588-89.

The fourfold use of the Greek word *hoti* and the step parallelism mark these six lines as a completed unit unto themselves. Regarding this text, N. T. Wright has written,

> This is the kind of foundation-story with which a community is not at liberty to tamper. It was probably formulated within the first two or three years after Easter itself, since it was already in formulaic form when Paul "received" it. We are here in touch with the earliest Christian tradition, with something that was being said two decades or more before Paul wrote this letter.[7]

The six lines need to be examined as a whole. Fear and trembling seem both appropriate and inevitable as one approaches this early theological diamond that reflects light in so many directions. Several points can be made:

1. The central focus of this creed is the doctrine of the atonement which is at the heart of the Christian faith. In 15:14-16 Paul affirms that without the resurrection, their faith is in vain and they are *still in their sins*. It is also unmistakable that the cross and the resurrection are linked. N. T. Wright is helpful when he writes, "Without the resurrection, there is no reason to suppose that Jesus' crucifixion dealt with sins, or with sin. But with the resurrection, the divine victory over sin(s), and hence over death, is assured."[8]

2. With the above in mind we are still obliged to ask, Why did the church, at this very early stage, conclude that the death of Jesus was different from the death of John the Baptist? The death of John (Mk 6:14-29) involved the following significant features:

- A proclaimer of the gospel made powerful enemies because of his proclamation.

- That proclaimer was unjustly imprisoned.

- A ruler admired the prisoner but was too weak to act on his scruples.

- That ruler acted to protect his own interests and ignored the demands of justice.

- Intrigue and power politics were involved.

- The wife of the ruler was also involved.

- Jewish law and the keeping of that law were at issue.

---

[7]Wright, *Resurrection*, p. 319; see Hays, *First Corinthians*, pp. 257-58.
[8]Wright, *Resurrection*, p. 320.

- An innocent man was brutally murdered (justice was violated).
- The ruler ordered the murder to please someone else.
- Soldiers were given the gruesome task.
- Disciples of the victim took the body and buried it.
- Resurrection was supposed by Herod, but nothing came of it.[9]

All of these features of John's murder were repeated when Jesus was executed with the exception of the last. Herod surmised that Jesus was John, who had been raised from the dead (Mk 6:14), but he was mistaken, and no one saw John alive after his murder. Jesus, however, appeared to the disciples after the cross, and that made all the difference. The fact of the resurrection brought unmistakable victory over sin and death. Their studied conclusion was, "Christ died *for our sins.*"

3. For the disciples it was not merely Rabbi Jesus who died but rather the *Messiah of God*, hence the confession, "Messiah [Christ] died for our sins."

4. Furthermore, this death "for our sins" and his resurrection were both events in history that took place "according to the scriptures." Isaiah 52:13–53:12 is often cited in this connection. With N .T. Wright, it is also appropriate to see the cross and resurrection as the culmination of Israel's history. The "return" that mattered was not the return to Jerusalem but the return to God, as is evident from the second of the servant songs in Isaiah 49:5. In that text the servant is formed in the womb "to bring Jacob back *to him*, and that Israel might be gathered *to him.*" The reader expects to read that the servant's task is to bring "Jacob back *to Jerusalem*, and that Israel might be gathered *to Judea.*" But the return is *to God.* Even so, in the death and resurrection of Jesus, the prophetic vision of salvation comes to its climax with victory over sin and death, not over the occupying forces of Rome. Isaiah 40:1-11, Jeremiah 31:31-34 and Ezekiel 36:22-32 have come to the minds of many. As regards the resurrection, Hosea 6:2 is often quoted.

5. Evidence for the historicity of both the cross and the resurrection are included in this brief creed. How do we know he died? Answer: He was buried. How do we know that he arose? Answer: He was seen by Peter and the Twelve. The fact of the resurrection was, from the beginning, on the edge of being unbelievable to many. The church was thus keen to affirm that there were witnesses to both of these historical events.

---

[9]Kenneth E. Bailey, *Jesus Through Middle Eastern Eyes* (Downers Grove, Ill.: IVP Academic, 2008), p. 228.

6. Paul is not the author of this creed. This is obvious for a number of reasons. First, the term *the Twelve* is common in the Gospels but appears only here in the writings of Paul. Second, Paul's widely used formula for quoting the Old Testament is "It is written." He never says, "in accordance with the scriptures." Third, Paul describes sin in the singular and understands it to be a power that holds people in bondage, not a series of individual acts. The use of the plural "sins" is a further indication that Paul did not write this creed. These three features (along with the fourfold use of *hoti*) are strong indications that Paul is quoting a text he did not compose. In short, Paul did not create the idea that Christ died for our sins; instead he confessed this early creed which came to him from the Christian tradition.

7. The issue is "our sins" not "my sins." Christians pray to "our Father" not to "my Father," and in this creed the community confesses its corporate sin. P. T. Forsyth affirms that reconciliation with God through the cross is not merely "the moving and attuning of individual men [and women] in their subjective experience."[10] He died for "our sins." God so loved "the world" that he gave his only son (Jn 3:16).

8. In the Gospels the primary witnesses to the resurrection are women. Here in 15:1-12 the women are missing. It is impossible to imagine that the witnesses were originally all men and that some time later the Gospel authors fabricated female witnesses. On the other hand, in a male-dominated society it is possible that the earliest church was concerned that if it rested the greater weight of its case for the resurrection on the testimony of women, such a witness might be dismissed by many listeners. In their *creed* they thus listed "Cephas" and "the twelve" as the primary witnesses to the resurrection (quietly leaving the women's names aside). They were describing a historical event, not a dream or a mystic vision, and they wanted to assure that their witness would be taken seriously by as many as possible (including those who would have dismissed the witness of women).

9. It is impossible to deal with this text without noting the work of the medieval theologian Anselm (b. A.D. 1033), who developed the widely influential substitutionary theory of the atonement. For Anselm "Christ died for our sins" meant that Christ was a substitute for sinful humankind. One of the major difficulties with this theory is that it has allowed the word *for* to take on commercial overtones. Someone can say, "I paid $15,000 *for* the car," meaning, I wrote a check and the car dealer gave me the car. In like manner, Christ

---

[10]P. T. Forsyth, *The Work of Christ* (London: Independent Press, 1958), p. 100.

died *for* our sins has a tendency to mean, A price for sin had to be paid. X amount of sin required X amount of suffering, and "Jesus paid it all." He endured the suffering required to pay the debt incurred by sin. Yes, Paul wrote, "You are not your own, you were bought with a price" (6:19). Such language is indeed *a part* of the larger mystery of the meaning of the cross. But that must fit into a larger whole as we contemplate the cross. Is such language adequate to understand the early Christian creed before us?

As a young man it came to me as a great theological shock when I discovered that Anselm developed this theory in the eleventh century. Assuming that the substitutionary theory of the atonement was the only possible option for understanding the cross, I naively wondered, *How then did Christians for the first millennium become believers when they did not have the substitutionary theory of the atonement to help them understand the cross?* The simple answer is, the early Christians did not need Anselm. They could ponder the good shepherd who lay down his life for the sheep (Jn 10:11-15) fighting the wolf. The good shepherd (Lk 15:4-7) acted out of his love for the lost sheep, went after it and struggled home with the animal over his shoulders. He did not say to himself, "The lost sheep has wandered five miles off the beaten track, so I must hike five miles across the open wilderness to pay for the sheep's mistakes." The focus is on the *rescue*, not the *penalty*.

The father in the parable of the prodigal son thought only of his love for his son when he humiliated himself in public by running down the crowded village street to reconcile his son before the son reached the hostile village.[11] As he ran he was offering a *costly demonstration of unexpected love.* He was not paying a debt. Granted, the prodigal would have been roughed up by the people in the village, and the father was running the gauntlet for him. But this is not a commercial exchange of, "So much sin requires so much suffering." Instead it is an outpouring of *costly* love made in the hope of achieving reconciliation.[12]

In Luke 15, along with other parables and dramatic actions, Jesus was indeed interpreting his own cross. The father in the parable was able to *reprocess*

---

[11]See Kenneth E. Bailey, *The Cross and the Prodigal* (Downers Grove, Ill.: InterVarsity Press, 2005); Kenneth E. Bailey, *Jacob and the Prodigal* (Downers Grove, Ill.: InterVarsity Press, 2003), pp. 95-117.

[12]In a thoughtful study, George Carey presents the entire sweep of the history of the doctrine of the atonement. He argues convincingly for a limited view of substitution as a part of the overall doctrine of the atonement. See George Carey, *The Gate of Glory* (Grand Rapids: Eerdmans, 1993), pp. 139-49.

*anger into grace* and offer a *costly demonstration of unexpected love* to his yet self-confident son. The son planned to "work and pay" for his sins. He thought the issue was the lost money, and surmised that if he could get job training he would one day be able to pay back everything that he had squandered. It was only when he saw the depth of his father's suffering love that he understood the depth of his sin, and only then could he *accept to be found* and restored by an act of pure grace.[13]

"Christ died because of our sins" is the preferred (legitimate) Arabic translation of this text. Our sins caused his death. The grave danger in much popular reflection on the atonement relates to the introduction of a third party. The theory, in its simplest form, is as follows: God is angry over sin, and he could justly punish us. But Jesus enters the picture and takes the punishment for us. So far, so good. In this sense Jesus is *rightly understood as a substitute* for us. But is Jesus a third party? Is God the Father a separate God from God the Son?

To affirm for this view is to create a strong whiff of Zoroastrianism, where there is a good god (Ahura Mazdah), and an evil god (Ahriman), a god of light and a god of darkness. The believer's task is to serve the good god, who protects us from the evil god. But not so the New Testament. Paul writes, "*God shows his love for us* in that while we were yet sinners *Christ died for us*" (Rom 5:8). He also wrote, "*God* was in Christ reconciling the world *to himself*, not counting their trespasses against them" (2 Cor 5:19). There is no third party. *God* is the one who acts *in Christ* out of love to reconcile us to *himself*. There is no split in the heart of God, with God the Father opposing God the Son.

I have created a parable to try to shed light on this great mystery. I know that this parable, as with all parables, has weaknesses. Like Thomas Friedman I am willing through the use of metaphor/parable to "trade a certain degree of academic precision for a much larger degree of explanatory power."[14] The parable (with some notes) is as follows:

A mother (who has a young son named Johnny) is preparing to host a social gathering for some of her friends. In her kitchen-dining room she spreads a tablecloth over the table and places a large glass pitcher of lemonade on top of it. She then tells her son, "Johnny, don't pull on the tablecloth, because if you do the pitcher will fall on you and you will get hurt." She turns to the kitchen sink to continue her preparations. As soon as her back is turned, Johnny grabs

---

[13]See Kenneth E. Bailey, "Jesus Interprets His Own Cross," DVD, www.cdbaby.com/cd/revdrbailey (13 half-hour lectures).

[14]Thomas Friedman, *The World Is Flat* (New York: Farrar, Straus & Giroux, 2007), p. x.

the tablecloth and starts pulling. Mom looks over her shoulder and to her dismay sees Johnny pulling on the tablecloth and the pitcher of lemonade just about to crash down on his unprotected head. Mom experiences a flash of deep disappointment and anger as she says to herself, *If Johnny had only listened to me, we wouldn't have this problem!*

[Note: The story has three possible endings.]

*Ending 1.* Mom is mad. Her anger drives her to rush across the room, grab the pitcher of lemonade and say: "Johnny, I told you *not* to pull on the table-cloth. Now you take this . . ." [*She dumps the lemonade on Johnny's head.*]

[Note: This is a familiar mindset. God gives the law. Humankind is told to obey and is warned that disobedience brings penalties. When humankind breaks the law, punishment results.]

*Ending 2.* A third actor in the drama is introduced. This is Billy, Johnny's older brother. Billy is in the next room working on his homework. Mom is again mad. She rushes across the room, grabs the pitcher and in anger says to Johnny, "Johnny, I should dump this on you because you deserve it for dis-obeying. But if I do, you will catch your death of cold."

In a loud voice she shouts over her shoulder, "Billy!"

Billy enters the room, and Mom dumps the lemonade on Billy and then says to Johnny, "See what you made me do!"

Feeling very guilty, Johnny crawls under the table and starts crying.

[Note: This is the third-party version of the substitutionary theory of the atonement.]

Ending 3: Mom notices that the pitcher of lemonade is about to fall on John-ny's head. Her anger at his disobedience does not lessen the intensity of her love for him. She reprocesses that anger into grace and rushes across the room. Just as she reaches the table, the pitcher begins to fall and she quickly knocks it aside. The pitcher shatters, and Mom sustains a deep cut in her arm. Her arm begins to bleed profusely. She quickly grabs the towel that is across her shoulder and winds it tightly around her arm. Blood continues to soak through the towel and drip onto the floor. Terrified, Johnny begins to cry.

Mom does *not* say: "Don't cry Johnny! *Don't be afraid.* I am not going to spank you. I am going to spank Billy instead."

Such a speech would do no good. Johnny is not crying because he is afraid he will get spanked. Thereby he will not be relieved or pleased if Mom tells him she will spank Billy. Johnny is crying because *he sees Mom getting hurt for him and he knows that it is his fault!*

In this third ending *there is no Billy in the next room*. Mom reaches out to the frightened Johnny, embraces him and says quietly, "It's all right Johnny. I love you anyway and I forgive you. It's all right Johnny—in three days I will be able to take off this ugly bandage. My arm will heal."

In Mom's all-encompassing embrace, and with the sound of Mom's offer of forgiveness penetrating his consciousness, Johnny's guilt melts away and with it his will to disobey her. He knows that *Mom got hurt for him—and she still loves him*. There is no third party. Mom *gets hurt for Johnny*, but there is no Billy in the next room. Johnny's disobedience makes it inevitable that someone will get hurt. Mom chooses to endure that suffering in place of Johnny, but her focus is on *redemption*, not *penalty*.

Johnny now realizes that Mom's initial admonition to leave the tablecloth alone was not an arbitrary exercise of will. There was no "You do what I say, because I say so!" Mom's will was an exercise of love for Johnny. Given the realities of glass pitchers, tables, little boys and the force of gravity, Mom's "law" was an expression of her love. Johnny only discovers the depth of that love when he sees Mom knock the pitcher aside and sustain a cut in her arm— for him! Witnessing that *costly* love *changes Johnny*.

Paul quotes the tradition, "Christ died *for our sins*." Interpreting that tradition he wrote, "God was in Christ reconciling the world *to himself*" (2 Cor 5:19). There is no third party.

Theologian Miroslav Volf has written,

> Let us beware that some accounts of what it means for Christ to have died on behalf of the ungodly—what theologians sometimes call his "substitutionary" death—are deeply problematic. If we view Christ on the cross as a third party being punished for the sins of transgressors, we have widely missed the mark. For unlike a financial debt, moral liability is nontransferable. But Christ is not a third party. On account of his divinity, Christ is one with God to whom the "debt" is owed. It is therefore *God* who through Christ's death shoulders the burden of our transgressions against God and frees us from just retribution. But since on account of Christ's humanity he is also one with us, the debtors, it is *we* who die in Christ and are thus freed from guilt. Christ's oneness with both creditor and debtors leaves only two categories of "actors" and thus negates the notion of his involvement as a third party.[15]

---

[15]Miroslav Volf, *The End of Memory: Remembering Rightly in a Violent World* (Grand Rapids: Eerdmans, 2006), p. 117.

William Temple points out that the New Testament always starts with the love of God, not his wrath. He writes,

> The slave has his orders and is punished if he disobeys; his only feeling when he has done wrong is fear. The son knows his father's love, and calls upon him by the name of endearment. So the forgiveness that Christ wins for us is not chiefly a remission of penalty; it is the restoration to the affectionate intimacy of sons with their Father. And it is for this that the Father longs.[16]

God is angry at sin, but, as Temple argues,

> [God's anger] is not anger, if by anger we mean the emotional reaction of an offended self-concern; it is anger, if by anger we mean the resolute and relentless opposition of a will set on righteousness against a will directed elsewhere. God must abolish all sinners; but He seeks to abolish sinners by winning them out of their sin into the loyalty and love of children in their Father's home. . . . It is only through preoccupation with thoughts of punishment that people have come to invent doctrines of transferred penalty. . . . The Atonement is accomplished by the drawing of sinful souls into conformity with the divine Will.[17]

Suffering is the divine choice in which we participate. Temple writes,

> There are two ways of expressing antagonism to sin; one is to inflict suffering on the sinner, the other is to endure suffering. . . . For St. Paul union with Christ is something so complete and intimate that whatever may be said to have befallen Him has befallen the disciples also.[18]

The issue is the reform of the sinner. Temple concludes,

> Fear of punishment might deter me from sinful action, but it could not change my sinful desires. . . . But to realize what my selfishness means to the Father who loves me with a love such as Christ reveals, fills me with horror of the selfishness and calls out an answering love. . . . We plead His Passion, not as a transferred penalty, but as an act of self-sacrifice which re-makes us in its own likeness.[19]

"Christ died for our sins," and "Mom got hurt for Johnny." Johnny can never be the same again; neither can we.

Paul continues by adding other witnesses to the resurrection. At the conclusion to his centerpiece, he lists himself. The creed has four principle affirmations, to which Paul adds four additional witnesses to the resurrection.

---

[16]William Temple, *Christus Veritas* (London: Macmillan, 1954), p. 258.
[17]Ibid., p. 259.
[18]Ibid., p. 261.
[19]Ibid., pp. 263-64.

## THE RESURRECTION AND THE VALIDITY OF THE FAITH (1 COR 15:12-20)

Having set out the creed with its affirmation of the resurrection (with witnesses) and having included himself among them, Paul presents a second homily that focuses on the critical nature of the resurrection. The text, a rhetorical masterpiece, is displayed in figure 5.1(5).

| | | |
|---|---|---|
| 1. | [15:12]And if *Christ is preached* <br> as *raised* from the *dead,* | CHRIST IS RAISED (+) <br> From the Dead |
| 2. | *how* can some of *you say* <br> "There is *no resurrection* of the dead"? | YOUR VIEW: <br> No Resurrection (-) |
| 3. | a.[13]And *if* there is *no resurrection* of the dead, <br> b. then *Christ* has *not been raised;* <br> c. [14]and *if Christ* has *not been raised,* <br> d. then *our preaching* is *empty* <br> e. and *your faith is empty.* | NO RESURRECTION (-) <br> Christ Not Raised <br> Preaching—Empty <br> Faith—Empty |
| 4. | [15]We are even found to be *misrepresenting God,* <br> because *we witness of God,* <br> "He *raised the Messiah,"* <br> whom *he did not raise* <br> *if it is true* that the *dead are not raised.* | WE—LYING (-) <br> Our Witness (+) <br> CHRIST IS RAISED <br> Not Raised (-) <br> No Resurrection (-) |
| 5. | a.[16]For *if* the *dead are not raised,* <br> b. then *Christ* has *not been raised.* <br> c.[17]And if *Christ has not been raised,* <br> d. your *faith is futile* <br> e. and *you* are *still in your sins.* | NO RESURRECTION (-) <br> Christ Not Raised <br> Faith—Futile <br> Salvation—None |
| 6. | [18]Then *those asleep* in Christ *have perished.* <br> [19]*If in this life* in Christ we have *hope only,* <br> we are of *all men most* to be *pitied.* | RESULT OF <br> Your View (-) <br> We Are Most Pitied |
| 7. | [20]But now *Christ has been raised from the dead,* <br> the *first fruits* of those *asleep.* | CHRIST IS RAISED (+) <br> First Fruits |

**Figure 5.1(5). The resurrection and the validity of the faith (1 Cor 15:12-20)**

### THE RHETORIC

This is yet another case of the prophetic rhetorical template of seven inverted stanzas with a climax in the center. In this case the beginning (cameo 1), the end (cameo 7) and the very middle (cameo 4) are *positives*. The other four stanzas are entirely *negative*.

Another striking feature of this homily is the chain-link connection that ties many of the cameos together. Cameo 2 closes with "no resurrection." Cameo 3 opens with "if there is no resurrection." Cameo 4 is linked to 5 in the same way and 5 is similarly linked to cameo 6. Extensive use of chain-link composition occurs only here in 1 Corinthians.[20]

The step parallelism that connects cameos 3 and 5 is also a prominent feature of this homily. Each of the five lines in 3 are matched by the five lines in 5. This step parallelism connecting two cameos within a prophetic rhetorical template is the precise pattern that appears in Isaiah 28:11-17[21] analyzed earlier.

The four outer cameos are so carefully matched that if the three cameos in the center were missing the reader would not notice their absence. The climax appears in the middle (as usual) with the bold affirmation, "We witness of God, 'He raised the Messiah.'"

## COMMENTARY

In this the final essay, Paul composes a joyful hymn to the resurrection that echoes and answers the hymn to the cross in 1:17–2:2. The hymn to the cross and the hymn to the resurrection are constructed as follows:

- *The hymn to the cross* (1:17–2:2)

    Opening (1):  I preach the cross of Christ.

                ( - negatives that deny that message)

    Middle (7):  We preach Christ crucified.

                ( - negatives that deny that message)

    End (13):  I proclaim . . . Jesus Christ and him crucified.

- The echoing *hymn to the resurrection* (15:12-20)

    Opening (1):  Christ is preached as raised from the dead.

                ( - negatives that deny that message)

    Middle (4):  We witness of God, "He raised the Messiah."

                ( - negatives that deny that message)

    End (7):  But now, Christ has been raised from the dead.

The hymn to the cross is composed of thirteen cameos and the hymn to the resurrection has only seven. Yet, both the cameos placed between the opening and the middle, and again between the middle and the end, are predominantly negative. Paul assumes that his thoughtful readers will be able to mentally follow the above parallels. Paul offers his readers history, theology, ethics

---

[20]Some of this type of chain-link composition appears in 11:28-32, as noted in the discussion.

[21]See figure 0.1(4) in "Prelude: Prophetic Homily Rhetorical Style and Its Interpretation."

and *art*. With this kind of artistry Paul ties together the first essay (on the cross) to the fifth essay (on the resurrection).[22] A Bach specialist is thrilled as he or she listens to the counterpoint in a great Bach fugue. That kind of thrill can also be ours as we listen to Paul's "music."

The Corinthians were theologically confused. Some of them were denying the resurrection (cameo 2). Using blunt language Paul makes uncompromisingly clear what is at stake. If there is no resurrection, their preaching is empty, they are lying about God, their faith is empty, there is no salvation and they are trapped in their sins (cameos 3-5). Furthermore, those who had died would have perished, and believers still alive would be without hope and of all people they would be the most pitiful (cameo 6).

This is another case where the third-party substitutionary theory of the atonement, with its focus on *penalty*, can lead astray. Imagine a scenario in which God takes Jesus to heaven seconds after the great cry, "It is finished." Had that happened, would there be any salvation for believers? If the focus is on *penalty*, then of course there is salvation, because "Jesus paid it all." Did he not cry out, "It is finished"? Does that not mean that the great work of salvation is completed? Not for Paul. For him, *without the resurrection* all faith is futile and believers are still in their sins. As noted, the *central* focus is *rescue*, not *penalty*. *Without the resurrection* the death of Jesus is like the death of John the Baptist. If there is no resurrection, Jesus is one more rabbi who tried to renew Israel and failed. In such a case Peter, James, Andrew and John would have returned to their boats, taken up their nets and lived out their lives in their village.[23]

The resurrection affirms that sin and death do not have the last word. At the cross the finest religion of the ancient world (Judaism), and the finest system of justice of the ancient world (Rome), joined to torture this good man to death. These were not evil forces. They were the best institutions the ancient world had to offer, *and yet* together they produced the cross. But that was not the end. After the cross came the victory of the resurrection. After the cross, no form of evil surprises us, no institutionalized brutality amazes us, because *we have been to the cross* and we know that beyond it is the resurrection. We have stood at the cross (the first essay) and have witnessed the empty tomb (the final essay)!

---

[22]In each case the hymn to the cross (1:17–2:2) and the hymn to the resurrection (15:12-20) appear as the second homily in their respective essays.
[23]For a detailed scholarly discussion of this chapter, see Wright, *Resurrection*, pp. 312-61.

The creed examined above (15:3-5) presents the cross and the resurrection as two sides of a single coin. The message of the gospel affirms "he raised the Messiah" (cameo 4) and the Messiah is "the first fruits of those asleep." Because he lives, we too shall live because of those first fruits (cameo 7).

This rhetorical and theological gem concludes the first section of Paul's presentation of the resurrection. The second concentrates on the first and the second Adam.

# Resurrection

*Adam and Christ—The End of All Things*

I CORINTHIANS 15:21-28

H AVING AFFIRMED THE CREED (15:1-11) and having stressed that without the resurrection all Christian faith is empty (15:12-20), Paul is ready to talk about *the broad sweep of history* and the *resurrection*. He does this in his first presentation of Christ and Adam [see fig. 5.2(1)].

**THE RHETORIC**

This homily also exhibits seven cameos. But in this instance Paul has fit the seven cameos into the "high jump format." The homily opens with two cameos for the approach, followed by two cameos for the jump. The climax (as always) is the crossing of the bar (the center), to which Paul adds a two-cameo descent on the far side. This format appears a total of twelve times in 1 Corinthians[1] and is one of Paul's favorite styles, which he uses with imagination and creativity.

The center is again filled with an Old Testament quotation, a feature that appears seven times in the epistle.[2] All seven of them are constructed using the high jump format.

---

[1] 1 Cor 2:3-10; 3:1-17; 6:13-20; 9:1-12; 9:12b-18 (modified); 10:1-13; 10:23–11:1; 11:2-17; 12:31–14:1 (modified); 14:13-25; 15:21-34; 15:35-40 (modified).

[2] 1 Cor 6:13-20; 9:1-12a; 10:1-13; 14:13-25; 15:1-11; 15:21-28; 15:35-50.

1. 15:21For as by a *man* came *death,*
    *by a man has come* also the *resurrection of the dead.*    ADAM AND
    22For as *in Adam all die,*    Christ
    so also *in Christ shall all be made alive.*

2.   23But each in his own order:
    *Christ* the *first fruits,*    CHRIST—FIRST
    24then at his *coming*    Then Those in Christ
    those who *belong to Christ.*

3.   Then comes *the end,*
    when *he delivers the kingdom* to *God the Father*    THE END—ALL
    after *destroying every rule*    To God the Father
    and every authority and power.

4.   25For he must reign until he has put    ALL ENEMIES
    all his *enemies under his feet.*    Under His Feet

5.   26The last enemy to be destroyed is *death.*    DEATH AND ALL
    27"For God has put *all* things *in subjection*    In Subjection
    *under his feet.*" [Ps 8:6]    Under His Feet

6.   But when it says,
    "*All things* are put in *subjection under him,*"    ALL THINGS
    it is plain that *he* is *excepted*    In Subjection
    who put all things under him.    Except: The Father

7.   28When *all things* are *subjected to him,*
    then the *Son himself* will also *be subjected*    THE END—ALL
    to *him who* put all things under him,    To the God/Father
    that *God* may be all in all.[3]

---

**Figure 5.2(1). Resurrection: Christ and Adam—The end of all things (1 Cor 15:21-28)**

## COMMENTARY

As he did in 3:21-23, Paul steps back to take a long view from the creation of Adam to the end of all things. It is a breathtaking vista that begins with cameo 1.

1. 15:21For as by a *man* came *death,*
    *by a man has come* also the *resurrection of the dead.*    ADAM AND
    22For as *in Adam all die,*    Christ
    so also *in Christ shall all be made alive.*[4]

---

[3]KJV, NRSV.
[4]Garland came to the same conclusion regarding the parallelism of these four lines. See Garland, *1 Corinthians,* p. 706.

Adam brought death and "in Adam all die." Two things are said about Adam and two about Christ:

- What happened: Adam brought death.
  Result: In Adam all die.

- What happened: Christ's resurrection.
  Result: In Christ all are made alive.

It is significant that Eve is not mentioned. Ben Sirach blames Eve for everything when he says, "Sin began with a woman, and thanks to her we all must die" (Sir 25:24). Like Paul, Ben Sirach's statement falls into two parts:

- What happened: Sin began with a woman.
  Result: Thanks to her, we all must die.

Paul does not follow Ben Sirach's lead, even though it was in the Jewish tradition. Yes, in 2 Corinthians 11:3 Paul notes in passing that Eve was deceived, but he does not blame her for introducing death.[5] In harmony with Romans 5:12-21 Paul places the blame squarely on Adam. One man (Adam) was responsible for bringing death into the world, and one man (Christ) brings life. This choice to blame Adam, and not Eve, is significant in any evaluation of Paul's attitudes toward women and men in the church.

Paul is talking about "those who belong to Christ." This is evident from verse 23 where that language is used. Cameo 1 is explained by Augustine as meaning, "No one comes to death except through Adam, and no one comes to life except through Christ."[6]

Cameo 2 continues the discussion.

2.　　　²³But each in his own order:
　　　　*Christ* the *first fruits,*　　　　CHRIST—FIRST
　　　²⁴then at his *coming*　　　　Then Those in Christ
　　　　those who *belong to Christ.*

The word "order" (*tagma*) is a military term that has to do with a corps or rank of troops.[7] A military image is again selected by Paul to communicate to a colony originally settled by retired soldiers. The first rank is the resurrected Christ, who is the "first fruits." The second rank, made up of "those who be-

---

[5]1 Tim 2:14 is a different problem. There the text claims that Adam was not deceived but Eve was.
[6]Augustine, quoted in *1 Corinthians: Interpreted by Early Christian Commentators*, trans. and ed. Judith L. Kovacs (Eerdmans: Grand Rapids, 2005), p. 351. See also Thiselton, *First Epistle,* p. 1227-28.; Robertson/Plummer, *First Epistle,* p. 353; Findlay, *First Epistle,* p. 926.
[7]Thiselton, *First Epistle,* p. 1229.

long to Christ," join the military parade at his coming. Paul is projecting ahead from the resurrection of Jesus to the end of all things.

There is no third rank. What about unbelievers? The text gives no answer. Findlay writes, "There is nothing to exclude O.T. saints (see x. 4; Heb. xi. 26, 40, John i. 11), nor even the righteous heathen (Acts x. 35, Matt. xxv. 32, 34, John x. 16), from the *tagma* (rank) of 'those who are Christ's.'"[8] Barrett leaves the question unanswered as he says, "nothing is said about the future life of those who are not Christians, and with this silence we must be content."[9]

The *parousia* (coming) is part of the discussion. In A.D. 66 Nero visited Corinth. The visit of an emperor or even a high official was called an *adventus*, which was the Latin equivalent to the Greek word *parousia*. For Nero's visit a special coin was struck inscribed with *Adventus Aug(usti) Cor(inthi)*. The other side of the coin read *Adventus Augusti*.[10] A great many such coins commemorating Hadrian's various visits have been recovered in Corinth. Such days were at times called "holy days," and Deissmann notes that some affirmed, "in Greece a new era was begun with the first visit of the Emperor Hadrian in the year 124."[11] The pomp and circumstance must have been extraordinary. The god was coming on a visit! What could be more worthy of worship and praise? Writing to a Roman colony, Paul invokes all adoration and honor for the *adventus* of the resurrected Christ.

With this grand setting Paul presents the five cameos that compose the high jump. Close examination of the parallel cameos is necessary in order to follow Paul's mindset as he uses this high jump format. Cameos 3 and 7 are the outside pair [see fig. 5.2(2)].

| | | |
|---|---|---|
| 3. | [24b]Then comes *the end*, | |
| | when *he delivers the kingdom* to *God the Father* | THE END—ALL |
| | after *destroying every rule* | To God the Father |
| | and every authority and power. | |

---

| | | |
|---|---|---|
| 7. | [28]When *all things* are *subjected to him*, | |
| | then the *Son himself* will also *be subjected* | THE END—ALL |
| | to *him who* put all things under him, | To the God the Father |
| | that *God* may be all in all. | |

**Figure 5.2(2). Cameos 3 and 7 (1 Cor 15:24b, 28)**

---

[8]Findlay, *First Epistle*, p. 927.
[9]Barrett, *First Epistle*, p. 355.
[10]Adolf Deissmann, *Light from the Ancient East* (Grand Rapids: Baker, 1980, c. 1909), p. 371.
[11]Ibid., pp. 371-72.

Cameo 3 mentions "every *arkhen* [rule] and every *exousian* [authority] and every *dunamin* [power]." These are not rare words that refer exclusively to secret societies or esoteric myths, Jewish or Greek. They are standard words used for governments and earthly rulers. When Paul writes the epistle to the Romans and discusses obedience to the Roman state (Rom 13:1-7), he refers to the authorities with the words *arkhontes* (rulers) and *exousia* (authority).

As observed, in 44 b.c. when the rebuilding of Corinth began, each of the retired soldiers settled there received a home and a piece of land from the Roman state. It is natural to assume that they and their descendants were solid supporters of their benefactor. When Paul wrote, "We have one Lord, Jesus Christ" (8:6), he was not only confessing his faith, he was also making a political statement. If Jesus is *kurios* (Lord), then Caesar isn't. In like manner, here in verse 24, even though Paul was writing about the climactic end of the age, he was at the same time de-absolutizing the rulers, authorities and powers around him. It was dangerous to even think let alone proclaim such things anywhere in the Roman Empire. But to write this kind of subversive literature and send it to the largest Roman city outside Rome was *extremely* risky. The apostle as much as announces that one of the goals of the resurrected Christ was the setting aside of eternal Rome. Paul was intimidated by no one, and by committing his vision to writing he surrendered control over who would discover these views.

As in previous homilies in this epistle, if these two cameos were side by side in the text and if cameos 4-6 were missing, no reader would observe any break in the flow of the argument. The Son delivers the kingdom to "God the Father" (cameo 3) and then subjects himself to the Father so that at the end God will be "all in all" (cameo 7). Paul's Christology never slides into tritheism. But this is not the totality of what Paul has to say. Three other cameos appear in the middle of the five cameos [see fig. 5.2(3)].

| | | |
|---|---|---|
| 4. | [25]For he must reign until he has put <br> All his *enemies under his feet.* | ALL ENEMIES <br> Under His Feet |
| 5. | [26]The last enemy to be destroyed is *death.* <br> [27]"For God has put *all* things *in subjection* <br> *under his feet.*" [Ps 8:6] | DEATH AND ALL <br> In Subjection <br> Under His Feet |
| 6. | But when it says, <br> "*All things* are put in *subjection under him*," <br> it is plain that *he* is *excepted* <br> who put all things under him. | ALL THINGS <br> In Subjection <br> Except: The Father |

**Figure 5.2(3). Cameos 4-6 (1 Cor 15:25-27)**

Death was *introduced* by Adam, *conquered* through resurrection by Christ (the first fruits), and will be finally *destroyed* in the ultimate victory of Christ at the end of history. The reign of Christ that began at the resurrection will eventually put all enemies under his feet (cameo 4). But more than that, as Scripture has affirmed (cameo 5) "all things" will be "in subjection under his feet"—ah yes, of course, with the single exception of the Father (cameo 6).

The climax is again a Scripture quotation. The psalmist used this metaphor about the feet in Psalm 8:6 and Psalm 110:1. For the psalmist God placed all animals (domesticated and wild) and all fish *under the feet* of humankind. Paul quotes the text but gives it a new meaning. Now *all things* are put under the feet of the messianic King, who has conquered death. The quote is from Psalm 8:6, but the range of the Messiah's rule is displayed in Psalm 110:1, where God is going to overcome kings, nations and chiefs for the Messiah. The image of "under the feet" that projects the extent of this victory is a powerful Middle Eastern metaphor.

In the Cairo Museum of Antiquity the contents of the tomb of Tutankhamen are on display. One of the striking exhibits is a life-size wooden statue of the Pharaoh seated on his throne with his feet elevated on a stool. The surface of the stool is filled with carefully carved bass relief images of the enemies of the king, all with their hands tied behind their backs. The enemies are "under the feet" of Pharaoh. Tutankhamen died in the fourteenth century B.C.

One of my colleagues, while I was teaching at the Ecumenical Institute (Tantur) in Jerusalem, was the late Sister Maria Nora of Italy. With two earned doctorates and the ability to teach theology in Latin, Italian, French and English, Sister Maria Nora had been sent to Eritrea by her order to build a university. She achieved that goal and in the process became a confidant of Emperor Haile Selassie. When the socialist regime of Mengistu Haile Miriam overthrew the country, Haile Selassie was murdered and his body disappeared. At that time Sister Maria Nora was obliged to flee for her life. After some years she joined our staff in Jerusalem and told us the following story.

After the fall of the socialist regime in Ethiopia, Sister Maria Nora was able to quietly contact some of her  highly placed Ethiopian friends. From them she learned that when Mengistu's government fell, the new rulers of Ethiopia wanted to find Haile Selassie's body. When the palace servants were questioned, they told the authorities, "Dig up the tiled floor under the desk in Mengistu's office." The authorities did so and found the body of Emperor

Selassie. Mengistu had secretly buried the emperor under the floor of his desk so that every day, as he sat at his desk, his "enemy" was "under his feet."

For Paul, *all things* will be *under the feet* of Christ. The language carries with it the image of total surrender and the impossibility of the enemies ever contemplating a "comeback."

Paul is thereby saying to his readers, "If Christ is not raised, then this vision of the end of all things is a lie. But Christ *is raised*, and we the apostles have seen him. If you deny him as the reigning Lord, you are the losers."

Having discussed this eagle's-eye view of the ages, Paul turns his attention to some of the immediate ethical issues critical to the resurrection.

# Resurrection and Ethics

1 CORINTHIANS 15:29-34

IN EACH OF THE FOUR PREVIOUS ESSAYS Paul placed his theological teachings in the center of the essay and positioned the ethical problem under discussion on the outside, around that center. For example, in the first essay the ethical problem was the Corinthian quarrel over Paul, Apollos and Cephas. After introducing that *ethical* problem, Paul discussed the *theology* of *the cross*, which was for all, both Jews and Greeks. He then presented a second *ethical* discussion of Paul, Apollos and Cephas. His pattern was ethics then theology and finally a return to ethics. He followed that pattern in each of the three following essays. But in this last essay, the order is reversed. On the outside there are two *theological* discussions centered on the resurrection. In the center, however, he points briefly to a series of concrete *ethical* issues that are profoundly related to the resurrection. The text of this central ethical discussion is displayed in figure 5.3(1).

## THE RHETORIC

This short passage is a simple five-cameo discussion of various ethical issues. The five cameos relate to each other using ring composition. As is customary, the climax is in the center, where Paul invokes the name of "Jesus Christ our Lord" and cries out in pain, "I die every day!" At the end there is a brief aside, such as appears on three other occasions in the epistle.[1]

If cameos 1 and 5 appeared in the text without the three intervening cameos the reader would not observe any break in the line of thought. The discussion of "if the dead are not raised" would flow seamlessly from 1 to 5. The

---

[1]The three previous asides appear in 1:14-15; 10:13; 11:34b.

same is true with 2 and 4. If the climax of 3 were not in the text, no one would detect its absence. These are signs of Paul's skillful use of ring composition.

1. [15:29]Otherwise, what do people mean
    by being *baptized for the sake of the dead?*    IF DEAD NOT RAISED
    *If the dead are not raised* at all,    Why Be Baptized for Their Sake?
    why are people *baptized for their sake?*

2.    [30]Why am I in peril    WHY ENDURE?
        every hour?

3.    [31]I protest, brethren, by my boasting in you    BY MY BOASTING
        which I have in Christ Jesus our Lord,    In Christ
        I die every day!    I Die Every Day!

4.    [32]What do I gain if, humanly speaking,    WHAT REWARD?
        I fought with beasts at Ephesus?

5.    *If the dead are not raised,*    IF DEAD NOT RAISED
    "Let us *eat* and *drink,*    Eat, Drink and Die!
    for *tomorrow we die.*"

---

[*Aside*]
6.    [33]Do not be led astray, "Bad company ruins good morals." [34]Come to your right mind, and sin no more. For some have no knowledge of God. I say this to your shame.

**Figure 5.3(1). Resurrection and ethics (1 Cor 15:29-34)**

## COMMENTARY

Cameo 1 presents a widely debated puzzle. The text reads:

1. [15:29]Otherwise, what do people mean
    by being *baptized for the sake of the dead?*    IF DEAD NOT RAISED
    *If the dead are not raised* at all,    Why Be Baptized for Their Sake?
    why are people *baptized for their sake?*

What does Paul mean when he writes "baptized for the sake of the dead"? In 1914 Robertson and Plummer were aware of thirty-five explanations of this verse.[2] Thiselton notes that the count is now over forty.[3] He then proceeds to set out the thirteen more notable interpretations (some of which offer multiple subdivisions).[4] But in spite of the complexity and multiplicity of interpreta-

---

[2]Robertson/Plummer, *First Epistle,* p. 359.
[3]Thiselton, *First Epistle,* p. 1240.
[4]Ibid., pp. 1242-48.

PAUL THROUGH MEDITERRANEAN EYES

tions, one option has had strong endorsement for more than a hundred years.

In 1900, G. G. Findlay wrote that Paul was referring to a common experience where

> the death of Christians leads to the conversion of survivors, who in the first instance "for the sake of the dead" (their beloved dead), and in the hope of reunion, turn to Christ—e.g., when a dying mother wins her son by the appeal, "Meet me in heaven!"[5]

Joachim Jeremias came (independently) to the same conclusion in 1960 when he wrote regarding 15:29,

> Take, for instance, a case in which a young woman belonging to the church, and engaged to be married, died, and whose heathen bridegroom had himself baptized "for her sake"—that is, in order to be united with her in the resurrection. This interpretation fits excellently into the context of the apologetic reflections of I Cor. 15.12-19. . . . The apostle had said in v. 18 that if Christ were not risen "they who are fallen asleep in Christ are perished." Now he adds that the same is true of their Gentile kinsmen (husbands, wives, lovers), who had themselves baptized in order to be united with them in the resurrection.[6]

After his own detailed discussion of the options, Thiselton describes the same alternative as follows:

> Baptism for the sake of ('υπερ) the dead refers to the decision of a person or persons to ask for, and to receive, baptism as a result of the desire to be united with their believing relatives who have died. This presupposes that they would share the radiant confidence that they would meet again in and through Christ at the resurrection of the dead.[7]

Thiselton goes on to conclude that this view is "the least problematic and most convincing of all."[8] Thus this view has had major champions across the twentieth century and beyond. I find it fully convincing.

The matching cameo 5 reads:

| | |
|---|---|
| 5. *If the dead are not raised,* | IF DEAD NOT RAISED |
| "Let us *eat* and *drink,* | Eat, Drink and Die! |
| for *tomorrow we die."* | |

---

Findlay, *First Epistle*, p. 931.

Joachim Jeremias, *Infant Baptism in the First Four Centuries* (London: SCM Press, 1960), p. 36, 36 n. 3.

Thiselton, *First Epistle*, p. 1248.

Ibid., p. 1249.

If there is no resurrection, give up! Hedonism is the appropriate way to shorten life and "get it over with." Drink yourself to death—why not? Paul borrows language from Ecclesiastes 8:15. Jesus appears to have used the same source for his parable of the rich fool (Lk 12:19).

The center of this ring composition is displayed in figure 5.3(2).

| | | |
|---|---|---|
| 2. | [30]Why am I in peril every hour? | WHY ENDURE? |
| 3. | [31]I protest, brethren, by my boasting in you which I have in Christ Jesus our Lord, I die every day! | BY MY BOASTING<br>In Christ<br>I Die Every Day! |
| 4. | [32]What do I gain if, humanly speaking, I fought with beasts at Ephesus? | WHAT REWARD? |

**Figure 5.3(2). Cameos 2-4 (1 Cor 15:30-32)**

The language Paul uses in the opening of cameo 3 is that of an oath. The Greek word *ne* occurs only here in the New Testament. It is also used in one text in the Greek Old Testament (LXX) where Joseph says to his brothers,

> It is as I said to you, you are spies. By this you shall be tested: *by the life of Pharaoh*, you shall not go from this place, unless your youngest brother comes here. Send one of you, and let him bring your brother, while you remain in prison, that your words may be tested, whether there is truth in you; or else, *by the life of Pharaoh*, surely you are spies. (Gen 42:14-16, italics added)

The phrase *by the life of Pharaoh* in the Greek Old Testament begins with the same Greek word *ne* that Paul uses in cameo 3. The standard use of this word is in an oath on a god or something exceedingly precious. Joseph's oath was "on the life of Pharaoh." (Pharaoh was divine for the Egyptians.) This is mirrored even today where an extremely common oath in modern Arabic is, "By my life" or "By the life of God." Paul is not declaring an oath "On the life of God" or "On the life of the resurrected Lord," but by something *extremely precious* to him, which is, "By my boasting in you, which I have in Christ Jesus our Lord." As noted in the earlier discussion of 13:3, Paul joins the idea of "boasting before God on the day of judgment" to the parallel idea of the hope to receive a reward from the judge. Here also the idea of "boasting in you—in Christ Jesus our Lord" is attached to the idea of "gain" that occurs in cameo 4.

Paul is not swearing an oath in the modern sense, but he uses the language of making an oath and says something like, "By that which is very precious to me I affirm: I die every day."

Paul knows full well the risks he is taking in Ephesus. Any foreigner who would dare enter a city like Ephesus and preach a message undermining the financial security of the "establishment" would be in grave danger. This was particularly true when the patron goddess of the city was involved. Because of Paul's preaching, the goddess of the city was under attack and income from "tourism" was threatened. Who would complain if the corpse of the foreigner who was causing this disruption was dumped into the harbor some moonless night? Yes, he is a Roman citizen, and that would help him if he made it to courts. But what if he never got that far? Paul uses the language of the fights to the death with wild beasts in the arena to describe his struggles in Ephesus.

Having lived through nine years of the Lebanese civil war and through the Israeli invasion of Lebanon the summer of 1982, I understand the affirmation "I die every day." This is the speech of someone who goes out each day wondering if it will be his last. Included in this is the never to be forgotten feeling at a rogue checkpoint when stopped by heavily armed militiamen. On such occasions one is convinced, "I will not be alive five minutes from now." The fall of 2009 I was privileged to meet Mr. Paul, the senior manager of "Hotel Rwanda" during the massacres that took place in Rwanda in 1994. For the three-month period of the massacres, Mr. Paul "died every day." It was the look in the eye. We understood each other. Paul the apostle breaks into *very strong language,* indeed the language of oath taking, as he declares, "I die every day."

If there is no resurrection—life is not worth it. Live it up and die—a natural conclusion to any denial of the resurrection, be it Saducean or secular![9] As Garland notes, "Resurrection means endless hope, but no resurrection means a hopeless end—and hopelessness breeds dissipation."[10]

This carefully structured homily is followed by a generalized aside that reads:

6. [33]Do not be led astray, "Bad company ruins good morals." [34]Come to your right
   mind, and sin no more. For some have no knowledge of God. I say this to
   your shame.

---

[9]Findlay, *First Epistle,* p. 932. This also fit popular Epicureanism.
[10]Garland, *1 Corinthians,* p. 721.

This aside may include a quotation from Menander's play *Thais*.[11] The reference to bad company and good morals may also have been a popular proverb. The same phrase reflects Isaiah 22:13. Is this a primitive error? At an early stage did someone insert a note on the margin of Paul's letter and the note was then transcribed as part of the original when the letter was copied? Or could it be a note that Paul added after his chosen scribe completed the requested "clean copy"? In the hymn to the cross (1:17–2:2) Paul managed to use language that would resonate both with Greeks and Jews. This may be a second example of that same extraordinary ability to speak to both communities by quoting from Menander and Isaiah *at the same time*. This is the fourth brief aside in the epistle that is attached to the end of a finely structured homily.[12]

After finishing these ethical reflections Paul is ready to continue his essay on the resurrection by presenting a balancing second homily on "Adam and Christ."

---

[11]Menander, *Thais*, frag. 218, cited in Wright, *Resurrection*, p. 339.
[12]The other three are: 1:14-16; 10:12; 11:34b.

# Resurrection

*Adam and Christ—The Nature of the Resurrected Body*

I CORINTHIANS 15:35-50

A GREAT DEAL OF thoughtful scholarship has gone into the interpretation of Paul's homily "Resurrection: Adam and Christ—The Nature of the Resurrected Body."[1] Our goal is to look carefully at the rhetorical style Paul uses, highlight a few conclusions, and at key points observe how the Oriental versions and commentators have dealt with the text.

The full text of this homily is displayed in figure 5.4(1).

## THE RHETORIC

The rhetorical devices used in this homily are both simple and sophisticated. They include:

1. The overall homily (15:35-50) is another case of the high jump format seen numerous times in the epistle except that in this case the high jump is also a double-decker sandwich. Summarized, the rhetoric of the homily is displayed in figure 5.4(2).

[1]Garland, *1 Corinthians*, pp. 725-38; Fee, *First Epistle*, pp. 775-95; Kistemaker, *1 Corinthians*, pp. 566-80; Wright, *Resurrection*, pp. 340-56; Thiselton, *First Epistle*, pp. 1275-92.

| | | |
|---|---|---|
| 1. | [15:35]But some one will ask, | HOW ARE THE |
| | "*How* are the *dead raised*? | Dead Raised? |
| | and with *what kind of a body* do they come?" | |
| | | |
| 2. | [36]You foolish man! | |
| | What you *sow* does not come to *life* unless it *dies*. | |
| | [37]And *what you sow* is not the body which is to be, | PLANTS |
| | but a *bare kernel*, perhaps of wheat or of some other grain. | |
| | [38]*But God gives it a body* as he has chosen, | |
| | and to each kind of seed its own body. | |
| | | |
| 3. | [39]For not *all flesh is alike*, | |
| | but there is one kind for humans, | HUMANS, ANIMALS |
| | another for *animals*, | Birds, Fish |
| | another for birds, | |
| | and another for *fish*. | |
| | | |
| 4. | [40]There are celestial bodies | |
| | and there are terrestrial bodies; | GLORY OF |
| | but the *glory of the celestial* is one, | Heavenly/Earthly |
| | and the *glory of the terrestrial* is another. | |
| | | |
| 5. | [41]There is one glory of the *sun*, | |
| | and another glory of the *moon*, | GLORY OF |
| | and another glory of the *stars;* | Heavenly Bodies |
| | for star differs from star in glory. | |
| | | |
| 6. | [42]So it is with the *resurrection of the dead*. | SO THE RESURRECTION |
| | What is sown is *perishable*, | Perishable |
| | what is raised is *imperishable*. | Imperishable |
| | | |
| 7. | [43]It is *sown* in *dishonor*, | |
| | it is raised in *glory*. | WEAKNESS TO |
| | It is sown in *weakness*, | Glory and Power |
| | it is raised in *power*. | |
| | | |
| 8. | [44]It is sown a *physical body*, | |
| | it is raised a *spirit-filled body*. | PHYSICAL |
| | If there is a *physical body*, | Spirit Filled |
| | there is also a *spirit-filled body*. | |
| | | |
| 9. | [45]Thus it is written, | |
| | "The *first man* Adam became a *living being*"; | 1st ADAM RECEIVES LIFE |
| | the *last Adam* became a *life-giving spirit*. | 2nd Adam Gives Life |
| | | |
| 10. | [46]But it is not the *spirit-filled* which is first | |
| | but the *physical*, and then the *spirit-filled*. | PHYSICAL |
| | [47]The *first man* was from the earth, a man of *dust*; | Spirit Filled |
| | the *second* is from *heaven*. | |
| | | |
| 11. | [48]As was the *man of dust*, so are *those who are of the dust;* | |
| | and as is the *man of heaven*, so are *those who are of heaven*. | |
| | [49]Just as we have borne the *image of the man of dust*, | DUST TO |
| | we *shall also bear the image of the man of heaven*. | Image of Christ |
| | | |
| 12. | [50]I tell you this, brethren: | |
| | flesh and blood cannot inherit the kingdom of God, | PERISHABLE |
| | nor does the *perishable* inherit the *imperishable*. | Imperishable |

**Figure 5.4(1). Adam and Christ—The nature of the resurrected body (1 Cor 15:35-50)**

1. How are the dead raised?
2.     Look at plants, people,
3.     animals, birds, fish,
4.     glory of celestial and terrestrial,
5.     glory of sun, moon, stars.
6a. This is how the dead are raised:
6b. perishable to imperishable,
7.     dishonor/weakness to glory/power,
8.       physical to spirit-filled,
9.         Adam and Christ (Scripture),
10.     physical to spirit-filled,
11.     dust to man of heaven,
12. perishable to imperishable.

**Figure 5.4(2). Rhetoric of 1 Corinthians 15:35-50**

The outer frame, composed of cameos 1, 6 and 12, creates the double-decker sandwich. Cameo 1, with its two questions, is the introduction to the homily while the conclusion appears in 12, with its rare reference to "inheritance" and "the kingdom of God."

2. Cameo 6 is used to close the first half of the homily and to open the second half. I have therefore chosen to print cameo 6 in each of them. This double use of the central cameo occurs eight times in the epistle. In three of these the center (of the double-decker sandwich) is composed of two closely related cameos.[2] The other five have a single cameo in the center.[3]

3. The first half of this homily has an introduction and a matching conclusion. In the middle of the first half, Paul presents another cluster of parables. This is the fifth time he has done so. In one case the parables were listed together (10:5-12). In three cases there was a list of parables, and the list was divided in the middle with an extra cameo (7:25-31; 9:1-12; 14:6-12). The homily currently under study is somewhat unique. Its list of parables can be seen in figure 5.4(3).

We can look at these four cameos in two ways. The first is to note that cameos 2 and 3 present the parables of plants, humans, animals, birds and fish. Cameo 5 continues the list of parables by adding sun, moon and stars. Cameo 4 does not introduce any new "bodies," instead it looks below to the first list (the terrestrial) and above to the second list (the celestial). From this vantage point this list fits into the collection of three previous texts (7:25-31;

---

[2] 1 Cor 1:1-9; 7:25-31; 14:1-12.
[3] See 1 Cor 6:13-20; 7:17-24; 9:12b-18; 15:21-28; 15:35-50. 1 Cor 15:58 concludes one discussion and begins a second unrelated topic.

2.    ³⁶You foolish man!
         What you *sow* does not come to *life* unless it *dies*.
         ³⁷And *what you sow* is not the body which is to be,         PLANTS
         but a *bare kernel*, perhaps of wheat or of some other grain.
         ³⁸But God gives it a body as he has chosen,
         and to each kind of seed its own body.

3.    ³⁹For not *all flesh is alike*,
         but there is one kind for humans,                  HUMANS, ANIMALS
         another for *animals*,                              Birds, Fish
         another for birds,
         and another for *fish*.

4.    ⁴⁰There are celestial bodies
         and there are terrestrial bodies;                   GLORY OF
         but the *glory of the celestial* is one,            Heavenly/Earthly
         and the *glory of the terrestrial* is another.

5.    ⁴¹There is one glory of the *sun*,
         and another glory of the *moon*,                    GLORY OF
         and another glory of the *stars;*                   Heavenly Bodies
         for star differs from star in glory.

**Figure 5.4(3). The parables of 1 Corinthians 15:35-50**

9:1-12; 14:6-12), where a list of parables is divided with an extra cameo in the center (or near the center). This would create the chiasm out of cameos 3-5 noted by Fee.[4]

But the four cameos also form a straight-line sequence of plants, then animals/humans and finally the glory of the heavens. Cameo 2 on plants is in sequence with cameo 3, with its discussion of humans, animals, birds and fish. Cameo 4 introduces the idea of "glory" for the first time, and this idea is developed in cameo 5 (reinforcing the straight-line sequence). Each cameo in 15:36-41 has its place in the broader literary framework of figure 5.4(3).[5]

4. The second half of the homily exhibits a further case of the prophetic rhetorical template with its seven inverted cameos.

5. Finally, the climax of the homily appears (as usual) in the center of the inverted second half. Again, *Scripture* occupies that important position. Also "the last Adam" (Christ) is introduced for the first time, and his presence resonates with the entire seven-cameo structure in which it is placed.

[4]Fee has chosen this option. See Fee, *First Epistle*, p. 783.
[5]It is also possible to see these four cameos as a list that is interrupted, but in this case not in the center. This would incorporate the homily into the list of four homilies which include a collection of parables that are split in the center.

## COMMENTARY

Cameo 1 reads:

1. [15:35]But some one will ask,
   *"How* are the *dead raised*?"                                 HOW ARE THE
   and "With *what kind of a body* do they come?"          Dead Raised?

With Wright, it is more helpful to see these as two questions. The first is, "How is resurrection possible?" and the second is, "What is the nature of the resurrection body?"[6] Paul answers the first question in the first half of the homily and deals with the second question in the second half.

The list of four cameos that provide Paul's answer to the first question says:

2. [36]You foolish man!
   What you *sow* does not come to *life* unless it *dies*.
   [37]And *what you sow* is not the body which is to be,          PLANTS
   but a *bare kernel*, perhaps of wheat or of some other grain.
   [38]*But God gives it a body* as he has chosen,
   and to each kind of seed its own body.

Corinth was a commercial, transportation and manufacturing center, yet the plain of Corinth supported significant agriculture, and the agricultural parable in this text is both simple and profound. The seed is a "body" that first must die. That body dies naked (bare) and *God gives it a new body* different from the one that dies, and yet it is the same in that each seed has "its own body." There is both continuity and discontinuity in this parable. God brings about resurrection *and* transformation.

Paul's mind then turns to:

3. [39]For not all *sarks* [flesh] is the same *sarks* [flesh],
   but there is one kind for humans,                        HUMANS, ANIMALS
   another *sarks* [flesh] for *animals*,                    Birds, Fish
   another *sarks* [flesh] for birds,
   and another for fish.[7]

Paul introduces the word *sarks* (flesh) and uses it four times. The *sarks* (flesh) dies, disintegrates and is gone. Humankind participates in this order of being along with animals, birds and fish. The fourfold repetition of the word

---

[6]Wright, *Resurrection*, pp. 342-43.
[7]My translation.

*sarks* (flesh) is striking in the Greek text. It is unfortunate that three out of the four occurrences of this word disappear in the RSV. The NRSV leaves two while the KJV preserves all four. Paul is making a pointed statement. No first-century Christian reading this text needs to worry about the bones of loved ones turning to dust in a rock-cut tomb.[8]

The reader can see the wisdom of beginning this list of four cameos with the parable of the seed. The new plant that arises from the soil is not created out of the vegetable matter found in the seed. Paul is not telling his readers that in the resurrection the *sarks* (flesh) will magically reform and arise using the same bone and flesh with which it died. This seems to be the main point of this particular cameo.

Paul uses three words to describe the *soma* (body) in this homily. These are:

- a *soma* (body) that has a *sarks* (a body that has *flesh*)

- a *soma* (body) as a *psychikos* (a body that is constituted as a *living, human person*)

- a *soma* (body) as a *pneumatikos* (a body that is *constituted* by the *Holy Spirit*)

These three aspects of the word *body* should be kept in mind as we proceed. Paul continues by "going celestial" and introducing the component of "glory" [see fig. 5.4(4)].

| | | |
|---|---|---|
| 4. | [40]There are celestial bodies | |
| | and there are terrestrial bodies; | GLORY OF |
| | but the *glory of the celestial* is one, | Heavenly/Earthly |
| | and the *glory of the terrestrial* is another. | |
| | | |
| 5. | [41]There is one glory of the *sun*, | |
| | and another glory of the *moon*, | GLORY OF |
| | and another glory of the *stars*; | Heavenly Bodies |
| | for star differs from star in glory. | |

**Figure 5.4(4). Cameos 4-5 (1 Cor 15:40-41)**

As in English, the Greek word *soma* (body) had a wide range of meanings. It could refer (1) to a physical body of a human or animal, or (2) to a person/ human being, or (3) to "any corporeal substance."[9] Paul appears to be stretching that third meaning a bit as he talks about the "body" of the sun, moon and

---

[8]In like manner, no twenty-first-century Christian needs to worry lest cremation damage the "resurrection body."

[9]LSJ, *Greek-English Lexicon*, p. 1749.

stars. With such a stretch he adds useful parables to his list. In English the stretch is easier when we recall the idiom "the heavenly bodies."

Although he does not mention it, the sun "dies" each night and is "reborn" every morning. To the eye, the moon and stars "die" each morning only to be restored to life every night. As a person looks to the sky, most mornings and evenings, something celestial is dying and something else is being resurrected. The continuity between what dies and what rises is very strong. But the new element Paul mentions is the question of "glory."

Not only do the various bodies that God created range from plants to celestial bodies, but they vary in glory (cameo 5). The glory of the heavenly bodies has to do with luminescence. But the Greek word *doxa* (glory) has the Hebrew word *kabod* (heavy) behind it, and *kabod*, when applied to people, has to do with honor, reputation and being held in high esteem.[10] Indeed earthly bodies have their own type of glory (honor) that differs from the glory (luminescence) of the sun, moon and stars.

After this list of parables, each with its own contribution to the understanding of "bodies" and their regeneration or rebirth, Paul completes the approach in his high jump format and starts the jump, which takes the form of another prophetic rhetorical template [see fig. 5.4(5)].

Paul is focusing on the "what" of resurrection. Again these seven cameos are so carefully composed and the relationships between cameos 6 and 12 are so close that if they stood alone and cameos 5-11 were missing, no reader would notice a break in Paul's argument. The theme of *perishable-imperishable* introduced in cameo 6 moves seamlessly to its conclusion in cameo 12.

Furthermore, whenever this tight relationship appears on the outside, the reader expects to find some special connection between that outside (cameos 6, 12) and the center (cameo 9). A quick glance at cameo 9 confirms that such a relationship is evident. In the center of the seven cameos (9), we read about the first Adam, who inaugurated the long chain of human bodies that are "perishable" (cameo 6). The second line of the same cameo (9) introduces "the last Adam" (Christ) who launched a new age where the incorruptible will inherit the eternal kingdom in the new creation (cameo 12). Paul is referring to the coming of the kingdom of God in its fullness at the end of the age.

---

[10]LVTL, *Lexicon*, pp. 418-19.

6.  [42]So it is with the *resurrection of the dead*.   SO THE RESURRECTION
    What is sown is *perishable*,                      Perishable
    what is raised is *imperishable*.                  Imperishable

7.  [43]It is *sown* in *dishonor*,
    it is raised in *glory*.                           WEAKNESS TO
    It is sown in *weakness*,                           Glory and Power
    it is raised in *power*.

8.  [44]It is sown a *physical body*,
    it is raised a *spirit-filled body*.               PHYSICAL
    If there is a *physical body*,                      Spirit-Filled
    there is also a *spirit-filled body*.

9.  [45]Thus it is written,
    "The *first man* Adam became a *living being*";    1st ADAM RECEIVES LIFE
    the *last Adam* became a *life-giving spirit*.      2nd Adam Gives Life

10. [46]But it is not the *spirit-filled* which is first
    but the *physical*, and then the *spirit-filled*.  PHYSICAL
    [47]The *first man* was from the earth, a man of *dust*;  Spirit-Filled
    the *second* is from *heaven*.

11. [48]As was the *man of dust*, so are *those who are of the dust*;
    and as is the *man of heaven*, so are *those who are of heaven*.
    [49]Just as we have borne the *image of the man of dust*,   DUST TO
    we *shall also bear the image of the man of heaven*.        Image of Christ

12. [50]I tell you this, brethren:
    flesh and blood cannot inherit the kingdom of God, PERISHABLE
    nor does the *perishable* inherit the *imperishable*.  Imperishable

---

**Figure 5.4(5). Cameos 6-12 (1 Cor 15:42-50)**


The "bare bones" of the seven stanzas are displayed in figure 5.4(6).

6.  Perishable/Imperishable
7.  Dishonor/Weakness to Glory/Power
8.  Physical to Spirit-Filled
9.  Adam and Christ (Scripture)
10. Physical to Spirit-Filled
11. Dust to Image of Christ
12. Perishable/Imperishable

---

**Figure 5.4(6). Summary of cameos 6-12 (1 Cor 15:42-50)**

*Each set* of parallel cameos requires reflection. The outer pair is composed of cameos 6 and 12 displayed in figure 5.4(7).

| | |
|---|---|
| 6.  [42]So it is with the *resurrection of the dead.* | SO THE RESURRECTION |
|     What is sown is *perishable,* | Perishable |
|     what is raised is *imperishable.* | Imperishable |

---

| | |
|---|---|
| 12.[50]I tell you this, brethren: | |
|     flesh and blood cannot inherit the kingdom of God, | PERISHABLE |
|     nor does the *perishable* inherit the *imperishable.* | Imperishable |

**Figure 5.4(7). Cameos 6 and 12 (1 Cor 15:42, 50)**

Cameo 6 also inaugurates a series of distinctions that differentiate the physical body of this life from the new resurrection body that awaits the believer in the resurrection. The first of these is, as noted, "imperishable versus perishable." Regarding this contrast N. T. Wright (who prefers the KJV terms *corruption-incorruption*) affirms,

> The contrast of corruption/incorruption, it seems, is not just one in a list of differences between the present body and the future one, but remains implicit underneath the rest of the argument, not least between the present humanity in its *choikos* ("earthy") state, ready to return to dust, and the new type of humanity which will be provided in the new creation.[11]

Wright's observation is reinforced by the connections between the beginning (cameo 6) and the end (cameo 12) observed earlier.

The second pair of cameos is 7 and 11, which are displayed in figure 5.4(8).

| | |
|---|---|
| 7.  a.  [43]It is *sown* in *dishonor,* | |
|     b.    it is raised in *glory.* | WEAKNESS TO |
|     a.    It is sown in *weakness,* | Glory and Power |
|     b.    it is raised in *power.* | |

---

| | |
|---|---|
| 11. a.  [48]As was the *man of dust,* so are *those who are of the dust;* | |
|     b.    and as is the *man of heaven,* so are *those who are of heaven.* | |
|     a.  [49]Just as we have borne the *image of the man of dust,* | DUST TO |
|     b.    we *shall also bear the image of the man of heaven.* | Image of Christ |

**Figure 5.4(8). Cameos 7 and 11 (1 Cor 15:43, 46)**

---

[11]Wright, *Resurrection,* p. 347.

An awareness of the parallels between these two cameos is helpful for a proper understanding of what Paul is saying. When he writes "sown in dishonor," he is not only thinking of the death of the human body in isolation, he is also looking ahead to the balancing cameo 11 where the first Adam, "the man of dust," left behind a heritage of "dishonor." Adam was guilty of disobedience before God, lying, trying to blame his wife and finally trying to blame God. Adam's final card was to say, "The woman *whom thou gavest* to be with me" (Gen 3:12 KJV) is responsible. The point is not simply "Blame her, not me!" but Adam is also saying, "If you had given me a *decent woman*, none of this would have happened! I didn't choose her! *You gave her to me*—it's all *your fault!*" Don't accept responsibility for your mistakes—blame someone else—even God! This was the record of "the man of dust," and every sinner is a part of that inheritance. "As was the man of dust, so are those who are of the dust," writes Paul. The "dishonor" is still with us.

The opposite of "dishonor" is "glory." Glory for humans has to do with the qualities of integrity, reliability and wisdom, not with splendor. Attached to the dishonor-glory contrasts are the weakness-power comparisons. This latter pair of contrasts throws the reader back to the definitions of weakness and power that Paul set forth in his hymn on the weakness and power of God seen in the cross in 1:17–2:2. Here in cameo 7 the "power" that is promised in the resurrection is the more perfect ability to express the life-changing power of love seen in the love of God demonstrated through the cross.

A careful a + b pattern runs through the eight phrases in these two cameos [see fig. 5.4(8)]. In each case "a" is negative and "b" is the balancing positive. The two cameos are precisely matched and balanced. Yet it is the three cameos in the center that bring the homily to its climax. These are:

8.  [44]It is sown a *physical body*,
       it is raised a *spirit-filled body*.          A HUMAN BODY
    If there is a *physical body*,                  A Spirit-Filled Body
       there is also a *spirit-filled body*.

9.  [45]Thus it is written,
       "The *first man* Adam became a *living being*";    1st ADAM RECEIVES LIFE
       the *last Adam* became a *life-giving spirit*.     2nd Adam Gives Life

10. [46]But it is not the *spirit-filled* which is first
       but the *physical*, and then the *spirit-filled*.  A HUMAN BODY
    [47]The *first man* was from the earth, a man of *dust*;  A Spirit-Filled Body
       the *second* is from *heaven*.

**Figure 5.4(9). Cameos 8-10 (1 Cor 15:44-47)**

These three cameos are easily misunderstood. Plato and the Greek philosophical tradition understood a human being to have a divine soul of pure fire that in this life was imprisoned in a body. At death, the soul escapes from that prison, returns to the divine fire from which it came, and becomes one of the stars. Resurrection of *the body* was deeply abhorrent to the Greek mind, and Paul's philosophical audience in Athens on Mars Hill listened to him politely until he mentioned the resurrection of Jesus from the dead. At that point the lecture was over. Some mocked, a small handful were willing to give Paul a second hearing, and he left town (Acts 17:22–18:1). As regards the body, the goal (for the Greeks) was to endure until death, at which time the body could be discarded with a sigh of "good riddance."

Paul's thinking started with the story of creation, where God created all things and declared them good (Gen 1–2). The body was not in itself evil, and thereby the problem was not the body but rather sin and death. What then does this have to do with the text before us?

Paul affirms that the body is sown a *soma psychikos* and raised a *soma pneumatikos*. Earlier we saw Paul describe the body three ways. Every human body has a *sarks* (a body of flesh). My *sarks* is this "thing" that I wash, feed, dress, exercise, put to rest and try to keep healthy. For Paul there was also a *soma psychikos*, which for him meant a *living human person*. Judith Kovacs has recently written, "The Greek word *psychikos* [is] an adjective derived from the word "soul" (*psyche*). It refers to what belongs to the natural world, apart from the Spirit of God."[12] As a *person* I am more than just a body, even though my person includes my body. But Paul had already emphasized that the *psychikos* was a person who by definition did not understand the things of God (2:14). Finally, for Paul there was also a soma *pneumatikos* (a body constituted by the Holy Spirit), and this is where the difficulties lie. The Corinthians thought they were already of the third type of being because, after all, did they not have spiritual gifts from the Holy Spirit? Paul told them that he could not call them *pneumatikois* (this highest type), but that they were *sarkinois* (the lowest type of all) because of their jealousy and strife (3:1-3). There were no "disembodied spirits" involved in any of these categories, either in Paul's mind or in the minds of the Corinthians. In the light of what Paul wrote in chapters 2–3, how are we to understand this language?

In cameo 8 Paul affirms that for the believer the resurrected body under

[12]Judith L. Kovacs, trans. and ed., *1 Corinthians: Interpreted by Early Christian Commentators* (Grand Rapids: Eerdmans, 2005), p. 271 n. 21.

discussion begins as a *psychikos* (a living human person with a body) who dies, and in death that *psychikos* is "sown" like a grain of wheat. But then it is raised as a *soma pneumatikos* (a body that is constituted by the Holy Spirit). The KJV translated this, "It is sown a *natural* body; it is raised a *spiritual* body" (italics added). The RSV changed this to, "It is sown a *physical* body, it is raised a *spiritual* body" (italics added). As Wright has ably pointed out, this latter language easily falls back into what he calls "Plato's ugly ditch."[13] We shed the body (good riddance) and from then on the resurrected body is a disembodied spirit, a "spiritual body." But this understanding violates Paul's discussion in chapters 2–3. It also disregards the resurrected body of Jesus which for Paul was the model, the first fruits, of what the resurrected body would be like. The resurrected Jesus left a tomb empty and his body was for Paul a reality that he had witnessed on the Damascus road when fully awake. He knew he was not talking to an angel or a *phantasm* (ghost). "Have I not seen Jesus our Lord?" he asks his Corinthian readers, with an edge of anger in his words (9:1). He did not claim to have seen "the spirit of the Christ" in a dream. He had seen *Jesus our Lord!* He then lists himself (last) among the *many witnesses* to the resurrection (15:8), along with Peter and the Twelve.

As early as A.D. 867 the Syriac scholar Bishr ibn al-Sari translated 15:44 into Arabic and commented on his translated text. He translated, "it [the body] is sown the body of a person, it arises a body of the Spirit."

Ibn al-Sari then commented: "It is here called 'a body of a person' because the person preserves it and directs it. And in the second part of the verse it is called 'a body of the Spirit' because the Holy Spirit preserves it and directs it."[14]

Ibn al-Sari understood the resurrection body to be a material, not an immaterial, body. That material body would be preserved and directed by the Holy Spirit. Across the centuries Oriental versions have endorsed this view. The Arabic reads *Yuzra' jasad nafsani* (it is sown a personal body). The Arabic *nafas* cognates with the Hebrew *nefesh*, which is an important Hebrew concept with many nuances. The Arabic form *nafsani* (having to do with humanness and personhood) turns this word into an adjective that describes personhood. The same is true with the second Arabic word, *ruhani* (having to do with the Spirit). Here too the word describes the character of the person who is filled with the Spirit. The word has nothing to do with the substance of the person

---

[13]Wright, *Resurrection*, p. 348.

[14]Bishr ibn al-Sari, *Pauline Epistles*, p. 85 with n. 46. (My translation with the assistance of Victor Makari of Egypt.)

but only with his or her character. A *physical person* who is *ruhani* is a *Spirit-filled physical person*. One or both of these two key words (describing character) appear in twenty of the Syriac, Arabic and Hebrew versions examined that stretch from the fourth to the twenty-first centuries, and in none of them are there any overtones of a "disembodied spirit."[15]

Chrysostom is helpful when he discusses this verse and explains that of course the Spirit is with us now, but sin causes the Holy Spirit "to fly away." Yet with the resurrected body things will be different. He writes, "Then the Spirit will continually remain in the flesh of the righteous and will be in control, with the soul also being present."[16]

Didymus of Alexandria (d. c. 396), in commenting on 15:42-44, wrote, "Somehow, then, what is raised is both other than and the same as the body that perishes."[17] Thiselton, Fee and Wright affirm the *material* nature of the resurrected body and the vital presence of the Holy Spirit that *reconstitutes that body*.

The climax appears (as expected in ring composition) in the center. The first man was created by God with a "living spirit." The account of creation in Genesis affirms that he thereby became the starting point for the first creation, and all humankind descended from him. He was a *recipient of life*. The second Adam was not a *recipient of life* but *the dispenser of life*. In the new creation the resurrection of Jesus stands at the point of origin in regard to the new Spirit-constituted and directed resurrection body.

This is indeed the climax of this homily, if not the central point of the entire discussion of resurrection. Scripture is quoted to affirm the continuity between the first creation and the new creation.

Perhaps Paul composed cameo 10 to balance his use of the prophetic rhetorical template format. If cameo 10 were missing his theological presentation would still be complete. Of course the man from the earth is first, and the man from heaven is second. Paul states this in cameo 9 and repeats it in cameo 11. But he needs four lines on the subject of "physical and spiritual" at this

---

[15]Peshitta Syriac (5th cent.); Vat. Ar. (8th-9th cent.); Sinai 151 (867); Sinai 155 (9th cent.); Sinai 310 (10th cent.); Erpenius (1616); London Polyglot (1657); Propagandist (1671); Shwair (1813); Martyn (1826); Shidiac (1851); Bustani-Van Dyck (1860, 1865); Jesuit (1880); Yusif Dawud (1899); Fakhouri (1964); New Jesuit (1969); Jerusalem Hebrew (n.d.). See appendix II, plate P.

[16]Chrysostom, quoted in *1 Corinthians: Interpreted by Early Christian Commentators*, trans. and ed. Judith L. Kovacs (Grand Rapids: Eerdmans, 2005), p. 272.

[17]Didymus of Alexandria, quoted in *1 Corinthians: Interpreted by Early Christian Commentators*, trans. and ed. Judith L. Kovacs (Grand Rapids: Eerdmans, 2005), p. 271.

point in the homily to match the four lines of cameo 8 that are on this subject and so he creates cameo 10.

Paul deals with his subject with great care. The physical body will decompose, but the resurrected body will not decompose (cameo 6). The latter is raised in glory and power (cameo 7) because it is constituted by and filled with the Holy Spirit (cameo 8) that proceeds from the resurrected second Adam (cameo 9). The body of the resurrected Christ is the "image" that "we shall also bear" (cameo 11).

In the resurrection the believer will have a Spirit-constituted physical body. The brokenness and decay of the old body will be gone. The new body will be a physical body like the resurrected body of Christ. Such a truly glorious vision and promise calls for an exuberant hymn of victory, which Paul offers in the next homily.

# Resurrection

*Victory*

1 CORINTHIANS 15:51-58

THE TEXT OF PAUL'S FINAL HOMILY, "Resurrection: Victory," is displayed in figure 5.5(1). N. T. Wright appropriately refers to this final paragraph as having "the sustained excitement of a celebration."[1] It can also be called "A Hymn of Victory." Having opened the epistle with a hymn to the cross, Paul closes it with a balancing hymn to the resurrection.

## THE RHETORIC

The overall structure of this final homily is artistically satisfying in its simplicity. It is composed of twelve cameos that break into three sections. In the epistle there are only five homilies that divide into three sections.[2] These are:

- On the Cross (1:17–2:2)
- On the Lord's Supper (11:17-33)
- On the Nature of Love (13:1-13)
- On the Victory of Resurrection (15:51-58)
- On Finance for Mission (16:1-14)

In each of these five homilies the section in the middle is critical to the beginning and the end. In all five, if the center were missing, the first and third sections would fit together hand in glove, and the reader would not notice any omission. This can be seen as follows:

---

[1]Wright, *Resurrection*, p. 356.

[2]The epistle has four homilies composed of two sections, and twenty-nine homilies with one section each. Isaiah 40–66 has eight homilies that divide into three sections. These include 43:14-24; 44:21-28; 45:14-19; 49:1-7; 56:1-8; 58:9-14; 61:1-7; 65:17-25. See www.shenango .org/Bailey/Isaiah.htm.

0.  <sup>15:51</sup>Lo! *I tell you a mystery.*                    A MYSTERY REVEALED

-------------------------------------       ----------

1.  We shall *not all sleep*,                              NOT ALL SLEEP
    but we shall *all be changed*,                         We—All Changed

2.      <sup>52</sup>in a *moment*,                              A MOMENT
        in the *twinkling of an eye*,                      A Twinkling

3.      at the *last trumpet*.                             THE TRUMPET
        For the *trumpet will sound*,                      Will Sound

4.  and the *dead* will be *raised imperishable*,      RAISED—IMPERISHABLE
    and we shall be *changed*.                              We—Changed

-------------------------------------       ----------

5.  <sup>53</sup>For this *perishable* nature            PERISHABLE
        *must put on the* imperishable,                    Imperishable

6.      and this *mortal* nature                              MORTAL
        must put on *immortality*.                         Immortal

7.  <sup>54</sup>When the *perishable*                   PERISHABLE
    puts on the *imperishable*,                            Imperishable

8.      and the *mortal*                                      MORTAL
        puts on *immortality*,                             Immortal

-------------------------------------       ----------

9.  then shall come to pass
    the saying that is written,                            VICTORY
    *"Death is swallowed up in victory."*                  Death Swallowed

10.     <sup>55</sup>"O *death*, where is thy *victory?*          DEATH
        O *death*, where is thy *sting?"*                  Defeated

11.     <sup>56</sup>The *sting of death is sin*,                DEATH
        and the *power of sin is the law.*                 Power Gone

12.<sup>57</sup>But *thanks* be to *God*
    who gives us the *victory*                             VICTORY
    through *our Lord Jesus Christ*.                        Through Our Lord Jesus Christ

--------------------------------------------------------------------------------

13.<sup>58</sup>Therefore, my beloved brethren, be steadfast, immovable
    always abounding in the work of the Lord,
    knowing that in the Lord                               CONCLUDING
    your labor is not in vain.                             Personal Appeal

**Figure 5.5(1). A hymn of victory (1 Cor 15:51-58)**

1. In the discussion of *the Cross* (1:17–2:2) the first section (cameos 1-3) connects smoothly with the third section (cameos 11-13). The center (cameos 4-10) contextualizes the message of the homily.

2. In the discussion of the *Lord's Supper* (11:17-33) the first and third sections deal with irregularities at the celebration. In the center Paul quotes the words of institution of the Eucharist. The key to the discussion lies in the center section.

3. In the *hymn to love* (13:1-13) Paul begins and ends with discussions of love and the spiritual gifts. In the center, between them, he *defines* love. That definition is the foundation on which the chapter rests.

4. Skipping ahead to the fifth example of a homily with three sections, we will see below that in chapter 16 Paul is *fundraising*. He presents three good places where the churches can spend their mission money. The first option is to support the Jerusalem church, the third is to finance Timothy. In the center he politely asks for funding for himself. He knows that he is the key figure in the "outreach team." If he can't visit the churches and reach out to new centers, the Christian movement will be seriously restricted. So he places his own travel budget request in the center of the three petitions.

5. In the *resurrection* text before us (15:51-58) the center is also essential to the other two, even though it is clearly not the climax of the homily. This homily is better viewed as a rare straight-line sequence, with the climax coming at the end in the great cry of victory over death. Yet there are three distinct sections, and again, if the second section were missing the omission would not be noticeable. This is evident in figure 5.5(2).

When the end of the first section is placed beside the beginning of the third section the connection between them is easy to discern.

4.  $^{52c}$and the *dead* will be *raised imperishable*,       RAISED—IMPERISHABLE
    and we shall be *changed*.                            We—Changed

-------------------------------------------------------------------------

9.  $^{54c}$Then shall come to pass
    the saying that is written,
    *"Death is swallowed up in victory."*       VICTORY
                                                Death Swallowed

**Figure 5.5(2). Cameos 4 and 9 (1 Cor 15:52c, 54c)**

The center section (cameos 5-8) also has unique features. Paul discusses:

(5) Perishable—imperishable  +  (6) Mortal—immortal

He then repeats himself with almost the same language in cameos 7-8. He could have dispensed with these last two cameos (7 and 8). Paul does not carelessly add extra verbiage. He was most likely aware of composing three sections with four cameos in each section, and he wanted to maintain a literary balance. If the first and third sections each had four cameos—then the second section should also have four. Furthermore, Paul certainly remembered the opening hymn to the cross (1:17–2:2) with its *amazing balance*. Should this concluding hymn on the resurrection not also be composed with artistic balance?

Finally, the two outside sections are constructed with eight cameos, each of which follows an A-B-B-A pattern. In the opening of the epistle (1:1-9) this identical rhetorical pattern of eight cameos appears. Paul may have composed the first and third sections of this "victory cry" deliberately modeling them after the beginning of the epistle and then opted to add cameos 5-8 in the center.

In the previous homily Paul told his readers about the new body that will be imperishable, raised with glory and power, filled with the Holy Spirit and fashioned after "the image of the man of heaven." What more need be said? Paul gives an answer.

## COMMENTARY

In this hymn to the resurrection it is impossible to separate rhetorical style from theological content. In the opening section [see fig. 5.5(3)], we read:

| | | |
|---|---|---|
| 1. | [51]We shall *not all sleep*, | NOT ALL SLEEP |
| | but we shall *all be changed*, | We—All Changed |
| | | |
| 2. | [52]in a *moment*, | A MOMENT |
| | in the *twinkling of an eye*, | A Twinkling |
| | | |
| 3. | at the *last trumpet*. | THE TRMPET |
| | For the *trumpet will sound*, | Will Sound |
| | | |
| 4. | and the *dead* will be *raised imperishable*, | RAISED—IMPERISHABLE |
| | and we shall be *changed*. | We—Changed |

**Figure 5.5(3). Section 1: Cameos 1-4**

Who are the "we" in this first section? If Paul is thinking strictly about his own age, then he obviously anticipates the coming of the Lord and the day of resurrection during his lifetime. Some have fallen asleep, but "we" are still alive. In this case Paul is arguing that both those who have died and those still

alive will experience transformation into the new resurrected state. Modern
scholars who hold this view understand Paul to have changed his mind by the
time he writes 2 Corinthians 5:1-10, where he does not expect to see the return of Christ in his lifetime.[3]

Anthony Thiselton argues convincingly that Paul is casting his glance
across the ages and that "we shall not all sleep" means that whenever the day
of Christ's return arrives (sooner or later), some believers will still be alive, but
it doesn't matter because "we shall *all* be changed." If "we" means all believers
from the beginning to the end of history, Paul does not change his mind before he writes 2 Corinthians.[4]

In the last cameo of this homily (12) Paul writes "thanks be to God who
gives us the victory." In this latter case he is looking across the ages. With
Thiselton, it is appropriate to see Paul taking the long view of history, both at
the opening and the closing of this homily.

In cameos 2 and 3 Paul emphasizes the suddenness of that final transformation into the Spirit-constituted body. It will happen in an instant. Every
believer knows that growth in becoming "conformed to the image of his Son"
is a slow, halting journey that lasts a lifetime. But the final transformation at
the resurrection into the new Spirit-constituted body will happen "in the
twinkling of an eye." It will be instantaneous. The trumpet image adds excitement and richness to the anticipation of that glorious moment. The first section closes with a repetition of the opening declaration that we shall be
changed. The second section is displayed in figure 5.5(4).

| | | |
|---|---|---|
| 5. [53]For this *perishable* nature | PERISHABLE | |
| *must put on the* imperishable, | Imperishable | |
| 6.    and this *mortal* nature | MORTAL | |
| must put on *immortality*. | Immortal | |
| 7. [54]When the *perishable* | PERISHABLE | |
| puts on the *imperishable*, | Imperishable | |
| 8.    and the *mortal* | MORTAL | |
| puts on *immortality*, | Immortal | |

**Figure 5.5(4). Section 2: Cameos 5-8**

This second section may not be the *climax*, but it is the *foundation* of the

---

[3]Wright, *Resurrection,* pp. 356-57.
[4]Thiselton, *First Epistle,* pp. 1293-95.

entire homily. As in 13:1-13, so here, Paul places the foundation of the hymn in the center. If the new resurrection body is not imperishable and immortal, then *we have not been changed* (result: cameos 1-4 are not true). Furthermore, if the new body is not imperishable and immortal, then *death is not conquered* (result: cameos 9-12 are not true). Paul is struggling to express the inexpressible. The transformation to the new body "in a moment" is a mystery, and he is doing his best to explain it. The old identity remains. The disciples recognized the resurrected Lord. He was the same, but different.

Two new components are added in this central section. For decades Lenin's body was kept by the communist authorities somewhat imperishable and on display in Red Square. But Lenin was dead; his corpse was not immortal. On the road to Damascus, in broad daylight, Paul did not just hear a voice, he saw a person, and he knew that the visible body of that person was both imperishable and immortal. A body that is imperishable does not decay, while an immortal person never dies. This foundation was critical to Paul's presentation, and thus he had theological (as well as literary) reasons for emphasizing it through repetition.

The second new component has to do with the language of investiture. The "perishable" must *"put on* the imperishable," and the mortal must *"put on* immortality." The picture is that of the investiture of a king, emperor or high official. The king has the same body, but after the investiture, with new robes, he is a new man. As with all metaphors, this picture of investiture has unsolvable problems. When all is said and done, Paul is still dealing with a mystery—regardless of how much of it he manages to reveal.

After the investiture we will be the same—and yet different.

The third section records Paul's cry of victory [see fig. 5.5(5)].

| | | |
|---|---|---|
| 9. | then shall come to pass<br>the saying that is written,<br>*"Death is swallowed up in victory."* | VICTORY<br>Death Swallowed |
| 10. | [55]"O *death*, where is thy *victory*?<br>O *death*, where is *thy sting*?" | DEATH<br>Defeated |
| 11. | [56]The *sting of death is sin*<br>and the *power of sin is the law*. | DEATH<br>Power Gone |
| 12. | [57]But *thanks* be to *God*<br>who gives us the *victory*<br>through *our Lord Jesus Christ*. | VICTORY<br>Through Our Lord Jesus Christ |

**Figure 5.5(5). Section 3: Cameos 9-12 (1 Cor 15:54-57)**

In this final section Paul quotes from Isaiah 25, which presents a vision of a great banquet that God will spread "on this mountain" (Jerusalem) for "all nations." The vision includes:

1.   $^{25:8}$He will swallow up death for ever.
            And the Lord Yahweh will wipe away tears
                from all faces.

2.        And the reproach of his people
            he will take away from upon all the earth,
                For Yahweh has spoken.

3.   $^{9}$It will be said on that day,
        "Lo, this is our God;
            we have waited for him
                that he might save us.

4.        This is Yahweh;
            we have waited for him;
                let us be glad and rejoice in His salvation."

**Figure 5.5(6). Death defeated (Is 25:8-9)**

Jesus built on Isaiah 25:6-9 (which includes these four cameos) as he created his parable of the great banquet (Lk 14:15-24),[5] and here Paul turns to the same text for his cry of victory.

To the Isaiah passage Paul adds textual content from Hosea 13:14 and fashions a taunt song. As N. T. Wright observes, "like a warrior triumphing over a fallen enemy Paul mocks the power that has now become powerless."[6]

He continues with a one-line summary of his views on death, sin and the law (cameo 11). This is well summarized by Robertson and Plummer:

> It was by sin that death acquired power over man, and it is because there is a law to be transgressed that sin is possible (Rom. V. 13; vii 7). Where there is no law, there may be faults, but there can be no rebellion, no conscious defiance of what authority has prescribed. But against law there may be rebellion, and rebellion merits death.[7]

To this we could add that for Paul the keeping of the law stimulates pride and a sense of superiority over those who fail to keep that law. Paul concludes by again taking the long view of history as he offers this ringing cry of victory.

---

[5]Kenneth E. Bailey, *Through Peasant Eyes* (Grand Rapids: Eerdmans, 1983), pp. 88-90.
[6]Wright, *Resurrection*, p. 358.
[7]Robertson/Plummer, *First Epistle*, pp. 378-79.

This final homily begins with the affirmation, "Lo! I tell you a *mystery*." In his hymn to the cross Paul reminded his readers that he came proclaiming "the mystery of God" (2:1) and later in the same essay he told them to look on him and his friends as *stewards of the mysteries of God* (4:1). As he closes, the "steward of the *mysteries* of God" is fulfilling his primary task by *unveiling a mystery!* The cross has its mysteries and so does the resurrection.

In the opening of the first essay, Paul also used the phrase *our Lord Jesus Christ* no less than four times, only to have it disappear from the text.[8] Here at the end of his final essay Paul returns to *this exact phrase* (15:57), and in the process adds one final stitch joining his discussion of the cross to his reflections on the resurrection.

It was "our Lord Jesus Christ" who died on the cross, and it was "our Lord Jesus Christ" who rose from the dead, the first fruits of those who sleep replacing the first Adam with the second Adam. If Paul's readers can reflect deeply on those four words, all will be well. He is discussing the resurrected *Jesus*, whom he met personally, not some departed historical figure out of the past. That Jesus is *Kurios* (Lord) in a way that Caesar is not. Let the Greeks and the Romans take note. Jesus is also *Messiah* (Christ). Let the Jews take note. Finally he is *our* Lord, not *my* Lord. Together we have one Lord and one Father.

Those four words can cause all the problems discussed in this epistle to disappear. The Corinthian divisions will disappear; their community-destroying sexual irregularities will stop; their offenses to the consciences of others will come to an end; their worship wars will be over; and their denials of the resurrection will be no more. The resurrected Jesus *is* "our Lord Jesus Christ."

As with the other four essays, Paul adds a final personal appeal to the end of the essay. He concluded three of the five essays with some form of the request to "imitate me" (4:16; 7:40; 11:1), and essay four concluded with a summary of the essay combined with a personal appeal (14:37-40). "Imitate me" does not fit when discussing the resurrection. Instead Paul offers a word of admonition that applies to all five essays. The text reads:

13.  [58]Therefore, my beloved brethren, be steadfast, immovable
     always abounding in the work of the Lord,
     knowing that in the Lord                    CONCLUDING
     your labor is not in vain.                   Personal Appeal

---

[8]For the others see 1:2, 7, 8, 10. The same words in different word orders appear in 1:9; 15:31.

The final personal appeal is remarkable for three reasons.

1. Paul opens this personal admonition by calling them "beloved." He had criticized them for their divisions, their trashing of the cross, their pride in their "spirituality," their immoral behavior, their indifference to the consciences of others, their quarrels over worship leadership, their drunkenness at the Lord's Table, their arrogance related to the spiritual gifts, their failures to love one another, their chatting in church and their denials of the resurrection. They had failed to be "steadfast and immovable" in both their theology and their ethics. Yet, they were his *beloved brothers and sisters*. Paul had kind words for his readers in the opening verses of the epistle (1:4-9). At its close he pens additional kind words in the form of a pastoral admonition.

2. Paul discusses labor that is "not in vain." In the opening of this essay on the resurrection he reminded his readers of the gospel "which you received, in which you stand, by which you are saved, if you hold it fast—*unless you believed in vain*" (15:1-2). In that same opening homily he affirmed "his grace toward me was *not in vain*" (15:10). Indeed, he worked harder than any of the apostles. A few verses later he warns his readers that if Jesus is not raised, "your faith is *in vain*" (15:14). As he concludes, what will he say about their deeply faulted discipleship? Does he think their faith is in vain?

The affirmation "not in vain" had two components. The first was faith in the historical fact of the resurrection of Jesus. The second was the believer's response in obedience to the risen Lord. Paul brings both of these factors into play. "Abounding in the work of the (risen) Lord" brings *sure knowledge* that their labor is "not in vain" (in the same way that Paul's labor was not in vain). He offers a word of assurance and of challenge.

3. This personal appeal is also amazing by reason of its challenge *in the present*. Paul had just revealed the mystery of the end of all things when death will be destroyed and "we shall be changed." His concluding remarks could easily have reflected some form of repose. Paul could have written, "Therefore let us wait with patience as we look to the future with hope, confidence and joy anticipating these great final events." But for Paul, the resurrection and all that it means for the *future*, rightly understood, empowers believers *to serve the risen Lord in the present*. Believers in Jesus as Lord were not part of a movement quietly awaiting its end. The gospel of the resurrection was not an escape mechanism from this life that left people passively anticipating the next. Paul was interested in *the now*. Final, total victory was already assured. The new age had dawned and the new creation had shown itself in the resurrection of

Jesus. Paul's efforts at establishing a church in Athens failed (as far as we know). Yet his labor "was not in vain" because it contributed to the larger goal of the coming of the kingdom of God *on earth*. Paul challenges his readers to engage "in the work of the Lord" *in the present*. As Bishop Bill Frey has said, "Hope is hearing the music of the future; faith is dancing to it today."[9]

This "concluding appeal" (15:58) is yet another instance of a cameo that Paul presses into service in both directions. It looks backwards *and* provides a finely crafted personal appeal with which to close the fifth essay (and bring resolution to all five essays). At the same time it looks forward and creates an introduction to his concluding remarks, to which we now turn.

[9]Bill Frey, from a sermon preached at The Trinity School for Ministry, Ambridge, Penn. September 2001.

# Concluding Notes

*Funding, Leadership, Greetings and Final Admonition*

I CORINTHIANS 16:1-23

Paul's concluding notes fall into three sections. The first is on "finance for mission" and is displayed in figure 6.1.

## The Rhetoric

This homily opens and closes with general admonitions. In between there are three appeals for funds. We will look briefly at the two general admonitions and then turn to the three requests for financial support, which we will examine in sequence. Each request uses ring composition with a climax in the center.

1. a. [15:58]Therefore, my beloved brethren, be steadfast, immovable,
   b. always abounding in the work of the Lord,
   knowing that in the Lord your labor is not in vain.     GENERAL
                                                           Admonition

-------------------------------------------------------------------

2.     [16:1]Now concerning the contribution *for the saints*:
       as I directed the churches of Galatia,
       so you also are to do.                              FINANCE
                                                           *For the Saints*

3.        [2]On the first day of every week,
          each of you is to *put something aside*
          and *store it up*,                               BASIS OF
          *as he may prosper*,                             Finance
          so that contributions need not be made when I come.

4.        [3]And when I arrive,
          I will send those whom you accredit *by letter*
          to carry *your gift to Jerusalem*.               FINANCE
          [4]If it seems advisable that I should go also,   *For Jerusalem*
            they will accompany me.

-------------------------------------------------------------------

| | | |
|---|---|---|
| 5. | ⁵I will visit you after passing through Macedonia, for I intend to pass through Macedonia, | THROUGH Macedonia |
| 6. | ⁶and perhaps *I will stay with you* or even spend the winter, | I VISIT You |
| 7. | so that you may *assist me on my journey, wherever I go.* | FINANCE *For Paul* |
| 8. | ⁷For I do not want to see you just now in passing; *I hope to spend some time with you,* if the Lord permits. | I VISIT You |
| 9. | ⁸But I will stay in *Ephesus* until Pentecost, ⁹for a wide door for effective work has opened to me, and there are many adversaries. | IN Ephesus |
| 10. | ¹⁰When *Timothy* comes, see that he has nothing to fear among you,[1] for he is doing the work of the Lord, as I am. ¹¹So let no one despise him. | VISIT OF Timothy (coming) |
| 11. | *Assist him on his way* in peace, that he may return to me; for I am expecting him with the brethren. | FINANCE *For Timothy* |
| 12. | ¹²As for our brother *Apollos*, I strongly urged him to visit you with the other brethren, but it was not at all his will to come now. He will come when he has opportunity. | VISIT OF Apollos (not coming) |
| 13.a. b. | ¹³Be watchful, stand firm in your faith, be courageous, be strong. Let all that you do be done in love. | GENERAL Admonition |

Figure 6.1. Finance for mission (1 Cor 15:58–16:13)

## COMMENTARY

The two general admonitions are bookends for the homily (see fig. 6.2).

| | | |
|---|---|---|
| 1. a. b. | ¹⁵:⁵⁸Therefore, my beloved brethren, be steadfast, immovable, always abounding in the work of the Lord, knowing that in the Lord your labor is not in vain. | GENERAL Admonition |
| 13.a. b. | ¹³Be watchful, stand firm in your faith, be courageous, be strong. Let all that you do be done in love. | GENERAL Admonition |

Figure 6.2. Two general admonitions (1 Cor 15:58; 16:13)

[1]NRSV.

As observed at the close of 15:58, again Paul has created a cameo that concludes the previous homily and at the same time opens the discussion that follows (cameo 1). First Corinthians 15:58 concludes the essay on the resurrection (15:1-57). It also opens Paul's discussion of financial gifts for Jerusalem and funds for apostolic travel.

The final admonition (cameo 13) includes five commands that read like a speech given by a commanding officer to his troops, with the exception of the last directive to do everything in love. The military flavor is strong in the first four commands. The final call to love provides a fitting conclusion to the homily.

Seen together each of these bookends (cameos 1, 13) is composed of two parts. The first part has to do with *character traits* and the second focuses on their *work in the Lord*. The character traits Paul lists are:

- be steadfast, immovable (1a)
- be watchful, stand firm in your faith, be courageous, be strong (13a)

In regard to their *work in the Lord*, he advises:

- be . . . always abounding in the work of the Lord,
  knowing that in the Lord your labor is not in vain. (1b)
- Let all that you do be done in love. (13b)

On reflection, the reader can connect the various character traits to some of the topics of the letter. The Corinthians need to be "steadfast, immovable" in their commitments to "Jesus Christ and him crucified." They must "stand firm in their faith and be courageous and strong" as they exercise discipline in the community and as they live out their lives in a pagan environment. They should be "watchful" as they await the "trumpet sound."

The second focus on "the work of the Lord" makes clear that awaiting the resurrection is not enough. They are to be engaged. The final appeal, to do everything in love, relates to the letter as a whole, not only to the final essay.

One recommended form for their "work of the Lord" is finance for mission. The text of the first financial appeal is displayed in figure 6.3.

2.      <sup>16:1</sup>Now concerning the contribution *for the saints*:
          as I directed the churches of Galatia,        A GIFT
          so you also are to do.                *For the Saints*

3.           <sup>2</sup>On the first day of every week,
               each of you is to *put something aside*     BASIS OF
               and *store it up*,                   Finance
               *as he may prosper*,
               so that contributions need not be made when I come.

4.          <sup>3</sup>And when I arrive,
           I will send those whom you accredit *by letter*    A GIFT
           to carry *your gift to Jerusalem*.         *For Jerusalem*
          <sup>4</sup>If it seems advisable that I should go also,
          they will accompany me.

**Figure 6.3. The collection for the saints in Jerusalem (1 Cor 16:1-4)**

In 9:1-18 Paul affirmed his right to receive financial support from the Corinthians and told his readers that they were responsible to pay the evangelists who came to them. Personally he refused such remuneration out of an eagerness to make the gospel free of charge and out of his desire to do more than what his commission required of him. Now Paul offers a contrast as he discusses the subject of "finance for mission."

It appears that Paul wanted to shape the Corinthian church (and all other churches that were reading this letter) as "missional churches." He did not tell them, "Be sure to pay your preachers." Nor did he say, "You have slaves among your membership. Be sure to take care of their special needs." Nor did he suggest, "Don't forget that Peter and Barnabas are married. You should pay a married man more than you give a single man," or, "Be sure to include a budget item to cover the extra expenses incurred by the owners of the homes in which your house churches meet." Instead, Paul offers three suggestions to his readers regarding their giving and all three have to do with *mission beyond their own community*.

Paul was not seated in a corner of the temple area in Jerusalem debating fine points of the Torah. He was on the move establishing new congregations. He wanted his readers to look beyond themselves and not merely pay their preachers. Paul did not suggest that they should first sort out who they were theologically and how they should live out the ethical requirements of the gospel, then some time in the future (with financial reserves in hand) they could consider contributing to the needs of others. Instead, in the midst of serious theological confusion and ethical aberrations, he urged them to contribute to needs *outside Corinth*. He looked first to Jerusalem, the "mother church."

The collection for Jerusalem has been studied carefully by Keith Nickle.[2] A full discussion of this topic is beyond the focus of this book. In passing we note that Paul's purposes included, at least:

1. a fulfilling of his pledge to the apostles in Jerusalem (Gal 2:10) that he would "remember the poor" (of Jerusalem),

2. a concern to unite the Jewish Christian and Gentile Christian elements into a wider fellowship,

3. an eagerness to publicly affirm Jerusalem's special status as the center of the church and,

4. a desire that each congregation might look outward and not inward.

Our concern is to note Paul's theology of mission giving and to observe his method in applying that theology.

Paul highlights his theology and methodology of giving by placing these two concerns in the middle of a simple ring composition (cameo 3). On the "first day of the week" each of them was to set aside some money for Jerusalem. He did not intend to "have a campaign" or even to "take up an offering" when he arrived. He suggested no set amount either for individuals or for the church in Corinth. Some of them were surely slaves with almost no income. Each person was to contribute "as he may prosper." Paul did not want anyone to ask, "How much money do you need, how much are other churches contributing and what is our fair share?" The church is not a country club and "mission" is not "putting a new roof on the clubhouse." Each is to contribute regularly "as he [or she] may prosper." Paul wanted the weekly, systematic giving to be collected before he arrived.

In cameo 4 Paul discusses the question of who will handle the money. By refusing to handle it he protects himself from criticism. He asks them to select their own financial representatives to carry the money (necessarily in cash) to Jerusalem. They knew who the honest people were in a way that he did not. Furthermore, he did not want anyone to take him aside and say, "You can trust so-and-so, but look out for so-and-so." Giving advice to an outsider on such matters is very complicated. The Corinthians (and others) had to decide who could be trusted to deliver the collected funds without taking a cut.

---

[2]Keith Nickle, *The Collection: A Study in Paul's Strategy*, Studies in Biblical Theology 48 (Naperville, Ill.: Allenson, 1966).

A further question was, did those who would deliver the money need letters, and if so from whom to whom? The text is ambiguous. The RSV (following the KJV) translates verse 3 as, "And when I arrive, I will send *those whom*
*you accredit by letter* to carry your gift to Jerusalem." That is, the *Corinthians*
must write letters for the delegation to take with them to Jerusalem (cf. NRSV,
JB). But the NIV reads, "I will *give letters of introduction* to the men you ap-
prove and send them with your gift to Jerusalem." This latter translation assumes that Paul will write letters introducing the delegation to his friends in
Jerusalem.

I am deeply convinced that the KJV, RSV, NRSV and JB are correct. In the
next verse Paul mentions the possibility of his accompanying them. He does
not say, "If I *do not go* with the delegation, I will be happy to write letters of
introduction to my friends." Obviously, if he accompanied the delegation
there would be no need for him to write letters of introduction to church leaders in Jerusalem. The letters Paul was talking about were important *even if he*
*went with them to Jerusalem.* The Middle Eastern versions, like the English
versions just quoted, are divided on this text. Some see the letters as documents written by Paul. Others read them as letters written by the Corinthian
leaders authorizing the delegation to handle their money.

The argument that Paul must be talking about a letter (or letters) that *he*
*will write* is voiced by Robertson and Plummer, who note that the delegation
will not leave until Paul arrives. "What need, therefore, for the Corinthians to
write letters?" ask Robertson and Plummer.[3] The assumptions behind this
point of view are clear: *If Paul goes*, no letter of introduction is necessary. *If*
*Paul does not go*, he will most certainly give the delegation letters of introduction to the apostolic leadership in Jerusalem. Thus (Paul or no Paul) there is
no conceivable need for the Corinthians to write anything.

But over a hundred years ago Findlay wrote, "Being chosen by the Corinthians, the delegates surely must have credentials from them (cf. 2 Cor. iii. 1,
and Acts xv)."[4] Building on that real need, there are compelling reasons for
Paul to insist that the delegation carry papers *from the donors* of the gift.

During the reign of Emperor Tiberius (d. A.D. 37) a case of theft was recorded by Josephus that relates to this topic. The story is about a man who
presented himself in Rome as a teacher of the laws of Moses. The man re-
cruited three others to join him in persuading a wealthy Roman woman by the

---

[3]Robertson/Plummer, *First Epistle*, p. 386.
[4]Findlay, *First Epistle*, p. 946.

name of Fluvia (a convert to Judaism) to give them "purple and gold for the temple at Jerusalem." Fluvia gave them the requested purple and gold, which they then stole. Her husband, Saturninus, discovered the theft and reported it to Tiberius, who responded by ordering "all the Jews to be banished out of Rome."[5] If this order was given, it must not have been carried out in a rigorous manner because, in A.D. 49, Claudius also "commanded all the Jews to leave Rome" (Acts 18:2). Yet the earlier incident was remembered. The question of a Jew collecting money in a Roman colony (claiming that the money was "for Jerusalem") was therefore a sensitive subject that could attract attention. The delegation *must have documentation* from responsible Corinthians (Romans?) who would sign for the donors. A letter from Paul was not enough!

Furthermore, the delegation would need such documentation to protect its own integrity. The entire gift had to be transported in cash. There was no other way. How much money was there originally? How much was stolen en route by the delegation? How much could legitimately be spent on travel? There had to be some written word from the donors declaring *the amount of the gift* and the *intentions of the donors*. This alone would demonstrate and preserve the integrity of the delegation. On arrival in Jerusalem the document, signed by the donors, would provide written proof to the apostles regarding the size of the gift and the donors' wishes.

With such donor documentation the delegation could not redirect a portion of the funds according to its whims. If on the way they found a needy fellow traveler, they could help him personally but they could not rechannel the church's gifts. The amount of the gift became public information when it was written in a public document. The congregation would know the amount collected. In the modern Middle East there is a well-known Arabic proverb that says, "Money left around loose teaches people to steal." The greater the distance between the givers and the receivers, the greater the possibility for part of the gift to disappear. Financial corruption is a known disease in cultures all around the world, and the Middle East is no exception. Paul understands this and his brief comments on *financial transparency and accountability* reflect careful thought and planning. He sets a standard for church finance that is a worthy model for the church in any culture and in any age.

Paul also knew that the Zealot movement was active in Judea. Both Roman and Jewish authorities could become *very interested* in a group of Gentiles (and

---

[5]Josephus, *Antiquities* 18.3.5, trans. William Whiston (Peabody, Mass.: Hendrickson, 1993), p. 481.

Jews?) who appeared out of nowhere with a large amount of cash for a minority organization in Jerusalem. Who *exactly* were they funding? The Zealots were active in Jerusalem. Dictators are *especially nervous* about cash moving across international borders. Precise documentation was critical for political reasons as well.

Paul wanted the donors to know that he trusted their messengers. He thus stated that he might or might not accompany them—leaving that option open. The scene in Corinth was too fluid at the time of writing. Paul appears to have thought of everything. At the heart of it all was a request for a sustained commitment to serve people beyond themselves. He wanted his readers to become *missional congregations*.

Paul's second financial request has to do with himself (see fig. 6.4).

| | | |
|---|---|---|
| 5. | ⁵I will visit you after passing through Macedonia, <br> for I intend to pass through Macedonia, | THROUGH <br> Macedonia |
| 6. | ⁶and perhaps *I will stay with you* <br> or even spend the winter, | I VISIT <br> You |
| 7. | so that you may *assist me on my journey*, <br> *wherever I go.* | FINANCE <br> *For Paul* |
| 8. | ⁷For I do not want to see you just now in passing; <br> *I hope to spend some time with you*, <br> if the Lord permits. | I VISIT <br> You |
| 9. | ⁸But I will stay in *Ephesus* until Pentecost, <br> ⁹for a wide door for effective work has opened to me, <br> and there are many adversaries. | IN <br> Ephesus |

**Figure 6.4. Paul's second financial request (1 Cor 16:5-9)**

## THE RHETORIC

The structure of these five cameos can be summarized as follows:

5. Paul's ministry beyond Corinth (Macedonia)
6.   His visit to Corinth
7.     His need for "travel funds"
8.   His visit to Corinth
9. Paul's ministry beyond Corinth (Ephesus)

## COMMENTARY

As indicated, Paul's ministry in Macedonia and in Ephesus is mentioned in the opening and closing of this section of the homily. The readers were familiar with Paul's statements "I die every day" (15:31) and "I fought with beasts at Ephesus" (15:32). There is no need for him to spell out the details. Stephanas, Fortunatus and Achaicus will probably carry his letter back to Corinth. They can explain everything orally. If Paul records the details—the wrong people might read them and things could get worse. He writes, "There are many adversaries" and that is enough.

After noting his ministry elsewhere (cameos 5, 9) he affirms and then reaffirms his desire for a long visit to Corinth (cameos 6, 8). He drops a hint that he might even spend the winter with them. We can surmise that Paul could find work more easily in Corinth than in any other city he visited. Tentmakers were naturally in demand for the spectators at the biennial Isthmian Games. Corinth also had two busy harbors. Tentmakers manufactured sails, and small ships that wintered in Corinth would naturally use the time to ready their vessels for the coming season. Paul had to winter somewhere and Corinth was a good place to do so.

Paul had not given up on them. In spite of their ethical and theological lapses, he loved them and wanted to live among them. His affection for them was not interrupted by the tough language he felt obliged to use as he discussed their failings.

His climax appears in the center. The key word *propempo* (help me on my journey)[6] is defined by BAGD as meaning to "help on one's journey with food, money, by arranging for companions, means of travel, etc."[7] Paul is seeking money and other assistance for himself and for Timothy. The detailed explanation of the extensive travel ahead for the three of them (Paul, Timothy and Apollos [16:5-12]) is not the casual news of the day; he is *fundraising for his travel budget*. He is saying indirectly, "Of course we need funding for travel—look at all of these journeys!"

Paul does not want any money for preaching the gospel to them. Nor does he ask them to arrange appropriate lodging in Corinth (now that Aquila and Priscilla, his former hosts in Corinth, have moved to Ephesus). Instead he (in effect) says,

I can earn my own keep—as I told you. But when it comes to travel—yes—

---

[6]Fee, *First Epistle*, p. 819.
[7]BAGD, p. 709.

while traveling I lose a lot of time and cannot make or mend tents while on the move. For travel expenses I (and my ministry team) need help, and for such costs I am eager for your financial assistance. I did not accept funds for my preaching. Surely you can help with my travel costs as I reach out to others.

Paul does not tell them where he is going, possibly because he simply had not yet decided. But it is also possible to see here a theology of mission that is exposed by this language. *He* will select his destination, *not the Corinthians.* Yes, he is asking for travel money, but no one in Corinth is allowed to say,

We don't think you gave Athens a fair try. We are very comfortable to see you return there, and (ahem) funding for an extended stay in Athens would be easy to collect. Athens is important to us. If you insist on going elsewhere, we could have a meeting and discuss your proposals. After all, if we are buying the ticket, we should have some say in where you are going!

In 4:1 Paul defined himself and his traveling friends as "servants of Christ." In 2 Corinthians 4:5 he further clarified his relationship to the Corinthians by adding, "(we are) your servants for Jesus' sake." Yes, he is a servant and will serve them (even free of charge), but *he will not surrender the right to choose the direction and nature of that servanthood.* Paul and his apostolic band will make those decisions.

Generally speaking the person you pay is in some sense under your control. Why were the Corinthians upset because Paul would not accept a salary from them when he was preaching in Corinth? Paul was obliged to make a spirited defense of his refusal to accept pay (9:3-18). I have a friend who served for some years as pastor to an English-language fellowship in a wealthy Middle Eastern country. On returning to America he had enough resources to pastor any congregation without a salary. He imagined that many struggling congregations would be eager to have him as their pastor. But he was mistaken. He is a fine pastor and a superb preacher, but churches were not interested. If they did not pay him they could not control him.

Paul probably had a plan, but did not want the Corinthians to imagine that they could determine his next move. "Please help fund my travel budget *wherever I go*" was his cry. This plea is the climactic center of his homily on funding.

When Paul divides a homily into three sections, the center has at least some prominence over the other two. At least partially, this principle may apply here as well. Paul told the Corinthians, "I became your father in Christ Jesus through the gospel" (4:15). With that special relationship, surely he could at least hint that *his mobility as an apostle to the Gentiles* had priority over Timothy's needs. A one-time collection for Jerusalem was very important to him (2 Cor 8–9) but his own mobility was critical to his continuing ministry.

Paul's third request for funding was also for mission outside the city of Corinth (see fig. 6.5).

| 10. | ¹⁰When *Timothy* comes,<br>see that he has nothing to fear among you,<br>for he is doing the work of the Lord, as I am.<br>¹¹So let no one despise him. | VISIT OF<br>Timothy<br>(coming) |
|---|---|---|
| 11. | *Assist him on his way* in peace,<br>that he may return to me;<br>for I am expecting him with the brethren. | FINANCE<br>*For Timothy* |
| 12. | ¹²As for our brother *Apollos*, I strongly urged him<br>to visit you with the other brethren,<br>but it was not at all his will to come now.<br>He will come when he has opportunity. | VISIT OF<br>Apollos<br>(not coming) |

**Figure 6.5. Paul's third request for funding (1 Cor 16:10-12)**

## THE RHETORIC

The rhetoric of this third section is straightforward. The request for additional funds appears in the center (cameo 11), while news of the ministry of Timothy and Apollos is placed on the outside.

## COMMENTARY

The opening reference to "fear" is revealing. Christian ministry from a position of powerlessness in a non-Christian world usually carries a serious component of risk and danger. Yes, Paul was a Roman citizen, but even that privileged status did not protect him from a public beating in the Roman colony of Philippi (Acts 16:19-24). In Corinth Paul was dragged before the Roman court and escaped unharmed, but Sosthenes, the new head of the synagogue, was beaten by his fellow Jews in public, with the Roman authorities watching and paying no attention (Acts 18:17). Paul's lists of hardships should never be passed over lightly (1 Cor 4:11-13; 2 Cor 6:4-6; 11:23-29). Paul Barnett makes the thoughtful suggestion that Paul's departure from Corinth was probably connected to the departure of Gallio from the city. Roman district judges served for one year and were then moved. Gallio ruled that the Christian movement was a part of Judaism and thereby legal (Acts 18:12-17). As long as Gallio was "on the bench," Paul was safe in Corinth. But Gallio stepped down

July 1, A.D. 51. A new judge might see things differently. When Gallio left town, so did Paul.[8] What will Timothy (a disciple of Paul) face when he enters Corinth?

When Paul admonishes the Corinthians to protect Timothy from fear, he could also mean that opponents of Paul in the church could threaten Timothy's ministry because he was close to Paul. I sense that the constant presence of danger (from beyond the church) was perhaps Paul's dominant concern.[9]

We are not told how Timothy supported himself. He could have accepted funding from the local congregations where he ministered, but evidently he also needed help with travel costs. Paul tells the Corinthians, "I/we (the apostolic band) can afford to send Timothy to you. But you must be responsible for sending him back to me. I am expecting him. Do not fail me!"

In his book *Jesus in Beijing*, David Aikman describes the house church movement in China. He tells of the outreach of the Tanghi Fellowship in the Henan province. In 1994 the Fellowship selected, trained and commissioned seventy young evangelists. They were given about $200 each and sent to twenty-two of China's thirty provinces. They were also given one-way tickets to their destinations and told to return after six months using the funds they would receive from the new house fellowships they were to establish. Exactly six months later, on October 10, 1994, all of them managed to meet the deadline and return to headquarters.[10] No one had died and there were only two short-term arrests. New communities of Christians were started in many places. Simultaneously, at five different locations, the young evangelists reported on their six months of ministry. Mr. Zing, one of the leaders of the fellowship, reported to Mr. Aikman,

> When we heard their testimonies, everybody was crying. They wore out their shoes, they were rejected by people. They lived in ditches and in forests. Some of them lived with pigs. In the meetings, God showed his love to us. We were joyful because they all came back alive.[11]

In the tradition of Paul, the new fellowships were invited to pay for the evangelists to return to the people who had sent them out.[12]

---

[8]Paul Barnett, *Jesus and the Rise of Early Christianity* (Downers Grove, Ill.: InterVarsity Press, 2002), p. 335.

[9]In the contemporary West there is a widespread mission-trip phenomenon. These efforts should be called "mission education trips." Often they take no risks, medical or physical.

[10]David Aikman, *Jesus in Beijing* (Washington: Regnery, 2003), p. 83.

[11]Ibid., p. 84.

[12]How many Western Christian "mission trips" follow this biblical precedent?

Paul concluded this threefold request for funding (cameos 5-9) with the second general admonition  examined above (cameo 13 [see fig. 6.2]).

As he continued to wind down, he offered a few words of commendation for the three men who came to him from Corinth and who most likely carried his epistle back to the congregation there (see fig. 6.6).

| | | |
|---|---|---|
| 1. | [15]Now brethren, you know that the *household of Stephanas* Were the first fruits in Achaia,[13] | HOUSE OF Stephanas |
| 2. | and they have *devoted themselves [tasso]* to the *service of the saints*; | DEVOTION Service to Saints |
| 3. | [16]I urge you to *be subject [hupo-tasso] to such men* and to *every fellow worker* and *laborer*. | BE SUBJECT To Such |
| 4. | [17]I rejoice at the coming of *Stephanas* and *Fortunatus* and *Achaicus*, | STEPHANAS Fortunatus, Achaicus |
| 5. | because they have *made up for your absence*; [18]for they *refreshed my spirit* as well as yours. | COMPENSATED Refreshed Me |
| 6. | Give *recognition* therefore *to such men*. | RECOGNITION To Such |

**Figure 6.6. Paul's words of commendation (1 Cor 16:15-18)**

## RHETORIC

Paul chooses step parallelism to express his views. Throughout the epistle he occasionally has two cameos, some distance apart, that are precisely woven together using step parallelism.[14] More often the two related cameos are side by side.[15] In this text Paul presents three closely connected topics, each of which is discussed twice, as shown in figure 6.6.

## COMMENTARY

The keys to these six cameos are the words *tasso* (devoted [themselves]) and *hupo-tasso* (be subject). No one elected or appointed the household of Stephanas to do anything.  They chose to *devote* themselves (*tasso*) to the service of the saints. Paul says, "Look for those who voluntarily give themselves in self-emptying service to others and follow them." The battle cry is, "Line up behind the servants." For Paul, the word *be subject* (*hupo-tasso*) is not about au-

---

[13]The KJV and the Greek text.
[14]1 Cor 3:5-9; 10:14-22; 15:13-17. This has a precedent in Is 28:15, 18, as noted earlier.
[15]1 Cor 5:9-11; 6:11; 6:13-14a; 7:36-37; 8:6; 11:4-5. This has a precedent in Is 55:10-11.

thority and power. It has to do with supporting those who voluntarily offer humble service to others. Leadership in this new fellowship called "the body of Christ" and "the new temple" is about finding the Mother Teresas of the world and joining them in their servanthood.

Paul is acting out the directive of Jesus when he said, "let the greatest among you become as the youngest, and the leader as one who serves. . . . I am among you as one who serves" (Lk 22:26-27). With Paul, as with Jesus before him, the system of patronage is reversed, and the one who voluntarily chooses to become a servant is the new leader.

These three men, writes Paul, have already "refreshed your spirits," and now they have done the same thing for him. Each of the first three cameos is repeated or completed in the matching final three. *Paul was the missionary*, not Stephanas and his friends. They did not have to "face wild animals" and "die every day." Paul did. Their task was to "refresh the spirit" of those on the ground in Ephesus who were engaged in mission. Stephanas and friends were engaged in a short-term "mission trip" and their efforts were much appreciated. But the larger task of mission was carried out by Paul and his team, not by short-term volunteers, and everybody knew it.

Paul continues to wind down as he extends greetings to the readers from the Christians in Asia Minor. These are:[16]

7.  [19]The churches of Asia send greetings.
    Aquila and Prisca, together with the church in their house,
    send you hearty greetings in the Lord.          GREETINGS FROM
    [20]All the brethren send greetings.              Brothers and Sisters
    Greet one another with a holy kiss.

The brief text opens a small window through which we are able to see many things. All the churches of Asia Minor were one fellowship (without email or Facebook!). Paul sends their greetings to the church in Corinth along with his own. He may again be staying in the household of Aquila and Prisca as he writes. Paul is careful to use her formal name (Prisca) rather than the more personal diminutive "Priscilla." He is very proper in so doing. The phrase "all the brethren" may refer to his apostolic band.

Paul concludes by urging the Corinthians to greet one another with a sign of authentic affection. Americans would say, "Give one another a hug." This

---

[16]Cameos 7 and 8 are "greetings" from various people. I have numbered them with cameos 1-6 because together these eight cameos fall under the general topic of "concluding remarks."

concluding directive harks back to the various party divisions he discussed in
the opening of his letter (1:10-13). Paul does not want a formal ceasefire between the warring parties, but rather a dissolving of all hostilities and a kin-
dling of genuine affection. Those who are "of Paul" and those who are "of
Cephas" are to greet each other with "a holy kiss."

Paul then takes the pen in his own hand and writes a postscript.

8.  a. [16:21]I, Paul, write this greeting with my own hand.
    b.  [22]If any one has no love for the Lord, let him be accursed.
    c.   Maranatha!                                    GREETINGS
    d.  [23]The grace of the Lord Jesus be with you.           From Paul
    e.  [24]My love be with you all in Christ Jesus. Amen.

Each of these five lines deals with a different topic and each deserves brief
comment.

*8a. "I, Paul write this greeting with my own hand."*

This first line of cameo 8 is often taken as evidence that Paul dictated
1 Corinthians. The argument is that after completing his dictation, Paul
takes the pen and scribbles his own final word. This view is usually built on
the widely held assumption that the epistle is a jumble, jumping from one
topic to another, composed in a hurry under pressure. Having found a great
deal of precision and thoughtful organization throughout, it is possible to
affirm that Paul composed the entire epistle with extraordinary care, using
both set pieces of composition already prepared and new material which he
had no doubt already taught in many churches. If he lectured in the hall of
Tyrannus every day for two years, he had a great deal of theological reflection on instant recall, some of which was in writing (Acts 19:9-10). Did he
never before discuss the cross, the Holy Spirit, Christian sexual behavior,
Christians in a pagan world, the Lord's Supper, spiritual gifts, the nature of
Christian love, the place of prophets in worship and the resurrection? Is it
possible to imagine that the hymn to the cross (1:17–2:2), the hymn on
Christian love (13:1-13) and the hymn on the resurrection (15:35-58) were
composed and dictated on the spur of the moment after a long day fighting
silversmiths?

Paul's eyesight may have been poor. At the end of Galatians he writes,
"See with what large letters I am writing to you with my own hand" (Gal
6:11). In his second letter to the Thessalonians he concludes, "I, Paul, write
this greeting with my own hand. This is the mark in every letter of mine; it
is the way I write" (2 Thess 3:17). His handwriting may have been both

large and hard to read. Before the days of printing, engaging a scribe with good handwriting was imperative for important documents. It is hard to take seriously a text that is barely legible. Having worked for forty years with many thousand-year-old, hand-copied Arabic and Syriac manuscripts, I know the innate tendency to pay more attention to those texts that have a clear, and at times beautiful, handwriting. Such handwriting is a precious gift that the author/scribe gives to the reader. How can Paul scribble "My love be with you all" (16:24) knowing that the reader is condemned to a frustrating struggle as she or he tries to read a long epistle written with the same almost illegible scrawl?

Paul must surely have composed 1 Corinthians with great care, spending long hours in composition to assure a nuanced statement of the truth of God. It is possible to assume a number of drafts. When the text was as precise and perfect as he could make it, he called in a brother with clear, attractive handwriting and said something like,

> Please make me a clean (fair) copy of this document. I want everyone in Corinth to be able to read it easily. Please do your best. This letter is important and may save a church. In fact, I would like to see that a copy reaches each of the churches. If there is anything you can't decipher, I'll read it to you. I love these people. Your beautiful handwriting will express that love to them indirectly on every page.

In Romans 16:22 the scribe (a believer) gives his name and sends his greetings to the church in Rome. Paul composed Romans with precision and, when he was finished, engaged a scribe. I pity any poor soul who has to read any lengthy document in my handwriting! Is it not possible that Paul's handwriting was both difficult to read and perhaps too large and thus too expensive for a long document? If transcribed with his large handwriting, such an epistle would require a much longer papyrus scroll. Knowing this Paul used a scribe/copyist.

*8b. "If any one has no love for the Lord, let him be accursed."*

"The Lord" for Paul was not an unknown person lost in the mists of the "oral tradition." Paul had listened to *eyewitness testimony*.[17] He had talked in person to hundreds of people who had seen and heard Jesus of Nazareth in the flesh before the cross. Jesus is Lord, and he is available to all who seek him through the indwelling Spirit and through the tradition of the church. At a

---

[17]Richard Bauckham, *Jesus and the Eyewitnesses: The Gospels as Eyewitness Testimony* (Grand Rapids: Eerdmans, 2006).

later stage, Gnostics did not like the Jesus of the Gospel records and created their own. Islam burst into the Middle Eastern world in the seventh century, conquering one district after another. Muslims were interested in Jesus because his name appears and is honored in the pages of the Qur'an. But they were not pleased with the Jesus they found in the Gospels, and thereby created what Muslim scholars have called "the Muslim Jesus."[18] The modern world, in turn, has created many different visions of Jesus.

Regarding Paul's curse on those who have no love for the Lord, Richard Hays notes astutely,

> The Christian community as a community of love is not infinitely inclusive: those who reject Jesus are not and cannot be a part of it. There is great danger to the church, in Paul's view, when some people represent themselves as Christians while rejecting the apostolically proclaimed gospel.[19]

For Paul there is no "other gospel" (Gal 1:8-9), and in this letter he has spoken his mind regarding those who say, "Let Jesus be cursed" (12:3). Through the use of a divine passive, Paul invokes the curse of God on those who do not love the Lord.

This is the third time that Paul presents opposing views and leaves his readers to sort out how he manages to live with the tensions of those opposites. (1) The first is in 4:9-13 where Paul records a list of hardships and wrongs that he has suffered. Then in 13:5 he writes love "keeps no account of wrongs."[20] (2) The second occurs in 10:19-22 when Paul states bluntly that idols do not exist and that those who worship them are *worshiping demons*. He sternly warns all Christians against such practice. A mere ten verses later he states, "Give no offense to Jews or to Greeks or to the Church of God" (10:32). If in Corinth he tells the worshipers of Jupiter and Athena, "Your gods do not exist and you are worshiping demons," is he not offending them? Yet, when lecturing on Mars Hill he quoted Greek literary sources sympathetically (Acts 17:28-29) and at the same time said, "we ought not to think that the deity is like gold, or silver, or stone." He is bold, and yet polite and respectful. (3) Cameo 8 showcases the third instance of what appears to be opposing texts. In 16:14 he writes, "Let all that you do be done in love." Six verses later he

---

[18]Tarif Khalidi, ed. and trans., *The Muslim Jesus: Sayings and Stories in Islamic Literature* (Cambridge, Mass.: Harvard University Press, 2001).

[19]Hays, *First Corinthians*, pp. 291-92.

[20]Under 13:5 there is an extended discussion of this first set of texts that can be read as opposites.

adds, "If any one has no love for the Lord, let him be accursed" (16:22). Paul is certainly not intending to call for love in all things and a few sentences later violate that call. The flash of anger expressed here is not an "emotional reaction of an offended self-concern"[21] but rather an unbending defense of Paul's deep commitment to his *Kurios*, his Lord. Later he will write to the Corinthians, "We destroy arguments and every proud obstacle to the knowledge of God, and take every thought captive to obey Christ" (2 Cor 10:5).

It is said that the classical British definition of a "gentleman" is someone who never insults anyone except on purpose. It is never by accident. But at the right time, faced with the right issue and confronted with the right person—an insult is the right thing to throw in the face of a representative of evil. Jesus' attack on certain types of Pharisees, recorded in Matthew 23:13-36, can be seen to fall into this category. Paul has already indicated that in Corinth there are those who claim to be inspired by the Spirit of God when they say, "Jesus be cursed" (12:3). Perhaps Paul is remembering that unthinkable claim, and responding to it. One is obliged to consider that Paul means to say, "There are times when invoking God's anger is an expression of love."

Paul's second letter to the Corinthians appears to be a collection of shorter letters. It is possible in that second epistle to see reflections of the first letter. In 2 Corinthians 2:4 Paul states, "For I wrote you out of much affliction and anguish of heart and with many tears, not to cause you pain but to let you know the abundant love that I have for you." Yes, he wrote some things that were hard for them to read, but those harsh words were written with tears and were intended to show his love. "Tough love," when called for, is a crucial component of deep and abiding love.

### 8c. "Maranatha!"

In this final cameo, Paul makes four statements about Jesus of which this is the second. The sudden appearance of two Aramaic words (*maran atha*) in a Greek document is startling. The earliest church incorporated a few key Hebrew-Aramaic words into its vocabulary. These include *amen, abba, halleluiah, mammon, hosanna* and *maranatha*.

As often observed, this last word can be read *maran atha* (our Lord has come). This translation addresses the readers and affirms a reality in the present (he is here). The two Aramaic words can also be divided to read *ma-*

---

[21]William Temple, *Christus Veritas* (London: Macmillan, 1954), p. 259.

*rana tha* (Our Lord—come!).[22] This is a request addressed to the risen Lord
that looks to the end of all things with the plea "Please come!" A variant on
this second option is, "Our Lord is coming." This also looks to the future, but
it is a statement of fact rather than a plea, and it is not addressed to Jesus. All
three options are linguistically possible, and all three fit Paul's theology.[23]
The only other occurrence of the Aramaic *maran atha* is in an early Christian
document called the *Didache* ("The Teaching"), where it appears in a chapter
on the Eucharist (*Didache* 10:6). Some have seen a relationship between
*maranatha* and the Greek of Revelation 22:20, "Amen, come, Lord Jesus!"
What can be said?

Many contemporary scholars have granted the validity of the two major
options (present and future) and have opted for the future.[24] Some have
granted that the word *atha* is a past that reads "has come" and have rejected
this option as reflecting ideas that Paul could not have intended.[25]

However, the past tense (has come) was preferred by the early fathers of the
church. John Chrysostom wrote, "But what does 'Maranatha' mean? Our
Lord has come. Why does Paul say this? To confirm what he has said about
God's plan for salvation, which is particularly evident in his discussion of the
seeds of resurrection (15:1-58)."[26]

Over the last fifteen hundred years Chrysostom's interpretations of Scripture have been highly regarded across the Middle East, and they continue to
impact the church there. Furthermore, Syriac, Arabic and Hebrew translations have consistently read *maranatha* as *maran atha* and translated it "our
Lord has come."[27] The Syriac Peshitta is particularly important, and its witness cannot be easily dismissed. Syriac is a sister language to Aramaic, and the
roots of the Syriac Peshitta are very early. Some of the early Arabic versions
leave the two Aramaic words in the text and divide them like the Syriac,

---

[22]All of the early copies of the New Testament have nodivisionsbetweenwords. The reader is
obliged to make them. Scholars across the board agree that we are dealing with two words and
both of the above divisions are possible.

[23]For a technical discussion of the languages involved, see K. G. Kuhn, "μαραναθα," in *TDNT*,
4:466-72.

[24]Fee, *First Epistle*, p. 839; Moffat, *First Epistle*, p. 284; Thiselton, *First Epistle*, pp. 1349-53;
Kistemaker, *1 Corinthians*, p. 612; Hays, *First Corinthians*, pp. 292-93; Barrett, *First Epistle*, p.
397.

[25]Findlay, *First Epistle*, p. 952; Orr/Walther, *I Corinthians*, p. 366.

[26]John Chrysostom, *1 Corinthians*, trans. and ed. Judith Kovacs (Grand Rapids: Eerdmans,
2005), p. 292.

[27]Both Hebrew versions concur with the Syriac. See London 1817; Jerusalem (Bible Society).

meaning "Our Lord has come."[28] Others have translated the two words into Arabic or written the Aramaic and then added an Arabic translation that reads, "Our Lord has come."[29] Among the twenty-three Semitic versions examined, there is no break in this tradition until the nineteenth century, when two individual efforts (one in India and the other in Lebanon) read the text as "Our Lord is coming."[30] Finally, two late-twentieth-century versions allow for "Our Lord—Come" as a marginal note, and the most recent version (1993) places this option in the text.[31] Matthew Black argued that the phrase was popular because of its "ambiguity and hence flexibility: it could be fitted into different contexts, in the Eucharist, as an imprecation, or as a confession ('The Lord has come')."[32] When all is said and done, for at least sixteen hundred years Middle Eastern churches have read this cry as a confession. Surely that option deserves serious consideration.[33]

In the light of the Aramaic origin and the enduring consistency of the Middle Eastern translation of these two words into "Our Lord has come," the following can be observed.

1. This is the only point in the epistle where Paul breaks into Aramaic. In 8:6 he refers to his Lord using the Greek word *kurios*. For us there is "one Lord [*Kurios*] Jesus Christ." So much for the ethnic Greek. But what about the Jew? For the Jew, Jesus was *Mar* (Lord). If it is right and true that God can be named *Abba* (Father/Our Father), then it is also right and true that Jesus can be called *Mar* and indeed *Maran* (Our Lord). Throughout his writings Paul managed nobly to express the deep things of God in the Greek language, yet in this text he (with his Jewish background) used his heart language to cry out *Maran* (Our Lord).

2. This use of *Mar* in connection with Jesus is an early Aramaic-Jewish cry from the heart. The fact that Paul uses Aramaic confirms that this was a

---

[28]Mt. Sinai 151 (867); Mt. Sinai 155 (9th cent.); Mt. Sinai 73 (9th cent.); Propagandist (1691); London Polyglot rev. (1717); Shidiac (1851); Martyn (1826); Bustani-Van Dyck (1865); Jesuit (1880); Yusif Dawud (1899); New Jesuit (1969).

[29]Vat. Ar. 13 (8th-9th cent.); Mt. Sinai 310 (10th cent.); London Polyglot (1657); Shawair (1813); Bustani-Van Dyck (1845-1860, as a note); New Jesuit (1969, as a note).

[30]Henry Martyn (1826); Shidiac (1851).

[31]Fakhouri (1964); New Jesuit (1969); Bible Society Arabic (1993). See appendix II, plate Q.

[32]Matthew Black, "The Maranatha Invocation and Jude 14, 15 (1 Enoch 1:9)," in *Christ and Spirit in the New Testament: Studies in Honor of Charles Francis Digby Moule*, ed. B. Lindars and S. S. Smalley (Cambridge: Cambridge University Press, 1973), p. 196.

[33]It is curious that appropriate deference is given in the literature to Matthew Black as an Aramaic scholar. But at the same time the fourth and fifth century translators of the Syriac Peshitta, whose first language was Syriac/Aramaic, are ignored.

"fixed term" in use among the churches.[34]

3. Chrysostom's point is well taken. If Jesus is *not raised*, then he is gone. But if he *is raised*, then he is still with us. Indeed "Our Lord has come" can mean incarnation and resurrection, as Chrysostom affirms.

4. It is not "My Lord" who is addressed here but "Our Lord," even as the Lord's Prayer opens with "Our Father." The community of faith utters this cry.

5. There is a relationship between this cry and the curse that Paul invokes against those who fail to love Jesus (16:22). It is like a group of protestors who gather at the gate of the palace shouting, "Down with the king!" Then a counter cry arises drowning them out saying, "Long live the king!" If there are those who do not like Jesus—so be it! But as for us: *Maran atha* (Our Lord has come). The very Lord Jesus, whom others so intensely dislike, is already here; he "has come," and because of his resurrection and the gift of the Spirit, he is among us—get used to it!

6. There is a strong possibility that this cry was used in connection with the celebration of the Eucharist. This is indeed the case, as noted, in the *Didache* (10:6) where the double word *maran atha* appears. At the Eucharist it is fully appropriate for worshipers to cry out "Our Lord has come" or "Our Lord is here."[35] "This is my body, which is for you" affirms his presence in a profound sense that reaches beyond all our attempts at definition.

7. It is true that in 1 Corinthians Paul expresses a heightened expectation for the return of Jesus. In 7:29 he writes, "The appointed time has grown very short." He also affirms, "Have I not seen the Lord?" (9:1). The Lord who appeared to him on the Damascus road had not abandoned him. The presence of Jesus, through the Spirit, is assumed throughout the epistle. The eight affirmations regarding the person of Jesus noted in 1:1-9 assume his continued presence. Indeed, "Our Lord is here!"

In light of these considerations, the centuries-old Middle Eastern Christian understanding of this text must surely be given serious consideration. Our Lord is here!

*8d. "The grace of the Lord Jesus be with you."*

Having found nothing else for which to be grateful, Paul opened the epistle with a prayer of thanks for the *grace* of God given to the Corinthians "*in Christ Jesus*" (1:4). At its close, he invokes *yet more* of *that same grace* upon

---

[34] K. G. Kuhn, "μαραναθα," in *TDNT*, 4:470.
[35] The Arabic *qad ja'a* (he has come) appears in Vat. Ar. 13 (8th-9th cent.); London Polyglot (1657); and Shawair (1813). This use of the particle (*qad*) carries overtones of "he has *indeed* come!"

them. Once more he selects a thread with which to sew the letter together.

*8e. "My love be with you all in Christ Jesus. Amen."*

After all the struggles he had come through with them—Paul's love remained. It was permanent; they could not break that bond, and he wanted them to remember its strength. They were quarreling among themselves and had taken offense at the cross. Immorality had broken out and some were offending others over idol meat. Celebrations of Holy Communion had become a disgrace, and there were disagreements over women leadership and spiritual gifts. Some had denied the resurrection, ignoring the creed. Yet in Christ Jesus—*he loved them all!*

Amen and amen!

After a very long journey in time and space with this great epistle, what can one say? A century ago Findlay concluded his introduction by writing:

> Within this stronghold of paganism and focus of Greek corruption [Corinth] Paul planted the cross of his Redeemer, rising out of his weakness and fear to a boundless courage. He confronted the world's glory and infamy with the sight of "Jesus Christ and Him crucified," confident that in the word of the cross which he preached there lay a spell to subdue the pride and cleanse the foulness of Corinthian life, a force which would prove to Gentile society in this place of its utter corruption the wisdom and power of God unto salvation. In "the church of God in Corinth," with all its defects and follies, this redeeming power was lodged.[36]

My prayer is that the Lord who inspired the apostle Paul to compose this masterpiece may move in our hearts and minds as we continue to struggle with many of the same problems that long ago he addressed so brilliantly.

---

[36]Findlay, *First Epistle*, p. 734.

# Common Themes in
# 1 Corinthians and Amos

THE BOOK OF AMOS CONCLUDES with a vision of the future when "the booth of David" will inherit "all the Gentiles upon whom my name is called" (Amos 9:12, my translation). This looks suspiciously like the opening of 1 Corinthians, where Paul affirms that he is writing to the Corinthians together with "all those upon whom my name is called in every place" (my translation). Are they related?

The prophecy of Amos and the epistle of Paul appear to be linked in four ways. These include (A) divine calling, (B) rhetorical style, (C) selection of metaphors and (D) theological/ethical content. Each of these points of comparison needs examination.[1]

## A. DIVINE CALLING AND EXPRESSIONS OF THAT CALLING IN AMOS AND 1 CORINTHIANS

This topic includes a number of aspects.

### 1. Both Amos and Paul affirm a divine calling.

When challenged by Amaziah, the priest of Bethel, Amos replies, "the LORD took me from following the flock, and the LORD said to me, 'Go, prophesy to my people Israel'" (Amos 7:15).

Paul defines himself as "called by the will of God to be an apostle of Christ Jesus" (1:1). Later, he asks the rhetorical question, "Am I not an apostle? Have I not seen Jesus our Lord?" (9:1). In the same passage he cries out "necessity is laid upon me" (9:16). He then defines himself as a person "entrusted with a commission" (9:17).

---

[1]Some of the points of comparison between Amos and 1 Corinthians here examined are found in other Hebrew prophets. My contention is that the overlap between 1 Corinthians and Amos is more extensive.

### 2. Both Amos and Paul are under attack.

Amos is under attack as a prophet. He is told to be silent and leave the country. He defends himself boldly and tells his accuser, Amaziah the high priest, that he (Amos) is under a divine commission *to prophesy* (Amos 7:10-17).

Paul is under attack as an apostle and he defends himself with vigor (9:1-18). He has a divine commission to *preach the gospel.*

### 3. Both of them have lowly professions.

Amos was a shepherd. When under attack by Amaziah, Amos fearlessly affirmed, "I am no prophet, nor a prophet's son; but I am a herdsman, and a dresser of sycamore trees" (Amos 7:14). Sycamore figs have a very low sugar content, almost no taste and are only eaten by the poorest of the poor. Amos's profession was not respected in the community but that fact did not faze him.

Paul supported himself as a tentmaker. Intellectuals and leaders among the Greeks were not expected to work with their hands. Part of the pressure on Paul to accept financial assistance from the Corinthians was probably related to the fact that they were not happy to have their founder working with his hands at "humdrum, often despised labor."[2]

### 4. Both Amos and Paul are missionaries.

Amos was a native of Judea (in the south) and was preaching in Israel (in the north).

Paul was a Jew preaching mostly to Gentiles outside of his own country.

## B. RHETORICAL STYLE IN AMOS AND IN 1 CORINTHIANS

Many commonalities can be demonstrated between the literary styles of Amos and 1 Corinthians. Amos uses the prophetic rhetorical template of seven inverted cameos with a climax in the center. An example of this appears in Amos 5:4-6 (see fig. I.1).

| | | |
|---|---|---|
| 1. [5:4]*Seek me* and *live;* | SEEK ME AND LIVE | |
| 2. but do not seek *Bethel,* | Bethel | |
| 3. and do not enter into *Gilgal* | Gilgal | |
| 4. or cross over to *Beer-sheba;* | Beer-sheba | |
| 5. for *Gilgal* shall surely go into exile, | Gilgal | |
| 6. and *Bethel* shall come to naught. | Bethel | |
| 7. [6]*Seek the* LORD and *live,* | SEEK THE LORD AND LIVE | |

**I.1. Prophetic rhetorical template of Amos 5:4-6**

[2]Thiselton, *First Epistle,* pp. 23-24.

Amos 2:14-16 with its two-line center exhibits a slight variation on the same template (see fig. I.2).

| | |
|---|---|
| 1.[2:14]*Flight* shall perish from the swift, | FLIGHT |
| 2.    the *strong* shall not retain his *strength*, | STRONG—STRENGTH |
| 3.      *nor* shall the mighty *save his life;* | NOT SAVE LIFE |
| 4a.        [15]who handles the bow *shall not stand*, | NOT STAND |
| 4b.          he who is swift of feet *shall not save himself*, | NOT SAVE SELF |
| 5.      *nor* shall he who rides the horse *save his life;* | NOT SAVE LIFE |
| 6.    [16]and he who is *stout* of heart among the *mighty* | STOUT—MIGHTY |
| 7.   shall *flee away* naked in that day. | FLEE AWAY |

**Figure I.2. Prophetic rhetorical template of Amos 2:14-16**

A second striking rhetorical style in the prophecy of Amos is the way he builds up a series of images in the form of questions. This appears in Amos 3:3-6 (see fig. I.3).

1.    [3:3]Do two walk together,
        unless they have made an appointment?
2.    [4]Does a lion roar in the forest,
        when he has no prey?
3.    Does a young lion cry out from his den,
        if he has taken nothing?
4.    [5]Does a bird fall in a snare on the earth,
        when there is no trap for it?
5.    Does a snare spring up from the ground,
        when it has taken nothing?
6.    [6]Is a trumpet blown in a city,
        and the people are not afraid?
7.    Does evil befall a city,
        unless the LORD has done it?

**Figure I.3. Series of questions in Amos 3:3-6**

Each of the seven questions in Amos 3:3-6 expects a negative reply. The first six put the reader into the mood of answering, "No, impossible!" Amos then makes his point in his seventh image/question. The Lord is in control of history.

A number of times in 1 Corinthians Paul also constructs lists. Sometimes they are lists of parables/metaphors (3:12-15; 9:7-10; 14:7-11; 15:36-41). Or they can be a list of sins (6:9-10) or a list of various kinds of people (7:29-31). A list of adjectives defining love (13:4-7) and lists of gifts (12:8-10, 28-29) also appear. The list of parables/metaphors in 9:7-10 reads:

⁹:⁷Who serves as a soldier at his own expense?

  Who plants a vineyard without eating any of its fruit?

  Who tends a flock without getting some of the milk?

    [⁹:⁸⁻¹⁰ᵃan interlude invoking the witness of the Torah]

¹⁰ᵇThe plowman should plow in hope.

  The thresher (should) thresh in hope of a share in the crop.

The first three, like Amos, expect negative responses. The last two are positive statements. In the middle of this list there is an interlude on the Torah. Yet in the five metaphors the soldier, the vineyard owner, the shepherd, the plowman and the thresher all expend energy expecting some return.

So much for rhetorical style. What of the selection of imagery?

## C. THE IMAGERY IN AMOS AND IN 1 CORINTHIANS

Amos and Paul use many of the same images. These include:

*1. Wild animals.* Amos talks about lions (Amos 1:2[3]; 3:4, 5, 8; 5:19), a bear (Amos 5:19) and a snake (Amos 5:19). Paul fought with "wild beasts" in Ephesus (1 Cor 15:32).

*2. The farmer.* Amos tells of those who plant vineyards and *do not* drink its produce (Amos 5:11). In his final vision of the future this order is reversed in that those who plant vineyards *will* drink their wine (Amos 9:14). Paul presents himself as a farmer who plants crops (3:6-8). He also mentions planting in general (9:7).

*3. The thresher.* For Amos, threshing is mentioned even though it is an image of cruelty (Amos 1:3). Threshing is one of the images Paul uses in 1 Corinthians 9:10.

*4. The shepherd.* Amos was a shepherd (Amos 1:1). The pastures of the shepherds "mourn" (Amos 1:2). The shepherd rescues a small part of a sheep (Amos 3:12). Paul notes that the shepherd (who tends a flock) has the right to some of the milk (9:7).

*5. Building and houses/temples.* Amos discusses houses and temples (Amos 3:15; 7:13; 8:3), and building or rebuilding them (Amos 5:11; 6:11; 9:11, 14). Corinth was destroyed in 146 B.C., and rebuilding started in 44 B.C.[4] Some of the city may have survived, yet the rebuilding must have been extensive. A contemporary Western wooden house can be built quickly. Stone houses, built

---

[3]Amos 1:2 affirms that the Lord "roars." He is thinking of the roar of a lion. This is evident from Amos 3:8.

[4]Thiselton, *First Epistle*, pp. 2-3.

without the benefit of power equipment, take years. Paul probably arrived in early A.D. 51, and due to the economic prosperity of that time, there must have been considerable construction underway across the city. Each construction project would have had a stonemason, called a "master builder," in charge. Paul used that image astutely to describe himself in this letter. He could not have reflected on Amos 9:11-12 without noticing the double reference to the rebuilding of ruined cities and the inhabiting of them (Amos 9:11, 14). Indeed, the labor of building and the resulting houses and temples are important images for Paul. He constructs a parable around this theme (3:9b-17; 6:19; 9:16).

*6. Fire of judgment.* The fire of God's judgment, and the image of burning, appear frequently in Amos (Amos 1:4, 7, 10, 12, 14; 2:2, 5; 5:6; 6:10; 7:4). Fire, for Paul, is an image of final judgment and testing (3:13-15).

*7. Light and darkness.* Light and darkness are images Amos employs (Amos 4:13; 5:8). In 4:5 Paul uses the same two metaphors.

*8. The trumpet.* Twice Amos hears the trumpet sound (Amos 2:2; 3:6). Twice Paul invokes a trumpet (14:8; 15:52).

*9. Musical instruments generally.* Amos refers to musical instruments (Amos 6:5). Musical instruments (other than the trumpet) are mentioned by Paul (13:1; 14:7).

*10. Mountains.* Mountains feature in Amos's prophecy (Amos 4:13). Mountains also appear in Paul's letter (13:2).

## D. THEOLOGICAL AND ETHICAL CONCERNS

A number of theological and ethical topics are dealt with by both Paul and Amos.

*1. Secrets/mysteries.* Amos tells his readers that God had revealed his "secret to his servants the prophets" (Amos 3:7). For Paul, God had revealed "secrets," "hidden wisdom" and "mysteries" to the apostles (2:7, 10; 4:1).

*2. Incest.* A case of incest appears in Amos (Amos 2:7). A man sleeping with his father's wife is the focus of an extended discussion for Paul (5:1-5). Both texts describe a man and his father (not a father and his son).

*3. Idol worship.* Amos is distraught over idolatry (Amos 2:4; 5:26-27; 8:14). Paul is also deeply concerned over idol worship and composed an essay related to the subject (8:1–11:1; 12:2).

*4. Sacrifices.* In the book of Amos the people bring their sacrifices "every morning" (Amos 4:4). Only in 1 Corinthians does Paul affirm, "Christ, our paschal lamb, has been sacrificed" (5:7). (This theme is dealt with differently by the two authors, but the subject of the atonement sacrifice links them together.)

**5. Slavery.** Amos condemns Gaza for enslaving a "whole people" (Amos 1:6). He also attacks Israel "because they sell the righteous for silver, and the needy for a pair of shoes" (Amos 2:6). Slavery is an important issue for Paul, who composes an entire sub-section on the question of how to cope with slavery (7:20-24). He tells his readers, "Do not become slaves of men" (7:23).

**6. The day of judgment.** "The day of the Lord" for Amos is a day of judgment (Amos 5:18-20). For Paul "the Day" (of the Lord) as a day of testing/judgment is important throughout 1 Corinthians (1:8; 3:13-15; 4:5; 5:5; 6:2-3; 7:26, 29, 31; 10:11; 15:24-28).

**7. The weak and the strong.** The book of Amos is famous for its defense of the poor and powerless against the rich and powerful. This theme permeates his prophecy. Paul is deeply concerned for "the weak" (in conscience) and the poor who "have nothing" and are humiliated by the rich (8:9-13; 11:22).

**8. Mourning over sin.** Amos is stricken over his people who "are not grieved over the ruin of Joseph!" (Amos 6:6). Paul is disturbed by the fact that his readers do not "mourn" over the gross sins being committed in their community (5:2, 6).

**9. Drunkenness.** Excessive drinking was condemned by Amos (Amos 4:1; 6:6). Paul faced the same problem in Corinth (5:11; 11:21).

**10. Desecrated sacramental worship.** Speaking for God, Amos attacks his readers sharply. "I hate, I despise your feasts," he declares. God will not accept or even look upon their offerings. Nor will he listen to "the noise" of their songs (Amos 5:21-23). Amos uses strong language in his rejection of the worship he observes. In like manner Paul is not pleased at what is happening at the Lord's Supper celebrations in Corinth. Their behavior is so unacceptable that he declares flatly, "it is not the Lord's supper that you eat" (11:20). One is hungry and another is drunk. The poor are humiliated. He will not commend them (11:22)! Paul also uses strong language as he criticizes the worship practices of the Corinthian church.

**11. Creation.** Creation was an important event for Amos. God "forms the mountains, and creates the wind. . . . [He] makes the morning darkness" (Amos 4:13). He also "made the Pleiades and Orion" (Amos 5:8).

Creation is high on Paul's agenda as well. It features prominently in the creedal formulation in 8:6. All things were created by God through Jesus. The creation story is the background to his discussion of men and women in worship leadership (11:7-13).

*12. The Gentiles.* Amos knows that God has a covenant with Israel. But Amos also writes, "'Are you not like the Ethiopians to me, O people of Israel?' says the Lord" (Amos 9:7). Yes, God brought Israel from the land of Egypt. But he also brought the "Philistines from Caphtor" (the Aegean islands) and "the Syrians from Kir" (Mesopotamia) and placed the Ethiopians in their land. Israel was not the only "family" that had received the grace of God in the form of the gift of a homeland. Furthermore, for Amos, "In that day . . . all the nations/Gentiles on whom my name is called" will become a part of the inheritance of "the booth of David that is fallen" (Amos 9:11-12).

Paul is deeply committed to the incorporation of the Gentiles into the people of God. The epistle is addressed to "all those on whom is called the name of our Lord Jesus Christ" (1:2). Many of those were Gentiles. The presentation of the gospel for both "Jew and Greek" is prominent in the great hymn to the cross (1:17–2:2) and elsewhere (9:19-23; 12:2; 16:1-19).

*13. God "knows" his people.* Amos writes, "You only *have I known* of all the families of the earth" (Amos 3:2). It was not simply that they knew God, but God knew them. Paul says, "But if one loves God, *one is known* by him" (8:3). The people of God are known by God in a special way. In the end "I shall know fully as I am fully known" (13:12).

## Summary

What then can we conclude from the extensive parallels between the book of Amos and 1 Corinthians? The following points can be made.

*1. The prominence of Amos 9:11-12 in the Jerusalem council meeting.* From Acts 15:16-18 it is clear that Amos 9:11-12 was an important part of the early apostolic reflection on the urgent question of the incorporation of the Gentiles into the people of God.

*2. Amos 9:11-15 and Paul.* Paul reflected deeply on Amos 9:11-15. This is apparent in three ways. (1) In the opening verses of his letter Paul affirms that he is writing to all those "upon whom my name is called." This language is very close to Amos 9:12. (2) Amos's vision of "in that day . . ." includes *repairing, raising up* and *rebuilding* of buildings. For Amos, God is going to "rebuild" (Amos 9:11) and the people will also "rebuild" (Amos 9:14). Paul makes extensive use of the image of *building* and creates an extended parable out of that image. Paul builds, and so do many others (3:9b-17). (3) Amos 9:11-15 is full of *farming* images. God is going to plant, and so are the people. These images tumble one after another like a waterfall in Amos 9:11-15. They include plowman, reaper, treader of grapes, sower, sweet wine dripping and flowing, planters of vineyards, makers of gardens, God's planting and the people never being uprooted. The connecting thread that runs through these images focuses on the farmer who *works* and *receives benefit* from his or her labor. Paul also uses farming images widely. He creates an extended parable built on "planting and watering" (3:6-9a). In his defense of his right to patronage he has four farming images, and all of them (like Amos) focus on work completed *and* benefit received (9:7-11). Paul turns again to a farming image when he explains the nature of the resurrected body (15:37-38, 42-43). With Amos, Paul focuses on sowing and the anticipated harvest that results.

**3. Acts 18:1-17 and Paul's first visit to Corinth.** Three events significant for this topic happened to Paul in Corinth during his eighteen-month stay in the city. (1) Paul was rejected by many in the synagogue, and he responded to that rejection by acting out Jesus' "sacrament of failure." He shook out his garments in the presence of his opponents.[5] (2) Paul then made an important move toward broadening his ministry among the Gentiles. This is confirmed by his recorded statement, "From now on I will go to the Gentiles" (Acts 18:6). (3) Paul had a vision of "the Lord" telling him, "I have many people in this city" (Acts 18:10). With the acceptance of the Gentiles by the Jerusalem Council, and James's quotation of Amos 9:12 in their deliberations, Paul would naturally have turned to the book of Amos as he contemplated further efforts among the Gentiles.

**4. In 1 Corinthians the Gentile believers are "no longer Gentiles."** At least at this stage in his ministry, Paul understood the new Gentile believers as people who had taken on a new identity. Paul never calls them "Jews." Instead he tells them that they are a part of the body of Christ and are built into the new temple. Abraham is their father and they are no longer "Gentiles." This appears in 12:2 where he writes, "when you were *Gentiles* (*ethne*), you were led astray to dumb idols."[6] This same assumption underlies 10:18 in the Greek text, where Paul refers to "Israel according to the flesh." The church in his mind is "the Israel of God" (Gal 6:16). In 10:1 Paul writes, "I want you

---

[5]In Antioch of Pisidia Paul carried out the same dramatic action (Acts 13:51). In Lk 9:5 Jesus instructs his disciples, when rejected, to shake off the "dust of the feet." This has to do with dust that arises from the feet and enters a person's outer cloak. The rejected messenger is told to take the cloak off and shake it as he or she departs.
[6]The RSV translates this word as "pagans." The Greek word is *ethne* (Gentiles).

to know, brethren, that *our fathers* were all under the cloud." In Paul's mind the "fathers" of the exodus were the ancestors of *the whole church*. He continues in verse 14 to address the same people and says, "Therefore, my beloved, shun the worship of idols." This language is pointedly addressed to believers with a Gentile background. The Gentiles, through faith and baptism, had joined the "Israel of God," even though they were not "Israel according to the flesh." This new Israel of God had a new temple, and they were part of it. That temple was the community, and the Holy Spirit had taken up residence in that new temple even though it was still in the process of being built (3:16-17). This means that Paul could have seen Amos 9:11-12 as being fulfilled in his day. Paul agreed with James. The incorporation of the Gentiles into the "booth of David," foreseen by Amos, was happening before their eyes.

In summary, Paul, like Amos, had a lowly occupation and was obliged to defend his calling as a messenger of God. Like Amos, Paul had to deal with drunkenness, incest, immorality, abuse of the weak, slavery, idol worship and perverted sacramental worship. Like Amos, he understood the secrets of God and reflected on creation and the coming of the Gentiles into the faith. Like Amos, Paul thought deeply on "the day of the Lord" and the fire of judgment. Many of Amos's concrete images and theological themes reappear in 1 Corinthians.

If the connection between these two texts is contemplated, new avenues into Paul's mind are opened. He does not start from scratch as he writes 1 Corinthians. The origin of significant parts of Paul's imagery, his ethics and his theology can be traced to the oracles of Amos, who faced many of the same problems. Paul looked far more to Jerusalem (Jewish sources) than he did to Athens (Greek sources). Observing the connections between Amos and Paul can help us better understand the prophetic roots of 1 Corinthians and more accurately interpret that letter for our day.

# Evidence from the Oriental Versions Used in This Study

Appendix II             *Oriental Versions: Plate A*           1 Cor 1:26

*The text under study:* (literal) Not many wise according to the flesh

*Greek*: ʽοτι ʼου πολλοι σοφοι κατα σαρκα

*Syriac: Peshitta*              ܕܠܐ ܣܓܝܐܐ ܡܢ ܚܕ ܚܟܝܡܐ ܣܓܝܐܐ ܒܒܣܪ

### Arabic: 8ᵗʰ to 16ᵗʰ centuries
Vatican Arabic #13 (8ᵗʰ -9ᵗʰ Cent.)         انه ليسوا كثير فيكم الحكماء الجسد
Bishr: Mt. Sinai 151 (867)                انه ليس الحكماء بالجسد كثير فيكم
Gibson, Mt. Sinai 155 (9ᵗʰ)               لأن ليس مثل الجسد حكماء كثير
Mt. Sinai #73 (9ᵗʰ)                       لأن ليس فيكم بالجسد حكماء كثيرون
Mt. Sinai Ar. #310 (10ᵗʰ)                 ليس فيكم من حكماء الجسد كثير
Ms. Bodl. Or. 712 (16ᵗʰ century?)     افما يوجد حكماء كثيرون فيما يخص بالبشر

### Arabic: 17ᵗʰ to 18ᵗʰ centuries
Erpenius (1616)                    يا اخوتى ليس فيكم من حكماء الجسد كثيرون
London Polyglot (1657)             افما يوجد حكماء كثيرون فيما يخص البشر
Propagandist (1671)                انه ليس حكماء كثيرون حسب الجسد
Revised London Polyglot (1717)     ان ليس حكماء كثيرون فيما يخص البشر

### Arabic: 19ᵗʰ century
Shawair, Lebanon (1813)            انه لا يوجد حكماء كثيرون فيما يخص البشر
Calcutta, H. Martyn (1826)         انه ليس فيه من الحكماء بالنسبة الى الجسد
Faris al-Shidiac (1851)            انه ليس بكثيرين حكماء حسب الجسد
Bustani-VD (MSS 1845-1860)         انه ليس كثيرون حكماء حسب الجسد
Bustani-Van Dyck (1860)            ان ليس كثيرون حكماء حسب الجسد
Jesuit (1880)                      انه ليس كثيرون حكماء بحسب الجسد
Yusif Dawud (1899)                 انه ليس كثيرون حكماء حسب الجسد

### Arabic: 20ᵗʰ century
Paulist – Fakhouri (1964)     المدعوين فيكم فليس كثيرون حكماء بحسب الجسد
New Jesuit (1969)             فليس فيكم كثير من الحكماء بحسب الجسد
Bible Society (1993)         فما كان فيكم كثير من الحكماء

### Hebrew
Hebrew: London, 1817              לא לחכמים רבים כבשר
Hebrew: Jerusalem (Bible Society)  שלא רבים החכמים מן הבשר

# Appendix II      *Oriental Versions: Plate B*     1 Cor 5:1a

***The text under study:*** Everyone has reported that there is immorality among you,

**Greek:** ὅλως ακουετι εν ὑμιν πορνεια

**Syriac:** *Peshitta*     ܡܟܠ ܡܫܬܡܥܐ ܒܝܢܬܟܘܢ ܙܢܝܘܬܐ

### Arabic: 8th to 16th centuries
Vatican Arabic #13 (8th -9th Cent.)     انه استمع ان فيكم الزناء
Bishr: Mt. Sinai 151 (867)     ثم بلغنى ايضا فيكم زنى
Gibson, Mt. Sinai #155 (9th)     يقينا قد سُمع فيكم الزتاء
Mt. Sinai #73 (9th)     قد سُمع يقينا الزناء
Mt. Sinai Ar. #310 (10th)     فالجملة انكم تعابون بالزناء
Ms. Bodl. Or. 712 (16th)     و بالجملة يُسمع ان فيكم زناء

### Arabic: 17th to 18th centuries
Erpenius (1616)     فان على جمله الامر انكم تعابون بالزناء
London Polyglot (1657)     وبالجملة يُسمع ان فيكم زناء
Propagandist (1671)     فان على جمله الامر شاع خبر ان بينكم زناء
Revised London Polyglot (1717)     بالجملة يُسمع ان فيكم زناء

### Arabic: 19th century
Shawair, Lebanon (1813)     وبالجمله يُسمع ان فيكم زناء
Calcutta, H. Martyn (1826)     قد اشتهر ان فيكم من الزناء
Faris al-Shidiac (1851)     لقد يُسمع و ذلك بالكليه ان بينكم زناء
Bustani-VD (MSS 1845-1860)     يُسمع بالجمله ان فيكم زناء
Bustani-Van Dyck (1865)     يُسمع مطلقا ان بينكم زناء
Jesuit (1880)     لقد شاع بين الجميع ان بينكم زناء
Yusif Dawud (1899)     على جمله الأمر قد شاع ان بينكم زناء

### Arabic: 20th century
Paulist – Fakhouri (1964)     لقد شاع ان بينكم حادث فُحش
New Jesuit (1969)     لقد شاع خبر ما يجرى عندكم من فاحشه
Bible Society (1993)     شاع فيى كل مكان حبر ما يحدث عندكم من زنا

### Hebrew
Hebrew: London, 1817     מכל נשמע על זנוה
Hebrew: Jerusalem (Bible Society)     הקול נשמע בכל מקום שזנות ביניכם

Appendix II          *Oriental Versions:  Plate C*          1 Cor 5:1b

*The text under study:* "Gentiles" or "pagans"?

*Greek*: 'εθνεσιν

*Syriac:* Peshitta                                                  ܠܥܡܡܐ

*Arabic: 8ᵗʰ to 16ᵗʰ centuries*
Vatican Arabic #13 (8ᵗʰ – 9ᵗʰ)                       ولا فى الشعوب يسمى
Bishr: Mt. Sinai 151 (867)                          لا فىالأمم يذكر أيضا
Gibson, Mt. Sinai #155 (9ᵗʰ)                         ليس فى الأمم مثله
Mt. Sinai #73 (9ᵗʰ)                                  ليس فى الأمم مثله
Mt. Sinai Ar. #310 (10ᵗʰ)                            لا يذكر من الوثنيين
Ms. Bodl. Or. 712 (16ᵗʰ)                             ما سمي و لا فى الأمم

*Arabic: 17ᵗʰ to 18ᵗʰ centuries*
Erpenius (1616)                                      فى الوثنيين
London Polyglot (1657)                               الأمم
Propagandist (1671)                                  ولا مثله بين الأمم
Revised London Polyglot (1717)                       ما سمي ولا فى الأمم

*Arabic: 19ᵗʰ century*
Shawair, Lebanon (1813)                              ما سمي و لا فى الأمم
Calcutta, H. Martyn (1826)                           لا فى العوام
Faris al-Shidiac (1851)                              لم يُسمَّ بين الأمم
Bustani-VD (MSS 1845-1860)                           الأمم
Bustani-Van Dyck (1865)                              الأمم
Jesuit (1880)                                        بين الأمم
Yusif Dawud (1899)                                   لا يذكر بين الأمم

*Arabic: 20ᵗʰ century*
Paulist – Fakhouri (1964)                            و لا بين الأمم
New Jesuit (1969)                                    عند الوثنيين
Bible Society (1993)                      لا مثيل له حتى عند الوثنيين

*Hebrew*
Hebrew: London, 1817                                 בגוים
Hebrew: Jerusalem (Bible Society)                    בנוים

Appendix II          ***Oriental Versions: Plate D***          1 Cor 7:1b

***The text under study:***   It is good for a man not to touch a woman.   (or)
Is it good for a man not to touch a woman?

***Greek***: καλον 'ανθρωπω γυναικος μη 'απτεσθαι   (Statement or Question?)

***Syriac***: *Peshitta*  ܫܦܝܪ ܗܘ ܠܓܒܪܐ ܕܠܐ ܢܬܩܪܒ ܠܐܢܬܬܐ

### Arabic: 8th to 16th centuries
Vatican Arabic #13 (8th -9th)      فإنه حسن للرجل ان لا يقرَب امرأة
Bishr: Mt. Sinai 151 (867)      فأعلمكم يا إخوة أنه حسن للرجل ألا يريد امرأة
Gibson, Mt. Sinai #155 (9th)      أخير للرجل ان لا يمس امرأة
Mt. Sinai #73 (9th)      أخير للرجل ان لا يمس امرأة
Mt. Sinai Ar. #310 (10th)      فإنه حسن بالرجل ان لا يقرب امرأة
Ms. Bodl. Or. 712 (16th)      فجيد للإنسان ان لا يلامس امرأة

### Arabic: 17th to 18th centuries
Erpenius (1616)      حسن بالرجل ان لا يدنو من امرأة
London Polyglot (1657)      فجيد للانسان ألا يلامس امرأة
Propagandist (1671)      فانه حسن بالرجل ان لا يدنو من امرأة
Revised London Polyglot (1717)      فجيد للانسان ألا يلامس امرأة

### Arabic: 19th century
Shawair, Lebanon (1813)      فجيد للانسان ألا يلامس امرأة
Calcutta, H. Martyn (1826)      فان الحسن للرجل ان لا يمسَ امرئة
Faris al-Shidiac (1851)      فيحسن بالرجل ان لا يمسّ امرأة
Bustani-VD (MSS 1845-1860)      فيحسن للرجل ان لا يمس امرأة
Bustani-Van Dyck (1865)      فحسن للرجل ان لا يمسَ امرأة
Jesuit (1880)      فحسن للرجل ان لا يمس امرأة
Yusif Dawud (1899)      فانه حسن للرجل ان لا يمسّ امرأة

### Arabic: 20th century
Paulist – Fakhouri (1964)      فحسن للرجل ان لا يمسّ امرأة
New Jesuit (1969)      فيحسن بالرجل ان لا يمسّ امرأة
Bible Society (1993)      خير للرجل ان لا يمسّ امرأة

### Hebrew
Hebrew: London, 1817      טוב לאיש לבל יגע באשה
Hebrew: Jerusalem (Bible Society)      לטוב לאד שלא יגע באשה

**Appendix II**     *Oriental Versions: Plate E*     1 Cor 7:20, 24

**The text under study:**
(20) each one in *the calling* in which he was *called* (24) in *that which* he was *called*

**Greek:** *(20)* ἕκαστος ἐν τῇ κλήσει ᾗ ἐκλήθη      (24) ἕκαστος ἐν ᾧ ἐκλήθη

**Syriac:** *Peshitta*    ܚܠܦ ܚܡܝܢܟܐ ܕܐܝܬܘܗܝ، ܗܘ ܡܢܗ ܐܠܗܐ    ܚܠܦ ܚܡܝܡ ܕܐܝܬܘܗܝ، ܐܝܢܐ

**Arabic: 8th to 16th centuries**     7:20     7:24

| | 7:20 | 7:24 |
|---|---|---|
| Vatican Arabic #13 (8th -9th Cent.) | الدعوة التى دُعي بها | الشي الذى دُعي به |
| Bishr: Mt. Sinai 151 (867) | أحد بالذي دُعي | فليثبت كما دعاه الله |
| Gibson, Mt. Sinai #155 (9th) | كل إنسان بما دُعي | الدعوة التى دُعي بها |
| Mt. Sinai #73 (9th) | الدعوة التي دعى بها | بالدعوة الذى دعى به |
| Mt. Sinai Ar. #310 (10th | كل امرئ منكم بما دعي يثبت | مرئ منكم على |
| Ms. Bodl. Or. 712 (16th) | الدعوة التى دُعي فيها | في الشي الذى دُعي اليه |

**Arabic: 17th to 18th centuries**

| | | |
|---|---|---|
| Erpenius (1616) | الحال التى دعى الى الأيمان عليها | الأمر الذى دعى عليه |
| London Polyglot (1657) | فى الدعوة التى دعى فيها | فى الشي الذى دعى اليه |
| Propagandist (1671) | الى الحال التى دعى الى عليها | الأمر الذى دعى عليه |
| Rev. London Polyglot (1717) | فى الدعوة التى دعى فيها | فى الشى الذى دعى فيه |

**Arabic: 19th century**

| | | |
|---|---|---|
| Shawair, Lebanon (1813) | دعاه الرب كذلك فليستمر | الدعوة التى دعى فيها |
| Calcutta, Martyn (1826) | فى حالة الاستدعاء التى دعى فيه | الدعوة التى دعى فيها |
| Faris al-Shidiac (1851) | على الدعوة التى دعى فيه | على ما دعى فيه |
| Bustani-VD (MSS 1845-1860) | الدعوة التى دعى اليها | ما دعى كل واحد فيه |
| Bustani-Van Dyck (1865) | الدعوا التى دعى فيها | ما دعى كل واحد فيه |
| Jesuit (1880) | على الدعوة التى دعى فيها | ما دعي فيه |
| Yusif Dawud (1899) | على الحال الذى دعي عليه | على الامر الذى دعى عليه |

**Arabic: 20th century**

| | | |
|---|---|---|
| Paulist – Fakhouri (1964) | على الحالة التى دعى فيها | على ما دعى فيه |
| New Jesuit (1969) | الحال اليى كان فيها حين دعاء الله | الحال التى كان فيها حين دعى |
| Bible Society (1993) | عندما مثلما كانت عليه حاله دعاه | حاله عند ما دعاه الله |

**Hebrew**

| | | |
|---|---|---|
| Hebrew: London, 1817 | בקראה אשר נקרא בה | עם אלהים באשר נקרא בה |
| Hebrew: Jer. (B. Soc) | משמרתו שמתוכה נקרא בה | משמרת שמתוכה נקרא בה |

Appendix II          *Oriental Versions:  Plate F*                    1 Cor 8:6

*The text under study*: (one F.) from whom are all things and we from him -
          (one Lord) through whom are all things and we through him

Greek: (one Father)'ἐξ οὗ τα παντα και ἡμεις εἰς αὐτον  (one Lord) δι' οὗ τα παντα και
                                                                        ἡμεις δι' αὐτου

|  | (One Lord) | (One Father) |
|---|---|---|
| *Syriac: Peshitta* | ܘܚܕ ܟܡܪܝܐ ܘܐܟ ܣܝ ܟܡܪܝܐ | ܚܠ ܡܢܗ ܘ ܣܝ ܟܡ |

### Arabic: 8th to 16th centuries

| | | |
|---|---|---|
| Vatican Arabic #13 (8th -9th) | كل شيء به ونحن بيده | منه كل شيء ونحن فيه |
| Bishr: Mt. Sinai 151 (867) | الكل بيده ونحن ايضا بيده | الكل منه و نحن به |
| Gibson, Mt. Sinai #155 (9th) | به كل سيء و نحن ب | منه كل شيء ونحن اليه |
| Mt. Sinai #73 (9th) | الكل به و نحن به | منه الكل و نحن اليه |
| Mt. Sinai #310 (10th) | فى قبضته و نحن به و فى يديه | الكل منه و انما نحن به |
| Ms. Bodl. Or. 712 (16th) | منه الكل و نحن به | منه كل البرايه و نحن لديه |

### Arabic: 17th to 18th centuries

| | | |
|---|---|---|
| Erpenius (1616) | كل بيده و نحن ايضا | كل شيء بيده و نحن به |
| London Polyglot (1657) | منه الكل و نحن به | منه كل البرايا و نحن لديه |
| Propagandist (1671) | كل الأشياء به و نحن ايضا | كل الأشياء منه و نحن اليه |
| Revised London Polyglot (1717) | به الكل و نحن به | نه كل البرايا و نحن اليه |

### Arabic: 19th century

| | | |
|---|---|---|
| Shawair, Lebanon (1813) | به الكل و نحن به | منه كل البرايا و نحن له |
| Calcutta, H. Martyn (1826) | تكوّنت به كل الكائنات و نحن به | منه جميع الموجودات و نحن له |
| Faris al-Shidiac (1851) | به كل شيء و نحن به | منه كل شيء و نحن له |
| Bustani-VD (MSS 1845-1860) | له جميع الأشياء و نحن | منه جميع الأشياء و نحن له |
| Bustani-Van Dyck (1865) | له جميع الأشياء و نحن به | منه جميع الأشياء و نحن له |
| Jesuit (1880) | به كل شيء و نحن به | منه كل شيء و نحن اليه |
| Yusif Dawud (1899) | كل شيء به ونحن ايضا | كل شيء منه و نحن اليه |

### Arabic: 20th century

| | | |
|---|---|---|
| Paulist – Fakhouri (1964) | به كل شيء و نحن به | منه كل شيء و نحن اليه |
| New Jesuit (1969) | به كان كل شيء و به نحن | منه كل شيء و اليه نحن راجعون |
| Bible Society (1993) | به كل شيء و به نحن | منه كل شيء و اليه نرجع |

### Hebrew

| | | |
|---|---|---|
| Hebrew: London, 1817 | בו הכל ואהנחנו בה | מנו הכל והנחנו לו |
| Hebrew: Jerusalem (B. S.) | הכל יבה ואנחנו על ידו | הכל ממהו ואנחנו אליה |

Appendix II          *Oriental Versions:  Plate G*          1 Cor 10:18

*The text under study*: Look at Israel according to the flesh

*Greek*: βλεπετε τον' Ισραηλ κατα σαρκα.

*Syriac:* Peshitta                          ܣܘܗ ܠܐܝܣܪܝܠ ܒܒܣܪܐ

### Arabic: 8th to 16th centuries
Vatican Arabic #13 (8th -9th Cent.)          انظروا اسرايل الذى بالجسد
Bishr: Mt. Sinai 151 (867)                   انظروا الى اسرائل الذى بالجسد
Gibson, Mt. Sinai #155 (9th)                 انظروا الى اسرائل الذى بالبشرية
Mt. Sinai #73 (9th)                          انظروا الى اسرائل بجسد
Mt. Sinai Ar. #310 (10th)                    انظروا الى اسرائل حسب الجسد
Ms. Bodl. Or. 712 (16th)                     ابصروا اسرائيل الجسدانى

### Arabic: 17th to 18th centuries
Erpenius (1616)                              انظروا الى ال اسرائل الجسدانيين
London Polyglot (1657)                       انظروا الى اسرائل حسب الجسد
Propagandist (1671)                          ابصروا اسرائيل الجسدانى
Revised London Polyglot (1717)               ابصروا اسرائيل الجسدانى

### Arabic: 19th century
Shawair, Lebanon (1813)                      ابصروا اسرائيل الجسدانى
Calcutta, H. Martyn (1826)                   فا نظروا الى اسرائيل الجسدانى
Faris al-Shidiac (1851)                      انظروا اسرائيل من جهة الجسد
Bustani-VD (MSS 1845-1860)                   انظروا الى اسرائيل حسب الجسد
Bustani-Van Dyck (1865)                      انظروا الى اسرائيل حسب الجسد
Jesuit (1880)                                فا نظروا الى اسرائيل الجسدانى
Yusif Dawud (1899)                           انظروا الى ال اسرائل حسب الجسد

### Arabic: 20th century
Paulist – Fakhouri (1964)                    فتأملوا اسرائيل حسب الجسد
New Jesuit (1969)                            أنظروا الى اسرائيل من حيث انه بشر
Bible Society (1993)                         انظروا الى بنى اسرائيل

### Hebrew
Hebrew: London, 1817                         ראו בעשרעל כבשר
Hebrew: Jerusalem (Bible Society)            הביטו אל ישראל שלפי הבשר

## Appendix II     *Oriental Versions: Plate H*     1 Cor 10:20, 27, 32

| *The text under study*: | The Gentiles | Unbelievers | Greeks |
|---|---|---|---|
| *Greek*: | (v. 20) τα 'εθνη[1] | (v. 27) 'απιστων | (v. 32) 'ελλησιν |
| *Syriac: Peshitta* | ܥܡܡܐ | ܥܡܡܐ | ܐܝܘܢܝܐ |
| **Arabic: 8th to 16th centuries** | | | |
| Vatican Arabic #13 (8th -9th Cent.) | الحنفاء | رجل ليس بمؤمن | الحنفا |
| Bishr: Mt. Sinai 151 (867) | الوثنيون | الوثنيون | للشعوب |
| Gibson, Mt. Sinai #155 (9th) | الامم | غير مؤمن | الحنفاء |
| Mt. Sinai #73 (9th) | الامم | غير المؤمنين | يونانيين |
| Mt. Sinai Ar. #310 (10th) | الوثنيين | الوثنيين | الرومان |
| Ms. Bodl. Or. 712 (16th) | الامم | الذين لم يؤمنوا | اليونانيه |
| **Arabic: 17th to 18th centuries** | | | |
| Erpenius (1616) | وثنييون | غير المؤمنين | سائر الشعوب |
| London Polyglot (1657) | الامم | الذين لم يؤمنوا | اليونانيين |
| Propagandist (1671) | الامم | غير المؤمنين | الامم |
| Revised London Polyglot (1717) | الامم | الذين لم يؤمنوا | اليونانيين |
| **Arabic: 19th century** | | | |
| Shawair, Lebanon (1813) | اليونانيين | الذين لم يؤمنوا | الامم |
| Calcutta, H. Martyn (1826) | العوام | غير المؤمنين | العوام |
| Faris al-Shidiac (1851) | الأمم | غير المؤمنين | للأمم |
| Bustani-VD (MSS 1845-1860) | الأمم | غير الؤمنين | للامم |
| Bustani-Van Dyck (1865) | الامم | غير المؤمنين | يونانيين |
| Jesuit (1880) | الامم | الكفرة | يونانيين |
| Yusif Dawud (1899) | الأمم | الغير المؤمنين | للأمميين |
| **Arabic: 20th century** | | | |
| Paulist – Fakhouri (1964) | الامم | غير المؤمنين | لليونانيين |
| New Jesuit (1969) | الأوثان | كافر | اليونانيين |
| Bible Society (1993) | الوثنية | وثني | غير اليهود |
| **Hebrew** | | | |
| Hebrew: London, 1817 | הגוים | לא יאמינו | עונים |
| Hebrew: Jerusalem (Bible Society) | הגוים | אינים מאמינים | יונים |

---

[1] Τα εθνη has strong attestation in many ancient manuscripts. Modern English versions include it. One Arabic version omits it.

Appendix II          *Oriental Versions: Plate I*          1 Cor 10:24

*The text under study*: the other

*Greek*: ἕτερος

*Syriac: Peshitta*                                    ܘܚܒܪܗ

*Arabic: 8th to 16th centuries*
Vatican Arabic #13 (8th -9th)                    لصاحبه
Bishr: Mt. Sinai 151 (867)                       لصاحبه
Gibson, Mt. Sinai #155 (9th)                     لغيره
Mt. Sinai #73 (9th)                              لغيره
Mt. Sinai Ar. #310 (10th)                        من شأن صاحبه
Ms. Bodl. Or. 712 (16th)              فليطلب ما ينفع قريبه

*Arabic: 17th to 18th centuries*
Erpenius (1616)              و يطلب كل امرئ نفع صاحبه ايضا
London Polyglot (1657)                           قريبه
Propagandist (1671)                              لصاحبه
Revised London Polyglot (1717)       بل كل أحد ما ينفع غيره

*Arabic: 19th century*
Shawair, Lebanon (1813)       بل كل احد فليطلب ما ينفع قريبه
Calcutta, H. Martyn (1826)                   فائدة غيره
Faris al-Shidiac (1851)                          لصاحبه
Bustani-VD (MSS 1845-1860)                       للآخر
Bustani-Van Dyck (1865)                          للآخر
Jesuit (1880)                                    لغيره
Yusif Dawud (1899)                               لغيره

*Arabic: 20th century*
Paulist – Fakhouri (1964)                        لغيره
New Jesuit (1969)                             مصلحة غيره
Bible Society (1993)                          مصلحة غيره

*Hebrew*
Hebrew: London, 1817                        את אשר לאחר
Hebrew: Jerusalem (Bible Society)                 רע

Appendix II                   ***Oriental Versions:  Plate J***               1 Cor 11:27

*The text under study*: *profaning* the body and blood

*Greek*: 'ενοχος 'εσται το σωματος και του αἱματος του κυριου

*Syriac: Peshitta*                         ܡܚܣܬ ܗܘ ܠܓܫܡܗ ܘܕܡܗ ܕܡܪܢ ܗ ܠܥܝܪܝ

### Arabic: 8th to 16th centuries
Vatican Arabic #13 (8th -9th Cent.)        فانه شاجب لجسد و دم الرب
Bishr: Mt. Sinai 151 (867)                 فهو شجب لجسد و دم الرب
Gibson, Mt. Sinai #155 (9th)               فانه محجوج فى جسد الرب و دمه
Mt. Sinai #73 (9th)                        غير مستوجبا فانه مدان فى جسد الرب و دمه
Mt. Sinai Ar. #310 (10th)                  فانه شجيب بجسد سيدنا و دمه
Ms. Bodl. Or. 712 (16th)                   فيكون غريما بطايلة جسد الرب و دمه

### Arabic: 17th to 18th centuries
Erpenius (1616)                            فهو مذنب الى جسد ربنا و دمه
London Polyglot (1657)                     فسبكون غريما بطايلة جسد الرب و دنه
Propagandist (1671)                        فهو مذنب الى جسد الرب
Revised London Polyglot (1717)   بلا استحقاق إنما يأكل و يشرب دينونه لنفسه

### Arabic: 19th century
Shawair, Lebanon (1813)   بغير استحقاق فسيكون غريما  بطايلة جسد رب و دمه
Calcutta, H. Martyn (1826)   بوضع غير مناسب يلزم بجسد الرب و دمه
Faris al-Shidiac (1851)                     مذنب إلى جسد الرب
Bustani-VD (MSS 1845-1860)                  مذنب إلى جسد الرب
Bustani-Van Dyck (1865)                     يكون مجرما
Jesuit (1880)                               يكون مجرماإلى جسد الرب
Yusif Dawud (1899)                          مذنب إلى جسد الرب

### Arabic: 20th century
Paulist – Fakhouri (1964)                   يكون مجرما الى جسد المسيح
New Jesuit (1969)                           فقد جنى على جسد الرب
Bible Society (1993)                        خطىء إلى جسد الرب

### Hebrew
Hebrew: London, 1817                        ירשע על גן ודם אדין
Hebrew: Jerusalem (Bible Society)           יאשם לגוף אדנינו ולדמו

Appendix II      *Oriental Versions: Plate K*      1 Cor 12:2

*The text under study*: When you were *Gentiles*, you were led astray

**Greek**: ʼεθνη

**Syriac** *Peshitta*                      ܥܡܡܐ ܗܘܝܬܘܢ ܐܝܟ

### *Arabic: 8ᵗʰ to 16ᵗʰ centuries*

Vatican Arabic #13 (8ᵗʰ -9ᵗʰ )      تعلمون انكم كنتم تساقون الى الأوثان
                             (key word is missing)

Bishr: Mt. Sinai 151 (867)        تعلمون انكم كنتم وثنيين

Gibson, Mt. Sinai #155 (9ᵗʰ)    تعلمون انكم حيث كنتم الى الاوثان --- تساقوا
                             (key word is missing)

Mt. Sinai #73 (9ᵗʰ)     انكم تعلمون ----- كنتم امم الى الأوثان ---

Mt. Sinai Ar. #310 (10ᵗʰ)              كنتم وثنيين

Ms. Bodl. Or. 712 (16ᵗʰ)      كنتم امم منقادين الى الأصنام

### *Arabic: 17ᵗʰ to 18ᵗʰ centuries*

Erpenius (1616)                  كنتم وثنيين

London Polyglot (1657)         أنكم كنتم أمما منقادين

Propagandist (1671)       فانتم تعلمون أنكم انتم وثنيون

Revised London Polyglot (1717)    علمتم انكم كنتم أمما منقادين الى الأ صنام

### *Arabic: 19ᵗʰ century*

Shawair, Lebanon (1813)    علمتم انكم كنتم أمما منقادين الى الأ صنام

Calcutta, H. Martyn (1826)    تعلمون انكم كنتم من العوام منساقين الى الأوثان

Faris al-Shidiac (1851)      كنتم من الأمم منساقين الى هذى الأوثان

Bustani-VD (MSS 1845-1860)         كنتم أمما

Bustani-Van Dyck (1865)           كنتم أمما

Jesuit (1880)                    كنتم أمما

Yusif Dawud (1899)              كنتم وثنيين

### *Arabic: 20ᵗʰ century*

Paulist – Fakhouri (1964)          كنتم وثنيين

New Jesuit (1969)               كنتم وثنيين

Bible Society (1993)             كنتم وثنيين

### *Hebrew*

Hebrew: London, 1817            הייתם גוים

Hebrew: Jerusalem (Bible Society)    לפנים גוים הייתם

Appendix II          ***Oriental Versions: Plate L***          1 Cor 12:19

***The text under study***: (literal) Where the body?

***Greek***: που το σωμα

***Syriac:*** *Peshitta*                        ܐܝܟܐ ܗܘ ܦܓܪܐ

### *Arabic: 8ᵗʰ to 16ᵗʰ centuries*
Vatican Arabic #13 (8ᵗʰ -9ᵗʰ Cent.)          أين كان يكون الجسد
Bishr: Mt. Sinai 151 (867)          أين كان الجسد (variant) أين يكون الجسد
Gibson, Mt. Sinai #155 (9ᵗʰ)          فأين الجسد
Mt. Sinai #73 (9ᵗʰ)          فأين الجسد
Mt. Sinai Ar. #310 (10ᵗʰ)          أين كان تكون الجسد
Ms. Bodl. Or. 712 (16ᵗʰ)          فأين الجسم

### *Arabic: 17ᵗʰ to 18ᵗʰ centuries*
Erpenius (1616)          أين كان الجسد
London Polyglot (1657)          أين الجسد
Propagandist (1671)          فأين كان يكون الجسد
Revised London Polyglot (1717)          فأين كان الجسد

### *Arabic: 19ᵗʰ century*
Shawair, Lebanon (1813)          فأين الجسم
Calcutta, H. Martyn (1826)          أين الجسم
Faris al-Shidiac (1851)          أين الجسم
Bustani-VD (MSS 1845-1860)          أين الجسم
Bustani-Van Dyck (1865)          أين الجسم
Jesuit (1880)          أين كان الجسد
Yusif Dawud (1899)          أين يكون الجسد

### *Arabic: 20ᵗʰ century*
Paulist – Fakhouri (1964)          فأين كان الجسد
New Jesuit (1969)          فأين الجسم
Bible Society (1993)          فأين الجسم

### *Hebrew*
Hebrew: London, 1817          איה הגו
Hebrew: Jerusalem (Bible Society)          איה הגוף

Appendix II          ***Oriental Versions: Plate M***          1 Cor 12:31b

***The text under study***: (literal) and still I will direct you to the *huperbolen* way

***Greek***: και 'ετι καθ' 'υπερβολην 'οδον 'υμιν δεικνυμι

***Syriac:*** *Peshitta*     ܐܶܢܳܐ ܕܶܝܢ ܚܰܘܶܐ ܐ݈ܢܳܐ ܠܟܽܘܢ ܐܽܘܪܚܳܐ ܡܝܰܬܰܪܬܳܐ ܕܬܶܗܘܽܘܢ

### Arabic: 8th to 16th centuries
Vatican Arabic #13 (8th -9th)         أيضا أُريكمم الطريق الفاضل الفايض
Bishr: Mt. Sinai 151 (867)            فأنا أيضـا أرشدكم إلى الطريق الأفضل
Gibson, Mt. Sinai #155 (9th)          ايضا اريكم الطريق الفاضلة
Mt. Sinai #73 (9th)                   ايضا اريكم الطريق الفاضلة
Mt. Sinai Ar. #310 (10th)             فانا ابصركم بالسبيل الفاضلة
Ms. Bodl. Or. 712 (16th)             لأريكم طريقا تختص بالتباهى فى الكمال ايضا

### Arabic: 17th to 18th centuries
Erpenius (1616)                       انا ايضا اريكم سبيلا آخر افضل جدا
London Polyglot (1657)               لأرينكم طريقا تختص بالتباهى فى الكمال ايضا
Propagandist (1671)                   انا ايضا أريكم سبيلا اخر افضل جدا
Revised London Polyglot (1717)     لأرينكم طريقا تختص بالتباهى فى الكمال ايضا

### Arabic: 19th century
Shawair, Lebanon (1813)              لأرينكم طريقا تختص بالتباهى فى الكمال ايضا
Calcutta, H. Martyn (1826)           اريكم الطريقة المثلى
Faris al-Shidiac (1851)               انا اريكم طريقا افضل
Bustani-VD (MSS 1845-1860)         سوف اريكم طريقا افضل
Bustani-Van Dyck (1865)             انا اريكم طريقا افضل
Jesuit (1880)                         انا اريكم طريقا افضل جدا
Yusif Dawud (1899)                   انا اريكم طريقا افضل جدا

### Arabic: 20th century
Paulist – Fakhouri (1964)            اريكم الطريق المثلى
New Jesuit (1969)                    إنى أدلكم على افضل الطرق
Bible Society (1993)                 انا ادلكم على افضل الطرق

### Hebrew
Hebrew: London, 1817                 ועדני אגיד לכם דרך עתרון
Hebrew: Jerusalem (B. Society)      ואני הנני מורה אתכם דרך נעלה על כלנה

Appendix II            ***Oriental Versions:  Plate N***            1 Cor 13:7, 8

***The text under study***:  (13:7)  Love *covers* all  &  (13:8)  Love never *falls*

**Greek**:  (v. 7) παντα στεγει    (v. 8) 'η 'αγαπη ουδεποτε πιπτει

**Syriac:** *Peshitta*            ܚܠ ܟܕܡ ܡܣܡܒܕܢ            ܪܗܠ

|  | (verse 7) | (verse 8) |
|---|---|---|
| **Arabic: 8<sup>th</sup> to 16<sup>th</sup> centuries** | | |

| | | |
|---|---|---|
| Vatican Arabic #13 (8th -9th Cent.) | كل شيء يصطبر | الحب منذ قط لا يقع |
| Bishr: Mt. Sinai 151 (867) | تصبر على كل شي | الحب لن تسقط ابدا |
| Gibson, Mt. Sinai #155 (9th) | كل يحتمل | الحب لا يسقط |
| Mt. Sinai #73 (9th) | كل يحتمل | الحب لا يقع أبدا |
| Mt. Sinai Ar. #310 (10th) | يصطبر على جميع الأشياء | الودّ لن تقسط البته |
| Ms. Bodl. Or. 712 (16th) | تحتمل كل شىء | المحبة ما تسقط اصلا |

**Arabic: 17<sup>th</sup> to 18<sup>th</sup> centuries**

| | | |
|---|---|---|
| Erpenius (1616) | تصبر على جميع الاشياء | المحبة منذ قط لا تسقط |
| London Polyglot (1657) | تحتمل كل شي | المحبة ما يسقط اصلا |
| Propagandist (1671) | تصبر على جميع الأشياء | المحبة منذ قط لا تسقط |
| Revised London Polyglot (1717) | تحتمل كل شيء | المحبة لا تسقط أصلا |

**Arabic: 19<sup>th</sup> century**

| | | |
|---|---|---|
| Shawair, Lebanon (1813) | تحتمل كل شي | المحبة ما تسقط أصلا |
| Calcutta, H. Martyn (1826) | تستر كل شيء | المحبة لن تزول |
| Faris al-Shidiac (1851) | تصبر على كل شيء | الحب لن تسقط ابدا |
| Bustani-VD (MSS 1845-1860) (Bustani)² | تستر | المحبة لا تسقط ابدا |
| Bustani-Van Dyck (1865) | تحتمل كل شيء | المحبة لا تسقط أبدا |
| Jesuit (1880) | تحتمل كل شيء | المحبة لا تسقط أبدا |
| Yusif Dawud (1899) | تصبر على جميع الأشياء | المحبة لا تسقط ابدا |

**Arabic: 20<sup>th</sup> century**

| | | |
|---|---|---|
| Paulist – Fakhouri (1964) | تتغاضى عن كل شيء | المحبة لا تسقط أبدا |
| New Jesuit (1969) | وهي تعذر كل شيء | المحبة لا تزول أبدا |
| Bible Society (1993) | المحبة تصفح عن كل شيء | المحبة لا تزول أبدا |

**Hebrew**

| | | |
|---|---|---|
| Hebrew: London, 1817 | נשאה עם כל | אהכה איננה נפלת |
| Hebrew: Jerusalem (Bible Society) | את כל תשא | האהבה לא תבל לעולם |

---

² Butrus al-Bustani translated: تستر while Eli Smith preferred: تحتمل

Appendix II　　*Oriental Versions: Plate O*　　1 Cor 14:3

*The text under study*: Upbuilding and encouragement and consolation.

*Greek*: οἰκοδομην και παρακλησιν και παραμυθιαν

| Syriac: Peshitta | (consolation) ܘܒܘܝܐܐ | (encouragement) ܘܠܘܒܒܐ | (upbuilding) ܒܢܝܢܐ |
|---|---|---|---|
| **Arabic: 8ᵗʰ to 16ᵗʰ centuries** | | | |
| Vatican Arabic #13 (8ᵗʰ -9ᵗʰ Cent.) | و الاعتصام | و العزاء | البنيان |
| Bishr: Mt. Sinai 151 (867) | و العزاء | و التشجيع | بالبنيان |
| Gibson, Mt. Sinai #155 (9ᵗʰ) | وعزا | طلبة | |
| Mt. Sinai #73 (9ᵗʰ) | للبنيان | وعزء | يتكلم كلمة |
| Mt. Sinai Ar. #310 (10ᵗʰ) | و تعزية | و قوة | بنيانا |
| Ms. Bodl. Or. 712 (16ᵗʰ) | و تسلية | او تعزية | توطيدا |
| **Arabic: 17ᵗʰ to 18ᵗʰ centuries** | | | |
| Erpenius (1616) | وتأييد | و تعزية | بنيان |
| London Polyglot (1657) | و تسلية | و تعزية | توطيد |
| Propagandist (1671) | و تعزية | و عظة | بنيانا |
| Revised London Polyglot (1717) | و تسلية | وتعزية | ببنيان |
| **Arabic: 19ᵗʰ century** | | | |
| Shawair, Lebanon (1813) | و تسلية | و تعزية | توطيد |
| Calcutta, H. Martyn (1826) | و التسلى | و الموعظة | باكتساب الرشد |
| Faris al-Shidiac (1851) | و تعزية | و موعظة | تشييدا |
| Bustani-VD (MSS 1845-1860) | وعزاء | و وعظ | بنيان |
| Bustani-Van Dyck (1865) | و تسلية | و وعظ | ببنيان |
| Jesuit (1880) | و تعزية | وموعظة | كلام بنيان |
| Yusif Dawud (1899) | و تعزية | و وعظ | البنيان |
| **Arabic: 20ᵗʰ century** | | | |
| Paulist – Fakhouri (1964) | و تعزية | وموعظة | كلام بنيان |
| New Jesuit (1969) | و يعزّي | ويعظ | كلام يبنى |
| Bible Society (1993) | و يعزّي | ويشجَع | كلام يبنى |
| **Hebrew** | | | |
| Hebrew: London, 1817 | ועל לבם | לונחמה | מבנה |
| Hebrew: Jerusalem (Bible Society) | ולנחמם | וליסרמ | לבנותם |

Appendix II                    ***Oriental Versions: Plate P***                    1 Cor 15:44

***The text under study***:  It is sown a *physical body*, it is raised a *spiritual body*.

***Greek***: πειρεται σωμα ψυχικον, 'εγειρεται σομα πνευματικον.

***Syriac***: *Peshitta*                        ܡܬܙܪܥ ܦܓܪܐ ܢܦܫܢܝܐ ܩܐܡ ܦܓܪܐ ܪܘܚܢܐ ܘܐܝܬ

### Arabic: 8ᵗʰ to 16ᵗʰ centuries
Vatican Arabic #13 (8ᵗʰ -9ᵗʰ Cent.)              يزرع جسد نفسانى يقوم جسد روحانى
Bishr: Mt. Sinai 151 (867)                       يزرع جسد نفسانى يقوم جسد روحانى
Gibson, Mt. Sinai #155 (9ᵗʰ)                     يزرع جسد نفسانى يقوم جسد روحانى
Mt. Sinai #73 (9ᵗʰ)                              يظرع جسد نفسانى يقوم جسد روحانى
Mt. Sinai Ar. #310 (10ᵗʰ)     تزرعون جسد ذو نفس و ينبعث و هو جسد روحانى ذوات نفس و ذوات روح
Ms. Bodl. Or. 712 (16ᵗʰ)                         نزرع جسم نفسانى فنقوم جسم روحانى

### Arabic: 17ᵗʰ to 18ᵗʰ centuries
Erpenius (1616)                         يزرع جسد ذو نفس و ينبعث و هو جسد روحانى
London Polyglot (1657)                  يزرع جسد نفسانى يقوم جسد روحانى
Propagandist (1671)                     يزرع جسد حيوانى و ينبعث جسد روحانى
Revised London Polyglot (1717)          تزرع جسد نفسانى فتقوم جسد روحانى

### Arabic: 19ᵗʰ century
Shawair, Lebanon (1813)                   يزرع  جسد نفسانى فيقوم جسد روحانيا
Calcutta, H. Martyn (1826)                يزرع جسدا نفسانيا و يبعث جسدا روحانيا
Faris al-Shidiac (1851)       يزرع جسما طبعيا فيبعث جسما روحانيه... طبيعى و... روحانى
Bustani-VD (MSS 1845-1860)                يزرع جسما حيوانيا و تقوم جسما روحانيا
Bustani-Van Dyck (1865)                   يزرع جسما حيوانيا و يقام جسما روحانيا
Jesuit (1880)                             يزرع جسدٌ حيوانيٌ و يقوم جسدٌ روحانيٌ
Yusif Dawud (1899)                        يزرع جسدٌ نفسانيٌ و يقوم جسدٌ روحانيٌ

### Arabic: 20ᵗʰ century
Paulist – Fakhouri (1964)                 يزرع جسدٌ حيوانيٌ و يقوم جسدٌ روحانيٌ
New Jesuit (1969)                         يزرع جسدٌ بشريٌ فيقوم جسماً روحانياً
Bible Society (1993)                      يدفن جسماً بشرياً و يقوم جسماً روحانياً

### Hebrew
Hebrew: London, 1817                      נזרע בגו הבשר ויקום בגו הרוח
Hebrew: Jerusalem (Bible Society)         יזרע גוף נפשי ויקום גוף רוחני

Appendix II          *Oriental Versions: Plate Q*          1 Cor 16:22

*The Text*: "Maran atha" (Our Lord has come)  or  "Marana tha" (Come Lord Jesus)
*Greek*:    μαραναθα

**Syriac** *Peshitta*                                    ܡܪܢ ܐܬܐ

*Arabic: 8ᵗʰ to 16ᵗʰ centuries*
Vatican Arabic #13 (8ᵗʰ -9ᵗʰ Cent.)              ربنا قد جاء
 Bashr: Mt Sinai 151 (867)                        مارن اثا
Gibson, Mt. Sinai #155 (9ᵗʰ)                      ربنا جاء
Mt. Sinai #73 (9ᵗʰ)                               ماران اثا
Mt Sinai Ar. #310 (10ᵗʰ)                          سيدنا جاء
Ms. Bodl. Or. 712 (16ᵗʰ)³              ماران اثا أي الرب قد جاء

*Arabic: 17ᵗʰ to 18ᵗʰ centuries*
Erpenius (1616)⁴   من لا يحب ربنا يسوع المسيح فليكن محروما من رجاء الرب
                                   (Key word missing)
London Polyglot (1657)               ماران اثا اى الرب قد جاء
Propagandist (1671)                            ماران اثا
Revised London Polyglot (1717)                 ماران اثا

*Arabic: 19ᵗʰ century*
Shawair, Lebanon (1813)      (note: اى الرب قد جاء )  موران ايتو
Calcutta, H. Martyn (1826)                     مارن اتى
Faris al-Shidiac (1851)                        ماران اتى
Bustani-VD (MSS 1845-1860)     (Smith noted: ياتى )  ماران اثا⁵
Bustani-Van Dyck (1865)                        ماران أثا
Jesuit (1880)                                  ماران أتا
Yusif Dawud (1899)                             ماران أثا

*Arabic: 20ᵗʰ century*
Paulist – Fakhouri (1964)                      مارانا ثا
New Jesuit (1969)                              ماران أثا
Bible Society (1993)        (note: يا ربّنا تعال )  ماران أثا

*Hebrew*
Hebrew: London, 1817                           מרן אתא
Jerusalem (Bible Society):                     מרן אתא

---
³ The Bod. Or. MSS 712 adds, "That is: the Lord has indeed come."
⁴ The Erpenius translation omits, "*maranatha*" and adds, "from the hope of the Lord" to the previous verse.
⁵ Bustani translated, "Our Lord has come." Eli Smith added a note translating, "Our Lord is coming."

# Glossary

THROUGHOUT THIS STUDY a number of words and phrases are used that carry specific meanings. Some of these terms are familiar. Others I have created myself. For the sake of clarity and ease of reference this list is included.

We will deal with three aspects of composition. These are (1) the smaller to larger units of composition, (2) the various ways Paul's homilies are compiled, and (3) various internal features of those homilies.

## 1. THE SMALLER TO LARGER UNITS OF COMPOSITION

*Hebrew parallelism*. This is a well-known ancient Middle Eastern literary style. During the biblical period and beyond, Middle Eastern authors often wrote using pairs of phrases or sentences. The second line may duplicate the first, present its opposite, illustrate the first, bring the first to a climax or simply finish the sentence. Multiple examples of all of these types of parallelisms are on display in the Psalms and the writings of the Hebrew prophets.

*Cameo.* I have chosen this word to refer to the clusters of phrases that form the essential building blocks out of which Isaiah, Paul and others construct homilies. Often the cameo is composed of one or more Hebrew parallelisms. These cameos are given numbers down the page for easy reference. The traditional chapter and verse numbers in our Bibles are included as raised numbers. These clusters of phrases could be called "stanzas," but I prefer "cameos" because the word *stanza* is too closely associated with hymns and poems. We are dealing with heightened prose, but I hesitate to use the word *poetry*.

*Homily.* A number of cameos together form a homily. As these appear in the Old Testament, I refer to them as *prophetic homilies*. In 1 Corinthians I call them *apostolic homilies*. In each homily presented, the cameos are numbered for easy reference. The key words or ideas in each cameo are printed to the right to highlight the themes that are repeated elsewhere in the same homily. The homilies form the building blocks for sections within an essay.

**Section.** One or more homilies together form a section (of an essay). Sometimes a longer homily is composed of two or three parts, which are also called sections (of the homily).

**Essay.** This word is used to describe each of the five major parts of 1 Corinthians. Each essay in 1 Corinthians is composed of four to seven sections.

## 2. THE VARIOUS WAYS HOMILIES ARE COMPOSED

*Ring composition.* This is a more recent term for what is often called "chiasm" or "inverted parallelism." All three of these designations refer to a common literary style where an author presents a series of ideas, comes to a climax and then repeats the series of ideas backwards, returning to the starting point and thus creating a "ring," hence the designation "ring composition." The climax of the ring composition is usually the center. Often the climactic center is in some important way related to the beginning and the end of the ring composition. At times these connections are bold and clear. At other times the connections are more subtle.

*Double-decker sandwich composition.* This designation refers to a homily that is put together like a double-decker sandwich. When using this style, Paul formulates an idea that he presents three times (like the three layers of bread in a double-decker sandwich). New material is then added between the three layers of "bread," thus creating the sandwich. Paul uses this format four times, with slight modifications among the four. This format appears in Isaiah 50:4-11.

*Prophetic rhetorical template.* When a biblical author presents a series of words, phrases, cameos, homilies or even sections using a 1-2-3-4-3-2-1 format (ring composition), I call the result a "prophetic rhetorical template." Seven is the perfect number in biblical literature. The prophets, the apostles and other New Testament writers often use this style. This particular format is so common with the prophets, the Gospels and in 1 Corinthians that it needed a name. After some years of reflection, *prophetic rhetorical template* seemed to be the best option.

*The high jump format.* Often Paul presents a short series of cameos in a straight line, and that series is used as an introduction to a finely crafted ring composition. This is like a high jumper who starts with (1) a short run, and then (2) comes the jump, which is (3) followed by the crossing of the bar. Finally (4) there is the arced fall on the far side. The arc of the fall is the reverse of the jump. Crossing the bar is the climax of the four movements. The close parallel between a high jump and this particular Pauline style of composition has led me to call this format the "high jump format." First Corinthians contains a number of fine examples of this style.

### 3. VARIOUS INTERNAL FEATURES OF HOMILIES

*Step parallelism.* This designation refers to a series of ideas that are presented on the page and then repeated in the same order. This creates a A-B-C, A-B-C format. Sometimes a series is composed of cameos and sometimes made up of single lines. Six cameos come together in 16:15-18 using step parallelism. More often a homily such as 3:5-9 is composed (in this case with four cameos) using ring composition. As the reader compares the *parallel cameos within* that ring composition, step parallelism appears. Isaiah 28:14-18 offers an early example of this style where cameos 1 and 7 are related together using step parallelism.

*Point of turning.* In ring composition the author presents a series of ideas, comes to a climax and then repeats the series of ideas backwards. Just past the center, as the ideas start to repeat (backwards), there may be a "point of turning." Something significantly different is introduced as the repetition begins. Paul occasionally uses this rhetorical device.

*Encased parable.* This phrase describes a metaphor, simile or parable (short or long) that appears in the center of a ring composition.

*Encased Old Testament quotation.* At times ring composition is constructed with an Old Testament quotation in the climactic center. The Old Testament quotation so placed is called an "encased Old Testament quotation." The quotation is given special prominence by being positioned thus.

# Bibliography

Aikman, David. *Jesus in Beijing.* Washington, D.C.: Regnery, 2003.

Aland, Kurt, ed., *The Greek New Testament.* New York: United Bible Societies, 1968.

Alford, Henry. *The Greek Testament.* Vol. 2. New York: Lee, Shepard & Dillingham, 1872.

Ambrosiaster. *Commentaries on Romans and 1-2 Corinthians.* Translated and edited by Gerald L. Bray. Downers Grove, Ill.: InterVarsity Press, 2009.

*The Anchor Bible Dictionary.* 6 vols. Edited by David N. Freedman. New York: Doubleday, 1992.

Aristotle. *The "Art" of Rhetoric.* Loeb Classical Library. Translated by J. H. Freese. Cambridge, Mass.: Harvard University Press, 2006.

Augustine. *Basic Writings of Saint Augustine.* 2 vols. Edited by Whitney Oates. New York: Random House, 1948.

Bailey, D. S. *The Man-Woman Relation in Christian Thought.* London: Longmans, 1959.

Bailey, Kenneth E. "Appendix A: The Oriental Versions, . . . " pp. 208-12. In *Poet and Peasant.* Grand Rapids: Eerdmans, 1980.

———. "Inverted Parallelism and Encased Parables in Isaiah and Their Significance for Old and New Testament Translation and Interpretation," pp. 14-30. In *Literary Structure and Rhetorical Strategies in the Hebrew Bible.* Edited by L. J. de Regt, J. de Waard and J. P. Fokkelman. Assen, The Netherlands: Van Gorcum, 1996.

———. *Jesus Through Middle Eastern Eyes.* Downers Grove, Ill.: IVP Academic, 2008.

———. "Methodology (2): Four Types of Literary Structures in the New Testament." In *Poet and Peasant: A Literary Cultural Approach to the Parables in Luke.* Grand Rapids: Eerdmans, 1976.

———. "Parallelism in the New Testament—Needed: A New Bishop Lowth." *Technical Papers For the Bible Translator* 26 (1975).

———. "Paul's Theological Foundation for Human Sexuality: I Cor. 6:9-20 in the Light of Rhetorical Criticism." *Theological Review* 3 (1980).

————. "Recovering the Poetical Structure of I Cor. i 17-ii 2: A Study in Text and Commentary." *Novum Testamentum* 17 (1975).

————. "The Structure of I Corinthians and Paul's Theological Method with Special Reference to 4:17." *Novum Testamentum* 25 (1983).

————. "Women in the New Testament: A Middle Eastern Cultural View." *Theology Matters* 6, no. 1 (January-February 2000).

Balakian, Peter. *The Burning Tigris: Armenian Genocide and America's Response.* New York: HarperCollins, 2003.

Barnett, Paul. *Jesus and the Rise of Early Christianity.* Downers Grove, Ill.: InterVarsity Press, 1999.

Barrett, C. K. *A Commentary on the First Epistle to the Corinthians.* New York: Harper, 1968.

————. *A Commentary on the Second Epistle to the Corinthians.* New York: Harper & Row, 1973.

Barth, Markus. *Ephesians.* Anchor Bible 34. New York: Doubleday, 1974.

Bauckham, Richard. *Gospel Women: Studies of the Named Women in the Gospels.* Grand Rapids: Eerdmans, 2002.

————. *Jesus and the Eyewitnesses: The Gospels as Eyewitness Testimony.* Grand Rapids: Eerdmans, 2006.

Bauer, Walter, W. F. Arndt, F. W. Gingrich and F. W. Danker. *A Greek-English Lexicon of the New Testament.* Chicago: University of Chicago Press, 1979.

Bengel, John A. *Bengel's New Testament Commentary.* 2 vols. Grand Rapids: Kregel, 1981.

Bertram, G. "παιζω." In *Theological Dictionary of the New Testament,* 5:625-36. Edited by Gerhard Kittel and Gerhard Friedrich. Grand Rapids: Eerdmans, 1967.

Betz, Hans Dieter. *2 Corinthians 8–9.* Philadelphia: Fortress Press, 1975.

Bishr ibn al-Sari. *Mt. Sinai Arabic Codex 151, I Pauline Epistles.* Corpus Scriptorum Christianorum Orientalium 453. Translated by Harvey Staal. Lovanii: Aedibus E. Peeters, 1983.

Black, Matthew. "The Maranatha Invocation and Jude 14, 15 (1 Enoch 1:9)." In *Christ and Spirit in the New Testament: Studies in Honor of Charles Francis Digby Moule.* Edited by B. Lindars and S. S. Smalley. Cambridge: Cambridge University Press, 1973.

Bligh, John. *Galatians in Greek: A Structural Analysis of St. Paul's Epistle to the Galatians.* Detroit: University of Detroit Press, 1966.

Boismard, M. E., and A. Lamouille. *Le Texte Occidental des Actes des Apotres: Reconstitution et Rehabilitation, Tome I Introduction et texts.* Paris: Editions Recherche sur les Civilisations, 1984.

Bonhoeffer, Dietrich. *The Cost of Discipleship.* London: SCM Press, 1954.

————. *Meditations on the Cross.* Louisville: Westminster John Knox, 1996.

Bornkamm, Günther. *Paul.* New York: Harper & Row, 1971.

Boys, Thomas. *A Key to the Book of Psalms*. London: L. B. Steely, 1825.

——. *Tactia Sacra*. London: T. Hamilton, 1824.

Bray, Gerald, ed. *1-2 Corinthians*. Ancient Christian Commentary on Scripture, New Testament 7. Downers Grove, Ill.: InterVarsity Press, 1999.

Bridgewater, W., and S. Kurtz. *The Columbia Encyclopedia*. 3rd ed. New York: Columbia University Press, 1963.

Bruce, F. F. *1 and 2 Corinthians*. New Century Bible. London: Oliphants, 1971.

——. *Paul, Apostle of the Heart Set Free*. Grand Rapids: Eerdmans, 1977.

——. *Paul and His Converts*. London: Lutterworth, 1962.

Bultmann, Rudolf. *Theology of the New Testament*. Vol. 1. London: SCM Press, 1952.

Burney, C. F. *The Poetry of Our Lord*. Oxford: Clarendon Press, 1925.

Calvin, John. *The First Epistle of Paul to the Corinthians*. Translated by J. W. Frazier. Edited by David W. Torrance and T. F. Torrance. Grand Rapids: Eerdmans, 1960.

Carey, George. *The Gate of Glory*. Grand Rapids: Eerdmans, 1993.

Chrysostom, John. *Homilies on the Epistles of Paul to the Corinthians*. Translated by Talbot W. Chambers. In *Nicene and Post-Nicene Fathers*, vol. 12, edited by Philip Schaff. Grand Rapids: Eerdmans, 1975.

——. "Homily IX [I Timothy ii. 11-15]," pp. 435-37. In *Nicene and Post-Nicene Fathers*, vol. XIII. Grand Rapids: Eerdmans, 1979.

Cohen, Shaye J. D. *From the Maccabees to the Mishnah*. 2nd ed. Louisville: Westminster John Knox, 2006.

Conzelmann, Hans. *1 Corinthians*. Hermeneia. Philadelphia: Fortress, 1975.

Cross, Frank M., David N. Freedman and James A. Sanders, eds. *Scrolls from Qumran Cave I: The Great Isaiah Scroll, the Order of the Community, the Pesher to Habakkuk from Photographs by John C. Trever*. Jerusalem: Albright Institute of Archaeological Research and the Shrine of the Book, 1972.

Dahood, Mitchell. "Pairs of Parallel Words in the Psalter and in Ugaritic," pp. 445-56. In *The Anchor Bible: Psalms III 101-150*. New York: Doubleday, 1970.

Dalrymple, William. *From the Holy Mountain*. New York: Henry Holt, 1998.

Daniels, Jon B. "Barnabas," pp. 610-11. *The Anchor Bible Dictionary, Vol. I*. New York: Doubleday, 1992.

Danby, Herbert, trans. *The Mishnah*. Oxford: Oxford University Press, 1980, c. 1933.

Darlow, T. H., and H. F. Moule, *Polyglotts and Languages Other Than English*. Vol. II in *Historical Catalogue of the Printed Editions of Holy Scripture in the Library of the British and Foreign Bible Society*. New York: Kraus Reprint, 1964.

Deissmann, Adolf. *Light from the Ancient East*. Grand Rapids: Baker, 1980.

Delling, Gerhard. "υπερβαλλω," 8:520-22. In *Theological Dictionary of the New Testament*. Edited by Gerhard Kittel and G. Friedrich. Grand Rapids: Eerdmans, 1979.

Dionesius ibn al-Salibi (d. 1164). *Kitab al-Durr al-Farid fi Tafsir al-ʿAhd al-Jadid* (The

Book of Rare Pearls of Interpretation of the New Testament). Edited by 'Abd al-Masih Dawlabani of the Syrian Orthodox Church. 2 vols. N.p., n.d. (assumed to be published around 1900). Written in Syriac and translated into Arabic in the monastery of Dair al-Za'farani in 1727.

Dio Chrysostom. *Discourses 8.* In Jerome Murphy-O'Connor, *St. Paul's Corinth.* Collegeville, Minn.: Liturgical Press, 2002.

Dunn, James G. D. *Jesus and the Spirit.* Philadelphia: Westminster Press, 1975.

Edersheim, Alfred. *The Life and Times of Jesus the Messiah.* 2 vols. New York: Longmans, 1906.

Evans, Craig A., and N. T. Wright. *Jesus, the Final Days: What Really Happened.* Edited by Troy A. Miller. Louisville: Westminster John Knox, 2009.

Fee, Gordon D. *The First Epistle to the Corinthians.* New International Commentary on the New Testament. Grand Rapids: Eerdmans, 1987.

Findlay, G. G. "St. Paul's First Epistle to the Corinthians." In *Expositor's Greek Testament.* Edited by W. Robertson Nicoll. Vol. 2. New York: George H. Doran, 1900.

Forbes, John. *The Symmetrical Structure of Scripture.* Edinburgh: n.p., 1854.

Forsyth, P. T. *The Work of Christ.* London: Independent Press, 1958.

Friedman, Thomas L. *The World Is Flat.* New York: Farrar, Straus & Giroux, 2007.

Furnish, Victor Paul. *2 Corinthians.* Anchor Bible. New York: Doubleday, 1984.

Garland, David E. *1 Corinthians.* Grand Rapids: Baker Academic, 2003.

Gerhardsson, Birger. *Memory and Manuscript: Oral Tradition and Written Transmission in Rabbinic Judaism and Early Christianity.* Copenhagen: Ejanr Munksgaard, 1961.

Godet, Frederic Louis. *Commentary on First Corinthians.* Grand Rapids: Kregel, 1977.

Gray, G. B. *The Forms of Hebrew Poetry.* Prolegomenon by David Noel Freedman. New York: KTAV Publishing House, 1972.

Griswold, Eliza. *The Tenth Parallel: Dispatches from the Fault Line Between Christianity and Islam.* New York: Farrar, Straus & Giroux, 2010.

Grosheide, F. W. *Commentary on the First Epistle to the Corinthians.* The New International Commentary. Grand Rapids: Eerdmans, 1976.

Guidi, Ignazio. "Le traduzioni degli Evangelii in Arabo e in Etiopico," pp. 5-37. *Atti della Reale Accademia die Lincei,* anno cclxxv [1888].

Hamilton, Edith. *The Greek Way to Western Civilization.* New York: Mentor Books, 1948.

Hays, Richard. *First Corinthians.* Louisville: John Knox, 1997.

Hering, Jean. *The First Epistle of Saint Paul to the Corinthians.* Translated by A. W. Heathcote and P. J. Allcock. London: Epworth, 1962.

*Herodotus.* Bk. 2. Loeb Classical Library. Translated by A. D. Godley. Cambridge, Mass.: Harvard University Press, 1946.

Holliday, William L. *A Concise Hebrew and Aramaic Lexicon of the Old Testament Based upon the Lexical Word of Ludwig Koehler and Walter Baumgartner.* Grand Rapids: Eerdmans, 1971.

Horst, J. "μακροθυμια," 4:374-87. In *Theological Dictionary of the New Testament.* Edited by Gerhard Kittel and G. Friedrich. Grand Rapids: Eerdmans, 1967.

Hughes, Philip E. *Paul's Second Epistle to the Corinthians.* Grand Rapids: Eerdmans, 1962.

Jebb, John. *Sacred Literature.* London: n.p., 1820.

Jeremias, Joachim. *The Eucharistic Words of Jesus.* New York: Charles Scribner's, 1966.

———. *Infant Baptism in the First Four Centuries.* London: SCM, 1960.

Jewett, Robert. *Dating Paul's Life.* London: SCM, 1979.

Josephus. *The Works of Josephus: Complete and Unabridged.* Updated ed. Translated by William Whiston. Peabody, Mass.: Hendrickson, 1987.

Kasch, Wilhelm. "στεγω," 7:585-87. In *Theological Dictionary of the New Testament.* Edited by Gerhard Kittel and Gerhard Friedrich. Grand Rapids: Eerdmans, 1979.

Khalidi, Tarif, trans. and ed. *The Muslim Jesus: Sayings and Stories in Islamic Literature.* Cambridge, Mass.: Harvard University Press, 2001.

Kistemaker, Simon J. *1 Corinthians.* Grand Rapids: Baker Books, 1993.

Koehler, L., and W. Baumgartner, eds. *Lexicon in Veteris Testamenti Libros.* Leiden: J. J. Brill, 1958.

Kovacs, Judith L., trans. and ed. *1 Corinthians: Interpreted by Early Christian Commentators.* Grand Rapids: Eerdmans, 2005.

Kugel, James L. *The Idea of Biblical Poetry: Parallelism and Its History.* New Haven: Yale University Press, 1981.

Kuhn, K. G. "μαραναθα," 4:466-72. In *Theological Dictionary of the New Testament.* Edited by Gerhard Kittel and G. Friedrich. Grand Rapids: Eerdmans, 1967.

Lampe, G. W. H. *A Patristic Greek Lexicon.* Oxford: Clarendon Press, 1961.

Lamsa, George M. *The Holy Bible, Translated from the Peshitta.* Philadelphia: Holman, 1957.

Lansing, G. *Egypt's Princes: Missionary Labor in the Valley of the Nile.* 2nd ed. Philadelphia: William S. Rentoul, 1864.

Layard, Austen Henry. *Nineveh and Its Remains: With an Account of a Visit to the Chaldaean Christians of Kurdistan, and the Yezidis or Devil-worshippers; and an Inquiry into the Manners and Arts of the Ancient Assyrians.* 2 vols. New York: George Putnam, 1848.

Lewis, C. S. *Letters: C. S. Lewis and Don Giovanni Calabria.* Ann Arbor, Mich.: Servant Books, 1988.

Liddell, H. G., Robert Scott and H. S. Jones. *A Greek-English Lexicon.* Oxford: Clarendon Press, 1966.

Lightfoot, John. *A Commentary on the New Testament from the Talmud and Hebraica: Matthew—I Corinthians.* Vol. 4: *Acts—1 Corinthians.* Grand Rapids: Baker, 1979.

Lowth, Robert. *Lectures on the Sacred Poetry of the Hebrews.* London: n.p., 1787.

Lund, N. W. *Chiasmus in the New Testament.* Peabody, Mass.: Hendrickson, 1992, c. 1942.

Manson, T. W. *The Sayings of Jesus.* London: SCM Press, 1964.

Marshall, I. Howard. *The Gospel of Luke: A Commentary on the Greek Text.* The New International Greek Testament Commentary. Exeter, U.K.: Paternoster, 1978.

Matta al-Miskin. *Al-Qiddis Bulus al-Rasul: Hayatu wa Lahutuhu wa A'maluhu* [(Arabic) St. Paul the Apostle: His Life, His Theology, His Ministry]. The Monastery of St. Maqar, wadi al-Natron, Box 2780, Cairo: The Monastery of St. Maqar, 1992.

Metzger, Bruce. *A Textual Commentary on the Greek New Testament.* New York: United Bible Societies, 1971.

Metzger, Bruce M. "A Survey of Recent Research on the Ancient Versions of the New Testament." *New Testament Studies* 2 (1955/56): 1-16.

Meyer, Heinrich August Wilhelm. *Critical and Exegetical Handbook to the Epistles to the Corinthians.* New York: Funk & Wagnals, 1884.

Midrash Rabbah, *Genesis.* Translated by H. Freedman. London: Soncino, c. 1983.

Moffat, James. *The First Epistle of Paul to the Corinthians.* Moffat Commentary. New York: Harper, 1938.

Moriarty, Frederick L. "Isaiah 1–39," pp. 265-82. In *The Jerome Biblical Commentary.* Vol 1., *The Old Testament.* Englewood Cliffs, N.J.: Prentice-Hall, 1968.

Morris, Leon. *The First Epistle of Paul to the Corinthians.* Grand Rapids: Eerdmans, 1958.

Moule, C. F. D. *An Idiom-Book of New Testament Greek.* Cambridge: Cambridge University Press, 1968.

Moulton, James H., and George Milligan. *The Vocabulary of the Greek Testament Illustrated from the Papyri and Other Non-literary Sources.* Grand Rapids: Eerdmans, 1963.

Muilenburg, James. "From Form Criticism and Beyond." *Journal of Biblical Literature* 88 (1969).

Murphy-O'Connor, Jerome. "Corinth." In *Anchor Bible Dictionary.* Vol. 1. New York: Doubleday, 1992.

———. *1 Corinthians.* Wilmington, Del.: Michael Glazier, 1982.

———. *St. Paul's Corinth: Texts and Archaeology.* Collegeville, Minn.: Liturgical Press, 2002.

———. *St. Paul's Corinth.* Collegeville, Minn.: Liturgical Press, 2002.

Nestle, Eberhard, ed. *Novum Testamentum Graece.* Stuttgart: Deutsche Bibelstiftung, 1979.

Neusner, Jacob, trans. *The Tosefta,* I-V. New York: KTAV, 1979-1986.

Newbigin, Lesslie. *The Open Secret.* Grand Rapids: Eerdmans, 1978.

Nickle, Keith F. *The Collection: A Study in Paul's Strategy.* Studies in Biblical Theology

48. Naperville, Ill.: Allenson, 1966.

Niles, D. T. *1 Corinthians.* Wilmington, Del.: Michael Glazier, 1979.

———. *This Jesus . . . Whereof We Are Witnesses.* Philadelphia: Westminster Press, 1965.

Orr, William F., and James A. Walther. *1 Corinthians.* Anchor Bible 32. New York: Doubleday, 1976.

Pappi, Ilan. *The Ethnic Cleansing of Palestine.* Oxford: OneWorld, 2007.

Plato. *The Dialogues of Plato.* Translated by B. Jowett. 2 vols. New York: Random House, 1937.

Pritchard, James B., ed. *The Ancient Near East: An Anthology of Texts and Pictures.* Princeton, N.J.: Princeton University Press, 1958.

Robertson, A., and A. Plummer. *First Epistle of St. Paul to the Corinthians.* International Critical Commentary. New York: Charles Scribner's, 1911.

Safrai, S., and M. Stern, eds., in cooperation with D. Flusser and W. C. van Unnik. *Compendia Rerum Iudaicarum ad Novum Testamenum.* Sect. 1. Vol. 2, *The Jewish People in the First Century.* Philadelphia: Fortress, 1976.

Safrai, S. "The Synagogue," pp. 908-44. In *The Jewish People in the First Century.* Vol. 2. Philadelphia: Fortress.

———. "Education and the Study of the Torah," pp. 945-70. In *The Jewish People in the First Century.* Vol. 2. Philadelphia: Fortress.

Saldarini, Anthony J. "Scribes." In *Anchor Bible Dictionary.* Vol. 5. New York: Doubleday, 1992.

Schweizer, E. "Dying and Rising with Christ." *New Testament Studies* 14 (1967-1968).

Swidler, Leonard. *Biblical Affirmations of Women.* Philadelphia: Westminster Press, 1979.

Talmud, Babylonian. *The Hebrew-English Edition of the Babylonian Talmud.* Edited by I. Epstein. London: Soncino, 1980. c. 1960.

Tasker, R. V. G. *The Second Epistle of Paul to the Corinthians.* Grand Rapids: Eerdmans, 1958.

Temple, William. *Christus Veritas.* London: Macmillan, 1954.

Theodoret of Cyr. *Commentary on the First Epistle to the Corinthians.* TLG database. CD-ROM.

Thiselton, Anthony C. *The First Epistle to the Corinthians.* New International Greek Testament Commentary. Grand Rapids: Eerdmans, 2000.

Thompson, Marianne M. "Jesus Is Lord: How the Earliest Christian Confession Informs Our Proclamation in a Pluralistic Age." Address delivered at the General Assembly of the Presbyterian Church (USA), June 19, 2002. Published privately.

Thrall, Margaret E. *1 and 2 Corinthians.* Cambridge: Cambridge University Press, 1965.

———. *The First and Second Letters of Paul to the Corinthians.* In *The Cambridge Bible Commentary.* Cambridge: Cambridge University Press, 1965.

Torrance, David W., and Thomas F. Torrance. *The Second Epistle of Paul to the Corinthians and the Epistles to Timothy, Titus and Philemon*. Grand Rapids: Eerdmans, 1964.

Trever, John C., photographer. *Scrolls from Qumran Cave I: The Great Isaiah Scroll, The Order of the Community, The Pesher to Habakkuk*. Jerusalem: The Albright Institute and the Shrine of the Book, 1972.

Vermes, G. *The Dead Sea Scrolls in English*. Baltimore: Penguin Books, 1973.

Volf, Miroslav. *The End of Memory: Remembering Rightly in a Violent World*. Grand Rapids: Eerdmans, 2006.

Walls, Andrew F. "Eusebius Tries Again: Reconceiving the Study of Christian History." *International Bulletin of Missionary Research* 24 (July 2000): 105-11.

Whale, J. S. "Christ Crucified: the Christian Doctrine of the Atonement." In *Christian Doctrine*. New York: Macmillan, 1941.

———. *Victor and Victim: The Christian Doctrine of Redemption*. Cambridge: Cambridge University Press, 1960.

Wiesel, Elie. *Night*. Translated by Marion Wiesel. New York: Hill & Wang, 2006.

Wills, Garry. *Lincoln at Gettysburg: The Words That Remade America*. New York: Simon & Schuster, 1992.

Wilson, J. M. *The Acts of the Apostles: Translated from the Codex Bezai with an Introduction on Its Lucan Origin and Importance*. London: SPCK, 1924.

Wilson, Victor M. *Divine Symmetries*. Lanham, Md.: University Press of America, 1997.

Wintermute, O. S., trans. *Jubilees*. In *The Old Testament Pseudepigrapha*. Vol. 2. Edited by James H. Charlesworth. New York: Doubleday, 1985.

Witherington, Ben. *Women in the Earliest Churches*. Cambridge: Cambridge University Press, 1988.

Wright, N. T. *The Resurrection of the Son of God*. Minneapolis: Fortress, 2003.

# Notations on the Oriental Versions
# Used in this Study[1]

## SYRIAC

*The New Testament in Syriac.* Noted as: Peshitta Syriac.
  Edited by John Gwynn. London: British and Foreign Bible Society, 1905-1920.
  This translation is the second of three Syriac New Testaments. It achieved its final form in the fourth to fifth centuries and is the authorized version of the Syrian Orthodox Church.

*The Holy Bible from Ancient Eastern Manuscripts Containing the Old and New Testaments Translated from the Peshitta.* Noted as: Lamsa Peshitta.
  The Authorized Bible of the Church of the East. Edited by George M. Lamsa. Philadelphia: A. J. Holman, 1957.
  This is an English translation of the Peshitta made by George Lamsa, a Deacon of the Syrian Orthodox Church (the Church of the East).

---

[1]Some of the notations in this index are gleaned from T. H. Darlow and H. F. Moule, *Polyglotts and Languages Other Than English*, vol. II in *Historical Catalogue of the Printed Editions of Holy Scripture in the Library of the British and Foreign Bible Society* (New York: Kraus Reprint, 1964). See also Ignazio Guidi, "Le traduzione degle Evangelii in Arabo e in Etiopico," *Atti della Reale Accademia die Lincei*, anno cclxxv [1888], pp. 5-37; Bruce M. Metzger, "A Survey of Recent Research on the Ancient Versions of the New Testament," *New Testament Studies* 2 (1955/56): 1-16. A more complete bibliography is available from Kenneth E. Bailey, *Poet and Peasant* (Grand Rapids: Eerdmans, 1980), pp. 218-19.

## ARABIC VERSIONS (CHRONOLOGICALLY ARRANGED)

## A. Ancient Manuscript Arabic Versions of the Epistles (printed and un-printed)

*Vatican Arabic 13.* Noted as: Vat. Ar. 13 (8th-9th cent.).

Generally recognized as the oldest extant Arabic New Testament. The last half of Luke and all of John are missing. The current manuscript is transcribed by five different people. The oldest parts of the Gospels may be pre-Islamic. In one text God is named "Elohim." The name for John is spelled three different ways on a single page. Many other distinctive features mark it as a very early version. There is some thoughtful early interpretation reflected in its readings. It includes influence from the Old Syriac.

*Mt. Sinai Arabic Codex 151 (I) Pauline Epistles.* Noted as: Mt. Sinai 151 (867). Translated and edited by Harvey Staal. Corpus Scriptorum Christianorum Orientalium 452. Scriptores Arabici Tomus 40. Lovanii: Aedibus E. Peeters, 1983.

This manuscript is the oldest extant copy of Acts and the Epistles. A Syriac scholar, Bishr ibn al-Sari, working near Damascus made a translation out of Syriac into Arabic and added his own thoughtful comments to the text. The manuscript is dated A.D. 867. Mt. Sinai 151 is the only extant copy.

*Mt. Sinai Arabic Codex 310.* Noted as: Mt. Sinai 310 (10th cent.).

The unknown translator of this manuscript adds brief explanatory words and phrases to the text which turns the work into a mini-commentary. It is thereby of great interest.

*Mt. Sinai Arabic 155. An Arabic Version of the Epistle of St Paul to the Romans, Corinthians, Galatians with part of the Epistle to the Ephesians from a Ninth-century Mss. in the Convent of St. Catharine on Mount Sinai.* Noted as: Mt. Sinai 155 (9th cent.).

Edited by Margaret D. Gibson. London: Cambridge University Press, 1894. Translated from Greek, this Arabic version is a copy of a yet older Arabic version. It is significant because of its antiquity.

*Mt. Sinai Arabic MSS No. 73, Epistles* (9th cent.).

This version is also important because of its age and the care with which it was translated from the Greek text. The early Kufic script is difficult to read.

*Bodleian Library Oriental MS 712*. Noted as: Bodl. Or. 712 (16th cent.).

This complete New Testament (on paper) is thought to be from the six-teenth century. It follows the chapter divisions of Western Christianity and the verse numbers have been added with some Latin notations on the inner margins. The handwriting is clear and beautiful. The origins of the copy and the version are not known.

## B. Printed Arabic Versions of the Epistles

*Novum Testamentum Arabice*. Noted as: Erpenius 1616. Edited by Thomas Erpenius. Leidae: n.p., 1616.

A seventeenth-century Dutch scholar, Erpenius relied on early Arabic versions made from Coptic, Greek and Syriac.

*Kitab al-ʿAhd al-Jadid, That Is the Holy Gospel of Our Lord Jesus the Messiah.*
Printed by the humble servant Richard Watson in London the Protected in the year 1823 from a copy printed in Rome the Great in the year 1671 for the benefit of the Eastern Churches.
Noted as: Propagandist 1671.
This version was composed by Sarkis al-Rissi, the Maronite Archbishop of Damascus who went to Rome in 1650 for the purpose of preparing this Arabic New Testament for the *Propagada Fide* Catholic order.

*The Holy Bible Containing Old and New Testaments in the Arabic Language.*
Newcastle-upon-Tyne: Sara Hodgson, 1811.
Noted as: London Polyglot rev. (1811).
This version was edited by Joseph Carlyle, Cambridge professor of Arabic.

*Greek Catholic Lectionary of the New Testament*. Schwair, Lebanon: Greek Catholic Monastery of St. John, 1813.
Noted as: Schwair (1813).
The Greek Catholic Monastery of St. John in Schwair, Lebanon, established the first Christian publishing venture in the Middle East. This version is an important milestone in the long Arabic language biblical tradition.

*Al-ʿAhd al-Jadid ila Rabbina wa Mukhullisina Yashuʾ al-Masih. (The New Testament of Our Lord and Savior Jesus the Messiah)*. Calcutta: Episcopal Press, 1826, c. 1816.

Noted as: Martyn (1816).

This translation was made in India by Nathaniel Sabat (a Christian scholar from Baghdad) under the supervision of the famous linguist Henry Martyn. It represents an early attempt to use Islamic-flavored words and phrases.

*Kitab al-ʿAhd al-Jadid liRabbina Yasu' al-Masih* [*The Book of the New Testament of Our Lord Jesus the Messiah*]. Translated by al-Shidiac. London: William Watson, 1851.

Noted as: Shidiac (1851).

Faris al-Shidiak of Lebanon completed this translation under the supervision of S. Lee and Thomas Jarrett of Cambridge. It is a fine work, overshadowed by the Bustani-Van Dyck version.

*Kitab al-ʿAhd al-Jadid liRabbina wa Mukhallisina Yasuʿ al-Masih* [*The Book of the New Testament of Our Lord and Savior Jesus the Messiah*]. Beirut: Bible Society, 1947. The New Testament was first published in 1860.

Noted as: Bustani-Van Dyck (1860).

This famous version was the combined effort of Butrus al-Bustani, Nasif al-Yaziji of Lebanon and Eli Smith and Cornelius Van Dyck, long-term American residents of Beirut. This version became and remains the most influential version ever produced in Arabic.

MSS worksheets of the Bustani-Van Dyck Version.

Noted as: Bustani-Van Dyck MSS (1845-1860)

*Kitab al-ʿAhd al-Jadid liRabbina wa Mukhallisina Yasuʿ al-Masih.* Photocopy of the original manuscripts of the Bible Society version of the Arabic New Testament translated from 1845-1860 and first published in Beirut, Lebanon, in 1860. These are in the handwriting of the translator Butrus al-Bustani, the stylist Yusif al-Yaziji and Eli Smith the linguist. The originals are held in the rare book room of the Near East School of Theology, Beirut, Lebanon. The notes and suggestions of each of the four scholars who created this translation are recorded and remain legible. An enormous amount of careful and meticulous scholarship is preserved in these documents. I was able to make clear photocopies of the New Testament volumes as sources for this study.

*Al-Kitab al-Muqaddas al-ʿAhd al-Jadid liRubbina Yasuʿ al-Masih* [The Holy Bible

the New Testament of Our Lord Jesus the Messiah]. Beirut: Jesuit Press, 1929.
    Noted as: Jesuits (1880).
    A high-quality translation completed by the Jesuits in Beirut using the
    Hebrew, Greek, Syriac and Latin texts. In critical passages the Vulgate is
    generally followed.

*Novum Testamentum Domini Nostri Jesu Christi Version Arabica.* Mausili: Typis
Fratrum Praedicatorum, 1899.
    Noted as: Yusif Dawud (1899).
    This version was translated by Yvusif Dawud, a Dominican Father, and
    published by the Dominicans in Mausil, Iraq. Father Yousif relied heavily
    on the Syriac Peshitta.

*Al-Kitab al-Muqaddas al-'Ahd al-Jadid* [The Holy Bible: The New Testament].
Harisa, Lebanon: Paulist Press, 1964.
    Noted as: Fakhouri (1964).
    George Fakhouri, a Paulist Father, produced this fine translation which
    was sponsored by and published by the Paulist Press in Lebanon.

*Al-Kitab al-Muqaddas al-'Ahd al-Jadid* [The Holy Bible: The New Testament].
Beirut: Dar al Mashriq, 1969.
    Noted as: New Jesuit (1969).
    The Lebanese Jesuit Order sponsored this new translation as an update of
    their earlier Bible published in 1880. The translation was done with great
    care consulting the original languages, contemporary scholarship, and the
    changes in the Arabic language over a hundred years.

*Al-Kitab al-Muqaddas* [The Holy Bible]. Beirut: Bible Society in Lebanon, 1993.
    Noted as: Bible Society Arabic (1993).
    This new united effort brought together scholars and church leaders of the
    Orthodox, Catholic and Protestant traditions to produce a version to be
    used in all the churches of the Arabic-speaking world. The result has been
    well received.

## HEBREW

*Brith Hdsha 'la Fi Mshih* [New Testament from the Mouth of the Messiah].
London: Macintosh Spitalfields, 1817.
    Noted as: Hebrew (1817).

*Hbrith hahdsha* [The New Covenant]. Jerusalem: Bible Society in Israel, n.d.
    Noted as: Jerusalem (Bible Society).
    This version of the New Testament was produced by the Bible Society in
    Israel in the recent past.

# Ancient Author Index

# Modern Author Index

# Ancient Text Index

# Scripture Index